Miscellanea Moreana
Essays for
Germain Marc'hadour

∽

Moreana 100: Volume XXVI
Mélanges Marc'hadour

medieval & renaissance
texts & studies

Volume 61

miscellanea moreana
essays for
Germain Marc'hadour

⁓

Moreana 100: Volume XXVI
Mélanges Marc'hadour

Edited by

CLARE M. MURPHY
HENRI GIBAUD
MARIO A. DI CESARE

medieval & renaissance texts & studies
Binghamton, New York
1989

© Copyright 1989
Center for Medieval and Early Renaissance Studies
State University of New York at Binghamton

Library of Congress Cataloging-in-Publication Data

Miscellanea Moreana: essays for Germain Marc'hadour
  (Medieval & Renaissance texts & studies ; v. 61)
A special issue of Moreana.
  1. More, Thomas, Sir, Saint, 1478-1535. 2. Authors, English—
Early modern, 1500-1700—Biography. 3. Humanists—Biography.
4. Erasmus, Desiderius, d. 1536. 5. Marc'hadour, Germain. I.
Marc'hadour, Germain. II. Murphy, Clare M. III. Gibaud, Henri.
IV. Di Cesare, Mario A. V. Moreana.
PR2322.M57 1989   942.05'2'0924   88-8925
ISBN 0-86698-045-8 (alk. paper)

This book is made to last.
It is set in Goudy text and Libra display,
smythe-sewn,
and printed on acid-free paper
to library specifications.

Printed in the United States of America

Assistants de Rédaction — Editorial Assistants

David & Mary Bradshaw, Huntsville, Alabama
Dorothy F. Donnelly, University of Rhode Island
Noëlle-Marie Égretier, Université du Maine
Ralph Keen, University of Chicago
Ruth H. Kossoff, URI Emerita
Robert P. Sorlien, URI Emeritus

Editorial and Documentary Assistant

Elaine C. Zajano, Wallingford, Pennsylvania,
and *Moreanum*, Angers

Assistante de Secrétariat et Photocomposition des Lettres

Béatrice Lemasson, *Moreanum*, Angers

Notes

L'illustration de couverture, due à la plume de Soeur Madeleine du Calvaire, s'inspire de *Mains d'apôtre*, de Dürer (1508). Utilisée pour la première fois dans la Gazette de 1980 (*Moreana* 65-66), elle a paru depuis dans les numéros 70, 73, 78, 83-84, et 93. La page 4 de *Moreana* 95-96 porte une notice nécrologique sur Soeur Madeleine, morte le 23 août 1987.

The cover illustration, fashioned after Dürer's *Hands of an Apostle* (1508) by Sister Madeleine du Calvaire, was first used for the 1980 Gazette (*Moreana* 65-66). It has since appeared as cover for numbers 70, 73, 78, 83-84, and 93. *Moreana* 95-96, page 4, carries an obituary for Sister Madeleine, who died August 23, 1987.

La *Prière Eucharistique A*, qui sert comme intertitres, émane du Comité international pour la langue anglaise dans la liturgie. La traduction proposée est de Harriet Dorothy Rothschild, URI, et Henri Gibaud.

Eucharistic Prayer A, which is used for the half-title pages, originates with the International Committee on English in the Liturgy. The French translation is by Harriet Dorothy Rothschild, URI, and Henri Gibaud.

Les dessins de Raymond Joly illustrant *L'Univers de Thomas More* par G. Marc'hadour (Paris: Vrin, 1963) sont reproduits avec l'autorisation de l'artiste et de l'auteur.

Raymond Joly's drawings are reproduced from *L'Univers de Thomas More* by G. Marc'hadour (Paris: Vrin, 1963) with the permission of the artist and the author.

Tabula Honoraria

Amici of the United Kingdom
Japan Thomas More Association
St. Thomas More Lawyers Guild
  of Hamilton, Ontario, Canada

Thomas More Society of
  America
University of Rhode Island

Tabula Gratulatoria

Agnes Albert
Hugh O. Albin
Manuel Alcalá
Elizabeth Alkaaoud
Jean Allard & Godeleine
  Allard-Gros
Ward S. & Peggy Allen
Hazel M. Allport
Un ami
Michael A. Anderegg
Charles Augrain, PSS
William J. Awalt

David & Sabine Baird-Smith
Dominic Baker-Smith
Mary Barbara, OP
Marie-Paule Bataille
Nicolas Barker
Ken Beckie
François Bellour
Charles Béné
Pierre Bercot
George M. Bernique
Thérèse P. Bernique
Mary Frances Berry

Tabula Gratulatoria

Marialisa Bertagnoni
André Berthout
La Famille Bervoets-Balthazaar
Alessandra Betta
Doris & Peter Bietenholz
Dale B. & Linda B. Billingsley
Claude-Charles Billot, OFM Cap.
Jeff Birren
Marcelle Blanc
Moïse Blatrix, OFM Cap.
William Blissett
Maurice Boisramé
Ann & Jackson Boswell
Daniel Bourgeois
Pierre-Auguste Boussard
Hermann Boventer
David & Mary Bradshaw
Piet, Thea, Piet Jr. & Paul Brouwer
Franklin W. Burch
Lorenza Butler
Brian F. Byron
Virginia Callahan-Corbett
Philip Caraman, SJ
Edward Carey
Kathleen Carroll
John R. Cavanaugh, CSB
Alphonse Chapeau
Jeanne Chauvel
Jacques Chomarat
Joseph Cinquino
Marion Clark
Cornelia Comorovski
F. Joseph Cornish
Jean & Yvonne Corrignan
Joseph & Monique Croizer
Yvon Croizer
Thomas W. Cunningham
In memoriam Bridget Curtin
Regina D'Arcy, CSCJ

Vincent F. Daues, SJ
Solange Dayras
José Maria de Arana
François de Cambolas
Gabriel F. de Freitas
Bob & Emilie De Graaf
Alfred M. M. Dekker
Marie-Madeleine de la Garanderie
Raymond Delatouche
René & Françoise Delattre
Charles de Lourmel
A.E. de Schryver
Lee DiCesare
Mario A. DiCesare
Margaret Lacy Dodds
Dorothy F. Donnelly
Mary Munson Donnelly
A.I. Doyle
Charles Clay Doyle
Paul Drochon
William Duffy
Philip & Kathleen M. Dust
Noëlle-Marie Égretier
A. Jean Elder
John X. Evans
Rosemarie Evans
Patricia Jane Fairhead
James K. Farge, CSB
In memoriam Arthur Fernée
Winifrede Fernée
Bernard C. Fisher
James J. Fitzpatrick
Roland Galibois
Yves-Claude Gélébart
Lucie Gérard
Albert J. Geritz
Aloïs Gerlo
Ursula M. Gerty
Henri Gibaud
Robert & Ellen Ginsberg

Tabula Gratulatoria ~ XI

James F. Glynn
Brian Gogan, CSSp.
Roger & Joan Gourin
Damian & Bernadette Grace
Hugh Green
Mark & Ellen Green
John Gueguen
Gabriel Guillaume
Jacques & Odile Gury
Alain Guy
Steven W. Haas
Barry Hagan, CSC
Edward B. Hanify
Henry Hassan
Cecilia Hatt
Dieter Hau
Dalton Haughey
Hans Heilen
Sam & Jacque Hornsby
Brenda M. Hosington
Robert Hughes
Amos, Martin, Paula &
  Seymour House
Robert Hubbard
Jorge Ipas
Juan José Iriarte
Edward & Karen Jacobs
Amand Jagu
In memoriam Paul F. Jaquet
In memoriam Catherine Jarrott
Gustave Jeanneau
Valerie & Harold Jewell
Robin & Joyce Johnson
Marie-Thérèse Jones-Davies
Elsie & Robert D. Kaiser
Béla & Ilona Kapótsy
Ralph & Mary Keen
Christopher A. Kelly
Lee Cullen Khanna
Arthur F. Kinney
James Daniel Kinney

Randy Klawiter
Mary Knowles
Jude Thaddaeus Koll, OSB
Johnemery & Gail Konecsni
Charles M. Kovich
Paul Oskar Kristeller
Maura & Joaquin Kuhn
Marion Leathers Kuntz
Amos Lee Laine
P. Terrence Lamb
Suzanne Lambert
Thomas M.C. Lawler
Anne Le Bars
Guy Le Bouédec
Étienne Ledeur
Rudolf Leinemann
Carmen & Jean-Joseph
  Lemasson
Lazare Lemonnier (Débora)
Simone Lemoyne
Marcel Le Ny
John Morrison Leonard
Francisco López Estrada
Hugh & Pat Loughran
Patricia Lusseau
Frank Manley
Mahmoud Manzalaoui
Gabrielle Marc
Anne-Marie Marc'hadour
Jean-Claude Margolin
Richard C. Marius
Louis L. Martz
William G. Marx
William A.M.J. McAllister
Patrick & Helen McCarthy
William G. McConalogue
James & Elizabeth McCutcheon
Thomas J. McGovern
Ruth E. McGugan
Robert B. McKeon
Andrew M. McLean

XII ~ *Tabula Gratulatoria*

Paul & Marianne Meijer
Thomas Merriam
Gérard Mesnet
G. Harold Metz
Patricia C. Metzner
Leland Miles
Clarence H. Miller
William Monihan, SJ
Denise Montalant
Jean-Pierre Moreau
Anne Mary Murphy, SHCJ
J. Clay Murphy
In memoriam Frank & Rufina Murphy
Francis G. Murray
Tohru Nakamura
Louis Neveu, PSS
M. Agnes Nolan
Lady Ruth Norrington
William V. Nuetzel
Arthur J. O'Dea
Anne M. O'Donnell, SND
Bernard O'Kelly
John & Marian Olin
Therese O'Neill-Madden
Walter J. Ong, SJ
Ray Ortali
Igor Ossinovsky
Pierre Ouvrard
Thomas & Edurne Pane
Monica Papazu
Angelo Paredi
Anne Payan
The Leeman L. Perkins Family
Giuseppe Petrilli
Arthur Petty
Alexandre Philippe
In memoriam Margaret Mann Phillips
Rainer Pineas
Raymond & Polly Plant

Marguerite Pohu
In memoriam C. Normand Poirier
Anne Lake Prescott
André Prévost
Edward A. Quattrocki
Henricus Queffelecus
Una & Sidney Ratcliff
Lord Rawlinson
David H. Reardon
Gerard D. Reilly
In memoriam George Rendel
Rosemary Rendel
Robert Adair Reynolds
Anne Maureen Richardson
Maurice Richomme
Marie-Claire Robineau, OP
Jean Rouschausse
Marie-Claude Rousseau
M. Madeleine Ruch
Albert J. Ruetz
Lawrence V. Ryan
Rita M. Ryan
Vincent J. & Monica H. Ryan
George M. St. Peter
Angele Botros Samaan
Upton A. & Caroline Savoie
John D. Schaeffer
Maria Schäfer
The Hans Schieser Family
Robert Schneebeli
Richard & Megan Schoeck
Marie-Claire et Jean Schoevaert-Brossault
Karl G. Schroeder
In memoriam Alice Schroell
Gabrielle Schroell
Hubertus Schulte Herbrüggen
Louis A. Schuster, SM
Anita, Lonny & Maryvonne Schwarz
Marie & Jean-Noël Scouarnec

Howard A. Seitz
Yvon Simard
Constance R. Smith
Malcolm C. Smith
Thurman L. Smith
Nancy Ruthford Sodeman
Robert Parker Sorlien
J.K. Sowards
Alfred B. Stapleton
Rudolf Sträter
Majie Padberg Sullivan
Raymond H. Sullivan
Yoshinori Suzuki
In memoriam Richard S. Sylvester
Michel Taillé
Bienvenido A. Tan III
Odile & Edouard Tellier
Marion Terrell
J.B. Trapp
Mel Tucker
Madeleine & Gabriel Turbé
Friedrich-K. Unterweg
John Murdo Urquhart
Louis Valcke
René Valtaud

Gustav van de Loo
Geert van den Steenhoven
Giuseppe Villa
Kazimir Vrljičak
Benjamin H. Walker
Robert Walter
Mildred Ware
James & Yolanda Warren
Yoshiko Watanabe
Peter M. Waters
J.B. Webb
Gerard Wegemer
James Michael Weiss
D'arne Welch
Franklin B. Williams
Jay Wilson
Leigh Winser
Nancy Cole Yee
Elaine C. Zajano
Halina Zak
Danila Zanibelli
Silvio & Huguette Zavala
Rosmarie Zell
Penny B. Ziemer
Lilijana Žnidaršič

Abbaye de Clervaux, Luxembourg
Abstracts of English Studies
Alexander Turnbull Library, Wellington, New Zealand
Ambrose Swasey Library, Rochester, New York
Arizona Center for Medieval and Renaissance Studies
Association Saint Yves
Bibliothèque de l'Institut Catholique de Paris
Bibliothèque Nationale de Luxembourg
Centre d'Etudes de la Renaissance, Université de Sherbrooke
Centre for Reformation and Renaissance Studies, Victoria University Library
Centre Thomas More, La Tourette
Centro Studi Antoniani, Padova

Chelsea Old Church, London
Dominicains de l'Albertinum, Fribourg, Suisse
E.M. Cudahy Library, Loyola University of Chicago
Fordham University
Gill Library, College of New Rochelle
Harvard University – "Villa I Tatti"
Donald Millus for the Independent Works of William Tyndale
Jesuit Community at Loyola University of Chicago
Keio University, Tokyo
LaGrange College
Llyfrgell Genedlaethol Cymrul/National Library of Wales
Memorie Domenicane, Pistoia
Monastère Notre Dame des Gardes, Chemillé
Monastère Saint Joseph du Bessillon, Cotignac
Poor Clares, Woodchester, Gloucestershire
Princeton University Library
Pontifical Institute of Medieval Studies
Renaissance Society of America
St. John Fisher College, University of Tasmania
St. John's Seminary Library, Brighton, Massachusetts
St. Thomas More Circle, New York City
St. Thomas More College, Crawley, Australia
St. Thomas More House at Yale University
St. Thomas More Society of Buenos Aires
Editors of *The Sixteenth Century Journal*, Kingdon, Kolb, & Schnucker
Thomas More Institute, Montreal
Thomas More Prep–Marian, Hays, Kansas
Thomas Morus Akademie, Bensberg
United Library of Garrett-Evangelical and Seabury-Western Theological Seminaries

CONTENTS

Tabulae Honoraria & Gratulatoria	ix
List of Illustrations	xix
Clare M. Murphy, Letter	xxi
Henri Gibaud, Lettre	xxix

I. PROLOGUE

Lawrence V. Ryan, Letter	1
Marie-Claude Rousseau, Les livres et les heures de Germain Marc'hadour: Bio-bibliographie	3
Nicolas Barker, The Ever-Widening Circle	9
Pierre Ouvrard, Lettre	13
J. B. Trapp, The Founding of the *Amici Thomae Mori*	17
Marie-Claire Robineau, OP, Lettre	21

II. TON VERBE SOMMA LA LUMIERE

Louis Neveu, Lettre	25
Ward Allen, King James's Translators and Words on the Wing	27
André Godin, Notes sur Érasme et le sacré	39
Brenda Hosington, "Quid dormitis?": More's Use of Sleep as a Motif in *De Tristitia*	55
Marie-Thérèse Jones-Davies, Lettre	71

III. THE CROWN OF ALL CREATION

Paul Oskar Kristeller, Letter	75
Louis Valcke, Jean Pic de la Mirandole lu par Thomas More	77

C. Normand Poirier, Letter	99
Marion Terrell, Letter	100
Michel Taillé, Lettre	101
J. K. Sowards, On Education: More's Debt to Erasmus	103
Caroline Chabot, Lettre	125
John C. Olin, Erasmus' *Adagia* and More's *Utopia*	127
Marianne S. Meijer, Lettre	137
Jozef IJsewijn, Erasmus in Rome: A Clash of Humanist Cultures?	139
Piet Brouwer, Letter	153
Friedrich-K. Unterweg, Letter	155
Jacques Chomarat, La philosophie de l'histoire d'Érasme d'après ses réflexions sur l'histoire romaine	159
Anne M. O'Donnell, SND, Cicero, Gregory the Great, and Thomas More: Three Dialogues of Comfort	169
Béla Kapótsy, Letter	199

IV. COMME UNE MERE RASSEMBLE TENDREMENT SES ENFANTS

Geert van den Steenhoven, Letter	203
Yvonne Marc'hadour Corrignan, Lettre	205
Hubertus Schulte Herbrüggen, Fletcher's Forgotten Play: *The Rising to the Crown of Richard III*	209
Jacques Gury, Lettre	221
Albert J. Geritz, John Aubrey's Brief Life of More: Facts, Half-Truths, or Fictions?	223
Clare Fitzpatrick, Letter	233
Marialisa Bertagnoni, Ironia e *pietas*: Alcune coincidenze fra *Utopia* e *I Promessi Sposi*	235
Arthur Petty, Letter	245
Anne Lake Prescott, Crime and Carnival at Chelsea: Widow Edith and Thomas More's Household	247
Peter Milward, SJ, Letter	265

V. A PEACE ... AND A JUSTICE

Angele B. Samaan, Letter	271

Damian Grace, *Utopia*: A Dialectical Interpretation	273
Jean-Claude Margolin, Sur l'insularité d'*Utopia*: Entre l'érudition et la rêverie	303
Andrew M. McLean, Letter	323
Marie-Madeleine de la Garanderie, Guillaume Budé, lecteur de l'*Utopie*	327
Mary O'Neill, Letter	339
Elizabeth McCutcheon, William Bullein's *Dialogue Against the Fever Pestilence*: A Sixteenth-Century Anatomy	341
Rosemary Rendel, Letter	361
Silvio Zavala, Aspects de la littérature utopique en Espagne et en Amérique latine	363

VI. FORTS DANS L'AMOUR

William J. Awalt, Letter	377
Krystyna Stawecka, Lettre	378
Michael Grace, SJ, Letter	379
Aloïs Gerlo, Érasme conciliateur	381
Rainer Pineas, Polemical Technique in Thomas More's *The Answere to ... the Poysened Booke*	385
Hugh O. Albin, Letter	395
Louis L. Martz, Thomas More: The Search for the Inner Man	397
Soeur Anne-Marie Marc'hadour, Lettre	417
Nancy Ruthford Sodeman, Letter	420
Léon-E. Halkin, Érasme contre la liturgie?	421
Thérèse Bernique, Letter	427
Brian F. Byron, From Essence to Presence: A Shift in Eucharistic Expression Illustrated from the Apologetic of St. Thomas More	429
Hazel M. Allport, Lettre	443

VII. INTO COMMUNION ... WITH ALL YOUR SAINTS

Paul Akio Sawada, Letter in More's Hand	447

Marion Leathers Kuntz, Angela da Foligno: A
Paradigm of Venetian Spirituality in the Sixteenth
Century 449
Przemyslaw Mroczkowski, Lettre 465
Jay Wilson, Letter 467
Charles Béné, Cadeau d'Érasme à Margaret Roper:
Deux hymnes de Prudence 469
Clarence H. Miller, Erasmus's Poem to St. Genevieve:
Text, Translation, and Commentary 481
Francisco López Estrada, Tomás Moro en un libro de
Fray Alonso de la Torre, cartujo sevillano 517
Anne Payan, Letter 533

VIII. EPILOGUE

Maryvonne Croizer Schwarz, Lettre 537
Richard J. Schoeck, Moreans from Chambers to
Marc'hadour: Some Recollections and Reflections 539
Jerzy Starnawski, Lettre 547
Majie Padberg Sullivan, Letter 549
Marie-Paule Bataille, Lettre 551
Joy Sylvester, Letter 553
Richard Marius, Looking Back 555
Thomas M. C. Lawler, Letter 563
John P. Marmion, Letter 565
Gabriel Guillaume, Décennies de voisinage et de
compagnonnage 567

ILLUSTRATIONS

Frontispiece, Photograph by Douglas C. Gamage	iv
Giovanni Pico della Mirandola, sketch by Raymond Joly	76
Etching by Jean Schoevaert-Brossault	126
Erasmus, sketch by Raymond Joly	158
Henry VIII, sketch by Raymond Joly	208
Signature of Christopher Columbus	244
Germain Marc'hadour holding wine cup made in London in 1656	322
G. Budé, sketch by Raymond Joly	326
Christopher Columbus, sketch by Raymond Joly	362
Hans Holbein the Younger, *Thomas More and His Family*	401
Hans Holbein the Younger, *Sir Thomas More*	402
Hans Holbein the Younger, *Sir Thomas More*	402
Wooden statue, 15th century, polychrome, artist unknown. Saint Anne holds the Virgin, who holds the infant Jesus. Photo par Pierre Gosselin.	419
William Roper, sketch by Michael Tunney, SJ	468
Part of a map of Paris (engraved by Visscher in 1618) showing the Abbey of St. Genevieve and Notre Dame	487
Part of a map of L'Isle de France. Johan Blaeu, *Le Grand Atlas* (Amsterdam, 1663; rpt. in 12 vols., Theatrum Orbis Terrarum, 1967), vol. 7	502
Anne de Bretagne, sketch by Raymond Joly	532
Thomas More, sketch by Raymond Joly	538

 The University of Rhode Island, Kingston, RI 02881-0812
Department of English, Independence Hall (401) 792-5931

Our beloved Abbé Germain,

Vere dignum et justum est: it seems indeed fitting and proper that this book have its beginning in a garden. And again, vere dignum et justum est: the garden is that of Thomas More's own home in Chelsea, the Allen Hall garden which boasts the mulberry tree planted by More. This garden scene takes place the final Sunday afternoon of the London More/Fisher Conference of July 1985. The principal player is a refreshingly humble person, and for that reason it is most gratifying for me to reveal that credit for the idea of this book belongs to your North American Secretary since 1973, Brother Michael Grace. Even his place in the Tabula Gratulatoria is subsumed in the fraternal anonymity of "Jesuit Community at Loyola University of Chicago." It is time, Mike tells me in that garden, for a volume of studies in honor of Germain.

The scene shifts to Wolfenbüttel, and the Neo-Latin Congress of August 1985. You, Ralph Keen, and I have shared an indoor picnic supper and you have gone to hear a plenary session paper. Ralph and I use the time to discuss a suitable occasion for the appearance of the volume, and Ralph suggests the end of the first twenty-five years of Moreana. When you return, we tell you that it would be a good idea, we think, to have a special volume to celebrate Moreana's silver anniversary. You are delighted.

The next scene is close to home for you, but you are in the US and I am on leave in Angers, for it is November 1985; and in the library of Moreanum, Henri Gibaud and I discuss the proposed homage volume. He is pleased to be editor in charge of articles in French. No one thinks of anything other than articles. But winter turns into spring and spring into summer, and it is July 1986. Dick Schoeck and I are sitting in a sidewalk café at Place de L'École Militaire in Paris. He has just come from a planning session for the 1988 Neo-Latin Congress in Toronto, and I mention to him the hope we then had of presenting the volume to you at that Congress. "We" now are three, for Mario Di Cesare has agreed to serve as managing editor, feeling honored by the invitation to his press to print the omaggio, as he likes to call it. Dick is immensely pleased at the idea of a festschrift to you. Scholarship, he remarks, is not created in a vacuum, but exists because of scholars; and a homage volume to a scholar presents to the world the human being behind the scholarship.

The academic year 1986-87 brings me home to URI and to Christ the King Parish that you now know so well from having lived and served there. You can picture the rectory living room where in the winter of 1987 I experienced the Genesis II program in spirituality. And I can picture the film screen and the face of the Trappist monk speaking of affirmation. Those who affirm the existence of others reflect the action of the God whose crucifixion affirmed the value of human existence. I do not know when the idea of the spiritual value of affirmation coalesced with my memories of the conversation with Dick in Paris, but when it did, I decided that there would be more than articles. There would also be letters affirming the man behind the scholarship.

One letter which arrived too late for inclusion illustrates well Dick's observation that scholarship is not produced in a vacuum. Father Richard Russell writes from Yale: "From my earliest days at More House in 1964 you have been my mentor and guide to the life of our patron. What a wonderful way to be introduced to such a great heritage! Years of reading and study could not match your living enthusiasm for the works, the times and the piety of St. Thomas More."

Henri speaks in his editorial letter of the affirmation of our efforts which so frequently accompanied the donations of *Amici* and others to this volume. Let me mention also the thrill with which even the most published of scholars responded to the invitation to submit an article. I choose one writer to speak for all: "I am so happy to be sending this article to you today. In many ways, being asked to submit an article to a volume in honor of Father Germain is the greatest professional experience of my life!"

The next scene is not a scene; it is a state of mind, a search that preoccupies me during the late winter of 1987, the search for suitable quotations or titles to introduce each section. Snatches come to me-- from More, from Erasmus, from Liturgy. But some sections remain without titles and there is no unity in the titles I do think of. It must be January of 1988, just before I am to take the complete typescript to Binghamton, that, hearing perhaps for the third time the new Eucharistic Prayer A, I realize that it is the perfect unifier of the sections.

It is one of those stunning winter days in the northeast that blesses the next scene, that of my long drive to Mario and Lee Di Cesare's home in late January 1988--clear blue sky, bright sun, fresh snow on the pine trees, shimmering cakes of ice on the ponds and rivers. And greeting me when I arrive are other winter delights--a blazing fire, a home-cooked meal, and of course a warm welcome. We sit around the fire to choose typefaces and dust jacket, I holding in my hand the choices Henri has sent. It is Lee who speaks so warmly of the Soeur Madeleine design for our cover. The adaptation of Dürer's praying hands, Lee quietly insists, is most suitable for the man being honored. I think of my choice of a Eucharistic Prayer for the half title pages, and I know we are both aware of a sentiment expressed by Thérèse Bernique in her letter: "Obviously, the most important role in your life has remained that of a priest, a minister to human spiritual needs."

<u>Miscellanea Moreana</u> now has a name, a name conceived by that inveterate Latinist Mario. <u>Vere dignum at justum est.</u> And <u>miscellanea</u> it is indeed, not only <u>Essays for Germain</u> Marc'hadour--the public title which is a compromise with the more personal

subtitle Mario would have preferred, *Essays for the Abbé*--but also a biography of the Abbé, and a history of the *Amici Thomae Mori*, of *Moreana*, of the Yale St. Thomas More Project, and of More Circle scholarship in general.

The Prologue introduces many of these subjects and gives an example of the influence of this Circle on our *Amici*, for just as later we will see Paul Akio Sawada's imitation of More's own hand, so in the Prologue, Soeur Marie-Claire pens her own Praise of Folly. This whole volume is, in fact, an *hommage* as well as a homage, for we, feeling your influence as well as that of the Circle, have adopted some of your kind editorial practices: using both American and British spellings as they suit the authors, allowing a certain personal latitude in footnoting practices, capturing the homespun touch of personal signatures on letters--not to mention my postscripts--and prefacing *Moreana* with editorial letters.

Ton Verbe somma la Lumière not only summons light, but also tells some of the story of your past and continuing Biblical study, and presents some aspects of this same study among our *Amici*.

Not surprising for a journal which specializes in studies of England's greatest humanist and not infrequently features the Prince of the Humanists, *The Crown of All Creation* is a long section. Its letters stress the humanist values of friendship and education. Jozef IJsewijn's study of

Northern humanism is followed by letters depicting two different contemporary views of Northern humanism, and Sister Anne's exploration of dialogues of comfort is accompanied by a contemporary Hungarian's gratitude for such comfort. My own thinking about Renaissance humanism has forever been affected by your residence on our campus as visiting distinguished professor of humanities and the many student/faculty conversation hours you led on the subject. Not surprisingly, you prefaced your discussions with spiritual considerations, pointing out that Christ's taking on of human flesh was the factor that gave humanity such value in Renaissance eyes. I mention this now because of John Olin's dedication of his article to a scholar who lived these ideals of humanism, Margaret Mann Phillips. In her letter of July 14, 1986, Margaret wrote: "The invitation to write for G.M.'s festschrift is an honour."

In "The Woman's Creed," Rachel Conrad Wahlberg proclaims: "I believe in Jesus / who spoke of himself / as a mother hen / who would gather her chicks / under her wings." When Henri was examining with me H. Dorothy Rothschild's French translation of Eucharistic Prayer A, he pointed out that this verse from Matthew 23.37 and Luke 13.34 is echoed in "as a mother tenderly gathers her children, / you embraced a people as your own." <u>Comme une mère rassemble tendrement ses enfants</u> gathers under its motherly wings letters from the Netherlands, France, Northern Ireland, Argentina, and Japan, including that of your one-year-older "big" sister who diplays her maternal pride. The articles amass the disparate characters of More's world or of that of our writers' interests: a conniving king and a conniving penniless wanderer, wandering victims of human frailty and witty gossipers. All are examined with the astute critical pens of some of our most literate Amici.

I had hoped for only a very few articles on Utopia. Enough has been said, I thought. Instead, writers I never thought would do so, wrote on Utopia, and I realized it was time to deconstruct my thinking on that work. It is not that all has been said; it is rather that all will never be said. The articles in A Peace . . . and a Justice--and there are still others elsewhere in this book on that book--illustrate Utopia's endless fascination for the critic. Angele Samaan's letter speaks of the second edition of her Arabic translation. The other letters describe their own Utopia, which for these writers seems to be Moreanum in Angers, even if for Rosemary Rendel that Utopian aspect expresses itself in the resemblances she finds between Angers and her (and More's) own London!

Forts dans l'amour is indeed a joyous section, focusing as it does on love as shown in liturgy and Eucharist, in ecumenism and conciliation. Its letters describe love in action from Washington to Texas, from Poland to Canterbury, from your own Angers to the French Guiana so strikingly evoked in the remembrances of one of your "little" sisters. Most gratifying in this section is its illustration of the progress the human race has made since More's time, the mutual hostility described in Rainer Pineas's article having given way to the beautiful ecumenism evidenced in the Reverend Hugh Albin's letter.

Vere dignum et justum est: in a volume celebrating a More scholar and things Morean, a section entitled *Into Communion . . . with All Your Saints.* Paul Akio tries his hand at our saint's hand; Marion Kuntz, Charles Béné, and Clarence Miller emulate you in studying holy women; Francisco López Estrada explores a Spanish manuscript concerning More's execution; the letter writers discover saintliness both in the past and the present.

Past and present meet with warmth in the Epilogue, beginning as it does with a letter from your third sister's daughter. Maryvonne's memories draw on the past while her references to her children suggest the future. In the Epilogue the wheel comes full circle in another way also. At the Toronto reception celebrating twenty-five years of *Moreana,* Larry Ryan read to you his letter opening *Miscellanea Moreana;* thus you knew that the "special volume" was really an *omaggio* to you. His letter is followed by the bio-bibliography from the pen of your colleague, Marie-Claude Rousseau. *Vere dignum et justum est:* the final article is from another colleague, a friend dear both to you and to many of us who frequent Moreanum, Abbé Gabriel Guillaume.

I know that I speak for all of your readers when I sign this letter

Your loving Clare

Clare M. Murphy

Moreanum - 29, rue Volney - B.P. 808 - F 49005 ANGERS CEDEX - FRANCE

Au Lecteur,

Le livre que vous avez entre les mains n'est pas tout à fait comme les habituels volumes de Mélanges, où les hommages proprement dits sont limités à la Préface ou à l'Avant-propos, à moins qu'un chapitre ne leur soit consacré. Parce que le dédicataire du présent volume, l'abbé Germain Marc'hadour, est plus qu'un "scholar"--lettré, érudit, cultivé, raffiné, savant ... autant d'équivalents donnés par le Robert et Collins et qui justifient l'emploi du mot anglais dans la circonstance--parce qu'il est un homme au grand coeur et un prêtre zélé, on trouvera, dispersés parmi les articles "doctoraux", des témoignages qui concourront à tracer de lui un portrait aussi complet que possible. Le prétexte de cet Hommage, ce sont les vingt-cinq ans de publication de la revue Moreana, qu'il dirigea pendant tout ce temps à la plus grande satisfaction des spécialistes de Thomas More et de son "milieu", mais également à celle de tous les membres de l'Amicale fondée sous l'égide du saint homme d'Etat anglais. Les dix ou douze mille pages que représentent les vingt-cinq volumes annuels de quatre numéros ne constituent qu'une partie de la production de son Directeur. Une bio-bibliographie offre d'ailleurs, dès l'ouverture, l'essentiel du "panégyrique".

"Panégyrique": c'est ainsi, en effet--avec ce que le mot comporte occasionnellement d'ironie-- qu'apparaîtra peut-être cette entreprise aux yeux d'un lecteur pressé qui tomberait par hasard sur certaines pages. Et pourtant, il serait bien dommage que l'on s'arrêtât à une telle impression et que l'on renonçât à explorer le reste. Car, d'abord, qui connaît un tant soit peu l'abbé Marc'hadour sait que les témoignages disent vrai, et sera vite rassuré quant aux éventuelles conséquences inflatoires, ou inflammatoires, sur son caractère ou son comportement, des éloges exprimés dans les "Lettres"; et d'autre part, l'ensemble des Lettres aussi bien que des articles récompensera abondamment, nous le pensons, une lecture assidue.

En tout cas, ce qu'il est possible d'affirmer sans redouter le moindre démenti, c'est que le projet d'un volume d'Hommages à l'abbé Marc'hadour a suscité une vive approbation parmi les abonnés de la revue et le vaste cercle des amis de son Directeur. Les spécialistes "classiques" de l'époque de More ont fourni de substantielles études, grâce auxquelles le présent volume d'Hommages est bien conforme à l'idée que l'on peut se faire de Mélanges en l'honneur d'un maître apprécié. En outre, comme en font foi les deux <u>Tabulae</u>, <u>Honoraria</u> et <u>Gratulatoria</u>, la souscription lancée pour couvrir, dans la mesure du possible, les frais importants du volume <u>Moreana</u> 100 a provoqué une grande générosité, souvent traduite par des dons dépassant largement la somme suggérée, et beaucoup d'envois de chèques étaient accompagnés d'un mot d'encouragement aux "éditeurs". Ces appréciations spontanées pourraient, elles aussi, faire l'objet d'un florilège, complémentaire des Lettres ici publiées. Il y aurait lieu de joindre à la liste un certain nombre de bienfaiteurs qui ont choisi l'anonymat.

    Voici le livre tel qu'il est. Comme tous les autres, il demande à être jugé sur sa globalité. Comme cela transparaît en le feuilletant ou simplement en consultant la Table de Matières, c'est avec une certaine admiration et une grande affection que nous le dédions à l'abbé Germain Marc'hadour, en souhaitant que le lecteur y trouve autant d'intérêt que nous, rédacteurs et auteurs d'articles et de Lettres, avons consacré de temps et d'efforts joyeux à sa préparation.

                                      Henri Gibaud

Blessed are you, strong and faithful God.
All your works, the height and the depth,
echo the silent music of your praise.

1 Prologue

Tu es béni, Dieu fidèle et fort,
Toutes tes oeuvres, la hauteur et la profondeur,
renvoient la musique silencieuse de ta louange.

SOCIETAS INTERNATIONALIS STUDIIS NEOLATINIS PROVEHENDIS
INTERNATIONAL ASSOCIATION FOR NEO-LATIN STUDIES

Seventh International Congress • Toronto, Canada 8–13 August 1988

Toronto, 8 August 1988

Reverend Germain Marc'hadour
Editor, *Moreana*

Dear Father Marc'hadour,

    As President of the International Association for Neo-Latin Studies, I offer you warmest congratulations on this occasion celebrating the appearance of the twenty-fifth annniversary issue of *Moreana*, quarterly journal of the association Amici Thomae Mori.

    The success of *Moreana* over the quarter-century of its existence has been mainly due to your loving and careful guidance of its fortunes. As a publication dedicated to studies of a major humanist author and of his illustrious circle, *Moreana* is appropriately honored at this Congress of Neo-Latin scholars. It is also fitting that this silver anniversary issue should be a *Festschrift* prepared by the Amici to honor you.

With all best wishes,

Lawrence V. Ryan

Professor Lawrence V. Ryan, President (Stanford)

MARIE-CLAUDE ROUSSEAU

Les livres et les heures de Germain Marc'hadour: Bio-bibliographie

I

Chronologie

1921: Germain Marc'hadour naît le 16 avril, à Langonnet, dans les collines du Morbihan. Second d'une famille de cinq enfants, il grandit dans un milieu bilingue, français et breton. Ses parents, Yves et Marie, sont artisans commerçants: leur patronyme "Marc'hadour," du latin *mercator*, signifie en breton "marchand."

Noël 1935: Premier contact avec Thomas More, dont le jeune G. M. découvre l'existence dans les pages du *Petit Larousse Illustré*, reçu en cadeau de Noël.

1937-1943: Après ses études au Petit Séminaire, G. M. entre au Grand Séminaire de Vannes. Il fait des intérims d'instituteur pendant la "drôle de guerre," sans interrompre la Théologie.

1943: Arrivé le 3 novembre à Angers pour y préparer, à la demande de son évêque, une licence d'anglais à l'Université Catholique de l'Ouest, il découvre le plaisir, insoupçonné, d'étudier les langues vivantes.

1944: Ordonné prêtre le 18 juin, quelques jours après le débarquement des forces alliées en Normandie. Le 4 août, il rencontre pour la première fois des Américains: des soldats du Général Patton venus libérer son village natal.

1945-1952: Muni d'une licence ès lettres, obtenue en juin 45, il enseigne l'anglais et un peu l'espagnol à Pontivy (Morbihan), où il est aussi aumônier de prison. Le dimanche, il sillonne le diocèse à moto pour aider ses confrères dans leurs tâches pastorales. *Août 1946:* premier séjour en Angleterre. Il passe les étés 48, 49 et 52 en Allemagne comme aumônier militaire par intérim auprès des Forces Françaises: Palatinat, Forêt Noire, Berlin-Ouest. Autant attiré par Newman et Chesterton que par More, avec lesquels il commerce lors de son premier été à Londres, c'est sur *Thomas More: Humanist and Educator* qu'il se décide à rédiger un mémoire en vue du Diplôme d'Etudes Supérieures obtenu à Rennes en janvier 1951. Ses premières recherches au British Museum lui révèlent que More y est plus ou moins méconnu.

1952-1953: La préparation du cours d'Histoire de la Langue que lui demande l'Université Catholique de l'Ouest à Angers ("la Catho") le conduit à Lyon pendant huit mois, et à University College, Londres, où il obtient un diplôme de Phonétique en décembre 53. Dans tout cela peu de temps pour la recherche pure.

1954: Le 2 février, premier cours à la Catho, dans le département d'anglais, où il enseigne, depuis ce jour, la philologie et la traduction. En 1958, paraîtra une version ronéotée en 292 pages de son cours sur l'*Histoire de la langue anglaise*, ouvrage maintenant épuisé.

Le 1er mars, il s'installe 49 rue Pascal avec sa mère—qui y mourra le 16 mai 1959—avant d'habiter, à partir du 1er mars 1960, au 29 rue Volney.

Avril 1955: Il lance la première d'une série de sessions pédagogiques qui réuniront, plusieurs années de suite, des professeurs d'anglais du secondaire à Angers, Rennes, Vannes. . . .

1956: Pendant deux ans, fera le trajet Angers-Tours pour y poursuivre, au Centre de la Renaissance, alors dirigé par Pierre Mesnard, son exploration du seizième siècle.

1956 est aussi l'année où paraît son premier article: "Thomas More et les Etats-Unis," *Etudes Anglaises*, Paris, suivi d'autres essais publiés dans *The Clergy Review* (Londres 1957, 1958).

Février 1959: Elizabeth F. Rogers ayant signalé ces travaux à Richard S. Sylvester, G. M. est invité à participer à l'édition des Oeuvres Complètes de More dont le projet vient de naître à Yale University.

Années 60

1960: Exposition Thomas More à Angers, en mai. Conférences. Le 1er juillet, G. M. assiste à la première de *A Man for All Seasons*, au Globe Theatre de Londres.

Septembre 1960-décembre 1961: Le 8 septembre, G. M. s'embarque pour les USA et séjourne quinze mois à Yale. Il y prépare l'édition critique de *Supplication of Souls*. Boursier "Fulbright," il en profite pour explorer les fonds moriens de Washington, San Marino, Los Angeles, San Francisco et Toronto. . . . Il publie, en février 1961, dans *Drama Critique* (Detroit), le texte de sa première conférence aux USA (Yale, octobre 1960) sur *A Man for All Seasons* que l'Amérique vient de découvrir. Il rentre en France à Noël 1961 avec la matière de deux livres: 1) des traductions de textes moriens anglais et latins, ce qui sera le *Saint Thomas More* publié en 1962 à Namur; 2) une chronologie de 588 pages: *L'Univers de Thomas More (1477-1535)*, qui paraîtra chez Vrin, Paris, en 1963.

Septembre 1963: Secrétaire International des *Amici Thomae Mori*, association fondée à Bruxelles le 29 décembre 62 avec six autres membres de diverses croyances et de divers pays, G. M. lance *Moreana*, bulletin bilingue (anglais-français), simple trait d'union qui prend vite de l'ampleur et devient une revue savante d'audience internationale, utilisant aujourd'hui une douzaine de langues, et diffusée dans une quarantaine de pays.

En hommage au travail de compilation et d'édition dont *Moreana* est le fruit, plusieurs spécialistes moriens dédieront leurs ouvrages à G. M. : E. E. Reynolds, *The Field Is Won*, Londres, 1968; Francisco López Estrada, *Tomás Moro*, Madrid, 1980; Fernando Mello Moser et José V. de Pina Martins, *Thomas More au Portugal*, Lisbonne, 1983.

A partir de cette année, conférences dans la plupart des grandes villes américaines ainsi qu'au Canada. Bénéficie de plusieurs bourses (Folger, 1963, 1966; Huntington, 1965). Son entrée dans le *Who's Who in Europe* de 1964-65 atteste sa réputation internationale. Il est interviewé en août 1965 à la télévision de San Francisco, avec R. S. Sylvester & R. J. Schoeck, à propos de More, Erasme et Luther. Il anime un séminaire "Early Tudor Humanism" à la Catholic University of America, Washington, dans l'été 67.

Jan. 1968: *Moreana* et son directeur font l'objet d'un reportage dans *Catholic Digest*. G. M., "Friend of the Saint" (pp. 63-68), y est représenté, en couverture, "a slight fortyish Breton with a boyish smile," avec pour toile de fond le portrait de More par Holbein.

Mai 1969: Docteur ès Lettres, Université de Paris-Sorbonne, avec "les félicitations du jury" pour sa thèse principale *Thomas More et la Bible* — sujet déposé en 1958, à une époque où le cercle universitaire français ignorait à peu près tout de More — et une thèse complémentaire, *Thomas More vu par Erasme*.

Années 70

Le temps libre que lui laissent son enseignement à la Catho où lui est conféré le grade de professeur en 1970, l'édition de *Moreana* et son ministère de prêtre, il le consacre à la publication de livres et articles, et à divers voyages à l'étranger, avec pour point culminant de ses activités les célébrations du cinquième centenaire de la naissance de More en 1977 et 1978.

1970: Il remplace pendant trois mois un missionnaire dans la brousse, en Guyane française, où enseigne sa soeur religieuse. Il y traduit quelques textes liturgiques en galibi, avec l'aide enthousiaste de jeunes écoliers amérindiens.

1972: Nouveau séjour à la Folger. Parution du *Guide to More's London*.

1973: Pèlerinage en Terre Sainte, comme aumônier d'un groupe scolaire.

1974: G. M. signe l'article de 3000 mots "Thomas More, Sir, Saint" de l'*Encyclopaedia Britannica*.

1975: "Visiting professor" à Sherbrooke, Canada, et à l'University of Georgia, USA.

1976: Co-éditeur avec R. S. Sylvester d'*Essential Articles for the Study of Thomas More*.

1977: Organise à Angers le Congrès International Thomas More, 13-20 avril, et rédige les 56 pages du Catalogue de l'Exposition.

1977-78: Tournée de conférences en Pologne, en Grande-Bretagne, aux USA, en Nouvelle-Zélande, en Australie, au Japon, en Belgique. La décennie du centenaire morien conduit également G. M. deux fois à Paris, à l'invitation de la télévision française, pour figurer au jury des Dossiers de l'Ecran avec, au programme, un film sur Henry VIII et un autre sur Thomas Becket, le martyr auquel More se réfère dans sa dernière lettre.

Années 80

1981-85: Parution du *Dialogue Concerning Heresies*, co-éditeur avec T. M. C. Lawler et R. C. Marius, Yale U. P., 1981. Puis séries de "pèlerinages moriens": Argentine, 1982; Espagne et Portugal, 1983; et en 1985, à l'occasion du cinquantenaire de la canonisation de More et John Fisher: mai, Rome; juillet, Londres; août, Wolfenbüttel (RFA) pour le Congrès néo-latin; septembre-décembre, les USA, dont cinq semaines à l'automne comme "distinguished visiting professor" à Auburn University, Alabama.

Edition, avec Roland Galibois, de *Erasme de Rotterdam et Thomas More: Correspondance*, Université de Sherbrooke, 1985.

1986: Il achève l'édition critique de *Supplication of Souls*, CW 7.

1987-88: Il figure dans la septième édition du *Nouveau Dictionnaire Biographique Européen* et il partage ses activités professionnelles entre un peu d'enseignement et beaucoup d'édition: non seulement celle de *Moreana*, qui totalise quelque 12.000 pages (sous l'égide du C. N. R. S. depuis une dizaine d'années), mais aussi celle de monographies "seiziémistes," issues du Moreanum, laboratoire qu'il dirige au sein de l'Institut de Recherche Fondamentale et Appliquée de l'UCO. Ces dernières années, sans refuser des conférences qui l'amènent à reprendre de temps à autre son bâton de pèlerin pour la cause morienne, il consacre une bonne partie de son temps ("Ceci est mon temps, prenez et mangez" est une de ses maximes) à accueillir dans son antre—"his lair" comme disait R. S. Sylvester—amis et chercheurs de passage. Adoubé chevalier dans l'Ordre des Palmes académiques, le 18 mai 1988, il participe, en août, au 7e Congrès d'Etudes Néo-Latines, à Toronto, et passe l'automne à l'University of Rhode Island comme Professeur invité. Il y est fêté par un colloque: *A Scholar for All Seasons*. A son retour en décember 88 il souhaite être libéré de ses tâches d'éditeur de *Moreana* pour cultiver, d'autres manières, son jardin morien.

II

Repères bibliographiques

1. *Saint Thomas More*: Son portrait par Erasme (1519); sa lettre à Dorp (1515); la Supplication des Ames (1529). Textes traduits et présentés. Collection "Ecrits des Saints," Soleil Levant, Namur, 1962, 280 pp. Epuisé.

2. *L'Univers de Thomas More: Chronologie critique de More, Erasme et leur époque (1477-1536)*. Collection "De Pétrarque à Descartes," Vrin, Paris, 1963, 588 pp.; dessins de Raymond Joly, Premier Grand Prix de Rome. Epuisé.

3. *Exile and Tenderness*. Traduction de Eloi Leclerc, *Exil et Tendresse* (Paris 1962), publiée par Franciscan Herald Press, Chicago, 1965, 184 pp. Epuisé.

4. *Thomas More et la Bible. La place des livres saints dans son apologétique et sa spiritualité*. Collection "De Pétrarque à Descartes," Vrin, Paris, 1969, 608 pp. (Thèse de doctorat ès lettres).

5. *Thomas More vu par Erasme*. Lettre du 23 juillet 1519 à Ulrich

von Hutten. Edition bilingue, avec présentation et commentaire. Ronéoté, Moreanum, Angers, 1969, 220 pp. (Thèse complémentaire). Epuisé.

6. *The Bible in the Works of St Thomas More*, B. De Graaf, Nieuwkoop, Pays-Bas:

Vol. 1. The Old Testament, 1969, 220 pp.
Vol. 2. The Four Gospels, 1969, 204 pp.
Vol. 3. Acts, Epistles and Apocalypse, 1970, 204 pp.
Vol. 4. Elements of Synthesis, 1971, 206 pp.
Vol. 5. Indexes, Concordances and Supplements, 1972, 266 pp.

7. *Thomas More ou la sage folie*. Collection "Philosophes de tous les temps," Seghers, Paris, 1971, 188 pp. Epuisé.

8. *A Guide to Thomas More's London*, Moreanum, Angers 1972, 32 pp.: promenade aux lieux de Londres où vécut et travailla Thomas More. Epuisé.

9. *Thomas More 1477–1977*: catalogue illustré, en anglais, de l'Exposition du Centenaire. Moreanum, Angers, 1977, 52 pages. Epuisé.

10. "Sir (Saint) Thomas More," *Encyclopaedia Britannica*, édition de 1974, 3000 mots.

11. *Essential Articles for the Study of Thomas More*, édité en collaboration avec R. S. Sylvester, Archon, Hamden (Connecticut), 1976, 700 pp. Epuisé.

12. *St. Thomas More: A Dialogue Concerning Heresies*, éd. critique, Yale University Press, New Haven, 1981, xiv–888 pp. en collaboration avec Thomas Lawler et Richard Marius.

13. *Erasme de Rotterdam et Thomas More: Correspondance*, traduction et commentaires avec Roland Galibois, Editions de l'Université de Sherbrooke 1985, 318 pp.

A quoi s'ajoutent des chapitres d'ouvrages collectifs, des préfaces, prologues et épilogues, des entrées dans diverses encyclopédies, sans compter une bonne centaine d'articles, anglais ou français, sur More, Fisher, Erasme, Newman, S. François d'Assise, dans plus de vingt revues de douze ou quinze pays, y compris le Japon, la Pologne et l'Australie. Plusieurs de ces articles ont été traduits en italien, japonais, néerlandais....

Université Catholique de l'Ouest

NICOLAS BARKER

The Ever-Widening Circle

IT IS HARDLY POSSIBLE TO IMAGINE a topic connected with any aspect of the life, times and subsequent *fama* of Thomas More that has not found its way into the pages of Moreana over the last twenty-five years. So far as I can see, however, no one has ventured on that odd but attractive work, Robert Southey's *Sir Thomas More, or Colloquies on the Progress and Prospects of Society*, first published in 1824. Few read it now, deterred by the mocking censure of Macaulay. Yet the improbable image of the ghost of Thomas More appearing to Southey—who disguises himself under the pseudonym "Montesinos" but remains clearly recognizable as the dweller among his beloved lakes—makes better reading than might be supposed. The theme, the improvement of a world recently gone mad, is not too distant from our own times, and Southey's stance, as well as his taste for dialogue, recall Peacock's dislike of the society of his time, as well as the combination of learning, contrivance and mockery with which he despatched it. There are plates, too, not only an engraving of More by Finden (unrecorded in *The Likeness of Thomas More*), but also, unexpectedly, of Lakeland scenery.

It is, at all events, a work which may be unfamiliar even to readers of the ensuing pages, and I venture therefore to inflict on them a passage which may serve as a preliminary text, an introduction to, if not an explanation of, the admiration always, the affection that springs from admiration, and (though I can hear his outraged denial) the veneration, that Germain Marc'hadour has inspired among his immeasurable friends all over the world. Here, then, is the passage. Southey, or rather Montesinos, has just quoted Thomas à Kempis, "In omnibus requiem quaesivi, sed non inveni nisi in angulis et libellis," and More replies:

> If wisdom were to be found in the multitude of books, what a progress must this nation have made in it since my head was cut off! A man in my days might offer to dispute *de omni scibile*, and in accepting the challenge I, as a young man, was not guilty of any extraordinary presumption, for all which books could teach was, at that time, within the compass of a diligent and ardent student. Even then we had difficulties to contend with which were unknown to the ancients. The curse of Babel fell lightly upon them. The Greeks despised other nations too much to think of acquiring their languages for the love of knowledge, and the Romans contented themselves with learning only the Greek. But tongues which, in my lifetime, were hardly formed, have since been refined and cultivated, and are become fertile in authors; and others, the very names of which were then unknown in Europe, have been discovered and mastered by European scholars, and have been found rich in literature. The circle of knowledge has thus widened in every generation; and you cannot now touch the circumference of what might formerly have been claspt.

One of the many miracles that *Moreana* has achieved in twenty-five years is to widen the circle of knowledge about More, without allowing its subscribers to lose touch with the circumference. I did not know, I suspect none of us knew, how widespread the international community of friends of Thomas More was. The silver jubilee of *Moreana*, however, is also the jubilee of Germain Marc'hadour's incessant pilgrimage, first to find and then to preserve and unite that community. No detail of the life and times and works of Thomas More, no detail of our own lives and work, has been too slight to escape his eager interest.

If he has been solicitous and protective of us, we have tried to do the same for him. We need him, not only for the bond that he preserves, but for himself. His enthusiasm enlivens our spirits, his faith illuminates our aspirations. He tries us, too, for no one ever took less care of himself, or for the morrow. As the unworthy successor of Dick Sylvester, a President of the *Amici* who was a fitting adversary (in the strict sense of the word) for the *Secrétaire International*, I know how often I have been beset with the feeling that I ought to have done more to "bless, keep and preserve" our fragile but indestructible, slight but indomitable, our universally beloved Abbé.

The introductory letter of *Moreana* 2 began "Amici omnes, and especially Mr. Barker": why I should have been singled out I cannot now remember, but I am proud, now, in the name of the same concatenation of friends, to be allowed to introduce this collection of essays.

The pages that follow are a tribute to the affection, admiration and veneration in which we hold Germain. *Ad multos annos*, let us now say, for our own sakes as much as his, well knowing that the spirit of Thomas More that has inspired him for so long will not desert him as long as he lives.

The British Library

UNIVERSITE CATHOLIQUE DE L'OUEST

3, PLACE ANDRE-LEROY B.P. 808

49005 ANGERS CEDEX   Tel. (41) 88.35.00

le Recteur

Angers, le 27 octobre 1987

Monsieur l'Abbé et cher ami,

    Ceux qui sont à l'origine de ce numéro spécial de Moreana ont souhaité que le Recteur de l'Université Catholique de l'Ouest parle, en tête de ces pages, de votre présence et de votre travail dans une institution où vous enseignez depuis 1952, c'est-à-dire depuis 35 ans ; je n'oublie pas les deux années (1943-1945) où vous étiez ici comme étudiant. Vous avez donc connu cinq Recteurs. Les Recteurs passent, l'Abbé MARC'HADOUR demeure. A vrai dire, ce dernier terme fera sans doute sourire plus d'un collègue en suggérant permanence et stabilité alors que vous avez acquis chez nous une solide réputation de voyageur. Mais j'y reviendrai.

    Votre naissance en Bretagne bilingue vous prédisposait peut-être aux études linguistiques. Je crois savoir, cependant, que vous auriez préféré la Théologie à l'Anglais. En véritable universitaire, vous refusez du reste les frontières : la Bible restera dans votre horizon, et vous ajoutez à une licence d'Anglais obtenue en 1945 des certificats de Latin et de Français.

Après sept ans de cette excellente école pédagogique qu'est le professorat dans le Secondaire, vous arrivez à "la Catho" en 1952, non sans une année de préparation aux Facultés Catholiques de Lyon. Vous avez enseigné, dès le départ, et jusqu'à l'an passé, la philologie, comme on disait alors, et le thème. En littérature que, depuis le décès en 1955 de M. le Chanoine JACQUART, vous partagiez avec votre "patron", M. l'Abbé CHAPEAU, celui-ci vous confiait les domaines de l'Anglo-Saxon et du Moyen-Age. Tous vos étudiants gardent le souvenir d'un professeur chaleureux, d'un pédagogue compétent et clair. Que dire de plus sinon évoquer "les travaux et les jours", corrections et préparations, mais aussi la richesse des contacts quotidiens avec les étudiants. Ceux-ci devenaient, pour la plupart, professeurs dans les établissements catholiques de cet Ouest français qui est le ressort académique de notre Université. C'est pour entretenir et renouveler les connaissances de ces enseignants, et former ceux qui n'avaient pas assez bénéficié d'études universitaires, que la Section d'Anglais organisait, pendant les vacances, des sessions. Celle de 1965, par exemple, a laissé un grand souvenir : la place manquant à l'U.C.O. où le "bâtiment des Lettres" n'était pas encore construit, c'est la toute récente construction de l'Ecole Supérieure d'Electronique qui vous accueillit.

Votre travail de recherche progressait pendant ce temps. Après avoir rêvé du côté de Newman, c'est vers Thomas More et son époque que vous vous êtes dirigé. En mai 1969, après votre soutenance à la Sorbonne vous devenez Docteur ès Lettres avec, comme thèse principale, Thomas More et la Bible, et Thomas More vu par Erasme, comme thèse secondaire. En 1970, le Conseil Supérieur des Evêques de l'U.C.O. vous confère le titre de Professeur.

C'est dès 1962 qu'avait été fondée l'Association des "Amis de Thomas More" dont vous deveniez, dès le départ, Secrétaire International. D'autres diront, sans doute, dans ce volume ce que vous avez fait pour l'Association et pour la revue Moreana. Permettez au Recteur de souligner qu'il n'y a pas deux domaines dans la vie d'un universitaire, dans votre vie : celui de l'enseignant et celui du chercheur. Vos fréquents séjours à l'étranger, pour travailler à l'édition critique des oeuvres de More à Yale University, pour des séminaires, des conférences, dans une cinquantaine d'Universités étrangères, vous conduisirent, bien sûr, à distinguer un semestre d'enseignement à Angers, et un semestre, dans le vaste monde, à la fois de recherche et d'enseignement. Mais, sans parler des retombées de ces voyages et de ces recherches sur le cours du professeur, comment ne pas souligner qu'avec le Centre "Moreanum" que vous animez -- c'est-à-dire dont vous êtes l'âme -- vous êtes de ceux qui ont fait connaître l'Université Catholique de l'Ouest à Angers bien au delà des frontières de la France. Vous figurez au Who's who depuis 1964 ! Combien d'universitaires, combien d' "amis" sont venus à Angers ! Ils y ont peut-être été surpris par la modestie des installations du "Moreanum" ; ils ont certainement été touchés par la chaleur de votre accueil, et ils ont apprécié, je le sais parce que plusieurs me l'ont dit, de rencontrer une communauté universitaire amicale.

Pour en revenir à vous-même tel que je vous vois, je suis frappé aussi de ce que votre grand homme, Thomas More, vous ait permis de ne pas séparer votre vocation d'universitaire et votre vocation de prêtre. Il faut, certes, distinguer l'une et l'autre, mais c'est pour les unir. S'il y a, dans vos travaux sur Thomas More, beaucoup de temps passé au travail d'érudition critique et aux activités d'enseignement, il faut noter aussi les innombrables prédications, voire retraites, sur celui qui ne fut pas seulement un homme d'Etat et un grand écrivain, mais un martyr et un saint. Je ne serais pas étonné que ce choix de Thomas More ait comporté consciemment, pour vous, dès le départ, l'avantage de cette double fidélité.

Comment conclure cette lettre que je ne vous envoie que par le détour de Moreana ? En vous disant tout simplement la reconnaissance de votre "Catho", à l'occasion de ces vingt cinq années de parution de la revue. Reconnaissance et félicitations. Nul n'ignore les soucis d'un responsable de publications, soucis multipliés, pour vous, par les distances et la diversité des langues. Votre temps est bien rempli, et c'est sans doute pour cela que vous courez plus souvent que vous ne marchez ! Ce qui ne vous empêche pas de demeurer calme et souriant. Est-ce la "douceur angevine" qui a déteint sur le breton que vous êtes resté ? Est-ce la douceur franciscaine ? Quoi qu'il en soit de ces hypothèses, le Recteur de l'Université Catholique de l'Ouest ne peut, notamment à l'occasion de ce 25ème anniversaire de Moreana, que se réjouir du travail que vous avez accompli et vous dire : merci ! continuez !

Je vous redis ma très cordiale amitié.

P. OUVRARD

J. B. TRAPP

The Founding of the Amici Thomae Mori

MY DEAR GERMAIN,
It is moving now, after twenty-five years, to hold in one's hands the first modest, cyclostyled number of *Moreana* and to remember the modest beginnings of an organization and a magazine that you alone can truly be said both to have brought into being and maintained by your own more than human efforts.

You will remember, I am sure, even more vividly than I, the foundation of the *Amici Thomae Mori*. Nevertheless, let me give myself at least the pleasure of recalling it, in perhaps superfluous and irrelevant detail. One day in the autumn of 1962 I received a letter from you and another, if memory serves, from the Abbé Jules Jacques in Brussels. He was writing on behalf of the *Compagnons de Thomas More*, a guild of Catholic students from Brussels and other universities in Belgium, to offer an invitation to attend as much as I could manage of a *Quinzaine Thomas More* that he and the *Compagnons* were organizing, under the exalted patronage of Cardinal Suenens, in honour of their patron and to mark the twentieth anniversary of their foundation. The *Quinzaine* was to begin on 22 December and would comprise a series of lectures, to be given — naturally and fittingly — by yourself, and by Louis Martz, the Chairman of the Yale St. Thomas More Project, the Abbé Jacques, and Léon-E. Halkin, together with an exhibition of Thomas More memorabilia in the original and in photocopies. There would also be a ceremonial dinner which was intended in part to mark the foundation of the international society that you were proposing. This society would be conceived on a larger plan than the *Compagnons de Thomas More*. It would be known as the *Amici Thomae Mori* and would consist of all those throughout the world with an interest in or a devotion to Thomas More. There could be no hesitation on my part: this was an occasion at which I would very much wish to be present. Not only, of course, for the occasion itself. I still had the pleasantest and most vivid memories of our meeting and our time together in New Haven in 1960–1961 and of an unforgettable day spent in Angers in July 1962, when David Foxon had driven me from Tours to Angers and both of us back to Tours that evening after a guided tour of Angers by you and Marie-Paule Bataille and the happiest of lunches with Marie-Paule's parents. It would be splendid to see you again.

What precisely was the *Amici*, however, and what the nature of its foundation ceremony? The late Garry Haupt was in London that year to prepare his volume for the Yale *Complete Works*. He too was invited. Louis Martz was also in England, though at Oxford, whence he would bring a book or two from the Bodleian Library for the exhibition. We put our heads together. Of course we would go to Brussels, but could we be sure to be well enough dressed and otherwise prepared for the occasion? Besides, there was the slight embarrassment of how to raise the fare. Garry and I were both fathers of young families and there was little to spare. He could be sure of being suitably dressed, having just managed to buy a new suit. I was not so sure. The problem of the fare was solved by Louis Martz and the late Richard Sylvester with their and the More Project's usual generosity: we were each given a travel grant. Thus secured, we set out on a chilly 27 December on the Dover-Ostend ferry and got to Brussels and the Pension Astoria (recommended by the Abbé Jacques) in good order. There Hubertus Schulte Herbrüggen was already installed. He had been a notable forwarder of the exhibition, but this was our first meeting and the beginning of an unbroken and much valued friendship.

Before we left, it may be worth recalling, Garry and I had been involved in a curious set of circumstances which might have resulted in the presence of More's *Psalter* and *Book of Hours*, now at Yale, in the Brussels exhibition. This was an exciting prospect. No one had seen the book for at least twenty years, and it had last been shown at Chelsea in 1929 and Oxford in 1935. Yale was already interested in acquiring it and Dick Sylvester had asked Garry to find out anything he could about its availability. He and I received an invitation to the flat of a St. James's dealer and were agog. Perhaps we should see and even handle the precious object. Not at all. It was in a bank vault and not even in London: the dealer was an agent for another, Swiss, dealer. On the other hand the prayer-book, which the dealer persisted in calling a manuscript, might be brought to Brussels for the exhibition. Alas, it was too late: the catalogue was printed, the exhibition open, the problems of insurance too great, so that the volume did not figure among the exhibition's four hundred items. All the same, it did get to Yale.

There was still plenty to be grateful for in Brussels: Louis Martz's splendid lecture on *A Dialogue of Comfort*, at which I found myself — well, shanghaied would be the word — into the chair. There was also the expedition which you and I at least — and perhaps Garry and Louis: I don't remember — made to a snowily beautiful and deserted *Maison d'Erasme* at Anderlecht. I do remember your successful hijacking of a passing motorist to get us back into town.

As for the foundation of the *Amici* itself, that was an engagingly modest affair. No fanfares, no ceremony, merely the serene statement by you of the purpose you had in mind to unite Moreans throughout the world and the request for help. Who could deny it? We sat in a circle, if I remember rightly, behind a screen in the Salle Ogivale of the Hôtel de Ville, where the exhibition was shown, seven of us, and found ourselves agreeing to be at once constituted national secretaries. I do not recall that we were characterized as the seven golden candlesticks from whom light would go out, but perhaps that was not absent from at least one mind among those present. At any rate you, of course, would be Secretary for France as well as Secretary General: we were all clear from the beginning that all would depend on you. The Abbé Jacques would deal with Belgium, Hubertus with Germany and Holland, Garry with the USA and I with Britain. So we went our ways home — Garry and I across a difficult Channel to a snowbound Folkestone (Dover had been closed) and no trains to London. Only memories, including that of the *Compagnons'* dinner, sustained us to London.

All this stands out clearly in the memory, as does the generous help offered in England by Dorothea O'Sullivan and Jon Harvey, who introduced me to the Thomas More Society, by Father Bernard Fisher and Monsignor George Tomlinson. Also clear in memory are my own shortcomings in the rôle that I had accepted. Only when the British secretaryship passed into successive more capable hands did the Amici prosper here. No one would deny that the credit for that was and remains yours.

May you allow yourself proper pleasure and even be tempted to a little pride in an association that you founded and have sustained with unremitting and loving care, in the journal that it (or rather you) publishes, in all that you have done to make that journal too a success, and in the opportunity you have given to so many to become friends through Thomas More.

With the warmest of thanks, congratulations and good wishes,

Yours ever,
J

Warburg Institute
University of London

Institution Sainte-Catherine de Sienne
32 rue de la Bastille
44000 NANTES

le 6 octobre 1987.

Cher Monsieur l'Abbé,

Il y a 35 ans, à cette heure précise, nous sortions de la chapelle de Notre-Dame de Joie après les premières Vêpres du Rosaire, et le Père Berto nous présentait l'un à l'autre. Récemment nommé professeur à l'Université Catholique d'Angers, vous passiez quelques jours près de lui, et j'arrivais au noviciat après deux ans en Angleterre. Peu d'Amis, sans doute, peuvent se vanter d'un aussi long bail d'amitié.

Et voilà que nous allons fêter les vingt-cinq ans de **Moreana**... Vais-je vous adresser votre propre éloge ? Votre humilité chrétienne et sacerdotale se rebifferait, et ces usages mondains sont si peu mon affaire que je vais me prévaloir de ces 10 + 25 années d'amitié pour découvrir plutôt ... vos défauts !

D'abord vous êtes très, mais TRÈS attaché à votre terre ancestrale. Vous rappelez-vous ce jour de septembre 1962 où vous regroupiez des amis pour visiter le cachot de saint Thomas More à la Tour de Londres ? Les présentations furent rapides : ... professeur allemand, prêtre canadien, missionnaire au Japon, etc., puis... : « Les deux Soeurs sont Françaises et moi je suis Breton ». Je protestai, mais c'était si vrai !

Vous vous fiez trop aux gens, tenant pour principe qu'il faut montrer de la confiance à tous et que les plus déshérités en ont le plus besoin. Alors, vous laissez le clochard dans votre bureau pendant que vous allez lui préparer un bon casse-croûte, et le clochard file, sans repas mais avec votre montre...

Vos comptes sont très curieusemenet tenus. Vous procédez à des échanges de livres, de publicatons, de timbres : la valeur de ce que vous offrez me semble toujours supérieure à ce que vous récupérez. Et je ne parle pas des cadeaux proprement dits ! Vous m'avez aussi raconté que vous recommandez à vos secrétaires de prendre tout le temps qu'elles désiraient pour regarder et lire tout ce qui les intéressait dans le Moreanum. - « Sur leurs heures de travail rétribué ? -- Bien sûr, cela les cultive. » Ah, le précieux comptable que vous faites !

Et vos déplacements ? Vous parcourez le monde en avion, chantant la gloire de saint Thomas auquel vous avez consacré votre vie, mais qui ne connaît à Angers la vieille bicyclette sans couleur sur laquelle, en vrai Franciscain, vous coltinez de lourds paquets, cahoté sur les pavés, parce que vous ne pouvez pas vous offrir une voiture ?

Vous avez toujours largement, trop largement, consacré à vos étudiants un temps précieux. Je me souviens, en particulier, de vacances de 1958, à Pontcalec : vous y aviez donné rendez-vous à tous les pauvres étudiants par correspondance de la région, pour leur offrir une journé de vrais cours : ils en tirèrent, ravis, joie et profit inestimables, mais la fin de vos vacances vous ramena aussi maigre à Angers.

Et les importuns, celui qui veut un renseignement historique, celle qui cherche une étymologie, l'autre qui réclame des documents, le futur savant que le vrai savant pousse et lance : travailleur acharné, avez-vous jamais su refuser quelque chose, ou même faire attendre une réponse ?

Vous avez un don pour l'amitié, à l'image de votre saint de prédilection. Mais ... quand on a réussi à trouver le moyen de venir passer une heure avec vous, une fois par an, vous avez, vous, jugé bon de convoquer tous les Amici et toutes les Amicae de la ville ; un joyeux, fantaisiste et cosmopolite goûter les réunit tous, mais ... on n'a pu avoir qu'un petit quart d'heure de conversation personnelle avec vous. Qui plus est, sur ce quart d'heure, vous avez invité l'Amica à réciter d'abord avec vous une des Heures du bréviaire : Dieu premier servi.

Voilà ce que vous êtes, un savant, certes, mais surtout un prêtre, c'est-à-dire, selon le mot du Bx Père Chevrier qu'aimait tant à citer le Père Berto, « un homme mangé » -- cela se voit ! -- un homme qui ne s'appartient plus, un homme tout donné, donné à Dieu, à saint Thomas More, aux autres. C'est ce qui résume tous vos défauts. Je me suis permis de les étaler, et j'attends celui, Amicus ou non, qui vous les reprochera...

J'attends aussi, sans crainte, votre pardon, et je vous redis, plus que jamais en cette occasion, mon affectueux et reconnaissant respect.

Soeur Marie-Claire Robineau, O.P.

Au commencement, ton Verbe somma la lumière:
la nuit se retira, et ce fut l'aube de la création.
A mesure qu'invisibles les siècles s'écoulaient,
les eaux se rassemblaient sur la face de la terre
et la vie apparut.

11 ton Verbe somma la lumière

In the beginning your Word summoned light:
night withdrew, and creation dawned.
As ages passed unseen,
waters gathered on the face of the earth
and life appeared.

Faculté de Théologie - Université Catholique de l'Ouest, Angers

le 10 octobre 1987.

Cher Collègue et Ami,

Certains Humanistes de la Renaissance connaissaient et pratiquaient la langue hébraïque. Thomas More était-il du nombre ? Son exemple a-t-il joué dans votre décision d'étudier, vous aussi, personnellement l'hébreu ?

Toujours est-il que vous avez établi un record dans la fréquentation des cours en cette matière à notre Faculté de Théologie : quatorze années d'assiduité, sauf une qui vous a retenu à l'étranger. Magnifique persévérance !

Durant ce cours, de temps à autre, il n'était pas insolite de vous voir intervenir pour un rapprochement linguistique, pour un parallèle biblique ou littéraire que savaient évoquer votre culture sacerdotale ou votre piété personnelle.

Vous goûtiez spécialement les Psaumes et j'avais plaisir à étudier, avec vous et vos compagnons de travail, la structure intime de ces pièces inspirées, la progression de la poésie sémitique à travers des procédés de composition que nous ne connaissons pas en Occident. Vous appreniez par coeur telle et telle pièce, et vous aimez, je le sais, les réciter en compagnie d'autres hébraïsants quand l'occasion se présente. De là vous passez aux versions anciennes, notamment à votre chère Vulgate.

J'en appellerai enfin à votre thèse sur «Thomas More et la Bible». Elle vous a permis d'examiner en profondeur, l'un appuyant l'autre, et le Livre inspiré et votre auteur de prédilection : vers la Bible par Thomas More, vers Thomas More par la Bible ! Vous avez érigé un monument à la mémoire du Chancelier britannique : le « MOREANUM ». Inversement, cette fréquentation vous a conduit à faire une large place au « Corpus Biblicum » des Ecritures sacrées : va-et-vient continuel et combien bénéfique !

En cette publication jubilaire, je suis particulièrement heureux de vous adresser mes félicitations et mes voeux.

L. NEVEU
(30 années Titulaire du
Département d'Hébreu Biblique)

WARD ALLEN

*King James's Translators
and Words on the Wing*

> For M. l'Abbé Germain Marc'hadour:
> Where words are the game, there is
> no hunter more clever than he.

THE FLIGHT OF WORDS ON THE WING is intricate and mysterious. The record of those flights in the *Oxford English Dictionary* evokes ghosts who in lonely study, no historical dictionary at hand, thought about words. Such were Renaissance readers. The words which Shakespeare wrote reveal much about how he read, how words scurried through his mind and imagination. But there is no map of the route words took through his mind. Was he conscious, as thanks to the OED we are, that when he wrote in *Troilus and Cressida*, "And the will dotes that is inclineable To what infectiously it selfe affects," he was introducing a verb, *affect*, from the Latin root, *afficere*, a verb that would overshadow the old *affect*, "To aim at . . . to be fond of . . . to make an ostentatious display of," which had come from the Latin root, *affectare*?[1] The ways of a solitary genius evade detection. A body of learned scholars, who may reveal what Renaissance scholars knew about the history, scope, and current status of English words, will be the object of our chase.

Those scholars were King James's translators of the Bible. Among them were scholars of languages and mathematics, a traveler to the new world who had sifted English for words to describe new experiences, scholars whose memories were filled with literary and theological words. Their translating required them to match in English Hebrew and Greek words, to consult English Bibles made during the sixteenth century, a century when English words were volatile. Although they tested their work against Latin, French, Spanish, Italian, and German Bibles, they were obliged to keep in mind words familiar to a common English reader. My aim is to peep at these translators at work on a few words which called for marginal glosses and to conjecture from these glosses what they knew about English words.

The word *quarrel* has a compact history, brief to tell. Its history begins with the Latin *querela*, man's ancient malady, "a complaint." When *quarrel* first reached English shores, by way of Frenchmen, it meant "a complaint." The last example in the OED for this sense, now obsolete, is dated 1641. The second division of the word is a use now rare, "A ground or occasion of complaint against a person, leading to hostile feeling or action." The history of this meaning spans four hundred years, 1340 to 1772. The third division is "An objection, opposition, dislike or aversion *to* a thing," a use introduced in 1581 and obsolete since the early eighteenth century. The fourth division is our common meaning, introduced in 1572, "A violent contention or altercation *between* persons, or of one person *with* another; a rupture of friendly relations."

Quarrel, used twice in the Authorized Version of the New Testament at Colossians 3:13 and at St. Mark 6:19, translates distinct Greek words. At each place there is a gloss.

St. Paul urges the Colossians to forgive "one another, if any man have a quarrel against any."[2] The gloss for *quarrel* is *complaint*, these two words translating St. Paul's μομφήν, "blame, reproof; cause of complaint."[3] To translate St. Paul's word Tyndale chose *quarrel*, pristine, as yet untouched by sixteenth-century growths. Coverdale, the Genevans, Bishops, and scholars of Rheims followed him. So did King James's men. But for them the word had doubled in size. Since St. Paul writes about complaints among human beings, there was no need to warn a reader about one of the new meanings, an "aversion to a thing." But there was every reason to warn a reader against the fourth meaning, introduced in 1572, "A violent contention or altercation *between* persons, or of one person *with* another." Shakespeare's plays show how rapidly this meaning had spread. Alert to the danger of this new meaning, these scholars added the gloss, *complaint*, which restricted *quarrel* to its etymological bounds. But why did they not, as important modern translations have done, promote *complaint* to the text? Perhaps the unanimity of tradition nudged them to keep the word. Perhaps the emphatic sound of "q" urged them to keep the word. Most likely the meanings of *complaint* which distract a reader from the Greek sense influenced their choice: "The action of. . .grieving" and an "expression of grief" (S). The upshot was that in the text stayed *quarrel*, restricted by *complaint* which has one meaning common to it and *quarrel*.

The other use of *quarrel* comes from Herodias's quarrel against John: "Therefore Herodias had a quarrel against him. . . ." The gloss is *an inward grudge*, which points to the second meaning of *quarrel*, "A ground or occasion of complaint against a person." Tyndale, followed by Coverdale and the Bishops, wrote that Herodias "laid wait for him," the scholars at Rheims that she "lay in wait for him." This phrase translates ἐνεῖχεν which means literally, "had it in" for him. By way of the Geneva Bible (1560) Herodias's quarrel made its way into the AV. A reader may regret that these translators did not elevate *grudge* and drop *quarrel*, a whining and to them troublesome word. But there were meanings of *grudge*, now obsolete, to avoid, such as "scruple, doubt, misgiving" (S). And *grudge* merely passes along information.

Quarrel is dramatic. While the restriction of *quarrel* to its second sense limits the denotation of *quarrel*, its connotations in this story are subtle. Inward grudges ride upon moods. Self-pity carries complaints. On scorn, which turns its enemy into a thing, rides dull aversion to objects. Vigor inflames the heart to scenes of violent altercation. In the connotations of *quarrel* King James's men have caught dramatically a truth of human experience, a truth which exposes Herodias's grudging spirit.

These denotations and connotations of *quarrel* evoke scholars who, with no historical dictionary at hand, knew inside out one English word. Four pairs of words from the first ten verses of Philippians will suggest that these subtle turns are no lucky chance. The words and glosses are *remembrance* and *mention*, *perform* and *finish*, *judgement* and *sense*, *approve* and *try*.

The history of *remembrance* stretches from the fourteenth century to today. One uses it yet in ways that Chaucer understood it, "Memory or recollection in relation to a particular object" or "The memory . . . which one has *of* a thing or person." With the passing of time the word accrued meanings unknown to Chaucer's age and dropped meanings familiar to that age. In 1565 it gained "The point at which one's memory of events begins." The first example of *remembrance* as "Mention, notice," is dated 1375. But that meaning ran thin and disappeared in 1631.

"I thank my God upon every remembrance of you." So goes the AV at Philippians 1:3. There is a gloss, *mention*. The Greek word means either *"remembrance"* or *"mention"* (L&S), as English *remembrance* once meant. Sir Thomas Elyot could write in the sixteenth century, "Gov. I.xviii. I can finde no .. remembrance that it was used of aunctent tyme." Scholars separate the two meanings of μνεία by the verb which governs it. When the verb ποιεῖσθαι governs the noun, the meaning is "to think of, to mention, someone" (K). When the verb ἔχειν governs the noun, the meaning is "to have in remembrance" (K). The murkiness of the distinction between "to think of" and "to mention" in the first definition reveals the uncertain borders of this distinction. King James's men followed the division which modern scholars follow. At Romans 1:9 the verb, ποιεῖσθαι, governs μνεία. So they translated, "I make mention of you." At 2 Timothy 1:3, where the verb ἔχειν governs the noun, they have translated, "I have remembrance of thee." There is no verb to govern μνεία at Philippians 1:3; therefore, it may mean both *remembrance* and *mention*. With a verb to govern the noun, one meaning overshadows, though both meanings are in the idea. Here both meanings are equal. Had they not realized that the sense of *mention* was at a trickle in *remembrance*, the translators would have needed no gloss. But realizing this falling off, they warned readers of the equal footing here of a meaning which ran dry in *remembrance* by 1631.

Perform, at Philippians 1:6, has the gloss, *finish*. The first entry, OED, for *perform* defines the obsolete meaning which these two words describe: "To carry through to completion; to complete, finish, perfect (an action, process, work, etc.)." Examples, which cover a span of two-hundred-and-fifty years, stretch from 1374 to 1620. The second of these includes this verse:

> 1382 Wyclif *Phil.* i.6 He that bigan in 3ou a good work, schal performe til into the day of Jhesu Christ [1611 will performe it (*marg.*) or will finish it; 1881 RV will perfect it].

St. Paul's word, translated by *perform*, is ἐπιτελέσει, "that he which hath begun a good work in you will perform it until the day of Jesus Christ." Tyndale had translated, "shall go forth with it," which Coverdale adopted in his Bible of 1535. But in the Great Bible Coverdale picked up Wyclif's *perform* which the Genevans and Bishops also chose. In the Rheims New Testament, there is *perfect*, but with the old spelling, "perfit."

With this meaning of *perform*, once again King James's scholars have sighted a word on the wing. The date for the last use of this obsolete meaning, 1620, makes clear the reason for the gloss. That the translators did not intend *finish* as an alternate reading for *perform* is clear, since no meaning of *finish* will fit the syntax of the sentence. "Finish this work until I return" does not make sense. Since the flow of this meaning for *perform* was dwindling in 1611, why did not the translators choose some other word, such as *make, do, accomplish,* or *perfect,* which in other places they had used for ἐπιτελέω? *Make* and *do* are unfit because they describe the work but suppress the end of the work; *accomplish* and *perfect* emphasize the end but suppress the work. Of the four words *accomplish* comes closest to *perform*. But there is a subtle difference between them. *Perform* emphasizes the "action, process, work." *Accomplish* emphasizes the "design, desire, promise."

The one other use of *finish* to translate St. Paul's ἐπιτελέω throws into clear light the difference between an emphasis on the work brought through to an end and the end itself:

> Insomuch that we desired Titus, that as he had begun, so he would also finish in you the same grace also. (2 Cor. 8:6)

All Tudor translators have emphasized the end here. Tyndale, Coverdale, the Genevans and Bishops, who had "shall go forth with it" and "perform" in Philippians, have translated here *accomplish*. The Rheims has here, as in Philippians, *perfit. Finish* in the AV carries a sense introduced in 1551 through T. Wilson's *Logike*: "To perfect finally or in detail; to put the final and completing touches to (a thing)." It is this meaning which the translators of the AV chose as a gloss to protect the sense in *perform* of "to complete, finish, perfect (an action, process, work, etc.)."

Judgement in the text and *sense* as its gloss are the English words at Philippians 1:9 for αἰσθήσει, which occurs this one time in the New Testament. St. Paul prays that for the Philippians "love may abound yet more and more in knowledge, and in all judgement." The Greek word means "*sense perception, sensation, . . . perception, . . . knowledge of a thing*" (L&S). St. Paul uses the word to denote "the power of moral discrimination and ethical judgment as distinct from religious" (K). This Greek word has tried translators. Tyndale has *feeling*. Coverdale, the Bishops, and Rheims have *understanding*. The Geneva has *judgement*. The Revised Version and the Revised Standard Version have *discernment*. Phillips, the New English Bible, and the New International Version have *insight*. The New American Bible has *perception*.

An understanding of why the AV has *judgement* in the text with *sense* as a gloss requires a history of these words. *Judgement* has a long and complex history in English; *sense*, a late-comer to English, has a complex history. Examples for *judgement* in the OED begin with 1225, for *sense*, 1400. Specimens for genera of *judgement* from the OED are an action, trial, assignment, decision, conclusion, pronouncing, formation, faculty, decree, ordinance, statute, and function. Its history covers three columns in the OED. The history of *sense* fills eight columns. This history begins with the classification, "Faculty of perception or sensation," under which there are eleven subdivisions. Words shadow man's assumptions. An age which explores feeling will come finally to see feeling as a way to knowledge. The third classification is "Meaning, signification," with eleven subdivisions. An example is from the Preface to Dr. Johnson's Dictionary: "The Solution of all difficulties . . must be sought in the examples, subjoined to the various senses of each word." Beside genera of feeling in the history of this word, the OED lists also genera of intelligence, mental apprehension, and faculties of the soul.

Of the twelve divisions of *judgement* in the OED one only has the genus of faculty. *Judgement* as a faculty came first into English in 1535. Examples prove how useful this concept has been to great literary men: Shakespeare (1599), Milton (1667), Pope (1709), Mackintosh (1832), and J. H. Newman (1870). While *judgement* occurs seventy- six times in the AV New Testament, this is the single use in which the word denotes a critical faculty. Therefore, the translators set this word apart, with a gloss, from *judgement* as "trial, sentence, decision, opinion, or notion." The gloss, *sense*, distinguishes this use of *judgement* as a faculty.

The gloss is not a synonym, for though *sense* may be an apprehension by the mind, the word is predominantly associated with feeling. In rejecting Tyndale's *feeling*, King James's men rejected here the notion of discernment primarily by the senses. By rejecting *understanding*, they rejected the notion of discernment primarily by the mind. *Judgement* as a critical faculty emphasizes the power of the faculty, not the source. As we have learned from Gerhard Delling, St. Paul describes "the power of moral discrimination and ethical judgement" (K). The gloss serves two functions. First, it directs the reader to the specific genus for *judgement*. Secondly, because it describes the faculties which respond to the bodily senses and the "faculties of mind and soul compared and contrasted with the bodily senses," *sense* supplies a sketch of the Greek word and of the complexity of faculties of discernment. But as a gloss it does not commit the text to this explication. *Judgement*, in this sense first used in 1535, became for the translators in 1611 the exact English word to convey St. Paul's meaning.

Approve and *try*, in the tenth verse, translate the Greek word, δοκιμάζειν, that the Philippians may "approve [or, *try*] things that are excellent [or, *differ*]." This Greek verb means to "*assay, test*" and to "*approve, sanction*" (L&S).

Approve is one of those rare instances where a single word comprehends two categories of meaning from two different roots. Obsolete meanings in the first category, "To make good . . . prove, demonstrate" and "To attest (a thing) with some authority . . . confirm" both enter the language with Wyclif. One of the meanings still current, "To pronounce to be good, commend," also has for a source Wyclif. Both meanings in the second category of *approve* are now obsolete: "To put to the proof or test of experience; to try, test" and "To find by experience." Examples of the first stretch from 1380 to 1770, of the second, 1578 until 1651.

Try came into English with a meaning now obsolete, but not obsolete in 1611, "To separate (one thing) from another." Like δοκιμάζειν, *try* once meant to refine metal by fire. Meanings for *try* match both of the obsolete meanings in the second category of *approve*: "To test the strength, goodness, value, truth, or other quality of; to put to the proof, test, prove"; "To have experience of; to undergo, go through," introduced by Lyly and last used by Gray.

Try is not an alternate reading for *approve*, for *try* carries but half of the meaning in δοκιμάζειν. It is rather a comment on *approve*, which in 1611 still carried the full meaning of the Greek, to *commend* and *test*. *Try* supports the idea of test in *approve*. Examples in the OED reveal how that idea had shrunk by 1611 to a trickle. While the last use of *approve* as test occurs in 1770, there are no examples to cover the intervening one-hundred-seventy-four years which follow Shakespeare's use of *approve* in this sense. Although the primary use for this gloss is to sustain *approve*, *try* also suggests the scope for the fundamental idea in the Greek verb of testing, an idea central to both classical and Christian thought.

King James's scholars have taken, in this gloss, the long view of assessing the history of a Greek word and the short view in addressing the current state of two English words. These two views, at hand for us through the OED, they purchased by their learning in languages and by their keeping sharp eyes for English words. John Bois, one of these scholars, showed his old Greek teacher, Andrew Downes, another translator for King James, to have had an eagle eye for words.[4] Bois has described, too, the violence with which Downes argued among the translators for his views. As a student, Bois formed the habit during the summer of continuing in the university library from four in the morning until eight at night. When Bois became chief Greek lecturer for his college, he read Greek lectures to fellows at four in the morning. Such habits and such passion, our examples have shown, may compensate for the lack of a historical dictionary. That deprivation, we may suspect, strengthened the will and sharpened the wits of scholars who had to make their own way through words.

Our last example will suggest an advantage purchased by those who weighed their words in lonely study. Dictionary study frames words analytically. For those who gathered words by reading and memory, there was no wall of analysis between word and life. Such a connection between word and life the word *honest*, at Philippians 4:8, illustrates.

Cicero's *De officiis* instructs his son in moral duties. In the first book of this essay Cicero sketched an intricate discussion, sections XXVII through XLV in scholarly texts, on *decus*, propriety. Propriety shows in our actions and in our surroundings, in our manner of walking and in our dwelling houses. It governs one's choice of words. Clothing reflects *decus*.

These specimens suggest the broad reach which *honestas* has. Cicero states emphatically, by a chiasmus, that *decus* and *honestas* are inseparable:

> Huius vis ea est, ut ab honesto non queat separari; nam et, quod decet, honestum est et, quod honestum est, decet; qualis autem differentia sit honesti et decori, facilius intellegi quam explanari potest.[5]

Examples from the OED show that Englishmen were at home with this idea from 1300 to 1566. Wyclif would have Ruth clothe herself decorously with "honest clothes," the AV with "raiment," the RSV with "your best clothes" (Ruth 3:3). For Wyclif there is a connection between decent clothing and honest character. With *raiment* the connection is between decent clothing and good order. *Your best clothes* is afloat from motive or character.

The breaking apart of *decus* and *honestas*, complete in our day, was a widening fissure in 1611. While the connection between *decus* and *honestas* broke asunder by 1566 for *honest* as "Decent or respectable in appearance," decency held in the adverb *honestly* until 1645. At Romans 13:13, Tyndale translated "Let us walk honestly." The Great Bible, Geneva Bible, Bishops' Bible, and Rheims New Testament follow Tyndale. But the translators of the AV, sensing that in a few years *honestly* and *decently* would cleave apart, placed a gloss for *honestly*, de-

cently. Modern versions illustrate the cleavage which King James's scholars foresaw: ". . . let us conduct ourselves becomingly" (RSV), "Let us live cleanly" (Phillips), "Let us behave with decency" (NEB), "Let us behave decently" (NIV). There is no hint in these versions that decent behaviour is inseparable from an honest heart.

In joining morality and propriety the Greek adjective καλός forms beauty. At Titus 3:14, St. Paul urges Christians to maintain καλῶν ἔργων "good works" as the AV has it, but with the gloss *profess honest trades*. This use of *profess*, now obsolete or archaic, was a brand new word in 1611. Entering English in 1577, this meaning denotes knowledge of and dedication to one's trade. Andrew Downes, a master of Greek, Latin, and English words and a violent contender for words, contributed both *profess* and *honest* to this gloss. The translators in using the adjective *honest* were using a meaning which was the last meaning of *honest* to hold together character and the rightness "Of things, conditions, actions." *Honest* in this sense had its last gasp in a kind of work where antique words linger, a translation of a classical epic, Pope's *Iliad*. But the dead return to life. The New English Bible has for this Greek phrase, "honest employment."

At Philippians 4:8, the AV has the adjective *honest* with yet another shade of meaning, " . . . whatsoever things *are* honest . . . think on these things." The gloss for *honest* is *venerable*. The Greek word for this English is σεμνός, "of human things, *august, stately, majestic*" (L&S). In this place the Greek word shades over into persons: "Only in Phil. 4:8 does σεμνός relate to man's conduct" (K). With this gloss the translators have turned a meaning of *venerable*, which had just entered the English language in 1601, into a gloss for explaining a weakened but noble word. Two words are caught on the wing, *honest* flying out, *venerable* flying in.

Each use of *honest* in these antique senses threads back to the meaning of noble character. St. Luke has described the fertile ground upon which God's word falls, "an honest and good heart," as the AV has it. If one takes *heart* to denote feeling, *honest* represents "Showing uprightness or sincerity of character or intention." If one takes heart to denote the whole person, *honest* signifies "marked by uprightness or probity." In either case the ground of honesty is character. Other uses in the AV of *honest*, which grow out of that ground, evoke Cicero's vision, *decus* and *honestas* bound in one. It is no wonder that King James's scholars held so tenaciously to the word.

Scattered throughout the works of St. Thomas More are biblical allusions, paraphrases and explication of passages, theological debates, and translations. The scholar whom we honor has gathered these references into a single work of five volumes.

The repertory of *The Bible in the Works of St. Thomas More*, compiled by Abbé Germain Marc'hadour, opens to a hunter of words the game in More's biblical translations.[6] More sometimes hit on words which have appeared in later biblical translations. His word "unreprovable," at I Timothy 3:2, reappears in the Geneva Bible. His "communications," at I Corinthians 15:33, found its way into the Rheims New Testament and into the AV. His "wrangling questions," from I Timothy 6:5, which More is quoting from Tyndale in the *Confutation*, reappears in the Revised Version, "wranglings," and the Revised Standard Version, "wrangling."

This phrase, "wrangling questions," translates the Greek word παραδιατριβαί which, as Andrew Downes pointed out, is equivalent to λογομαχίαι, "strifes about words." Some Greek texts have here διαπαρατριβαί, which John Bois thought to signify "continual janglings, or, brablings." In arguing for διαπαρατριβαί Andrew Downes cited St. John Chrysostom, who defines this word as σχολὴ, ἢ Διατριβή, "an academic disputation, wherefore, a School of Philosophy." Beza translated παραδιατριβαί as *perversae exercitationes* and connects this word with schools: *Porro διατριβὰς vocant Graeci quas Quintilianus scholarum exercitationes appellat*. Tyndale caught this academic echo in his New Testament of 1526 where he Englished the Greek as "superfluous disputing." He strengthened the echo in 1535 with "vayne disputacions," a phrase found in the Great, Geneva, and Bishops' Bibles. The AV preserves the academic echo, though muted, with "perverse disputings." But in the margin there is an alternate reading, suggested by Andrew Downes, which denotes John Bois's sense of the word divorced from academic disputations, "continual janglings." The marginal gloss is "gallings one of another." This view wins the day in modern versions: "wranglings" (RV), "wrangling" (RSV), "endless wrangles" (NEB), "constant friction" (NIV), "mutual friction" (NAB). Tyndale's original translation, "superfluous disputings," suggests academic disputes. But his revision, "vayne disputacions," amplifies that echo and puts into clear relief the παρα—which suggests the byways of academic disputes that lead beyond the subject under dispute. Since by 1551 *disputation* had appeared in written English to describe "An exercise in which parties formally sustain, attack, and defend a thesis" (S), we may assume that the word had an academic ring by Tyndale's day. *Wrangle* also had an academic ring. A meaning first found in written English in 1570, but now obsolete, is "to dispute or discuss publicly, as at a university, for or against a thesis" (S). Thus, in appending "wrangling" to "questions" More and Tyndale caught an academic echo as well as the sense "to bicker" (S). So in a single word they have caught the two parts denoted in text and margin of the AV.

This brings us to a warning for all hunters. The "wrangling" in More's *Confutation* is not the same as "wrangling" in modern versions. While of the same genus, it lacks one characteristic of More's. It does not suggest in the least an academic dispute. A hunter of words in flight must keep a keen eye. On the wing a quail and a partridge look alike.

The evidence of this essay leads, I hope, to a tentative assumption that Renaissance men, despite their not having a dictionary assembled on historical principles, had nonetheless a grasp on the status of English words.

Auburn University

Notes

1. All definitions, etymologies, and illustrations for words in this essay are from the *Oxford English Dictionary* or *The Shorter Oxford English Dictionary*. An "S" following a definition will denote the latter.
2. All quotations from the AV are from a 1612 Quarto, Imprinted at London by Robert Barker. I have modernized spelling and the old use of the letters i, u, v, and long s. All quotations from other Tudor Bibles and the Revised Version are from *The New Testament Octapla*, ed. Luther A. Weigle (New York, n.d.). Quotations from the Revised Standard Version are from *The New Oxford Annotated Bible* (New York, 1977). Quotations from *Phillips* and the *New English Bible* are from *The New Testament in Four Versions* (Washington D.C., 1966). I have used the *New International Version* (Grand Rapids, 1984) and *New American Bible* (Iowa Falls, 1986).
3. All definitions of Greek words are from Liddell & Scott, *A Greek-English Lexicon* (Oxford, 1948), or from Gerhard Kittel, *Theological Dictionary of the New Testament* (Grand Rapids, 1983). Quotations from each will be identified in the text by (L&S) or (K). Lists of English words used in the AV to translate a single Greek word come from Ethelbert W. Bullinger, *A Critical Lexicon and Concordance to the English and Greek New Testament* (Grand Rapids, 1975).
4. References to the work of John Bois and Andrew Downes come from Bois's notes, reproduced in Ward Allen, *Translating for King James* (Nash-

ville, 1969). A delightful and rich account of the lives of the translators is found in Gustavus S. Paine's *The Learned Men* (New York, 1959), reprinted as *The Men Behind the King James Version* (Grand Rapids, 1977). Gustavus Paine discovered the copy of John Bois's notes which is in the Bodleian Library.

5. Cicero, *De officiis*, ed. Walter Miller (Cambridge, Mass., 1975).

6. Germain Marc'hadour, *The Bible in the Works of Thomas More* (Nieuwkoop, I, II 1969, III 1970, IV 1971, V 1972).

ANDRÉ GODIN

Notes sur Érasme et le sacré

EN PRÉAMBULE À CES QUELQUES pages offertes à un ami dont l'idéal constant, inscrit dans *Moreana*, est d'unir l'*eruditio* et la *pietas* en une démarche d'humanisme intégral, précisons que notre but n'est pas de rouvrir le débat largement dépassé sur l'orthodoxie du catholicisme érasmien, mais d'éclairer la spécificité d'un humanisme chrétien à partir d'une enquête lexicale en cours sur le mot *sacer* et d'autres vocables exprimant la religion décrite et vécue par Érasme de Rotterdam.

I

Eléments de l'enquête

Les *Adages* fournissent un intéressant point de départ. Lecteur dévorant, Érasme n'a cessé d'enrichir, sa vie durant, ce livre qu'on ne lit plus guère aujourd'hui, recueil pratique de sagesse antique, parsemé d'éclatants morceaux de la *philosophia Christi* chère à son auteur.[1] Dans une lettre de 1514 adressée à son prieur, Servais Roger, le Rotterdamois présente la collection comme "un livre profane à la vérité, mais des plus utile à toute instruction" (Allen 296/570/147). D'une édition à l'autre, le chiffre des proverbes expliqués comprenant le mot *sacer* est passé de six à huit: total infime sur la masse des adages rassemblés, supérieur pourtant aux trois ou quatre attestations d'emploi qu'on finit par trouver, en cherchant bien, dans les 7334 notes de la dernière édition (1535) des *Annotations sur le Nouveau Testament*.

Il est vrai que dans celui-ci, *sacer*, ἱερός, est un hapax: "sacras litteras," ἱερά γράμματα (2 Tim. 3:15) pour désigner l'Écriture sainte. De plus, comme le dit Érasme lui-même en concluant un commentaire psalmique sur lequel nous reviendrons: "l'Écriture ne met guère de différence entre *sacra* et *sancta*."[2] A propos d'un dérivé de *sacer*, *sacramentum*, utilisé par la Vulgate en Eph. 5:32, on observera seulement ici que l'exégète, pour des raisons philologiques et contextuelles évidentes, lui a préféré *mysterium*. Par cette substitution, Érasme allait à l'encontre d'une tradition interprétative erronée qui lisait dans le verset paulinien l'attestation scripturaire du mariage-sacrement. Sans nier la sacramentalité du mariage, à laquelle il croyait *cum Ecclesia*, Érasme déclarait, au terme de son annotation, avoir voulu "examiner si l'on pouvait, à partir de ce passage, enseigner que le mariage est proprement un sacrement, comme on le dit du baptême" (*LB* VI, 855E). Sa réponse était évidemment négative: on devine le tollé et les controverses qu'elle souleva.[3]

Pour en rester aux *Adages*, essayons de repérer les réactions d'Érasme aux prises avec ces reliques vénérables de l'histoire culturelle gréco-latine. Certes, il n'ignore pas le sens primitif du mot "sacré": ce qui appartient à la sphère du divin et diffère radicalement du domaine de la vie profane. On peut le vérifier à propos du proverbe "miscebis sacra profanis," *i.e.*, "tu feras tout pareillement en mêlant ce qui est permis et ce qui ne l'est pas. Les anciens mettaient beaucoup de différence entre les affaires humaines et celles des dieux, au point qu'Homère distingue les mots humains de ceux que les dieux ont l'habitude d'utiliser. Et Pythagore, d'après ce qu'on dit, aurait ordonné qu'on s'abstienne de ce qui avait été consacré aux divinités" (*Ad.* 82, *LB* II, 142D).

On constate un processus de mise à distance critique à propos de l'adage "a sacris abstinendae manus." "Le commun des mortels croit qu'il y a danger de mort si l'on met la main sur des objets sacrés et dédiés à Dieu, si l'on s'attaque à des hommes pieux ou du moins qui exercent des ministères sacrés, par exemple le pontife romain, des évêques, des abbés, même s'ils laissent à désirer quant à la piété des moeurs" (*Ad.* 2845, *ASD* II-6/533/424-27). Sont bien relevés l'aspect tabou, terrible, de ce qui est sacré (objets et personnes), l'instinctif mouvement de recul, analysés maintes et maintes fois par les historiens de la notion;[4] mais ces réactions élémentaires, paniques, sont réservées au *vulgus*. Érasme refuse la "chosification" du sacré et ne manque pas l'occasion d'égratigner les mauvais ministres du sacré, fonctionnaires dévoyés du culte. Il faut souligner ce déplacement d'accent sur l'éthique: les spécialistes chrétiens du sacré ne le sont effectivement qu'en raison de leur sainteté personnelle de vie. L'habit ne fait pas le moine![5]

L'emploi récurrent par Érasme du fameux vers de Virgile "auri sacra fames"[6] confirme cette visée moralisatrice de l'humaniste. L'idée de vouer aux dieux infernaux, encore présente chez le poète latin, fait place à une connotation purement morale. La citation vient spontanément sous la plume d'Érasme pour stigmatiser toutes les formes de cupidité à l'égard des richesses, au premier chef chez les mauvais pasteurs[7] uniquement soucieux de s'enrichir sur le dos de leurs crédules ouailles, en exploitant sans vergogne leur sentiment de culpabilité au moment de la mort[8] ou leur attrait superstitieux pour les objets et les lieux de sacralité les plus chers à la piété médiévale: reliques et pèlerinages. Indépendamment des sentiments personnels d'Érasme, les conséquences objectives de cette volonté critique de moralisation prennent tout leur sens dans une perspective large d'histoire des religions. Analysant un colloque d'Érasme qui aborde l'ensemble du thème pèlerin à partir d'une connaissance directe, j'ai pu y repérer les traces multiformes d'un processus complexe de désacralisation qui, antérieur à Érasme, s'accélère avec les Lumières du dix-huitième siècle, le positivisme du dix-neuvième siècle, et caractérise en profondeur l'histoire culturelle de l'Occident dans sa longue durée.[9]

Pour en revenir aux *Adages*, on observe d'autres glissements de sens dans le commentaire de trois d'entre eux. L'effet de désacralisation s'y trouve précisé, privilégiant le rôle du sujet responsable et minimisant celui des forces extérieures contraignantes censées commander, dans l'antiquité païenne, la force exceptionnelle, la puissance, la sublimité de l'être revêtu de ἱερός. Soit par exemple, l'adage "sacram ancoram solvere," proverbe utilisé chaque fois qu'on se réfugie dans les ultimes secours. Prêchant sur Lazare en son quatrième sermon, Jean Chrysostome appelle ancre sacrée le sanctuaire de la conscience "parce que celle-ci ne supporte jamais que l'homme soit emporté, comme dans une tempête, par la violence des passions."[10] Bien plus, conclut Érasme, elle s'y oppose de toutes ses forces.

Pour autant, il ne s'agit pas d'exalter une personnalité autonome et prométhéenne, coupée de ses enracinements divins, comme l'attestent tant de passages tirés des écrits de notre humaniste chrétien. Mais si Érasme ne met jamais en doute que le Christ et son Évangile soient, pour l'Église secouée par la tempête du Luthéranisme, l'ancre indéfectible de miséricorde,[11] il n'en exprime pas moins son scepticisme sur l'efficacité apostolique de certains de ses serviteurs, en commentant l'adage "sacer manipulus", variante du précédent. Il en rappelle d'abord l'origine supposée. "Il existait autrefois à Thèbes une partie de l'armée nommée ἱερὸν λόχον,[12] constituée par les amants et leurs amantes." Les Thébains voyaient dans ce corps d'armée un fer de lance décisif en cas de guerre. L'amour en effet rend les gens extrêmement forts; il les pousse même à mépriser la mort. Et de conclure ironiquement: "Il sera fait usage du proverbe si quelqu'un dit que la Cause chrétienne de nos jours dépend des moines comme d'un manipule sacré" (*Ad.* 3551, *LB* II, 1088B). Par ce coup de griffe final, Érasme suggère les conséquences néfastes d'une religion formaliste et sans amour pour les combats de l'Église.

Plus allusivement, un autre adage, "sacra haec non aliter constant," dénonce les minuties du ritualisme religieux voisin de la magie et fondé sur la peur. "Le proverbe provient des actes sacrés qui sont accomplis jusqu'au bout par des cérémonies précises: si vous en modifiez un seul détail, vous êtes réputé comme ayant perpétré un sacrilège" (*Ad.* 1388, *LB* II, 548F).

Faisant écho à une critique, très explicite dans l'*Enchiridion militis christiani*[13] et l'*Éloge de la Folie* (*ASD* IV-3, 160/531), du formalisme religieux qui mesure l'intensité de la prière à la quantité de psaumes débités sans comprendre, à la façon des perroquets, l'adage "sacra celerius absolvenda" (*Ad.* 2848, *ASD* II-6, 534/445-55) stigmatise à mots couverts l'attachement scrupuleux à "la lettre qui tue." En matière spirituelle, application et concentration de l'esprit valent mieux que longueur et respect maniaque des formules prescrites. Ce qui compte avant tout c'est la pureté d'intention, l'élan de l'âme priante, à la différence de certains prêtres qui s'attardent trop longtemps à leur messe et à leur bréviaire.

En terminant notre parcours sémantique dans les *Adages*, nous relevons des attestations d'usages franchement profanisés. Ainsi dans l'adage "sacrum sine fumo," Θυσία ἄκαπνος, éclairé par une citation de Lucien (*Amoribus*, 4), auteur grec favori d'Érasme et de More, réputé pour ses qualités littéraires au service d'une oeuvre décapante de démystification religieuse. On désignait par ce proverbe un sacrifice où l'on ne brûlait aucune offrande. L'expression en est venue à désigner un repas trop parcimonieux, quand on ne sert aucun aliment cuit. L'adage fait référence en effet à une pratique sacrificielle des "pauvres qui offrent seulement de la farine sacrée, un peu d'encens, du lait, des guirlandes alors que les dieux, d'après Homère, réclament cette fameuse odeur qui s'élève jusqu'au ciel avec la fumée" (*Ad.* 911, *LB* II, 371C).

Cité d'après Suidas, le proverbe "sacra nihil sunt" signale des victimes maigres qui n'ont rien d'autre que la mâchoire et les cornes. "Non sans art, conclut Érasme, on l'applique à un mets dégoûtant" (*Ad.* 2493, *ASD* II-5, 342/335-38).

De ce piquetage impressionniste dans les *Adages*, il ressort donc que, lorsqu'il n'est pas purement et simplement enregistré comme une catégorie profanisée, le vocabulaire du sacré, en son vêtement aphoristique, escamote les signifiés archaïques – crainte et fascination mêlées face à un objet de sacralité plus ou moins magique, extérieur au sujet – et leur substitue ceux d'un christianisme personnaliste, intériorisé. Les *Adages*, ce livre apparemment le plus éloigné des questions religieuses, dessinent déjà la plupart des traits essentiels de la religion érasmienne.

II

L'Écriture sainte et le sacré

Sous réserve d'un inventaire exhaustif, on peut d'ores et déjà avancer qu'il est rare de trouver, sous la plume d'Érasme, *Scriptura* ou *Scripturae* pour désigner les livres de la Bible. S'impose à lui le recours à l'épithète *sacer*, précisant le sens de différents substantifs plus ou moins synonymes. La dénomination la plus courante reprend la formule paulinienne citée plus haut, "sacrae litterae," par exemple dans la *Vita Hieronymi*: "Jérôme savait par coeur les lettres sacrées."[14] On trouve aussi fréquemment les variantes: "sacri libri, sacra volumina, sacra scriptura, scriptura canonica." Les expressions "litterae divinae, litterae arcanae, mysticae litterae" paraissent moins attestées et relèvent plutôt du cursif rédactionnel ou de la *copia verborum*.

Retraçant le cheminement intellectuel et spirituel du jeune Jérôme,[15] l'un de ses modèles patristiques avérés avec Origène,[16] Érasme écrit dans sa biographie du saint exégète: "Parmi tant d'excellents auteurs qui, par leurs talents, ont défendu et illustré la religion du Christ, ont fait défaut aux uns les lettres séculières, aux autres la connaissance de la sainte Écriture."[17] Le seul des latins qui se puisse comparer aux pères grecs, c'est Jérôme. "Après s'être formé pleinement aux lettres profanes que certains appellent séculières," il appliqua son esprit "aux études de plus de poids."[18]

Si le biographe distingue les ordres d'autorité, ce n'est pas pour les opposer mais pour mieux les unir dans une hiérarchie englobante qui atténue – si elle ne les supprime pas tout à fait – les effets séparateurs habituels du sacré et du profane. Ce que confirme un passage du *Convivium religiosum*,[19] maintes fois commenté par les érasmisants. A quoi tient en effet la sacralité ou la sainteté de l'Écriture? A son auteur divin, certes, mais également au fait qu'elle a puissance de rendre pieux et bons ceux qui en font l'étude et la lecture en une approche respectueuse de son mystère. A ce résultat moral décisif, ont tendu de leur côté plus d'un auteur païen dont les livres ne sont nullement déplacés auprès de ceux de la Bible judéo-chrétienne. C'est tout l'idéal humaniste des *bonae litterae*, littéralement des lettres capables de rendre l'homme meilleur, qu'il faut ici évoquer. Dans le *Banquet religieux*, dont on connaît surtout la fameuse invocation "Saint Socrate, priez pour nous,"[20] l'un des convives, qui était resté silencieux jusque-là dans l'amicale discussion sur des péricopes scripturaires, prend soudain la parole: "Si je croyais permis de mêler à une conversation aussi sainte (*sacris colloquiis*) un extrait des auteurs profanes (*prophanis autoribus*), je vous proposerais moi aussi un passage que j'ai lu aujourd'hui et qui loin de me tracasser m'a procuré d'incomparables délices" (ll. 611-13).

Le maître de maison, Eusèbe (le pieux), porte-parole d'Érasme, lui répond du tac au tac: "Allons! On ne doit pas appeler profane ce qui est pieux et sert la morale. Il est vrai que les Saintes Lettres (*sacris literis*) ont partout l'autorité la plus haute, mais il m'arrive quelquefois de rencontrer des choses dites par les Anciens, ou écrites par des païens, même poètes, et qui ont un caractère si pur, si saint, si divin, que je ne puis croire qu'au moment où ils les écrivaient leur intelligence n'était pas animée par quelque bon génie. Peut-être l'Esprit du Christ se répand-il plus largement que nous ne l'admettons" (ll. 614-19).

Suggérer ainsi l'élargissement indéfini du champ de l'Inspiration divine, n'est-ce pas implicitement dilater à l'extrême l'espace du sacré et réduire considérablement, à la limite rendre caduque, l'idée de séparation radicale entre les sphères du sacré et du profane? En l'occurrence, c'est de toutes façons récuser l'existence de deux couples antagonistes, celui du christianisme annexant tout le sacré en un quasi monopole et celui du paganisme relégué dans les ténèbres du profane.

Légitimés doctrinalement par leur hôte, les amis se mettent alors à commenter un dit de Caton rapporté par Cicéron dans son *De senectute*: problèmes d'authenticité, explication proprement dite assortie de remarques grammaticales et stylistiques, sens et portée du passage, rien ne manque à cet exercice d'exégèse mené exactement comme l'avaient pratiqué les convives dans la séquence précédente à propos d'une péricope paulinienne. Nous touchons peut-être ici à l'explication ultime, on oserait dire structurelle, des audaces ou innovations exégétiques d'Érasme, traducteur et annotateur controversé du Nouveau Testament.

Si l'on peut tenir pour sacrée n'importe quelle écriture, païenne ou chrétienne, qui provoque l'homme à la conversion spirituelle et morale, on peut et on doit en faire l'étude selon d'identiques critères qui sont ceux de l'exégèse humaniste. Les instruments d'analyse en sont la grammaire, la stylistique, la comparaison des manuscrits originaux en vue de retrouver le texte dans sa fraîcheur et sa pureté primitives, voire d'en fournir une traduction. On sait assez que ce travail de restitution critique entraîna dans l'oeuvre aboutie d'Érasme des effets de désacralisation par rapport à la Vulgate que certains adversaires du Rotterdamois, rivés à une conception momifiée du sacré, tenaient pour un texte inspiré, quasiment intangible. Autant que les irrévérences ou indifférences dogmatiques chez l'annotateur chrétien du Nouveau Testament, les antagonismes existentiels au sujet d'une catégorie religieuse fondamentale expliquent l'âpreté de la querelle entre les tenants de l'une et l'autre herméneutique.[21] Et il ne serait peut-être pas sans intérêt de relire, avec ce fil conducteur, les péripéties de la tumultueuse histoire de l'exégèse catholique jusqu'à nos jours.[22]

III

Personnes, actes, lieux et temps sacrés

L'idéal de piété visé par Érasme exclut tout ce qui, de près ou de loin, ressemble à une captation automatique du mystère de Dieu par des rites accomplis sans une adhésion personnelle, transformante,[23] de tous les participants, ministres du culte ou laïcs adonnés aux divers actes de religion. L'essentiel de son effort de critique décapante tendait à purifier les "cérémonies"[24] du caractère superstitieux, formaliste, "judaïque"[25] qu'elles conservaient à son époque et non à les supprimer, en vue d'atteindre peu à peu (*paulatim*) à la religion "en esprit et en vérité" dont parle l'évangile de la Samaritaine (Jn. 4:1–42).

Ainsi en va-t-il par exemple de la messe, acte liturgique essentiel du catholicisme. Dans le colloque Ἰχθυοφαγία (*ASD* I–3, 495–536) qui traite du problème des règles ecclésiastiques concernant le jeûne et l'abstinence, un passage très significatif est consacré à la célébration eucharistique, aux fidèles astreints d'y assister et aux célébrants indignes. Érasme exprime son point de vue par le truchement de deux laïcs, vrais "théologiens populaires,"[26] un poissonnier et un boucher: "Alors que nous lisons que le jour du Seigneur a été institué principalement pour que le peuple chrétien se rassemble afin d'entendre la parole évangélique, celui qui n'écoute pas la messe[27] est abominable; celui qui néglige le sermon, préférant le jeu de paume, celui-là est pur" (ll. 1165-68). Et quelques lignes plus loin: "Qu'ils sont nombreux les prêtres qui aimeraient mieux mourir sur le champ que de sacrifier avec un calice et une patène non encore consacrés par l'évêque ou s'ils sont revêtus du vêtement de tous les jours. Mais parmi ces gens qui sont dans de telles dispositions, qu'ils sont nombreux à oser s'approcher de la sainte table (*sacram mensam*) après une nuit de beuveries et de débauche! Quel trouble, s'il leur arrive de toucher fortuitement le *Corpus Domini* avec une partie de la main qui n'a pas été frottée d'huile sainte (*sacro oleo*)! A plus forte raison, devons-nous veiller à avoir le même scrupule religieux pour ne pas offenser le Seigneur par une âme profane (*animus prophanus*)" (ll. 1172-78).

Et le boucher de renchérir: "Nous ne touchons pas aux vases sacrés (*vasa sacra*), et si d'aventure cela nous arrive, nous pensons avoir commis un sacrilège et entre temps nous violons impunément les temples vivants de l'Esprit saint!" Le poissonnier: "Un décret humain interdit d'admettre aux saints ministères (*sacra ministeria*) un bâtard, un boiteux ou un borgne. Ici, comme nous sommes intraitables! mais par contre nous admettons en vrac des ignorants, des joueurs de dés, des ivrognes, des soldats et des assassins!" (ll. 1179-83).

Sans récuser les médiations humaines de la religion et ses conditions d'exercice, Érasme ne les confond pas avec la réalité divine dont ils ne sont que les instruments contingents. Il ne cesse de renvoyer les chrétiens, clercs et laïcs, à l'essentiel: la pureté d'intention, l'appropriation personnelle, libre et révérante, du Mystère. Le sacré chrétien est intérieur à l'homme: il le porte toujours avec lui. Bien plus, il est en lui. Dès lors, le temps et l'espace humains tout entiers peuvent devenir le cadre d'une sainte liturgie, perpétuelle et universelle.

Commentant, dans l'*Ecclesiastes* (LB V, 792C, F), un passage du *Lévitique* (21:12) qui interdisait au prêtre de quitter le Temple durant l'exercice de sa fonction liturgique, Érasme applique la prescription à la situation présente: "Il s'en éloigne celui qui, la messe dite ou le sermon achevé, vaque à des affaires humaines et profanes." Mais l'injonction s'adresse avant tout à l'évêque, qu'il soit à la Cour, dans un banquet, en bateau ou en chariot: si, par sa vie et ses paroles, il appelle au zèle de la piété, il ne s'éloigne pas de sa sainte fonction, il ne quitte pas le temple.

L'incident des épis arrachés en chemin par les disciples de Jésus le jour du sabbat (Marc 2:26) suscite ce commentaire d'Érasme dans la *Paraphrase* correspondante: "Autrefois il y eut un temps où n'existait pas la religion du sabbat. Il viendra un temps où, pour tous les hommes vraiment pieux, n'importe quel jour sera également sacré. En effet, jamais n'a cessé et jamais ne cessera le temps sanctifié par le fait de porter secours au prochain dans le besoin."[28]

Sanctification du Temps valorisé par la charité, loi immémoriale et éternelle des hommes, mais aussi affirmation du caractère sacré de n'importe quel chrétien, vraiment pieux, susceptible de devenir un temple vivant qui l'emporte sur tous les édifices matériels, et d'abord sur le temple de Jérusalem: telle est également la conviction du paraphraste commentant la rencontre de Jésus avec la Samaritaine (Jn. 4:21). Le culte "en esprit et en vérité" que le Christ a définitivement inauguré "s'opère en des temples plus sacrés (*sacratioribus templis*) que celui de Jérusalem, à savoir dans l'âme pure des hommes."[29]

Par la grâce du baptême en effet, qui fait de lui un prêtre, tout homme devient capable d'accomplir en sa personne l'acte par excellence de religion: le sacrifice.

> Que chacun d'entre nous veille donc, dans son temple intérieur, à sacrifier parfaitement des victimes pures avec pureté, des victimes chastes dans la chasteté. Que dites-vous? Celui qui éteint en lui les brûlures du désir charnel immole à Dieu un bouc excellent et inflige du même coup à Satan son ennemi une blessure mortelle. Celui qui coupe court en son âme aux mouvements de la jalousie offre une hostie agréable. Celui qui comprime en lui la colère bouillonnante immole un lion . . . [30] car, en vérité, pour ce genre de sacrifice il n'est pas d'animaux qu'on ne puisse offrir, soit qu'ils deviennent figure de quelque vice, soit qu'ils deviennent image d'une vertu. Ainsi l'homme qui vit chastement avec son épouse légitime, immole au Seigneur un couple de tourterelles; celui qui gémit dans son désir de la vie céleste et s'attache à être simple envers tous, celui-là offre un couple de colombes . . . Tel est le sacrifice de louange dont Dieu aime être honoré. Tel est le sacrifice de justice qu'il requiert de nous. Tel est le sacrifice de miséricorde qui appelle sur nous la miséricorde du Seigneur. Celui qui, pour l'amour du Christ, vient en aide aux indigents, pardonne à son offenseur, celui-là offre au Seigneur un don tout à fait précieux. Et si, selon le conseil de l'Apôtre (Eph. 5:19), nous chantons sans cesse au Seigneur dans nos cœurs des hymnes et des cantiques spirituels, cette mélodie surpassera

toutes les musiques d'orgue. Sacrifions donc de cette manière et continuellement à Notre Seigneur, avec son aide guerroyons de même contre Satan, afin de passer de ce tabernacle-ci au tabernacle du ciel où nous régnerons tous ensemble avec le Christ.[31]

Telles sont donc les dernières lignes du *Commentaire sur le Psaume quatorze*, écrit six mois avant la mort d'Érasme (1536) à la demande de Christophe Eschenfelder, officier de douanes à Boppard sur le Rhin, marié et père de famille. Un autre passage de ce même commentaire, qui précède de quelques lignes l'extrait cité, évoque lui aussi "la pureté du tabernacle, *i.e.*, de l'Église chrétienne," pour reprendre le sous-titre de cet ouvrage-testament. S'il n'est pas moins fervent que le précédent, le texte que je vais citer me paraît laisser pointer une critique à laquelle Luther aurait pu souscrire; il marque, en tout état de cause, la limite extrême ou une dérive dangereuse (on se gardera de trancher) dans la recherche érasmienne du sacré trop souvent réduit selon lui, par la faute de ses dépositaires, à ses aspects matériels extérieurs, et encombré par les surcharges contingentes accumulées au cours des siècles par un christianisme intempérant en matière de "cérémonies."

En quelques brèves remarques lexicographiques, inscrites dans un magnifique couplet sur la dignité de l'homme chrétien et suscitées, à ce qu'il semble, par l'évocation du fameux verset de la *1ère Epître de Pierre* (2:9: "nation sainte, sacerdoce royal"),[32] le vieil humaniste rappelle le sens courant des trois vocables-clefs du sacré avant de les appliquer aux actes de la vie chrétienne:

> D'après les jurisconsultes, est *saint* ce qu'il est criminel de violer, par exemple les remparts, les portes de ville, le sénat et autres choses semblables; *sacré* ce qui est consacré à une Divinité; *religieux* ce que nous nous abstenons de violer par une sorte de crainte, ainsi les tombeaux. Toutes ces caractéristiques, dans leur ensemble, t'appartiennent en propre, ô chrétien. Avec le Christ tu as été enseveli dans le baptême et tu es mort au monde; tu violes la religion si tu livres ton sépulcre à la dissipation du monde. Tu as été consacré à la sainte Trinité, tu es devenu le temple du Saint Esprit . . . Tu es cordonnier ou foulon, il (*i.e.* ce temple) n'est pas violé par la saleté des peaux ou par le savon mais il est profané par l'orgueil, l'impudicité, la colère, l'avarice et autres immondices de l'âme . . . Tout ce qui jadis s'accomplissait dans le Temple de Salomon ou qui aujourd'hui encore s'accomplit par des rites extérieurs, s'opère spirituellement en chacun de nous, et de façon

plus éminente et plus efficace parce que cela s'opère spirituellement, parce que cela s'opère au-dedans dans la partie la plus éminente de l'homme, parce que cela s'opère divinement. C'est à nous tous qu'est dit ce qui a été dit aux prêtres: "Soyez saints puisque moi le Seigneur votre Dieu je suis saint" (Lev. 19:2). On consacrait non seulement Aaron lui-même, mais aussi ses vêtements et tous les vases du temple. Nul n'était assez téméraire pour oser employer l'un d'eux à des usages domestiques: avec combien plus de scrupule religieux devons-nous prendre garde de rien détourner à un usage je ne dis pas profane, mais honteux, de ce qui a été consacré au culte divin. Les vases de notre temple sont tous nos membres, toutes les forces de notre âme; les vêtements sont nos actions dont nous sommes parés pour la gloire de Dieu. Tu admires un temple bâti de marbre blanc, éclatant de pierreries et d'or: mais tu es un temple plus précieux. Tu es saisi d'un respect religieux quand tu te trouves dans un temple qu'un évêque a consacré par une onction: toi, tu es plus sacré. Tu n'as pas été oint de l'huile sacerdotale. Et alors quoi? Le Christ non plus n'a jamais été oint de l'onction mosaïque, bien qu'il soit roi des rois et prêtre pour l'éternité. Ta tête et tes mains n'ont pas été oints de l'huile que fabriquent les droguistes, mais tu as été oint tout entier du sang de Jésus Christ l'agneau immolé. Heureusement oint qui a le coeur oint de l'Esprit. Du reste, l'onction extérieure ne te fait pas défaut. Tu as été oint lors du baptême, tu as été oint lors du sacrement de confirmation, là pour le sacerdoce, ici pour le combat. Le Seigneur proclame par le Prophète: "Ne touchez pas à mes christs" (Ps. 105:15), *i.e.* à mes oints. Et Jean déclare: "Son onction vous instruira de tout" (cf. 1 Jn. 2:27), en parlant non seulement aux prêtres, mais aussi à tous les baptisés.[33]

Soit qu'on y découvre en chrétien l'annonce prophétique des documents libérateurs du concile Vatican-II, soit qu'on les relise en référence à une époque qui multiplie les manifestations d'une sécularisation à outrance en même temps que les traits multiformes, anarchiques même, d'un retour au sacré, les textes érasmiens, ici rassemblés pour marquer le "jubilé d'argent" de *Moreana* et remercier son infatigable animateur, sont assurément — en leur foisonnante complexité — autant de pierres vives qui édifient ce temple sacré, l'homme en quête de lui-même et de son dépassement.

Centre National de la Recherche Scientifique
Paris

Notes

Références brèves incorporées dans le texte.
Ad. = Erasme, *Adagia*, numéro . . . (+ source).
Allen = P. S. Allen éd., *Opus Epistolarum Des. Erasmi*, Oxford, 1906-58, lettre numéro . . ./page/ligne.
ASD = *Erasmi Opera Omnia*, Amsterdam, 1969–, tome, page/ligne.
LB = J. Leclerc, *Erasmi Opera Omnia*, Leyde, 1703-09, tome, colonne, lettre.

1. Margaret Mann Phillips, *The Adages of Erasmus: A Study with Translations* (Cambridge University Press, 1964). Voir aussi plus bas, p. 135 n. 1.
2. *Enarratio psalmi* XIV, ASD V-2, 314/947.
3. J. B. Payne, *Erasmus, His Theology of the Sacraments* (Richmond, VA, 1970), 112-21.
4. Par ex., R. Otto, *Le Sacré* . . . , trad. A. Jundt (Paris, 1949); A. Dumas, art. "Sacré" in *Encyclopaedia Universalis*, 14, (Paris, 1985), col. 335-38. Dans une lettre de 1527, Erasme formule ainsi la bipolarité du sacré qu'organise la religion: "Religio sonat proprie venerationem cum horrore tremoreque coniunctam," le mot "religion" signifie proprement la vénération jointe à l'horreur et à la crainte (Allen 1877/178/326-27).
5. Cf. H. Holborn éd., *Erasmus . . . Ausgewählte Werke* (Munich, 1933, repr. Munich, 1964) = . . . *Enchiridion militis christiani*; . . . *Ratio seu methodus . . . ad veram theologiam*; Enchiridion 135/8: "Monachatus non est pietas," l'état monastique n'est pas la sainteté.
6. Virgile, *Énéide* 3, 57; Allen 1211/512/186.
7. Évêques ou prêtres dont le comportement répond si mal à leur nom. "Ils oublient que leur nom d'évêque signifie labeur, vigilance, sollicitude, mais, surveillants clairvoyants, ils fonctionnent tout à fait épiscopalement en prenant l'argent au filet!" Cf. Mc 1:17; *Moriae Encomium*, ASD IV-3, 170/750 sq. Quant aux prêtres (*Ibid.*, 176/841-85), ils feraient bien de se souvenir que "sacerdos non a saccis (bourses) sed a sacris tractantibus dictus est" (*Ecclesiastes*, LB V, 914 B).
8. Voir, entre autres, le colloque *Funus*, ASD I-3, 539-44/85-254.
9. A. Godin, "Érasme et le Sacré: *Peregrinatio religionis ergo*" in *1536-1986. Dix conférences sur Érasme. Éloge de la Folie–Colloques* (Paris-Genève, 1988), 121-46.
10. Ad. 24, LB II, 35 F. Cf. aussi Ad. 3564, LB II 1091 C.
11. Allen 1977/365/6-7. De même: *Enchiridion* (n. 5 supra), 7/30; *Ratio* (ibid.) 204/12. Cf. M. O'Rourke Boyle, *Erasmus on Language and Method in Theology* (Toronto, 1977), 60-61.
12. Cf. Denys d'Halicarnasse, *Dinarque* 99, 25; Plutarque, *Pelop.* 18, etc. Erasme renvoie uniquement au livre 13 du *Banquet des Sophistes* d'Athénée, écrivain grec qu'il appréciait et dont il possédait un exemplaire aujourd'hui conservé à la Bodléienne.
13. *Enchiridion*, (n. 5 supra), 30/1-10.
14. *Eximii doctoris Hieronymi Stridonensis Vita*, in W. K. Ferguson, *Erasmi opuscula. A Supplement to the Opera Omnia* (La Haye, 1933), 151/490. De

même, *Vitae Origenis Adamantii epitome*, LB VIII, 438 B. Cf. A. Godin, *Érasme. Vies de Jean Vitrier et de John Colet* (Angers, 1982), 29, n. 44.

15. C'est par l'héroïcité de sa vie "pieuse et sainte" que Jérôme a bien mérité son nom sacré: Ἱερώνομος, précise Érasme, en un jeu de mots qui déporte à nouveau vers l'éthique la notion de sacré, *Hieronymi Vita* (cf. n. 14), 140/155-64. Cf. *supra*, n. 7 et G. Marc'hadour, "Thomas More, les arcanes d'un nom," *Moreana* 5 (1965): 73-75.

16. A. Godin, *Érasme lecteur d'Origène*, "Travaux d'Humanisme et Renaissance," n CXC (Genève, 1982).

17. *Hieronymi Vita* (n. 14 *supra*), 187/1451-54.

18. *Ibid.*, 144/264-65.

19. *ASD*, I-3, 231-66. A défaut d'y déceler l'idéal érasmien de la messe, comme le suggèrent certains commentateurs (v.g. J. Chomarat, *Grammaire et Rhétorique chez Érasme*, I (Paris, 1981), p. 705), le fond et la forme de cet admirable colloque, avec—entre autres—son ordre de préséance quasi liturgique des lectures (Ancien Testament, Épîtres de Paul, Évangile), permettent au moins de dire qu'Érasme, par son fervent biblicisme, a esquissé dans le *Banquet religieux* un modèle plus scripturaire de célébration eucharistique: voir A. Godin, "La Bible et la philosophie chrétienne," in *Bible de tous les Temps*, t. V, dir. G. Bedouelle et B. Roussel (Paris, 1989), 580-86.

20. *ASD* I-3, 254/710. Voir R. Marcel, " 'Saint Socrate,' Patron de l'Humanisme," *Revue internationale de philosophie*, t. I, (Bruxelles, 1951), 135-43. Traductions empruntées à *Érasme. Cinq banquets*, dir. J. Chomarat et J. Ménager (Paris, 1981), 85.

21. Voir J. Chomarat (*supra* n. 19), I, 502, et A. Godin (cf. *supra* n. 16), 170-74.

22. Sujet tabou pour la haute hiérarchie catholique, il est probable que la question du célibat ecclésiastique a beaucoup à voir avec une certaine conception du sacré, assez étrangère à Érasme mais très répandue en son temps. Voir là-dessus les pénétrantes analyses de J. P. Massaut, "Vers la Réforme catholique. Le célibat dans l'idéal sacerdotal de Josse Clichtove," in *Sacerdoce et célibat*, éd. J. Coppens (Louvain-Gembloux), 463-78.

23. Sur l'importance de ce verbe et de ses synonymes (v.g. *transfigurari*) dans l'oeuvre érasmienne, voir A. Godin (n. 16 *supra*) 42, 66-67, 258-59, 390-91.

24. Terme générique et récurrent pour désigner n'importe quel acte du culte, liturgique ou non, public ou privé. Cette dénomination englobe également les divers sacrements de l'Église. "Je ne blâme aucunement les cérémonies corporelles des chrétiens et les dévotions des simples, celles-là surtout que l'autorité ecclésiastique a approuvées. Elles sont en effet quelquefois soit des signes, soit des adjuvants de la piété," *Enchiridion* (cf. *supra* n. 5), 76/29-31. Elles ont un rôle pédagogique, provisoire peut-être dans l'utopie religieuse d'Érasme, qui reproche sans trêve aux laïcs et aux clercs (plus coupables que les premiers, *ibid.*, 77/14-15) de placer en elles la fin, "le faîte de la religion" (77/1).

25. Voir A. Godin, "L'antijudaïsme d'Érasme: Équivoques d'un modèle

théologique," in *Bibliothèque d'Humanisme et Renaissance*, t. XLVII (1985):537-53.

26. *Methodus*, Holborn (n. 5 *supra*), 155/27.

27. Érasme écrit indifféremment "audire missam" ou "audire sacrum" (*Ratio*, cf. *supra* n. 5, 274/8). On aura noté la minimisation de l'aspect proprement sacrificiel, à tout le moins l'insistance sur la table de la Parole qui comprend évidemment le sermon, dont Érasme se fait une si haute idée que dans la *Ratio* (301/11-12), il s'exclame: "Pourquoi ne dirais-je pas sacrées les prédications, alors qu'autrefois elles faisaient partie du sacrifice?" En 1533, effrayé par le radicalisme des Protestants, il en revient aux positions traditionnelles: la messe, renouvellement du sacrifice unique du Christ sur la Croix; affirmation de la Présence réelle, assortie cependant de remarques critiques, entre autres sur la dévotion superstitieuse des fidèles à l'égard de l'élévation, pratique inconnue du christianisme ancien. Distinguant l'essentiel de l'accessoire, il propose en somme un "aggiornamento" des rites et laisse au concile à venir le soin de trancher sur les questions controversées entre théologiens, v.g. le mode de présence du Christ dans l'Eucharistie: *De sarcienda Ecclesiae concordia*, ASD V-3, 307/747, 310/862. A lire l'ensemble de ce traité irénique, oecuménique avant la lettre, on comprend mieux comment il a pu inspirer, dans les années 1540, la politique impériale dite des "Colloques."

28. *Paraph. in Mc*, LB VII, 178 C. Voir aussi le commentaire, très détaillé, du verset 27: "temple, victimes, nourriture, vêtement, jours de fête, jeûnes, voeux, dons," bref toute la religion, expression visible du sacré, se mesure uniquement à l'aune de la charité, dont la dynamique est elle-même réglée, selon Erasme, par l'incessant passage du visible à l'invisible, du charnel au spirituel. On observe "irreligiose" les cérémonies "corporelles" (*corporalia*), chaque fois qu'elles blessent tout ce qui concerne "le salut du prochain." L'observance "la plus religieuse" consiste donc à les subordonner au service d'autrui et à intérioriser constamment ces "ombres" des biens à venir. Telle est "la maxime catholique" que le Christ oppose à la fausse (*perverse*) religion des Pharisiens: *Ibid.*, 179 A-D. Avec A. Dumas (art. "sacré" col. 338 – cf. *supra* n. 4) paraphrasant le célèbre verset de l'Évangile selon saint Marc, on dirait volontiers que pour Érasme aussi "le sacré demeure fait pour l'homme et non l'homme pour le sacré." Ou, avec Bernanos (*Dialogues des Carmélites*): "Ce n'est pas la règle qui nous garde; c'est nous qui gardons la règle." La liberté humaine fonde et justifie la Loi comme le sacré.

29. *Paraphr. in Ioh.*, LB VII, 528 F.

30. Érasme énumère ici tout un bestiaire allégorique qui doit autant à sa culture biblique qu'aux représentations populaires: sacrifier une brebis, c'est rejeter la sottise et l'ignorance; un veau, l'insolence; un renard, la fourberie; un porc, la débauche; une pie, les sots bavardages.

31. *Enarr. psalm.* XIV, ASD V-2, 315/971, 316/999.

32. Est-ce tout à fait un hasard si l'essai sémantique d'Érasme intervient seulement à propos d'un passage qui sert à Luther de bélier scripturaire majeur pour abattre "la première muraille," ce cloisonnement traditionnel entre les spécialistes du sacré et les autres, i.e. les laïcs appelés au "sacerdoce univer-

sel?" Pour de plus amples développements sur l'apport, décisif, de la Réforme à la constitution d'une société occidentale de l'homogénéité sociale, avec— organisatrice de ses valeurs— la triade neuve individu-liberté-conscience, voir A. Dupront, "Réformes et 'modernité' " (Leçon finale), in *Les Réformes, enracinement socio-culturel*, éds. B. Chevalier et R. Sauzet (Paris, 1985), 415-34.
33. *Enarr. cit.* (n. 31), 314/927, 315/970. Noter le martèlement des termes "onction" et "oindre," qui signale, de toutes les façons possibles, la sacralisation éminente de l'homme chrétien devenu prêtre. Pour éclairer par contraste ce passage, qui pose indirectement le problème du pouvoir hiérarchique dans l'Église mais où l'on se gardera de lire anachroniquement l'utopie contemporaine d'un sacerdoce sans cléricature, consulter J. P. Massaut, "Thèmes ecclésiologiques dans les controverses antiluthériennes de Clichtove: pouvoir-ordre-hiérarchie," in *Les Réformes*, (cf. n. 32 *supra*), 331-32. Ici encore (cf. *supra*, n. 22), l'auteur a bien perçu à quel point sont imbriquées, pour les tenants d'une certaine conception du sacré/séparation, les questions nodales du pouvoir et du célibat ecclésiastiques. En outre, une investigation psychanalytique du trio sacré-sexualité-pouvoir, en oeuvre chez Érasme et dans l'histoire de l'Église, donnerait probablement leur pleine assise anthropologique à nos analyses fragmentaires.

BRENDA   HOSINGTON

"Quid dormitis?":
More's Use of Sleep
As a Motif in De Tristitia

THOMAS MORE'S FINAL WORK, *De Tristitia, tedio, pauore, et oratione christi ante captionem eius*,[1] the third of what have come to be known as "The Tower Works," recounts the gospel narrative of Christ's agony in the Garden of Gethsemane and his subsequent betrayal and arrest. It is both an exegetical commentary and a devotional treatise, both a public and a private composition.[2] Like the accounts in Matthew, Mark, Luke, and in Jean Gerson's *Monotessaron*, More's avowed source, *De Tristitia* divides naturally into two parts: Christ's agony and his arrest. Unlike Matthew, Luke, and Gerson, however, More chose to concentrate more attention on the first part (roughly sixty per cent). Of the 310 folio pages of the Valencia manuscript roughly one third contain references to sleep and related concepts such as sloth (*desidia, ignavia, segnitia*), laziness (*pigricia*), sluggishness (*socordia*), and apathy (*torpor*), and to their opposites, wakefulness (*vigilantia*), watchfulness (*pervigilium*) and diligence (*diligentia*). The vast majority of these occur in the first part of the work, which is not surprising since it recounts Christ's injunctions to stay awake and pray and his discoveries of the disobedient apostles sleeping. What is surprising, however, is the number of references to sleep and watchfulness and the way in which they develop. Germain Marc'hadour has pointed out how the two phrases, "stay awake and pray that you may not enter into temptation" and "for the spirit indeed is willing but the flesh is weak" (159/5–7), "fournissent à More la matière d'une trame serrée, où s'entrecoupent des fils majeurs : prière et vigilance, infirmité de la chair et allégresse d'esprit, tentation et tentateur."[3] In fact, the metaphor of the tightly-woven web can be applied equally well to the phrases, "[Christ] went to the disciples and found them sleeping" and "he found them sleeping for sadness," and to the question, "Why are you sleeping?" In the network of sleep and waking images these phrases inspire in the first part of the *De Tristitia* there is also an intersecting of major "threads": slothful disregard for God's orders, the wrongness of seeking consolation in sleep, and the folly of sleeping when danger is at hand. It is the purpose of the present article to discuss the thematic significance of the sleep motif, but also to explore the way in which the various images form a structural pattern in the first part of the work and contribute to its literary qualities.

The two central topics of concern to More in *De Tristitia* are the fear which Christ and the martyrs felt when faced with suffering and death, and the importance of good praying habits. Related to this second theme is the more general question of man's spiritual sloth and its dangers. The motif of sleep is used in discussing all three.

A reference to sleep appears only once—and this briefly—in relation to the theme of martyrdom. The need to sleep serves as a sign of Christ's humanity, says More, along with other bodily needs like hunger and thirst, or with normal emotions like weariness and fear (51/5-7, 53/1, 89/6). The *lassitudo* Christ felt (89/6) should not be interpreted as "slackness" or "sloth" (*socordia*) in accepting martyrdom and quoted as a precedent by fearful and hesitant martyrs. Rather, they should emulate Christ's victory over such human needs as sleep, won by means of prayer. Sleep is not in itself bad, for it is a natural function;[4] it becomes an instrument of evil only when it interferes with our accomplishment of duty or acceptance of martyrdom.

In the discussion of prayer, his second major theme, More leans much more heavily on images of sleep and sloth to make his points. From the opening words of Gerson's narrative, "Hec quum dixisset Iesus / hymno dicto exierunt in montem Oliueti" (3/3), More extracts two ideas: how to pray and when to pray. Whereas Christ and the apostles sang a hymn of thanks for the meal, we just manage to mumble grace through our yawns. And where they went out into the night, "and not to bed," we turn our thoughts to sleeping (7/5-7). More then introduces a figure who stands midway between Christ and us: the prophet of the Psalms who rises at midnight to pray and who thinks of God even when he is in bed.[5] The contrast between good and bad praying habits is elaborated upon a little later (33/1-2). Christ had the *custom* of spending whole nights in prayer, whereas those who sacrifice a little sleep to pray on special occasions pride themselves on their virtue (31/3-6, 33/1- 2). He also prayed at night in the open air, whereas the hypocritical pharisee "molli stertebat in lecto" (35/3-4). This leads into a comment on Christians in general that echoes the earlier observation concerning the prophet: even if too lazy to emulate Christ, we should at least remember his all-night vigils and offer a moment of prayer when, More says with a touch of wry realism, we turn over in our beds, half-asleep (35-37).[6]

The discussion on how to pray continues with the gospel words, "et progressus pusillum procidit in faciem suam super terram et orabat" (111/5-6). More invites his readers to contemplate Christ's posture and thereby correct their lazy, sleepy way of approaching God (*segniter*, 115/8, and *sompnocenti*, 117/1). He uses an analogy to reinforce his point that we must concentrate while praying. The minds of those who pray negligently are besieged by fantasies, as the mind of the sleeper is besieged by dreams (119/8-123/3).[7] As one should prepare one's mind for prayer by concentrating, so one should assume an appropriate stance. In a passage whose direct and almost bantering tone is reminiscent of the *Utopia*, More asks if we would yawn and stretch in the presence of a temporal prince as we do in the presence of God (133/4). Again, he sets up the three-figure contrast to illustrate his point: Christ lay prostrate to pray, the prophet of Psalm 62 lay on his bed thinking of God but rose to pray, we lounge, or need cushions to support us. The vocabulary chosen points up the difference in the three postures: Christ, we are told, "procidit", denoting a posture of humility; the prophet simply "fuit super stratum"; we however lie back, "corporis incuria et supinitate." It is acceptable to pray lying down (*cubantem*) but only as long as we are thinking on God.

If we must pray diligently, we must also pray constantly, night and day, because prayer is both useful and extremely necessary in order to combat the temptations of the flesh, one of which is sleep (167/9-11). More reminds us that Christ said not just *vigilate* but *vigilate et orate*, not just occasionally but constantly, and not just in the day, as we doze and yawn, but even at night-time when we would usually be asleep (171/7-11, 173/1-3). Constant prayer is also a powerful aid when we weary in following God's path. The verb More uses is not the *tedere* of the work's title, which means to become spiritually weary or discouraged, but *languere*, to be physically tired, or sluggish (205/5). Sometimes we progress so slothfully (*segniter*) or are hampered by weak irresolution (*mollici*), and laziness (*pigricia*), so that we need to beg God to pull us along with him. We must however pray earnestly, not lazily or carelessly (227/6) if we are to be given the right kind of consolation.[8] Lastly, prayer will ensure forgiveness of past sins, help us deal with the present, and act as a surety for the future, but again our prayers must be said not lazily and yawningly (*oscitanter*) "but incessantly and fervently" (311/9-10).

More insists on the need for diligent and constant prayer because the sleep of the Apostles in the Gethsemane narrative represents for him the spiritual sloth into which we all slip on occasion. The dangers of such sleep are many and appear throughout the *De Tristitia*. Drowsiness (*sompnolentia*) prevents us from understanding the significance of biblical names, which in turn causes us to misinterpret God's purpose in the world (17/5). When sloth (*desidia*) overtakes us, fondness for prayer is the first of our virtues to disappear.* (209/1-2). Laziness (*pigricia*) makes us neglect our prayers. Sleep blunts our feelings, even for Christ whom we should love most (159/3-4), as the narrative clearly shows when Christ returns to the Apostles to find them sleeping. It also prevents us from holding firm and obeying God's will, as is sharply emphasized in Jesus' words to Peter: "Simon, dormis? non potuisti una hora uigilare mecum?" (159/5-6). The double "sting" in Christ's use of "Simon" rather than "Peter" is directed at the Apostle's having fallen asleep, More asserts. Peter means "firmness," hardly applicable for one so "infirm" that he cannot keep awake; "Simon" means "listening" and "obedient," no less inappropriate, for Peter has made himself deaf with sleep and in so doing has disobeyed. Furthermore, he has laid himself open to another danger: sleep has made him defenceless at the very moment that Satan is "seeking to sift the Apostles like wheat" (167/1). The readiest of the band to defend Christ, he will deny his Master thrice before the night is out.

The traditional association of sleep with the traps and snares of the devil and the workings of evil at night, found both in the Bible and patristic and exegetical writings, must have influenced More's imagination very strongly, for it appears seven additional times in the *De Tristitia*, as well as in several of his other works. Evil never sleeps; rather, it keeps watch while we sleep. Thus while the Apostles slumbered, Judas was "so wide awake that the idea of sleep never entered his mind" (259/3-5). Later, More says that we stumble into temptations and traps (*insidia*) set by the devil because our eyes are closed, yet we slumber on, "watching the dream visions induced by mandragora," rather than praying (307). The association of sleep with the devil is elaborated upon in the metaphor of the castle of the soul, to which we deny prayer entry when we sleep and into which we consequently allow the "besieging troops of the devil to break" (311/1-2). The Apostles overestimated their power to overcome these troops, as witnessed in their succumbing to sleep while danger was at hand (333/5-9).[9] The question is revived in the second half of the work. Sleep enabled the devil to weaken the will of all the Apostles, "nutantes et incogitantes"; thus unprepared to face the imminent danger with forbearance, they either fought or fled (563).

Again in the tradition of exegetical and homiletic writings, More uses sleep, in both *De Tristitia* and his other works, as a metaphor for man's state of sinfulness and vice.[10] As we are "slumbering on the pillow of our sins," God in his goodness . . . "shakes us, strikes us, and does His best to wake us up" (203/1-3). Sometimes, however, we are "so fast asleep in our vices" (211/7) that even God's calls cannot arouse us; like Jesus in the Garden of Gethsemane, he leaves us to sleep. More then passes from the general to the specific by associating sleep with the type of sin that threatens the very church itself through the administrations of unworthy prelates and priests, and of heretics. He suggests that the scene contrasting the sleeping apostles and vigilant traitor clearly projects "as if in a mirror" (259/7-8) an image of the state of the church throughout the ages: sleeping and apathetic bishops too slothful to protect the truth or defend their flocks from Christ's vigilant enemies. Some are even worse than the apostles, for their sleep is induced not by sadness but by "the new wine of the devil, the flesh and the world" (259-263). Others are so overcome by dejection (*maestitia*) and sleep that they neglect their duty (265/3-8). No better are priests who administer the sacrament unworthily and neglect their duty to stay awake and pray for their people (351).[11] Worst, however, are the heretics. Like the devil and Judas, they are constantly awake, ready to spread evil and betray Christ.[12] Again, More interprets the scene of the sleeping apostles tropologically, calling it an "imaginem ac mysterium temporis futuri" (341/5). The added "dormientibus discipulis quum traderetur filius hominis" (341/4-5), as Miller points out (p. 917), introduces the sleep-betrayal association in preparation for the following section, where it becomes an important theme. We must not sit and sleep or be caught snoring, cautions More, if we are to combat the threat to Christians by Turks from without and by heretical sects from within. Christ's question, "Quid dormitis?" applies to us all: Why are we sleeping in the face of heresy, that "creeping disease" which, like a slowly but surely spreading cancer, betrays Christ and his followers? (347-51).

The description of sleep as a disease had been used a little earlier. Christ offers a remedy for "that sluggish disease of somnolence" (*ignavam sompnolentiae morbum*), one More wishes we would apply occasionally: getting up and praying (303). The disease metaphor leads into a passage containing two other figures of speech that describe the dangers of sleep, both found in exegetical and devotional writings. More had spoken earlier of the Apostles being "buried" in sleep (*sepultos*) (259/1), and the bishops being "lulled to sleep and buried" (*sopiti et sepulti*) in destructive desires, sleeping, "like pigs sprawling in the mire" (263/1–2); now he explicitly calls sleep the "very image of death"[13] and warns us to resist its seductive powers:

> Itaque non est lucta sensim superandus sompnus sed illecebrosa brachia quibus nos amplectitur et reclinat semel impetu diuellenda sunt nobisque protinus ab eo proruendum. Tum uero ubi semel sompnum desidem mortis uidelicet imaginem reiecerimus uitae succedet alacritas. (305/2–6)

Casting off sleep is also the only way to fight one final danger: sadness, the *tristitia* of the work's title. While recognizing the source of the Apostles' sadness—the knowledge that their Master was in imminent danger—More criticizes the fact that they succumbed to it by falling asleep.[14] Such sadness leads to heavy-heartedness (*maestitia*) and then despair, for we abandon hope and seek refuge in sleep. Ultimately, it will lead to hell, as More tells us in his criticism of the dejected, sleeping bishops who neglect their duty (265/3–7), for God gives sinners chances that, if asleep, they cannot but ignore (283/1–2). Consolation in sleep, unlike the true consolation prayer provides, fails to relieve our troubled minds and, weary, we fall unseeingly (*oculis clausis*) into the devil's traps (287).

The three-part structure of the account of the agony in the garden was imposed on More by the Gospel narrative: Christ three times leaves the apostles in order to pray, telling them to do likewise, but returns to find them sleeping. Within this overall structure, however, More was free to elaborate on or condense his materials, shift emphasis, and establish a more complex pattern or "sub-structure" of references to sleep. The characteristic feature of this pattern is the establishment of balanced parallels and contrasts, or polarities.[15]

The pattern of sleep references develops in a tightly-ordered sequence. The first ten folios constitute a type of introduction: Christ and the apostles recite a hymn, cross the brook Cedron, and enter the Garden of Gethsemane, where Judas knew they often went. More sets up a series of polarities revolving around sleeping and watching in order to present his two subjects: the need for constant and proper prayer and the evils of sleep and sloth. Thus he contrasts Jesus and the vigilant prophet with us slothful Christians; the ever-vigilant Jesus with the sometimes-vigilant pharisee; the hymn-singing Christ and his apostles with us, mumbling our grace yawningly; the care taken by the evangelists to include in their narrative significant biblical names with the drowsiness that prevents us from comprehending that significance.

More begins Part I of the narrative by quoting Jesus' exhortation, "Sustinete hic et uigilate mecum" (39/3-4). Again, he presents the twin subjects of praying properly and avoiding the dangers of sleep in a series of parallels and contrasts: Christ's humble praying posture and ours, lazy and irreverent (115-117); our behavior when petitioning a temporal prince and when praying to God; the careless worshipper and the sleeping dreamer. The section concludes with Christ's discovery of the sleeping apostles, which provides More with a final contrast: their "giving into sleep" indicates the limited nature of their love for their Master whereas his returning to see them demonstrates his ever-vigilant love (157-59).

The next stage of the narrative opens with Christ's question to Peter, "Simon dormis?" and his second injunction, "uigilate et orate" (159/5-6). This time, More reverses his previous order by speaking, first, of the dangers of sleep that prevent us from behaving like Christians, then of the role sleep plays in distracting us from praying properly. The contrasts start with an etymological one: Peter's sleep represents his infirmity, deafness and disobedience rather than the true significance of his names (161-163). Sleep represents the weakness of the flesh; if the apostles, those "young green branches," could not resist, how can we, "sapless sticks"? (169). God's kindness in waking us up is contrasted with our negligence in slumbering on the "pillow of our sins" (203/1-3), his vigilant care for us with our laziness and softness as we travel life's road (205-207), and his mercy in stirring us from our deep sleep of vice (211-13). Similarly, contrasts are set up between Christ's instruction on prayer and our unsatisfactory execution of it (173) and between his agonized praying that will bring true consolation in the form of an angel and our lazy, hurried and sluggish efforts that deprive us of true comfort and leave us troubled (255-57).

Christ's second discovery of the sleeping apostles, his question, "Quid dormitis?" (this time addressed to all the apostles as seen in the plural verb form), and his third exhortation, "surgite et orate," introduces the third but this time more complex sequence of references to sleep and waking (257). Sleep is used as an image of heresy and betrayal, extreme sadness leading to despair, and disease; there follows a repetition of "surgite et orate." It is then used to symbolize death and evil in the form of the devil's troops; this too is followed by "surgite et orate." The section continues with instructions on praying properly, expressed in sleep images, and then ends as it had begun, with the question of heresy, which flourishes while we sleep (345/5–361/5).

The first part of this third section, discussing betrayal and heresy, is built on both contrast and analogy: the apostles buried in sleep are unlike the wakeful Judas; on the other hand, heretics resemble the archtraitor in that they are constantly awake, and negligent bishops and priests resemble the slothful apostles. The subsequent points More makes are also centred around figures of contrast. The apostles' and bishops' reaction to sadness (283 ff.) is to escape into sleep whereas Christ's is to pray: the consolation they receive contrasts sharply with the true consolation offered by prayer. If sleep is a disease, to get up and pray is an instant remedy (303); if it is the image of death, to be wide awake is to allow life to begin anew (305). A final contrast is drawn between the busy troops of evil battering the castle of the sleeping soul (309-11) and the nocturnal activities of heretics and the snoring insouciance of slumbering Christians.

This carefully and densely constructed pattern of images of sleep and waking thus forms one of the underlying structures in the first part of the *De Tristitia*. It also illustrates the fact that More composed this his last work in much the same way as he had all his previous writings. He announces his themes early in the work; then, lawyer-like, he explores them by arguing for and against before returning to his theme and restating the case; next he departs in a new direction — but without losing the thread of his argument — often in a seeming digression, only to return to his theme once more. As Louis Martz has demonstrated, such was More's writing procedure in the *Confutation of Tyndale's Answer*, *Dialogue of Comfort* and *Treatise on the Passion*.[16] In the third part of this article, I shall discuss the literary aspects of More's use of the motif of sleep with a view to demonstrating that here too More was faithful to his habits of composition. Although working under great duress and with little time to spare, he carefully revised his manuscript as he wrote, as the Valencia manuscript reveals, and many of his revisions were made not only in order to sharpen his arguments and clarify his points, but also to make stylistic improvements. As a result, I shall argue, the *De Tristitia* is of literary as well as exegetical and homiletic value, despite Alistair Fox's comment that "it does not rate very high as literature."[17] In the passages containing references to sleep, we discover examples of More's sense of drama, and of his use of irony, digression, repetition, and rhetorical questions.

One of the contributing factors to the "public" character of *De Tristitia* is the way in which More imparts a sense of drama. He does this in several ways. First, he uses set speeches, some of which are paraphrases of Jesus' words. Two of the most striking are related to the subject of sleep. The first is inspired by the five-line speech to Peter taken from the Gospel and beginning, "Simon, dormis?" This is expanded into a paraphrase of what Jesus could have said had he been more reproachful (163–67). It comprises a series of nine questions following immediately one upon the other and ending with a variant of the verb *dormire*: *dormis, dormitans, indormias*. The last four all end with "et tu Simon dormis?" (165). The repetition of "Simon" nine times in the speech underlines the irony that More says is intended in Christ's use of the name, while the volley of questions emphasizes the sense of urgency. At the same time, the passage underscores More's point that underlying Jesus' "gentle words" was a feeling of sharp disappointment.

In the second paraphrase of Jesus' final injunction to his apostles, "Sleep on, Take your rest" and then in the next breath, "Get up," the rhetorical pattern is elaborately developed around the basic polarity of sleeping and waking (289–91). The tone is set by More's opening words: Jesus grants permission to stay asleep but intends to take it away. The passage that follows is built upon a rapid succession of antitheses: *dormite, dormiatis, vigilare; dormitastis, dormiendi, ne sedendi, surgendum*. Jesus' final contradictory and almost sarcastic statement forms a fitting conclusion: "sleep . . . rest — you have my permission — that is, if you can. But you will certainly not be able to." A final wry antithesis reminds us of More's point that evil-doers are always active while the slothful sleep: "For there are people coming . . . / who will *shake* the *yawning sleepiness* [italics mine] out of you." The sense of drama is heightened throughout the passage by the use of connectives like "now" and adverbs like "immediately" and "soon" which impart a sense of urgency and build up to the final emphatic "for the hour has almost come." The paraphrase is repeated some sixteen folios further on but this time revolves round the orders "stay awake" and "get up" (337–39). Again, "now," "straight away," and "at this very moment" are used effectively to increase the tension.

Two other favourite literary devices of More's are used in *De Tristitia* to create a sense of drama: rhetorical questions and the introduction of a fictional adversary, whose role is to argue points of doctrine or biblical interpretation. The devices are used side by side in a passage discussing the veracity of the Gospel statement that the apostles were all asleep while Jesus prayed (189–99). How could the apostles relate what Jesus said if they were truly asleep? Why did Jesus return to see if they were awake? If he wanted them to stay awake, why didn't he make them? After suggesting answers, More creates a character who might still not be satisfied concerning the third question: an officious investigator of the divine plan, as More rather mockingly calls him (197/3–4). The "investigator's" question and More's reply are both couched in direct speech, with More calling him "bone vir" (the flattery is of course ironical). All these techniques, used in the *Utopia*, *Dialogue of Comfort* and several of the polemical works, further animate the passage.

The figure of irony manifests itself in two ways in those *De Tristitia* passages containing sleep references. Firstly, there is an ironic and at times even sarcastic tone in some of More's own words and comments. In his paraphrase of Jesus' reproach (165/1–2), he has Jesus say: "As for that old name of yours, Simon, you live up to that very well, that's certain!" (*scilicet*).* As Monsuez has pointed out, *scilicet* is used at the end of a sentence in exactly that ironic way in the *Utopia*.[18] Elsewhere, More ironically tells the reader in direct speech: "Now imagine if you talk carelessly and lazily" (*supinus*, which can also mean lying on one's back) and, he continues, "loll, yawn and stretch in the presence of a temporal prince!" (131–33). Again, the tone is reminiscent of the *Utopia*, where Hythloday imagines himself in the French King's Council and starts his description in exactly the same way: "Age."[19] The second type of irony in *De Tristitia* comes directly from the Gospel account. According to More, Jesus' final, cutting words to the apostles, "Sleep on now. Take your rest. That is enough. Get up. Let us go," is not irony of the "trivial and jesting variety" (*leuicula et iocosa*) enjoyed by "idle and witty men" (289/5–6). Rather, it is "serious and weighty" and thus quite in order in Scripture, despite some opinions to the contrary.[20] Interestingly enough, More seeks to support his defence of biblical irony with yet another sleep image, this time taken from the Old Testament. Elias ridiculed the prophets of Baal by telling them: "Call louder! For your god is sleeping, or perhaps he's away on a journey somewhere!"* (295/6–7). The image of the sleeping god is doubly rich. The statue of Baal was deaf, More says; he thereby reminds us of Simon Peter's deafness, which as he had pointed out contradicts the etymological significance of his name, and of the deafness that assails us when asleep and prevents us from hearing God's voice. More completes his argument about irony by giving Saint Augustine's contrasting view that Jesus' words were not ironic, "in order to put forth both sides of the question," and he concludes with a final ironic twist of his own: "It is not for a nobody like myself to render a decision as if I were an appointed arbitrator"* (301-3). The self-mocking pun on *arbiter honorarius* (appointed arbitrator) and *onorarius* (beast of burden) heightens the irony contained in the statement: More of course had often been called upon to render decisions in court. It is also perhaps yet another echo of the passage in *Utopia* describing the French King's Council, where Hythloday had made a similar tongue-in-cheek statement that it was not for him, an *homuncio*, or little man, to express opinions.

The *De Tristitia*, an exegetical and devotional work sometimes thought to be very different from More's previous compositions in both subject and tone, in fact shares many of their features. Some of these manifest themselves in the various references to sleep, as has been shown in this article. Themes like the value of prayer and good praying habits, the need to be constantly on guard against evil, and the dangers of falling into spiritual sloth, figured forth here in images of sleep and wakefulness, are discussed by More in his various works. The use of an underlying pattern of imagery built on polarities and serving to explore those themes and formulate arguments, and the careful attention to style are familiar features of his writings. This consistency is made further apparent by the fact that More had used images of sleep and sloth in similar fashion in his previous writings, particularly in the *Dialogue of Comfort*, although nowhere had he been given the opportunity to weave them into such a close fabric as in his discussion of Christ's agony in the Garden. Nor must it be forgotten that like More's first great work, the *Utopia*, the *De Tristitia* was written in Latin. As Louis Martz says, it is a "moving and appropriate thought that in the somber close of his career More should have sought to communicate with the audience that had admired his *Utopia*."[21] Lastly, the *De Tristitia* in many ways completes the group of "Tower writings." It combines the thematic concerns of the *Dialogue of Comfort* and the exegetical and devotional nature of the *Treatise upon the Passion*, and like them exploits certain literary devices which enabled More to express both his public and private thoughts.[22]

As Alistair Fox notes, *De Tristitia* is thematically the "logical, climactic conclusion to [More's] whole opus."[23] I would also add that More's final work demonstrates a continuation of the various literary techniques and stylistic strengths that characterize his whole body of writings. This is certainly true of his concern with both the physical and spiritual aspects of sleep and of the way in which he weaves appropriate images of sleep and waking into his writings. As he awaited execution, he no doubt had to fight not only the fear of pain and death but also the heavy-heartedness that he confessed in one of his last letters to Margaret had kept him lying "longe restles and wakying, while my wyfe had went I had slept . . ."[24] However, by describing the sleep of the apostles and the agony of their Master, he prepared himself to face—honorably and bravely—the final "sleep of death."

Université de Montréal

Notes

A shorter version of this article was given at the Thomas More-John Fisher International Conference in London, July, 1985.

1. This is the title that More gave to his work. Clarence H. Miller discusses the various titles of *De Tristitia* in the Introduction to his edition, *De Tristitia christi*, Volume 14 of *The Complete Works of St. Thomas More*. (New Haven and London: 1976), 739-40. All quotations will be taken from this edition and the page and line references will be indicated in parentheses in the text. Most English translations are also from this edition; my own translations are indicated by an asterisk.

2. Garry Haupt discusses this dual aspect of the *Treatise upon the Passion* and *De Tristitia* in his Introduction to the *Treatise upon the Passion*, CW 13, pp. li-cxxii; Clarence Miller touches on the question in his Introduction to CW 14, pp. 741-43; Louis Martz writes at some length on the question of the public humanistic audience and the private meditative nature of *De Tristitia* in "The Tower Works" in *St. Thomas More: Action and Contemplation*, edited by R. S. Sylvester (New Haven: Yale University Press: 1972), and "Thomas More: The Sacramental Life," *Thought* 52 (1977): 300-18.

3. Germain Marc'hadour, *Thomas More et la Bible* (Paris: 1969), 342.

4. In *The Confutation of Tyndale's Answer*, More specifies that God provides sleep for man's refreshment; the problem with David (and us) is that "we slepe when we shulde not." *The Confutation of Tyndale's Answer*, edited by Louis A. Shuster, Richard C. Marius, James P. Lusardi and Richard J. Schoeck as Volume 8 of the *Collected Works* (1973), 535. In *A Dialogue of Comfort Against Tribulation*, Antony tells Vincent that although "Waking in good business is much more acceptable to God than sleeping, yet God wills us to sleep." *A Dialogue of Comfort Against Tribulation* edited by Louis L. Martz and Frank Manley as Volume 12 of the *Collected Works* (1976), 57.

5. Psalms 119:62 and 63:6. The vigilant prophet had also appeared in one of More's earliest works, the *Life of John Picus* where, in the Seventh Rule, Pico had praised him. More translated Pico's "super custodiam meam stabo" by "Thou must with the prophet stand and keep watch." *The Life of John Picus* in *The English Works of Sir Thomas More*, edited by W. E. Campbell and A. W. Reed (London: 1931), 383. The Utopians, it will be remembered, devoted eight hours to sleep, six to work, and expelled all idle persons from the commonwealth. *CW* 4, 126/31-32. The editor notes Stapleton's statement that More himself devoted no more than four or five hours to sleep, p. 405.

6. In *A Dialogue of Comfort*, More describes with equal realism the plight of the sinner who instead of grasping the help God offers in the form of prayer lies awake at night "amending his pillow," engaging his bed-partner in conversation, and so on. *CW* 12, 60.

7. While More possibly drew this analogy from Gerson's *De oratione et ejus valore*, a work he quotes later in the *De Tristitia* (327/1), (*Opera omnia*, edited by Louis Ellies du Pin, 5 vols. Antwerp: 1706. Vol. 3, p. 250), he goes beyond his source. The wandering thoughts of the "waking dreamer" are not simply "useless" but "unnatural," and "abominable" and, More adds as a final touch, would not be recounted "apud pueros" even if they had been dreams. Waking illusions and dreams had been compared by Antony in the *Dialogue of Comfort* although within the context of a discussion on divine revelation, *CW* 12/141-43.

8. In his *Dialogue Concerning Heresies*, More reminds Tyndale that Jesus exhorted us to watch and pray at all times, which is harder than any church-inspired commands on prayer; the rest and ease Christ offered in return is not a "lewd liberty of slothfull rest" but "a pleasaunt taste of heaven." *A Dialogue Concerning Heresies* edited by Thomas Lawlor, Germain Marc'hadour and Richard Marius as Volume 6 of the *Collected Works* (1981), 106.

9. Miller includes in his edition the cancelled folio 23[v] in which More had elaborated upon the danger of the devil's setting snares while we sleep (pp. 690-91).

10. In *The Confutation of Tyndale's Answer*, More had disputed Tyndale's explanation of David's adultery and his murder of Uriah in a section entitled "One who sins does not sleep" (pp. 534 ff.). He accuses Tyndale of using sleep as an excuse for his heretical belief that since the elect do not sin wilfully, any sins they do commit while asleep are not in fact sins because they take place in a trance. In the *Dialogue of Comfort*, Antony warns against sleeping away the day in the secure hope that God will wake us at the last minute; in other words, we must not idle away our lives in sin in the hope of last-minute grace (p. 95).

11. G. R. Owst has pointed out the association of sloth and the clergy in medieval homilies and literature but remarks that Sleuthe in *Piers Ploman* is both cleric and layman. *Literature and Pulpit in Medieval England: A Neglected Chapter in the History of English Letters and of the English People* (New York: Barnes and Noble, 1961), 88-89, 278-89, 554-69. Incidentally, Sleuthe shares several specific characteristics with More's description of sloth: he needs a

hassock to pray (V. 382), his heart is miles away from the words when he says the rosary (V. 400), and he has to be woken and shaken out of his despair by *Vigilate* (420). More also discussed sloth, sister of Gluttony because they both muddle people's thinking and make men "lye down like swyne," and cautioned against underestimating its power in *The Four Last Things. The Workes of Sir Thomas More Knyght, Sometyme Lord Chancellor of England, Wrytten by Him in the Englysh Tonge* edited by William Rastell (London: 1557), 80 ff. On the church's attitude toward idleness, see More, *The Answer to a Poisoned Book*, Stephen Merriam Foley and Clarence H. Miller, Volume 11, The Complete Works of St. Thomas More (New Haven and London, Yale UP, 1985), pp. 33-34.

12. Contrasting the apostles' sleep and Judas' wakefulness in *The Confutation* (*CW* 8, p. 36), More had already likened the traitor to heretics always writing "ungracyose bookes" and the apostles to sad, slumbering defenders of the faith.

13. More had used the metaphor in *The Four Last Things* (*EW*, 80 ff.) where he had called sleep a "swowne" in which we "lye like dead stokes," and added, "Among al wise men of old it is agreed that slepe is the very ymage of death." The metaphor appears in several places in the New Testament: Mark 13.36, Romans 13:11, 1 Cor. 11:30, 15:20, et cetera.

14. The "sleeping for sorrow" excuse in Luke 22:45 that More rejects here is glossed by Chrysostomus in the *Catena*: the Apostles' sleep is "somnus in torporis sed maevoris." Some kinds of sadness are unacceptable, namely those that we find so unbearable that we escape in sleep, as did the apostles. St. Thomas Aquinas, *Catena aurea in quatuor evangelica* in *Opera omnia*, 25 vols. (Parma: 1852-73), Vol. 12, p. 234. Nicholas De Lyra also explained the relation between sadness and sleep, as Miller points out (p. 1029). Erasmus makes it clear in his Paraphrases that the apostles' sleep was induced by the "weakness of their nature" and "grievous mental suffering." *Complete Paraphrases* (Basel, 1523), 2 vols. More himself had developed the sadness-bodily weariness contrast in a folio that he subsequently cancelled in preference for the sadness-sleep theme (p. 691). Earlier, in the *Dialogue of Comfort*, he had had Antony explain the various kinds of consolation for sadness, one of which is a "careless, deadly dullness . . . the comfortless kind of heaviness in tribulation [which is] the highest kind of the deadly sin of sloth" (*CW* 12/14). In the *Dialogue Concerning Heresies*, More had related this wrong kind of repose and consolation to heresy, calling it a "lewd liberty of slothfull rest" and comparing it with the "easy yoke" of the "sweetness of hope" (*CW* 6/106).

15. Miller (pp. 763-69) discusses the parallels and contrasts both in More's style and in the larger structural patterns of the *De Tristitia*, singling out some of the "dominant polarities" such as body and soul and eager and fearful martyrs. He does not however mention the contrasting images of sleep and waking.

16. Louis Martz, "More as Author: The Virtues of Digression," *Moreana* 62: 105-19.

17. Alistair Fox, *Thomas More: History and Providence* (Oxford: Blackwell,

1982), 243. See also Clare M. Murphy's comment on Fox's charge in her review of his book, *The Catholic Historical Review* 72, 1 (January 1986): 85–86.

18. R. Monsuez, "Le Latin de Thomas More dans 'Utopia,'" *Caliban* 3, 35–78. See page 44, note 6.

19. CW 4, 86–88. Monsuez points out that of all Cicero's interjections, More retains only three, one of which is *age* (p. 42).

20. Throughout his life, More had highly apprized wit but had differentiated between various forms of it. He had also expressed the humanist belief that wit must be tempered by decorum: in the story of the jester and the friar in *Utopia*, in his Letter to John More, and in the *Dialogue of Comfort*. The same held true of the use of wit in religious contexts, as he states clearly in the *Confutation* and *Responsio ad Lutherum*. The statement in *De Tristitia* is thus in accordance with the opinions that he had expressed earlier. As for irony in biblical texts, More espoused Erasmus' view, which differed from that of the church fathers. See Miller's note to this (p. 1030).

21. Louis Martz, "Thomas More: The Sacramental Life," 307.

22. For a detailed discussion of this, see Garry Haupt, CW 13, cxlviii–clxxxi.

23. Fox, 244.

24. Letter No. 211 (1534), in *The Correspondence of Sir Thomas More*, Elizabeth Frances Rogers, ed. (Princeton: Princeton UP, 1947), 546.

UNIVERSITE DE PARIS - SORBONNE

1, rue Victor-Cousin 75230 PARIS CEDEX 05

CENTRE DE RECHERCHES
SUR LA RENAISSANCE

Cher Ami,

Le Centre de Recherches sur la Renaissance de Paris-Sorbonne (devenu S.I.R.I.R. = Société Internationale de Recherches Interdisciplinaires sur la Renaissance) a bénéficié, depuis une douzaine d'années de l'appui efficace et amical du Directeur de *Moreana*. La publication de nos premiers volumes fut même rendue possible grâce à votre aide et à celle de l'équipe d'Angers. Des liens solides se forgèrent, renforcés par la participation active de divers membres de l'Association *Amici Thomae Mori* à nos colloques en Sorbonne. N'est-ce pas déjà un motif suffisant pour que S.I.R.I.R. figure parmi vos admirateurs reconnaissants dans ce livre d'hommage qui vous est dédié ?

Mais en rester là serait ne pas tenir compte de souvenirs plus lointains ou plus personnels, qui, pour moi, n'ont jamais disparu dans « la besace de l'oubli » que le Temps porte sur son dos... (Comment ne pas citer Shakespeare ?)

Je me rappelle avoir entendu parler de vous en Angleterre avant même de vous rencontrer pour la première fois à Rennes, où vous êtes venu me voir en 1960 à propos de l'Exposition Thomas More que vous organisiez à Angers. Puis, dès 1966, j'ai suivi avec un intérêt croissant les dernières étapes de la rédaction de votre thèse *Thomas More et la Bible,* étapes importantes puisqu'il nous fallut prendre ensemble plusieurs décisions en vue de votre soutenance.

Le coup de vent malicieux, qui emporta aux quatres coins de mon jardin de Sceaux, où je résidais alors, les nombreux feuillets, encore non reliés et non paginés de la première mouture de votre thèse est comme le symbole de ce qu'allait être le rayonnement de vos écrits sur More à travers le monde.

Dans *Thomas More et la Bible,* fruit d'un patient travail de recherche, vous avez réussi « par le fil d'or des Saintes Ecritures » à coudre ensemble une série d'essais « rédigés pour la plupart avant que ne se précisât le dessin d'ensemble ». Vous êtes en cela, vous nous l'expliquez, l'émule de More : « Ainsi travaillait Thomas More, utilisant les bribes de ses oeuvres et réservant pour la fin, lorsqu'il y en avait une, l'effort d'architecture. » Le résultat, dans votre cas, est l'un de ces ouvrages qui méritent d'être « ruminés et digérés », pour reprendre les mots de Francis Bacon. C'est ce que je vous disais dans la Salle Louis Liard quand j'étais votre « rapporteur », le jour où vous avez reçu votre titre de Docteur ès Lettres.

Cette thèse, et beaucoup d'autres de vos publications, comme *L'Univers de Thomas More,* sont des mines d'érudition. Le lecteur ne se lasse pas de s'y reporter et sa curiosité est sans cesse renouvelée.

Si l'on aime vous lire, on aime tout autant vous écouter. Les qualités de More, « penseur, écouteur et parleur » que vous énonciez au cours d'une conférence à Paris (« De la Conversation au Dialogue ») sont aussi les vôtres, tant vous êtes uni à votre compagnon de route. Et ceux qui ont eu la chance de vous entendre savent avec quelle intelligence fine et quelle sagesse souriante vous faites revivre l'humanisme de More.

Vous avez récemment apporté votre contribution à un colloque sur « Le Roman de Chevalerie au Temps de la Renaissance ». Serait-ce exagéré de dire que parfois vous apparaissez aux yeux de vos amis comme un chevalier dont l'audace et la générosité sont inlassables. Et un certain 7 juillet, date qui vous est chère, puisqu'elle unit les souvenirs de More et de Becket, où je vous rencontrai par hasard devant le mémorial de saint Thomas Becket dans la cathédrale de Cantorbéry, c'est à un chevalier errant que vous me faisiez penser. Car ainsi vous allez de par le monde, mince silhouette, combien vibrante de vie, d'énergie, de sincérité et de foi pour semer les paroles de ce « Man for all Seasons » qu'est votre « ami si proche et si attachant ».

C'est bien cette vérité de l'amitié que par vous toujours le Temps continue à nous révéler. Et pour cela, avec tout mon coeur, je vous redis « merci ».

M.T. Jones-Davies

When the times at last had ripened
and earth grown full in abundance,
you created in your image man and woman,
the crown of all creation.

III The Crown of All Creation

Les époques enfin mûries et la terre devenue abondante,
tu créas à ton image l'homme et la femme,
couronnement de toute la création.

Sept. 30, 1987.

Dear Father Marc'hadour,

On the occasion of the 25th anniversary of Moreana, I should like to send you my warmest congratulations. Like all Renaissance scholars, I have long admired your great contributions to the study of Thomas More and his circle.

Your studies, editions and translations, and especially your great work L'Univers de Thomas More, have been an invaluable and indispensable source of precise information for numerous scholars including myself. At the Université Catholique de l'Ouest, you have been teaching for decades and have transmitted your wide knowledge to numerous students. The institute founded by you at the University, the Moreanum, with its large specialized library, has been a leading center of research on More and Northern Humanism and has attracted many visitors. The society founded by you, the Amici Thomae Mori, has been active in promoting More studies all over the Western world, and its periodical, Moreana, which is now celebrating its 25th anniversary, has published over the years an impressive number of important articles by scholars from different countries, all of them indebted to you for your kind encouragement and editorial help. I am myself grateful to you because you were interested in my own modest paper on Thomas More as a Renaissance humanist, agreed to publish it in Moreana where it would attract the attention of all More scholars, and allowed me to reprint it elsewhere.

I remember with great pleasure your visit in New York, your kind hospitality when I and my wife Edith visited Angers, and our pleasant and interesting conversations on both occasions. You showed us not only the Moreanum and its great library and the famous medieval tapestries displayed in the Palace Museum, but also the magnificent weeping beech tree in the university garden of which you recently sent us a beautiful and much appreciated photograph.

I wish to send you on this happy occasion, also in the name of my wife Edith, our warmest regards and best wishes for your own health and continued activities and for the future of your institute, of your society, and of your periodical Moreana.

Sincerely yours, *Paul Oskar Kristeller*
Paul Oskar Kristeller
Frederick J.E. Woodbridge Professor Emeritus of Philosophy
Columbia University

Giovanni Pico della Mirandola, sketch by Raymond Joly

LOUIS VALCKE

Jean Pic de la Mirandole lu par Thomas More

I

Choix et intention de More

On a souvent noté que Thomas More s'est limité à ne traduire qu'une sélection des écrits les plus édifiants de Jean Pic de la Mirandole, omettant tout ce qui a trait à sa formation intellectuelle et à ses préoccupations philosophiques, métaphysiques, théologiques.[1] C'est ainsi que, dans l'oeuvre de Pic, More n'aborde ni les *Conclusiones*, proprement scolastiques, ni le *De ente et uno*, oeuvre spéculative particulièrement importante, ni l'*Heptaplus*, savant commentaire de la Genèse, ni les *Disputationes*, cette critique de l'astrologie, qui, sur le plan théorique, fut de première importance.

En guise de présentation, Thomas More fait précéder son choix de textes par la traduction de la célèbre *Vita* écrite par Jean-François Pic, le neveu biographe.[2] Le lecteur moderne verra dans cette brève anthologie, selon ses dispositions propres, ou bien l'affirmation émouvante d'une foi sincère, ou bien l'expression banale d'une spiritualité assez fade. En aucun cas n'y reconnaîtra-t-on l'originalité ni, surtout, cette structuration intellectuelle rigoureuse dont Jean Pic fait preuve dans la majorité de ses autres oeuvres.

On ne fera pas grief à Thomas More de l'orientation de cette compilation, car son intention n'était certes pas de présenter aux lecteurs anglais un résumé autorisé ou une synthèse tant soit peu complète de la vie et de l'oeuvre de Jean Pic. Tout au contraire voulait-il, prenant occasion de ce choix de textes, produire une oeuvre de dévotion destinée à un large public, oeuvre dont il n'était pas nécessaire qu'elle fût le reflet exact de son origine première. Comme le remarquait Germain Marc'hadour, "clearly, from first page to last, the Pico volume is a spiritual nosegay, specifically Christian, resolutely geared toward the increase in 'godliness' of both compiler and reader."[3]

Cette intention exhortative et didactique ressort non seulement du choix auquel Thomas More s'est limité, mais encore de la présentation même de l'opuscule. La lecture en est rendue plus aisée par la division en paragraphes et par l'insertion de sous-titres. En outre, les marges donnent un bref résumé du texte ainsi que les références bibliques. Les citations des Ecritures sont en latin, mais chacune d'elles est suivie de sa traduction en langue anglaise, manifestant ainsi l'intention évidente de faire oeuvre de vulgarisation.

On mesurera par là toute la distance qui sépare l'humanisme anglais de ses origines italiennes, surtout si l'on tient compte d'une brève remarque de Jean-François. Se référant à quelques écrits platonisants que son oncle avait rédigés en toscan, il se promet, si le loisir lui en est donné, de les traduire en latin "de crainte que la très éminente doctrine . . . qu'un si grand homme a consacrée à ces arcanes, ne soit donnée en pâture à tout venant."[4]

II

Intellectualisme néoplatonisant de Pic

Dans le texte de Jean-François, la *Vita* est déjà un panégyrique, beaucoup plus proche de l'hagiographie que de la biographie, et l'intention du neveu est assurément de tracer de son oncle une image très idéalisée.

Pourtant cette image reste conforme à son modèle, au moins en ce sens que le caractère, les intérêts fondamentaux, le cadre existentiel, la démarche intellectuelle, l'évolution spirituelle de Jean Pic s'y trouvent décrits de façon vivante et détaillée: si idéalisé soit-il, le portrait brossé par Jean-François reste le portrait d'un personnage concret.

Il en va tout autrement dans la traduction que More nous présente.

On comprend, en fonction du public auquel il s'adressait, que Thomas More ait cru bon d'omettre les nombreux passages décrivant le cadre de vie de Jean Pic, ou les allusions historiques et géographiques que seul un familier de l'Italie pouvait comprendre et apprécier. Néanmoins, si justifiées soient-elles sur le plan didactique, ces omissions ont pour effet de déshumaniser Jean Pic de la Mirandole, d'en faire le modèle abstrait et paradigmatique de l'homme vertueux, qui, après une jeunesse insouciante, tout entière tournée vers les gloires et les plaisirs terrestres, cependant grandi par une épreuve providentielle, se libère des vaines amours, distribue ses biens aux pauvres, se détourne du monde, pour enfin se convertir à une vie de dévotion et d'ascèse tout entière orientée vers Dieu. . . .

A vrai dire, ce tableau n'est pas faux: dans ses grandes lignes, il correspond sans doute à une dimension réelle de la vie de Jean Pic. Il s'agit cependant d'un tableau partiel, profondément tronqué, qui a perdu toute la coloration vivante que son modèle pouvait encore avoir dans le texte original de Jean-François.

Beaucoup plus grave que cette distorsion littéraire est, par rapport au modèle historique, l'omission systématique et presque complète de tout ce qui, dans l'existence réelle de Pic, avait trait à la vie philosophique: ses études constantes, ses recherches inquiètes, la somme de ses écrits. . . .

Ces omissions aussi résultent du souci de ne pas alourdir un texte destiné à la vulgarisation. Mais qu'on y prenne garde! Si nous avons signalé plus haut que, dans l'esprit de More, l'utilisation de la langue vulgaire correspondait certainement à un souci pédagogique – en quoi il se montrait beaucoup plus "progressiste" que Jean-François – on constate ici, par l'omission des références philosophiques, que cette vulgarisation se paye d'une moindre rigueur, d'une évidente perte de qualité et de profondeur. Les arcanes philosophiques ne sont peut-être pas à la portée du tout venant – c'est ce que supposait Jean-François – encore est-ce induire en erreur que de laisser croire qu'elles soient gratuites ou superflues.

Le neveu, quant à lui, insiste très longuement sur cet aspect essentiel de la carrière de son oncle, et, dans la *Vita*, la description qu'il en donne représente environ un tiers de la longueur totale de son texte.[5]

Or, si tous les interprètes s'accordent aujourd'hui pour reconnaître que le souci constant de la vie et de la pensée de Pic fut toujours un souci essentiellement religieux,[6] il apparaît tout aussi clairement que cette vision religieuse et chrétienne ne peut être dissociée d'une démarche intellectuelle dont elle est en quelque sorte le couronnement et l'aboutissement logique. Contentons-nous ici de citer le témoignage de Paul O. Kristeller selon qui "Pico seems to regard religion as a fulfilment of philosophy."[7]

En cela, Pic se montre fidèle néoplatonicien, car le néoplatonisme est avant tout une doctrine de salut. On peut en être assuré, cet aspect salvifique du néoplatonisme est à l'origine de l'enthousiasme du philosophe pour la doctrine de Plotin.

Contrairement à Aristote, en effet, Plotin enseignait que la philosophie ne doit pas être poursuivie pour elle-même: elle est une démarche ascétique qui purifie l'âme, et la connaissance *intellectuelle* qu'elle permet d'atteindre n'est à son tour que médiane par rapport à la fin ultime que l'âme atteint dans la vision béatifique (*Enn.* I–1 c.3; VI–4 c.16). Mais, et ce point est essentiel, cette *démarche intellectuelle* est aussi *la seule* qui, à travers la pure contemplation et au-delà de celle-ci, permette à l'âme de retrouver son origine et de s'unir à l'Un.

C'est cette vaste perspective que le jeune Pic exaltera dans les pages les plus brillantes de l'*Oratio de hominis dignitate,* où, par exemple, il reprend l'interprétation classique qui, depuis le Pseudo-Denys, a été donnée à l'image biblique de l'Echelle de Jacob.

C'est aussi cette conception intellectuelle que l'on retrouve jusque dans la structure même des *Conclusions,* car la succession des 900 thèses s'échelonne selon une démarche ascendante qui, partant des problématiques philosophiques les plus traditionnelles, conduit graduellement le lecteur à la révélation de la Cabale – il va sans dire que Pic croit y retrouver les grands dogmes chrétiens.[8] Or, en cette ascèse tout intellectuelle, le néoplatonisme est situé au plus haut niveau que la raison humaine puisse atteindre par ses forces propres, à l'*interface* entre la philosophie et les révélations ésotériques, passage obligé, donc, entre l'un et l'autre niveau.[9]

C'est, très succinctement, cette même conception que Pic résume dans une lettre célèbre adressée à Aldo Manuzio: "Philosophia veritatem quaerit, theologia invenit, religio possidet."[10]

∼

En tout cela, donc, l'influence du néoplatonisme sur la pensée de Pic est évidente, et l'intellectualisme qui lui est propre laissera sa marque même après que Pic, dans le *De ente et uno* (1491), aura passé la doctrine de Plotin au crible d'une critique rigoureuse.

A la demande d'Ange Politien, à qui il est dédié, Pic examine dans cet écrit la question des relations entre l'*Un* et l'*Etre*. Faut-il, selon l'interprétation (néo)platonicienne, reconnaître la primauté de l'Un sur l'Etre, ou doit-on, au contraire, à la suite d'Aristote, admettre la convertibilité, c'est-à-dire l'équivalence ontologique, des deux concepts?

De prime abord, il peut paraître qu'il s'agisse là d'une question académique, relevant de la spéculation la plus gratuite. C'est ce que semble avoir cru Thomas More, puisqu'il ne souffle mot de cette question dans ses traductions.

L'enjeu, cependant, est de taille car c'est de la réponse à cette question que dépend la convergence ou la divergence entre platonisme et aristotélisme. Or, une discordance radicale entre les deux grandes traditions philosophiques entraînerait une discordance du même ordre entre, par exemple, S. Thomas et S. Augustin, donc entre les deux grandes traditions théologiques de l'Eglise.[11] A quoi on ajoutera également que, dans sa logique extrême, c'est encore de cette réponse que dépend la possibilité d'une théologie qui ne soit pas seulement négative.

Or, dans le *De ente*, Pic s'emploie à prouver la concordance fondamentale des deux doctrines. Pour ce faire cependant, s'il prétend "défendre Aristote en le rendant conforme à Platon son maître,"[12] c'est en fait le processus contraire qu'il suit, puisque c'est Platon qu'il reconduit à Aristote et non l'inverse.[13] C'est donc en son fondement même que Pic critique toute la tradition néoplatonicienne.

Si Jean-François ne parle que brièvement du *De ente*, il en résume cependant fort bien le thème fondamental.[14] Dans sa traduction, More omet ce résumé—mais il reproduit fidèlement le commentaire édifiant par lequel Jean-François, en un contexte distinct, présente la célèbre exclamation qui interrompt le développement du *De ente*, et que Pic adresse au Politien:

> Sed vide, mi Angele, quae nos insania teneat. Amare Deum dum sumus in corpore plus possumus quam vel eloqui, vel cognoscere; amando plus nobis proficimus, minus laboramus, illi magis obsequimur; malumus semper tamen per cognitionem numquam invenire quod quaerimus, quam amando possidere id quod non amando frustra etiam invenitur.[15]

Ce passage a fait couler beaucoup d'encre. Le P. de Lubac, après l'abbé Marc'hadour, y lit le rejet par Pic de la démarche intellectualiste et le choix de "la voie de l'amour."[16] Cette lecture s'oppose à celle de Cassirer qui, au contraire, prétendait trouver là l'orgueilleuse affirmation selon laquelle "la recherche est l'unique forme sous laquelle il est concédé à l'homme de connaître le vrai."[17]

Bruno Nardi également avait maintenu qu'en un premier temps l'accord entre Pic et "les averroïstes du courant sigérien" aurait été complet, mais que, par après, le jeune philosophe se serait détourné de la "mistica averroistica" parce qu' "il ne tarda pas à se rendre compte que, dans ce mirage de félicité, conçu intellectuellement, il y avait quelque chose de froid et d'artificiel qui ne pouvait satisfaire les aspirations spirituelles nourries dans l'âme par quinze siècles de vie chrétienne."[18]

C'est la même leçon que Jean-François veut, lui aussi, tirer de ce passage. Il y voit en effet l'affirmation par Pic de la prépondérance absolue de la voie affective sur la voie intellectuelle.[19]

Mais cette interprétation que, par sa traduction, More fait sienne,[20] correspond-elle bien à ce qui fut l'esprit authentique de Jean Pic, après comme avant la "conversion" du *De ente?* Rien n'est moins certain.

En effet, l'apostrophe de Pic est probablement une paraphrase de S. Augustin qui, dans ses *Confessions* s'était lui aussi exclamé: "Quid ad me si quis non intelligat? . . . Gaudeat etiam sic et amet non inveniendo invenire potius quam inveniendo non invenire te."[21]

Cependant, s'il y a paraphrase, elle est en quelque sorte inversée par une nuance significative: pour Augustin, la "voie de l'amour" est la seule qui importe, et elle est possible dès ici-bas. Pour Pic au contraire, même s'il reconnaît que cette voie de l'intellect est "folie," c'est néanmoins en toute lucidité qu'il se sent en quelque sorte contraint de l'adopter. Il semble en effet avoir considéré qu'elle était la conséquence, malheureuse certes, mais inévitable, de la déchéance humaine: ". . . malumus enim *semper*. . . ." Non pas donc exaltation de la recherche intellectuelle pour elle-même, comme le voulait Cassirer, mais résignation du *viator* à accepter un substitut dont il sait l'inadéquation, mais dont il voudra néanmoins explorer et exploiter toutes les possibilités.

D'ailleurs, un peu sur le ton dont on dirait "Et maintenant, passons aux choses sérieuses," Pic ferme la parenthèse pour reprendre le développement rigoureux du *De ente:* "Sed redeamus ad nostra."[22]

Pic a souvent été évalué au seul vu d'une brève citation sortie de son contexte. Ce fut le cas, hélas, pour tout ce que, depuis Burckhardt, on a voulu lire dans son *Oratio.* Méfions-nous, ici aussi, de toute extrapolation hâtive: ce n'est qu'en la situant dans son contexte qu'il sera possible de mesurer la portée réelle de cette apostrophe. Or, le *De ente* est précisément l'ouvrage le plus abstraitement métaphysique qui soit issu de l'esprit de Jean Pic, comme il en est aussi le produit le plus rationnellement théologique, signe sans doute que son exclamation n'était que l'expression d'une nostalgie sans conséquence ou d'une velléité éphémère.

Après le *De ente*, la spiritualité de Pic ne cessera de s'affirmer selon ses voies propres. C'est de cette période que datent la plupart de ses oeuvres d'édification religieuse, mais c'est aussi durant cette période que Pic travaille d'arrache-pied à ce qui allait devenir les célèbres *Disputationes adversus astrologiam divinatricem*, oeuvre monumentale qu'il ne put mener à terme et dont les brouillons furent colligés par Jean-François, pour être édités en 1496, deux ans après la mort de Jean Pic.

Quoique inachevés, les douze livres des *Disputationes* témoignent de l'importance que Pic attachait à cette entreprise monumentale. Il y consacrait toutes ses énergies, tous ses talents et toute la puissance de son intelligence, comme l'atteste Jean-François.[23]

A sa façon, cette oeuvre est bien dans la manière de Jean Pic.

Elle devait, nous dit Jean-François, être la cinquième section d'un vaste ouvrage "ad debellandos septem hostes Ecclesiae":[24] c'est donc bien parce que l'astrologie et les sciences occultes représentent un péril pour la religion qu'il importe d'en faire la critique, et en ce sens, les *Disputationes* sont intégralement portées par une intention religieuse et chrétienne. D'autre part, c'est précisément parce qu'elles sont de fausses sciences que les sciences occultes minent la religion. Par conséquent, la critique que Pic en fera sera une critique strictement rationnelle, s'appuyant exclusivement sur une argumentation à la fois philologique, philosophique et scientifique, comme l'observait Giovanni Di Napoli.[25]

Les *Disputationes* témoignent donc, elles aussi, de cette constance de la conception de Jean Pic, où la religion s'inscrit dans la continuité d'une recherche intellectuelle, l'une ouvrant la voie et donnant sa finalité à l'autre.

III

Les parallélismes textuels entre More et Pic

Reprenons notre constatation initiale: de tous les matériaux que les écrits et la vie de Jean Pic mettaient à sa disposition, More n'a retenu que ce qui lui convenait, et qu'il a aménagé dans une intention qui n'était ni celle de l'historien, ni celle du philosphe. Dans ces conditions, More gardait une liberté entière à l'égard de ses sources, et, dès lors, on ne pourra lui reprocher d'avoir, par sa traduction, donné une vue tronquée de la vraie personnalité de Jean Pic de la Mirandole.

Il est au demeurant ironique de constater que More sera à son tour victime de certaines "réorientations idéologiques," comme en témoignent quelques-unes des traductions de l'*Utopie*. D'autre part, en ce qui concerne Pic, More ne fait que lui rendre la monnaie de sa pièce, lui qui avait, sans scrupule aucun, pillé les auteurs qu'il s'était appropriés par sa vaste érudition, pour leur faire dire ce qui lui convenait. En cela, d'ailleurs, Pic comme More reflètent simplement la mentalité et les habitudes de leur époque, et ils s'inscrivent ainsi dans une tradition qui remonte aux Pères de l'Eglise.

Reste néanmoins la question de savoir si, malgré ou à travers le prisme de cette lecture, la méditation sur la vie et l'oeuvre de Jean Pic a pu avoir une "seminal influence" sur l'esprit de l'humaniste anglais, comme le pensait Vittorio Gabrieli?[26] Sans nier qu'une telle influence, dans le sens vague et général du terme, ait put exister, les arguments apportés pour étayer la thèse d'un impact spécifique peuvent paraître insuffisants.

Gabrieli croit retrouver "a number of striking echoes from and parallels to Pico's ideas . . . scattered throughout More's other writings,"[27] et il souligne également "the recurrence of certain themes and attitudes in More's writings," ce qui semblerait indiquer qu'il existait "a deeper continuity of spiritual influence"[28] de Pic à More. Mais, d'une part et on l'a vu, ce sont précisément les écrits de Pic qui respirent la spiritualité la plus traditionnelle que More a repris dans ses traductions, comme c'est aussi une image particulièrement conventionnelle qui ressort de la *Vita* après les coupures que More lui fit subir. D'ailleurs Gabrieli en convient indirectement, puisqu'il note lui aussi que ce sont "les lieux communs de la piété chrétienne"[29] que More emprunte à Pic.

De plus, il n'y a évidemment pas lieu de s'étonner que les thèmes de la lutte contre la tentation, de la fuite hors du monde, vallée de larmes ou prison de l'âme, se retrouvent parallèlement chez les deux auteurs, profondément chrétiens l'un et l'autre et nourris d'une même tradition, quelles que soient par ailleurs les différences déjà fondamentales qui commençaient à séparer leurs époques et leurs cultures respectives. Ceci vaut également pour certaines similitudes textuelles. Lecteurs assidus de la Bible, interprétant dans un même esprit les mêmes références scripturaires, il est *a priori* probable que les commentaires de More rejoindront ceux de Pic, sans qu'il soit aucunement nécessaire de supposer entre les deux auteurs une quelconque filiation.[30]

IV

La spiritualité de Pic

Comme on vient de le signaler, les deux lettres adressées à Jean-François ressortissent, essentiellement, à cette même littérature pieuse, et n'ajoutent donc pas grand'chose à l'image d'une spiritualité assez conventionnelle qui se dégage des autres traductions faites par More.

La première de ces deux lettres cependant, qui date du 15 mai 1492, mérite d'être notée, car on peut y lire la confirmation de certaines orientations fondamentales de la pensée de Pic, telles qu'elles s'exprimaient déjà dans ses diverses oeuvres antérieures, en particulier dans l'*Oratio*. On sait que cette "hymne à la liberté" fut diversement interprétée. On voulut y voir le cri de révolte de l'homme prométhéen, revendiquant enfin sa pleine autonomie. Nous ne reviendrons pas sur ces lectures étonnantes: la critique en a été faite entre autres par le P. de Lubac[31] et, de façon radicale, par William G. Craven.[32]

Dans sa lettre à Jean-François, Pic réaffirme cette liberté en termes qui font écho à ceux de l'*Oratio*: ". . . nous n'avons pas besoin d'autres forces pour vaincre que de vouloir, nous-mêmes, vaincre. Il est grand, le bonheur du chrétien, puisque la victoire dépend de sa libre volonté. . . ."[33] Voilà certes une citation qui, hors contexte, fera resurgir toutes les imputations de pélagianisme qui furent adressées à Pic! Mais quelques paragraphes plus loin, reprenant cette question, Pic précise les rôles réciproques de la liberté et de la grâce dans l'économie du salut: "Que pouvons-nous faire, en effet, sans l'aide de Dieu? ou comment nous aidera-t-il sans être invoqué?"[34] Ici encore nous retrouvons une orthodoxie sans faille où résonnent les paroles augustiniennes: "Qui ergo fecit te sine te, non te iustificat sine te."[35]

Intrinsèquement plus importante et significative est la seconde lettre traduite par More, que Pic adressa à l'humaniste Andrea Corneo. Comme le rappelle More dans sa présentation, l'humaniste avait conseillé à Pic d'abandonner l'étude de la philosophie pour se mettre plutôt au service de quelque prince italien. Ainsi, prétendait Corneo, ferait-il enfin oeuvre utile. . . .[36] Touché au plus profond de son être et de son orgueil, Pic réplique sans faire la moindre concession, en exaltant la vie retirée et contemplative qu'il a choisie:

> Tu écris qu'il est temps que je me mette au service de l'un des princes régnant en Italie. C'est que tu ne sais pas quelle opinion les philosophes ont d'eux-mêmes, eux qui, comme le dit Horace, s'estiment rois parmi les rois. Ils ne peuvent se soumettre aux coutumes serviles; ne quittant guère leurs cénacles, se satisfaisant de la paix de leur esprit, ils se suffisent à eux-mêmes; ils ne cherchent rien hors d'eux-mêmes; ce qui est honoré par le vulgaire, eux le méprisent, et tout ce vers quoi aspirent les désirs humains ou l'ambition, ils le négligent ou le dédaignent. . . . C'est donc cette "aurea mediocritas" qu'il nous faut rechercher, elle nous portera telle une monture sûre, soumise à notre volonté. . . . Fidèle à cette vision des choses, j'ai toujours, aux cours princières, aux offices publics, au désir de vous plaire et aux faveurs des curies, préféré ma cellule et mes études, les délices de mes livres et la paix de mon âme.[37]

Que More ait choisi de traduire cette lettre si caractéristique montre qu'en certains points au moins, il existait une réelle affinité entre le saint et le philosophe. More en effet avait longuement hésité. Lui aussi s'était senti attiré par la vie contemplative: ne fut-il pas l'hôte régulier de la Chartreuse de Londres? On sait que, de prime abord, il ressentit une vive répugnance à accepter les honneurs, les charges et les responsabilités de la vie publique. La lettre que Pic adressait à Andrea Corneo a dès lors pu trouver chez More une résonance profonde, un écho de ses propres interrogations.[38] Peut-être aussi était-ce par humilité, ou à titre de mémento personnel, que More exaltait la valeur exemplaire de cette vie contemplative dont lui-même s'était détourné pour mettre ses talents au service d'un prince chrétien, appliquant en cela les conseils de Corneo. Jean Pic, pour More, c'était la voie qui aurait pu être. . . .

Mais ici encore, il faut poser la question: Pic correspond-il à ce portrait idéalisé? En le brossant, More ne s'est-il pas laissé induire en erreur, à force de vouloir que son héros réalise le type de spiritualité dont lui, More, avait gardé la nostalgie? Certains indices permettent de le supposer.

Il y a d'abord une assez étrange confusion de date. More fait expédier cette lettre de Paris, le 15 octobre *1492*, alors que Jean-François donne Pérouse, 15 octobre *1486*. Sans doute le neveu est-il loin de respecter toujours une exacte chronologie;[39] il est néanmoins certain que cette missive a été écrite dans les mois qui précédèrent immédiatement la venue de Pic à Rome, car elle fait allusion au débat public où Pic avait l'intention d'affronter les plus éminents docteurs de la chrétienté.

On sait que cette Dispute, qui aurait dû avoir lieu "après l'Epiphanie" de 1487, fut reportée, puis finalement interdite par Innocent VIII. Pour Pic, cette interdiction, et surtout la disgrâce qui s'ensuivit, furent un choc terrible, et c'est à partir de cet échec qu'il allait progressivement changer son mode de vie. C'est la "conversion" dont Jean-François fait état, et qu'attestent plusieurs contemporains, parmi lesquels Laurent le Magnifique dans ses lettres du 11 août 1488 et du 13 juin 1489. Dans ce contexte, les dates sont importantes, car c'est avant cet échec et avant le revirement auquel il conduisit, que Pic écrivit à Andrea Corneo. A cette époque, il était loin d'être l'humble contemplatif retiré du monde que More voulait voir en lui. Bien au contraire, le jeune comte – il a à peine 24 ans – aspire à la gloire et veut faire un coup d'éclat. C'est pourquoi il décide que le débat aura lieu à Rome: d'exercice académique qu'il aurait été à Paris, il devient, à Rome, événement universel.

Pic ne cache ni son arrogance, ni sa vanité. Il les étale sans vergogne dans cette même lettre à Corneo. Qu'on en juge:

> Je me rendrai prochainement à Rome où je passerai l'hiver, à moins que quelque événement imprévu ou quelque nouvel incident ne me conduise ailleurs. De là te parviendra sans doute l'écho de tout ce que ton Pic a pu réaliser par sa vie contemplative, caché dans sa cellule. Tu peux t'attendre à ce qu'une foule de docteurs aille à sa rencontre, et, pour le dire de façon plus arrogante, tu te demanderas en quoi les oeuvres d'autrui pourront désormais, dans le domaine des lettres, encore lui être utiles.[40]

Par charité chrétienne, ou pour ne pas ternir l'image idéale de son héros, More omet la totalité de ce passage, qui, pourtant, jette une lumière crue sur l'état d'esprit qui était celui de Pic avant que ne le frappe la fortune, par la mesquinerie d'Innocent VIII.

Dans sa *Vita*, et donc indépendamment de la lettre à Corneo, Jean-François avait raconté en détail tout cet épisode. More le rapporte fidèlement tout en y ajoutant encore quelques lignes dans l'intention de faire ressortir l'esprit de soumission dont Pic aurait fait preuve à cette occasion. En effet, selon la version de More, Pic lui-même, reconnaissant le danger que la présentation de ses *Conclusiones* pouvait présenter pour un public non averti, aurait demandé que la lecture en soit interdite. Et Thomas More souligne la portée exemplaire de l'événement: "Picus himself desired, that it should not be readde. And so was the reading thereof forboden. Lo, this ende had Picus of his hye mynde and proud purpose: and where he thought to have gotten perpetuall praise, there had he muche werke to kepe himself upright: that he ranne not in perpetual infamy and sclaundre."[41]

⁓

Il est vrai que, par après et graduellement, Pic perdra son arrogance initiale; de plus en plus, il voudra se retirer hors du monde pour s'adonner à une contemplation plus pure et moins ostentatoire. Est-ce à dire que, lors de cette seconde phase de son évolution spirituelle, Pic ait plus authentiquement correspondu au portrait que More s'en fera? En particulier, sera-ce sans arrière-pensée, sans réserve et par humilité vraie, que Pic voudra se libérer des tentations mondaines?

On notera d'abord qu'au dire même de Jean-François, c'était à une retraite dorée que Pic se préparait. S'il se défait au bénéfice de son neveu des terres qu'il possédait à Mirandole et à Concordia, c'était, note son biographe, pour "posthabitis dominandi curis,"[42] jouir plus librement d'une pleine quiétude. Et s'il distribue aux pauvres des sommes importantes, ce sera après avoir pris la sage précaution de se bâtir une résidence champêtre à Corbula,[43] où, entouré d'une bibliothèque en laquelle il avait investi, au bas mot, quelque 7.000 écus d'or, il allait pouvoir enfin se livrer aux plus hautes méditations. . . .

A ce tableau virgilien, Jean-François ajoute une touche fort significative: c'est son ami Girolamo qu'il chargera de distribuer ses biens aux pauvres, se libérant ainsi de contacts sans doute trop directs. Plus tard, Benivieni confirmera ce point à Jean-François, ajoutant qu'il se considérait comme le "buffetier" de Jean Pic. . . .[44]

On sait également, et More le reprend de Jean-François, que Jean Pic "avait en horreur les dures obligations qu'impose le siècle, comme il avait horreur des liens conjugaux. Un jour qu'on lui demandait en manière de plaisanterie lequel des deux maux lui semblerait plus tolérable, s'il était mis en demeure de choisir, il hésita quelque peu en hochant la tête, et répondit en souriant: 'Le lien conjugal, qui n'impose pas une égale servitude, ni autant de danger que les obligations publiques.' "[45]

⁓

Charles Trinkaus observait que "solitude is a heaven on earth reserved for those few individualists who put their own salvation before that of others and live the dream life of perpetual vacation in their country retreat."[46] C'est Pétrarque que Trinkaus décrit ainsi, mais combien ce portrait sera-t-il encore celui de Pic, quelque cent années plus tard! Quant à Thomas More qui, lui, a choisi l'engagement social, il signale, en une prise de conscience qui aurait réjoui Emmanuel Kant, le danger de la "fuite hors du monde":

> Alors qu'un peu hâtivement tu envisages de te soustraire à l'emprise des pernicieuses voluptés en cherchant refuge en une pieuse solitude, sous le regard de Dieu . . . peut-être te convaincras-tu d'avoir refusé les affaires publiques, de t'être dérobé aux obligations et d'avoir, sous prétexte de piété, recherché la douceur du repos et voulu échapper à l'accablement des soucis.[47]

Pic semble ne s'être jamais posé de telles questions, ni avoir ressenti de telles hésitations. Aussi n'éprouve-t-il jamais le besoin de justifier son choix—ce qui étonne de la part d'un homme très porté à l'introspection, surtout en matière religieuse.

Comparant donc les types de spiritualité exemplifiés respectivement par Pic et par More, et dans la mesure où il est légitime d'opposer l'orientation plus sociale de la conscience religieuse humaniste à celle plus intimiste des temps médiévaux, c'est Thomas More, bien évidemment, qui représente une spiritualité nouvelle, tandis que la religiosité de Pic était radicalement tournée vers les modèles des temps passés. Combien plus proche en effet devait-il se sentir d'un Gundissalinus qui, au douzième siècle exprimait son idéal de vie religieuse et contemplative en cette formule lapidaire: *in secreto cordis, soli sibi loqui et Deo*.[48]

Weiss prétendait que "ciò che di Pico attraeva specialmente il Moro era che nei suoi scritti egli troveva non così tanto una nuova filosofia, quanto l'espressione di *quel nuovo tipo di sentimento religioso* a cui annelava."[49] Craven s'en étonne et ironise: "It is difficult to understand how these writings could provide the slightest evidence of a new worldly asceticism, or even the 'new type of religious sentiment' which Roberto Weiss claimed that More had found in them."[50] Au vu de ce qui précède et en ce qui concerne les textes traduits par More, on ne peut que se déclarer pleinement d'accord avec Craven, si souvent iconoclaste soit-il.

V

Le théologien laïc

Cela dit, il est un aspect de l'oeuvre et de la personnalité de Pic que Thomas More aurait pu prendre et citer en exemple. Pic en effet, et malgré le caractère intimiste de sa religiosité, préfigure un trait essentiel de ce nouveau type de chrétien laïque qui allait s'affirmer aux temps de la Réforme et de la Contre-Réforme—mais c'est là un aspect qui n'apparaît d'aucune façon dans la sélection de textes faite par More.

Intégralement croyant, apportant toutes les ressources de sa réflexion et de sa vaste culture aux discussions théologiques, dont il reconnaît par là-même l'importance capitale, c'est d'égal à égal qu'il prétend y participer, en toute fidélité, certes, mais aussi en préservant jalousement son indépendance intellectuelle. Tel apparaît Pic, et à cet égard il fut une des figures-clés de la culture religieuse humaniste: Erasme lui-même n'hésitera pas à le prendre pour modèle. Car la théologie est au centre des préoccupations de Pic et motive toutes ses recherches.

C'est en effet d'abord aux théologiens de son temps que Pic lance le défi de son débat public; l'*Heptaplus* est un commentaire exclusivement théologique; on a signalé plus haut quelques-unes des plus évidentes implications théologiques du *De ente*; de larges sections de ses *Conclusiones* traitent de questions théologiques, et l'*Apologia* en reprend plusieurs, qui y sont traitées selon le style, dans la perspective, et avec les ressources de la scolastique. Or, en toutes ces matières, Pic revendique la plénitude de son droit de parole, et veut faire oeuvre originale. Si on le voit dans son *Apologia* qui prend plaisir à souligner les nombreuses contradictions échappées à la plume de "Thomas,"[51] et s'il n'hésite pas à invoquer l'autorité d'Augustin, à grand renfort de citations textuelles, c'est précisément pour battre en brèche l'argument d'autorité, même et surtout en théologie. Et Pic de souligner: "En dehors du canon de la Bible, il n'y a pas de vérité infaillible."[52] Aussi n'accepte-t-il de soumettre son jugement, en matière théologique, qu'à l'autorité du pape, parce que le pape "agit en vicaire de celui-là même qui est la vérité."[53]

Par ailleurs, comme en témoigne l'arrogance de son attitude et les sarcasmes qu'il leur adresse, il se considère très évidemment supérieur aux membres de la Commission d'enquête, pourtant choisis par Innocent VIII parmi les théologiens les plus réputés de ce temps, et c'est sur leur propre terrain qu'il entend les mettre en déroute. Ajoutons encore qu'en ce qui concerne sa démarche religieuse personnelle et le développement de sa vie spirituelle, Pic a toujours tenu à préserver son entière autonomie. Même face à la personnalité puissamment dominatrice d'un Savonarole, Pic ne s'est jamais laissé détourner de ce qu'il pensait être sa voie. Malgré les vives incitations du Dominicain, malgré le respect que Pic lui voua, toujours et jusqu'à la fin, il refusa d'entrer dans les Ordres, parce qu'il estimait que telle n'était pas sa vocation.

Sur ce point, il existe un évident parallèle entre l'attitude de More et celle de Pic.

Une dernière remarque s'impose. Pic exige avec force et constance de participer en égal aux discussions des théologiens. Cependant cette exigence ne signifie en aucune façon que, dans ces discussions, il se soit fait le porte-parole de positions d'avant-garde ou simplement novatrices: on note même que la plupart des conceptions théologiques qu'il défendait étaient plus traditionnelles ou conventionnelles que celles habituellement reçues au sein de la *via communis*, ce qui explique, au moins en partie, les difficultés que lui firent subir les autorités romaines.[54]

La Commission chargée par Innocent VIII d'enquêter sur l'orthodoxie des 900 Conclusions était constituée de théologiens qui se réclamaient presque tous de la *via moderna*, à forte dominance scotiste et occamiste. A de nombreuses reprises et dès la première discussion, Pic s'oppose explicitement à cette "voie courante," précisant bien qu'il "appelle 'voie courante des théologiens' celle qui est communément admise aujourd'hui à Paris où règne principalement l'étude de la théologie. Or en cette ville, presque tous . . . marchent sur les traces des scotistes et des nominalistes."[55] Garsia, qui se faisait le porte-parole de ses collègues et était l'adversaire le plus acharné de Pic, lui opposa explicitement la thèse fidéiste, selon laquelle la foi est d'abord un acte de la volonté libre, et que par conséquent elle ne demande ni ne présuppose aucune intervention de l'intelligence: "Deo digna credulitas est illa et sola talis qua si creditur sine omni pignore rationis aut probationum coactione, gratis scilicet et oboedienter . . . et omnis alia credulitas est irreligiosa et Deo contumeliosa."[56]

Or, dans sa conclusion *De libertate credendi*, Pic avait précisément défendu la thèse opposée, et cette conclusion avait été jugée *heresim sapientem*. Il la reprendra longuement dans son *Apologia* où il précisera entr'autre qu' "il n'est pas au libre pouvoir de l'homme de faire apparaître à son intelligence la vérité ou de faire apparaître la non-vérité d'une chose; donc il n'est pas au pouvoir de l'homme de croire, de telle ou de telle façon, que telle chose est vraie ou non."[57] L'insistance de Pic sur ce point montre à l'évidence que selon sa thèse, l'intellect a au moins une primauté de fait sur la volonté, ce qui confirme encore l'orientation antifidéiste et antivolontariste de sa pensée.

Réapparaît ainsi l'antique controverse qui, depuis Augustin et Plotin, oppose "volontarisme" et "intellectualisme." Cette controverse, au centre des débats de l'humanisme depuis Pétrarque, allait marquer les âpres disputes de la Réforme, le paradoxe étant que Thomas More, l'homme d'action, se trouvait sur ce point beaucoup plus proche de la Réforme que Pic, le contemplatif, aurait jamais pu l'être. Ce n'est pas le lieu ici de développer cette question; ce qu'on en a dit cependant permet de souligner à quel point il est faux d'inscrire Pic dans cette lignée qui, partant à la fois de l'occamisme et de la mystique rhénane, aboutit à Luther en passant par la *devotio moderna*. Telle était cependant la thèse de Ed. Zeller, qui prétendait mettre "en évidence la parenté entre la pensée de Pic et la *theologia germanica* que Luther devait particulièrement apprécier, à côté de la Bible et des écrits de S. Augustin."[58]

En fait, dans cette accélération de l'histoire que connut le début du seizième siècle, Thomas More, contemporain d'Erasme et de Luther, participe d'une mentalité "pragmatique" où l'action et la transformation du monde l'emportent sur les considérations théoriques. Concluons donc qu'entre Pic et More, une cassure irréversible est survenue. Ils représentent, dans le cadre d'une même foi chrétienne, l'affrontement de deux types de spiritualités qui, si elles empruntent parfois le même langage, sont enracinées, à une génération de distance, dans des époques déjà profondément différentes.

Université de Sherbrooke

Notes

Les références renvoient aux éditions suivantes: *Oratio* et *De ente et uno*: — G. Pico della Mirandola, *De hominis dignitate, Heptaplus, De ente et uno*, a cura di Eugenio Garin (Firenze: Vallecchi Editore, 1942); *Apologia* et *Lettres*: — *Ioannis Pici Mirandulani Opera Omnia*, reproduction anastatique de l'édition de Bâle (1557), avec introduction de Cesare Vasoli (Darmstadt: Wilhelm Weihert); *Ioannis Pici Mirandulae Vita*: —Edition de Tommaso Sorbelli (Modena: Aedes Muratoriana, 1963). Sera par la suite abrégé en *Vita*.

Pour les citations de l'*Oratio*, de l'*Apologia* et de la *Lettre* à Jean-François, nous utilisons, parfois librement, les traductions de R. Galibois, du Centre d'études de la Renaissance, Université de Sherbrooke (non encore publiées).

The Life of John Picus Erle of Myrandula . . . est citée dans l'édition des *English Works of Sir Thomas More*, reproduced in facsimile from William Rastell's edition of 1557, and edited . . . by W. E. Campbell, (London and New York: Eyre and Spottiswoode, Lincoln Mac Veagh, 1931). Sera par la suite abrégé en *Life*.

1. Cf. Roberto Weiss, "Pico e l'Inghilterra" in *L'opera e il pensiero di Giovanni Pico della Mirandola nella storia del umanesimo* (Firenze: Istituto nazionale di studi sul Rinascimento, 1965) vol. I, p. 141–58; dans le même sens: Myron Gilmore, "More's Translation of Gianfrancesco Pico's Biography," Ibid. vol. II, p. 301–4; Eugenio Garin, *Pico della Mirandola* (1963), pp. 52–53.

2. Le total ne représente que 34 pp. des *English Works*.... De ces 34 pp., les 10 premières contiennent la traduction de la *Vita*; suivent trois lettres, dont la première et la troisième sont adressées à Jean-François Pic et la seconde à l'humaniste Andrea Corneo. Viennent ensuite quelques-unes de ces oeuvres d'édification que Jean-François mentionne globalement comme étant "*quaedam item minutula non tornata* . . ." [*Vita*, p. 54]. De ces "oeuvrettes inachevées," More traduisit le *In psalmum XV commentarius* ainsi que les *Regulae XII partim excitantes, partim dirigentes hominem in pugna spirituali*. Suivent encore les *Duodecim arma spiritualis pugnae*, que Thomas More développe longuement. Il en va de même des *Duodecim conditiones amantis* et de l'élégie *Deprecatoria ad Deum*. Excluant donc la *Vita*, dont l'auteur est Jean-François Pic, excluant aussi les présentations, les additions et les commentaires que More ajoute à sa traduction, il ne reste finalement qu'une vingtaine de pages qui sont vraiment attribuables à Pic. C'est peu de chose, surtout en tenant compte de la prolixité de ce dernier.

3. Germain Marc'hadour, "Thomas More's Spirituality" in *Saint Thomas More: Action and Contemplation*, ed. Richard Sylvester (New Haven and London: Yale University Press, 1972), p. 130.

4. *Vita*, p. 46: "Vidimus etiam nonnulla platonica vernaculo sermone ab eo digesta . . . quae forsan maius ocium nacti latina reddere tentabimus ne tanti hominis supereminens doctrina hisce de rebus maxime pervia quibusque vulgi ante ora feratur."

5. Dans l'édition Sorbelli, le texte latin avec traduction italienne comprend 58 pp., et les références à la démarche philosophique de Jean Pic, entièrement omises par Thomas More, comportent à elles seules 18 pp.

6. C'est ce que le livre du P. de Lubac établissait de façon définitive: Henri de Lubac, *Pic de la Mirandole* (Paris: Aubier-Montaigne, 1976).

7. Paul O. Kristeller, "Pico della Mirandola," in *Encyclopedia of Philosophy* (New York and London: Macmillan and Free Press).

8. *Oratio*, p. 160: ". . . vidi in illis [libris scientiae Cabalae] — testis est Deus — religionem non tam Mosaicam quam Christianam. Ibi Trinitatis mysterium, ibi Verbi incarnatio, ibi Messiae divinitas, ibi de peccato originali, de illius per Christum expiatione etc. . . . eadem legi quae apud Paulum et Dionysium."

— ". . . j'y ai vu [dans les livres savants de la cabale] — Dieu m'est témoin — une religion non pas tellement mosaïque que chrétienne. Là le mystère de la Trinité, là l'Incarnation du Verbe, là la divinité du Messie, là la doctrine du péché originel et de son expiation par le Christ, etc. . . . me sont apparus exactement comme chez Paul et Denys."

9. Nous nous permettons de renvoyer le lecteur à notre article "Entre raison et foi: le néoplatonisme de Jean Pic de la Mirandole," dans *Recherches*

94 ～ *Pic de la Mirandole*

de Théologie ancienne et médiévale, Tome LIV (Louvain: Abbaye du Mont-César, 1987), pp. 186-237.
10. *Opera omnia*, p. 359.
11. En un livre par ailleurs très inégal, Jacques Quéron souligne à ce propos qu'"il y va . . . de la cohérence de cette théologie bicéphale que ses garants disent très profondément la même chose, au moins en tout ce qui regarde le cheminement vers Dieu et sur ce qui peut être articulé de sa nature." Jacques Quéron, *Pic de la Mirandole, contribution à la connaissance de l'humanisme renaissant* (Aix-en-Provence: Université de Provence, 1986), p. 56.
12. *De ente et uno*, p. 386: ". . . quomodo et defenderetur . . . Aristoteles et Platoni magistro consentiret."
13. Voir en particulier le deuxième chapitre du *De ente*: "In quo quaerit ubi Plato de ente et uno sit locutus ostenditque illius verba favere sententiae dicenti unum et ens aequalia, quam his qui volunt unum esse ente superius."
– "On se demande où Platon a parlé de l'être et de l'un, et l'on montre que ses paroles sont plutôt favorables à l'opinion que l'un et l'être sont égaux, qu'à ceux pour qui l'un est supérieur à l'être."
14. *Vita*, p. 44; ". . . opusculum etiam *De ente et uno*, decem capitulis distinctum, absolvit, breve quidem corpore, sed amplum viribus, sed altissimis et Philosophorum dogmatis et Theologicis sensibus undequaque respersum quo superius Ente non esse Unum, sed sibi invicem respondere, aequalique esse ambitu ostendit."
– ". . . l'opuscule, divisé en dix chapitres, traite également à fond de l'Etre et de l'Un, dans un exposé bref mais vigoureux, mais mis en lumière tant par les théories philosophiques que par les positions théologiques les plus hautes, par quoi l'on montre que l'être n'est pas supérieur à l'un mais qu'ils se répondent l'un à l'autre et que les deux sont commensurables."
15. *Vita*, p. 70; l'apostrophe interrompt le cinquième chapitre du *De ente*, p. 418.
– "Mais vois, mon cher Ange, quelle folie nous tient. Nous pouvons aimer Dieu, tant que nous sommes dans notre corps, plus que nous ne pouvons parler de lui, ou même le connaître; l'aimer nous est plus profitable et demande moins d'effort; nous l'honorons alors davantage; et pourtant nous préférons toujours, par la connaissance, ne jamais trouver ce que nous cherchons, plutôt que de posséder dans l'amour ce que nous trouvons en vain sans l'amour."
16. Cf. H. de Lubac, pp. 281-82.
17. Cité par H. de Lubac, ibid.
18. Bruno Nardi, "La mistica averroistica e Pico della Mirandola," *Umanesimo e Machiavellismo* (Padova: Ed. Liviana, 1969), p. 71.
19. *Vita*: ". . . hortabaturque ut ad Deum amandum converterent et incitarent mentes. Quod opus praeponderaret cuicumque, quam in hac vita habere possemus, cognitioni hoc etiam in libello ipso *De Ente et Uno* luculentissime est executus, quando ad Angelum Politianum . . . in ipsa disputatione, conversus haec verba effatus fuerit: 'Sed vide, mi Angele . . . ,'" p. 70. Cf. *Life*, p. 7.
– ". . . et il les exhortait à tourner et à stimuler leur esprit vers l'amour

de Dieu. Cette enterprise était plus urgente que toute connaissance offerte en cette vie, comme il l'a exposé lumineusement dans le livret *De ente et uno*, lorsque, dans cette dissertation même . . . il s'adresse à Ange Politien en ces termes: Mais vois, mon cher Ange . . ."

20. Cf. *Life*, p. 7.
21. *Conf.*, I vi, 10.
22. *De ente*, p. 418.
23. *Vita*, p. 48, 54.
24. Ibid., p. 46.
25. Giovanni Di Napoli, *Pico della Mirandola e la problematica del suo tempo* (Roma, Parigi, Tournai, New York: Desclée-de Brouwer, 1965), p. 237.
26. Vittorio Gabrieli, "Giovanni Pico and Thomas More," *Moreana* 15/16 (1967): 44.
27. Ibid., p. 43.
28. Ibid., p. 46.
29. "Echoes and analogues of Pico's commonplaces of Christian piety . . . crop up. . . . The echoes chiefly regard the problems of virtue and sin, of death and doom, of temporary pleasure and everlasting joy." Ibid., p. 50.
30. En particulier en ce qui concerne l'exemple donné, puisque l'auteur reconnaît que le thème de *The Four Last Things* (*Les Quatre Fins Dernières*) est inspiré de "Quoi que tu fasses, souviens-toi de ta fin et jamais tu ne pécheras," et que "Pico had probably the same passage of Scripture in mind. . . ." La référence Ecclésiastique 7.27 comme source de ce texte est une coquille; c'est Ecclésiastique 7.40 selon la Vulgate, Siracide 7.36 dans les bibles modernes.
31. V. n.6.
32. William G. Craven, *Pico della Mirandola, Symbol of His Age* (Genève: Librairie Droz, 1981).
33. ". . . neque aliis nobis ut vincamus viribus opus est, quam ut vincere ipsi velimus. Magna Christiani felicitas, quando & in eius arbitrio posita est victoria." *Opera omnia*, p. 340–41.
34. "quid enim possumus sine auxilio Dei? aut quomodo ille auxiliabitur non invocatus?" Ibid., p. 343.
35. *Sermo* 169.
36. "Wherefore he counseiled Pycus to surceace of study, and put himself with some of the great princes of Italie, with whom (as this Andrew said) he should be much more fruitfully occupied, then alway in the study and lernyng of philosophie." *Life*, p. 14.
37. "Scribis appetere tempus, ut me alicui ex summis Italiae principibus dedam. Adhuc illam philosophantium de se opinionem non nosti, qui iuxta Horatium se regum reges putant, mores pati, & servire nesciunt, secum habitant, & sua contenti animi tranquillitate, sibi ipsis ipsi supersunt, nihil extra se quaerunt; quae in honore sunt apud vulgus, inhonora sunt apud illos, & omnino quaecumque vel humana sitit libido, vel suspirat ambitio, negligunt et contemnunt. . . . Aurea illa optanda mediocritas, quas nos uti man(n)us vehat aequabilius, & imperii patiens nobis vere serviat non dominetur. In

hac ego opinione perstans cellulam meam, mea studia, meorum librorum oblectamenta, meam animi pacem, regiis aulis, publicis negociis, vestris aucupiis, curie favoribus, antepono." *Opera omnia*, p. 377.

On note que c'est en des termes fort semblables que Pic s'adressera à Jean-François, dans sa lettre du 15 mai 1492: "In principum gratia promerenda, in aequalium amicitiis conciliandis, in honoribus ambiendis, quae moles molestiarum, quantum anxietatis, quantum sit sollicitudinis ex te rogo discere potius possum quam te docere, qui meis libris meo ociolo contentus, a pueris usque infra fortunam vivere didici, & (quantum possum) apud me inhabitans, nihil extra meipsum suspiro vel ambio." *Opera omnia*, p. 341.

—"Mériter la faveur des princes, gagner l'amitié de ses égaux, rechercher les honneurs; le poids des peines, le foisonnement des inquiétudes et le foisonnement des soucis . . . je ne demande qu'à apprendre tout cela de toi plutôt que je ne saurais que te l'enseigner, car moi, si je me contente de mes livres et de mes loisirs, c'est que j'ai appris dès l'enfance à vivre en-deça de mes moyens, et autant que possible, dans la solitude; je ne souhaite et ne recherche rien hors de moi."

38. Cf. Gabrieli, p. 48; Weiss, 146–47.

39. Cf. Eugenio Garin, *La cultura filosofica del Rinascimento italiano* (Firenze: Sansoni Ed., 1979), p. 254.

40. "Romam prope diem proficiscar inibi hyematurus, nisi vel repens casus, vel nova intercidens fortuna, alio me traxerit. Inde fortasse audies quid tuus Picus in vita umbratili & cellularia contemplando profecerit, aut quid tandem (dicam enim quamquam arrogantius) quid inquam, quando tu illi isthuc accedenti doctorum copiam polliceris, aliorum opere indiget in re literaria." *Opera omnia*, p. 378.

41. *Life*, p. 4.

42. *Vita*, p. 62–64: "Triennio igitur priusquam diem obiret, ut, posthabitis dominandi curis, in alta pace degere posset, securus quo sceptra caderent, cuncta patrimonia, quae Mirandulae, Concordiaeque possidebat, hoc est tertiam partem earum, mihi nescio an dono an venditione tradidit."

—"Et donc, trois ans avant sa mort, ayant renoncé à tout souci de domination et afin de vivre dans une paix totale, assuré du côté où tomberaient les sceptres, il me remit en don ou à titre onéreux, je ne sais pas, toutes les terres qu'il possédait à Mirandole et à Concordia, c'est-à-dire le tiers de ses biens."

43. Ibid., p. 64: "Corbula in agro Ferrariensi multis aureorum milibus nummum sibi comparavit." Thomas More ne parle pas de ces "milliers d'écus," et prétend corriger Jean-François en affirmant que l'achat, fort modeste, ne portait que sur "a little lande" *Life*, p. 6.

—"A Corbula, dans la région de Ferrare, il fit une acquisition pour des milliers et des milliers d'écus d'or."

44. Giovanni Di Napoli le dit fort bien: "I poveri, cui Pico sovveniva, venivano talora a bussare alla sua casa, ma più spesso egli non li conosceva; aveva dato incarico a Girolamo Benivieni di provvedere ai bisogni in genere e alle giovani che non avessero i mezzi necessari per le loro nozze; egli, Pico,

avrebbe poi rimborsato al Benivieni le somme errogate; non aveva torto il Benivieni di considerarsi lo "armario" dell amico Conte." Giov. Di Napoli (n. 25), p. 227.

45. *Vita*, p. 72: "Militiam quoque saeculi et conjugale vinculum perosus fuerat; interrogatusque inter iocandum quid ei ad alterum subeundum onus ferendumque et necessitate cogente et optione data, levius videretur haesitabundus aliquantum nutabundusque necnon pauxillum subridens coniugium, respondit, cui non tantum esset et servitutis annexum et periculi quantum militiae subeundum onus." Cf. *Life*, p. 8.

46. Charles Trinkaus, *The Poet as Philosopher, Petrarch and the Formation of Renaissance Consciousness* (New York and London: Yale University Press, 1979), p. 83.

47. Elizabeth Frances Rogers, *The Correspondence of Sir Thomas More*, (Princeton University Press, 1947), pp. 203-4, 1443-59 ("To a Monk" No. 83); v. aussi tr. fr. de ce passage par Henri Gibaud et Germain Marc'hadour, *Moreana* 27/28 (1970): 79-80.

48. Cité par Eugenio Garin, *Medioevo e Rinascimento* (Bari, Ed. Laterza, 1981), p. 21.

49. Weiss, p. 146.

50. Craven, p. 86.

51. *Apologia*, Opera omnia, pp. 136-38.

52. Ibid.: ". . . extra canonem Bibliae non sit veritas infallibilis. . . . Ipsimet doctores de dictis suis dubitant, an in eis erraverint an non." *Opera omnia*, p. 144.

53. Ibid.: "Examinabunt haec deinde alii viri docti & insignes & apud nostras & apud exteras Academias iudicabit sancta sedes, et sedens in ea Innocentius octavus, cuius iudicium neglegere aut violare, nephas & flagitium, ipse iudex supraemus in terris, qui eum refert, qui iudex est vivorum & mortuorum, ipse, promptuarium arcanumque veritatis, qui eius agit vices qui est ipsa veritas, & caro factus habitavit in nobis, ut veritatem nobis annunciaret." *Opera omnia*, p. 125.

—"Ensuite, d'autres esprits éminents examineront ce dossier et, en présence des universités d'ici ou d'ailleurs, le Saint-Siège, avec Innocent VIII son occupant, portera jugement; jugement qu'il serait impie et ignominieux de négliger ou d'enfreindre: lui-même est ici-bas le juge suprême, représentant de celui qui est juge des vivants et des morts; lui-même est, de la vérité, la secrète chambre-forte, et il agit en vicaire de celui qui est la vérité même, et qui, s'étant fait chair, a demeuré parmi nous pour nous annoncer la vérité."

54. A propos de la Commission d'enquête et de sa composition, cf. Giovanni Di Napoli, parte prima, cap. II et III.

55. *Apologia*: "Communem viam theologorum appellans, quae communiter nunc tenetur Parisiis, ubi praecipue viget studium theologiae. Ibi autem fere omnes incedunt in ista materia de praesentialitate animae ad locum cum Scotistis et Nominalibus." *Opera omnia*, p. 135.

56. Cf. Giovanni Di Napoli p. 183. Cette formulation rappelle la thèse

de Holkot, successeur d'Occam à Oxford, qui poussa le nominalisme à ses conséquences extrêmes.

57. *Apologia*: "Non est in potestate hominis libera, facere apparere aliquid suo intellectui esse verum, et facere apparere non esse verum, ergo, non est in potestate hominis, sic vel sic credere esse, vel non esse verum." *Opera omnia*, p. 226.

58. Cf. *Conclusiones...*, éd. Bohdan Kieszkowski (Genève: Librairie Droz, 1973), p. 26.

C. Normand Poirier
9117 Hamilton Drive
Fairfax, Virginia 22031

Dear Germain,
November 20, 1987

This is a happy occasion. Not often enough do we express our sentiments for one whom we have long admired and for whom respect and regard have provided fertile soil for a wonderful friendship.

Our association dates from the Thomas More symposium held in Washington in 1978. I was pressed by friends whom we have both held in affection, Therese and Roger Bernique, to introduce myself to you on that occasion. I did so little realizing how this association would deepen and lead to activities undertaken with others to promote knowledge of Thomas More.

Your unselfish support helped those of us who organized the Thomas More Society of America to recruit our first members. Following a conference held in Angers, you launched the Gazette which our Society adopted as its official bulletin and which constantly wins the praise of those who are active in the Society's affairs. Your support has been continuing and without any element of self aggrandizement to blemish the generosity with which it has always been characterized.

I would be remiss if I failed to note your personal qualities of winsomeness, friendship and the splendid luster of your character which combine to earn for you a depth of affection and respect that few command. For these and for your many kindnesses given over these years I express my deep appreciation and regard.

Sincerely,

Normand

(C. Normand Poirier : April 18, 1927 - June 28, 1988.)

Washington, D.C.
Nov. 4, 1987.

Dear Father Germain,

If my memory is correct, I believe we first met in the summer of 1966 when you and Yvonne Batard and Noëlle Marie Egretier all converged in Washington. What happy gatherings we had. You will remember one day when we took Father Laurentin to the airport for his flight to Dayton!

Among my most treasured memories are those times when you said Mass in my living room for some of our friends. And then there was the memorable -- for me! -- August of 1979 which I spent in Angers, thanks to you.

May I simply say: Thank you with all my heart for all you have given me over these years. You have enriched my life enormously.

May God continue to bless you and help you in good health.

With love,

Marion Ferrell

```
Marion was again able to have Abbé Marc'hadour
preside at a liturgy in her home, during his
visit to Washington in April 1989.  This visit
also provided an opportunity for a rendezvous
with Monsignor Awalt.  (See his letter in
Section VI.)
```

Département d'Anglais
Institut de Perfectionnement en Langues Vivantes
Université Catholique de l'Ouest
Angers

Cher Ami,

Je ne sais pas si j'ai bien le droit d'utiliser ce vocatif, puisque les circonstances n'ont pas fait de moi un Amicus Thomae Mori, – ou ne m'ont fait abonné de Moreana que peu d'années (les premières, il est vrai) : mais peut-être l'ancienneté de nos relations m'excusera-t-elle de l'usurper ?

On me dit que quelque célébration se prépare pour marquer à la fois le jubilé d'argent de Moreana et le fait que tu transmettes quelques-unes de tes responsabilités à de plus jeunes. Bien que la cérémonie doive avoir lieu à Toronto, sache que, par-dessus l'océan, je me joindrai bien sincèrement par la pensée à tout ce qui s'y passera d'agréable pour toi. Depuis environ trente ans que je te connais, j'ai trop souvent eu l'occasion d'apprécier ton dynamisme, la serviabilité et tes compétences culturelles, pour ne pas profiter de la circonstance pour te dire quelle admiration et quelle gratitude je porte à ton égard.

Comme étudiant, j'ai pu profiter, agréablement et utilement, de ton goût communicatif, sinon de ta passion, pour la philologie, et, trente ans après, je me réjouis encore d'avoir été ainsi touché par cette grâce, si le mot n'est pas trop fort. Mais le serait-il quand il s'agit de faire allusion à une discipline qui met l'esprit contemporain en contact avec l'esprit de nos ancêtres dans la culture ? Comme collègue, j'ai particulièrement apprécié l'aide que tu m'as apportée dans la préparation d'une thèse de Doctorat sur des questions à la fois linguistiques et religieuses. Dans de tels moments laborieux et parfois angoissants, l'intérêt, les encouragements et le conseil d'un spécialiste sont proprement inappréciables. Comme responsable actuel du Département d'anglais, j'apprécie souvent ta disponibilité à nous rendre service, cette année à nouveau, bien que tu eusses aimé à être déchargé de tout enseignement.

Pour tout cela et bien d'autres circonstances de la vie dont celles évoquées ici, compétence, solidarité et dévouement, ne sont que la partie visible d'un iceberg, je saisis l'occasion qui m'est donnée pour t'exprimer publiquement mes remerciements et mon amitié. Je les confie aussi à Dieu, avec les vœux que je forme pour toi en union avec tous les Amici : Il saura, mieux que moi et avec une efficacité plus réelle, leur donner une vraie valeur.

Michel TAILLÉ

J. K. SOWARDS

On Education: More's Debt to Erasmus

ERASMUS WAS THE MOST important and influential educational writer of the sixteenth century.[1] His ideas about education and schools, about language, about the nature and nurture of children radiated out to his friends and fellow humanists to influence their views and often to be influenced by their suggestions and practices. Among these was the great English humanist and statesman Thomas More. It will be the subject of this paper to examine the relationship and influence of Erasmus as an educational writer upon the ideas and educational practices of More.

The celebrity of Erasmus as an educational writer and theorist derived, to some extent, from the more general celebrity in the world of contemporary letters of the "Prince of Humanists." It derived as well from the fact that Erasmus stood at the end of a long process of evolution in educational theory that stretched back through his fifteenth-century Italian humanist predecessors to the revered ancient authorities—Cicero, Plutarch, and especially Quintilian.[2] But it also derived from the liveliness, good sense, and practicality of what he had to say about children and the process of instructing them.

His interest in the educative process began in an intensely practical way, when in the late 1490s, as a theological student at the University of Paris, he was forced to take private tutorial pupils to supplement his income. When he looked around for texts and manuals from which to teach them he found none that satisfied him—indeed he was appalled by what he did find. This forced him to search back into his own experience of education and to replicate it. The first edition of his later famous *Adagia* was almost certainly suggested by his own practice of note-taking and was dedicated to one of his English pupils, Lord Mountjoy, intended as an aid for him, and other pupils, in "searching for greater elegance and more refined style."[3] The earliest form of the *Colloquia* was "a few daily conversational sentences such as we use on meeting each other at table,"[4] which Erasmus prepared for the use of two other pupils, the Northoff brothers, from northern Germany, little dialogues as examples of good spoken Latin. The original version of his great textbook on letter writing, *De conscribendis epistolis*, was dedicated to another young English pupil, Robert Fisher.[5] It was the same with the earliest version of his most important textbook, *De copia*.[6] The "ordered course of study," that would later be published as *De ratione studii*,[7] was written for Thomas Grey, yet another English pupil.

All these young men were regular students at the University of Paris at various stages in various curricula. But there is no evidence that any of them sought Erasmus' tutorial help with their regular university courses or that he was interested in providing such help. They and he were interested rather in improving their command of colloquial humanistic Latin, not only to put them in touch with the leading intellectual fashion of the time, but in order to get along better in the academic and professional world. Hence the focus of Erasmus' attention was upon pre- and non-university education in practical eloquence and "good letters," especially for teen-agers. It was a focus he never lost in his later educational writings. He always considered university studies as professional in nature, to be entered upon only after the kind of secondary schooling or tutorial instruction he advocated. The center of his educational writings was to be the adolescent years and what we would today call upper primary and secondary education.

It was surely the purest chance that several of Erasmus' pupils in Paris were young Englishmen—Mountjoy, Fisher, Grey. One of them, Lord Mountjoy, invited his tutor to come to England with him in the summer of 1499 and Erasmus accepted. Mountjoy introduced Erasmus to the circle of English men of letters, scholars, humanists, and patrons who were to be counted among his closest friends and who were to exert such a powerful influence upon his life. They included the teacher and rhetorician William Grocyn, the humanist physician and Greek scholar Thomas Linacre, the theologian John Colet, and, not least, young Thomas More, who was to become his dearest friend.

In those few months of his first visit to England Erasmus was preoccupied with his emerging educational ideas and must have discussed them with his new English friends, for such ideas were of perennial interest in the humanist community. Erasmus returned to England in 1506 and, after a brief visit to Italy, came back to England in the summer of 1509 for his longest stay there, until 1514. His ideas about education continued to develop and were furthered by his association with John Colet's work at St. Paul's school. Colet had been appointed dean of St. Paul's in 1504 and, in 1510, as part of his effort to reform the chapter, he used his own sizable family fortune to re-endow the cathedral school. Erasmus became Colet's chief educational advisor in this enterprise.[8]

Thomas More was also interested in Colet's school and the innovative humanist program that was being set in place there—to the discomfort of many conservative theologians and scholastics. In a brief note to Colet, probably written in the spring of 1512, he said:

I don't much wonder if *they* are bursting with jealousy of your excellent school. For they see that, just as the Greeks who destroyed barbarian Troy came out of the Trojan horse, so from your school come those who reprove and overthrow *their* ignorance.[9]

These were the years of the closest personal association between More and Erasmus, during which they shared their enthusiasm for the new Greek studies and were perfecting their own knowledge of Greek.[10] They were also the years during which More's children were born— Margaret in 1505, Elizabeth in 1506, Cecily in 1507, John in 1508. Within less than a decade these children, along with a handful of More's wards and other members of his household, would constitute his own "school." It was, thus, during the years between 1505 and 1520 that More was most intensely interested in Erasmus' educational ideas and most closely associated with them.

For some years before he even met Erasmus there is every reason to believe that More already subscribed to the revived study of classical authors which had long been the central tenet of humanism.[11] But when he did meet Erasmus he was exposed to a sharper and more specific argument for this traditional liberal program. One of the most substantial pieces of Erasmus' work in 1499 was the manuscript which would later be published as *Antibarbarorum liber*. At least two of the proposed four books were available in some form by this time:[12] we know that Colet was "quite persuaded" by the argument of the second book.[13] But we can be certain too that More read the work and discussed it with Erasmus. That he was as captivated by it as Colet is indicated by a reference in a later letter from More to Erasmus in which he refers to his "perceiving that you intended to set up a monument to our friendship in that work." This is, in all likelihood, a reference to Erasmus' intention to make More the main speaker in the dialogue.[14] While this did not, in fact, occur, it is clear that More wholeheartedly subscribed to the views expressed in the *Antibarbari*. For those views are quite specifically paralleled in works of his own over the next few years, in particular his long treatise-letters to Martin Dorp, to Oxford University, to Edward Lee, and to a monk, and in his great imaginative work *Utopia*. The general theme of the defense of the classics runs through all these works. But Erasmus' spirited advocacy of the study of Greek is picked up with equal zeal by More, particularly in his *Letter to the University of Oxford*. It was written on March 29 of either 1518 or, more likely, 1519 and carried not only the authority of More's arguments and connections at court, but the implied endorsement of the king, Henry VIII.[15]

More himself, in the letter, cites the circumstances of its composition—the formation at Oxford of a group of scholars and students opposed to Greek studies and calling themselves the Trojans. More specifically, "a scholar in his own estimation, a wit of the first water in that of his friends, though slightly deranged in that of anyone observing his actions, has chosen during Lent to babble in a sermon against not only Greek but Roman literature, and finally against all polite learning, liberally berating all the liberal arts."[16]

More observes that such "an attack on humane letters" is totally inappropriate for a Lenten sermon and indeed is a "defamation of the preaching office." What is appropriate, he continues, is that "this education which he calls secular does train the soul in virtue." It is, after all, chiefly for these studies that men come to Oxford. But,

> even if men come to Oxford to study theology, they do not start with that discipline. They must first study the laws of human nature and conduct, a thing not useless to theologians; without such study they might possibly preach a sermon acceptable to an academic group, without it they would certainly fail to reach the common man. And from whom could they acquire such skill better than from the poets, orators, and historians?

His opponent, More notes, wants to do away with all language study in favor of old-fashioned scholasticism. No, More responds, theology is properly based on the ancient fathers of the church and their Latin and Greek texts. He continues,

> Further, this fellow, just to show how immoderate *he* could be in a sermon, specifically called students of Greek "heretics," teachers of Greek "chief devils," and pupils in Greek "lesser devils" or, more modestly and facetiously as he thought, "little *devils*"; and the zeal of this holy man drove him to call by the name of devil one whom everybody knows the Devil himself could hardly bear to see occupy a pulpit. He did everything but name that one (D. Erasmus), as everybody realized just as clearly as they realized the folly of the speaker.

Not only is Greek not heretical, More goes on, but "to the Greeks we owe all our precision in the liberal arts generally and in theology particularly; for the Greeks either made the great discoveries themselves or passed them on as part of their heritage." The New Testament is in Greek, he points out, the best New Testament scholars were Greek and wrote in Greek. All the Latin fathers felt compelled to know Greek.

More closes by urging the university authorities not to listen to the detractors of Greek study but to protect it. It is in the interest of the university for, "in fact, it is in part from these studies that your university had acquired its pedagogical prestige both at home and abroad." And he assures them that their chancellor, the Archbishop of Canterbury (William Warham), supports Greek studies, as does the Archbishop of York (Thomas Wolsey), and even "his sacred majesty."

More had adapted for this particular occasion nearly all the arguments Erasmus had earlier formulated in more general terms in the *Antibarbari*. In that work Erasmus began by noting the persistent resistance to the classics, especially Greek, as the basis of true education. "To know Greek is heresy and to speak like Cicero is heresy too," he reports.[17] Out of their abysmal ignorance the opponents of good learning bring forth their specious arguments that such learning harms religion.[18] Rather, it is the other way round: it is ignorance that makes men insolent and proud.[19] And there is a positive linkage between good learning and sound religion. In what Margaret Mann Phillips calls "the central passage of the *Antibarbari*," Erasmus contends, "everything in the pagan world that was valiantly done, brilliantly said, ingeniously thought, diligently transmitted, had been prepared by Christ for his society." A bit later on, he continues, "None of the liberal disciplines is Christian, because they neither treat of Christ nor were invented by Christians; but they all concern Christ." This belief that all that is good comes from God and that the pre-Christian classical age was inspired by the Holy Spirit for his own purposes is what Mrs. Phillips calls the basis of the Christian humanism to which both Erasmus and More were profoundly committed.[20] And, of course, Erasmus has reference throughout the work tc the age of the church fathers and to the classical learning of Augustine, Jerome, Chrysostom. For example, he writes,

> Who could be holier than Ambrose? let us imitate him. Who could be more pious or more cultured than Jerome or Augustine? let us try to be like them. In the works of all these men how much there is in the way of literary art, of languages, philosophy, history, antiquity, Latin and Greek style, how much familiarity with authors! And all this up to that time was pagan.[21]

More, in his letters to the Louvain theologian Martin Dorp, in 1515, just as in his later letter to Oxford, had not only defended his friend Erasmus and his work but the principles of classicism and Greek study so important to them both: "it is from Greek," he writes, "that the rest of mankind has received every variety of knowledge and that we have been fortunate enough to receive nearly all the books of the New Testament."[22] In his letters to the conservative English theologian Edward Lee and to a monk, in 1519-20 – though they deal largely with the tumult over Erasmus' Greek New Testament – More again not only defended Erasmus and his work but defended their common commitment to the classics and to Greek studies.[23]

Even in *Utopia*, the composition of which dates from 1515-16 and which had many linkages with Erasmus,[24] More manages to make some of the same arguments about the classics and the study of Greek that we have already identified in others of his works. For example, he makes Hythlodaeus, his narrator, observe the close tie between Utopian philosophy and religion, that "they [the Utopians] never have a discussion of philosophy without uniting certain principles taken from religion as well as from philosophy,"[25] and that "they carry on the same debates as we do."[26]

He makes Hythlodaeus and his companions introduce the Utopians to the study of Greek and to record their remarkable progress and great enthusiasm for it so that "in less than three years they were perfect in the language and able to peruse good authors without any difficulty."[27] And Hythlodaeus further reports that on his fourth voyage to Utopia he took "most of Plato's works, several of Aristotle's, as well as Theophrastus on plants."[28] It is hardly accidental that, in Erasmus' *De ratione studii*, he lists "Plato, Aristotle, and his pupil Theophrastus" as "the best teachers of philosophy."[29] For the study of Greek grammar, Hythlodaeus continues, "they have only Lascaris, for I did not take Theodore with me"[30]: this reference is to the grammar of Theodorus Gaza which Erasmus had translated and which he had lectured on at Cambridge.[31] Again, in *De ratione studii*, Erasmus had expressed exactly the same sentiment as More, "among the Greek grammarians everyone assigns first place to Theodorus Gaza; Constantine Lascaris, in my opinion, rightly lays claim to second place."[32] Further, the Utopians' favorite Greek authors are precisely the same as Erasmus': "they are very fond of the works of Plutarch and captivated by the wit and pleasantry of Lucian. Of the poets they have Aristophanes, Homer, and Euripides, together with Sophocles in the small Aldine type. Of the historians they possess Thucydides and Herodotus, as well as Herodian ... some small treatises of Hippocrates and the *Ars medica* of Galen." [33]

By the time *Utopia* was published More's children had already reached school age and he had established his "school" for them in his own household. Once again, in virtually every aspect of this enterprise, More was indebted to Erasmus' educational ideas. Erasmus had long argued that it is best if fathers themselves oversee the education of their children—on the classical models of Pliny the Younger and Aemilius Paulus.[34] And this is precisely what More did. Erasmus commented on it in *De pueris instituendis*: "In England there is the illustrious Thomas More, who despite his commitments to the affairs of state did not hesitate to serve as a tutor to his wife, son, and daughters, beginning with their religious education and then advancing to their Greek and Latin studies."[35] It is clear from the charming letters More wrote to his children and their tutors between 1518 and 1523 that he supervised their curriculum and the regimen of their instruction. That he was deeply and personally committed to their education is revealed in a passage from one of his letters to Margaret. He wrote,

> I beg you, Margaret, tell me about the progress you are all making in your studies. For I assure you that, rather than allow my children to be idle and slothful, I would make a sacrifice of wealth, and bid adieu to other cares and business, to attend to my children and my family, amongst whom none is more dear to me than yourself, my beloved daughter.[36]

But, of course, More could not personally "attend" to the education of his children. He was a busy public figure, much occupied at court and often out of the country. Hence he had to make use of tutors. There was no subject to which Erasmus devoted more attention in his educational writings than that of choosing a tutor for one's children and there is substantial evidence that he was deeply involved not only in the choice of several of More's household tutors but in prescribing their qualifications. Erasmus had already done this for Colet's school. He was probably instrumental in the selection of William Lily as high master of the school—who had been an early companion of More's in Greek studies. And he was also involved, at Colet's request, in the search for a competent surmaster.[37] The involvement in this search for schoolmasters for Colet overlapped with his assistance to More.

More's first house tutor was John Clement. While Clement was known to Erasmus—who admired his gifts—he was chosen by More himself. Clement had been one of the first students at St. Paul's. By 1514 he had become a servant-pupil of More and accompanied him to Bruges in 1515, then to Antwerp, where plans for *Utopia* were being discussed with Erasmus.[38] In 1516 he was tutoring Colet in Greek[39] and in 1517 he was appointed tutor to More's children and wards. He served in this capacity about a year before entering the service of Wolsey,[40] who appointed him first reader of rhetoric and humanity at his newly-founded Cardinal College Oxford. Clement continued to be fondly mentioned by both More and Erasmus.[41] About 1530 he married Margaret Gigs, More's ward and one of his former pupils in the More household.

The next tutor, William Gonnell, was a protégé of Erasmus, who undoubtedly recommended him to More. Erasmus had known him and his family at Cambridge in 1513-14 when Gonnell was a schoolmaster at Landbeach, a village nearby, and served Erasmus as a copyist.[42] By the summer of 1517 he was a member of More's household and, when Clement left for the cardinal's service, probably took over the duties of tutor.[43] More wrote him a long letter, in May 1518, about his teaching duties.[44]

Of the next tutor, one "Master Drew," almost nothing is known except that More included him among "so many and such excellent tutors" as his children had enjoyed, in a letter of 1521 "to his whole school."[45] In the same letter he refers to their no longer needing the services of "Master Nicholas" "since you have learned whatever he had to teach you about astronomy."[46] Master Drew was apparently not known to Erasmus. But he was acquainted with "Master Nicholas," Nicholas Kratzer, a German whom he may have commended to More. Kratzer was an established scholar, and in his mid-thirties by this time. Some years earlier, in 1517, he had delivered a letter to Erasmus from Pieter Gilles in Antwerp.[47] He was an astronomer who caught the fancy of Henry VIII and remained a court astronomer for most of the rest of Henry's reign. He continued to have ties with Erasmus. He was present in Antwerp in 1520 when Dürer made a drawing of Erasmus.[48] While there he also met, and apparently impressed, Cuthbert Tunstall, the English cleric and diplomat who was a friend of both More and Erasmus. In 1521 Kratzer was one of More's household tutors. He apparently was retained as a special tutor in astronomy, and More slyly suggests, in the letter cited above, that he was not as impressed with Kratzer's astronomical knowledge as Henry was. In any case Kratzer seems shortly to have left the More household. In 1523, in addition to his court duties, he became a professor at Oxford. He was also acquainted with Erasmus' friend Hans Holbein, who did his portrait as well as the sketch for a projected painting of the More family. It was Kratzer "who wrote the notes on Holbein's sketch, identifying the family members."[49]

The last full-time tutor in the More household was Richard Hyrde, who had taken his degree at Oxford in 1519 and was "a young man learned in physic, Greek and Latin."[50] Like John Clement, Hyrde was a protégé of More rather than of Erasmus. More was, in some way, responsible for his rearing and education: Hyrde later referred to him as "my singular good master and bringer-up."[51] But he was, nevertheless, an admirer of Erasmus. He wrote a preface indicating as much to Margaret More's translation of Erasmus' *Precatio dominica*, entitled *A Devout Treatise upon the Paternoster*.[52] He was a vigorous advocate for the education of women, doubtless influenced by More's views on the subject—as was Erasmus, as we shall see. He later translated the important work of the Spanish humanist Juan Luis Vives on the same subject, *De institutione feminae christianae*, as *Instruction of a Christian Woman*, which More proofread and corrected and commended to the reading public.[53]

The tutors named above were listed by Thomas Stapleton in his *Tres Thomae*, one of the important pieces of exile literature pertaining to More, published in 1588.[54] There may have been other tutors. Certainly there were some who taught specialized subjects, like Kratzer. And in the light of More's love of music, there must surely have been music teachers.[55] There may also have been one or more instructors in medicine considering that Margaret Gigs took special interest in that subject and that many years later, as the wife of John Clement, who had become a physician, she was competent enough to assist him in his researches and writing.[56]

All the tutors who passed through More's household were full-fledged members of it, treated as friends and equals, taking part in those conversations and discussions that so delighted More, and were intimate with the learned friends who often visited him. This was exactly as Erasmus wished a learned tutor to be treated in a great house and, though More's treatment of his house tutors was largely a function of his own generous nature, it may have owed something to the prescriptions of Erasmus on the subject. And there were other notions of Erasmus on the choosing of a tutor that were reflected in More's choices. Erasmus would have the ideal "learned and honourable" teacher be a man of mature years, preferably a layman, industrious and reliable, of good family, and with as much experience as possible, preferably one who had spent the greater part of his life in literary pursuits.[57] And, he insists, a good teacher must have "a certain friendliness and flexibility," he must "make allowance for what the child does not know," and he must encourage his pupils by a kind and charming manner and not alienate them by harshness. Under such instruction, he says, "young minds exposed to a congenial programme of studies that is assimilated in gradual stages and intermingled with play will soon adapt themselves to a more substantial course of learning."[58] Although, in the list of More's tutors, only one, Nicholas Kratzer, was a man of mature years, all were laymen, all were apparently industrious and reliable, all were of respectable family. Certainly all of them were trained in literary pursuits and Gonnell and Kratzer, at least, had prior experience. The evidence of More's letters to his children and tutors suggests that the tutors had the friendliness and flexibility that Erasmus wanted and that they did indeed make allowance for what the children did not know. In the case of Gonnell, at least, it is clear that he was extremely reluctant to chastise or discipline Margaret, that her "lofty and exalted character of mind should not be debased."[59]

In dozens of other instances, trivial and important, systematic and incidental, the opinions of Erasmus on educational matters were reflected in the precepts and practices of education in More's household. For example, in Gonnell's reluctance to discipline Margaret and thus debase her character of mind we see Erasmus' passionate hatred of corporal punishment in schools and of flogging schoolmasters. In *De pueris instituendis* he writes: "I maintain that nothing is more damaging to young children than constant exposure to beatings. When corporal punishment is applied too harshly, the more spirited children are driven to rebellion while the more apathetic ones are numbed into despair."[60] More would have his tutors "warn my children to avoid as it were the precipes of pride and hautiness, and to walk in the pleasant meadows of modesty" and to teach them "in their studies to esteem most whatever may teach them piety towards God, charity to all, and modesty and Christian humility in themselves. . . . These I consider the real and genuine fruits of learning." Later on in the same letter he urges "that this plague of vainglory may be banished far from my children, may you, my dear Gonnell, and their mother and all their friends, sing this song to them, and repeat it, and beat it into their heads, that vainglory is despicable, and to be spit upon, and that there is nothing more sublime than that humble modesty so often praised by Christ."[61] But he quite agreed that such lofty ends were not to be gained by cruelty or actual beatings. In a Latin poem addressed to his children and written long before this letter to Gonnell, he reminds them, ". . . how often I kissed you, how seldom I whipped you. My whip was never anything but a peacock's tail. Even this I wielded hesitantly and gently so as not to mark your tender backsides with painful welts. Oh, brutal and unworthy to be called father is he who does not himself weep at the tears of his child."[62]

The subjects the pupils of More's "school" studied are listed by Stapleton.

> The subjects of study were not only Latin and Greek literature but also logic and philosophy, in which subject disputations were arranged, and also mathematics. Sometimes, too, the writings of the Fathers were read, as I will show from More's correspondence. The pupils exercised themselves in the Latin tongue almost every day, translating English into Latin and Latin into English.[63]

Erasmus presents us with almost exactly corresponding lists of the subjects he recommends, most succinctly in his dialogue on *The Right Way of Speaking Latin and Greek, De recta latini graecique sermonis pronuntiatione dialogus*, in which he lists Latin and Greek, in which instruction is to be begun as soon as possible; "enough dialectic to have some acquaintance with it"; rhetoric which "must be studied with care" but within limits, "the point of it is to help in writing and speaking, not to instil an anxious obedience to teachers' rules." Geography should be mastered while arithmetic, music, and astronomy "need only be sampled." Medicine and physics should be treated mainly as practical subjects to enhance good health and the knowledge of the nature of things; finally "ethics will be taught by means of aphorisms, especially aphorisms that refer to the Christian religion and to one's duties toward society."[64]

Erasmus was a firm believer in starting education at an early age and his writings are full of references to this conviction. Indeed, it is the principal theme of *A Declamation on the Subject of Early Liberal Education for Children, De pueris statim ac liberaliter instituendis*, one of his most important and influential educational works: Gerald Strauss calls it a "pedagogical best-seller."[65] The leading principle for Erasmus is that instruction should begin at the earliest point at which a child can benefit from it: ideally "as soon as a child is born, he is ready for instruction in right conduct, as soon as he is able to speak he is ready for learning his letters."[66] The precise age is not important; what is important is that instruction begin "while his mind is still uncorrupted and free from distractions, while he is in his most formative and impressionable years, and while his spirit is still open to each and every influence and at the same time highly retentive of what it has grasped."[67]

More knew this book and subscribed to its views.[68] Though we do not know when he began the instruction of his own children, we may presume that he followed Erasmus' advice and began the process early. In his letter to Gonnell of 1518 he still refers to "the tender years of my daughters,"[69] although Margaret would have been thirteen and Cecily, the youngest, eleven. Of his Utopians, however, More observes, in very Erasmian terms, that

> they take the greatest pains from the very first to instill into children's minds, while still tender and pliable, good opinions which are also useful for the preservation of their commonwealth. When once they are firmly implanted in children, they accompany them all through their adult lives and are of great help in watching over the condition of the commonwealth.[70]

Another often stated Erasmian educational principle was that of teaching by game-playing. As early as 1497, in a letter to his former pupil Christian Northoff, Erasmus wrote, "a constant element of enjoyment must be mingled with our studies so that we think of learning as a game rather than a form of drudgery, for no activity can be continued for long if it does not to some extent afford pleasure to the participant."[71] Later, in *De pronuntiatione*, he advocates giving children letter-shapes to hold or pin on their clothes,[72] and in *De pueris instituendis* he advocates the practice of teachers in antiquity of baking cookies in the shape of letters or using carved ivory letters as toys. Then, as an example of contemporary devices of the same sort, he writes:

> The English are very partial to archery, which is the first thing they teach their children. One clever father, therefore, seeing how fond his son was of the game, had a beautiful set of bow and arrows made, decorated all over with the letters of the alphabet. As targets he used the shapes of letters of the Greek and Latin alphabets (starting with the Greek); when the boy hit a target and pronounced the letter correctly he would be applauded and be rewarded in addition with a cherry or something else that children like. I might add that even better results are obtained with this game if there are two or three well-matched contestants competing with each other, the reason being that hope of victory and fear of disgrace will make each of them more alert and enthusiastic. It was by means of this stratagem that the boy in question learnt in a few days of fun and play to identify and pronounce his letters—something which the majority of teachers, with all their beatings, threatenings, and insults, could scarcely have accomplished in three years.[73]

In all likelihood this "clever father" was More and the boy his son John. Seebohm thought so,[74] and it is certainly in character. In the annotation to the Yale edition of *Utopia*, 180/2, "animi studijs," the editors point out that it is implied that for study to have a lasting effect, it must be joined to pleasure: and Erasmus is cited.[75]

The handful of letters More wrote to his children and their tutors between 1517 and 1523, to which we have often referred in this paper, represent not only More's most substantial writings on educational matters and demonstrate many connections with Erasmus' educational ideas, but in themselves show many connections with Erasmus' important textbook on letter writing, *De conscribendis epistolis*, and the concepts and practices elaborated in it. The letters to his children—written in Latin—were clearly meant to be models of style. And, equally clearly, he enjoined the children to use their letters to him as literary exercises. He expects them to write every day, on any subject—or none at all! "How can a subject be wanting when you write to me, who am glad to hear of your studies or of your games, and whom you will please most if, when there is nothing to write about, you write just that at great length."[76]

He further tells them,

> whether you write serious matters or the merest trifles, it is my wish that you write everything diligently and thoughtfully. It will do no harm if you first write the whole in English, for then you will have much less trouble and labor in turning it into Latin; not having to look for the matter, your mind will be instead only on the language. That, however, I leave to your own choice, whereas I strictly enjoin you that whatever you have composed you carefully examine before writing it out clean; and in this examination first scrutinize the whole sentence and then every part of it. Thus, if any solecisms have escaped you, you will easily detect them. Correct these, write out the whole letter again, and even then do not grudge to examine it once more, for sometimes, in rewriting, faults slip in again that one had expunged.[77]

These injunctions exactly parallel Erasmus' advice on model letters to be prepared by teachers of letter writing.[78]

In the letter just cited above, More observes that "there is nothing in itself so insipid that you cannot season it with grace and wit if you give a little thought to it."[79] This reflects Erasmus' advice to make use of recantations: "to sharpen their wits [the teacher] should propose disagreeable subjects," even outlandish or trivial subjects, for "nothing is so inherently good that it cannot be made to seem bad" by a gifted speaker or writer of letters.[80]

In another charming letter addressed simply "Thomas More to his whole school greeting," he begins by talking about this salutation:

> See what a compendious salutation I have found, to save both time and paper, which would otherwise have been wasted in listing the names of each of you in salutation, and my labor would have been to no purpose, since, though each of you is dear to me by some special title, of which I could have omitted none in an ingratiating salutation, no one is dearer to me by any title than each of you by that of scholar.[81]

This is exactly the sort of commonsense advice Erasmus gives in his several chapters in *De conscribendis epistolis* on the salutation—which had become, in contemporary epistolary practice, burdened with pompous multiple titles and grandiose epithets.[82] Erasmus and More are obviously of a single mind in this matter.

There remains one final aspect of educational theory and practice in which the lead was taken not by Erasmus but by More, the education of women. Erasmus freely admits his debt to his friend. In a letter to Budé, of 1521, in which Erasmus is describing More and his family, he says, "It was not always believed that letters are of value to the virtue and general reputation of women. I myself once held this opinion: but More completely converted me."[83] More's position on the education of women is natural enough. As Richard Marius observes, "He was driven to this position by his own lifelong devotion to the ideal of self-improvement for everyone and also by the accident that God had given him an unusual number of daughters and female wards to educate."[84]

More's earliest writing on the subject occurs in a Latin poem, "To Candidus: How to choose a wife." This poem parallels Erasmus' treatment of the theme of the persuasive letter in *De conscribendis epistolis*, in which his primary example of the genre is a long letter persuading a friend to marry. It was written, probably as a declamation in its earliest form, by 1499[85] and probably read by More early on in their association. More's poem was among those that Erasmus had urged Froben to print in the spring of 1518.[86] It had likely been written earlier, though how much earlier it is impossible to say. While the parallels exist between Erasmus and More in the matter of matrimonial advice, More's poem takes a rather different tack and emphasizes not so much the duty of the prospective husband as the attractiveness of the prospective wife. And among the attractions is that of learning:

Happy is the woman whose education permits her to derive from the best of ancient works the principles which confer a blessing on life. Armed with this learning, she would not yield to pride in prosperity, nor to grief in distress — even though misfortune strike her down. For this reason your lifetime companion will be ever agreeable, never a trouble or a burden. If she is well instructed herself, then some day she will teach your little grandsons, at an early age, to read.

You will be glad to leave the company of men and to seek repose in the bosom of your accomplished wife, the while she attends to your comfort, and while under her dexterous touch the plucked strings resound, while in a sweet voice (as sweet, Procne, as your sister's) she sings delightful songs such as Apollo would be glad to hear. Then you will be glad to spend days and nights in pleasant and intelligent conversation, listening to the sweet words which ever most charmingly flow from her honeyed mouth.[87]

A bit later, in *Utopia*, he reports that among the Utopians "a large part of the people . . . men and women alike, throughout their lives, devote to learning the hours which, as we said, are freed from manual labor."[88] In the less idealized setting of his own time, More had to deal with the received tradition of the natural inferiority of women. He accepted that tradition as essentially true. But, in his long letter to Gonnell, the tutor of his daughters, and using the extended metaphor of "the harvest of good learning," he turned the assumption of inferiority into a practical case for the education of women: "But if the soil of a woman be naturally bad, and apter to bear fern than grain, by which saying many keep women from study, I think, on the contrary, that a woman's wit is the more diligently to be cultivated, so that nature's defect may be redressed by industry." It is the result, not the instrumentalities, male or female, that counts. "Nor do I think that the harvest is much affected whether it is a man or a woman who does the sowing. They both have the name of human being whose nature reason differentiates from that of beasts; both I say, are equally suited for the knowledge of learning by which reason is cultivated, and, like plowed land, germinates a crop when the seeds of good precepts have been sown." It is "a new thing," this business of the education of women, he admits to Gonnell, and apt to be misunderstood, but "on the other hand, if a woman (and this I desire and hope with you as their teacher for all my daughters) to eminent virtue of mind should add even moderate skill in learning, I think she will gain more real good than if she obtains the riches of Croesus and the beauty of Helen, not because that learning will be a glory to her, though learning will accompany virtue as a shadow does a body, but because the reward of wisdom is too solid to be lost with riches or to perish with beauty, since it depends on the inner knowledge of what is right, not on the talk of men, than which nothing is more foolish or mischievous."[89]

More, as we have seen, developed and put into effect in his "school" a full-fledged program of learning for his daughters and female wards. Erasmus, though he shared More's convictions about education of women, devoted relatively little attention to it in his own educational writings.[90] He did, however, have a genuine regard for learned women, especially for the daughters of Thomas More, most especially for Margaret, the eldest, whom he had known all her life. In an affectionate Christmas letter of 1523 he dedicated to her his commentary on Prudentius' hymns for Christmas and Epiphany, ending with best wishes not only to Margaret but to her sisters, "that whole choir" of More's "school."[91] Margaret exchanged letters with Erasmus in 1529.[92] And it is almost certain that she was the model for the saucy Magdalia, the "learned lady" of his Colloquy, "The Abbot and the Learned Lady."[93] We have already noticed her translation of his treatise on the Lord's Prayer.

In conclusion, then, we have argued and attempted to demonstrate at some length, the close association between Erasmus' ideas on education and the educational ideas and practices of Thomas More. In this area, as in so many others, the two friends who shared "one soul between . . . [them]" shared also their convictions about the ideals, the means, and the ends of education.

Wichita State University

Notes

1. No inconsiderable claim in the century that produced Melanchthon, Sturm, Cordier, and the Jesuit *Ratio studiorum*. But the claim can be sustained. See the extended argument in the introduction to vols. 25-26 of *The Collected Works of Erasmus*, ed. J. K. Sowards (Toronto/Buffalo/London: University of Toronto Press, 1985), especially pp. xli-li, hereafter cited as CWE.

2. For Erasmus' standing in this evolutionary process see *ibid*, pp. xxx-xxxiii.

3. Ep. = P. S. Allen ed., *Opus Epistolarum Des. Erasmi*, Oxford, 1906-1958, Ep. 126: 30-1.

4. Ep. 130: 108-9.

5. Ep. 1284, CWE 25, pp. 2, 10-11.

6. Epp. 95: 39-40; 136: 57-9; 138: 188-9. See also CWE 24, p. 280.

7. Ep. 66: 12-3. See also CWE 24, p. 662.

8. CWE 24, pp. 450, 662; Epp. 230: 10-6, 227: 5-16 and n.6, 17-9, 341; and C. Reedijk (ed.), *The Poems of Desiderius Erasmus* (Leiden: Brill, 1956), pp. 291-92, 297-300. Erasmus' colloquy "The Whole Duty of Youth" (1522) was undoubtedly meant to reflect the values of Colet's school and one of the two speakers, Gaspar, can probably be identified as Thomas Lupset, a former student at St. Paul's, protégé of Colet's, and a friend of More's. See *The Colloquies of Erasmus*, tr. and ed. Craig R. Thompson (Chicago: University of Chicago Press, 1965), p. 31.

9. *St. Thomas More: Selected Letters*, ed. Elizabeth F. Rogers (New Haven and London: Yale University Press, 1967), p. 6. There is an interesting linkage among More, Erasmus, and Colet's school in the great textbook, *De copia*, that Erasmus wrote for the school. One of the stunning demonstrations of *copia* was the sentence *semper dum vivam tui meminero*, "always, as long

as I live, I shall remember you." It was a sentiment expressed for Erasmus' friend More—and he created two hundred variations on it—as in such refined expressions as "your memory will be so enduring that I myself will not endure any longer" and "More's memory will never perish within me, unless I perish myself." CWE 24, p. 361.

10. To a great extent by entering a friendly competition translating the dialogues and essays of Lucian and composing, each, a response to his declamation *Tyrannicida*. See Craig R. Thompson, *The Translations of Lucian by Erasmus and St. Thomas More* (Ithaca: Cornell University Press, 1940), Craig R. Thompson (ed.), *Translations of Lucian* (New Haven and London: Yale University Press, 1974), Vol. 3 Part 1, and Erika Rummel, *Erasmus as a Translator of the Classics* (Toronto/Buffalo/London: University of Toronto Press, 1985), pp. 49–69.

11. Erasmus tells us, in his famous biographical letter on More and his family, written to Ulrich von Hutten, July 23, 1519, Ep. 999, that More, even as a boy applied himself to the study of "Greek literature and philosophy" until his father forced him into the study of law. In an important critical article a generation ago, William Nelson, "Thomas More, Grammarian and Orator," *PMLA*, 58 (1943), 337–52, Nelson argued that More was not simply a humanist and humanist advocate but actually a professionally trained teacher of grammar and rhetoric. Though it seems doubtful if he ever practiced as such, it does strengthen the tie between More and Erasmus in matters of education.

12. These drafts were among the works Erasmus left in Italy in 1509 and only parts of them, notably Book I, ever found their way back to him prior to the eventual publication of Book I in 1520. See the account in CWE 23, in the introductory note to the *Antibarbari*, by Margaret Mann Phillips, pp. 4–5.

13. *Ibid.*, Dedicatory Letter to Johann Witz, p. 16.

14. Ep. 706, 32 n. The conclusion was drawn by P. S. Allen, the editor of *Opus Epistolarum Des. Erasmi Roterodami*, 11 vols. (Oxford: Clarendon Press, 1906–58) and is endorsed by the annotator of the letter, Peter G. Bietenholz, in CWE.

15. *In Defense of Humanism*, vol. 15 of *The Complete Works of St. Thomas More*, ed. Daniel Kinney (New Haven and London: Yale University Press, 1986), intro. pp. xxix–xxxi.

16. For speculation as to the identity of this Lenten preacher see *ibid.*, pp. xxviii–xxx. This quotation and those that follow from the same letter are from More, *Selected Letters*, ed. Rogers, pp. 95 ff.

17. The text cited here is CWE 23, edited and translated by Margaret Mann Phillips, p. 32.

18. *Ibid.*, pp. 35–8, 49–50.

19. *Ibid.*, pp. 61–71.

20. *Ibid.*, pp. 9–10, 60. Much earlier, More in his dedicatory letter to Thomas Ruthall, of the 1506 edition of his translations from Lucian, points out that these ancient pagan works do not harm Christians but do more to

induce them to "eschew superstition, which obtrudes everywhere under the guise of religion," to "live a life less distracted by anxiety; less fearful, that is, of any gloomy and superstitious untruths" than many well intentioned Christian works that mix truth with pious fiction, *Translations of Lucian*, ed. Thompson, pp.. lxxiii–lxxiv, 5.

21. CWE 23, pp. 91 ff; the quotation is on p. 108.
22. *In Defense of Humanism*, ed. Kinney, p. 99.
23. Ibid., passim, but see especially pp. 221–3, 227.
24. See, for example, Richard Marius, *Thomas More, A Biography* (New York: Knopf, 1984), pp. 152–70.
25. *Utopia*, vol. 4 of *The Complete Works of St. Thomas More*, ed. Edward Surtz, S. J. and J. H. Hexter (New Haven and London: Yale University Press, 1965), p. 161. Hereafter cited as CW4. This sentiment generally parallels Erasmus in *Antibarbari*: cf. n. 20 above, and specifically in *Hyperaspistes*, in Desiderii Erasmi Roterodami *Opera Omnia*, ed. P. Clericus (Leiden 1706), X, 1294, hereafter cited as LB.
26. CW 4, p. 161.
27. CW 4, p. 181.
28. Ibid.
29. CWE 24, *De ratione studii*, ed. Brian McGregor, p. 673.
30. CW 4, p. 181.
31. Ep. 233: 11–12.
32. CWE 24, p. 667.
33. CW 4, p. 183. For parallel lists of authors in Erasmus see CWE 25, pp. xiv–xv.
34. CWE 25, pp. xviii–xix.
35. CWE 26, pp. 322– 3.
36. More, *Selected Letters*, ed. Rogers, p. 109.
37. CWE 25, p. xxxix. E. E. Reynolds, *The Life and Death of St Thomas More, The Field is Won* (London: Burns and Oates, 1978 [1968]), p. 157, suggests that More's association with Lily during his all-too-brief headmastership at St. Paul's "had strengthened their common interest in education."
38. Ep. 388.
39. Ep. 468.
40. Epp. 820, 1138.
41. Epp. 820, 907.
42. Epp. 274, 276, 279, 287, 289.
43. Ep. 601. Reynolds, *The Field is Won*, pp. 158–9, cites a letter of his preserved in L. P. II. ii. Ap. 17. in which he refers to Clement's still being a member of the More household.
44. More, *Selected Letters*, ed. Rogers, No. 20.
45. Ibid., No. 29.
46. Ibid.
47. Ep. 515.
48. Ep. 1132, intro.
49. E. E. Reynolds, *Saint Thomas More* (New York: Kenedy, 1953), p. 150.

50. Cited from a statement of Stephen Gardiner in *ibid.*, p. 151.
51. In the dedicatory epistle to his translation of Vives' *De institutione feminae christianae*, as cited in Reynolds, *The Field is Won*, p. 159.
52. Published in London by W. de Worde, n.d.
53. *Saint Thomas More*, p. 151. The work is listed in STC as 24856.
54. Thomas Stapleton, *The Life and Illustrious Martyrdom of Sir Thomas More*, tr. Philip E. Hallett, ed. and notes E. E. Reynolds (New York: Fordham University Press, 1966 [1928]), pp. 91–2.
55. Reynolds, *The Field is Won*, p. 159.
56. R. W. Chambers, *Thomas More* (London: Cape, 1935), pp. 184–5. Margaret More also seems to have had more than a passing interest in medicine and apparently broached the subject of her studying it to her father. More did not entirely close the door to that study but advised her first to gain a complete mastery of the "liberal authors" as a basis for later, more professional work. See More, *Selected Letters*, ed. Rogers, No. 31. For the parallel views of Erasmus see *De pronuntiatione*, CWE 26, p. 387 and *Adagia* 3401, LB II, 1054, and Ep. 542.
57. *De pronuntiatione*, CWE 26, p. 379.
58. *De pueris instituendis*, CWE 26, p. 335.
59. More, *Selected Letters*, ed. Rogers, No. 20.
60. CWE 26, p. 331. There is no theme that Erasmus dealt with more often in his educational writings. See also *De pueris instituendis*, CWE 26, pp. 326–30, *De conscribendis epistolis*, CWE 25, p. 41, *De pronuntiatione*, CWE 26, pp. 385–6.
61. More, *Selected Letters*, ed. Rogers, No. 20. In his discussion of crime and punishment in *Utopia*, p. 61, Hythlodaeus observes, "In this respect not your country alone but a great part of the world resembles bad schoolmasters, who would rather beat than teach their scholars."
62. *The Complete Works of St. Thomas More*, Vol. 3 Part 2, *Latin Poems*, ed. Clarence H. Miller, Leicester Bradner, Charles A. Lynch, and Revilo P. Oliver (New Haven and London: Yale University Press, 1984), No. 264, p. 281.
63. Stapleton, *Life of Sir Thomas More*, p. 92. The list is incomplete, omitting astronomy, which we know was taught.
64. CWE 26, p. 387. In a letter to John Faber, Ep. 2750, probably written in 1532, Erasmus characterized More's "school" in terms of the subjects taught and the emphasis placed on them, "You say that his house was another Platonic academy. Rather I think it was a reproach to Plato's academy: in the latter were carried on disputes over numbers and geometric figures and moral virtues; but More's house you would more correctly call a school of the Christian religion. Nothing went on there that was not redolent of the liberal disciplines, especially and primarily those that concerned piety. There was no quarreling there, no wantonness, no laziness."
65. In his *Luther's House of Learning: Indoctrination of the Young in the German Reformation* (Baltimore: Johns Hopkins University Press, 1978), p. 53.
66. CWE 26, p. 319.
67. *Ibid.*, p. 297.

68. Erasmus had left the first draft of the work in Italy and it was finally returned to him by More, who had gotten it from Lupset. He had obviously read it because he wrote to Erasmus that it is "in your writing" but a first draft only, "nothing really complete," Ep. 502, dated in December 1516.
69. More, *Selected Letters*, ed. Rogers, No. 20.
70. CW 4, p. 229.
71. Ep. 56.
72. CWE 26, p. 400.
73. CWE 26, p. 339.
74. Frederic Seebohm, *The Oxford Reformers* (London: Longmans, Green, and Co., 1887), p. 500. The only other possibility is Charles Blount, the son of Erasmus' former student and benefactor William Blount, Lord Mountjoy. Erasmus certainly took an interest in this boy's education and dedicated a number of books to him. On the other hand, the identification of the ingenious father as Lord Mountjoy is less likely because he did not know Greek. See the entries in *Contemporaries of Erasmus, A Biographical Register of the Renaissance and Reformation*, ed. Peter S. Bietenholz and Thomas B. Deutscher (Toronto/Buffalo/London: University of Toronto Press, 1985-87).
75. CW 4, p. 465.
76. More, *Selected Letters*, ed. Rogers, No. 32.
77. *Ibid.*
78. CWE 25, pp. 33-4.
79. More, *Selected Letters*, ed. Rogers, No. 32.
80. CWE 25, pp. 145-6.
81. More, *Selected Letters*, ed. Rogers, No. 29.
82. CWE 25, pp. 45-62.
83. Ep. 1233.
84. Marius, *More*, p. 223.
85. CWE 26, pp. 528-9.
86. More, *Latin Poems*, pp. 3-4.
87. *Ibid.*, pp. 187-9.
88. *Utopia*, p. 159.
89. More, *Selected Letters*, ed. Rogers, No. 20.
90. In fact, only the passage from Ep. 1233, cited above, and a slightly longer one in his *Christiani matrimonii institutio*, LB V, 712 B-713 A, 716 C-717 A. See J. K. Sowards, "Erasmus and the Education of Women," *Sixteenth Century Journal*, 13 (1982), 77-89.
91. Ep. 1404. See also Allen I, p. 13.
92. Epp. 2212 and 2233.
93. See *Opera Omnia* Desiderii Erasmi Roterodami (Amsterdam: North Holland Publishing Co., 1972), I/3 ed. L.-E. Halkin, F. Bierlaire, and R. Hoven, pp. 403-8, and *The Colloquies of Erasmus*, ed. Thompson, p. 218.

Caroline CHABOT
53, rue Delacroix
49000 ANGERS

Angers, le 1er Octobre 1987.

Cher Monsieur l'Abbé Marc'hadour,

Vous savez sans doute que je suis devenue professeur d'anglais à la Catho. A cette occasion, je tiens à vous remercier de l'enseignement et de l'encouragement que vous m'avez apportés lors de mes études. Je garde un excellent souvenir des cours de thème anglais, où vous saviez donner la passion du mot juste et le goût de la langue -- qu'elle soit anglaise ou française. Plus récemment, c'est à vous que je dois la bourse d'études qui m'a été offerte par le A.C. DUNCAN Catholic History Trust et qui m'a permis d'effectuer des recherches en Angleterre pour mon D.E.A.. A la suite de ce séjour d'études, j'ai encore bénéficié de votre soutien pour publier, dans *Moreana*, un article sur R.W. Chambers.

Je suis donc heureuse de partager avec vous la joie de ma nomination et je vous assure que votre exemple de dévouement me reste présent à la mémoire.

Avec les sincères salutations de

Caroline

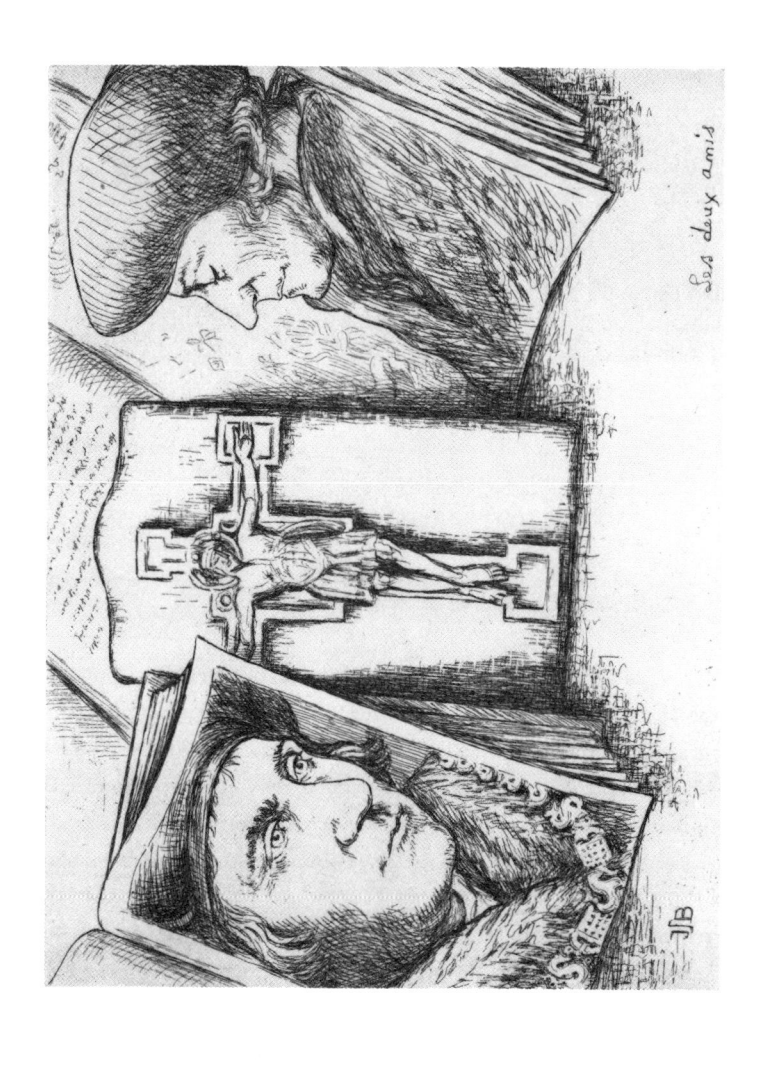

Etching by Jean Schoevaert-Brossault Inscribed "à l'Abbé Germain Marc'hadour, Bien Amicalement"

JOHN C. OLIN

Erasmus' Adagia and More's Utopia

In memoriam Margaret Mann Phillips

MONTAIGNE REMARKED IN HIS ESSAY "On Repentance" that if he had met Erasmus he would have expected him to speak in proverbs. He was thinking most probably of the collection Erasmus had gathered from the ancient classics and had published in numerous editions, the *Adagia* or more descriptively the *Adagiorum chiliades*, "thousands of adages," containing not only the proverbs themselves, but also essays, long and short, explaining the proverbs, recounting their literary sources, and enunciating themes dear to the heart of Erasmus.[1] Indeed it can be called at least in part a book of essays, and although they are of a different character and tone than Montaigne's, there is some kinship perhaps in the genre.

I am going to translate here one of the shorter adage-essays and comment on it. My purpose is to call attention to a significant theme in the reform humanism Erasmus represented. I am struck by the affinity between this theme and that great masterpiece of the Renaissance, Thomas More's *Utopia*, and I want particularly to discuss the character and significance of their relationship.

The *Adagia* saw many editions and revisions during Erasmus' lifetime. First published in Paris in 1500 at the outset of his career it was greatly expanded in 1508 and published in Venice by the famous printer Aldus Manutius with whom Erasmus was working at that time. The next important edition, further revised and enlarged, appeared in 1515, issuing from the press of Johann Froben in Basel where Erasmus had recently gone and where he was henceforth regularly to publish. This revised *Adagia* has been called the "Utopian" edition because of the affinity of several themes prominent in it with Thomas More's *Utopia* which was first published in 1516.[2] There were several subsequent Froben editions of the *Adagia* while Erasmus lived and many reprints both during and after his lifetime. The volume grew to be a formidable collection of 4151 adages, a vast treasure house of classical erudition and a compendium of Erasmian comments, opinions, and critiques.

The adage-essay that I have selected for translation and discussion here is the first one in the collection, the proverb *Amicorum communia omnia*, "Friends have all things in common." In essay form it dates from the 1508 Aldine edition, and there are significant additions to it in the 1515 and 1526 Froben editions. It had appeared in embryo in the Paris edition of 1500, but it became proverb number one only in the expanded edition of 1508, a place of honor and importance it retained thereafter. Let me now present the English translation of the complete text.[3]

Friends Have All Things in Common

Τὰ τῶν φίλων κοινά, that is, Friends have all things in common. Since there is no proverb more wholesome or more famous I have chosen it as a good omen to begin this book of adages. And indeed if it were as fixed in the hearts of men as it is ever on their lips, certainly most of the evils of our life would be averted. Socrates inferred from this proverb that all things belong to good men just as they do to the gods. For all things belong to the gods, he said. Good men are the friends of the gods, and friends have all things in common. Therefore good men possess all things.

The proverb is quoted in Euripides' *Orestes*, *Phoenissae*, and *Andromache*, and in Terence's *Adelphoe*. It is said that it was also in Menander's play of the same name. Cicero quotes it in the first book of *De officiis*, and Aristotle cites it in Book VIII of the *Ethics* and Plato in Book V of the *Laws*. In the latter passage Plato attempts to show that the best state of the commonwealth consists in the sharing of all things. "The first society then," he declares, "the one with the best constitution and laws, is where the old saying will be observed as far as possible throughout the whole society. I mean the saying that friends have all their possessions in common." *He also says that a society will be happy and blessed where the words 'mine' and 'not mine' are never heard. But it is amazing how displeasing, yes, how hateful that community of Plato's is to Christians, although nothing ever said by a pagan philosopher is more in keeping with the mind of Christ.*[4]

Aristotle in Book II of the Politics *modifies the view of Plato, saying that ownership and property belong to specific individuals but otherwise for the sake of use, virtue, and civil fellowship everything is common according to the proverb.*[5] Martial in Book II of the *Epigrams* jests about someone called Candidus who always had this adage on his lips although he shared nothing with his friends:

Candidus, O Candidus, pompously you echo this adage
    Night and day, "Friends have all in common."

And he concludes his epigram:

You give naught away, yet you say, O Candidus,
    "Friends share all."

Theophrastus in Plutarch's essay 'On Brotherly Love' elegantly remarks: "If the goods of friends are held in common, it is very fitting that the friends of friends also be shared in common."

Cicero in the first book of the *Laws* seems to attribute this adage to Pythagoras when he says: "For whence comes that Pythagorian dictum, the goods of friends are held in common and friendship is equality." Moreover Diogenes Laertius has Timaeus relate that this saying had its origin with Pythagoras. *Aulus Gellius in his* Attic Nights, *Book I, chapter 9, claims that Pythagoras not only was the author of this proverb but also introduced a community of life and resources, even such as Christ wishes all Christians to practice. For whoever Pythagoras had admitted into that band of his disciples gave whatever money and property they possessed to the common fund. This practice is called in Latin* coenobium, *a word undoubtedly derived from the fellowship of life and possessions.*[6]

˜

The development of this adage-essay is remarkable. In 1500 Erasmus had limited himself to a few lines. He simply stated that the proverb was quoted by a character in one of Terence's plays and was cited also in Plato "under the name of Euripides." In 1508 a major expansion of its classical sources took place, and drawing on Cicero and Diogenes Laertius Erasmus attributes its origin to Pythagoras. In 1515 came further revision. Several new sentences were added which radically changed the character of the essay. The adage now took on greater thrust as a reform concept, and by the same token its affinity with the teachings of Christ was affirmed. The correspondence of its presentation in such incisive form in this edition with More's description (and Hythloday's defence) of Utopian society is also striking. More's book in fact, we might say, is a dramatic commentary on this adage. And the emphatic references to what Christ thought and desired not only heighten the proverb's role as a principle of moral and social reform but demonstrate that harmony between the classical heritage and Christianity which Erasmus and other humanists perceived. Finally in 1526 Erasmus somewhat qualified the full Platonic ideal of community by adding a restraining note from Aristotle. He retreated slightly, it would seem, though his citation from the *Politics* hardly does justice to the fundamental critique which the great Peripatetic launched against his former teacher's communalism.

The theme of this adage-essay and its correspondence with More's *Utopia*, as I have indicated, especially intrigue me. Both Erasmus and More present and develop the same basic idea: the best social order is one in which all possessions are held in common and a close community of living and sharing prevails. Both men appear most certainly to be advocating communism, albeit without the Marxist dialectic or any modern political overtone. They are aware that their prescription has its roots in classical as well as Christian antiquity—a factor, it would seem, that makes it an integral part of their humanist inheritance. The question I should now like to pose is how should we understand this espousal of so radical a moral and social concept, how literally should we take it as a reform proposal.

The question is often asked of More's *Utopia*, but it is one not easily or definitely answered in view of the character of that work—its fictive as well as its dialogue form, its occasional irony, the ambiguity of its proper names. Is Utopia really Noplace? Is Hythloday simply spinning a yarn? If not, what lesson are we to draw from this "best state of a commonwealth"? That question perhaps can be better approached through Erasmus' *Adagia*. If the same theme is struck in both works, the more direct and straightforward expression of it should be the simpler to analyze, the clearer to grasp.

In the introduction to the *Adagia* which first appeared in the Aldine edition of 1508 Erasmus discusses the nature and use of proverbs, and to show how a very short adage can contain deep philosophical and religious truths he cites the dictum "Friends have all things in common." His extended comment proving this point runs as follows:[7]

> If anyone more diligently and deeply analyzes that saying of Pythagoras "Friends have all things in common," he will certainly find the sum and substance of human happiness expressed in this brief remark. What else is Plato driving at in so many volumes save to promote community and its foundation, friendship? If he could convince mortals of these things, war, envy, fraud would immediately depart from our midst; in short a whole army of evils would march out of our lives once and for all. What other aim had Christ the prince of our religion? Truly He gave to the world only one precept, the rule of charity, and He stressed that everything in the Law and the Prophets hangs on that alone. Or, what else does charity urge save that all have all things in common? Namely, it urges that joined in friendship with Christ and bound to Him by the same force that unites Him with the Father and imitating as far as we can that perfect communion by which He and the Father are one we also become one with Him and, as Paul says, are made one spirit and one flesh in God, so that by right of friendship all that is His is shared with us and all that is ours is shared with Him. Then it urges that joined with one another in equal bonds of friendship as members of the same Head, as one and the same body, we come alive with the same spirit and weep and rejoice at the same things. That mystical bread gathered from many grains into one flour also reminds us of this, as does the draught of wine fused into one liquid from the clusters of many grapes. Finally charity urges that since the sum total of all created things is in God and God in turn is in all things the whole universe, as it were, be restored to unity. You see what an ocean of philosophy or rather theology has been opened up for us by so small a proverb.

What strikes us most about this explanation of Erasmus is how he relates the proverb to Scripture and to basic Christian doctrine. In the adage-essay of 1515 he had indicated that the Platonic-Pythagorian dictum was in harmony with the teaching of Christ, but here seven years earlier he had spelled out that agreement in considerable detail. (These introductory remarks of course prefaced the adage-essay in 1508.) Plato's *communitas* is equated with Christ's *charitas*, and the peace and well-being of society is made to coincide with membership in the mystical body of Christ and with universal reconciliation, both of which St. Paul so often speaks.[8] The proverb is given a fundamentally religious meaning, or at least its social thrust is confirmed and reinforced by religion and rooted in a profound theology of unity.[9] It is an impressive statement. It is clear proof, I think, of Erasmus' religious seriousness and depth, and it corroborates an observation of John O'Malley that the doctrine of the mystical body of Christ "must be taken as one of the fundamental strands in the fabric of his thought."[10]

What does this explanation tell us about this axiomatic prescription as a social reform, about Utopian communism as an example to imitate? I think we begin to realize that what both Erasmus and More are presenting is an ultimate moral and religious ideal—a way of life millenial, or practically so, in its fulfillment of the demands of Christian charity and its achievement of that unity for which Christ prayed. The pagans with the light of reason may have glimpsed the possibility and may even have elaborated their vision, but its actual attainment will be the product of Christian virtue and brotherhood as it is the object of Christian hope. This seems to be the message Erasmus conveys in his introductory remarks. More in *Utopia* is not so explicit, but his work lends itself to this understanding.

A true expert on *Utopia*, Edward Surtz, interprets More's attitude in this way.[11] In his view Utopia is an ideal that exists only in More's mind and heart, and its realization must depend on the moral rectitude of those who would create and maintain such a commonwealth. More's "ideal will always remain that of a common Christian life for a whole Christian nation, but the realization of this ideal depends upon the character of its citizens, who must be as perfect in their Christianity—or as eager in their pursuit of Christian perfection—as the Utopians are in their rationality."[12] That's a tall order indeed. Such perfection on a broad scale, whether Christian or rational, is out of reach, for the nature itself of man and the conditions of his earthbound existence stand in the way. The Utopian ideal then is a millenial dream; the concrete circumstances and practical problems of man in society require other arrangements.

Does this interpretation render *Utopia* as well as Erasmus' adage-essay a futile, not to say meaningless, exercise? I think not, but before I answer that question I want to say a few more words about More's famous book. I would like to take note of three passages in *Utopia* that are particularly relevant, I believe, to what we have been discussing.

In Book II of *Utopia* in the description of Utopian religions we are told that when the citizens of that mythical commonwealth heard about

Christ and His teaching many were disposed to become Christian.[13] Hythloday, More's narrator, speculates that it may have been "because they thought it [Christianity] nearest to that belief which has the widest prevalence among them." And he adds: "But I think that this factor, too, was of no small weight, that they had heard that His disciples' common way of life had been pleasing to Christ and that it is still in use among the truest societies of Christians."[14] This comment echoes especially the concluding remarks which Erasmus added to his adage-essay in 1515. The whole passage of course asserts the affinity between pagan, that is, rational, and Christian ideals in so far as the Utopian scheme of things is concerned.

A similar point is made in a passage near the end of *Utopia*, though an extremely interesting qualification is appended that underlines the difficulty in making good the ideal. Hythloday summing up the communal order that prevails in Utopia declares:

> Nor does it occur to me to doubt that a man's regard for his own interests or the authority of Christ our Saviour—who in His wisdom could not fail to know what was best and who in His goodness could not fail to counsel what He knew to be best—would long ago have brought the whole world to adopt the laws of the Utopian commonwealth, had not one single monster, the chief and progenitor of all plagues, striven against it—I mean, Pride.[15]

The linkage of Utopia with a Christian paradigm is asserted, but the great stumbling block is seen as man himself—his imperfection, his sinfulness. "This serpent from hell," Hythloday continues, "entwines itself around the hearts of men and acts like the suckfish in preventing and hindering them from entering on a better way of life."[16]

This realism finds even more pointed expression in a memorable and oft-quoted passage in Book I. In the dialogue that is the central theme of that Book about serving as a councilor to a prince More counters Hythloday's high-minded disdain for such a post with these remarks:

> So it is in the commonwealth. So it is in the deliberations of monarchs. If you cannot pluck up wrongheaded opinions by the root, if you cannot cure according to your heart's desire vices of long standing, yet you must not on that account desert the commonwealth. You must not abandon the ship in a storm because you cannot control the winds. On the other hand, you must not force upon people new and strange ideas which you

realize will carry no weight with persons of opposite conviction. On the contrary, by the indirect approach you must seek and strive to the best of your power to handle matters tactfully. What you cannot turn to good you must make as little bad as you can. For it is impossible that all should be well unless all men were good, a situation which I do not expect for a great many years to come.[17]

Hythloday objects and makes his reply, but More's hardheaded and pragmatic approach to political reality in this instance is certainly striking and has the ring of simple truth. "The author of *Utopia* was no Utopian," observes Professor Hexter in discussing this remarkable passage.[18] It is the last sentence however to which I would like to call attention: "It is impossible that all should be well unless all men were good . . ." Since they are not and their vices like the suckfish hold them back the Utopian dream per se is unrealizable. What then is its purpose? Why do More and Erasmus both advance this lofty ideal?

I have already stressed that the ideal they have in mind is a spiritual one. It has to do with men being good, it has to do with Christ's command to love one another, it has to do with the values men live by, it has to do with changing and reforming lives. Obviously the social dimension is paramount. The health of society depends on how men behave. Greedy landlords, ambitious princes, fawning courtiers cause suffering and disorder. It is they who bear the brunt of the criticism in the first Book of *Utopia*, and it is their absence in the commonwealth described in the second Book that makes that happy land Utopia. There the vices so prevalent in the Europe of More's time have been eradicated. Utopian laws and institutions supposedly have eliminated them, but it is actually the moral philosophy of the Utopians and their many virtues that have triumphed. Good people have built a good society. More's message, I think, is contained therein. Erasmus wrote that More "published *Utopia* to show what the cause of our civil problems are, having England which he knows and understands so well particularly in mind."[19] The conciseness and precision of that statement are admirable. If we read it in the context of what both men have written it means that the causes lie within man himself and that a better world awaits man's moral reformation. It means that the redress of the social and political ills besetting Christian Europe in those critical times will only proceed from a change of heart in its peoples. More has dramatized that theme in *Utopia*, Erasmus has expounded it with special emphasis in the *Adagia*. Together they have raised a beacon on the margin of a stormy sea.

Fordham University

Notes

1. Margaret Mann Phillips, *The 'Adages' of Erasmus, a Study with Translations* (Cambridge, 1964). See also Thomas M. Greene, "Erasmus's 'Festina lente': Vulnerabilities of the Humanist Text" in *Mimesis, From Mirror to Method, Augustine to Descartes*, eds. John D. Lyons and Stephen G. Nichols, Jr. (Hanover and London, 1982), pp. 132–48. The first 500 adages have so far been translated and published in *Collected Works of Erasmus*, Vol. 31: *Adages Iii to Iv100*, trans. Margaret Mann Phillips, annotated by R. A. B. Mynors (Toronto, 1982). The complete *Adagia* is in the Leiden *Opera Omnia* of Erasmus (1703–06), volume II. A new critical edition will appear in the Amsterdam *Opera Omnia*, now in progress. Vol. II, nos. 5 and 6, of this series, containing the third thousand of the adages, *Adagiorum chilias tertia*, was published in 1981.

2. Phillips, *The 'Adages' of Erasmus*, pp. 106 ff. More began writing *Utopia* at Antwerp in the summer of 1515 and finished the book in London the following year. Erasmus arranged for its publication by Dirk Martens at Louvain later that year. See J. H. Hexter, *More's* Utopia (Princeton, 1952), pp. 15 ff.

3. I have used the text in the *Adagiorum chiliades* published by the heirs of Sebastian Gryphius at Lyons in 1559. Additions to the text as it was expanded and revised by Erasmus in earlier editions are in italics and are footnoted. I have not always repeated in my translation the proverb as quoted by Erasmus from the ancient author he cites.

4. The above two sentences in italics were added in the 1515 Froben edition. The second citation is from the *Republic*, Book V (462c).

5. This sentence in italics was added in the 1526 Froben edition. Book II of Aristotle's *Politics* contains an extensive critique of Plato's community ideal. Chapter 5 of Book II is especially relevant here.

6. The above three sentences in italics were added in the 1515 Froben edition. The term *coenobium* which Erasmus also gives in its Greek form κοινόβιον literally means "common life."

7. I have made the translation from the 1559 Lyons edition, col. 11. The text is the same as the original 1508 text.

8. Romans 12:4–5, 1 Corinthians 12:12–27, Ephesians 1:9–10, Colossians 1:20.

9. See John 17:20- 23.

10. In "Erasmus and Luther, Continuity and Discontinuity as Key to Their Conflict," *Sixteenth Century Journal* V, 2 (October 1974):55.

11. In *The Praise of Pleasure* (Cambridge, Mass., 1957), Chap. XV: "Thomas More and Communism: the Solution."

12. *Ibid.*, p. 182.

13. St. Thomas More, *Utopia* in *The Complete Works of St. Thomas More*, vol. 4, eds. Edward Surtz, S.J., and J. H. Hexter (New Haven, 1964), 217-19. Hereafter cited as CW 4.

14. The reference is to Acts 2:42-45 and 4:32-37, the *locus classicus* for the existence of a community of goods, a κοινωνία, among early Christians, and also to religious orders who practiced a community life.

15. CW 4, 243.

16. CW 4, 243-45.

17. CW 4, 99-101. German Arciniegas hits the bull's-eye when he states in his *America in Europe* (New York, 1986), p. 54, that "Utopia presupposes a government in the hands of good men." Chapter 3 of this work presents an excellent discussion of More's classic in its historical context.

18. *More's Utopia*, p. 131.

19. My translation of Erasmus' reference to *Utopia* in the sketch of Thomas More he wrote in a letter to Ulrich von Hutten July 23, 1519, in *Erasmi epistolae*, eds. P. S. Allen and H. M. Allen, vol. 4 (Oxford, 1922), 21 (Ep. 999, 11.256-59).

Washington, le 20 septembre 1987.

Cher Germain,

C'est avec joie que je profite de cette occasion pour exprimer publiquement ma gratitude envers vous. Quand j'ai fait votre connaissance, j'étais encore plongée dans la rédaction de ma dissertation. L'intérêt que vous avez pris à mon étude et votre enthousiasme contagieux pour les travaux de recherche en général ont eu une influence décisive sur ma carrière, et je ne l'ai pas oublié. Chacune de vos visites à Washington a renouvelé le plaisir d'avoir fait votre connaissance il y a quinze ans. J'aimerais rappeler deux incidents particuliers. Je vous dois la publication de mon tout premier article, et cette preuve de confiance à ce moment précis ne peut être sous-estimée. Et puis, vous m'avez envoyé un beau jour la page d'un catalogue indiquant la vente d'un exemplaire du livre de François de Billon, sujet de ma thèse. Je n'ai pas pu résister à la tentation d'acquérir ce livre ancien, et me voilà lancée en tant que bibliophile ! Ce détail montre l'intérêt que vous portez aux occupations d'autrui. Vous avez influencé ma vie et je vous en suis reconnaissante. Mais le plus important, c'est que votre énergie infatigable et votre bonté inspirent ceux qui vous connaissent. Merci, Germain ! Je vous souhaite à l'avenir une vie moins épuisante, plus détendue, et j'espère de tout coeur que nous vous verrons souvent à Washington !

Marianne S. Meijer

Les Meijer ont reçu Abbé Marc'hadour chez eux pour un petit séjour pendant le mois d'avril 1989.

JOZEF   IJSEWIJN

*Erasmus in Rome:
A Clash of Humanist Cultures?*

IN HIS DIALOGUE *Ciceronianus* (1528) Erasmus discusses some fundamental questions concerning language, literature and culture in general in the world of Renaissance humanism. In a well-known passage of this dialogue he draws a particularly dark image of the humanist and, in his eyes, unchristian culture in the Rome of the popes and the Curia.[1]

Erasmus' story connects, he says, with his stay in Rome in April 1509. First he mentions two famous humanist orators, Petrus Phaedra Inghiramus and Camillus, probably Delminius, the first from Volterra in Tuscany, the second from Friuli. Without any apparent coherence, he recalls a Good Friday sermon preached *coram papa* by a humanist he does not name, but who cannot be one of the two men mentioned before, since Erasmus expressly states that the orator was a real Roman. Erasmus had received an invitation to attend the sermon with Julius II, many Cardinals, bishops and humanists. The orator, says Erasmus, was a real Ciceronian:

> His preface and his peroration—which was almost longer than the entire speech— were taken up with singing the praises of Julius II, whom he called Jupiter Optimus Maximus, describing him as grasping and hurling with his omnipotent right hand the three-forked, unerring thunderbolt and with a mere nod having his will performed. All that had been done in the preceding years

in France, Germany, and Spain, Portugal, Africa, and Greece, had come about, he maintained, by the nod of his will and his alone. In all of which to be sure, he spoke as a Roman in Rome, using Roman speech and a Roman accent.

Erasmus then asks what all this had to do with Christendom and a Christian religious service. Nobody in the audience was moved to sadness or mourning, although the cruel passion and death of Christ were described in a highly colourful oratorical manner. As a matter of fact, Christ was put on the same footing with ancient pagan heroes who had given their lives for their peoples, Greek or Roman. In short, the rhetorical model everywhere was Cicero and not St. Paul, as would have been becoming to a Christian orator. Erasmus thus reaches this conclusion:

> This Roman spoke so Romanly that I heard nothing about the death of Christ. Yet this eager aspirant after the Ciceronian idiom was judged by the Ciceronians to have spoken marvellously; though he said practically nothing on the subject, which he seemed neither to understand nor care for. . . . The only thing he could be praised for was for speaking in Roman fashion and recalling something of Cicero.

The full story is a good illustration of Erasmus' own loquacity: most of the time he is too long in his exposé, as he admits himself several times. More important, however, is what the dialogue says and the influence it exercised throughout the centuries and sometimes still continues to exercise.

The text introduces us to two entirely opposed worlds: on one side the Roman Renaissance, where it was imperative to be first and foremost a well-trained humanist before devoting oneself to theology; on the other, the transalpine world of the Devotio Moderna, in which one had to be first and above all a theologian or at least a pious man in order to be allowed to pursue humanist studies. At the same time the text reminds us of a mostly forgotten fact, viz., that a skilled rhetorician — as Erasmus was! — can force upon his readers a certain image of men and the world with no less efficacy than today a good journalist can do. Let me illustrate both points, the second one first, the effect of Erasmus' gripping *ars suasoria*.

Ever since the publication of the *Ciceronianus*, Italian and especially Roman humanism has had a bad press, even in much scholarly literature: it is called void and vain and its main roles are played by caricatural popes and prelates. In some ways, it reminds me of those old Roman emperors treated by Tacitus "sine ira et studio." The few humanists from the north who had shown some predilection for southern humanism got the same black stamp put upon them and their work. This overdrawn picture has, of course, been strengthened since the sixteenth century by the Reformation conflicts and their concomitant propaganda campaigns. It could maintain itself in our age because only a few specialists of Erasmus have studied Italian humanism thoroughly and, vice-versa, hardly any students of Italian humanism look very long to the other side of the Alps. Finally not many scholars today seem really to enjoy reading Latin texts for the sake of their specific textual beauty – a prerequisite for a good understanding of what humanism really was and wanted to be.

The image of the Roman preacher *coram papa* as depicted by Erasmus has recently been the subject of a critical evaluation by two eminent scholars: the American Jesuit John O'Malley, a specialist in both Roman and Erasmian humanist rhetoric,[2] and Lucia Gualdo Rosa of Rome, who is perfectly familiar with the problems of Italian humanism and is keenly aware of the fact that humanism does not stop at the southern ridge of the Alps.[3]

O'Malley has carried out a careful and systematic analysis of the sermons *coram papa* held between 1450 and 1521, i.e., from the pontificate of Nicholas V to the death of Leo X, both key figures in the development of Vatican humanism. Gualdo has added to this investigation a microanalysis of one such sermon, viz., the *De morte Christi Domini Deique nostri deque eius tormentis*, delivered by Thomas Phaedra Inghiramus on Good Friday, April 4, 1504. Erasmus most probably had that man in mind when he wrote his *Ciceronianus* passage, but it is utterly impossible that he is the decried orator since Inghiramus was not a Roman, but a Tuscan.

What is now the result of both studies? From the historical point of view Erasmus' story is pure fiction, yet it contains just enough fact to make the caricature acceptable to readers not better informed, and who was among Erasmus' Northern readers? It is still unknown who was the actual preacher whom Erasmus heard in April 1509. It is just possible (and nothing more!) that it was the Roman Joannes Baptista Casalis, one of Julius II's favourite preachers. A disturbing detail in this connection is the fact that this man had written an invective against Erasmus four years before the *Ciceronianus*, something which the latter would hardly have appreciated. A literary settlement of accounts *inter doctos* thus seems to be a possible background of the whole story.

O'Malley finds so far over fifty sermons *coram papa*. On the basis of a close screening of their contents his verdict is clear: not a single sermon corresponds to the Erasmian description. The arguments are not classical and profane, but evangelical; praise of the pope is hardly ever given. In sermons of a few preachers, such as precisely Inghiramus and Casalis, one sometimes comes across a short passage which may be indicated as the origin of Erasmus' exaggeration. A good example to the point is the sermon studied by Gualdo. That unedited text is preserved in ms. 7352B in the Bibliothèque Nationale, Paris, on fols. 221-236. Its *Peroratio* is on fols. 234v-236 and certainly not as long as the rest of the text, as Erasmus would make us believe. In that *peroratio* exactly one sentence describes Julius' power and glory, but it is formulated in such a rhetorical way that it serves to move the pope to an attitude of pious humility. Inghiramus puts it as follows:

> And in the first place You, Julius, Pontifex Optime Maxime, by whose will and whose authority the world is ruled; by whose word heaven is opened and the underworld shut; whose power is the closest to that of the immortal God; you, Julius, lay off your majesty to the extent that you surpass the other men in virtue, dignity and glory; forget your pomp and majesty and come in public to the Crucified at whose feet you have kneeled so often alone in prayer.[4]

Surely to modern ears this sounds bombastic if not downright ridiculous, but it does not say more than do scores of common late mediaeval descriptions of a pope and his unique position above men.

O'Malley has found more. In sermons preached in Rome in other places than the papal chapel and outside Rome, preachers sometimes indulged in the exaggerations ridiculed by Erasmus. And apart from that, the sermon had undergone an important evolution under humanist influence: the language had adopted a greater classical elegance, yet not to the extent Erasmus suggests. On the contrary, there were humanists in Rome who blamed Erasmus himself for using too classical language when he wrote about religious matters. As a matter of fact, Erasmus often enough says "tingere" instead of "baptizare," "retincti" for "anabaptistae," "concionator" and not "praedicator" and so forth.

The contents of the sermon had changed also. The medieval usage of discussing the *essentia Dei* in a didactic vein—we may also wonder what that meant to the greater part of the audience—had given way to epideictic oration in praise of the *magnalia Dei*. This change demanded quite naturally a rhetorical style colliding with the opinion of those who find the core of Christianity in an attitude of self-humiliation and sorrow for one's sinfulness rather than in a more vital and triumphant approach to life and faith. The former attitude was fostered by the Devotio Moderna. It shines through Erasmus' words and, in a sense, also in the final conclusion of Gualdo, who for the greater part supports Erasmus' point of view. In her opinion an orator who speaks in a triumphant style and offers beautiful sentences about Christ to his audience cannot elicit more than a superficial emotion, no real conversion, and therefore, such a person can possess neither true faith nor internal richness.

I am not convinced by that argument. In my opinion that conclusion is a *latius hos*, perhaps anachronistically influenced by certain recent postconciliarian beliefs. In any case, it does not take into account the quite obvious fact that Christians, depending on time, place and milieu, at one time tend to be triumphalist and at another self-deprecating in an almost masochistic manner. I do not think a historian has to decide on the quality of the faith of Christians, whatever their tendency may be. He only has to try to understand and to explain what happened. If we look at our problem in that way we will notice that a preacher in Rome about 1500 would not even have found an audience among the cultivated humanist intellectuals if he had spoken in the antiquated scholastic manner and, in particular, in "gothic" Latin. To explain more clearly this situation we must try to describe the world and ideals of those Roman humanists; if then we confront it with the world of Erasmus as a Northerner, we will see why they necessarily came to a clash.

Humanism in its origin is a restoration movement of Italian artists and intellectuals. The country which had ruled the world in Roman times had been torn to pieces in the Middle Ages; it was dominated largely by foreigners and riven by countless civil quarrels as well as battles and scuffles between little local potentates. For centuries the emperor had been a German, i.e., a transalpine barbarian; in the fourteenth century even the pope was no longer in Rome, but in Avignon and most of the time an abhorred Frenchman to boot. The first humanists dearly wanted to restore Italy's old glory, in a first stage by a revival of classical Latin against the Gothic degeneration, later also by a restoration of Rome's prestige. To get back the emperor soon proved to be an impossible dream, as Petrarch's nasty experience showed. The pope, however, ultimately came back, was, with few exceptions, an Italian again, and soon enough it was understood in Rome what an enormous help humanism could be in the process of rebuilding the papal power and authority after its catastrophic decline during the late Middle Ages. The humanists were indeed well-trained Latinists in a world with one international language, Latin. They also could provide the necessary ideological substructures to Rome's glorious privileges by reviving ancient symbols and ideals. As early as the mid-fifteenth century, under Nicholas V, the sun became the symbol of the pope, as it had been of ancient Roman emperors (and two centuries later, following in the footsteps of the popes, of "le roi-soleil" in France). About 1500 Annius of Viterbo, Vatican court theologian, conceived the theory of an archpriesthood established in Rome since the primitive age of the god Ianus, who was equated to Noah. Again, one has to consider all this in the context of its time: the pope was a feudal lord and the greater and the more powerful the impression he could give to the outside world, the better it was—so a very common belief held—for the Church.

Hence a conscious and at times ruthless cultural policy from the fifteenth century through the eighteenth, changed completely the medieval village outlook of Rome to make it one of the most splendid art cities in the whole world, which today continues to make happy both art lovers and travel agents. From L. B. Alberti to G. L. Bernini or Alessandro Galilei for that matter, humanists and artists under humanist influence have planned and built that city at the service of the popes and cardinals, to make it a visible terrestrial foreshadowing of the heavenly glory. In many a humanist oration and verse that purpose is explicitly underlined. The spirit of a triumphant development of Christendom permeated Rome in those centuries. Despite the Turkish threat and despite the growing problems with the Reformation (initially considered a monks' quarrel, as there had been so many throughout the centuries) Rome saw the Church in an age of expansion never known before. The discovery of America and Asia was interpreted as a manifest proof of God's help in that perspective. Against that spirit the complaints of Erasmus, who thought that the Church was shrinking and in regression, offer a glaring contrast.

The situation just described and the intellectual climate in Rome in the early sixteenth century make it perfectly understandable that a rich rhetorical eloquence in the classical vein matched that atmosphere in a precise and unique way. To that may be added the well-known extroverted Mediterranean exuberance that does not please many a Germanic northerner. How, therefore, could a strong pope like Julius II, a man who hired the service of artists such as Bramante, Raphael and Michelangelo, ever have found pleasure in sombre meditations of one preaching penitence in doggerel Latin? From a certain point of view, the Roman style of living has been condemned as particularly unchristian. Many visitors to Rome, such as the German Fichardus, found it unacceptable that Clement VII, the Medici successor of the stern Dutch theologian Hadrian VI, had his bathroom in Castel Sant' Angelo adorned with frescoes representing pretty, nude classical nymphs, and Venus and Mars.[5] But all this suited perfectly well the joyous outlook on life among pretridentine Roman humanists, who loved to read Ovid, to imitate Martial, and, in any case, did not wish — as other humanists like Budé and Vives did — that their works might have perished. At that time Rome still had to invent the *Index* and Jesuits were not yet at work producing an expurgated Horace and similar schoolbooks used until far into the twentieth century!

Anyone who wants to condemn that Roman way of life on moralistic grounds must not forget, however, that enjoying life did not prevent humanists from doing serious work. Long before Erasmus, the Roman Lorenzo Valla had applied his philological acumen to the study and the improvement of the New Testament Vulgate. Most Latin translations of the Greek patristic authors were made in Rome, often ordered by the popes. When Erasmus published his Origen he could use freely the Latin version made by the Roman canon Christophorus Persona in the late fifteenth century. Still, Roman thinking about the badly needed reformation of the Church was certainly not lacking. Several times criticism voiced in Rome was not less harsh than that from the other side of the Alps. Julius II has been the first pope in about four hundred years to launch the idea of a Church reform Council and even Erasmus had great expectations regarding the policy of Clement VII, as one can see in his *De amabili Ecclesiae concordia*. Today, of course, we can see that all this fell entirely short of what was really needed to eradicate some centuries-old abuses, but it is always easier to see shortcomings *post factum*. Finally, speculative theology certainly was an area of small interest in Rome. The number of strictly theological works printed in Rome is insignificant in total book production, whereas in northern Europe at certain moments they threatened to eliminate all other publications. It is not difficult to explain that situation. Theology does not belong to the areas of direct humanist concern, and since the Curia was composed for a good part by humanists and for the rest mainly by jurists and canonists, one could not expect much theological, or even purely philosophical work, for that matter. Theology belonged to the universities and the monasteries and one could say, therefore, that the *Sapienza* did not fulfill all its duties.

We now turn our eyes to northern Europe, where humanism was a typical imported culture. At Rotterdam, Deventer or Louvain it was hardly thinkable to dream of a restoration of Rome's grandeur as a possible means of promoting local culture and prestige. Humanism was a rather esoteric affair of restricted circles or even isolated individuals among the university and Church personnel who used Latin on behalf of their professional duties and sometimes were attracted by the spell and charm of the new Latin of their Italian colleagues. They had come into contact with that new Latin either in Italy during their study time and business visits or – and this is the case with Erasmus – in Italian books now multiplied and widely diffused thanks to the new printing technology. They found that Latin much more palatable than the barbarous late scholastic jargon their teachers were using or was found in *modist* or similar schoolbooks. The *Invectiva in Modos significandi* of Alexander Hegius, the enlightened school director of Deventer, bears witness to the profound paedagogical change going on under Italian influence in the Low Countries in the second half of the fifteenth century.

The majority of the first northern humanists were young and enthusiastic teachers and students in the arts faculties and some Latin schools, i.e., beginners at the bottom of the academic hierarchical scale. One easily imagines what was going to happen when these "underdogs" began to tell the highly respected and infallible *Magistri Nostri*, the professors of divinity on the top of the tree, that they were ignorant barbarians, who knew nothing of good Latin, did not understand the Latin authors and adhered to unsound scholarly methods. Furthermore, humanism hardly had any base or support outside the classroom. Culture at the Burgundian Hapsburgian court was feudal and French and for a long time humanist influence did not proceed beyond the reading of a few classical texts, mostly those of historians, in French translation. Generally speaking, the higher nobility did not understand or care for Latin.

An early sixteenth-century exception, and only a short-lived one, was the court of Margaret of Austria in Mechlin. There we find the only profane humanist poets of the Netherlands, the *Tres Fratres Belgae*, Johannes Secundus and his brothers. But these young men were the sons of the highest officer in court, youth with a solid social and economic independence living in circles where theology was not the all-dominating and oppressing power. Compared to them, Erasmus belonged not only to a much older generation, born when humanism was at its very first attempts to penetrate into the Low Countries, but he was also a bastard and an orphan, stowed away in a monastery, a young man without economic independence who as a monk and a priest had to look for patrons within the ecclesiastical establishment. Even at an older age such reasonably good income as he had derived for the greater part from ecclesiastical benefices and preferments. He had, moreover, been submitted in his young years to the spiritual brainwashing of the Devotio Moderna – and who ever rids himself completely of youthful impressions? Neither had Erasmus a chance to study in Italy in his younger and impressionable years. He knew the homeland of humanism only after the shape of his mind had already become more rigid. Erasmus, without doubt, had inborn talents for a real humanist literary career, but he never had the liberty to develop these talents fully, and all his life long he had to give and take in a position somewhere between literature and theology.[6] Facts speak clearly: as a schoolboy he became enticed by Latin poetry and very soon he applied himself to the writing of Latin verse, perhaps the most characteristic of all humanist activities. But barely had he written a few poems when he received a strong admonition from the slightly older Cornelius Aurelius: it is all very well to write verses but only if they be pious and Christian. Otherwise they are a pure waste of time. Such is not, of course, the best possible means of encouraging budding humanist talent. How did Erasmus cope with the situation? If I am not mistaken, in two ways.

First he sometimes adopted a camouflage strategy, disguising specifically humanist activities as religious and theological work. There are telling examples of those tactics. As a true humanist Erasmus translated a few tragedies by Euripides. It was, however, not merely translating. Erasmus toiled much at transferring into Latin the rich and difficult metrical variety of the Greek originals. That did not prevent him offering his work to Archbishop Warham as a preparatory exercise to his studies of the Bible and the Greek patristic authors. A more typical excuse *pour les besoins de la cause* cannot be found. In fact, if one wants to study Koinê Greek or patristic prose, the last thing to do is to tackle metrical problems in a poetic language several centuries older. Can we imagine an American today trying to make a highly poetic translation of Vondel's tragedies in order to study Schillebeeckx? To put the question is to answer it. Another example: in 1523 Erasmus composed in classical Latin a mass in honour of Our Lady of Loretto. Its *sequentia* is a poem of thirty verses divided into fifteen distichs, each of them in a different and sophisticated metre, paroemiacs, archilochians, elegiambi. I find it hard to interpret such a poem as an exercise in pious devotion but rather as a proof of a profound affection for dear old Horace.

And can we avoid this question when we read such a text: does the man who wrote it still have the right to be scandalised only five years later by the Roman preaching style? What have we to think then of his piety? if Ciceronian prose style cannot move our religious feelings, then how can Horatian verses do so? If a Ciceronian orator cannot have true faith, how can a Horatian poet have it? Our suspicions that Erasmus' Ciceronian vexation ultimately must be explained, at least in part, by his bad feelings against some Italian humanists are strengthened. Possibly it had hurt him very deeply that Italians and Romans had not been prepared to praise and to celebrate him as the unique prince of humanism, although they had not spared their praise for his predecessor Agricola and sometimes also his challenger Longolius. Erasmus, one must be reminded, was very touchy on that point. Think of his absolutely exaggerated reaction, in 1531, against a Roman philosopher, Augustinus Steuchus from Gubbio. That serious scholar had pointed out that Erasmus' etymology of the name Adam was wrong and it made him very angry. The psychological factor must indeed not be underestimated. In his homeland Erasmus could fiercely attack the "barbarians," i.e., the non-humanist Latin authors, whom he tore to pieces with his sarcasm. But in the Italy of the high Renaissance quite a few purists and chauvinists were easily inclined to consider Erasmus as a semi-barbarian. He was very learned, to be sure, but not really and perfectly eloquent according to their sophisticated tastes. And it is a fact that Erasmus, in contrast to Agricola, never dared to speak in public in Italy. Perhaps he lacked sufficient volubility at a spoken performance or simply a good Italian accent.

In Erasmus' time many German humanists were keenly aware of the fact that they could not match the Italians in the field of Latin eloquence. Henricus Bebel (1472–1518), a professor at Tübingen and a staunch propagator of humanist ideals, as late as 1510 – about the time of Erasmus' Italian experiences – wrote in his *Commentarii de abusione linguae Latinae*: "The Latin of the Germans is so poor that when they are in Italy and Rome their language reminds people of that spoken by shoemakers and bakers in ancient times."

I am coming now to Erasmus' second way of surviving as a humanist in his scholastic environment. Disguising was not the only and not even the most important means. The best way to survive was to put his humanist skill and knowledge in the field of languages and philology at the service of biblical and patristic studies. Italian humanists had shown the way: Laurentius Valla had corrected the Vulgate gospels; the Florentine Giannozzo Manetti (1396-1459) had translated the psalms from the Hebrew, and many others were making Latin versions of Greek patristic authors.

Yet, even here Erasmus was walking on slippery ground. Most theologians felt little respect for humanists and never did consider Erasmus as a colleague on equal footing with themselves. Even his good friend and assistant, the Augustinian monk Martinus Lipsius of the Louvain Sint-Maartensdal monastery, once characterised him as a "humanist and only a very little theologian" – "poeta rhetorque, at theologus perexiguus."[7] By tackling textual problems of the bible, Erasmus exposed himself to criticism that was not long in coming. At this point it is fair to say that Erasmus has shown courage and perseverance. Many a young humanist has given way to theological pressure. There is no better example than Erasmus' fellow countryman Martinus Dorpius, who was a very promising literary artist in his student years, but who was lost to humanist literature under such a pressure. J. L. Vives, although a layman (but poor, and therefore dependent on others) swore solemn oaths to Louvain theologians to prove that he was not a humanist (*poeta*), but a decent Aristotelian philosopher. Yet, in private he loved classical poets not less than Erasmus.

Such were the limitations and specific leanings imposed upon northern humanism in general and Erasmian humanism in particular due to its largely unhumanist if not anti-humanist surroundings: monasteries without much classical culture, universities dominated by scholastic theologians, nobility without clear classical interests.

All this does not imply, however, that I nourish doubts about Erasmus' sincerity in matters of religion. I believe him unconditionally when he says that his life was at the service of a double ideal, to foster good classical literature and simple, sincere theology. As a matter of fact, that ideal is basically an application of a general humanist dream: let us go back to the unspoiled sources, even in a non-humanist area. It is probably thanks to this combination of the humanist and Christian ideals by men such as Erasmus, Budé, More, and Melanchthon that some humanist principles after all influenced broad areas of northern culture in spite of the overpowering theological disputes. In its purely Italian outlook, humanism had little chance in the north, except with a few individuals like the strongly Italianised Agricola and a few poets such as Celtis and Secundus. In the north scholasticism and Devotio Moderna had impregnated the intellectual life too deeply. During the whole of Erasmus' lifespan the visual arts there remained gothic and pious, hardly touched by the classical renewal. Only Latin began to change thoroughly under humanist influence, but it was more or less an isolated phenomenon in a Gothic environment.

One must not conclude from my exposé either that Erasmus was working on the New Testament or the Fathers only grudgingly. On the contrary, this work gave him the opportunity to live in a world of his philological preferences and, moreover, it gave him the feeling that he was contributing to the well being and the purification of the Church which was dear to his heart. The situation is different as it concerns the theological-philosophical disputes into which he was drawn very reluctantly, because he disliked them wholeheartedly. On several occasions he vented his vexation and said these disputes were a mere waste of time.

In early sixteenth century Rome, Cardinals paid for the annual printing of Pasquillus' gibes and taunts directed at the pope, at prelates, and at the Church, a healthy exercise in self-criticism one might say. But can we imagine even for a moment a theologian in Louvain, Paris or Cologne in precisely the same years paying for an edition of Pasquillus' sister *Moria*? The answer to this question marks the difference between the worlds of Roman and transalpine humanism.

I am keenly aware of the fact that I have drawn rather sharp lines and that historic reality is much more complex. It is, however, my purpose to underline some undeniable differences in the various "brands" of humanism in order to arrive at better discerning *Wahrheit* and *Dichtung* in Erasmus' overdrawn satire on Roman humanism and to explain why he wrote in such a way and why so many took his word at face value for so long a time.[8]

Katholieke Universiteit
Leuven

Notes

An earlier version of this essay was published in Dutch at Utrecht in the series *Utrecht Renaissance Studies* 5 (1986), pp. 25–40.

1. The Latin text is found in the ASD edition of Erasmus, *Opera Omnia* I, 2 (Amsterdam 1971), pp. 637, 15 to 639, 11. For some corrections in that text, see *Humanistica Lovaniensia* 27 (1978): 302-4. Another edition was made by A. Gambaro, Brescia 1965. An English translation, from which I quote a few lines, has been published by Betty I. Knott in the *Collected Works of Erasmus*, vol. 28 (Toronto 1986) = *Literary and Educational Writings*, vol. 6, ed. A. H. T. Levi. See pp. 384-86.

2. John O'Malley S. J., *Praise and Blame in Renaissance Rome. Rhetoric, Doctrine and Reform in the Sacred Orators of the Papal Court, c. 1450-1521* (Durham, N.C., 1979).

3. Lucia Gualdo Rosa, "Ciceroniano o Cristiano? A proposito dell'Orazione *De Morte Christi* di Tommaso Fedra Inghirami," *Humanistica Lovaniensia* 34A (1985) = *Roma Humanistica. Studia . . . J. Ruysschaert*, ed. J. IJsewijn, pp. 52-64.

4. "Tuque in primis, Iuli, Pontifex Optime Maxime, cuius nutu ac dicione sola terrarum gubernantur, cuius auctoritate celum patet, Tartara reserantur, cuiusque potestas proxime ad Deum immortalem accedit, quantum ceteris virtute, dignitate, gloriaque prestas, tantum de maiestate submitte, ac decori maiestatisque oblite, cui privatim sepe supplex ad pedes iacuisti, nunc publice accede." Quoted by Gualdo, o.c. (note 3), p. 60.

5. See (Autori vari), *Quando gli dei si spogliano. Il bagno di Clemente VII a Castel Sant'Angelo e le altre stufe del primo Cinquecento* (Roma 1984), pp. 55, 68-69. The author did not correctly understand, however, the Latin of Fichardus: whereas Fichardus in his description of the bath uses "tangere" in a spiritual sense, he understands it as "to touch" in the literal sense, which makes nonsense of the whole passage.

6. See Erika Rummel, *Erasmus' Annotations on the New Testament. From Philologist to Theologian*. Erasmus Studies 7 (Toronto 1986).

7. Allen 922, 11.10-11

8. An entirely different problem is, of course, the relation between Erasmus and the Italian theologians, which I do not feel competent to discuss. On that point see, e.g., Silvana Seidel Menchi, "La Discussione su Erasmo nell'Italia del Rinascimento: Ambrogio Flandino vescovo a Mantova, Ambrogio Quistelli teologo padovano e Alberto Pio principe di Carpi" in *Società, Politica e Cultura a Carpi ai tempi di Alberti III Pio*. Medioevo e Umanesimo 46 (Padova 1981), pp. 291-382.

Rotterdam, 22-09-87.

Pater Reverendissime,

About a year ago you were our charming guest during the Erasmus Congress in Rotterdam. In about one year you will read this letter, avec nos souvenirs de votre séjour dans une famille hollandaise, speaking in a home-made way French and English in one sentence, and trying to pray with you in Dutch.
Et ce que nous avons respecté le plus profondément dans votre personne pendant ces jours c'est votre préférence of being a priest above all.
Every day you would say Mass, et vous étiez très heureux quand nous assistions à votre Messe. Je me rappelle surtout the day you said Mass in Latin -- Concelebration was for you too : Praying in Dutch -- et dans la Messe particulière en latin l'Evangile était dans la traduction d'Erasme, and you gave an excellent comment on it. Mais comme 'Epistle' nous avons lu un passage du *De Imitatione Christi*, le livre de notre compatriote Thomas à Kempis, quoique St Thomas More l'ait attribué à Gerson.
Et c'est ce passage que je propose volontiers as a homage to this scholar who is a priest above all, et que l'on reconnaît si bien dans ces mots, written about the life of a priest, five hundred years ago.

Duo namque mihi necessaria permaxime sentio in hac vita, sine quibus mihi importabilis foret ista miserabilis vita. In carcere corporis hujus detentus duobus me egere fateor : cibo scilicet et lumine. Dedisti itaque mihi infirmo sacrum Corpus tuum ad refectionem mentis et corporis, et posuisti lucernam pedibus meis verbum tuum. Sine his duobus bene vivere non possum : nam verbum Dei lux animae meae, et sacramentum tuum panis vitae. Haec possunt etiam dici mensae duae, hinc et inde in gazophylacio sanctae Ecclesiae positae. Una mensa est sacri altaris, habens panem sanctum, id est Corpus Christi pretiosum, altera est divinae legis, continens doctrinam sanctam, erudiens fidem rectam, et firmiter usque ad interiora velaminis, ubi sunt Sancta Sanctorum, perducens gratias tibi, Domine Jesu, lux lucis aeternae, pro doctrinae sacrae mensa, quam nobis per servos tuos Prophetas et Apostolos, aliosque Doctores ministrasti. O quam magnum et honorabile est officium Sacerdotium, quibus datum est Dominum majestatis verbis sacris consecrare, labiis benedicere, manibus tenere, ore proprio sumere et ceteris ministrare.

Prophetas et Apostolos et Alios Doctores : Thomas More - Erasmus -- et : Germain Marc'hadour ? Wij weten het, wij hopen het, wij hebben het ondervonden. U groeten in oprechte en ware vieindschap de door U tot 'Mater Amabilis' uitgeroepen Thea, U groeten Piet en Paul, en U groet hij, die Uw gastheer wezen mocht in Rotterdam, Nijmegen ne Roosendal en Uw gast in Angers en Parijs .

Thea Brouwer - Kroon
Piet Brouwer Jr.
Paul Brouwer.
Piet Brouwer Sr.
Esdoornlaan 1
3053 WS
Rotterdam.

Piet again visited Moreanum, Angers, in March 1988, and in June he joined Abbé Marc'hadour and other Amici in Paris for the annual celebration of the feast of Saints Thomas More and John Fisher.

Friedrich-K. Unterweg
Buchenweg 24
4006 Erkrath 2

29 Oct. 1987.

Dear Father Marc'hadour,

Yesterday evening I returned from Rotterdam, where I had read a Dutch lecture about « Thomas More in Nederlandse dramas » to the students of PABO Thomas More -- the Teacher Training College, where you spoke about « My life with Thomas More » and planted a mulberry tree (which is doing very well !) on their 1986 « academie-dag ». On my way back, the lecturers' and students' appreciative reports of your visit and the fact that it was (once again) your recommendation which made Meneer Brouwer invite me to speak on their third « academie-dag » recalled to mind the occasions on which we had met in the past six years. First of all, the Brixen Thomas More Symposium in July 1981 where we got to know each other. Do you remember the day when we two made a little tour into the beautiful hills above Brixen and visited the « Kirchlein » with the « Amaza's-kiss fresco », while all the others were on a coach tour ? This « hermit day » (as you called it) with our conversation about your studies, friends, journeys and lectures and about my preparations for a thesis on Thomas More dramas assured that my studies would not lead into a cul-de-sac and gave me the calmness and self-confidence which I badly needed for my first public lecture ever on the following day. Moreover, I think it was your and Prof. Herbrüggen's positive criticism of my lecture and the manifold exchange of ideas during this stimulating week which encouraged me to go on with my research on Thomas More (and made me join the Amici Thomae Mori).

Years passed with a letter or a phone call now and then (all beginning with your very friendly and cheerful -- almost musical -- « allo ?! ») before I finally managed to visit you and your Moreanum in Angers in March 1985. In the course of this visit I spent fascinating hours browsing through the numerous books and other Moreana you have collected or which have been sent to you from all over the world. The conversations we held about the desiderata of More research and More studies in Germany, the numerous bibliographical hints you gave me and the discussion of our further projects and my edition of the Four Last Things were both interesting and stimulating. Finally, my acquaintance with Marie-Claude Rousseau -- which you initiated -- has led to a cooperation in the project of establishing a « chronology of More adaptation », which you favoured in one of your letters.

Your and Clare Murphy's visit to our home before and after our journey to the Neo-Latinists' Congress and the week we spent at Wolfenbüttel belong to my most impressive experiences since we got to know each other. According to your wish, our journey began in the Mettmann Thomas More church, where you, together with Father Buter, celebrated a moving mass, almost without ever needing to resort to the little piece of cardboard, onto which you had in the early morning noted down a few key words and some difficult German words or phrases : weil ich (as you told us the evening before) nur ein klein bißchen Deutsch spreche. To my greatest suprise and very much to the delight of the parishioners, you spoke very good German throughout the entire service, and -- a week later -- also introduced the parish's new Vicar with an effective German address to the public. On both occasions I was once again impressed by your ability to adapt yourself to your audience and to awaken their interest for your ideas, and the friendly family atmosphere that spreads among scholars, students, parishioners, young people and even children, while you talk.

Thinking of Wolfenbüttel, I remembered how you (after you had meditated a while in the back of my van, where the luggage left you hardly enough room to stretch out) shortened the long hours of travel for Clare and me by commenting on the symposium's programme, by giving us information about numerous scholars from all over the world who were personnally known to you, or by telling anecdotes from your journeys to foreign countries. Not long after our arrival, you had (as in Brixen) converted your hotel room into a study where you worked *on articles, corresponded with your friends, or meditated before, between or after the lectures. During that week I once again became very conscious of your moderate, even ascetic way of life (I remember that you refused to take anything but a few plain biscuits and a small bottle of water for your long journey back to Angers). As before, I thought that your little rucksack which usually contains more books and papers than personal things is a kind of symbol for your attitude to life. It is carried by a merry and lovable man, who tries to grasp the essentials of life instead of burdening himself with basically useless things, and who is, as my wife put it after his departure to Angers, « in many respects very much like Thomas More. »*

My stroll down memory lane whilst on my homeward journey has strengthened my wish to meet you again and has made me hope that you -- despite your « retirement » in 1988 -- might further accompany my research on Thomas More with your advice and cr..icism. With best wishes and love from Beate, Julia Katharina, Malte Sebastian and 'Oma'.

Yours

Friedrich

Friedrich and Abbé Marc'hadour met again at the International Neo-Latin Congress in Toronto, August 1988.

Erasmus, sketch by Raymond Joly

JACQUES CHOMARAT

La philosophie de l'histoire d'Érasme d'après ses réflexions sur l'histoire romaine

L'EXPRESSION "PHILOSOPHIE DE L'HISTOIRE" n'apparaît qu'au dix-huitième siècle,[1] mais la chose a existé bien avant le mot; historiens et philosophes, poètes et prophètes se sont posé des questions telles que: quels sont les événements importants, à quel domaine appartiennent-ils, quelles en sont les causes, obéissent-ils à des lois, dépendent-ils de la nécessité, du hasard, d'une Providence, préparent-ils un état final de l'humanité stable et satisfaisant? De telles réflexions nourrissent les divers messianismes et millénarismes, les analyses de Thucydide ou de Polybe, la grandiose synthèse de *La Cité de Dieu*. Érasme n'a consacré à ces problèmes que quelques *Préfaces*: en 1517 il place en tête de son édition de Suétone et de l'*Histoire Auguste* des considérations sur l'Empire romain; la même année la *Paraphrase* de l'*Epître aux Romains* est précédée d'un parallèle entre la Rome païenne d'autrefois et la Rome chrétienne d'aujourd'hui. La *Paraphrase* de l'*Epître aux Ephésiens* en 1520, celles des *Evangiles* de Luc et de Marc en 1523 sont préfacées par des méditations sur histoire et religion chrétienne.[2] C'est une synthèse des idées exprimées dans ces textes voisins chronologiquement—ce qui est un gage de leur cohérence—que l'on voudrait esquisser.[3]

Il apparaît aussitôt que l'histoire, pour Érasme, se déroule sur trois plans, ou dans trois domaines, entre lesquels existent des rapports complexes. Il y a l'histoire politique des États et des Empires, l'histoire religieuse, enfin celle des lettres en donnant à ce mot un sens très étendu rassemblant poésie, éloquence, philosophie, sciences, langues et grammaire. L'histoire de l'art en est donc absente; certes, dans la *Paraphrase* de l'*Epître aux Romains*, Érasme évoque les monuments encore visibles dans la Rome de son temps, les arcs et les pyramides, la statue dite d'Hadrien qui en fait est sans doute le Marc-Aurèle de la place du Capitole, les thermes de "Domitien" (en réalité, comme le dit Allen,[4] de Dioclétien), mais il ne regarde pas ces ouvrages d'un point de vue esthétique. Il y voit seulement des vestiges qui perpétuent le souvenir des empereurs de jadis, de leur puissance et de leur gloire évanouie, et de ce fait ils appartiennent pour Érasme à l'ordre du politique.

◈

C'est à celui-ci qu'est consacrée la *Préface* du Suétone; de biographies, individuelles par définition, Érasme tire des réflexions d'ensemble sur l'Empire romain. La vision qu'il en a, pourrait-on objecter, est sans doute biaisée par un dessein politique: contrecarrer les projets de ceux qui souhaitaient restaurer ou plutôt instaurer une monarchie universelle;[5] mais n'est-ce pas plutôt parce qu'il connaît bien ce que fut l'Empire romain qu'il rejette l'idée de le voir renaître autrement que comme un vain nom?[6] Car le jugement d'Érasme sur l'Empire est tout à fait péjoratif, il en peint une image affreuse. Pas trace chez lui de l'idée issue de saint Augustin et si répandue au Moyen-Age que l'Empire a été voulu par la Providence pour que le monde fût unifié quand paraîtrait son Sauveur, afin que l'Évangile se répandît dans tout le genre humain. Érasme note avec sagesse que si cet Empire a été le plus étendu et le plus durable de tous ceux qu'on ait connus (586/182-83), il avait laissé en dehors de lui une grande partie des terres habitées connues en ce temps-là sans compter celles qu'on venait de découvrir au temps d'Érasme (586/195-96), et qu'il a fini par s'effondrer (586/185-93); l'unité politique n'est donc pas nécessaire à l'expansion de la vérité religieuse.

En elle-même l'histoire de Rome est un fort bon exemple de la variabilité, de la fluctuation incessante qui est la loi des choses humaines, surtout dans l'ordre politique; Érasme compare leur va-et-vient à celui de l'Euripe:[7] rien de permanent, ascension, puis déclin, et ainsi sans fin (586/70; 1062/3-9); à Rome la monarchie initiale a été suivie de la démocratie ou plutôt de l'oligarchie; mais les abus (*licentia*) de celle-ci ont suscité un retour au principe monarchique avec les tribuns de la plèbe, puis des dictateurs, enfin des *imperatores*, mais bientôt sous l'Empire naquit le regret des formes antérieures de la vie politique (*pristini reipublicae status*) (1062/9-13). Alternance ou cycle où l'on croit déceler un écho de la *République* de Platon (VIII, 546 sq.); l'insatisfaction de l'état présent semble le seul élément durable à travers ces changements.

En outre, plus que tout autre régime l'Empire romain a été fondé sur la violence: despotisme du maître (586/75-76), despotisme des soldats qui l'ont fait maître par cupidité (586/144-45, 156 sq.); crimes à sa naissance, les guerres civiles au temps de César, puis d'Octave (586/128), assassinats et incestes (586/31), barbarie et avidité insatiable des soldats (586/134), tandis qu'étaient opprimée l'autorité du sénat, opprimées les lois, opprimée la liberté du peuple romain (586/163-64). On peut ajouter à cela l'idolâtrie dont les empereurs étaient l'objet, puisqu'ils avaient des temples et étaient élevés au rang de dieux après leur mort, alors même qu'ils étaient parvenus au trône par le crime et avaient régné en tyrans (586/78-83).

Est-ce à dire que ce régime, le pouvoir des Césars, était illégitime? Non, dit Érasme, énonçant une loi générale de l'histoire: "un pouvoir acquis par la force et le droit de la guerre et même par le crime prend peu à peu racine par le consentement de la multitude (*consensu multitudinis*) et devient légitime" (586/174). On ne saurait trop considérer ce principe, fondement de toute l'histoire politique. C'est la violence (la guerre, le crime) qui est à l'origine de tous les régimes (par politesse Érasme dit: presque tous) (586/175-78), mais il y a transformation de l'illégitime en légitime, passage du fait au droit, et ce qui assure cette légitimation c'est le *consensus multitudinis*. Il n'y a pas de définition en quelque sorte objective de la légitimité: est légitime ce que la majorité des gens en un pays donné à une époque donnée considèrent comme tel. Le droit est un simple fait. Ce qui confirme cette constatation quelque peu ironique c'est que les lois les plus sages, les plus justes, ne s'exportent pas: ni Solon, ni Lycurgue, ni Minos, ni les décemvirs à Rome n'ont rédigé de lois valables en dehors de leur pays d'origine. Platon n'a pu faire adopter celles qu'il avait composées. Celles de Moïse, malgré le prosélytisme des Pharisiens, ne sont jamais sorties de la nation juive (1381/250-70). Seules celles du Christ font exception, mais justement elles appartiennent à l'ordre religieux et non pas politique (1381/271 sq.).

L'histoire effective est-elle donc absurde? Pour qu'on la juge telle, il faut avoir présente à l'esprit une idée, même confuse, de ce que pourrait être une histoire sensée, c'est-à-dire aboutissant à un état où chaque être humain est pour les autres son prochain, où la violence n'a plus de place. Érasme écarte l'idée que cet achèvement de l'histoire pourrait être atteint par une monarchie universelle; celle-ci, dit-il, ne ferait que superposer un despotisme universel aux despotismes monarchiques déjà existants (586). Pour que cesse le va-et-vient de l'Euripe politique, les guerres et révolutions, il faut que les gouvernants cessent d'être animés par les *humanis cupiditatibus*,[8] qui jusqu'ici ont été le ressort de leurs actions: désir du pouvoir, amour des richesses, orgueil, colère, vengeance, plaisir de nuire (1400/331-33). Il faut que leur conduite soit inspirée par la recherche du bien de leurs sujets, par l'abnégation de soi-même. Platon voulait des rois philosophes, Érasme souhaite des rois chrétiens de coeur et non pas seulement de titre. L'un des premiers devoirs de ces monarques fidèles aux enseignements du Christ serait de s'entendre entre eux sur des frontières stables, seul vrai moyen d'empêcher les contestations et les guerres qui en résultent (586/245-51). Bref l'histoire politique laissée à elle même, au jeu des passions *humaines*, n'a aucune chance d'aboutir à un état satisfaisant, elle n'est que ressassement sanglant. Pour qu'elle devienne sensée, il faudrait qu'elle disparaisse, qu'elle s'élève du politique au religieux.

∽

La nature de l'histoire religieuse est donc toute différente de celle de l'histoire politique et elle n'apparaît nulle part mieux que dans l'expansion du christianisme sous l'Empire romain. Cette expansion a été universelle,[9] alors que celle de l'Empire ne l'était pas; elle a touché à la fois *Graecos et barbaros, doctos et indoctos, plebeios et reges* (1381/272-73); elle s'est faite dans des régions extrêmement diverses par leurs coutumes, leurs moeurs, leurs traditions religieuses (1381/286-89); or, alors que sur le plan politique la diversité est source de discorde, donc de conflit ou de despotisme, le christianisme en ces temps-là a fait naître la concorde entre les mondes les plus variés (1381/287-88).

Érasme insiste sur le caractère paradoxal de cette expansion si on la considère selon les normes politiques de la puissance. Car tout s'est passé comme si les forces entières de ce monde s'étaient liguées dans une guerre à outrance contre la nouvelle religion. Aux princes et magistrats persécuteurs s'unissaient les philosophes avec leurs préceptes, les rhéteurs, les poètes (1381/305-12). Or bien que cette religion ait une doctrine plus paradoxale que les plus grands paradoxes des philosophes

(1381/295-96), elle a triomphé alors que les oeuvres de ses adversaires ont en grande partie disparu et ne doivent leur survie partielle qu'aux citations qu'en ont faites les chrétiens.[10] Ce triomphe ne peut s'expliquer par des ressorts purement humains, mais seulement par la *virtus diuina* (1381/385-87); non point que Dieu ait troublé par des miracles le jeu des forces naturelles, mais parce que sa grâce a donné aux apôtres et aux disciples le courage de résister aux menaces et aux séductions (1381/331, 335). Il vaut la peine de considérer la figure typique de cette expansion, celle du martyr, car elle est en quelque sorte le contrepied de celle du soldat, qui caractérise l'ordre politique; le guerrier risque certes sa vie, mais son rôle est de donner la mort, il représente même en temps de paix la menace de mort pour qui ne se soumet pas à sa loi. Il est la violence toujours possible. Le martyr est celui qui refuse tout à la fois de se plier à cette loi et de recourir lui-même à la violence pour se défendre. Il accepte de bon coeur la mort, comme fait le vaillant soldat, mais il ne la donne pas.[11] Érasme ne nomme aucun martyr à proprement parler, mais il conte un exemple dont la signification est aussi nette, l'histoire du moine Télémaque sous l'empereur Honorius. Venu d'Orient à Rome et entré dans un amphithéâtre, il vit deux gladiateurs (car ce genre de spectacles subsistait) qui marchaient l'un contre l'autre pour un combat à mort, image éclatante de la guerre; il bondit entre les deux et s'écrie: "Que faites-vous, frères? pourquoi vous élancez-vous à votre perte mutuelle, comme des bêtes?" La foule, furieuse d'être frustrée de son cruel plaisir le lapida. Mais quand il apprit l'événement l'empereur interdit désormais les combats de gladiateurs et Télémaque fut canonisé (1400/205-26). On a ici sous une allégorie transparente les deux formes de l'histoire, la politique et la religieuse, l'une étant la négation de l'autre.

Cependant, si le christianisme a triomphé par le refus de la violence, il a eu par la suite une histoire moins glorieuse, car il n'est pas resté fidèle à lui-même. Pourquoi, demande Érasme, le domaine de la chrétienté s'est-il rétréci au cours des siècles récents (1381/391-96)? Il pense, ce disant, aux territoires abandonnés par les chrétiens devant les Arabes, puis les Turcs. Son explication est paradoxale, mais logique: les chrétiens ont laissé leur piété s'affaiblir. Ce ne sont pas les menaces extérieures qui affaiblissent le christianisme, ni les guerres, ni les persécutions, mais le refroidissement de la ferveur religieuse. A la Rome du temps de Jérôme d'une foi si pure et si éclatante s'oppose la Rome d'aujourd'hui (710/88-95): le pape est adoré comme une sorte de divinité terrestre (710/100-1), il prétend commander à tous les princes du monde (710/97-98) et se mêler de toutes les affaires des mortels (710/101-2).

En recherchant la puissance et la domination, il redescend du religieux au politique ou plutôt en ramenant le religieux au politique, comme avant le Christ, il le corrompt. On se souvient du courroux d'Érasme contre Jules II, le pape guerrier.[12] Nulle part il n'a parlé de Constantin, mais il n'est pas malaisé de conjecturer ce qu'il pouvait penser de ce despote qui a le premier confondu les domaines du religieux et du politique.

∾

Il est une autre raison du déclin moderne du christianisme, qui tient aux relations entre l'histoire religieuse et celle des *studia*, de la culture et du savoir qui constituent le troisième élément dans l'histoire des hommes. Érasme n'étudie guère son influence sur l'histoire politique, sinon par quelques indications rapides, mais importantes, sur le rôle des historiens dans la formation des gouvernants, car, peignant avec exactitude ceux qui ont régné ils proposent des exemples à fuir ou à imiter et agissent ainsi indirectement à leur tour sur le cours de l'histoire politique: qui consentirait à être un nouveau Néron (586/12-42, surtout 29-36)?

Érasme s'étend davantage sur les relations entre histoire religieuse et histoire des lettres au sens large. Elles ont tantôt combattu, tantôt servi l'Évangile; combattu lorsqu'aux premiers siècles du christianisme philosophes, poètes et rhéteurs réfutaient, critiquaient, calomniaient la nouvelle doctrine et ses adeptes (1381/307-9); plus tard les mêmes disciplines ont été utiles aux Pères de l'Église dans leur tâche de prédication et d'apologétique (1062/22-27). Mais à nouveau par la suite les doctrines philosophiques avec leurs argumentations tout humaines, voire ennemies du Christ, ont souillé les sources limpides de la doctrine évangélique (1062/27-39); en revanche d'autres érudits se sont efforcés de rétablir la pureté première des sources par la connaissance des langues et des bonnes lettres (1062/39-44); on doit hélas! regretter que certains d'entre eux aient attaqué avec violence, en ennemis, les partisans obstinés de la tradition corrompue.[13]

Cet abrégé, dont toute l'oeuvre d'Érasme à certains égards constitue le développement, montre que les lettres, au point de vue religieux, sont tantôt bonnes, tantôt mauvaises, ou encore qu'elles sont divisées en elles-mêmes. Ailleurs, Érasme examine la relation dans l'autre sens et considère l'influence de la religion sur les lettres. Dans sa *Préface au Sénèque* de 1529, il stigmatise la piété mal éclairée de certains chrétiens de jadis qui ont fait disparaître maintes oeuvres païennes de l'Antiquité (2091/133-87) et même falsifié le texte de l'Écriture.[14] C'est là une déplaisante caricature du vrai sentiment religieux. En tout cas les lettres aux yeux d'Érasme n'ont pas seulement un rôle instrumental; elles ont une certaine autonomie et une histoire à part qui ne se réduit ni à celle des États où elles sont nées, ni à celle de la religion.

∼

Dans l'*Enchiridion militis christiani* Érasme reconnaît trois parties en l'homme : *spiritus, anima, caro*, l'esprit, l'âme, la chair.[15] Entre la chair, source des passions et du péché, et l'esprit, par lequel nous ressemblons à Dieu, se trouve l'âme qui se rallie à l'une ou à l'autre en toute liberté, mais sans pouvoir rester neutre. Il est manifeste que l'opposition entre la chair et l'esprit se retrouve dans l'histoire sous forme de l'opposition entre politique, domaine de la violence née des passions, et religion chrétienne, qui est en quelque sorte la présence ici-bas de l'éternité; aussi, en prenant les termes à la rigueur, n'y a-t-il pas à proprement parler d'histoire religieuse; sous ce nom il n'y a que l'histoire des fluctuations dans la lutte entre les passions et la vraie piété, des conquêtes et des reculs de l'esprit depuis qu'a eu lieu la Révélation. Quant aux lettres il n'est pas arbitraire de leur reconnaître un rôle analogue à celui de l'âme, tantôt entraînée par les passions charnelles, tantôt liant sa destinée à l'esprit.

∼

Cette conception de l'histoire, foncièrement dualiste, peut d'abord faire penser aux deux cités de saint Augustin, celle des hommes et celle de Dieu. Pourtant sur un point décisif les deux doctrines se séparent. Pour le docteur d'Hippone, "même nos péchés sont nécessaires à la perfection de la totalité qu'a créée Dieu;"[16] des pires péchés, celui d'Adam, celui des frères de Joseph, celui de Judas, Dieu tire de plus grands biens;[17] il y a ainsi une sorte de sanctification de l'histoire par la considération de l'*uniuersitas*, la totalité; les guerres servent le dessein de Dieu, l'Empire romain, oeuvre de pillards[18] comme tous les autres Empires, est en quelque sorte béni par le choix qu'a fait le Christ d'y naître. Rien de tel chez Érasme, qui ne fait pas intervenir la notion de totalité; comment le mal pourrait-il servir au bien, comment pourrait-il lui être nécessaire? Le mal est le mal, la violence est la violence, une croisade est une guerre, le pouvoir temporel des papes ne soutient pas l'Église, mais la corrompt. Si l'on ne craignait d'abuser des rapprochements on pourrait dire que dans la descendance de saint Augustin se situe Hegel, alors que du côté d'Érasme on rencontrerait Kant.[19] Dans l'histoire au sens courant, c'est-à-dire politique, il n'y a rien de divin.[20]

Université de Paris
— Sorbonne

Notes

Les parenthèses du texte renvoient à P. S. Allen, *Opus Epistolarum* (Oxford, 1906–58); elles indiquent le numéro de la lettre et celui de la (des) ligne(s).

1. Voltaire, *Fragments sur l'Histoire*, art. X, *Oeuvres*, ed. Didot, t. 5, p. 239; une phrase en est citée dans Littré, s.v. "Philosophie."
2. Suét.: Allen 586; Rom.: 710; Eph.: 1062; Luc: 1381; Marc: 1400. Les autres textes auxquels on pourrait penser (*Préfaces à La Cité de Dieu*, aux autres *Paraphrases*) se sont révélés sans intérêt pour le sujet.
3. On notera que dire "*la* pensée d'Érasme (ou de n'importe qui) sur tel sujet" renferme l'hypothèse, qui reste à vérifier, de l'unité et de la cohérence de cette pensée; voir Raymond Boudon, *L'Idéologie* (Paris, 1986), 211.
4. Allen (710/58–61) identifie ("probably") la "statue d'Hadrien" avec la tête colossale du Musée du Vatican, mais le mot *statua* employé par Érasme convient-il pour une tête? L'erreur d'Érasme sur les thermes rend plausible une autre confusion, entre les deux empereurs, également barbus, tous deux appartenant à la "dynastie" des Antonins; au reste la statue équestre du Capitole était censée au Moyen-Age représenter Constantin, ce qui la sauva de la destruction.
5. Allen 586/208 sq.; voir le colloque *Puerpera*, ASD I-3, 454/46 et Allen 2126/12–40.
6. Allen 586/127: *inanem magni nominis umbram*; l'expression vient de Lucain.
7. Allen 586/68–71 ; 1062/1 sq.; *Adage* 862, LB II 357AD.
8. Allen 586/233; v. aussi 1381/312, où Érasme parle des *daemones huius mundi dominos*.
9. Allen 1381/271 sq. L'affirmation d'Érasme est évidemment tout à fait excessive.
10. Allen 1381/297–304. Érasme pense peut-être au *Contre Celse* d'Origène.
11. Devant ce personnage qui semble n'être ni maître ni esclave, un hégélien

dirait qu'il est esclave d'un maître tout-puissant et qu'il n'accepte la mort qu'en apparence, étant assuré de son immortalité.

12. Voir surtout *Julius exclusus*.
13. Allen 1062/45-65; sans doute allusion à des Luthériens tels que Hutten; voir Allen 951/29-36.
14. Pour mieux réfuter les Ariens.
15. Ed. Holborn, p. 52 (*LB* V 19; tr. Festugière, p. 123).
16. "Etiam peccata nostra necessaria sunt perfectioni universitatis quam condidit Deus" (*De libero arbitrio*, III, 9, 26); cf. *Cité de Dieu* (= *C.D.*) XI. 23,1. Sur cette question: F. Chatillon, *Revue du Moyen-Age latin*, IX (1953) 281-88 et G. Foillet, *Revue des études augustiniennes*, V (1959):540.
17. *Sermo*, X, 5 (*P.L.* V.95) ; *Contra Iul. op. imperf.* V, 11 (*P.L.* X.1142), etc.
18. *C.D.* IV, 4, 1: "Latrocinia"; *C.D.* V, 21: "Haec plane Deus unus et verus regit et gubernat, ut placet; et si occultis causis, numquid iniustis ?" Voir encore *C.D.* XVIII, 22: "condita est ciuitas Roma, velut altera Babylon, etc."
19. Kant admire les *Colloques*, voir *Kant intime*, textes réunis et traduits par Jean Mistler, Paris (1985), 26. Mais bien sûr Érasme aurait été choqué par les thèses de Kant sur le rôle éducateur de la guerre (*Conjectures sur les débuts de l'Histoire humaine*, p. 169 de *La Philosophie de l'Histoire*, opuscules traduits pas Stéphane Piobetta, Paris, 1947).
20. Il arrive cependant à Érasme plus tard, devant les violences déchaînées, de faire allusion au rôle caché de Dieu.

ANNE   M.   O'DONNELL,   SND

Cicero, Gregory the Great, and Thomas More: Three Dialogues of Comfort

O F THE THREE MAJOR WORKS that Thomas More completed in the Tower, *A Dialogue of Comfort Against Tribulation* is the most recognizably humanist because of its use of the dialogue, a favorite classical and patristic genre. K. J. Wilson and Germain Marc'hadour have noted correspondences between More's dialogues and those of Cicero[1] and Gregory the Great.[2] This study will examine Cicero's *Tusculan Disputations*, Gregory's *Dialogues* and More's *Dialogue of Comfort* more extensively, focussing on the following points: 1) their authors, 2) the dialogue form, 3) the settings, 4) the times, 5) the double speakers, both mentors and disciples, 6) major themes and moral exempla, and 7) general resemblances.

I

Although separated from each other by many centuries, Cicero, Gregory and More resemble each other as political leaders and moral philosophers. Cicero (106–43 BC) was in his public career the most outstanding Roman orator and in his private life, the father of a beloved daughter Tullia. Her death in childbirth and his political danger as a loyal republican prompted Cicero to write the *Tusculan Disputations* in 45 BC, the year before the murder of Julius Caesar and two years before his own assassination.

Elected to the papacy in an era of social and political turmoil, Gregory (ca. 540–604) saved the city of Rome from attack by the Arian Lombards. When no help was forthcoming from the Byzantine emperor, he allegedly placated King Agilulf by paying a huge sum of money and a yearly tribute drawn from church sources.[3] Gregory expressed an apocalyptic view of his age in the commentaries on Job in the *Moralia* and in his *Homilies on Ezechiel*, as well as in his *Dialogues* (593–94). In a more hopeful spirit, he sent Augustine of Canterbury to evangelize the Anglo-Saxon invaders of Celtic Britain.

After a long career as a royal councillor, Thomas More (1478–1534) was appointed Lord Chancellor, the highest political office under the king. Like Cicero, he had a favorite daughter, Margaret. Arrested on April 17, 1534 because he refused to take an oath implying England's ecclesiastical independence from Rome, More was confined in the Tower of London for about fifteen months. There he completed three books, including *A Dialogue of Comfort*. Finally he was condemned to death for treason and beheaded five days later on July 6, 1535. Challenged by the political revolutions of their age to write about moral courage in the face of death, More and Cicero put their principles into action while Gregory was, at least, a martyr in spirit.

Each of these authors pretends that his book is a spoken discourse later written down. Cicero begins each of his five subdivisions with a dedication to "the noblest Roman of them all" (*Julius Caesar*, 5.5.68) and thus presents the *Tusculan Disputations* as a direct address to Brutus. At the beginning of his *Dialogues* Gregory notes that he will record the conversations with Peter the Deacon that had taken place earlier (Prologue 1, p. 5).[4] At the end of More's *Dialogue of Comfort* Vincent declares that he will write down his conversations with Antony in Hungarian and German, his two vernaculars (p. 326, CW 12:320).[5] The half-title at the beginning of the work claims, however, that this book was "Made by an Hungarian in Latin, and Translated out of Latin into French, and out of French into English" (p. 3, CW 12:3). In his edition of *A Dialogue of Comfort*, Leland Miles suggests that the version we have is only a first draft and that More would have removed these inconsistencies if he had had the opportunity to revise his work.[6] The three authors probably did discuss suffering and death with their friends, though More prudently sets his conversation in another country. In any case, the urgency of real exchange is preserved under the guise of dialogues transcribed.

The two Catholic authors wrote their books to give strength to others, while Cicero hoped to assuage his grief for the death of his daughter Tullia and the downfall of the Roman Republic. He explains to Brutus at the conclusion of the *Tusculan Disputations* that in composing this book, "I cannot readily say how much I shall benefit others; at any rate in my cruel sorrows and the various troubles which beset me from all sides no other consolation could have been found" (5.41.121).[7] Gregory wrote his *Dialogues* to give encouragement especially to the clerics, monastics and devout lay people which his narratives describe.[8] His interlocutor Peter gives the proper interpretation of Gregory's numerous exempla, "Even when we are in great distress we can be certain that our Creator does not abandon us. These amazing miracles are proof of it" (3.30, p. 166). In his fictional role as interlocutor, Gregory never acknowledges fear. Perhaps he felt it incumbent upon himself as chief pastor to provide an image of confident leadership to his flock. Antony, too, presents an image of cheerful fortitude to Vincent, even though More confesses his "heauy fearfull heart" in a Tower letter to Margaret.[9] In his biography of More written in 1557–58, Nicholas Harpsfield explains More's purpose in composing the Tower Works:

> [H]is principall drifte and scope was to stirre and prepare the mindes of englishe men manfully and couragiously to withstande, and not to shrinke at, the imminent and open persecution which he fore[sawe] and immediatly folowed, against the vnitie / of the Churche and the catholike faythe / of the same.[10]

Thus Cicero, Gregory and More demonstrate a fortitude that is an inspiration to their weaker fellows.

Because Cicero and More both wrote their dialogues in a time of public and personal crisis, it is not surprising that they treat similar topics: the prospect of poverty, disgrace and death weighed against the supreme value of a virtuous life. Yet there is more than an accidental resemblance between the two books. An examination of his Tower Works, Latin writings and other dialogues will demonstrate More's knowledge of Cicero's *Tusculan Disputations*.

Scattered references to the *Tusculan Disputations* occur in the *Responsio ad Lutherum*, *A Dialogue of Comfort* and the *De Tristitia*. But the *Utopia* contains the most striking reference (1.43.104), a paraphrase of the saying of Anaxagoras, "From all places it is the same distance to heaven" (CW 4:51), *Vndique ad superos tantundem esse uiae* (CW 4:50). The commentary notes "the characteristically humanistic and Christian change of *ad inferos* (to the lower world) to *ad superos* (to heaven)."[11] Nearly twenty years later More would defend his contentment with his prison cell to his exasperated wife Dame Alice, "Is not this house . . . as nighe heauen as my owne [manor in Chelsea]?"[12] Thus it is possible that More consciously modelled aspects of his dialogue on a similar composition of his classical predecessor.

One of many witnesses for traditional Catholic teaching, Gregory appears in numerous litanies of Fathers and Doctors in the *Dialogue Concerning Heresies* and the *Confutation Against Tyndale*. According to Germain Marc'hadour, Gregory is quoted more frequently than any other Father, except Augustine, in these two works of controversy.[13] In the *Dialogue Concerning Heresies*, Gregory's *Dialogues* (4.42, pp. 249–50) are directly named as the source of the miracle performed by the deacon Paschasius while still in purgatory:

> And so fynd we (as I remember) in the dyaloges of saynt Gregory / that one had helpe by prayer made vnto an holy man late deceaced whiche was hym selfe yet in purgatory. So lyked it our lorde / to let the worlde knowe / [that] he was in his specyall fauour / thoughe he were yet in payne of his purgacyon.(CW 6:215)

The many miracle stories in Gregory's *Dialogues* offer a precedent for More's defense of miracles in his *Dialogue Concerning Heresies*.

In the *Confutation Against Tyndale* Gregory is praised as proof that, contrary to the Reformers' assertion, the Church's teaching maintained its continuity from the patristic era through its so-called period of degeneracy:

> And syth they call that tyme the tyme of thys .viii. hundred yeres last passed: lette vs take the tyme in whyche saynt Gregory was pope / for that is now more than .ix. hundred yere a go. And saynte Gregory was a good man and a good pope, and so good that I thynke none heretyke dare for shame saye the contrarye.
> (CW 8:925)

More's *Confutation* also recounts a miracle from Gregory's life in which the saint persuades a matron to believe in the Real Presence of Christ in the eucharistic loaves she herself had made (*CW* 8:276). The transformation of the bread into a bleeding fragment of finger has the same literalism as many of Gregory's exempla. The source of this miracle is not the *Dialogues*, but the Latin biography of Gregory (Chap. 20), written by an anonymous monk of Whitby in the early eighth century.[14] The story was eventually incorporated into the thirteenth-century *Legenda Aurea* by Jacobus de Voragine, later translated into English and published by William Caxton in 1483.[15]

More held Gregory in special veneration because this pope had initiated St. Augustine of Canterbury's missionary expedition to the Anglo-Saxons. In the last speech at his trial, More emphasized this filial relationship of the English Church to Rome:

> So might St Gregorye, Pope of Roome, of whom, by St Austyne, his messenger, we first receaved the Christian faithe, of vs Englishmen truly saye: "Yow are my children, because I haue geuen to you everlasting salvacion, a farr [higher and] better inheritaunce then any carnall father can leaue to his child, and by [re]generation made you my spirituall children in Christe."[16]

Given his devotion to this sixth-century pope and his knowledge of Gregory's *Dialogues*, More could have indeed modelled his *Dialogue of Comfort* on elements in the *Dialogues* of his spiritual father.

II

A Dialogue of Comfort is humanist chiefly because of its dialogue form, a literary mode created by Plato. In fact, Plato's Epistle 7 offers a helpful definition of "dialogues" as "benevolent disputations by the use of question and answer without jealousy" (344B).[17] Plato's dialogues, however, usually imitate the mental process of searching for the truth instead of the conversion of a disciple to the truth that the master presents. This latter type of dialogue clearly does not follow the Platonic model but adopts the method of Aristotle in his lost dialogues. As G. L. Hendrickson explains, "Aristotle and his school modified the Socratic form by assigning to a leading speaker a larger and more continuous role, lightened by interludes, interruptions, and transitions, shared in by other speakers."[18] Thus Cicero, Gregory and More all follow the Aristotelian and not the Platonic form of dialogue.

During the Summer of 45 BC Cicero composed a dialogue in five books called the *Tusculan Disputations*. The second word of the title, "Disputation," can be misleading since the organization of the work is more formal than the older meaning of "conversation" but less polemical than the modern meaning of "controversy." A. E. Douglas, in his comprehensive essay on "Cicero the Philosopher," remarks that the work would be more inviting to prospective readers if it were called simply "Discussions at my country-house at Tusculum."[19] After an exchange of pleasantries between the interlocutors, the discussion moves into a straightforward refutation by "M." of a thesis proposed by "A."

Each discussion concludes with the expression of satisfaction volunteered by "A." at the end of Books I and II or presumed by "M." at the end of Books III, IV and V. Of the three dialogues we are considering, this work is the most intellectually challenging because of its predominately abstract material.

As a sequence of short narratives, Gregory's *Four Books of Dialogues on the Life and Miracles of the Italian Fathers and on the Immortality of the Soul* are easy to read. Their intellectual challenge lies in recognizing the biblical antitypes on which his many saints' lives are patterned. Although Gregory received a typical Roman education in grammar, rhetoric and law,[20] his literary antecedents are the Christian classics. From the piety of his family background and his monastic training, Gregory became familiar with Christian dialogues based on the Ciceronian model. These include the *Dialogues* of the Gallic Father Sulpicius Severus and the *Collations* of Cassian on the teachings of the Egyptian Monks.[21] If Gregory knew anything of Plato's theories or dialogue form, it was probably through the philosophical writings of Cicero or Boethius.

More had read Plato's dialogues, preeminently *The Republic*, and with the collaboration of Erasmus had translated five of Lucian's dialogues from Greek into Latin.[22] Unlike More, Plato and Lucian usually present half a dozen characters in their dialogues. Boethius was also one of More's favorite authors. In her letter to Alice Alington describing her visit with More in the Tower, Margaret relates how her father quoted from the work written while the Roman consul was himself in prison (Book 2, Prose 6, 1.147).[23] Like More's *Dialogue of Comfort*, *The Consolation of Philosophy* has two interlocutors, the austere Lady Philosophy and the distraught Boethius. While not claiming that More had actually read Petrarch's *Secretum*, Howard B. Norland notes another use of two interlocutors, the accusatory Augustine and the remorseful Petrarch.[24] Yet Antony's avuncular sallies and Vincent's respectful replies are more congenial in tone than the exchanges related by Boethius or Petrarch. The mentor-disciple relationships depicted in Cicero and Gregory are closer analogues to More's *Dialogue of Comfort*.

III

The settings of these three works are each a place of leisure, where deeper questions can be probed. Cicero's dialogues are set at his country villa at Tusculum outside the city of Rome. Gregory is not at the monastery which he founded in his family home on the Caelian Hill but in "a quiet spot" (Prologue 1, p. 3) in Rome, perhaps a room in the Lateran Palace, his papal home. More's dialogue is set in Antony's sickroom within the city of Buda in Hungary.

The traditional title of Cicero's *Tusculan Disputations* tells much about the ambience of this dialogue. Cicero's favorite villa was located at Tusculum, about ten miles south-east of Rome near modern Frascati.[25] Among the amentities of his country house were two gymnasia, the upper called the "Lyceum" after Aristotle's school of philosophy[26] and the lower called the "Academy" after Plato's (2.3.9). One wonders why the upper gymnasium was named for Aristotle and not Plato since Cicero declares that Aristotle "far excels everyone—always with the exception of Plato" (1.10.22). At least, Cicero indicates his preference for Plato by setting all five books of discussion in the "Academy."

Gregory's *Dialogues* take place in some generalized locale within Rome. Although the immediate setting is not described, Gregory provides numerous descriptions of rural life in his first three books and several allusions to churches in Rome in his fourth book. Like biblical narratives, Gregory's miracles are intended to be expounded for moral lessons, yet they also offer illuminating glimpses of economic arrangements and anthropological rituals in sixth-century Italy.

In his triad Gregory gives us a series of eclogues and georgics. It is not surprising that contemplative monks would have the solitude necessary for pastoring sheep (3.22, p. 154), but even a subdeacon with responsibilities for the social welfare of the local church watches his own flock (3.17, p. 145). The agricultural setting offers Gregory occasion for constructing analogues of biblical miracles. When his cellarer refused to give away the monastery's last flask of oil to a poor man, the prayers of St. Benedict filled an empty oil-cask to overflowing in imitation of Elias (1 Kings 17:7–16) and Eliseus (2 Kings 4:1–7) (2.29, p. 97).[27] A primitive fertility rite was performed by seven naked women dancing in a monastery garden near Subiaco (2.8, p. 71). These vignettes succinctly depict the rural world of late antiquity.

As the Acts of the Apostles conclude with Paul's arrival in the imperial capital (Chap. 28), so too the last book of Gregory's *Dialogues* ends at Rome. The noblewoman Galla (4.14, p. 206) led a saintly life in a monastery near the Constantinian basilica of St. Peter's, where the humble shoemaker Deusdedit gave his surplus away every Saturday to the poor (4.38, p. 242). Three holy women led a monastic life in their home near Saint Mary Major's (4.16, p. 208), while the paralytic Servulus devoted himself to prayer in his home near St. Clement's and the Coliseum (4.15, p. 207). Thus countryfolk and city-dwellers both continued the tradition of holy lives and deaths established by the apostolic martyrs Peter and Paul.

Because the fictional setting of A *Dialogue of Comfort* is a sickroom in Buda, More avoids the problem of describing an unfamiliar city. Yet he was not unfamiliar with the Hungarian political situation. Frank Manley writes that More, as unofficial personal secretary to Henry VIII, had been privy to the diplomatic correspondence about the Turkish conquest of Buda in 1526 (*CW* 12:cxxv-vi). This distant setting was not chosen simply as a ploy to move the scene of action as far away from England as possible. Enduring mental suffering on the Western edge of Christendom, More empathized with his fellow Catholics persecuted on the Eastern edge of the Empire.

Although the generalized setting of More's dialogue is Buda, reminiscences of Tudor London add realistic details to the scene. More's New Building, which he had constructed on his estate in Chelsea, was a model retreat for prayer and study. Antony recommends such a hermitage as a place for the tempted Christian to pray, "Let him also choose himself some secret solitary place in his own house, as far fro noise and company as he conveniently can, and thither let him sometime secretly resort alone" (p. 167, *CW* 12:164). Antony's reference to the maze with hell in the center (p. 171, *CW* 12:167) recalls the maze at Hampton Court. Antony's admiration of the Carthusians and the Brigittines (p. 283, *CW* 12:276) recalls the London Charterhouse and the Brigittine monastery of Syon, which produced More's fellow martyrs. Antony's sickroom in Buda is as little confining as is More's cell in the Tower.

IV

Not only does each author indicate a specific place, but he gives some reference to the passage of time as the conversation unfolds. Cicero imagines the dialogue taking place on five different days with one book of discussion per day. Gregory depicts the exchange occurring in three meetings with an intermission for rest occurring after Books I (1.12, p. 53) and II (2.38, p. 110). More's dialogue supposedly takes place on three occasions: Book 1, on an unspecified day; Book II, a few days later before dinner; Book III after dinner when Antony has awakened from a nap and Vincent completed an errand (pp. 190-91, *CW* 12:187). Perhaps Books II and III are set on the same day because their material is closely connected. In Book II More analyzes three temptations found allegorically in Psalm 90 (91), vv. 5-6a; in Book III he develops the fourth temptation found in v. 6b. This passage of time is necessary to accommodate the interlocutors to the hard truths they face.

There are few references to fictional time in Cicero's *Tusculan Disputations* besides the general proposal that the interlocutors spend their mornings in rhetorical exercises and their afternoons in philosophical discussions (2.3.9). Cicero alludes to this time element after his address to Brutus at the beginning of each book. At the end of the second day, he wittily promises to meet on the morrow to "practise declamation by the water-clock" (2.27.67). Appropriately, all five days' discussion is recalled at the conclusion of the work (5.42.121). References to Cicero's political contemporaries add particularities to the dimension of time. Crassus' death in the Parthian campaign of 53 BC (1.6.12), Pompey's assassination after his defeat at Pharsalus in 48 BC (1.6.12) and the survival of the dictator Julius Caesar (1.36.88), all depict the troubled background which makes the discussion of equanimity in the face of death a timely topic for philosophical inquiry.

If Cicero knew that the Roman Republic had been replaced by a dictatorship, Gregory believed that the end of the world was approaching. Specific references to events in Rome indicate that Gregory's *Dialogues* were composed in the interval between July 583 and November 594.[28] The four horsemen of the Apocalypse can be used to categorize the trials from which Italy suffered during the fifth and sixth centuries. Most obvious are the onslaughts of the various barbarian tribes, represented by the white horse (Revel. 6:2) whose rider went "from victory to victory" and the red horse (Revel. 6:4) whose rider carried "a huge sword." A hermit's vision witnesses the damnation of Theodoric, King of the Ostrogoths, whose harsh imprisonment of Pope John I had led to his death in 526 (4.31, p.228). Shortly before the Lombard invasion in 568, a martyr appears in a vision to Bishop Redemptus, announcing three times "The end of all flesh has come!" (3.38, p. 186). These successive waves of invasion are not the only disasters. The black horse of famine (Revel. 6:5) ravaged Italy in 537-38 (2.21, p. 88 and n. 47). The flooding of the Tiber in 589 (3.19, p. 149) called forth the "deathly pale" horse of plague (Revel. 6:8) which wasted Rome the next year (4.37, p. 239). These events confirmed Gregory's apocalyptic view of his age.

The general time of More's *Dialogue of Comfort* is the two and a half years between the fall of 1526 and the spring of 1529; the particular

178 ∾ *Three Dialogues of Comfort*

fictional time is approximately one week within this period. On August 29, 1526 the Turkish army under Suleiman the Magnificent had decimated the Hungarians at the battle of Mohács. On September 9, Suleiman entered Buda and killed everyone over the ages of 13 or 14 (*CW* 12:cxxv–vii). In the spring of 1529 Suleiman invaded Hungary again and accepted as a vassal John Zapolya, the rebel leader who had kept his troops in reserve during the battle of Mohács. Hungary was then divided into areas of Christian and Moslem control, but this political compromise could not be accepted as a theological position by Antony and Vincent. Although Gregory's Rome was spared pillage by the Lombards, the political storm that raged outside Cicero's villa and Antony's sickroom would eventually engulf the ex-consul and the two Hungarians.

V

Within each of these books written in a time of crisis there are two interlocutors. Cicero calls his speakers simply "M." and "A.", probably representing "Magister" and "Adolescens."[29] Pope Gregory converses with Peter the Deacon, who has a filial relationship to him. More creates the characters of the elderly Antony and his nephew Vincent. Of Cicero's two speakers, indicated simply by the letters "M." and "A.", Rockwood notes that "So far as can be determined by manuscript authority, the letters were not in the original text, but were inserted by a copyist."[30] "M." stands for "Marcus," Cicero's personal name or for *magister* ("teacher"). "A." stands for *adolescens* as in the phrase of direct address, *At tu, adolescens* (2.12.28) or for *auditor* as indicated in the clause, *qui audire vellet* ("who would wish to hear") (1.4.8).

While "A." is a rather neutral interlocutor, "M." is an historical personality. He obviously represents Cicero himself, as we can conclude from numerous references to his earlier political career, present political inactivity, paternal grief for Tullia and other writings. The earliest public office that Cicero held was the quaestorship in 75 BC. During his year in Sicily, he had discovered the forgotten tomb of Archimedes the geometrician. For Cicero the moral value of the scientist's life outshines that of the tyrannical ruler, Dionysius the Elder (5.23.64–66). Recalling his most important political achievement, Cicero asserts that he did not act in anger when he had Catiline and his fellow conspirators executed without benefit of trial (4.23.51–52). Rejecting popular acclaim as ephemeral (5.36.104), Cicero remembers his exile following this emergency intervention and his forced retirement after the rise of the First Triumvirate. Now a private citizen, the elder statesman serves his country by making the treasures of Greek philosophy accessible in Latin.

Plato's belief in the immortality of the soul became a personal consideration for Cicero after the death of his daughter Tullia. Five times he recalls the *Consolatio*, which he wrote to assuage his grief. In addition to this now lost essay, Cicero mentions three of his dialogues, the lost *Hortensius*, the *Academica* and the *De Re Publica*. Writing the *Tusculan Disputations* within the year after Tullia's death and during the dictatorship of Julius Caesar, Cicero exclaims, "I have been robbed of the consolations of family life and the distinctions of a public career" (1.34.84). Cicero acknowledges his emotional vulnerability (5.1.4) while striving manfully to feel that virtue is sufficient for a happy life (5.1.1).

Much less vividly rendered than "M.," "A." keeps the *Tusculan Disputations* from being purely expository. In Book I "A." speaks on eight occasions, in Book II, on seven. In Books III and IV he speaks only three times each; the dramatic interest in Book III arises from "M.'s" three apostrophes to the philosopher Epicurus (3.16.35, 3.17.37, 3.18.41) and from the imagined address of the more revered Pythagoras and Plato to Cicero (3.17.36). The character of "A." achieves greater prominence in Book V where he speaks up six times, even with wit and a touch of impudence. When "M." asserts that the virtuous man can be happy even in prison, "A." objects that "M.'s" arguments are hackneyed (*pervulgata*) (5.5.13) and not persuasive. "A." playfully raises objections by quoting Cicero's friend Brutus (5.8.21) and Cicero's own *De Finibus* (5.11.32) against "M.'s" distinctions between goods and advantages. Except for this surge of individuality in the last book of the *Tusculan Disputations*, "A." represents a generalized listener to "M.'s" philosophical lectures.

Like Cicero, Gregory puts himself into his dialogue *in propria persona*. His earlier life was shaped by the wealth received from his patrician father (4.36, p. 234) and the example given by his monastic aunts (4.17, p. 211). His admiration for St. Benedict, who adopted the eremetical life in youth (2.1, p. 56), stands in silent contrast to Gregory, who did not adopt the monastic life until 574, when he was in his middle thirties.[31] Having left a secular career as Prefect of Rome to follow a contemplative life, Gregory was called back to active service as papal nuncio at Constantinople (3.36, p. 177). His election to the papacy in 590 gave him a special consciousness of its dignity. He mentions six popes of the preceding century, including his grandfather Felix III (4.17, p. 211), "whom by the grace of God I had the honor to succeed to the throne of Peter here in Rome" (3.3, p. 116).

In spite of his increased administrative duties, the pope does not neglect the office of teaching. Although his temporal and spiritual responsibilities leave him "deeply dejected" (Prologue 1, p. 3), Gregory becomes confidently magisterial once he begins to converse with Peter. Vogüé describes their exchange as a liturgical ritual, "Le pontife, assisté de son diacre, exerce imperturbablement sa fonction doctrinale. Jamais il n'apprend, jamais il n'est pris en défaut, jamais il n'hésite."[32] To reinforce his instruction of Peter, Gregory makes five specific references to his *Homilies on the Gospel* preached to the people of Rome. Gregory is the most imposing of the three mentors by reason of his ascetic discipline and pontifical authority.

Like Pope Gregory I, Peter the Deacon is a historical rather than a fictional person. Vogüé has traced his service in administering church property from Ravenna (Ep. 6.24), to Sicily (Ep. 1.1 and 3), to Campagna (Ep. 3.1) and finally to Rome (Ep. 3.56).[33] A capable manager in real life, within the *Dialogues* Peter is Gregory's spiritual son, "dear friend" and "companion in the study of sacred Scripture" (Prologue 1, p. 3). Vogüé has counted Peter's interventions in each book: 31 in Book I, 28 in Book II, 39 in Book III and 47 in Book IV.[34] Peter's initiatives can be straightforward expressions of the proper emotional reaction to Gregory's miracle-stories: tears (3.1, p. 115), "fear and hope" (3.7, p. 123), "awe and wonder" (3.32, p. 169). Sometimes Peter's reactions are mistaken. When he declares that raising the dead to life is the greatest miracle, Gregory counters that converting a sinner is greater (3.17, pp. 146–47). Sometimes Peter's questions afford Gregory the opportunity to expound a central idea. When he asks how St. Benedict lived "with himself," Gregory explains, "By searching continually into his own soul he always beheld himself in the presence of his Creator" (2.3, pp. 62–63).

Like Cicero's "A." and More's Vincent, Gregory's disciple becomes more self-assured and articulate as the dialogue progresses. Thus Peter argues more vigorously with Gregory in the last, most abstract book of the *Dialogues*. He resists the argument from the soul's activity after death because "the mind rebels at believing what it cannot see with bodily eyes" (4.5, p. 198). He questions the presence of physical fire in hell (4.30, p. 226) and queries the justice of punishing finite sins with eternal pains (4.46, p. 255). In the end, however, Gregory wins perfect acquiescence as Peter declares: "I am pleased with your answer" (4.25, p. 217); "I agree with what you say" (4.26, p. 219); "I have no more questions to ask" (4.39, p. 244). Respectful of Gregory's office, Peter the Deacon maintains a more formal relationship with his mentor than either Cicero's "A." or More's Vincent.

About the time of his first marriage, More had translated into English the life of Pico della Mirandola written by the Italian humanist's nephew, Gianfrancesco. Thirty years later, More depicts in Antony another uncle whose piety inspires the literary production of his nephew.[35] Probably named after St. Antony Abbot, a centenarian when he died, this Antony is also a venerable patriarch. Born shortly before the fall of Athens in 1452 and of Constantinople in 1453, he was imprisoned by the Turks twice during the period of 1470-1490 (CW 12:336 and 332). In his comprehensive essay, "Here I Sit," Marc'hadour notes that Antony is old enough to be More's father.[36] The senior More (1451-1530) was nearly 80 years old when he died, while Antony is at least in his middle seventies. His patron saint had hoped to be martyred during the persecution of 311 when he left his desert solitude to bring food and comfort to imprisoned Christians.[37] Although he was not arrested, the Egyptian hermit could claim to be a martyr in desire. The Hungarian Antony is at least willing to die for his faith even if the Turks should break into his sickroom (p. 321, CW 12:315).

Confined to his bed, Antony reminiscences about his earlier life. Like Shakespeare's Theseus, he knows that "in the night, imagining some fear, / How easy is a bush suppos'd a bear! (*Midsummer Night's Dream*, 5.1.21-22). During his soldiering days, scouts for the Hungarian troops once mistook a hedge for the approaching Turkish army (pp. 113-14, CW 12:109-10). In his middle age Antony, like More, had suffered from a tertian fever that made him feel simultaneously hot and cold. Thus can the Christian under tribulation experience both pain and consolation from God (p. 91, CW 12:88). Now in his old age Antony's life flickers like a burnt-down candle (p. 89, CW 12:85). He occasionally suffers from memory lapse in the midst of his narrative (p. 93, CW 12:90). But his sense of humor never fails him, and he confesses himself to be "even half a giglet [jokester] and more" (p. 86, CW 12:83). Remembering the characteristic humor of the author, we find here a witty pun on his own name, "half a giglet and More."

The name of Antony's nephew Vincent comes from the Latin verb *vincere*, meaning "to conquer." Antony's arguments are so cogent we can be assured that, in the end, Vincent will overcome his fears and become a martyr if need be. While Antony is as old as More's father, Vincent is the same age as More's son John (1508-1547). At the time when this dialogue was composed, the junior More was about 26 or 27 years old. Then married for half a dozen years, he was a young householder such as Vincent describes himself to be (p. 207, CW 12:202). Like Gregory's deacon, Vincent faces a violent death at the hands of marauding invaders. As nephew to Antony, he resembles Gianfrancesco Pico, who helped spread the teachings of his uncle.

It has been suggested that the younger Hungarian is named for St. Vincent of Lérins, who articulated the famous definition of orthodoxy, "Quod ubique, quod semper, quod ab omnibus creditum est."[38] While this link to a defender of the faith is appropriate, there is an earlier Vincent, martyred in Saragossa in AD 304. A deacon like Stephen and Lawrence, with whom he is joined in the Litany of the Saints, this Vincent was arrested with his bishop Valerius. The elderly churchman was exiled, but the younger was racked, torn with iron hooks and burnt on a grill. When his executioners tried to dispose of his corpse by throwing it into the sea, it was cast up on the shore and given a honorable burial by devout Christians. Augustine commemorates this martyr in four sermons, punning on the name in his inimitable style, "Vicit in verbis, vicit in poenis; ... vicit exustus ignibus, vicit submersus fluctibus; postremo vicit tortus, vicit mortuus."[39] The Spanish poet Prudentius celebrated his fellow countryman in a lengthy hymn in which the saint fearlessly defies his pagan judge and torturers.[40] Both these authors are quoted in the *Legenda Aurea* for the feast of January 22. The separate judgments for Bishop Valerius and Vincent the Deacon are analogous to the probable fates of the two Hungarians. Arguably, the aged Antony will die a natural death, but the youthful Vincent will be martyred.

Vincent's character is not so fully portrayed as Antony's, but certain details are given. In Book I Vincent regards Antony as more like a father than an uncle (p. 4, CW 12:4); therefore, he is especially considerate of Antony's age and poor health (pp. 66, 79, CW 12:64, 77). This same concern is shown at the end of Book II (p. 190, CW 12:186) when Vincent welcomes the arrival of Antony's dinner. Like the celebrants of Erasmus' "Godly Feast," Vincent seeks counsel from another layman, not from a priest. In Book II Vincent reports a sermon he had heard in Reformation Saxony, wittily exaggerating its opposition to justification by works (p. 97, CW 12:94).

Just as Peter the Deacon temporarily adopts the role of a weak Christian fearing the Lombards (4.4, p. 196), so Vincent pretends to be a wealthy Christian lord facing the Turks (pp. 235-43, CW 12:229-37). Recovering his courage, Vincent grows in independence as the dialogue unfolds. When Antony argues that the whole world is a prison, Vincent protests against his "sophistical fantasy" (p. 269, CW 12:262). All in all, Vincent makes five objections to Antony's arguments in Book I and four each in Books II and III. While not contentious, their verbal exchange reveals that A *Dialogue of Comfort* was written by a lawyer and that it does have a firm logical substratum.

Antony addresses Vincent by his Christian name for the first time in Book II, that is, about 40% through the book (pp. 127, 141, CW 12:123, 136). Since Vincent is becoming more autonomous, he is more worthy of being addressed by his proper name. In Book III Antony uses this proper name six times, a sign that Vincent has now found his true spiritual identity. At the end of Book III Vincent takes the initiative for writing their conversation down so he can recall Antony's counsel later and in turn share it with others (p. 326, CW 12:320). Because of his wit, Antony is the most humanly appealing of the three mentors, while among the three disciples Vincent has achieved the most self-direction.

VI

To a literary critic the fictional elements of the three dialogues are most revealing, but to a moral philosopher the contents are most significant. Each book of the *Tusculan Disputations* discusses a major theme: 1) death, 2) physical pain, 3) psychological distress, 4) the remaining disorders of the soul and 5) the principle that virtue is of itself sufficient for leading a happy life. Gregory's *Dialogues* are not so logical or thematic in their presentation as they are narrative and anecdotal. Book I discusses the Italian saints of the sixth century, Gregory's near contemporaries; Book II, the monastic patriarch St. Benedict (ca. 480–543); Book III, saints of the more distant past, such as St. Paulinus of Nola (354?–431). With its discourse on the soul's existence after death, Book IV is the most philosophical. In More's *Dialogue of Comfort* Book I defines tribulation in terms of its sources. Book II further examines three kinds of tribulation, while Book III discusses the worst type, open persecution. Although Cicero did not share the assured religious belief of Gregory and More, all three authors maintain their moral integrity in the face of death and affirm their hope in a blessed hereafter.

Because his dialogue is a philosophical investigation and not religious instruction, Cicero will try, not always successfully, to conceal his personal opinion (5.4.11). Four times he rejects the philosophy of Epicurus, who prefers the body to the soul and pleasure to virtue. He is more approving of the Peripatetics, although he considers that their doctrine of the golden mean (3.10.22) countenances limited disorders in the realm of feelings (4.17.38). He does not urge emotional insensibility (3.6.12), but adopts the Stoic position that the wise man is always happy. Gregory and More agree with Cicero on the relativity of pain and death. The Roman pontiff also urges emotional sobriety, even for children (4.18, p. 212), but the Englishman finds room for merry tales in a study of tribulation.

Referring frequently to the ideas of the Peripatetics, Academics and Stoics, Cicero makes direct quotations only from the texts of Plato. Like the exterior walls of a Roman basilica, Books I and V contain the weightiest themes of the *Tusculan Disputations*: 1) that death is not an evil, 5) that virtue is sufficient for leading a happy life. Book I repeats the lengthy argument for the immortality of the soul found in the *Phaedrus* 245 (1.23.53-54) and Socrates's address to his judges (1.41.97-99) quoted in the *Apology* 40C. Book V recounts Socrates's doubt that the oppressive kings of Persia and Macedon are happy (*Gorgias* 470D, E) (5.12.35) and his affirmation that the happy life rests on virtue alone (*Menexenus* 247E) (5.12.36). Superb orator that he is, Cicero positions his most important material at the beginning and end of his discourse.

Like the window-filled clerestory of a Roman basilica, the middle books are distinguished by numerous literary allusions which illuminate Cicero's philosophical principles. Among the Greek authors Euripides (fragments of four lost plays and *Orestes*, 11.1-3) and the *Iliad* (9.646-47, 4.201-2, 19.226-29) are quoted more frequently,[41] but Sophocles and Aeschylus are quoted at greater length. The wild exclamations of Hercules in his mortal agony (*Trachiniae* 1046 ff.) (2.8.20-2.9.22) are contrasted with the sober assessment by Prometheus of his eternal torment (from the lost *Prometheus Unbound*) (2.10.23-25). With pleasant irony the author includes the long selections from Sophocles and Aeschylus and another from Ennius (2.16.38-2.17.39) in the very book where "M." agrees with Plato that poets should be banished from the ideal commonwealth (cf. *Republic* 2.398A) (2.11.27).

In addition to these literary allusions, Cicero gives exempla from ancient history. Even though condemned unjustly, Theramenes showed that he did not fear death when he toasted the health of his enemy with the cup of hemlock (1.40.96). Marius courageously underwent surgery for varicose veins without an anesthetic and without being tied down (2.22.53). The political danger of the tyrant Dionysius, who banqueted under the sword of Damocles (5.21.61–62), proves that virtue is necessary to happiness. Though more serious in tone, Cicero's moral illustrations provide the reader with the same respite from intellectual concentration as More's merry tales.

The major theme of Gregory's *Dialogues* is the continuing power of God demonstrated through the outward miracles and inward holiness of the saints. This topic is not easily isolated from the more than 200 miracles which Gregory relates. Vogüé counts ca. 45 each in Books I and II, ca. 70 in Book III and ca. 50 in Book IV.[42] The high number of exempla is soon taken as normative for each book. In Book IV, which begins as a more theoretical defense of the immortality of the soul, the reader is not surprised when the discussion returns to the anecdotal level. Vogüé offers a pictorial image to organize this multiplicity of miracles. Book II with its single figure of St. Benedict is like the central section of a triptych, flanked by two panels of grouped saints, twelve in Book I, thirty in Book III.[43] Like a tableau of the Last Judgment, Book IV crowns the other three books as it epitomizes the goal toward which they tend.[44]

Perhaps the most effective method for interpreting Gregory's *Dialogues* is to skim the miracle stories but to scrutinize the pontiff's brief exegesis of the moral. Early in Book I, Gregory enunciates his basic principle: "The soul that is really filled with the Spirit of God will easily be recognized by its miraculous powers and humility" (1.1, p. 8). For Gregory, a miracle is a quasi-sacrament in which the outward sign indicates an inward grace in the human agent. It usually causes a recognition of God's power in Arian witnesses or an increase of devotion in Catholic ones. The virtues which these saints demonstrate are primarily contempt for the world and humility before God's power at work in them. Gregory teaches an exalted ideal of piety but in a much simpler mode than either Cicero or More.

Although Gregory's exempla are by no means confined to incidents connected with the Lombard invasion, we will focus on these as most related to the theme of public persecution. Out of approximately 24 stories involving conflicts between Arians and Catholics, the latter suffer imprisonment or death in only seven incidents. Otherwise, the monks of Monte Cassino are saved from death through the prayers of St. Benedict (2.17, p. 86); the executioner cannot strike off the head of the priest Sanctulus who substituted himself for a captured deacon (3.37, p. 182); Bishop Cassius cures the sword-bearer of the Gothic King Totila (3.6, p. 120). The fundamental virtues of prayerfulness, love of neighbor and forgiveness of enemies illuminate these exemplary tales.

As Cicero is inspired by the philosophy of Plato, and Gregory by the example of St. Benedict, so More derives his spiritual teaching from patristic and medieval theology as well as from independent reflection. The first third of the *Dialogue of Comfort* reads like a categorization of typical human experience. In Book I Antony defines "tribulation" as "a kind of grief, either pain of the body or heaviness of the mind" (p. 10, *CW* 12:10). Next, he divides the topic into three kinds of tribulations: 1) those stemming from our own fault, 2) those coming from other people or events, 3) those sent directly from God to test our patience. In Book II Antony modifies this threefold division. Difficulties that are brought on by our own fault become those that are willingly chosen; those not brought on by our own fault become those willingly endured; those sent to us directly from God become those that cannot be avoided. Later in Book II, Antony subdivides the genus of tribulation into the ordinary distress of temptation and the grievous affliction of persecution.

The final two-thirds of More's dialogue describe four types of persecution based on a traditional exegesis of Psalm 90 (91), vv. 5–6. The fear of the night (v. 5a) is tribulation when the cause is dark and unknown. More derives his treatment of the elements of fear from Bernard's *Commentary on Psalm 90* (*PL* 183.197) and of mental confusion from earlier commentaries by Jerome (*PL* 26.1099) and Augustine (*PL* 37.1153–54). Jean Gerson contributes a method for discerning the source and goal of one's inspirations.[45] The arrow flying in the day (v. 5b) is pride in worldly prosperity, More's original exegetical contribution (*CW* 12:398). Again following Bernard (*PL* 183.198), More interprets business walking in the darkness (v. 6a) as worldly prosperity before the dawn of our conversion or after the sunset of our rejection of God's grace. In Book III More concurs with Augustine (*PL* 37.1153–56) in defining the noonday devil (v. 6b) as open persecution. Thus More's themes are derived from Scripture and traditional Catholic theology (cf. *CW* 12:379, 380, 398, 413), while his exempla are drawn from folklore and personal experience.

At the beginning of Book II, the merry interlude in More's Tudor drama, Vincent raises the issue, "Whether a man may not in tribulation use some worldly recreation for his comfort" (p. 85, *CW* 12:82). Antony answers in the affirmative, appropriately so because Book II is the most humorous of the three books. Throughout the whole work Vincent recounts three merry tales, but Antony tells fourteen.

Some of Antony's best tales are animal fables, purportedly taken from Aesop. Two describe the Christians of Hungary threatened by Suleiman, the wolf (p. 193, CW 12:189) or the dog which steals the bone fought over by two other dogs, Ferdinand I and John Zapolya (p. 8, CW 12:8). One fable minimizes the rumors of persecution when the lion's roar turns out to come from an ass (p. 114, CW 12:111). Another reverses the Utopian attitude toward capitalism, the hen that laid the golden egg of employment for the working class (p. 184, CW 12:181). The last two refer perhaps to the English scene. Is More the snail that refused to leave his house to attend the wedding feast of Henry VIII and Anne Boleyn (p. 292, CW 12:285)? Are More and Fisher the two deer that fear the yelping of the ill-tempered bitch (pp. 300-301, CW 12:294-95)? By reducing these problematic human situations to animal tales, More humorously gains control over his anxiety.

Besides these animal fables, of which there are six, five other merry tales have been identified as referring to More's indomitable wife, Dame Alice. A sixth refers to a timorous housemaid whose mistress was "a very wise woman (which is in women very rare), very mild also and meek" (p. 116, CW 12:113). Could this forebearing homemaker be Dame Alice? Perhaps. Whereas she might feel the need to assert her domestic capabilities against her husband's political and literary achievements, she could afford to be more accommodating with subordinates. With their Roman sobriety, neither Cicero nor Gregory can compare with the affirmative humor of More.

VII

Having examined the morphological features which all three dialogues share, we will make some general conclusions about the resemblances between More and his two predecessors. Besides the references to the *Tusculan Disputations* noted by the Yale commentary, the *Dialogue of Comfort* also examines Cicero's themes of integrity, tribulation, suicide, and death in general. While spurring his audience on to achievement in public life, Cicero distinguishes between popular acclaim and true honor:

[T]o my mind all things seem more praiseworthy which are done without glorification and without publicity, not that this is to be avoided—for all things done well tend to be set in the light of day—but all the same there is no audience for virtue of higher authority than the approval of conscience. (2.26.64)

In rejecting the Royal Supremacy, the ex-chancellor differed with most of his English contemporaries. Yet, as he told Margaret when she visited him in the Tower, More clung to the minority position approved by his conscience:

> [S]ith this conscience is sure for me, I verelie trust in God, he shall rather strenght [sic] me to bere the losse [of all worldly goods], than against this conscience to swere and put my soule in peryll, sith all the causes that I perceyue moue other men to the contrary, seme not such vnto me, as in my conscience make any chaunge.[46]

Thus the Roman and the Tudor statesmen both maintain their personal integrity in extreme political situations.

In discussing the means of alleviating distress, Cicero lists the method that a comforter may use. He may deny that any evil exists or say that the evil is not serious. He may attempt to turn the sufferer's attention away from evil to focus on the good. He may say that the evil is not upsetting because it was unforeseen or deny that we have an obligation to grieve. Finally, the comforter may try all of the above, as Cicero did in writing the *Consolatio* immediately after Tullia's death (3.31.76).

Faced with the demand to renounce his basic religious commitment, More could not deny the option of evil or say that it was not serious since he believed that his choice meant either damnation or salvation. He could agree with Cicero's comforter that nothing unforeseen had happened to him. Roper later recounts how More tried to strengthen the family before his arrest by telling them stories of the patience of martyrs "that when he after fell into the trouble indeede, his trouble to them was a greate deale the lesse."[47] Since More maintains an attitude of Christian hope, the emotional tone of the Tower Works is cheerful, even impersonal. The *Dialogue of Comfort*, especially Book II, is remarkable for the number of merry tales and grim jokes that it contains, some even on the topic of suicide.

Both Cicero and More raise the possibility of suicide as a way out of an intolerable situation. Cicero admired Cato's reaction to his defeat by Julius Caesar at Thapsus in 46 BC. After reading Plato's *Phaedo* throughout the night, the republican committed suicide at dawn "with a feeling of joy in having found a reason for death" (1.30.74). His scorn for adversity proves to Cicero that human virtue does indeed exist (5.1.4). Antony disagrees, referring to Augustine's judgment in *The City of God* (1:23, PL 41.36–37) that Cato's suicide was "but plain pusillanimity and impotency of stomach [spirit]" (p. 134, CW 12:130). Although Cicero approved of suicide as an escape from disgrace, he refrained from taking his own life after his banishment in 58 BC, due to consideration for his family.[48]

Entrusted with responsibility for the whole Church, Pope Gregory never considers the possibility of suicide, but More devotes a long section to it in Book II of the *Dialogue of Comfort*. Three examples of gallows humor explore this theme: a nagging wife goads her husband into beheading her (pp. 128–31, CW 12:124–127); a Viennese widow tries to bribe a neighbor to behead her so she will be canonized (pp. 131–33, CW 12:127–29); a man entreats his wife to crucify him in an attempt to follow Christ too literally (pp. 147–48, CW 12:143–44). More describes the second case so graphically that it seems he is mentally rehearsing his own death. Pretending to comply with the widow's wish, her neighbor

> made her lie down and took up the ax in his own hand, and with the tother hand he felt the edge and found a fault that it was not sharp, and that therefore he would in no wise do it till he had grounden it sharper. He could not else, he said, for pity, it would put her to so much pain.   (p. 132, CW 12:128)

Equally probable in a life-threatening situation is the recurrence of obsessional thoughts about suicide:

> Some have, with holding a knife in their hand, suddenly thought upon the killing of themselves, and forthwith in devising what an horrible thing it were, if they should mishap so to do, have fallen in a fear that they should so do indeed, and have with long and often thinking thereon imprinted that fear so sore in their imagination, that some of them have not after cast it off without great difficulty, and some could never in their life be rid thereof, but have after in conclusion miserable done it indeed.   (p. 154, CW 12:150–51)

Although Walter M. Gordon rejects the inference that More was personally tempted to commit suicide,[49] his extensive treatment of this topic seems to suggest otherwise. How hard it must have been to reject pathological depression during the fifteen months of isolation in the Tower. Perhaps More was tempted to do actual physical violence to himself; at least, he could fear that his resistance to the king was an indirect form of self-destruction.

While Cicero could not foresee the exact circumstances of his death, he realized that it was a dangerous course to champion the traditional Roman values of political freedom in an era of dictatorship. Because they contain no mention of Julius Caesar's assassination, the *Tusculan Disputations* were presumably written before the famous Ides of March.[50] Four explicit references to the opposition between the despotic Tarquin and Lucius Junius Brutus suggest that Cicero was subtly urging the current Brutus to eliminate the contemporary Tarquin.[51] But the murder of Julius Caesar did not restore the Republic. In retaliation for Cicero's Philippics, Marc Antony demanded his execution in the proscriptions of the Second Triumvirate. When Cicero saw his assassins approach, he ordered his slaves to set down his litter. Then he thrust his head out the window to give their swords an unobstructed swath. Cicero's praise of the defeated gladiator unwittingly foretells the manner of his own death, "Who after falling has drawn in his neck when ordered to suffer the fatal stroke?" (2.17.41).[52] The exercise of writing philosophical works in the penultimate year of his life enabled Cicero to die with dignified courage and thus illustrate the dictum of his master Plato, "For the whole life of the philosopher . . . is a preparation for death" (*Phaedo* 67D, quoted in 1.30.74). Not an admirer of the Stoics like Cicero, More allows an emotional response to the human condition. Yet both statesmen follow their consciences in spite of tribulation and death.

Writing about religious persecution, the two Catholic authors also discuss the themes of tribulation and death. Gregory's *Dialogues* allude to the sufferings inflicted by the Ostrogoths in Italy (e.g., 2.14, p. 79), the Visigoths in Spain (3.31, p. 168) and the Vandals in North Africa (e.g., 3.1, p. 111). The Roman pontiff particularly recalls the devastation caused during the Lombard invasion of Italy a generation before in AD 568:

> Cities were sacked, fortifications overthrown, churches burned, monasteries and cloisters destroyed. Farms were abandoned, and the countryside, uncultivated, became a wilderness. The land was no longer occupied by its owners, and wild beasts roamed the fields where so many people had once made their homes.(3.38, p. 186)

Nearly a millennium later, Antony describes the harsh treatment of faithful Christians in Greece and Macedonia, which had been conquered by the Turks in the mid-fifteenth century:

For lands, he suffereth them to have none of their own; office or honest room they bear none. With occasions of his wars he pilleth them with taxes and tallages unto the bare bones. Their children he . . . taketh . . . fro their parents, conveying them whither he list, where their friends never see them after.
(p. 195, CW 12:191)

The Turks thus tried to pressure Christians into renouncing their faith when they did not slay them outright.

Just as Gregory and More describe comparable situations of persecution, so they have similar understandings of laying down one's life for Christ. Gregory discusses two kinds of martyrdom, the public and the secret (3.26, pp. 160–61). The first is a literal dying for one's faith, but the second is a hidden renunciation of selfishness in the daily events of life. More understands analogously that tribulation can be of two kinds, physical and psychological:

[S]ith tribulation is not only such pains as pain the body, but every trouble also that grieveth the mind, . . . the temptations of the devil, the world, and the flesh soliciting the mind of a good man to sin . . . [are] a great inward trouble and secret grief in his heart[.]   (pp. 52–53, CW 12:51)

In particular, More would have known the mental suffering of a judge who would not render a false judgement in behalf of the powerful (pp. 35–36, CW 12:34). Yet as Antony's very last quotation from Scripture affirms, "The sufferings of this life are not to be compared with the future glory which will be revealed in us" (Romans 8:18).
(cf. p. 325, CW 12:319)

One of the most striking resemblances between the dialogues of Gregory and More is the way in which both authors rework Plato's Parable of the Cave (*Republic* 7:514 ff.). Plato uses this allegory of prisoners in a dark cave lacking knowledge of the daylit world to explain how the ordinary person can scarcely conceive of such abstractions as Ideal Forms. Gregory describes how a little boy, born in prison, cannot believe his mother's description of the beauties of the outside world:

So it is with men born into the darkness of this earthly exile. They hear about lofty and invisible things, but hesitate to believe in them, because they know only the lowly, visible things of earth into which they were born.   (4.1, p. 190)

The reader with even a modest acquaintance with Plato will interpret Gregory's parable as an adaptation of the Allegory of the Cave. Even though he lived six years at the Byzantine court, however, Gregory confesses that he did not know Greek.[53] Vogüé cites a possible Latin source for Plato's allegory in Cicero's *De natura deorum* (2.37), but it is a luxurious subterranean land. Vogüé also refers to St. Gregory of Nyssa's comparison of our mortal life to incarceration in his "De mortuis" (PG 46.505-8), but this sermon is another Greek text.[54] The motif of imprisonment is a recurrent one in the psalms and the prophets; for example, Yahweh addresses the Suffering Servant in Isaiah 42:6-7: "I have appointed you ... to free captives from prison, and those who live in darkness from the dungeon." Thus Gregory could have shaped his parable from scriptural material. Furthermore, Boethius describes death as freeing the soul "from this earthly prison" in his *Consolation of Philosophy* (Book 2, Prose 7).[55] Although Gregory never mentions the author of *The Consolation of Philosophy* in his *Dialogues*, the pope does mention Boethius' father-in-law Symmachus, who was also executed by Theodoric (4.31, p. 228). Another possible source for Gregory's knowledge of Plato is oral tradition as posited by Joan M. Petersen.[56]

More, of course, knew Plato's *Republic* thoroughly, as his own ideal commonwealth testifies. Although he does not compare earthly life to a prison, Raphael explains the Utopians' view of death as an entrance into greater freedom, which "like all other good things, they conjecture to be increased after death rather than diminished in all good men" (CW 4:225). In the *Dialogue of Comfort*, More imitates Gregory in depicting the whole world as a prison:

> [I]f there were some folk born and brought up in a prison, that never came on the wall, nor looked out at the door, nor never heard of other world abroad, but saw some for their shrewd turns done among themself locked up in some strait room, [they would think that those in greater confinement were prisoners but the other inmates were free]. (pp. 281-82, CW 12:275)

Thus More in the Tower relativizes his limited freedom by considering himself to be confined in a maximum security cell within the prison of the world.

Unlike Cicero and More, Gregory positively yearned for death, which he "cherished as the entrance into life and the reward for labor" (Prologue 1, p. 4). With his positive outlook on eternal life, he encourages his audience with stories of St. Scholastica, whose soul departed for heaven in the form of a dove (2.34, p. 104), and of her brother St. Benedict, whose road to heaven was covered with rich carpets (2.37, p. 108). The deathbeds of various monks and nuns are attended by choirs of saints chanting antiphonally (4.16, p. 210), by St. Peter (4.14, p. 206), by angels (4.20, p. 214) and by Jesus himself (4.17, p. 211). Heavenly singing (4.15, p. 208) and fragrant odors (4.28, p. 224) grace the deaths of holy laymen. One of these, Count Theophane, anticipates the virtues of St. Thomas More since he was "a man given to acts of mercy, always ready to undertake a good work, zealous in practicing hospitality, and actively engaged in performing the duties of his office as count" (4.28, p. 223). The souls of sinful laymen, however, depart for hell, depicted as "open pits burning with fire" near Sicily (4.36, p. 236). Ten years after he completed the *Dialogues*, Gregory died in Rome, worn out by ill health and his administrative labors.

Immediately faced with the prospect of a violent death, More resembles Cicero rather than Gregory. Thomas Stapleton recounts the full rigor of the original sentence pronounced against More:

> [H]e shall be hanged, cut down while yet alive, ripped up, his bowels burnt in his sight, his head cut off, his body quartered and the parts set up in such places as the King shall designate.[57]

Besides anticipating the pain of beheading in his tale of the Viennese widow, More also considers the usual death for treason. The invalid Antony weighs the pain of a terminal illness lasting a week or two against the short pain of a violent death taking less than half an hour. The sick man's repeated spasms of heart or lungs would be more excruciating than the condemned man's pain of having "a knife to cut his flesh on the outside fro the skin inward" (p. 309, CW 12:302). Antony comments dryly that "a man may have his leg striken off by the knee and grieve him not, if his head be off but half an hour before" (p. 299, CW 12:293). In the end, the king commuted More's sentence to beheading, a mercifully short death compared to the agony of being hanged, drawn and quartered. After discerning that his refusal to accept the Oath of Supremacy did not stem from spiritual pride, More was able to face his executioners with cheerful courtesy and even with a quip.

In concluding our assessment of this Tower Work, we marvel that More can write so masterfully in such adverse circumstances. *A Dialogue of Comfort* is well organized, especially if one accepts the hypothesis that it is a first draft; furthermore, it is emotionally warm and witty. Even though More fears a violent death, his attitude is not self-dramatizing or uncontrolled. This is the man who heartens the courtier bringing him the message that he will be executed that morning:

> Quiet your self . . . and be not discomforted; For I trust that we shall, once in heaven, see eche other full merily, where we shalbe sure to live and loue together, in ioyful blisse eternally.[58]

Not only does More imitate the dialogue form of his classical and patristic forebears, but the humanist in the Tower becomes a victim of tyrannical power like Cicero and, like Gregory, a saint.

The Catholic University of America

Notes

This paper is an expanded version of a presentation made at a conference on The Humanism of Thomas More: Continuities and Transformations, Barnard College, Columbia University, November 16, 1985.

1. K. J. Wilson, *Incomplete Fictions: The Formation of English Renaissance Dialogue* (Washington, D.C.: Catholic University of America Press, 1985), 28–45.

2. Germain Marc'hadour, "Here I Sit: Thomas More's Genius for Dialogue," in *Thomas More: Essays on the Icon*, ed. Damian Grace and Brian Byron (Melbourne: Dove Communications, 1980), 30.

3. Bertram Colgrave notes that Gregory never mentions this intervention and suggests that it was created by popular legend on the analogue of Leo the Great's meeting with Attila the Hun, in his edition, *The Earliest Life of Gregory the Great*, by an Anonymous Monk of Whitby (Lawrence: University of Kansas Press, 1968), 154 n. 94.

4. Saint Gregory the Great, *Dialogues*, trans. Odo John Zimmerman, O.S.B., the Fathers of the Church 39 (New York: Fathers of the Church, Inc., 1959). Book and chapter numbers are followed by page references to this translation.

5. All quotations from *A Dialogue of Comfort Against Tribulation* are taken from the modern-spelling version, ed. Frank Manley, in the Yale Selected Works series (New Haven and London: Yale University Press, 1977); the second references in the parentheses are to the original-spelling edition in *The Complete Works*, vol. 12, ed. Louis L. Martz and Frank Manley (New Haven and London: Yale University Press, 1976), henceforth designated as "CW 12."

6. Saint Thomas More, *A Dialogue of Comfort Against Tribulation*, ed. Leland Miles (Bloomington and London: Indiana University Press, 1965), ciii–iv.

7. Cicero, *Tusculan Disputations*, trans. J. E. King, Loeb Classical Library (Cambridge: Harvard University Press; London: William Heinemann Ltd, 1966), hereafter cited as "King."
8. Grégoire le Grand, *Dialogues*, ed. Adalbert de Vogüé, trans. Paul Antin (Paris: Les Éditions du Cerf, 1978-80), 1:45.
9. *The Correspondence of Sr Thomas Moore*, ed. Elizabeth Frances Rogers (Princeton: Princeton University Press, 1947), Letter 211, p. 546, 1. 83.
10. Nicholas Harpsfield, *The Life and Death of Sr Thomas Moore*, ed. E. V. Hitchcock, Early English Text Society, Original Series, 186 (London: Oxford University Press, 1932), 133-34.
11. *Utopia*, ed. Edward Surtz, S. J., and J. H. Hexter, *The Complete Works of St. Thomas More* 4 (New Haven and London: Yale University Press, 1965), 303.
12. William Roper, *The Lyfe of Sir Thomas Moore*, ed. E. V. Hitchcock, Early English Text Society, Original Series, 197 (London: Oxford University Press, 1935), 83.
13. *A Dialogue Concerning Heresies*, ed. Thomas M. C. Lawler et al., *The Complete Works of St. Thomas More*, vol. 6 (New Haven and London: Yale University Press, 1981), Part II, p. 531 and n. 1.
14. *The Confutation of Tyndale's Answer*, ed. Louis A. Schuster et al., *The Complete Works of St. Thomas More*, vol. 8 (New Haven and London: Yale University Press, 1973), Part III, p. 1561. The Commentary cites a fourteenth-century sermon for this miracle. The original source, however, is *The Earliest Life of St. Gregory the Great*, 107.
15. Jacobus de Voragine, *The Golden Legend*, trans. Granger Ryan and Helmut Ripperger (New York: Longmans, Green and Co., 1941), v-vii, 185-86.
16. Roper, 94.
17. Wilson, 16.
18. G. L. Hendrickson, introduction, *Brutus*, by Cicero, The Loeb Classical Library (Cambridge: Harvard University Press; London: William Heinemann Ltd, 1939), 9.
19. A. E. Douglas, "Cicero the Philosopher," in *Cicero*, ed. T. A. Dorey (London: Routledge & Kegan Paul, 1965), 147.
20. F. Homes Dudden, *Gregory the Great: His Place in History and Thought* (London: Longmans, Green, and Co., 1905) 1:72-79.
21. Joan M. Petersen, *The Dialogues of Gregory the Great in Their Late Antique Cultural Background* (Toronto: Pontifical Institute of Medieval Studies, 1984), 23-24.
22. *Translations of Lucian*, ed. Craig R. Thompson, *The Complete Works of St. Thomas More*, vol. 3, Part I (New Haven and London: Yale University Press, 1974).
23. Rogers, Letter 206, p. 519, 11. 203-205.
24. Howard B. Norland, "Comfort through Dialogue: More's Response to Tribulation," *Moreana* 24.93 (1987): 53-66.
25. Cicero, *Tusculan Disputations, I . . .* , ed. Frank Ernest Rockwood (1903;

196 ～ *Three Dialogues of Comfort*

Norman: University of Oklahoma Press, 1966), 4.7 n., hereafter cited as "Rockwood."
26. King, 154, n. 2.
27. Maximilien Mahler, "Evocations Bibliques et Hagiographiques dans la Vie de Saint Benoît par Saint Grégoire," *Revue Bénédictine* 83 (1973): 417.
28. Vogüé, 1:25.
29. King, xviii.
30. Rockwood, xxviii.
31. Vogüé, 2:127 n. 4.
32. Vogüé, 1:79.
33. Vogüé, 1:44, nn. 75-79.
34. Vogüé, 1:79, n. 152.
35. Wilson, 137-39.
36. Marc'hadour, "Here I Sit," 36.
37. St. Athanasius, *The Life of St. Antony*, trans. Robert T. Meyer, Ancient Christian Writers, 10 (Westminster, Md.: Newman, 1950), 59.
38. Wilson, 149, n. 12, PL 50.640.
39. *Sermo* 274, PL 38.1252.
40. "The Passion of the Holy Martyr Vincent," *The Poems of Prudentius*, trans. Sister M. Clement Eagan, C. C. V. I., The Fathers of the Church, 43 (Washington, D.C.: Catholic University of America Press, 1962), 146-67.
41. King, Appendix I, "Cicero's Translations from the Greek," passim.
42. Vogüé, 1:85 n. 2.
43. Vogüé, 1:51.
44. Vogüé, 1:52-54.
45. Jean Gerson, *De Probatione Spirituum* in *Opera Omnia*, ed. M. L. Ellies du Pin (Antwerp, 1706), 3:37-42, cited in CW 12:389-93.
46. Rogers, Letter 206, pp. 528-29, 11. 552-56.
47. Roper, 56.
48. Torsten Petersson, *Cicero: A Biography* (Berkeley: University of California Press, 1920), 318.
49. Walter M. Gordon, "Suicide in Thomas More's *Dialogue of Comfort*," *American Benedictine Review* 29.4 (1978): 361.
50. Cf. Rockwood, xxv.
51. King, 382 n. 1.
52. King, 192 n. 2.
53. *S. Gregorii Magni Opera*, ed. Dag Norberg, Corpvs Christianorvm, Series Latina, 140, 140A (Tvrnholti: Typographi Brepols Editores Pontificii, 1982), Registrvm Epistolarvm VII, 29 and XI, 55.
54. Adalbert de Vogüé, OSB, "Un Avatar du Mythe de la Caverne dans *Les Diagogues* de Grégoire Le Grand," in *Homenaje a Fray Justo Perez de Urbel*, OSB, Studia Silensia, 4 (Abadía de Silos, 1977), 2:19, nn. 3 and 4.
55. Boethius, *The Consolation of Philosophy*, trans. Richard Green, The Library of Liberal Arts (Indianapolis: The Bobbs-Merrill Company, Inc., 1962), 39.
56. Petersen, 190.

57. Thomas Stapleton, *The Life and Illustrious Martyrdom of Sir Thomas More*, trans. Philip E. Hallett, ed. E. E. Reynolds (London: Burns & Oates, 1966), 176.
58. Roper, 101–02.

10/16/87, the 132nd day of the Marian Year.

Dear Reverend Abbé Marc'hadour,

Having seen the demise of a good number of magazines, I am convinced that *Moreana*'s longevity is due, above all, to two factors : 1) the heavenly care and patronage of our Saint, Sir Thomas More, and 2) your devotion, zeal, and unbounded love for our Saint and for his cause throughout the world.

For these, we are all grateful to you -- eternally. For Hungarians -- in Hungary and outside of Hungary -- a special, most grateful « thank you » for your interest in More's *A Dialogue of Comfort against Tribulation*. Modern « Turks » are at large in the world now, and our Saint's -- and *Moreana*'s -- focus on *The Dialogue* is a sure spiritual help in our twentieth-century predicament.

Gratefully yours,

Béla & Ilona Kapótsy
Assoc. Prof. (retired)
Hunter College/CUNY

Dieu très saint,
Qu'elle est merveilleuse, l'oeuvre de tes mains !
Tu restituas la beauté de ton image
quand le péché eut déparé le monde.

Comme une mère rassemble tendrement ses enfants,
tu as accueilli un peuple qui soit tien...

IV Comme Une Mère Rassemble Tendrement Ses Enfants

All holy God,
how wonderful the work of your hands!
You restored the beauty of your image
when sin had scarred the world.

As a mother tenderly gathers her children,
you embraced a people as your own...

G. van den Steenhoven
Herregaard
NL 6616 AE Hernen

Hernen, August 1988.

My dear Germain,

To think of *Moreana* means also to think of you, its founder, editor, animator. At the approach of its silver jubilee, a warm and grateful feeling prompts me to congratulate you, and ourselves the *Amici*, with your achievement. Inevitably, my words will sound a little more solemn than is usual in our correspondence.

From the various aspects of your achievement I would like to choose one which I regard as equally remarkable and admirable : your talent of uniting into a common ground, both in *Moreana* and in the Amicale as such, scholars *and* mere « aficionados » like myself. Among the Amici and in *Moreana* you have brought about a « humanising » tendency, refraining scholars from immoderate professionalism and amateurs from indulging in naïvety. To St. Thomas More's intercession, I attribute this happy situation first, and second to the unifying strength of your personal approach and indefatigable input.

At this time I am writing to you as founder and editor of *Moreana* . I could equally (but will leave that to others) honour you as a true and inspiring Roman Catholic priest, as a personal friend always ready to encourage and help, as a scholar from whose works on Thomas More and his period we have profited so much.

Vivat *Moreana*, vivat the Amicale, vivat our dearly treasured Germain Marc'hadour !

Totus tuus

Geert.

JEAN CORRIGNAN
YVONNE CORRIGNAN
KREIZ AR HOËD - MERLEVENEZ
56700 HENNEBONT

Le 1er décembre 1987.

Très cher Germain,

Il n'est pas sûr que notre projet d'aller au Canada te rejoindre pour le Congrès d'Août 1988 aboutisse, comme je le souhaitais.

Aussi, en cet ultime moment du Jubilé d'argent de « Moreana », je veux venir te témoigner notre joie profonde et notre fierté de t'avoir comme frère, notre chance inouïe, en vérité.

Dans cette existence plus courte que la mienne, tu as vu tant de pays, rencontré tant de gens divers, tant parlé, tant écrit, que je me demande parfois comment ton cerveau fait encore pour « tenir le coup ». Tu lui demandes beaucoup d'efforts, cher Germain, ainsi qu'à ton pauvre corps usé par les veilles prolongées, les voyages multiples et souvent épuisants..., très récemment Mr Bercot nous racontait que déjeûnant chez eux boulevard Suchet -- voici des années, -- tu t'infligeais un parcours très compliqué dans Paris, pour profiter des conditions plus avantageuses pour l'Amérique. Tu étais chargé de trois grosses serviettes de cuir et, dédaignant l'ascenseur, tu prenais l'escalier en courant, et sur le boulevard tu courais encore ; par la suite ils ont appris que dans ce charter spécial tu n'avais pu, étant trop inconfortablement installé, réaliser le travail projeté ! Avec un pincement de coeur, je me disais : « Nul ne pouvait donc le conduire à l'aéroport ? »

Ce fait, Germain, n'est qu'une infime poussière parmi les mille et mille péripéties que tu auras connues le long de ta vie professionnelle si emplie.

J'ai souvenance aussi de te voir arriver, le visage défait, le corps brisé de fatigue par ce décalage horaire depuis New York, pour la mort brutale de notre bien-aimé Louis, en Juin 1961.

A chaque rencontre, Jeannette Coantic me dit ceci : « Quel honneur pour Langonnet d'avoir ce Germain si savant, si cultivé, et toujours si simple ! » Et d'évoquer notre enfance, notre adolescence dans ce petit bourg breton, et de parler du beau Germain rieur et rayonnant avec son vif regard bleu, ses cheveux courts, ses grosses cuisses dans ses culottes courtes hiver comme été, toujours batailleur au foot, toujours premier en classe, où il restait abasourdi et ahuri de découvrir que ses voisins ne comprenaient rien de ce qu'expliquait le maître, restaient muets au tableau, et chantaient à la récitation imposée « Un pommier est un homme qui donne des pommes » au lieu « d'un arbre » bien sûr.

Tous ces souvenirs me ramènent au père Bourc'his de l'école publique qui était venu voir nos parents, leur disant : « Confiez-moi Germain, ne l'inscrivez pas à la nouvelle école privée ; laissez-moi le diriger sur Quimperlé ou Lorient, je vous promets d'en faire quelqu'un, avec ce certificat d'études à 10 ans, il ira loin ». Papa et maman cependant t'ont laissé choisir un autre chemin, et cela a été le séminaire et l'accomplissement de la vocation sacerdotale.

Très vite, ce fut l'Angleterre et d'autres vacances d'études et de travail !

Souvenir de ta prêtrise aussi, et de la maman de Jean qui racontait avec beaucoup d'émotion ton arrêt à Bodion en cette Saint Jean ♯♯ où tu la bénissais pour la première fois. Elle ne l'oublia jamais.

Puis ce fut St Ivy tout près de nous huit années durant. Et en 1952, ta nomination à l'Université Catholique d'Angers où depuis 36 ans tu vis, environné de livres, de documents, de paperasseries innombrables mais tous si précieux.

Ah oui, il avait raison le père Bourc'his : tu es devenu quelqu'un

- quelqu'un qu'on attend à travers le monde,
- quelqu'un qu'on écoute,
- quelqu'un qui a guidé tant d'esprits à faire leur chemin,
- quelqu'un qu'on aime surtout, et là est l'essentiel.

Nul de ceux qui ont pu croiser ta route ne t'oubliera, Germain.

Nous sommes très humbles, Jean et moi, quand nous parlons de cette oeuvre magistrale :te Moreana, conçue par toi, portée à bout de bras, si vaillamment, à travers toutes les difficultés financières et autres, ignorées de nous la plupart du temps car tu ne sais pas gémir ni te plaindre.

Tu peux passer le flambeau, Germain, et envisager de te reposer un peu maintenant.

Vive toi !

Jean et Yvonne Errignan

Henry VIII, sketch by Raymond Joly

HUBERTUS
SCHULTE HERBRÜGGEN

Fletcher's Forgotten Play:
The Rising to the Crown of Richard III

Time

MEMORIES OF SIR THOMAS MORE, London's great hero, were still flourishing in the 1590s in spite of all Henry VIII's efforts to erase them, in spite of John Foxe's wild tales of cruelty and of Edward Halle's sneers. This was the decade when Rowland Locky painted his two well-known composite copies of Hans Holbein's group portrait of the family of Sir Thomas More, one a monumental wall-covering oil painting (formerly at Burford Priory and now at the National Portrait Gallery) dated 1593,[1] the other, dating perhaps a few years later, a watercolor on vellum miniature (now at the Victoria and Albert Museum).[2] Those were the years, too, when Anthony Munday, Henry Chettle, Thomas Heywood, William Shakespeare and Thomas Dekker composed their *Book of Sir Thomas Moore,* a play which incorporates the London tradition of "the best friend that the poor e'er had."[3]

Title

About the same time, probably in 1593, a small quarto volume of 80 pages was published anonymously and without indication of place, year or printer's name. It appeared under the title

LICIA,
or
POEMES OF
LOVE, IN HO-
nour of the admirable
and singular virtues of his Lady,
to the imitation of the best
Latin Poets, and others.
whereunto is added the Rising to the
Crowne of RICHARD
the third.
Auxit musarum numerum Sappho ad-
dita musis.
Faelix si saevus, sic voluisset Amor.[4]

The title-page border[5] is made up of four woodcuts with allegorical figures of virtues. They are taken from John Day's *Book of Christian Prayer*, 1569, 1578, 1581.[6] In the later London edition of 1590,[7] these four woodcut virtues are characteristically wanting.[8] The small volume is dedicated to "Ladie Mollineux, wife to the Right Worshipfull Syr Richard Mollineux Knight." The dedication is dated 4th September and the preface to the reader 8th September 1593. On the unnumbered page after page 69 we find a new title-page

THE RISING
TO THE CROWNE
of RICHARD the
third.
VVritten by him selfe.

The border has the same four woodcuts of virtues as the book's title page at the front, though here in a different order. The verso is blank. Page (70) (= sig.L1) is headed again by the title and then begins with the text: "The Stage is set, for Stately matter fitte. . . ." Then follow twelve pages with four six-line stanzas each (except for this first page [70], which has only three). They end on p. 80 (= sig.M3v): ". . . I vvore no garland but a golden Crovvne." The ensuing[9] note "To the reader" on p. [81]r offers corrections of errors in *Licia* and has no bearing on "Richard III." The verso is blank.

The history of the Richard III plot in English literature after More is dealt with by R. S. Sylvester in his fine critical edition of More's English and Latin versions of his unfinished *The History of King Richard*

III[10] and mentioned in Daniel Kinney's recent presentation of a new Latin text;[11] both editors, however, make no mention of Giles Fletcher and his narrative poem. Although George B. Churchill includes a brief paragraph on it in his dissertation,[12] Fletcher's piece is not mentioned in the latest (red) edition of the BL Catalogue, s.v. "Richard III,"[13] nor in such standard publications as Oscar James Campbell's and Edward G. Quinn's *A Shakespeare Encyclopedia*,[14] in Wolfgang Clemen's impressive *Kommentar zu Shakespeares Richard III. Interpretationen eines Dramas*,[15] in Ina Schabert's *Shakespeare Handbuch. Die Zeit – das Leben – das Werk – die Nachwelt*,[16] in Pamela Tudor-Craig's *Richard III*, in E.M.W. Tillyard's *Shakespeare's History Plays*, in Lilly B. Campbell's *Shakespeare's Histories*.[17] nor does the title occur in printed catalogues of the libraries of the *Deutsche Shakespeare Gesellschaft* or in the pages of *Moreana. Bulletin Thomas More*.[18] Thus it might not be amiss to draw the modern reader's attention to Fletcher's work.

The Author

In the first of the "Piscatorie Eclogs" in *The Purple Island*,[19] Phineas Fletcher describes the life and writings of his father, Giles the elder, under the name of Thelgon, of whom he says in the tenth stanza: ". . . (I) raised my rhyme to sing of RICHARD'S climbing." On the basis of this allusion it has been generally accepted that Giles Fletcher was the author.

Giles Fletcher "the elder" (1549?-1611), civilian lawyer, diplomatist, and author, was born in Watford (Hertfordshire), the son of Richard Fletcher, later vicar of Bishops Stortford. Giles was educated at Eton and, from 1565, at King's College, Cambridge; 1568 fellow; 1573 M.A.; 1581 LL.D.; 1581 M.P. for Winchelsea. In 1580-1581 he married Joan Sheaf, by whom he had two sons, Giles ("the younger") and the aforementioned Phineas; he also had a nephew, John Fletcher. All three were poets. Sent to Scotland in 1568 in the company of the English ambassador, he was later employed by Queen Elizabeth as a minister in her negotiations with Hamburg and Stade. He served as a diplomatic envoy to Russia in 1588. An account of his mission, *Of the Russe Common Wealth*, was published in 1591 and dedicated to Queen Elizabeth. It led to remonstrances from English Eastland merchants and was quickly suppressed as being likely to give offense to the Czar; it was later printed in an abridged form in Richard Hakluyt's *Diuers voyages*. . . (London, 1582) and in *Hakluytus Posthumus or Purchas his pilgrimes* (London, 1625). In 1590 he made plans for an extensive Latin history of Queen Elizabeth. Besides *Licia, or Poems of Love...*, he published other poems and three "Eclogues."[20]

Thus Fletcher's "The Rising to the Crown of Richard III" stands at or near the end of the literary career of an experienced lawyer and diplomat who over the years had himself been able to glean an inside knowledge of the political stage and who knew the ups and downs, the glamour and the downfalls, of those appearing on it.

The Printer

The printer, John Legate "the elder" (d. 1620?), was made free of the Stationers' Company, London, in 1586, and served, from 1588 to 1609, as a printer to the University of Cambridge, where *Licia* and "The Rising" were printed. In 1609 he left Cambridge and carried on his business in London.[21]

The Book

Licia, or Poems of Love,[22] is one of the then flourishing sonnet sequences (plus additional poems and elegies), composed in emulation of Sir Philip Sidney's *Astrophel and Stella*,[23] which had been published only two years earlier and had become an inspiring model for many other poets, including Shakespeare. However, his conventional sonnets, praised by some and rejected by others, need not concern us here.

Fletcher's "Rising to the Crowne of Richard the third" is a poem of 47 stanzas of six decasyllabic lines each, consisting of two interlacing or crossed rhyme pairs and a concluding heroic couplet (*ababcc*). In poetic genre, the poem combines the elegiac complaint with narrative lyric.

The structure of the poem shows three major parts: stanzas 1–6 serving as a general preface, stanzas 7–43 being devoted to the "rising to the crown" and stanzas 44–47 constituting final reflections. The general preface of the first six stanzas "sets the stage," as it were, for a princely play, of which three parts are said to have been acted already, those of the rise and fall of Shore's Wife (stanza 2),[24] of Fair Rosamond (3)[25] and of Queen Elstred (4).[26] Their downfalls, we are told, however great they may have been, were trifles compared with his own. Now Richard makes Lady Fortune his partner at a tennis-match of two games for the crown in which he wins the first, and loses the second (5).

The main part (stanzas 7 to 43) is devoted to the 'rising to the crown' in the form of Richard's reflections on the various stages ("stations") of his career up to its climax. Anticipating, perhaps,[27] Shakespeare's opening monologue, Fletcher begins with Richard's self-introduction (7-9). We are told that "Tyme-tyrant Fate" has fitted him for a Crown to which his father's fall taught him to aspire. Richard also introduces his family: his father, Richard Duke of York, his brothers Edward (later Edward IV) and George Duke of Clarence. His ambition seems revealed (9) when he, the youngest, gives himself precedence over his brothers. In stanza 10 the unnamed "Sad Muse" (probably Melpomene, muse of tragedy) is invoked to set down his "sable fortunes" and his "mournful tale" ending with a resigned *sic transit gloria mundi* motif.

Each stage of his career is marked by his victims. As in a procession all those turn up, one by one, who stood between him and the crown and whom he disposed of in cold blood. Or, as he calls it, "all my lettes full soundly were remoov'd" (stanza 12), euphemistic "soundly" being indicative of the cunning by which he brought about such bloody deeds. The dance is led by his brother Clarence (12), followed by King Henry VI (13), whom "men say" or "fame does report" were slain by him, Clarence by having been "given wine" in a brotherly fashion (i.e., drowned in a butt of Malmesy), Henry as a result of "a dagger's stab." Being resolved to obtain the crown for himself (16), Richard rejoiced when his elder brother, King Edward IV, died (17), leaving two sons of an infant age, which was convenient for Richard. Having removed one of them, young Edward V, to the Tower (19), he then put Rivers and Grey to death (21). Next he went out of his way to bring the other prince, young Richard, under his control too. This part of the story takes the form of a narrative digression of sixteen stanzas in two parts or about one half of the main part (22-37).

The first part of the digression (22-29) recounts how the widow queen (Elizabeth Grey, relict of Edward IV) on hearing of Richard's activities, takes refuge in a sanctuary (22). She turns to the Archbishop of York and Lord Chancellor (Morton's name remains unmentioned) for help (23), laments her fortunes (24) and explains her fears (25). The Archbishop tries to comfort her (26 ff.), leaves his Great Seal with her (28), returns home and is reproached and dismissed by Richard (29).

The digression is interrupted by a short interlude of two stanzas, in which Richard remembers how he gained political strength by promoting his friends and depriving his adversaries (30), and how he planned in council to bring young Richard under his control (31) as a "playmate" for his royal brother.

The second part of the digression shows "the Cardnall" being sent to persuade the Queen to surrender Prince Richard (32-33). The Queen, in spite of her fears, finally gives in and bids him a motherly farewell (34–37). Hypocritically, Richard "kist the child, and took it in (his) arme" (38). Being "Lord Protector" of the royal brothers, he sees himself as "the wolfe" (18, 39) defending "the harmless sheepe." With them both safe in the Tower, he "both at once did smother" (39). His next victim is Hastings (40), then he wins Buckingham over "through favours" (40). By using London's lord mayor (42) and "a learned doctor" (Dr. Shaa, 43) as his mouthpiece, he at last succeeds in bringing about that "all did cry, Heavens let King Richard live" (43). Here the story of his "rising" ends.

The last four stanzas of the poem (44–47) are reserved for Richard's final reflections, after having achieved his aim. Interwoven with retarding elements like a reassuring "live Richard long, the honour of thy name" (46), they nevertheless fully reveal his failure and indicate his fall by showing his unrest "till all friends were dead" (45), by his remaining without any remorse (46), by his torments and sleeplessness "because I got which long I could not keep" (47), until, in the last line, he has to admit, "I wore no garland, but a golden Crowne." The disillusioned, diminutive *but* is revealing. The crown has lost its glamour.

In its tone, the poem combines the individualism of the lyric with the elegiac self-reflection (in the first person singular) of a deceased Richard III who has lost "a Crowne, mine honour, and my life" (stanza 3, line 6) and is now (the poet does not say whence) reconsidering his rise and how relentlessly he has removed everyone standing between him and the crown. The poem shows already some of those elegiac characteristics which were not developed fully until later: subjective mournful or resigned mood, invocation of a muse, expression of grief or lament felt in his loss (of the crown), a procession of persons and events on his way up, and some digressions, here in the form of narrative lingering at one of his stages while the dramatic events are related partly in direct speech. The connection with death (here in the figure of the dead speaker himself) is clearly present, as is the subjective sequence of thoughts.

Sources

The *sujet*, *Stoff*, subject matter or material deals with a certain period of English history leading to the end of the "Wars of the Roses" between Lancaster and York, in particular with the machinations and attempts of Richard Duke of Gloucester to obtain the crown of England for himself. Extra-literary in itself, taken from real life, it nevertheless has a long literary tradition in English historiography, dating back to near-contemporaries of the protagonist. Under the Tudors, Richard's historiographers began to mold the material into a structured "plot," acted as it were, on a stage by equally stylized characters. Thus from the very beginning we find an invariable historical core, tied to certain historical persons and events, existing (or having existed) in their own right, independent of literature, *plus* factors modified by authors who took license in shaping their material according to their political, historiographical or literary ideas. Here, as with many of the ancient accounts of history, it is difficult to draw an exact line between historical truth and literary formgiving.

A detailed textual history of Fletcher's "Rising" must needs lie beyond the scope of the present article. May it suffice to state that Fletcher as well as Shakespeare took most of the Richard story from a literary tradition, of which More's unfinished English and Latin versions, *The History of King Richard III* and *Historia Richardi regis Angliae eius nominis tertii* (written between 1513 and 1518),[28] mark the beginning, and the second edition of Raphael Holinshed's *Chronicles* the end.[29] From these and, perhaps, the chronicles of the intermediary stages (John Hardyng,[30] Edward Halle[31] and Richard Grafton)[32] Fletcher, like all historians and playwrights throughout the sixteenth century, freely borrowed many features of Richard's life.

Apart from most of the narrative stages of Richard's career already mentioned, Fletcher borrowed from More many historical details, including the following:

—the early beginnings of Richard's plans for usurping the crown (8),[33]
—Clarence's treason in plotting to gain the crown for himself (11),[34]
—his brother Clarence's death, which favours Richard's plot (17),[35]
—Richard as the "butcher" of Henry VI (12),[36]
—Fletcher's repeated dependence on rumour ("men say," twice; "fame doeth report") in relating Richard's part in both their deaths (12, 13),[37]
—his "carelessness" in slaying "how or who" in gaining the kingdom (13),[38]
—Richard's pleasure over Edward IV's death and becoming Lord Protector of the two royal princes, "both under age, unfitte to guyde the land" (17),[39]
—his double role as Protector and wolfe (18),[40]
—the Queen's four arguments for keeping young Richard with her in sanctuary (35),[41]

—Richard's attempt at winning over Buckingham by plans to match their children and grant him the Earldom of Herford (*sic*, i.e., Hereford [40]).[42]

—the crown won, his tormented sleeplessness (47).[43]

Having borrowed from More in so many instances, Fletcher, however, omits the many structural prognostications employed by More in knitting together his plot (e.g., Richard's monstrous birth, Stanley's dream, Hasting's horse stumbling, his meeting with a priest and a pursuivant), *except* one, the ominous swelling of the sea before a storm, portending imminent evil. Fletcher's

> Nowe the Sea before a storme doeth swell,. . . .
> I dem'd it danger, speech for to despice,
> For after this I knew a storme would rise   (41)

echoes More's

> were it that before such great thinges, mens hartes of a secret instinct of nature misgiueth them. As ye sea w^{t}out wind swelleth of himself somtime before a tempest: or were it that some one man happely somwhat perceiuing, filled mani men w^t suspicion, though he shewed few men what he knew.[44]

Later the same omen was employed by Shakespeare:

> By a divine instinct men's minds mistrust
> Ensuing danger; as by proof we see
> The water swell before a boist'rous storm.[45]

Finally, it should be noted that Fletcher has the mayor of London making his fellow citizens "eye" Richard "as the rising sun" (42), anticipating (?) Shakespeare's famous punning in the introductory monologue of *Richard III*, "this son/sun of York."[46] Whereas Fletcher relates the sun image to Richard himself,[47] Shakespeare's pun refers to Edward IV.[48] At any rate, the underlying meaning of "son of York" applies to both Edward and Richard, both being sons of Richard Plantagenet, Duke of York.

The sun image, shared by Fletcher and Shakespeare, seems to have no direct verbatim equivalent in More's *History of Richard III*, although the gist of both Dr. Shaa's and the Duke of Buckingham's eloquence employed in debunking Edward and his kin and promoting Richard centres around the chief idea of Richard being the only true "son of York," arising as it were, sun-like out of the Edwardian darkness.[49]

In borrowing almost his entire material from his antecedents, Fletcher also inherited their views, above all their deliberately hostile view of Richard's character as a Machiavellian villain, as a blood-thirsty, merciless tyrant and monster who spared neither children nor his own brother. This view had been developed by More and was employed as a substantial part of the "Tudor myth" by which the young dynasty sought to support their claim to the throne. Fletcher thus conforms very much to the political climate and ideological context of the age in which he worked and is yet another writer within the Tudor machine to dutifully propound the Tudor court propaganda.

Rise and Fall

As Fletcher's title indicates, his poem confines itself almost entirely to the story of Richard's rise, from his parental origins to his eventually being crowned King. There, characteristically, his reflected story ends without relating the stages of his "fall," too.

Even so, the part of his "fall" is by no means absent. Although missing from the narrated "plot," it nevertheless is present in the ego of the poem's speaker, Richard himself. It is the *fallen* Richard who muses on his fate after having lost Crown, honour and life (3).

Thus Fletcher has Richard appear before our eyes as a tragic figure in a double sense. When viewed with secular eyes, his tragedy lies in the fact that his highest goal, the crown, bought with so many unscrupulous killings of friends and relatives, quickly brings about his own downfall, since he cannot wear it long (47). From a religious perspective Richard is a tragic figure, because, being steeped in the blood of his victims, he remains without remorse even after the deed. As if finally summing up *sub specie aeternitatis*, he says in the last stanza, "where I doe end, my sorrow did begin."

Universität Düsseldorf

Notes

1. National Portrait Gallery, 2765; J. B. Trapp and H. Schulte Herbrüggen, *The King's Good Servant: Sir Thomas More 1477/78-1535* (London, 1977), no. 1 (quoted as KGS with number).

2. Victoria and Albert Museum, 15-1973; KGS 170.
3. British Library: MS Harl. 7368; KGS 275.
4. *A Short-Title Catalogue of Books Printed in England, Scotland, & Ireland* ed. W. A. Jackson, F. S. Ferguson and Kathrine F. Pantzer, Second edition, 2 vols., London, 1976-86, no. 11055 (quoted as STC with number). British Library: Huth 41. Bodleian Library: Douce fragm. 836 (has an early stage of some pages). Modern editions: *Miscellanies of The Fuller Worthies' Library. In four volumes*, ed. Alexander B. Grosart, vol. III (London, 1872, 586-99; repr. New York, 1970). *An English Garner: Ingatherings from our History ad Literature*, ed. Edward Arber, vol. VIII (Westminster, 1896), 465-75.
5. Apparently not in R. B. MacKerrow and F. S. Ferguson, *Title-page Borders used in England & Scotland, 1485-1640*. Bibliographical Society, London, Illustrated Monographs, 21 (London, 1932).
6. STC 6428, 6429, 6430.
7. Printed by Richard Yardley and Peter Short for the assignes of Richard Day. STC 6431.
8. Cf. James Kennedy, W. A. S. Smith and A. E. Johnson, *Dictionary of Anonymous and Pseudonymous English Literature*, vol. III (Edinburgh & London, 1928), 347.
9. In the Huntington Library copy, apparently a binder's fault as the catchword "To" at the foot of the preface page indicates, it precedes the dedicatory letter in the front.
10. *The Yale Edition of the Complete Works of St. Thomas More*, vol. 2, (New Haven and London, 1963). Cited as *CW* 2 with page number.
11. *Ibid.*, vol. 15, *In Defense of Humanism . . . Historia Richardi Tertii*, (New Haven and London, 1986). Cited as *CW* 15 with page number.
12. *Richard the Third up to Shakespeare*, Palaestra, X (Berlin, 1900, repr. New York & London, 1970), 529 ff.
13. *The British Library Catalogue of Printed Books*, vol. 275 (1985), pp. 157-58.
14. London, 1966.
15. Göttingen, 1969.
16. Stuttgart, 1972.
17. Catalogue of an exhibition at the National Portrait Gallery, London, 1973; Tillyard (London 1944), repr. in Pelican Books (1986); Campbell was first published 1947, repr. London 1964.
18. Angers (France), 1963–.
19. Cambridge, 1633. STC 11082. Cf. Joseph Hunter, *The Illustrations of the Life, Studies, and Writings of Shakespeare. Supplementary to all Editions*, vol. II (London, 1845), 77f.
20. *Dictionary of National Biography*, London, 1885 ff., s.v. (quoted as *DNB*); C. H. & T. Cooper, *Athenae Cantabrigienses*, vol. III (Cambridge, 1913), 34.
21. *DNB*.
22. Starting on p. 1 = sig. B2r ending on p. 69 = sig. K4v.
23. STC 22536.
24. From the edition of 1563 onward, the tragedy of "Shores wyfe" had been included in William Baldwin's *Mirror for Magistrates* (STC 1248). It was

reissued in 1571, 1574, 1575, 1578, 1587 and again in 1593. In the same year, 1593, Anthony Chute published his *Beautie dishonoured written under the title of Shores wife* (STC 5262). A ballad, "Jane Shore" (Roxburghe Collection, I, 63) has been attributed "without any evidence and with no apparent reason" to Thomas Deloney (cf. Francis Oscar Mann, ed., *The Works of Thomas Deloney* [Oxford, 1967], 503). For Jane Shore cf. Nicolas Barker's and Sir Robert Birley's articles in *Etoniana* (Eton, Berks.), nos. 125, 126 (1972): 383–414.

25. In 1592 Samuel Daniel's 'Complaint of Rosamond' was published in his *Delia* (STC 6243.2 and .3).

26. Cf. Thomas Lodge's, *Phyllis, where-vnto is annexed, the tragicall complaynt of Elstred*, 1593 (STC 16662), where the sonnet sequence is followed, as in Fletcher's, by a didactical poem on a historical legend after the "rise and fall" pattern from the *Mirror for Magistrates*, 1574 (STC 13443).

27. Shakespeare's *Richard III* was first performed, it appears, in 1594; it was entered into the *Stationers' Register* 20 Oct. 1597; first printed in quarto 1597. Many scholars assume 1592/3 as a possible date of origin.

28. More's English text ("fro the copie of his own hand") was available to the Elizabethans in William Rastell's (More's nephew) monumental folio volume of *The vvorkes of Sir Thomas More Knyght . . . wrytten by him in the Englysh tonge* (London, 1557), 35–71 (sig. c.ii.r–e.iiii.r). STC 18076. More's Latin text, "Historia Richardi regis. . . ," was available in *Thomae Mori . . . Omnia Latina Opera. . .* (Louvain, 1565 & 1566), 44–56.

29. *The first and second volumes (the third volume) of chronicles* (London, 1587). STC 13569. For the literary tradition of Richard III cf. Churchill (supra notes 12) and the introductions to the Yale volumes (supra notes 10, 11).

30. *The chronicle . . . from the firste begynnyng of Englande . . . in metre*, (London, 1543), sig. DD^8–L1^6. STC 12767. Second edition, 1543, DD^7–L1^5. STC 12768.

31. *The Vnion of the-two noble and illustrate famelies of Lancastre & Yorke. . .*, London, 1548, AA^1–FF^1. STC 12721. Second definitive edition 1550, AA^1–bb^2 (repr. Menston 1970). STC 12723.

32. *A chronicle at large . . . of the affayres of Englande . . . vnto the first yere of queene Elizabeth* (London, 1568). STC 12147.

33. ". . . he long time in king Edwardes life, forethought to be king," CW 2.8.

34. "at the lest wise heinous Treason was there layde to his charge," CW 2.7.

35. "he was gladde of his brothers death," CW 2.9.

36. "he slewe with his owne handes king Henry the sixt," "that boocherly office," CW 2.8.

37. "as menne constantly saye," "somme wise menne also weene," "as menne demed," "they that thus deme," CW 2.8.

38. "Frende and foo was muche what indifferent, where his aduantage grew, he spared no mans deathe, whose life withstoode his purpose," CW 2.9.

39. "putte in hope by the occasion of the tendre age of the young Princes . . . he contriued their destruccion," CW 2.9.

40. "to bee protectoure of the king and his realme, so . . . the lamb was betaken to the wolfe," CW 2.24.

41. Echoing the long debate between her and the archbishop and later the "Cardnall," CW 2.22, 26 ff.

42. "that the protectours onely lawful sonne, should mary ye dukes daughter, and that the protectour shold graunt him the . . . Erledome of Hertford" (sic, i.e., Hereford). Whereas the English text of 1557 has "Hertford" the Latin text of 1565 and the Arundel MS correctly have "Herfordiae comitatum," CW 2.44, 123. Similarly the Paris MS has "Herfordiae conuentum," CW 15.400. Cp. Churchill, op.cit., 530, 126 ff.

43. "he neuer hadde quiet in his minde,. . . he took ill rest a nightes, lay long wakyng & musing, sore weried with care & watch, rather slumbered then slept, troubled wyth fearful dreames, sodainly sommetyme sterte vp, leape out of his bed. . . ," CW 2.87.

44. Ed. Sylvester, CW 2.44. Similarly More's Latin version (ibid., 44, 123; ed. Kinney, CW 15.402) in which More echoes Seneca's Thyestes 434 ff., 957–60 (cf J. W. Cunliffe, The Influence of Seneca on Elizabethan Tragedy [London, 1893], 77 ff.; Churchill, op.cit., 126 ff.; ed. Kinney, 620).

45. Richard III, II. iii. 43–5.

46. The sun-in-splendour was the badge of the House of York.

47. Cf. C. W. Scott-Giles, Shakespeare's Heraldry (London, 1950), 172 ff., who sees the emerging sun as the special emblem of Richard III.

48. Other scholars associate it in particular with Edward IV, e.g., Richard Adams, ed., Richard III, The Macmillan Shakespeare (London, 1974), 46.

49. (Shaa:) "But ye lord protectour he said, y^t very noble prince, ye special paterne of knightly prowes, as well in all princely behaueour as in ye lineamentes & fauor of his visage, represented the verye face of ye noble duke his father. This is quod he, ye fathers owne figure, this is his owne countenance, ye very prent of his visage, ye sure vndoubted image, ye playne expresse likenes of that noble Duke" (CW 2.67). (Buckingham:) ". . .ye most excellent prince ye lord protector as to ye very lawfully begotten sonne of the remembered duke of Yorke" (CW 2.74).

Brest, le 22 Décembre 1987.

Cher Monsieur l'Abbé,

Voici vingt ans, jour pour jour, vous avez béni mon union avec Odile, en l'église Saint-Etienne de Rennes, Et depuis, vous avez été présent dans notre foyer, comme, je le suppose, auprès de nombreux couples que vous avez bénis ou qui se sont rencontrés sous le patronage de Thomas More.

Lettres, billets, circulaires, *Moreana*, arrivant régulièrement, sans oublier les livres à recenser, les articles à évaluer, les épreuves à relire, tout cela a tissé un lien solide entre le Moreanum et notre famille au fin bout de la Bretagne. Elizabeth et Jean-Philippe, nos enfants, ont tant entendu parler de l'Utopie que l'île d'Hythlodée est pour eux plus réelle que bien des pays lointains, et ils savent que se retrouvent sur cette terre mythique ceux qui partagent les mêmes valeurs.

Nous nous sommes bien sûr retrouvés depuis 1967, à Brest, à Angers, à l'occasion de colloques, mais ces rencontres « were few and far between », tandis qu'il n'y a guère de semaine où le hasard de la conversation ou l'arrivée du courrier ne vous aient pas fait entrer chez nous, en compagnie de Thomas More, et d'*amici*, vivants, ou disparus comme Dick Sylvester, de cette immense famille spirituelle et intellectuelle.

Grâce à vous, nous avons souvent échappé à l'isolement, relatif, où nous nous trouvons, pour participer par la pensée à la communion que vous avez établie sous l'invocation de Thomas More. J'en suis sûr, chaque foyer d'*amici* trouve, dans la grande fraternité morienne qui s'est tissée autour de vous, à s'épanouir et à se conforter, et chaque famille sait que son bonheur est l'objet de votre discrète sollicitude et de votre affectueuse attention.

Merci encore pour tout ce que vous nous avez apporté depuis vingt ans.

Croyez, Cher Monsieur l'Abbé, à nos sentiments respectueusement et cordialement dévoués.

Jacques GURY

ALBERT J. GERITZ

*John Aubrey's Brief Life of More:
Facts, Half-Truths, or Fictions?*

JOHN AUBREY IS OFTEN VIEWED as that quaint, amusing chap who traveled about England in the seventeenth century collecting all that colorful but decidedly erroneous biographical trivia.[1] Aubrey's detached, objective desire to depict "the thing as it is" (Kite 112), however, gives his *Brief Lives* some importance as a historical document. In fact, the *Lives* is frequently cited on the pages of twentieth-century biographies of early political and literary figures, because it provides information not found elsewhere. Thomas More, about whom Aubrey tells five stories, is among those figures.

But are these stories based on facts, half-truths Aubrey and his contemporaries believed to be facts, or fictions? What are we to make of these glimpses of More's life? Do we expurgate the one about Roper's choice of a bride as did Andrew Clark when he edited the *Lives* for his Victorian audience in 1898? Or do we add them to the long list of fictions about More as did Anne Manning in *The Household of Sir Thomas More?*

Whether Aubrey's amusing anecdote about More convincing others that he saw a "prodigious Dragon in the skye" (214) actually occurred cannot be verified. That the More who was labeled the "wisest fool in Christendom," who had translated Lucian, who had written dozens of witty epigrams, *A Merry Jest*, and *Utopia*, and who had created Antony's sense of humor in *A Dialogue of Comfort Against Tribulation*, would pull the verbal prank Aubrey describes as typical of More's "extraordinary facetious ... discourse" (214) is not unlikely, though. Choosing to believe this episode might have taken place depends upon how willing we are to have Aubrey or Aubrey's More impose it "on [our] phantasies" (214).

The *Lives* is, of course, full of funny anecdotes similar to this one, and it is evident to anyone opening the book at random that amusing himself, Anthony à Wood, or anyone else who might see the manuscript, was also Aubrey's motive in writing. Nevertheless, what we can see in Aubrey is his adherence to the truth as he knew it and his exactitude, for almost always his intention is to get the facts down on paper as faithfully as possible. If he is to be faulted with including hearsay in his *Lives*, as the anecdote about More and the dragons might well be, he is to be applauded for not falling to the temptation of disguising such stories with the thin film of specious authority as did other biographers (Kite 136). On the other hand, Aubrey, great storyteller that he was, might have "made up" this anecdote (and many others) — a probability Kite seldom stresses.

Aubrey's inclusion of this and other anecdotes about More, however, must be viewed in another light — that of literary tradition. Heir to prevalent notions about the nature of biography at his time, Aubrey was inclined to draw characters in the style of Theophrastus rather than portray individuals (Kite 90-91). Because the method of the character is deductive instead of inductive, Aubrey set some subjects (particularly those who, like More, had died long before Aubrey was born) in preconceived molds, and this habit of mind and procedure hampered the development of empirical and inductive reasoning. Since More's reputation for wit outlived him and was soon shaped into a stereotype, Aubrey naturally found or invented stories to fit the mold of that generalization. Even though Aubrey was often at a loss for detailed information about his subjects — a fact making the method of drawing characters all the more appropriate to his task (perhaps making it the only way to proceed in some cases), it must be remembered that his story of More telling his companions he saw a "prodigious Dragon in the skye" adds to our notion of how More's personality may have been seen during Aubrey's time.

Whether we accept the anecdote about Tom of Bedlam and More (213-14) is again left to our senses of humor and our conceptions of More's wit; that such an event could have happened is not impossible. The location of that event and More's customary use of that place, however, may well supply us with another look at not only the "Countrey-howse ... at Chelsey, in Middlesex, where Sir John Danvers built his howse" (213), but also More's habits. Aubrey sets the scene of More's encounter with "Tom of Bedlam" at the "Gate-house, which was flatt on the top, leaded, from whence [the roof] there is a most pleasant prospect of the Thames and the fields beyond." "On this place," Aubrey continues, "the Lord Chancellour More was wont to recreate himself and contemplate" (213).

This "Gate-house" may have been part of the portion of More's estate to which Roper gives the name "New Building."[2] In his biographical tribute to his father-in-law, Roper enlarges Aubrey's report as he writes:

> And because he was desirous for godlye purposes sometyme to be solitary, and sequester himself from worldly company, A good distaunce from his mansion house builded he a place called the newe buildinge, wherein there was a Chapell, a library and a gallery; In whiche, as his vse was vppon other dayes to occupy himself in prayer and study together, so on the Fridaie there vsually contynewed he from morning till evening, spending his time only in devoute praiers and spirituall exercises. (25–26)

When we consider the number of those residing at the Chelsea estate,[3] More's retreats to New Building are easy to understand.

Aubrey's account not only reinforces Roper's, but it may also supply some details about the appearance of the gateway at the estate when More lived there. In addition to the statement that "the chimney-piece of marble in Sir John's chamber [may have been] the chimney-piece of Sir Thomas More's chamber, as Sir John [Danvers] himself told me,"[4] Aubrey writes that the gate "is . . . adorned with two noble Pyramids" (213). E. E. Reynolds speculates, on the basis of John Thorpe's plan and Leonard Knyff's "careful topographical drawing of Beaufort House and its grounds," that "there may have been no considerable changes" to this gateway "up to the end of the seventeenth century" ("Right Fair House" 7). Some of what Aubrey saw on the grounds of Danver's House then may help us to see parts of the estate as it may have been in More's day.

The story Aubrey tells about the trunk of More's body being buried in the Chelsea parish church is erroneous, though Aubrey is not entirely at fault for following a tradition of his times rendered believable by the presence of the "slight Monument erected . . . neer the middle of the South wall" (214) of that church. Never intended to be a tomb, the stonework on this "Monument" was purely decorative, and what looked like a tomb was empty. Aubrey and some of his contemporaries thought, but never certainly knew, that Margaret Roper obtained permission to transfer her father's body to the tomb he himself had prepared in the parish church of Chelsea, and on which is inscribed the epitaph he composed after he resigned the chancellorship in 1532 (Reynolds, *Saint Thomas More* 188).[5]

Although More surely wished to be buried in his vault (which was under the church's floor, not in its wall) with other family members, that was not to be. The only information contemporary with More's burial comes from Thomas Stapleton whose account is based on the story of a witness (a method of recounting events not unlike Aubrey's). Stapleton records Dorothy Colley's recollections about the day she and Margaret Roper made their way to the place of More's burial, the Church of St. Peter-ad-Vincula within the Tower (192). Reynolds reports that, during a "thorough restoration" of this little church in 1876, the bones of hundreds were discovered when the flagstones of the floors were removed. Not all these dead were victims of Henry VIII's tyranny; some were members of the Tower parish, and St. Peter-ad-Vincula was their church. Among these bones, which were carefully removed and reburied in a new vault (north of the chapel), were those of More and John Fisher. Almost a hundred years later, on Sunday, 26 April 1970, in the crypt of St. Peter's was dedicated this memorial to More:

THOMAS MORE, knight, scholar, writer, statesman,
Lord Chancellor of England 1529–1532,
Beheaded on Tower Hill, buried in this Chapel, 1535
Canonised by Pope Pius XI, 1935.
("In the Tower")

Portions of Aubrey's story about "one of [More's] daughters" obtaining his head "now preserved in a vault" (214) in Canterbury are true; the spectacular, grotesquely-comic, manner Aubrey describes it falling into the lap of that nameless daughter and its place of preservation in the "Cathedral Church of Canterbury" (214) are not. As that of other convicted traitors, More's head was displayed on London Bridge. Margaret Roper, nearly a month after the execution, when she knew her father's head would be thrown into the Thames (as John Fisher's had been), bribed the executioner to let her have it. During her lifetime (she died in 1544), she kept the head. Tradition has it that she left it to her eldest daughter, Lady Elizabeth Bray, who died in 1558 (Reynolds, *Field* 381; Albin and Schulte-Herbrüggen).[6] She, "it is assumed" (Reynolds, *Field* 381), placed it in the Roper vault in St.

Dunstan's Church, Canterbury, where it was last viewed in 1837 (Reynolds, Field 381) and 1978 (Albin, "Opening" 31-32). Today what is probably More's skull remains in that church, in a lead box, shaped like the mail coif of chain armor, behind an iron grill in a niche.[7] A tablet set in the floor of the chapel of St. Nicholas reads:

BENEATH THIS FLOOR
IS THE VAULT OF THE
ROPER FAMILY IN WHICH
IS INTERRED THE HEAD OF
SIR THOMAS MORE
OF ILLUSTRIOUS MEMORY
SOMETIME LORD CHANCELLOR
OF ENGLAND WHO WAS
BEHEADED ON TOWER HILL
6TH JULY 1535.
ECCLESIA ANGLICANA LIBERA SIT.

To his account of More's burial, Aubrey adds a word about one of More's descendants. Among "a great many things of value" owned by "Mr. More, of Chilston, in Herefordshire" (214) was More's "Chap, which" was "kept for a Relique" (214). Although this story of a jawbone and other relics of value is suspect to the unreliability of hearsay or tradition, some of it may be true, since it is not unlikely More's descendants might have treasured some of their famous ancestor's possessions.

The remark that " 'tis strange that all this time he is not Canonised, for he merited highly of the Church" (214) is typical of Aubrey, whose religious beliefs were surprisingly liberal considering his times and his aristocratic background. Because Aubrey had no religious allegiances, disapproved of religious controversy and fanaticism, and lamented the Restoration laws that deprived suspected Catholics of civic honors and public preferment (Kite 95-98), his statement about More's religious merits is honest and one of the early expressions voicing the desire for More's canonization.[8]

Aubrey's most memorable, most outrageously funny, story is, of course, about Roper's selection of his bride.[9] Prefaced with the statement, "in his Utopia his lawe is that young people are to see each other stark-naked before marriage," this tale, in which literature shapes life, reduces "all the trouble of wooeing" to "one morning, pretty early when More carrie[d] Sir William into the chamber [where his daughters were asleep] and [took] the Sheete by the corner and suddenly whippe[d] it off" (214). Awakened by this disturbance, the girls, with "their smocks up as high as their arme-pitts," turned over. Roper, having seen both sides, gave one of them "a patt on the buttock," and "made choice of, sayeing, 'Thou art mine' " (214).

Ironically, the concluding sentence of this section, in which Aubrey cites his sources in order to give this story veracity, renders it all the more suspect of fabrication. When Aubrey writes "this account I had from my honoured friend old Mris. Tyndale, whose grandfather, Sir William Stafford, was an intimate friend of this Sir W. Roper, who told him the story" (214), we not only think of the four times it had been passed around, but also of the number of years between sometime before 1521 (the date of Roper's marriage) and when Aubrey first heard it, made it up, or wrote it down.

If this distance of well over a hundred years and the number of storytellers are not sufficient to call this tale's truth into question, the nature of storytelling itself casts further doubts upon it. The art of storytelling cannot be separated from the notion that so-and-so told so-and-so who told so-and-so such-and-such a story. But the problems of passing a story along—not to mention the problems of the storytellers' memories (even those with first-hand knowledge)—are compounded by the additions and subtractions with which they embellish their materials for various audiences. When another story in the *Lives* told by the same "old Mris. Tyndale," Aubrey's "honoured friend" and direct source for this story, is a bawdy one about Dean Overall's lovely wife who "was so tender-hearted that (truly) she could scarce denie any one" (226), our doubts about this story of Roper's choice are augmented.[10]

In addition, certain facts about the association of the Mores and Ropers make this tale untenable. These families had been involved in law at Lincoln's Inn and Westminster for over a quarter of a century. John Roper, William's father, and Sir John More were old friends who often served on commissions together. That one of John More's granddaughters would be matched with his friend's son was to be expected. The year William Roper entered the More household is not certain, but it must have been some time before he married Margaret. Since their marriage took place on 2 July 1521, and since More went to the Tower on 17 April 1534, the opening paragraph of Roper's biography of his father-in-law provides an estimate. As Roper had been "xvj yeares and more in house conversant with" More (Hitchcock edition), Roper probably came to live at Chelsea in 1517 or 1518. In 1518, Roper was admitted to the Society of Lincoln's Inn, and the living arrangement at More's household was convenient for the young law student. During these four or five years, Roper chose Margaret for his bride. Given the marriage customs of the times (Hogrefe 17-21; Warnicke 16-25), that Margaret was More's eldest daughter made it likely that Roper would be expected to choose her before her younger sisters. Although these simple, straightforward facts lack the humor, excitement, and character of Aubrey's anecdote, they supply a more plausible picture of how Roper probably made his choice (or had it made for him).[11]

Filled with facts, half-truths, and fictions—Aubrey's stories of More—what do we make of them? Aubrey's facts, of course, give more proofs of what we already know. Without the appearance of new evidence, to separate the half-truths from the facts and fictions is virtually impossible; but, since these half-truths bear such resemblances to the More we discover in reliable accounts, they are not without value. Perhaps the results of his acceptance of hearsay, the traditions of his times, or his love of creating or passing on "good" stories, his fictions not only add to the lore about More but also to our knowledge of how an individual, some of his contemporaries, and his age viewed More. Hence, Aubrey's character sketch of More commands more attention than what it seems, at first glance, to deserve.

Fort Hays State University

Notes

1. Although the text of *Brief Lives* used in this essay is taken from Dick's edition unless otherwise noted, the notes and texts of Barber and Clark's editions also proved helpful. Kite's dissertation provides the most recent evaluation of the literary and historical merits of the *Lives*. However, since Kite is mainly concerned with the seventeenth-century literary and political figures Aubrey sketches, it is no surprise he fails to mention More.

2. Richard Marius uses this name to speculate upon the notion that the main house may already have been in being when More moved there and that he did not have it built himself (230-31). E. E. Reynolds discusses New Building and other aspects of More's estates in *Saint Thomas More* (185-86), *The Field is Won* (181-82), "More's Manors," "A Right Fair House," and "Butclose." Bernard Basset contributes to the discussion in *Born for Friendship* (138-39), while Germain Marc'hadour transcribes and examines the deed whereby More sold Crosby Place in an article entitled "1966."

3. Estimates vary, but Holbein's portrait, a 1532 letter Erasmus wrote to John Faber, Bishop of Vienna, reports from More's pupil-secretaries and others show that family sometimes included his wife, son and daughter-in-law, three daughters and their husbands, and eleven grandchildren.

4. This passage is taken from Barber's modern English version of *Brief Lives* (213).

5. Albin, Basset, Reynolds, and Schulte Herbrüggen discuss the questions of the burial of More's trunk and the whereabouts of his head, along with the identities of those in the More vault at the Chelsea parish church (which was blitzed in 1941).

6. Schulte Herbrüggen questions this tradition.

7. See Albin and Schulte Herbrüggen for pictures of the vault and grille.

8. Greene argues that More's "authorship of *Utopia* may have played no small part in his ambiguous status among his co-religionists for four centuries" (201).

9. Surtz and Hexter in the notes of their edition of *Utopia* (480) and Wilson are among those who discuss the sources and analogs of the "open-eyed spouse selection" *topos*. In his article, "Baring Some Facts," Charles Clay Doyle adds to this growing list of sources and analogs.

10. Clare M. Murphy makes the same assessment: "The circuitous fashion in which Aubrey claims to have heard the tale, and the mistake in the number of More's daughters, would seem to render this report fictitious even if its unsuitability to More's character did not." Noting that the same story had been told about King Arthur (wrongly—see Doyle, p. 17) as a suitor, she concludes: "Like Aubrey's anecdote, this one has passed through several tellers. Such reoccurrence of a narrative demonstrates that it is a folkloric scenario into which any given narrator may insert whatever actors strike the moment's fancy" (113).

11. For further information about the relationship of the Mores and the Ropers, see Hitchcock's introduction to her edition of Roper's *Lyfe*.

Works Cited

Albin, Hugh O. "Canterbury: More's Head and a More Window." *Moreana* 37 (1973): 51–52.

———. "Opening of the Roper Vault in St. Dunstan's Canterbury and Thoughts on the Burial of William and Mary Roper." *Moreana* 63 (1979): Tome 2, 29–35.

——— and Hubertus Schulte Herbrüggen. "Thomas More's Head Revisited." *Moreana* 78 (1983): 47–49.

Aubrey, John. *Brief Lives* [A modernized English version]. Ed. Richard Barber. Totowa, NJ: Barnes and Noble, 1975.

———. Ed. Andrew Clark. 2 vols. Oxford: Clarendon Press, 1898.
———. Ed. Oliver Lawson Dick. London: Secker and Warburg, 1950.
Basset, Bernard. *Born For Friendship: The Spirit of Sir Thomas More.* New York: Sheed and Ward, 1964.
Doyle, Charles Clay. "Baring Some Facts." *Moreana* 95-96 (1987): 17-19.
Greene, James J. "*Utopia* and Early More Biography." *Moreana* 31-32 (1971): 199-208.
Hogrefe, Pearl. *Tudor Women: Commoners and Queens.* Ames: Iowa State UP, 1975.
"In the Tower of London." *Moreana* 25 (1970): 4.
Kite, John Bruce. "A Study of the Works and Reputation of John Aubrey, with Emphasis on his *Brief Lives.*" Diss. University of California, Santa Barbara, 1977.
Manning, Anne. *The Household of Sir Thomas More.* New York: Dutton, 1906.
Marc'hadour, Germain. "1966." *Moreana* 12 (1966): 107-11.
Marius, Richard. *Thomas More: A Biography.* New York: Knopf, 1984.
More, Thomas. *Utopia.* Eds. Edward Surtz, S. J. and J. H. Hexter. *The Complete Works of St. Thomas More.* New Haven: Yale UP, 1965.
Murphy, Clare M. "On the Women in More's Life: Two Recent Works." *Moreana* 82 (1984): 109-17.
Reynolds, E. E. "Butclose." *Moreana* 59-60 (1978): 5-8.
———. *The Field is Won: The Life and Death of Saint Thomas More.* Milwaukee: Bruce, 1968.
———. "More's Manors and Other Notes." *Moreana* 12 (1966): 81-86.
———. "A Right Fair House." *Moreana* 47-48 (1975): 5-10.
———. *Saint Thomas More.* New York: Kennedy, 1953.
Roper, William. *The Lyfe of Sir Thomas Moore, Knighte.* Ed. Elsie Vaughan Hitchcock. Early English Text Society, Old Series, Vol. 197. London: Oxford UP, 1935.
Stapleton, Thomas. *The Life and Illustrious Martyrdom of Sir Thomas More.* Trans. Philip E. Hallett. Ed. E. E. Reynolds. Bronx, NY: Fordham UP, 1966.
Warnicke, Retha M. *Women of the English Renaissance and Reformation.* Westport, CT: Greenwood, 1983.
Wilson, Katharina M. "Thomas More and Theophrastus—An Idea Put to Work." *Moreana* 67-68 (1980): 35-37.

49 Adelaide Park
Belfast
BT9 6FZ

Dear Father,

Before July 1987 « Moreana » meant very little to me ; it was simply another of my Dad's 'peculiar' hobbies ! Now however it evokes some of my happiest memories.

My stay at number 29 was quite different from any holiday I've had before, but it was one of the most enjoyable and certainly the most enriching.

Meeting you was an experience in itself. I remember being slightly baffled by Elaine and Clare's excitement the night you were returning from England. As you said yourself, one o'clock in the morning is 'a most ungodly hour' to meet someone at a train station. Now that I know you however, I understand just how they felt.

As you know the warmth and hospitality of 'les angevins' have succeeded in enticing me back to Angers for a whole year. I greatly look forward to seeing you again soon.

Je vous embrasse,

Clare Fitzpatrick

MARIALISA BERTAGNONI

Ironia e pietas: *Alcune coincidenze fra* Utopia *e* I promessi sposi*

6 LUGLIO 1535–22 MAGGIO 1873: quasi tre secoli e mezzo dividono le due morti; tragica e prematura la prima, naturale, a conclusione di una lunga vita tranquilla,[1] la seconda (ma non è detto che, se non fosse sopravvenuta la crisi religioso-dinastica, le aspirazioni di More non si sarebbero concretate in una serena longevità simile a quella del proprio padre; né che, messo di fronte ad un'eguale, inderogabile alternativa, il creatore di fra' Cristoforo e dell' Innominato non avrebbe operato la stessa scelta).

Diversi, certo, nella storia personale – e nella personale incidenza nella storia – l'umanista inglese e il romanziere italiano. Ma per alcuni versi anche simili. Per il "cattolicesimo liberale," ad esempio, di cui, a ragione o a torto (e più o meno anacronisticamente), entrambi sono ritenuti rappresentanti; e almeno e soprattutto per una caratteristica: che, entrambi autori di molte opere (Manzoni pubblicò varie tragedie, poesie, saggi di filologia letteraria, di analisi religiosa e di ricerca storica),[2] sono tuttavia correntemente noti per un solo libro: *Utopia* e *I promessi sposi*.

Ed anche questi due libri diversissimi (quanto possono differire una parabola fantapolitica e un "romanzo romantico") hanno molte più cose in comune di quanto si potrebbe supporre. Innanzitutto, il loro stesso carattere: pseudostorico, ma anche saldamente radicato nella storia in un intrecciarsi assolutamente plausibile dei fatti e dei personaggi reali con quelli di fantasia; affidato a un narratore-testimone (il manoscritto anonimo secentesco, "novellamente ritrovato" – come l'isola di Utopia nella prima edizione italiana – nel caso di Manzoni), che non è il solito espediente letterario per dare maggiore credibilità al racconto, ma al contrario (in More come in Manzoni) serve piuttosto a *fingere* di darla, chiamandone complice il lettore, e soprattutto a esprimere con mistificante candore – direttamente o *a contrario* – la propria opinione, o a sottolineare l'assurdità di quella corrente. E poiché l'ambientazione storica delle due narrazioni (almeno ai nostri occhi di posteri) non è molto distante – l'Europa del 1516-1517 come quella del 1628-1630[3] era percorsa da guerre di prestigio e dinastiche, attraversata da eserciti mercenari, devastata da epidemie, governata da intricati machiavellismi, amministrata da leggi tanto minatorie quanto inefficaci – le consonanze nella rappresentazione e nel commento sono frequenti. Espresse dai due autori attraverso una stessa ironia e una stessa *pietas*.

"Emigrant miseri ... e notis atque assuetis laribus ...":[4] la pagina famosa in cui Itlodeo descrive con vibrata commiserazione l'esodo dei contadini dalle chiudende, forzati a lasciare le loro povere cose dall' avidità di "unus helluo inexplebilis" (*CW* 4, 66/11), sembra prolungarsi nell'altrettanto famosa pagina manzoniana dell' "Addio, monti ..." (cap. VIII), che descrive lo stato d'animo di Lucia, costretta ad abbandonare la propria casa e il proprio paese per sottrarsi all'arrogante Don Rodrigo, "sbalzata lontana, da una forza perversa," dai luoghi amati verso un oscuro avvenire. E il doloroso drappello di quei "miseri" – "viri, mulieres, mariti, uxores, orbi, viduae, parentes cum parvis liberis, et numerosa magis quam divite familia ..." (*CW* 4, 66/15-17) – sembra solo precedere di pochi passi quegli altri poveri contadini "scompagnati, a coppie, a famiglie intere, mariti, mogli, con bambini in collo o attaccati dietro le spalle, con ragazzi per la mano, con vecchi dietro ..." (cap. XXVIII) che nei *Promessi sposi* lasciano i loro villaggi devastati dai saccheggi o ridotti alla miseria dalle requisizioni e i taglieggiamenti per la guerra di Successione al ducato di Mantova.[5]

Allo stesso modo, gli immaginari (ma quanto verosimili !) complicatissimi e ingegnosissimi machiavellismi che Itlodeo suppone escogitati dai Consiglieri del re di Francia per suggerirgli "quibus machinamentis Mediolanum retineat, ac fugitivam illam Neapolim ad se retrahat, postea vero evertat Venetos ac totam Italiam subijciat sibi ..." (*CW* 4,

86/26-9)[6] troverebbero i loro più convinti estimatori e più puntigliosi commentatori nei convitati al banchetto di Don Rodrigo che con infiammata saccenteria discettano sulle arti politiche del conte di Olivares, così sottili che "quando accenna a destra, si può esser sicuri che batterà a sinistra": sicché "quelli stessi che devon mettere in esecuzione i suoi disegni, quegli stessi che scrivono i dispacci, non ne capiscon niente," a scorno e scapito di "quel pover'uomo del cardinale di Riciliù" che "tenta di qua, fiuta di là, suda, s'ingegna," ma non riuscirà mai a stanare la preda.

È la saggia opinione di Itlodeo, che avrebbe invece suggerito al re di Francia "omittendam Italiam et domi . . . esse manendum" (*CW* 4, 88/21-2) per accontentarsi di amministrare bene il proprio regno senza mettersi in testa di conquistare gli altrui, è riflessa come in uno specchio (ma con un gioco di duplice ironia che potrebbe essere tipicamente moriano) dai ragionamenti del pusilanime don Abbondio, a guerra terminata, ("Se la prendeva col duca di Nevers, che avrebbe potuto stare in Francia a godersela, a fare il principe, e voleva esser duca di Mantova a dispetto del mondo; con l'imperatore, che avrebbe dovuto aver giudizio per gli altri, lasciar correre l'acqua all'ingiù, non istar su tutti i puntigli. . . . ; col governatore [di Milano], a cui sarebbe toccato a far di tutto, per tener lontani i flagelli dal paese, ed era lui che ce gli attirava: tutto per il gusto di far la guerra") (cap. XXIX)[7]: che, proprio per essere espressi da un pusillanime, e per motivi soltanto egoistici, acquistano un'ironia ancora più pungente, contrabbandando sotto l'aspetto di ottusa incomprensione delle nobili ragioni della gloria militare l'effettiva, tragica futilità di quella gloria.

༄

La "conspiratio divitum" (*CW* 4, 240/20) e la sopraffazione degli umili protagonisti della "storia milanese del XVII secolo" (come recita il sottotitolo dei *Promessi sposi*) muovono dunque i due autori ad un eguale giudizio di moralità offesa, portandoli alla compassione o al sarcasmo. Più divertita, anche se altrettanto netta, l'ironia con cui l'uno e l'altro rappresentano (e giudicano) tutta quella folla di adulatori, arrampicatori e parassiti che pullula intorno ai grandi (o creduti tali) e ne è insieme complice e vittima.

Tutti i lettori di *Utopia* ricordano i convitati del cardinale Morton che fanno a gara nell'approvare le opinioni del giurista, salvo contraddirle non appena si accorgono che non sono condivise dal Cardinale;

che plaudono alla battuta del parassita solo dopo essersi assicurati che anche il Cardinale ne sorride; che si affrettano ad esaltare perché sostenuto dal Cardinale quello stesso provvedimento che tutti erano d'accordo a disapprovare quando lo aveva proposto Itlodeo (CW 4, 80/6-7 e 18-19, 82/21-2, 84/26-9). Quei commensali potrebbero benissimo scambiarsi il posto con i "due convitati oscuri" del banchetto di Don Rodrigo "che non facevano altro che mangiare, chinare il capo, sorridere e approvare ogni cosa che dicesse un commensale, e a cui un altro non contraddicesse" (cap. V), o con quegli altri alla tavola del contezio "i quali cominciando dalla minestra a dir di sì con la bocca, con gli occhi, con gli orecchi, con tutta la testa, con tutto il corpo, con tutta l'anima, alle frutta v'avevan ridotto un uomo a non ricordarsi più come si facesse a dir di no" (cap. XIX).

E la coincidenza nell'invenzione (e nel giudizio) dei due autori si estende anche al principale argomento di conversazione dei convitati. La leggerezza con cui i commensali del Cardinale si fanno assertori dell'impiccagione dei ladri (CW 4, 60-80), mentre quasi sempre era la necessità a spingerli al furto, collima con la vacuità con cui i commensali di Don Rodrigo si fanno zelatori dell'impiccagione per i fornai presunti incettatori del grano (cap. V), mentre la penuria di grano era conseguenza delle devastazioni e le requisizioni della guerra. Si potrebbe quasi scommettere che, se il Cardinale non fosse intervenuto a dar ragione al parere contrario di Itlodeo e, più saggio e più sobrio di Don Rodrigo, non avesse congedato presto i suoi ospiti (CW 4, 84/19-20) e li avesse invece trattenuti per avere la loro opinione sul vino servito a fine tavola, anche il suo convito si sarebbe concluso press'a poco come quello: "Si andava intanto mescendo e rimescendo di quel tal vino; e le lodi di esso venivano, com'è giusto, frammischiate alle sentenze di giurisprudenza economica; sicché le parole che vi s'udivan più sonore e più frequenti erano: *ambrosia* e *impiccarli*" (cap. V).

⁂

Per la sua stessa più ampia struttura narrativa, il romanzo appare spesso quasi una illustrazione o una esemplificazione delle storture che gli utopiani rilevano nei nostri costumi e hanno voluto bandire dalla loro repubblica.

"Leges habent perquam paucas" (CW 4, 194/6) in Utopia, dato che "hoc in primis apud alios improbant populos, quod legum interpretumque volumina, non infinita sufficiunt" (CW 4, 194/7-9); e nei *Promessi sposi* Manzoni si diverte ironicamente a enumerare e a citare per esteso sempre più lunghe, complesse e minatorie "gride" contro i misfatti dei "bravi" e dei loro protettori (o mandatari), la cui stessa *escalation* in prolissità, minacciosità e frequenza è la più chiara dimostrazione di inefficacia (cap. I & III).

Gli utopiani non vogliono avvocati nella loro isola (*CW* 4, 194/12-14), perché questi (come talvolta anche i giudici) (*CW* 4, 92/18-25) con i loro cavilli "nihil minus ac fortuna ipsa summis ima permiscunt" (*CW* 4, 156/26-27): e l'Azzeccagarbugli manzoniano rassicura l'incolpevole Renzo: "All'avvocato bisogna raccontar le cose chiare: a noi tocca poi a imbrogliarle" (cap. III).[8]

L'astrologia e la sillogistica (entrambe onorate e coltivate coscienziosamente nei circoli intellettuali del Cinquecento) sono considerate dagli utopiani con aperta insofferenza. La prima, come un'autentica impostura (*CW* 4, 160/2-6); la seconda, come una capziosa futilità, che More si diverte a ridicolizzare fingendosi stupito che un popolo in altri campi tanto evoluto sia poi così sprovveduto da non aver saputo inventare nessuna di quelle sottigliezze dialettiche che qui da noi sono familiari anche agli scolaretti (*CW* 4, 158/20-29).

Identica è l'invenzione umoristica usata da Manzoni per prendersi gioco delle stesse due discipline (anche se, scrivendo in epoca postilluministica, la sua ironia è più scontata, e non ha la dirompente impertinenza di quella di More) nel personaggio dell' erudito Don Ferrante (cap. XXVII & XXXVII), le cui convinzioni culturali e le cui scelte bibliofile sono descritte attraverso gli apprezzamenti dell'Anonimo secentesco e le candide dichiarazioni del personaggio stesso. Se in Utopia "amicitiam atque errantium dissidia syderum, ac totam denique illam ex astris divinandis imposturam ne somniat quidem" (*CW* 4, 160/2-6), Don Ferrante si riteneva un esperto "d'influssi, d'aspetti, di congiunzioni ... di transiti e di rivoluzioni" degli astri: insomma "de' princìpi ... più certi e più reconditi della scienza" (cap. XXVII); e se More si meravigliava che fra gli utopiani, con tutto il loro sapere, "ne hominem ipsum in communi quem vocant, quamquam (ut scitis) plane colosseum et quovis gigante maiorem, tum e nobis praeterea digito demonstratum, nemo tamen eorum videre potuit" (*CW* 4, 158/26-29), Don Ferrante avrebbe potuto obiettargli quel che egli stesso "più di una volta disse, con gran modestia: che l'essenza, gli universali, l'anima del mondo, e la natura delle cose non eran cose tanto chiare quanto si potrebbe credere" (cap. XXVII).

E nel personaggio di Don Ferrante l'esemplificazione paradossale della cieca fede nell'astrologia e nella sillogistica viene portata, si può ben dire, alle estreme conseguenze. Di sillogismo in sillogismo, di astro in astro, Don Ferrante, al diffondersi della peste, si convince che, non possedendo nessuna delle proprietà di sostanza né di accidente, il contagio non poteva esistere, e che l'epidemia era solo effetto di una congiunzione di pianeti: sicché, stimando inutile ogni precauzione, si era esposto tranquillamente al morbo, e ne era morto "come un eroe di Metastasio, prendendosela con le stelle" (cap. XXXVII).[9]

∽

Nella biblioteca di Don Ferrante non si trova *Utopia*. Sullo scaffale degli statisti, accanto (e in contrapposizione) al *Principe* e ai *Discorsi* di Machavelli, "mariolo sì, ma profondo," egli aveva posto la *Ragion di Stato* di Giovanni Botero, "galantuomo sì, ma acuto" (dove tutta l'ironia è in quei due "ma," che sembrerebbero presupporre l'incompatibilità tra morale e politica), e "quel libro piccino, ma tutto d'oro . . . Lo *Statista Regnante* di Don Valeriano Castiglione" (cap. XXVII).[10]

Ma, nonostante questa grave lacuna (di cui Manzoni è da rimproverarsi o da ringraziarsi?), c'è ancora qualche ragione per concludere con Don Ferrante questo breve (e ben altrimenti lacunoso) *excursus*.

"Uomo di studio, non gli piaceva né di comandare né d'ubbidire." E la moglie, cui rimaneva affidato tutto l'andamento della casa, dopo avere invano tentato di tirarlo dalla sua parte, "s'era ristretta a brontolare spesso contro di lui, a nominarlo . . . un uomo fisso nelle sue idee, un letterato; titolo nel quale, insieme con la stizza, c'entrava anche un po' di compiacenza" (cap. XXVII).

Non c'è un'eco abbastanza familiare, in queste parole, per i lettori di More e dei suoi primi biografi? Forse, ritrovandosi con Manzoni nel Paradiso dei letterati, sir Thomas More e Dame Alice avranno sorriso con lui anche di questa coincidenza.

Vicenza

∽

Note

*I promessi sposi è la storia di due giovani fidanzati, il tessitore Renzo e la filatrice Lucia, abitanti in un paesino vicino al lago di Como, in Lombardia, il cui matrimonio è impedito, alla vigilia della celebrazione, dall'arroganza del nobile Don Rodrigo e dalla pavidità del curato don Abbondio (dove il primo "Don" è la particella nobiliare spagnolesca e il secondo l'attributo del sacerdote), che si piega alle sue intimidazioni. I due fidanzati sono quindi costretti a dividersi e a lasciare il paese; la riunione avverrà dopo varie vicissitudini in cui hanno parte anche il passaggio degli eserciti per la guerra di successione al ducato di Mantova, la sollevazione di Milano e la epidemia di peste del 1630.   M. B.

≈

I promessi sposi (ou *Les Fiancés*) sont un tisserand, Renzo, et une fileuse, Lucia, qui habitent un village près du Lac de Côme. La veille de leur mariage, on annule la cérémonie à cause de l'arrogance du seigneur, Don Rodrigo, et la lâcheté de Don Abbondio, leur curé obséquieux. (Le premier "Don" est la particule nobiliaire en espagnol, le second "Don" s'emploie pour les prêtres.) Obligés de se séparer et de quitter leur pays, Renzo et Lucia finissent par se retrouver après des fortunes diverses, la guerre, et la peste de 1630.
                                                                C. M. M.

≈

I promessi sposi, or *The Betrothed* as the title is usually translated in English, are the weaver Renzo and the spinner Lucia, who live in a village near Lake Como in Lombardy. On the eve of the ceremony, their wedding is cancelled because of the arrogance of the landlord Don Rodrigo and the cowardice of the subservient parish priest Don Abbondio. Forced to separate and leave Lombardy, Renzo and Lucia are eventually reunited after diverse vicissitudes complicated by the war of succession to the Duchy of Mantua, the uprising of Milan, and the plague of 1630.   M.-P. B. & C. M. M.

≈

1. Alessandro Manzoni era nato a Milano il 7 marzo 1785. La sua vita si svolse nell'ambiente familiare, nell'agiatezza, nella considerazione di tutti. Gli unici avvenimenti salienti furono soltanto interiori e familiari : la conversione al cattolicesimo (passata forse attraverso il giansenismo) nel 1810, dopo una giovinezza alquanto dissipata e areligiosa, e la morte della prima, amatissima moglie, Enrichetta Blondel, nel 1833.

2. Le tragedie *Il conte di Carmagnola* e *Adelchi*; gli *Inni Sacri*; alcune poesie ispirate ad avvenimenti storici contemporanei, quali *Marzo 1821* sui primi moti risorgimentali in Italia, e *Il 5 maggio* in morte di Napoleone (con atteggiamento insieme ammirativo e critico); le *Osservazioni sulla morale* cattolica,

la *Storia della colonna infame*, le *Lettere sul Romanticismo*, i saggi *Del romanzo storico* e *Dell'unità della lingua*, etc.

3. La vicenda de *I promessi sposi* ha inizio il 7 novembre 1628, e si conclude nell'ottobre 1630 : un periodo che comprende la guerra di successione al ducato di Mantova e la terribile epidemia di peste che attraversò tutta l'Europa.

4. *Utopia*, Tomo IV, *The Complete Works of St. Thomas More* (New Haven and London: Yale University Press, 1964), 66/15 sgg. Tutte le citazioni seguenti sono date fra parentesi nel testo, *CW* 4.

5. Alla morte di Vincenzo Gonzaga, nel 1527, la successione al ducato di Mantova venne disputata fra i discendenti di due rami della famiglia, Carlo duca di Nevers, sostenuto dalla Francia di Luigi XIII (e di Richelieu), e Ferrante principe di Guastalla, sostenuto dalla Spagna di Filippo IV (e del conte di Olivares). Per l'uno o per l'altro dei due pretendenti si schierarono Carlo Emanuele di Savoia, l'imperatore di Germania Ferdinando II d'Asburgo, papa Urbano VIII e la Repubblica di Venezia.

6. Per tutti i suggerimenti machiavellici del Consiglio del re di Francia, 86/22-88/19.

7. Don Abbondio è il pavido curato che, cedendo all'intimidazione dei 'bravi' di Don Rodrigo, si era rifiutato di celebrare il matrimonio di Renzo e Lucia, costringendo i due giovani fidanzati alla separazione e alla fuga.

8. "Azzeccagarbugli" (=*pettifogger*) è il soprannome coniato da Manzoni per il personaggio di questo avvocato abilissimo a escogitare cavilli per aggirare le leggi a tutto vantaggio dei prepotenti e dei loro scherani.

9. Pietro Metastasio (1698-1782), poeta arcadico autore di molti libretti di celebri melodrammi.

10. Il milanese Valeriano Castiglione (1598-1668) pubblicò il suo libro a Venezia nel 1628, rifacendosi, e quasi compendiandola in cinquanta massime, alla ben più celebre opera di Botero.

Résumé

Bien que différentes, la vie de Thomas More et celle d'Alessandro Manzoni présentent certaines similitudes. En particulier, l'un et l'autre ont écrit de nombreux ouvrages dont un seul a fait connaître leur nom. A l'image de leurs auteurs, ces oeuvres, dissemblables de prime abord, offrent plus d'une analogie. En effet, leur caractère pseudo-historique ne les empêche nullement de s'enraciner dans une Histoire qui ne varie guère d'un récit à l'autre; de plus, on remarque une imbrication des personnages réels avec ceux du mythe et, dans l'un et l'autre cas, un truchement fait appel à la complicité du lecteur; celui-ci ne tarde pas à noter qu'Ironie et *Pietas* alternent chez More et chez Manzoni. Des situations parallèles se rencontrent dans les deux ouvrages. Peut-être, conclut l'auteur, Manzoni, More et sa seconde épouse auront-ils, au paradis des hommes de lettres, souri de ces coïncidences.   M.-P. B.

Summary

Although Thomas More and Alessandro Manzoni wrote voluminously, both their names have been made known by single works, which themselves offer some similarities. Each work has a pseudo-historical blending of real and fictional characters and places, and each presents a narrator who demands the complicity of the reader. Dottoressa Bertagnoni herself concludes by wondering if Manzoni, More, and Lady Alice laugh together in heaven over the resemblances between the two men and the two books.

C. M. M.

Signature of Christopher Columbus

ST. THOMAS MORE SOCIETY,
CONESA 2120, (1428) BUENOS AIRES,

London, July 6th, 1988.

M. l'Abbé Germain Marc'hadour,
ANGERS.

Dear Abbé,

Time seems to fly ! Please accept this short epistle extending our Society's humble congratulations as a tribute to the magnificent work you initiated way back in 1962 at Brussels with the foundation of Amici Thomae Mori, dedicated to promoting the life and works of our illustrious Patron.

In Argentina, every since your visit in 1982 there has developed a growing interest in St. Thomas More in both Spanish and English circles ; many lectures have been organised in this respect. Opportunity is taken to thank you for your many kindnesses during my recent visit to Paris and Angers, where I again had the privilege of meeting members of Amici & your team at 29 rue Volney.

Arthur Petty,
Honorary President.

ANNE LAKE PRESCOTT

Crime and Carnival at Chelsea: Widow Edith and Thomas More's Household

HUMAN BEINGS HAVE ALWAYS FELT a little nervous about jokes, and rightly so, for jokes are both a subversive recourse when we cannot respectably hate or safely dissent and a handy method of repressing those who might hate or dissent from us. Anthropologists understand our ambivalence, as do literary critics, yet we still resist humor that offends us almost as much as the Sorbonne resisted Rabelais or Ben Jonson's Justice Overdo resisted Bartholomew Fair. For example, Linda Woodbridge, the author of a lively and valuable study of women and the English Renaissance, frowns over *The Wydow Edyth*, a collection of twelve "mery gestys" describing in often vigorous if rugged verse the career of a marginally competent petty thief and swindler; they were composed by Thomas More's servant Walter Smith and published in the spring of 1526 by More's brother-in-law, John Rastell.[1] Admitting with some sarcasm that "We shall probably have to accept that these palpable gross jests were very appealing to high-minded Tudor humanists," Woodbridge with some justice calls *Wydow Edyth* "an offensive book, which delights in the disgrace and punishment of one of the most pitiful tricksters of all time."[2] Nevertheless, in this article I will argue that *Wydow Edyth* is more wittily conceived and structured than one might guess from its heartlessness or crudity. Its overtones and playfulness do not diminish the text's seeming "realism," but they do invite us to read Edith as at least partially allegorical and hence, maybe, not merely "pitiful."

She herself is weak; the powers and principalities she represents or serves are strong indeed.

As Woodbridge says, Edith makes a pathetic crook, seldom winning more than a few coins, some clothes, and a bed for the night (although usually without a deluded man in it to keep her company, for despite the frequency with which the widow becomes betrothed this is a curiously chaste book: Edith is often called a whore, but usually after being revealed as a thief, seldom because of some strictly sexual misdoing). On occasion she is discovered and stripped of the garments she has persuaded someone to give or lend her, and sometimes she must leave her bed before dawn to avoid capture. Yet the stories at times seem to hint at something more than Tudor England's problems with rogues, vagabonds, and sturdy beggars. To be sure, the widow may have been in some sense "real." Smith implies that she was, and the 1573 edition's prefatory poem calls these tales "No fayned Stories" (29); the concrete detail and the specificity of the names and places, furthermore, give the impression of actuality. More participated during these years in several plans to diminish crime and vagabondage in and around London, and since Smith lived in More's household his twelve "gests" could derive from what he heard there.[3] Possibly Edith or someone like her did find a way into More's house to precipitate the disgraceful events described in the tenth "gest."

It may be significant, however, that among the book's few characters who remain unidentified as actual people are Edith, her father, and her husband.[4] I suspect that this widow is fictional, or perhaps a composite. If I am right, her true identity is not far to seek, for although as a real woman Edith would be (at least to others) a social nuisance, a symptom of a national economic and moral malaise, as a literary figure she is closely related to the more ambiguous Trickster, a figure of ancient and sometimes even noble lineage. Like her ancestors in myth and jest, she is marginal yet forever threatening to move front and center, cunning, peripatetic, an eiron (witting or not), slippery, mendacious, inventive, polluting the neighborhood not only because of her criminality but because she is in several ways anomalous in status or situation and by her society's definitions always out of her proper place. What chiefly distinguishes her from her more famous analogues, besides her gender, is her ineffectiveness, the frequency with which she is caught (although tricksters can be stupid too), and her more tenuous connection to liminality and transition.

Edith is not, in any case, a mere victim, and indeed this social anomaly is not a widow at all, having deserted her husband. That she is nonetheless *called* a widow comments amusingly on role-playing and on the problematic relationship between our names for things and the nature of the things named. But her "title" also allows Smith to signal a complex of issues concerning widowhood and what it may symbolize. After all, Edith is now far more married to the world and flesh — perhaps, indeed, representing the world and the flesh — than to the bridegroom she left westward in Exeter when she directed her wandering steps to the big city. Does she deserve the compassionate protection of men like More? Even More's Utopian-minded Hythloday might hesitate. St. Paul says that we should honor widows "which are widdowes in dede" (Geneva trans. here *et seq.*), that is to say, genuinely bereft, well behaved, and at least sixty. But the church owes no welfare to younger ones: "for when they have begonne to waxe wanton against Christ, they wil marie, Having damnation, because they have broken the first faith. [Paul does not repressively object to all remarriage; what he fears is a broken promise to be faithful to the dead spouse and to give up the world; faithless widows are in effect 'dead.'] And likewise also being ydle they learne to go about from house to house: yea, they are not onely ydle, but also prattelers and busibodies, speaking things which are not comelie" (1 Tim 5:3-13). Witness Edith, not a true widow in any sense except that she lacks a husband and was brought up fatherless. Luckily, her mother treats her with natural affection:

> Her Mother aye dyd her busy cure,
> As Mothers done by course of nature:
> And vertuously, as I have hard say,
> She brought up her daughter night and day,
> Charging her upon her blessyng,
> That she ne should medle with anything,
> That sowned unto good huswyfry;
> But aye study to forge and lye.... (34)

Edith responds, as a good child should, with loving obedience:

> Mother, she sayde, I am your Daughter,...
> My study shalbe how I may conclude
> In things the people to delude.

And she promises to keep her mother's parting advice:

> Daughter, make mery, whiles thou may,
> For this world wyll not last alway. (34-35)

Smith was not alone in stressing a matrilineal sinfulness; Aretino, Du Bellay, and Buchanan, for example, all found a dark fascination in whorish mothers teaching their daughters to follow suit. Doubtless there are many reasons for this image of bad mothers in a series like disreputable nesting dolls: patriarchal suspicion of the unguided feminine, anxiety about what the sexual "other" is plotting when the masculine back is turned, and so forth. But Smith may also remember the harlot Jerusalem, to whom God says, "Beholde, all that use proverbes, shal use this proverbe against thee, saying, As is the mother, so is her daughter. Thou art thy mothers daughter, that hathe cast of her housband and her children" (Ezek 16:44–45; admittedly, Edith has cast off only her husband, for her child has died). This harlot, who appears in Lamentations 1:1–2 as a widow deserted by her lovers, is thus a bad mother and, like Edith, an oathbreaker—although, being Jerusalem, she will of course be restored and forgiven some day, a fate we can only hope awaits Smith's Widow. To hear such associations as these may be fanciful, yet a number of Smith's details here and elsewhere, while hardly adding up to full-scale allegory, seem to solicit a second look. In this regard, as in others, reading *Wydow Edyth* is not unlike reading *The Canterbury Tales*.

The stories themselves usually repeat the same pattern: Edith's claim to wealth (hers or her fictive daughter's), her willingness to share her own goods and invitation to others to entrust theirs to her, her extraction of a little money, even the promise of marriage, some clothes, next the discovery of her fraud, often for reasons we are not told, then either a fairly brief spell in jail (punctuation, but not a full stop) or flight—unless the flight precedes the discovery—and last the statement that no man knew where she had gone. This almost ritualistic repetition diminishes the book's narrative excitement but completes its satirical and moral argument: Edith's world has one story only—like the carnal world itself, she offers seduction, betrayal, then disappearance. If her winnings are paltry, this well shows how the fruits of our errancy are not worth what they have cost us. As for her victims, they are, as the 1573 edition was to put it in the prefatory poem,

> men and women of every degree,
> As wel of the Spiritual, as temporalitie:
> Lordes, Knights, and Gentlemen also:
> Yemen, Groomes . . . (29)

And all are duped through misdirected longing, for by keeping faith with literary tradition, if not with her gulls, Edith reveals the world's cupidity even as she relies on it for her keep. Smith's own views of crime and disorder are not radical and environmentalist like Hythloday's in *Utopia*, and indeed the injustices examined in Book I of that work cannot explain Edith, but he was far too satirical, too alive to the world's sinfulness, to think Edith's victims innocent; she and her predatory, greedy society deserve each other.

Quitting her husband and home, Edith sets forth on her adventures. Soon, though, she is in turn deserted by the lover who had ("in avoutry" [adultery]) given her a son who died; this widow, Smith may imply, is the opposite of true womanhood, unable to bring forth new life by her husband or by anyone else. Never at a loss, however, she convinces a Wiltshire gentleman that she has a rich daughter, thus furthering one of Smith's recurrent images of fraud and anomaly: the widow with a husband is also the mother of a fiction. Yet her claims are not without overtones, for her frequent pretence that she has given birth to one who will inherit a treasure makes this particularly fallen woman the opposite of Mary, true mother and true spouse. Discovered but unabashed, Edith now moves to Kew, near where, says Smith, the Lord Chamberlain lay. This was Charles Somerset, born the bastard son of the third Duke of Somerset but now Earl of Worcester, whose responsibilities until his retirement in February of 1526 put him in charge of court revels, disguisings, and role playings; perhaps Smith's juxtaposition of Chamberlain and trickster is not accidental.

Edith takes lodging with a poor man, lying about her wealth. Her host is amazed by her condescension and "with his knees flexed" wonders how so great a lady has deigned to visit "this poore cotage" (39). Edith replies that she prefers for a time to keep incognito ("I wil not be kno, / What I am as yet"). Soon the Lord Chamberlain's barber comes to call and hears rumors about Edith's thousand pounds. After greeting her, with a respectful concern inspired by greed and professional curiosity (barbers were also surgeons) he edges closer to examine an ulcer on her chin; Smith identifies it as a *noli me tangere*. Edith is willing to encourage his advances, but she wants no attention to her sore; it is

> A thing (quod she), that I wyll take no great cark
> [i.e., anxiety or care]
> For surgery therto: for I was borne so,
> I thank God whether I ryde or go.
> It doth not greve me otherwise than you see.

And it is no great blemysh, so mote I thee [i.e.,
so may I prosper]. . . .   (42)

Edith is unlikely to prosper with a *noli me tangere* on her chin, for the ulcer is in fact a sort of cancer (or was then thought so) and medical authorities considered it probably fatal, particularly if not treated fast.[5] It results, like most tumors or sores, from an excess of some humor or corruption in the blood trying to make its way out. A different diet (low in salty foods and stressing whatever is cold and moist) would help, as would a more ordered life and, if the sore is in its early stages, a poultice made with lettuce or sorrel juice. Surgery is indicated when possible, but such tumors put down roots and soon cannot be eradicated because the patient would bleed to death. Despite Edith's defiant unconcern, then, the prognosis is not good. Nor is the barber likely to give her the best advice, for he himself does not live well, telling his friend the host that he can eat anything he likes because if he has trouble digesting it "I drinke a little lamp Oyle, and cast up my gorge" (40).

Taken by itself, the name *noli me tangere* would be unlikely to recall ironically the risen Christ's words of warning to Mary Magdalene (John 20:17), for the medical term was fairly common, but Edith's spottedness may have other implications besides the medical (these implications were more readily seen as moral before the discovery of microbes because many diseases, including those visible on the skin, were assumed to be the result of internal imbalance, not of invasion from without; a *noli me tangere* could readily symbolize a hidden spiritual rottenness, whereas modern germs can suggest the enemy "other"). Sores are fairly common in the Bible, falling on those who bear the mark of the beast (Revel. 16:2), causing David's friends to stand well away from him (Psalms 38:11; "plague" in Geneva, "sore" in KJV), and in 2 Chron 6:29 each of God's servants, unlike Edith, will "knowe his owne plague ['sore' in KJV], and his owne disease, and shal stretche forthe his hands toward this house [i.e., the Temple]." Edith refuses, though, to see her sore as a "blemysh." She says she has had it from birth, which while medically implausible is symbolically true of us all, for it is that congenital spot that must be cured before Christ's bride can be brought to him "not having spot or wrincle, or anie suche thing: but that it shulde be holie and without blame ['blemish' in KJV]" (Eph. 5:27). Christ himself is "a Lambe undefiled, and without spot" (1 Peter 1:19); but Edith's sort, "they which counte it pleasure to live deliciously for a season," are themselves blemishes: "Spottes they are and blottes, deliting them selves in their deceivings, in feasting with you, Having eyes ful of adulterie, and that can not cease to sinne, beguiling unstable soules: they have hearts exercised with covetousnes, cursed children, Which forsaking the right waye have gone astraye . . . For in speaking swelling wordes of vanitie [Edith is a great boaster], they beguile with wantonnes . . ."(2 Peter 2:13-18).

Edith's emphatic refusal of medical attention, then, seems symptomatic of a darker spiritual rejection of the cure available in the Temple to which the Israelites turn for help with their sores or from the spotless Lamb for whom we should become "without spotte and blameles" (2 Peter 3:14, cf. Song of Songs 4:7). That there may be something like this implication in Smith's comedy is further indicated by the curious promise Edith makes her host that she will have his roof redone in lead. After Edith has spent time "dalliyng both day and night" with her barber and even while the pair is becoming betrothed "in holy Churche, / Where Christ's workmen do wurche" other workmen pull the thatch of the house down. Why this detail? Perhaps for more trickster comedy and concrete imagery, but perhaps also to echo parodically Mark 2:4, in which a sick man's friends uncover the roof so they can lower him down to be healed by Christ. No, we should not overburden Smith's cheerful verse with pious significance, yet the very arbitrariness of his sharply realized details seems to signal a request for ironic scrutiny.

Having deceived some innkeepers in the London suburbs, Edith meets a priest to whom she confides her plans to become a nun. He is sympathetic, and no wonder, for he has a reputation to keep up:

> A Doctor he was of hie devinytie,
> Called devote and ful of charitie:
> A good publysher of God's word
> In Church and Towne, and sitting at the Bord:
> This world dispising night and day:
> All mundayne glory, he wold saye,
> I wholy defye, and utterly forsake. . . .   (47)

The hypocrite, whose tirelessness in rejecting the world seems all the more suspect for the dinner invitations he apparently accepts, preaches her a sermon lamenting clerical greed for benefices. *He*, however,

> could be wel pleased
> With iiii. such promocions: and hold me wel eased
> As for a certayne time, tyl an other fall . . . .   (49)

Does Edith want to confide in him? "Dispayre not," he assures her, "what so ever the matter bee: / I shall go betwene the Feend and thee." That "betwene" gives one pause. The priest means her to fancy him defending her against Satan, protectively interposing himself, but the reader can also, by rereading "betwene," suspect a reversed sense in which he is an obliging pander or "go-between"; and we can also imagine a threesome moving arm in arm as the greedy divine goes "betwene" his two friends, World holding Flesh holding Devil (or perhaps Flesh, World, and Devil), amicably joined on the roads of England.[6] Either deaf to this irony or understanding it all too well, Edith makes a lying confession to him, telling him of her treasure, and he gives her an equally false absolution: "Ego absolvo te: / Forte sic, forte non" (49). The entire scene is nearly worthy of Chaucer's Pardoner, although *he* would not have lost five nobles to Edith (the doctor believes her when she says he will see them again "within three dayes" [50]). Before leaving him, Edith promises him a scarlet gown and a "nest" of goblets if he will walk with her; it seems appropriate that this diabolically hypocritical priest should befriend a "quean" in possession of scarlet raiment and wine cups (cf. Revel. 17:4).

Next, while walking near the Thames, Edith encounters a husband and wife on pilgrimage, inducing them to dismount "to the cold ground" by acting "as she wold her selfe drownd" (51). She further plays on their sympathy by telling them and some others who hope to help her that she is a potentially rich widow, wronged by a nameless wicked knight but trusting that God will "sende me once a frende"; she would even sell her jewelry to get help in recovering her property (53–54). Like God pitying the faithless Jerusalem who has used her jewels for whoredom and idolatry, but with mixed motives and unconscious of what they are really doing, the widow's new friends clothe her nakedness with fine garments. And, like Jerusalem and other Biblical harlots, when the "arrand quen" [arrant whore] is discovered she is stripped "sterk belly naked" (57) and threatened with dogs (cf. Ezek. 16 and for the dogs see the treatment of Jezebel in 2 Kings 9.36). By now the pilgrims have found both her distress and her purported wealth distracting. Quite so. Hers is a tangled path with no end (not in this world anyway), and it cuts across or blocks the main road. Living a life that is one long digression, Edith is the cause of digression in others, so even after discovering her fraud, her dupe "went to Fullam [upriver from Chelsea] on the next day, / Deferryng his pylgremage to Caunterbery" (57).

This moment in the sequence of tricks makes fairly clear, I think, why Smith gives no geographical design to Edith's wanderings once she is near London: this trickster, whose most reliable technique is to fool other worldlings into thinking her rich, is going nowhere, and those who for a time accompany her go nowhere too. They do move around, for Edith's lies not only fool people for a time but set them into rapid motion on fruitless searches for her wealth or hopeless errands at her request. She is a wanderer who in turn sets the world scampering with misguided pity and desire. That she stays in so many inns, especially in her early and last "gests," emphasizes her fleeting slipperiness and marginality, her typical trickster's preference for the neither-here-nor-there and what a modern authority calls a "peripheral and interstitial pattern of residence," but there is also a moral point to her inability to find a direction, and Smith's impression of very specific but aimless motion from one named town or inn to another can only be deliberate.[7] It also, of course, adds to the work's "realism."

Back in London, Edith cheats a draper and then, during the seventh "gest," something happens to the book's social world. So far, the widow has come to and wandered around London, duping a variety of folk without approaching the great. Now she starts climbing, not unlike one of the little kings saying "regnabo" on Medieval wheels of fortune; she seldom fools the magnates themselves, but she does slip further into their households to hoodwink their servants.

Her first victim in this second part is a servant of Sir Thomas Neville. Neville was a privy councillor and member of Star Chamber who had a town house in Bridewell, near where in 1525 a palace was built for the visiting Charles V; a few years later Edith might have been sent there, for it was soon to become the notorious reformatory. Neville sometimes served as a commissioner of the peace for Surrey, where this "gest" takes place, and in 1517 he had been appointed to investigate enclosures in Middlesex county; one wonders if his homework included Book I of *Utopia*, published the year before. In February of 1525, a year before the probable publication date of Smith's book, he had been put on a commission in charge of searching out "suspicious characters in London" (*DNB*), and was thus one of More's colleagues in the endless struggle to do something about the city's unwanted. Now one of those unwanted has come to him. Once again, Edith plays the mother of an heiress, and Neville merrily reminds his man that he might relish the daughter more than the widow. "By God, sayd the servant," before setting out "joly and amorous" on a Friday, Venus' day, "and peradventure so / I wyll yet doe, when I have seene both" (67). The councillor's worldly humor does not, however, save his household from undesirables.

In a very brief episode, Edith next fools, "with cogging and boastyng," a servant of John Fisher, Bishop of Rochester. She promises him her wealth and her hand:

> On that condition he wolde her wed,
> And keepe her company at boord & in bed. (70)

The young man is "glad and light," thinking innocently—or cynically—that

> I shalbe made a knight
> By the meanes of this gentlewomans store
> Gramercy, Fortune I can no more.

So he arranges "in hast" to be wed, joining

> in one flesh that is dying,
> And two soules evermore livyng.

For once, though, there seems little satire beyond the fun of having Edith near so revered a man as Fisher (it is true that he has a worldly servant, but God himself has those in abundance); one has the impression that Smith hesitated to push his rough-house comedy very far into this particular episcopal household. The episode seems hurried, unlike those set at Chelsea or Hampton Court, and there is something resistant about Fisher's world: the trickster irony decreases precisely because he and even his servant are able to pause before any damage is done, to suspect mere assertion. Thus the servant takes Edith to meet "his Lorde,"

> Before whom they were at accorde
> Upon a condition maryed to be,
> Which condition was, if that she
> Could performe all that she had sayd. . . .
> He wolde then marry her, it should not be delayd.

Edith is already headed for trouble, but it is the threat of an investigative conversation with the bishop, who sends for her "to commen [converse] further," that sends her flying. Edith is a fast talker, but she cannot risk talking to a wise listener. There is a serious point here, for in an earlier jest the victim had handed his goods to Edith "without any interogation" (59). Fisher knows how to delay, how to question. Smith could not then guess what tragedy and triumph that independence of spirit was to bring the bishop, but he knew how to praise it.

Now on and upwards (socially, at least) to the household of the late Earl of Arundel, dead in 1524, where for a time the earl himself is deceived by lies about a rich daughter. And thence (after being yet once more stripped "of her array: / Walke, hore, they all gan say," 74) to Chelsea and the household of the famous and increasingly powerful Thomas More, recently settled in; we may deduce this chronology, I think, because Arundel is alive in the ninth jest and More's family did not complete the move to Chelsea until the second half of 1524.[8] Here, says Smith smoothly, "she had best cheare of all" (75).

Once installed, Edith beguiles three servants including, we hear after some teasing postponement, none other than Walter Smith. The others serve Masters Alington and Roper. It seems appropriate that this text should acquire self-referentiality at just this point with just this family, headed by a man who despite his recent turn to angry polemics was still well known for merry tales, practical jokes, and ironic paradoxes with self-reflective and infinite regression. More himself does not appear, which may hint that in the absence of his patriarchal guidance the World and its deceptions can infiltrate even his domestic school of virtue. Or maybe Smith simply wanted to detach his master from what follows, from comic but dirtying mess. At first all goes well, Edith lying as usual about her wealth. But her lies, to my perhaps over-receptive ear, suggest not only plenty but Adam's curse, a world of almost frantic work and bustle, unlike the golden festive world of Chelsea (festive, that is, in this particular story): she has, she says, two looms, two mills "that went night and day," a busy brewery, four plows, fifteen great knaves, and seven woman servants to spin, card, and milk (76). The three young men are "cast in a heat" just listening and compete in courting her. One of them stands so close behind her at supper that "if she had let a crack / Never so styll, he must have had knowledge; / But all is honycombe, he was in such dotage" (77). Not an elegant way to indicate affection but a good introduction to the story's impressive scatology. This scatology is not directed exclusively at Edith, who indeed collaborates with it when she "let[s] a great fart" in the lap of William Roper's servant Thomas Arthur, saying, "And I loved you not . . . I wold not geve you this" (80). Thus when Smith praises Thomas he stops himself in mid-eulogy and says, "Peace, no more! he standeth at my backe; / And yf he here me praise him, he wil we[n]e I flatter" (78). Coming hard upon the description of the fart-sensing wooer at Edith's back, the equation of flattery and flatulence is amusingly clear.

After some quiet inquiries Alington's servant Thomas Croxton discovers Edith's dishonesty. Unlike some of her earlier victims who merely grab off her borrowed clothes and shout insults, he controls his temper and "kept al this within his owne brest, / Because his felows should not at him jest" (80). Edith guesses, perhaps, that something is wrong, for when she asks him why he keeps glancing at her he replies in words with considerable resonance, "on this world, I think." Edith's solution for too much thinking about the world is just what the World itself would advise: "Tut, a straw! quod she; take the cup and drink" (80). The next day Smith himself proposes to her; whatever the real sources of his love, his proposal is sweet, pious and naive:

> And yf ye can finde in your hart to love me
> As wel, sweet darlyng, as I love you,
> Than I trust there shalbe such seeds isow
> Betwixt us both, that it shalbe principally
> To Gods pleasaunce and to our comfort secondly.

When the widow asks the "yong woer" if he really means it he promises her a gold crucifix "for a token and a remembrance" (83). Walter may be just a little confused himself about what the crucifix is meant to make us remember (not unlike, say, the ambiguous love tokens of the Prioress and the Monk in *The Canterbury Tales*), but we may assume Edith will know what to do with it.

Soon Thomas Arthur returns with the news that Edith is a crook. More's household does not get upset; it plots revenge. The revenge is singularly appropriate: the family's perimeter, so to speak, has been breached by trickery so that seductive worldly falsehood could have passage in. What better response than to open up the perpetrator's own perimeter so as to dirty the dirt-bringer against her will? But Smith does not merely show us a trickster tricked, for the scene incorporates carnival elements as well.[9] He sets the scene at Sunday supper, a communal gathering on a feast day: "To Chelsay againe she came the same night, / But than the world was changed; al was cum to light." As in a carnival, "her dyet was chaunged"—but not with fat food. Rather, "Her potage and eke her ale were well poudred / With an holsome influence" (some might hear a possible pun on "holesome"): a laxative and purgative medication that makes her "greatly mistempered, and far out of frame."

> All that sate at Supper had good game
> Her to behold, and they laught all aboute.
> Quod she: for Goddes love let me come out;
> Let me come, let me come, for our Ladies sake;

My belly rumblyth, and my hart doth ake. . . .
But she was ay kept in, that she could not start,
Tyll my Lady [Dame Alice More] gan to have
pytie in her hart,
And for womans honestie, bad that she should
ryse. . . .   (84)

Edith races to the privy, leaving a trail behind her and creating such steam that a servant thinks the place on fire. The poor woman even gets a nosebleed. Edith's "lodging" is also "changed" and as she does a three-week stretch in jail, her clothes are removed to be "restored to the owner," and "w[h]ere gret Estats [persons of importance and power] were chaynes about theyr necks, / She had dis[d]ayne to were them on her legs," another image of reversal, one that reverses the customary pattern of misrule in which the lowly for a time take on the trappings of authority (86). In *Utopia*, More had mocked the chains of office (CW 4.154), but Smith's concluding irony is even more complex and considerably crueller: the irons Edith wears are displaced downward from statesmen to crook, from neck to legs, but not — from the victim's point of view — in a festive or tricky undoing of authority. The irony (a sad one for radicals from Hythloday on) is that her chains really are those of authority, the authority that has immobilized her in prison more firmly than her mockers at Chelsea had penned her in at the dinner table before Alice More pitied her. Thus in one sense the reversal is no reversal at all, but a revelation of how the king's law that threatens to hang about our legs is the same law that hangs in golden ambiguity around the necks of the king's great men.

Edith's punishment, however, remains also a revision and inversion of Carnival's rough justice, at once a purgation (of Edith's body and of the domestic society she infects) and a comic twist on the usual relationship between the shifty trickster and the stable world of political and social rules.[10] Poor Edith. Mobile con artist among respectable if greedy gulls, she goes to one of the most famous households in the kingdom and finds herself defeated *in her own terms*. Tricking her way into the home of a man famous for learning, piety, and virtue, her normal course of action as a paler and cleaner Tyl Eulenspiegel would be to bring disorder, upending, and perhaps even a trace of Bakhtin's "lower bodily stratum." Instead, she discovers that More's household already had that kind of wisdom too: it is festive as well as Utopic, whether because of More's influence or thanks to his absence, and it can outfox the devious and deviant, outjest the eiron.[11] In other words, Edith's generic being as well as her body are humiliated in a household that claims both the official and the subversive or serpentine worlds. Poor Edith indeed, for if Chelsea as seen from within is all the more attractive for combining the marginal and central, the tricky and the honest, the riotous and the lawful, when seen from without its very totality and faintly self-congratulatory inclusiveness render it both impervious to lasting penetration or subversion and, in a curious way, oppressive (not dialogic but omnilogic), closed to a transformation it considers unnecessary. Smith's humor, like his treatment of vagabondage, finally serves a vision less challenging and skeptical than More's own had once been and perhaps still was.

What saves Smith's Chelsea from being merely smug in its punitive festivity, though, is the cheerful admission that Edith had, for a time, managed to dupe all but the (presumably) absent More himself. The tenth "gest" is thus both self-referential and self-implicating. This is, I think, important, for Smith admits that trickery, delusion, the marginal and parasitic can enter even here. The trickster is not just that "other" in other peoples' houses but may sometimes be among ourselves, may even be inside ourselves. It is this awareness that allows Smith's book to be what some have called the Trickster and his world: a *speculum mentis* reflecting the world within and without.[12] Is the episode in any sense liminal or initiatory? Smith had not read Victor Turner or Paul Radin but it still seems somehow right that this scatological moment should happen, if my chronology is correct, fairly soon after the More household had finished its slow move to a new location.[13]

The comic harshness of Chelsea's rude justice is modified, furthermore, by the compassion that Alice More eventually shows her desperate guest. The "pytie in her hart" (84) bespeaks a depth not found in the boisterous young servants (as Smith had read in Chaucer, "pitee renneth soone in gentil herte"), and her concern for "womans honestie" indicates not only a lady's decorum but a sense of feminine kinship. It is refreshing to find Dame Alice behaving with command and dignity. Smith might have hesitated to have her act otherwise, for she was, after all, his master's wife. Still, not everyone in More's circle was so admiring. Dame Alice, the respectable married widow, is in some ways a perfect foil for Edith the disreputable invader and disrupter. Although presumably fooled for a while herself, she presides over the family feast with prudent watchfulness, indulging misrule until charity and a sense of what is fitting require her to overrule it. She exemplifies, Clare Murphy suggests to me, the wife of Proverbs 31 who "stretcheth out her hand to the poore, and putteth forthe her hands to the nedie. . . . She overseeth the waies of her housholde, and eateth not the bread of ydlenes" (vv. 21, 27; one might add that her husband—like More—"sitteth with the Elders of the land," v. 23).

Was More amused by *Wydow Edyth*? Probably so. He had married a (genuine) widow himself, after all, and, as Germain Marc'hadour has reminded me, widows were to play a part in his polemic: on several occasions he cites the passage from 1 Tim. 5 on widows. In the *Dialogue Concerning Heresies* (1529) Paul's words support some bitter mockery of Tyndale's views on marriage and More quotes them again in explaining how to read the statement "Faith without works is dead" (*CW* 6.306; 386). Here and in the 1533 sections of the *Confutation* (*CW* 8.404; 413; 716) the passage serves arguments concerning interpretation, the nature and role of faith, and clerical marriage as infidelity. But More might also have taken pleasure in seeing a jestbook version of his own interest in the marginal, the mobile and displaced. He was, as I have said, officially concerned by now with vagrancy and undesirables (hence his servant's clever mischief in introducing Edith into Chelsea, whether the episode is fictional or not); and of course Book I of *Utopia* explores the causes of criminal wandering even as Book II immobilizes the potentially deviant with a few good laws (including prohibitions against pointless travel), social engineering, and, as a penultimate resort, enslaving chains that merge into one symbol: irons like those Edith wears in jail, the coin cherished by worldlings like her victims, and the signs of office or status around the necks of men like More. Some would call Richard III a trickster, and More himself has been linked by one recent and very clever critic to the same marginal and parasitic energies or negations that with another part of his imagination he thought dangerous.[14] And, of course, More had some years earlier written a lively poem about role playing, deception, and the trickster tricked: "A mery gest how a sergeaunt wolde lerne to be a frere." So I doubt very much that he dismissed his servant's "mery gestys" as idle entertainment with nothing for a witty and learned statesman to examine and laugh at beyond the popular comedy that appealed to everyone.

Where can the widow go after Chelsea? Who is even more important than More? Edith now moves to the palace of Cardinal Wolsey and the usual pattern reasserts itself, from deception to discovery and disappearance ("but no man can tel, / Where she is become, with walk queane walk . . . the feend be her gyde!" 91). And then . . . from a privy councillor to a learned bishop, to an Earl, to the celebrated Thomas More, to Cardinal Wolsey, second man in the kingdom, to. . .?

Exactly. One might expect some attempted trickery in at least the lower reaches of the royal household, but after thus clearly gesturing at the pinnacle and center of the kingdom, Smith suddenly reverses direction, sending Edith tumbling down, in this mirror for magistrate-troublers, to bilk a mere innkeeper, flee, and now roam to no one knows where, still ahead of the law, still on the move: "God save the Wydow, whereso ever she wende" (108). Edith is back where she started: her epic twelve chapters or *gesta* are, after all, merely a minimally patterned calendar—if even that; in them we see only the perpetual motion of a circling world that goes nowhere, at least not yet. Perhaps further rotations will for a time bring Edith back up, though, for this widow we always have with us.

Smith's book is thin stuff in some ways and one could wish that he had had more compassion for rogues and vagabonds, a more radical understanding of why a woman might leave her husband and take to the road, but in its structure, its irony, and its Chaucerian use of symbolic or symptomatic detail, *Wydow Edyth* is ingenious. And Smith's compliment to More's family, far from merely vulgar, is both disquieting and profound.

Barnard College
Columbia University

Notes

This article elaborates a paper read at the Columbia Renaissance Seminar in 1986 and, in a revised version, at the 1987 Sixteenth Century Studies Conference.

1. Rastell gives the publication date of *The Wydow Edyth: .xii. mery gestys of one callyd Edyth* as March 23, 1525. Since this was before Easter, we may probably read 1526; see Germain Marc'hadour, *L'Univers de Thomas More* (Paris: Vrin, 1983), p. 363. Nothing in my argument depends on either date, but 1526 would make a few of Smith's ironies less tightly timed. I have not examined the 1525/6 edition. The 1573 edition with the 1525/6 variants is in *Shakespeare Jest-Books*, ed. W. C. Hazlitt (London, 1864), III; my page references cite it. On Smith see A. W. Reed, *Early Tudor Drama* (London: Methuen, 1926), chapter 6. Reed stresses Chaucer's influence (Smith's will left "Chauscer of Talles and Boccas" to John More; see p. 154) and identifies

many of the characters. For the "real" people in the jestbook I have relied on Reed and the *DNB*. Reed does not describe the scene at Chelsea, saying only that the reader will "learn . . . things that are not suggested in Roper, but may not be the less true for all that" (p. 153). See also Fernando Ferrara, *Jests e Merry Tales: Aspetti della narrativa popolaresca inglese del sedicesimo secolo* (Rome: Edizioni dell'Ateneo, 1960), pp. 70–80.

I have modernized j and i, u and v, and expanded a few contractions. When quoting the Bible I have used the Geneva version of 1560 – Protestant, to be sure, but available in modern facsimile and preserving the diction of Smith's time better than does the King James or the Douai.

2. "New light on *The Wife Lapped in Morel's Skin* and *The Proud Wife's Paternoster*," *ELR* 13 (1983): 35.

3. See J. A. Guy, *The Public Career of Sir Thomas More* (New Haven: Yale University Press, 1980), p. 13. Smith's "realism" need not preclude literary mediation; "realism" has its own traditions. One small example: Ferrara, p. 72, credits to Smith's powers of everyday observation the moment when Edith enters a room and the hostess "therewith . . . drove the Cat of the borde, / And made rome for a dish or two more." Yes, but in Chaucer's *Summoner's Tale* a friar enters a house where he expects good cheer and a little easy money: "And fro the bench [table] he droof awey the cat." Anyone who lives with cats spends some time shoving them around, but clearly Smith remembers Chaucer quite as much as actual felines.

4. My understanding of the Trickster derives primarily from Paul Radin, *The Trickster*, with commentaries by Karl Kerenyi and C. G. Jung (1972 ed., New York: Schocken Books); Mary Douglas, *Purity and Danger: An Analysis of Concepts of Pollution and Taboo* (1970 ed., London: Penguin Books); and Barbara Babcock-Abrahams, " 'A Tolerated Margin of Mess': The Trickster and his Tales Reconsidered," *Journal of the Folklore Institute* 11 (1975): 147–86. Less immediately relevant but helpful theoretically are Warwick Wadlington, *The Confidence Game in American Literature* (Princeton: Princeton Univ. Press, 1975), 3–23, and Carroll Smith-Rosenberg, "Davy Crockett as Trickster: Pornography, Liminality, and Symbolic Inversion in Victorian America," in *Disorderly Conduct: Visions of Gender in Victorian America* (New York: Knopf, 1985), 90–108. Edith differs significantly from traditional tricksters like Hermes, Loki, or the Winnebago Wakdjunkaga, though: she is female, not supernatural or legendary, and has little generative or salvific potential beyond the inadvertent or parodic. Not on the Trickster himself but for a relevant discussion of liminality see in particular Victor Turner, *The Forest of Symbols* (Ithaca: Cornell Univ. Press, 1967), Chapter 4 ("Liminality may perhaps be regarded as the Nay to all positive structural assertions, but as in some sense the source of them all . . . ," p. 97) and *The Ritual Process* (Chicago: Chicago Univ. Press, 1969), Chapter 3. Many of the characteristics Turner applies to liminal *personae* do not appear in Edith because liminality is only part of her job as a character and she is not involved in collective rituals, but her mobility, taste for disguise, poverty, and frequent nakedness take on a new meaning in view of his discussion.

5. Peter Lowe, *A discourse of the whole art of chyrurgerie*, 1634, especially sigs. F2 and I2v. Lowe writes more than a century after Smith but uses traditional authorities.

6. My thanks to my Columbia colleague, Howard Schless, for noting that "go betwene" also suggests pandering.

7. Babcock-Abrahams, 155.

8. Marc'hadour, *Univers*, 347; the 1524 move took some time and was over by October at the latest. Smith's word "servant" need not mean a menial, and in any case even in important households the "upstairs/downstairs" division was less rigidly drawn at meals than in later centuries.

9. The current starting place for thinking about carnival is of course Mikhail Bakhtin's seminal *Rabelais and His World*, trans. Helene Iswolsky (Cambridge, Mass.: M. I. T. Press, 1968). About his historical generalizations I nevertheless have many reservations. Indeed, *Wydow Edyth* in its small way indicates the difficulty of defining the genuinely "popular" in the early sixteenth century and of separating the festive and official worlds.

10. Tricksters, needless to say, are scatological too. For an exemplary study of scatology, irony, and trickery see Wayne Rebhorn, "Jonson's 'Jovy Boy': Lovewit and the Dupes in *The Alchemist*," *JEGP* 79 (1980): 355-75.

11. Bakhtin and others sometimes speak of carnival as "utopian," but despite carnival's comic dreams of egalitarian plenty or utopia's satirical images of reversal, and despite shared sources in the imagination of hope and play, the two seem to me finally quite distinct. The former's fertile milling disorder, festive mocking indecency, and ambiguous disguisings are worlds away from most utopias' sharply linear arrangements, abstract rationality, clarity, and concern for justice—ironically presented though these may be.

12. Radin, xxiv.

13. The tenth "gest" is intriguingly unlike an episode with More and a trickster in *The life and pranks of Long Meg of Westminster* (1635), sig. C1. We hear of a dinner with guests including More and Skelton at which the host, a knight from Spain (thus doubtless proud, inviting humiliation), has just lost a fight with a "desperate gentleman." More kindly reminds him that even Caesar tasted defeat. When the "gentleman" enters and literally lets her hair down to reveal her gender, the abashed Spaniard must join in the general laughter as Meg is made "master of the feast." The passage includes More, I assume, because of his reputation for jesting. The narration, unlike Smith's, is self-consciously jolly and distanced from the events it recounts; the reversals are merry but unproblematic and the atmosphere relaxed with no darker tones. Jackson Boswell quotes the episode extensively in his forthcoming collection of STC Moreana; my thanks to him.

14. John Perlette, "Of Sites and Parasites: the Centrality of the Marginal Anecdote in Book I of More's *Utopia* [i.e. *CW* 4.80]," *ELH* 54 (1987): 231-52.

S. J. HOUSE
7-1 Kioicho, Chiyoda-ku
Tokyo, 102 Japan
TEL. (238) 5111 Information.

S. J. ハ ウ ス
〒102 東京都千代田区紀尾井町7-1
電 話 (238) 5 1 1 1 受付

November 10, 1987.

Dear Father Germain,

    Let me begin by congratulating you on the Silver Jubilee of *Moreana* and your own editorship of that great little journal. Can it be really twenty-five years since you brought out its first issue ? No, I can't believe it. But yes, I have to face the fact. Still, as Shakespeare puts it so well -- in his inimitable manner -- « To me, fair friend, you never can be old. »

    First, let me emphasize what I regard as the distinctive feature of *Moreana* among all the academic journals of today's world. It is not so much the assemblage of learned articles listed in the table of contents, such as appear in almost all academic journals. No, it is rather the array of odds and ends, bits and pieces, that look like space-fillers to prevent any gaps in the pages, as it were following on the opening editorial handwritten and signed by yourself. It is such glosses and comments that, in my opinion, constitute the essence of *Moreana* and make it the appropriate organ -- I almost said mouth-organ -- for the *Amici Thomae Mori*. Other journals are all too often merely academic, parading that knowledge which (as St. Paul says) merely puffs up ; but this journal has its knowledge suffused with the charity that edifies. And it is in all these little titbits that its charity most appears.

    Now let me say a little more about the source of that charity. I may say I first encountered it in the very home of *Utopia*, Bruges, in the fifth centenary year of Thomas More, 1977, when you came to that great little city to give an unforgettable talk to my Japanese group on « Thomas More and Bruges ». I am afraid I have quite forgotten the contents of that talk ; but I can never forget the way you spoke in such intimate and loving detail of all the people connected in any way with Thomas More. For as your interest in him is a deeply personal interest, so you extend this interest in an equally personal way to everyone else, till all are somehow united in an invisible network of charity -- like the « communion of saints ».

I again encountered it here in Tokyo, whither you came the following year in the course of what seemed a whirlwind world tour ; and you gave another talk here at Sophia University to the members of the Thomas More Association of Japan, under Professor Sawada. Again I quite forget the contents of your talk -- a fate that seems to attend all the talks I attend ! -- but I remember the lecture-room here (on the fifth floor of our tower building) and the restaurant to which we subsequently adjourned, as vividly as if it all happened yesterday. Or rather, what I remember are not so much the places as your personality and your way of speaking that filled the places with your sweet charity.

I encountered it yet again when I happened to be in the city of Washington (D.C.) in the spring of 1982, and you unexpectedly turned up, to give a lecture to a group of *Amici* in the capital. Then I was unexpectedly invited by you to make a minor contribution to the occasion -- I only remember it was some kind of translation you asked me to produce on the spur of the moment. It was a privilege, and a pleasant surprise.

Lastly, I encountered it, after all these various places around the world, at your home base in Angers this very summer, when I brought yet another Japanese group on a Renaissance tour « in search of the Middle Ages ». How well we found what we were searching for, when we met you and enjoyed your warm hospitality -- in whom the mediaeval-Renaissance spirit of Thomas More lives on so vividly ! There we were happy to meet your co-workers, Clare and Elaine, to look round your offices in the rue Volney, and above all to concelebrate Mass with you in that little chapel, where we were united in the memory not only of Thomas More but also of his divine Master who at the last supper gave us his new commandment of charity : « Love one another ! »

Such are the memories that come crowding in on my mind, as I pen (or rather type) these few words of congratulation to you -- and through you to Thomas More -- and through Thomas More to Our Lord himself. So may God bless you and keep you actively involved in *Moreana* -- even in your retirement -- for at least another twenty-five years, so that you may celebrate another, Golden Jubilee ! *Ad Multos Annos* !

Peter Milward, S.J.
Sophia University,
Tokyo.

Since Father Milward presented a paper at "A Scholar for All Seasons: a Renaissance Colloquium in Honor of Germain Marc'hadour," the two had still another meeting--at the University of Rhode Island, November 18 and 19, 1988.

...and filled them with longing
for a peace that would last
and for a justice that would never fail.

V a peace...and a justice

...et tu l'as rempli
d'une aspiration ardente
après une paix qui dure
et une justice qui jamais ne faillirait.

15a Haroun Street
Dokki
Cairo
Egypt

Oct. 24, 1987.

Dear Father Marc'hadour,

Now that the second edition of the Arabic translation of *Utopia* is out, I feel that it should be put on record that without your constant encouragement and generous assistance, the only Arabic translation of *Utopia* so far might have never seen the light.

I recall how you kindly sent me a copy of *Moreana* and invited me to join the *Amici Thomae Mori* when you first heard, through Professor Mahmoud Manzalaoui, of my intention of embarking on the project of translating More's masterpiece into Arabic.

Not only did you continue to send me *Moreana* even when, for some reason or other, I did not pay my subscription, but you also continued to enquire about the progress of my work and, in a truly scholarly spirit, to provide me with more valuable material.

As you may remember, it took me years to make the final effort of completing the job, which was repeatedly put aside for more urgent, and lesschallenging commitments. The translation of the two last thirds of the book, I confess, was largely the result of a sense of shame at having had repeatedly to answer your enquiries by making some kind of excuse for my lack of progress.

Through reading *Moreana* and many of the articles and books written by you and other *Amici* scholars, my interest in and knowledge of Thomas More have increased. Without this, I might have never ventured into the field of Morean scholarship -- however modestly -- my own field of specialization being the modern utopian novel.

Joining the *Amici* at your invitation, participating in More conferences in Angers and London, and making friends with a number of Morean Amici, I've had an enriching influence introduced into my life.

Your own passionate and scholarly devotion to Thomas More and your friendly concern for all the Amici have been, since I had the pleasure and privilege of knowing you, a subject of wonder, admiration and great respect.

May you continue the good work for many many years to come.

Yours sincerely,
Angele B. Samaan

Angele B. Samaan

DAMIAN   GRACE

Utopia: *A Dialectical Interpretation*

I N A FINE STUDY OF MORE'S "genius for dialogue," Germain Marc'hadour has shown how this capacity draws from both the character of its exponent and his education in humanism and the law.[1] This is the More "born for friendship" whose dialogues are conducted in intimate, civil and persuasive conversation, qualities often denied him in controversies of a more public and intense nature. It is to this subtle, beguiling More that we must attend, in the spirit of Abbé Marc'hadour, if we are to grasp the meaning of so compact a text as Utopia.[2] This paper essays such a reading suggesting that the tactical ambiguities and paradoxes characteristic of Utopia make it dialectical in a sense understood by its immediate audience, and productive of a wide variety of interpretations since.

The puzzles of Utopia extend from the lexical to the formal. The names of the island, its places, cults, and officials have elusive etymologies;[3] the topography and demography are specified in contradictions;[4] a favourite authorial device is litotes;[5] and in form, the book is a combination of dialogue and discourse. The author places himself inside the text, both as interlocutor and narrator, and yet remains the creator of the whole. And, if we follow Hexter's brilliant reconstruction of the composition of Utopia, it appears to be the result of at least two sets of intentions, which correspond roughly to Books I and II.[6] The wise traveller, Raphael Hythlodaeus, is a Portuguese yet possesses a fittingly Utopian name,[7] perhaps to indicate that Utopia is not so far from Europe as might be supposed. His journey to an antipodean Nowhere lies somewhere between the voyages of discovery of Vespucci and the interminable navigations of the ships of fools, yet the book's parerga invite favourable comparison with Plato.[8]

The response of the interpreter to these ironies and ambiguities is also a response to the politics of Utopia. It may be viewed as a conventional critique of the issues of the time wedded to a *jeu d'esprit*, calculated perhaps to win preferment for the author with the reform-minded Cardinal Wolsey;[9] or as a radical critique of nascent bourgeois society anticipating a Marxist solution in the common ownership of property;[10] or as a warning against idealism, rationalism and the abuse of God's providence;[11] or, most recently, a methodologically sophisticated imitation of a Greek best-commonwealth exercise.[12] Such variety should be something of a critical scandal, for Utopia manages quite well to accommodate all manner of contrary readings. It is a mirror not only of aspects of early sixteenth century Europe, but of the social, religious and political views of later interpreters. Its curious open-endedness invites readers to join issue with Hythlodaeus at the conclusion of his discourse. More does not deny us that opportunity by foreclosing: Utopia remains, in the coinage of K. J. Wilson, an "incomplete fiction."[13]

In order to appreciate the nature of this open-endedness, it is necessary to identify the problems with which More was concerned as he wrote his *libellus*. The obvious place to look is Book I, even though its critique of Europe has long worn the burnish of familiarity.

Book I contains two dialogues, one within the other. The outer dialogue recounts a conversation amongst Raphael, Peter Giles and Morus during the latter's visit to Antwerp in 1515. Raphael's widely informed conversation prompts Peter to ask why he does not become counsellor to some king and thereby bring profit to himself, his friends and relations, and, not least, to the commonwealth. Raphael replies with a stinging attack on the foolishness of kings and courtiers, thus raising the problem of good counsel in a wicked world (55–59). This problem is illustrated in Raphael's account of a conversation at the table of Cardinal Morton, itself replete with a variety of topics and sub-themes.

This inner dialogue begins with Raphael challenging the views of a lawyer who is puzzled that the strict punishments for theft have not reduced its rate. Raphael denounces capital punishment for property crimes as too harsh, and proceeds to an analysis of social decay which relates crime not to personal fault so much as to structured abuses.

Eventually all evils will be identified as the progeny of pride (243), but here Raphael argues that sin is the consequence, not the proximate cause, of social abuses.

Stealing is shown to be the only course open to increasing numbers of people who have no other means to secure a livelihood. Many of them have been maimed in wars, and being now useless for their former occupations, must beg or steal to get by. Yet, as Raphael remarks, "You never have war unless you choose it" (65/32–33). The problem lies in persuading belligerent rulers that they and their kingdoms are better served by renouncing violence (89–91).

To the hardships imposed by war must be added those of idleness in peace. The retinues which mark the status of noblemen produce nothing of value to society, and are not fitted by training or habits of life to do so. When their masters have no use for them or they fall sick they swell the numbers of vagrants, beggars and robbers (63). Nor are these the only sources of social blight. High prices for fine wool have led an oligopoly of rich men – "noblemen, gentlemen, and even some rich abbots" – to buy up their neighbours and dispossess their tenants so that farm land might be enclosed for pasture. Whole families whose livelihood depended on tillage are thus forced from their useful occupations into penury, beggary and crime. They are gaoled for vagrancy or hanged for theft, but they cannot follow the callings which they know. To their number are added spinners and weavers who cannot afford to buy expensive wool, the more valued because of its scarcity and the control of the market by the oligopoly. The same class has been using agistment as a means of making quick profits, waiting for high prices before selling fattened cattle. So food prices rise, servants cost more to feed and their employers dismiss them to join the ranks of the vagrants and thieves. Meanwhile, others are ruined in the pursuit of luxury and must rob to pay their debts (67–69). So it is that vice and crime are products of the social environment, brought about by the misrule of the few to the ruin of many.

It is through the few, then, that social evils are to be mended. Enclosers and farm-wreckers must be made to restore what they have damaged.[14] The right of the rich to control commodities must be limited. Idleness must be curbed, and farming and cloth-working encouraged. These are the proper remedies for crime, vagrancy and poverty, not harsh laws which exact the ultimate penalty. "Such justice," says Raphael, "is more showy than really just or beneficial" (71/10–11).

Morton is impressed rather than offended by Raphael's analysis and silences the lawyer as he begins an inflated reply. What lesser penalties, asks the Cardinal, are appropriate to crimes of property if even death is no deterrent? This is an extremely odd question to raise after Raphael's extended discussion of the causes of crime: it shifts the whole matter back to regulation through punishment rather than the reformation of law and society. Raphael replies with an attack on capital punishment which argues from classical authority (73/15-21), utility (75/5-15), but most tellingly from Scripture. This is the first of the two occasions in Book I where Raphael gives classic moral summations of all that is wrong in the commonwealth. The death penalty exemplifies socially sanctioned deviations from God's law.

> God has withdrawn from man the right to take not only another's life but his own. Now, men by mutual consent agree on definite cases where they may take the life of one another. But if this agreement among men is to have such force . . . will not the law of God then be valid only so far as the law of man permits? The result will be that in the same way men will determine in everything how far it suits them that God's commandments should be obeyed. (73/26-36)

If men do not scruple about adjusting God's law with respect to killing, then, *a fortiori* they will not worry about bending its other provisions. The importance of this argument goes beyond the issue of capital punishment: it stands as the paradigmatic criticism of the commonwealth. Raphael repeats it at the end of Book I in reply to Morus' argument that the wise man can at least ameliorate the policies of wayward rulers. Raphael finds such a position compromising and defends his principles against accommodation.

> Truly, if all the things which by the perverse morals of men have come to seem odd are to be dropped as unusual and absurd, we must dissemble almost all the doctrines of Christ. (101/23-26)

A courtier who took Christianity seriously would be out of place at court, and in failing to support "the worst counsels" and "the most ruinous decrees" would be reckoned "almost a traitor." He would merely expose himself to corruption or be used as "a screen for the wickedness and folly of others" (103/1-14).

More presents these criticisms with such remarkable economy that they are readily identified as the problems to which his book is a response. While in substance they were common enough, the manner of their presentation was not. Indeed, so powerful is the structural analysis which More gives to Raphael, that Russell Ames, R. P. Adams and, most recently, George Logan have taken it to be the truly distinctive feature of Book I.[15] Important as the structural account is, however, Hexter is right both in stating that More "does not ultimately ascribe the troubles of the world to impersonal forces" and in identifying the chief personal cause of social mischief as pride.[16] For Hexter, pride is a sinful propensity in human nature whose evil consequences More reveals in the Dialogue and contrives to restrict in the Discourse on Utopia. But More's conception of pride is more complex than Hexter's discussion allows. It is not only a postlapsarian affliction of the will, as St. Augustine argued, but a defect of judgement as well. In More's use of *superbia* a mistake about the nature of things is always implied. Counsellors who regard novel ideas as threatening are the victims of "proud, ridiculous, and obstinate prejudices" (57/31-59/17). Rulers who believe that idleness and pride are the marks of majesty are warned that they are mistaken and risk being despised or hated by their peoples (97/5-7). Those who glory in gems and finery have succumbed to counterfeit pleasures (167/27-39, 169/15-29). In Utopia only children take pride in precious stones and pearls. As maturity comes, however, they leave these toys behind (153/23-30). By contrast, the Anemolian ambassadors to Utopia reveal themselves as "more proud than wise" in their rich attire, which seems to the Utopians more in the manner of slaves or clowns than that of men of judgement (155/3-28). Similarly, those whose pride "counts it a personal glory to excel others by superfluous display of possessions" (139/5-9) have been deceived by false pleasures (169/30-171/5). And in his peroration, Raphael extols Utopian institutions arguing that either self-interest or the authority of Christ would have led to their wholesale adoption "had not one single monster, the chief and progenitor of all plagues, striven against it—I mean Pride." He pictures pride seizing the hearts of men, "preventing and hindering them from entering on a better way of life" (243/25-245/2).

Pride is a complex condition rather than a class of specific actions like the carnal sins of gluttony or lechery.[17] As More makes clear in *The Four Last Things*, it is a spiritual malaise. In *Utopia* it has a broader and more flexible usage. It encompasses the corruption of spirit, will and judgement. It is dangerous not only because it generates a host of other sins, but because it is self-disguising.[18] In this respect it is analogous to the concept of ideology adapted by Karl Mannheim from Marx.[19] Ideology, like pride, is a systematic but plausible distortion of reality; a pattern of ideas which justifies and thereby conserves the interests of those in power, enabling even the most anomalous states of affairs to seem reasonable.

This is well illustrated in the inner dialogue. The pride depicted at Morton's table is peculiarly the sin of the rich and powerful. In cataloguing the ills of commonwealths, Raphael explicitly lays the blame upon the privileged seven times,[20] and his narrative culminates in the observation that the commonwealths of Europe are "nothing else than a kind of conspiracy of the rich, who are aiming at their own interests under the name and title of commonwealth" (241/27-29). But throughout the inner dialogue the critique is implicit, and it permeates the book. This minority of rich men is not only slothful and greedy, but, being proud is blinded to its own faults and to the misery inflicted upon the majority. Each of the speakers, with the exception of Raphael and Morton, is the victim of a false position. The lawyer fears for his reputation unless he finds something to criticise in the speech of another (59/3-6). The flatterers vary their opinions with their anticipations of the Cardinal's responses to Raphael's criticisms. The friar has an anger which is born of pride though he protests that it is righteous.[21] It is only the genuine humility of Morton which allows the dialogue to proceed and Raphael to make any criticism at all. The other listeners are all too ready to rebut arguments they have barely heard and not appreciated. Pride has dimmed their intellects, and it is clear from this microcosm of a royal court, that the good man's counsel will fall upon deaf ears. The refusal of all but Morton to attend to his analysis confirms for Raphael the incorrigibility of rulers and their ministers, and the inevitability of the good counsellor being compromised at court.

The twin lights of reason and faith have been dimmed in the minds and hearts of rulers and courtiers by their indoctrination in false values. The propensity to vanity inherent in human nature is accentuated in political life.[22] Hence the absurdity that an abbot can engross his lands at great social cost while standing for the teaching of Christ. In a society whose values rest upon the teaching of the Gospel but whose practices reflect a devotion to the world a wide gap must be disguised. Hence, God's word is interpreted to legitimise the conduct of the ruling group and the real extent of their departure from the Gospels is hidden. What is neither reasonable nor Christian has become ideologically sustaining in a world of distorted values.

So the fundamental problem for the wise counsellor is not to devise better laws or advocate more just policies. The first problem is to penetrate to those who control social resources, to gain access to the minds of those who decide. In order to come to grips with the besetting ills of the commonwealth, the reformer must first deal with the ideological problem. This is the issue raised in the Dialogue of Counsel, which, above all others elicited More's response in *Utopia*.

Of course, if Hexter's persuasive account of the book's composition is correct, then this identification of the problem encounters a difficulty. It would suggest that More wrote Book II without originally intending to clarify its purpose. While it is not impossible that More later explicated his intentions in the enlarged Book I, this explanation is less satisfying than looking for evidence of the "ideological problem" in Book II. And there it can be found, in the work of More's putative first intention, in the central discussion of Utopian ethics.

The Utopians order their social life according to nature, which they believe has provided pleasure as an incentive to virtue. Edward Surtz and M.-M. Lacombe, in common with most commentators, locate the Utopian view of pleasure against a revaluation of Epicureanism.[23] An obvious source for More would have been Cicero's *De Finibus*, but there were a number of others available to him. It is clear that More was well acquainted with Epicureanism,[24] although Judith Jones has suggested that parallels with the *Philebus* are more apt. The issue, however, is not which source has priority, but what More made of ideas that would have been familiar to his audience. He departs from the antireligious stance of Epicurus and the opposition of intelligence to pleasure in Plato to give prominence to the question of discerning true pleasure from false. The Utopians hold that only true pleasures are truly productive of happiness and these are found in following nature and right reason. Like Epicureanism, Utopian ethics place friendship high on the list of true pleasures, and in contrast with European practices prescribe a duty to distribute "vital commodities" equitably, for no one's pleasure has more rights than another's. To deprive others of pleasure is injustice. To pursue false pleasures is contrary to nature, and is therefore irrational. Hence honour is condemned:

> What natural and true pleasure can another's bared head or bent knees afford you? Will this behaviour cure the pain in your own knees or relieve the lunacy in your own head? (169/2-5)

And what true pleasure is there in hunting? The "expectation of a creature being mangled under your eyes ... ought rather to inspire pity" (171/18-20).

As with honour and hunting, so too with dicing, possessions and wealth. Those things most esteemed in Europe are measured according to their true value in Utopia. The irony here is that the privileged classes of Christendom devote themselves not to pleasures at all but to mere *simulacra* of what is truly pleasurable. Those who feed on *simulacra* have become habituated to them and are no longer able to discriminate the genuine from the counterfeit. So it is impaired judgement which leads men to satisfy their desires in unworthy pursuits. Their justification cannot affect the character of their desires: "it is impossible for any man's judgement, depraved either by disease or by habit, to change the nature of pleasure any more than that of anything else" (173/5-8).

Moreover, according to Epicurean psychology, the pursuit of false pleasures produces appetites which are of their nature insatiable. As D. Konstan puts it, "It is not that certain *simulacra* arouse limitless desire; rather, desires are limitless when they feed on *simulacra*." The reason is simple: "Irrational passions, unlike natural needs, have an unreal object, an empty *simulacrum*, and therefore cannot be allayed."[25] The corrective is to banish "opinion" falsely added to the data of the senses, to seek security in "a stable condition of soul and body" and not through the acquisition of property, status and honour.[26] Hythlodaeus' utopianism is wholly consonant with Epicurean ideals. It posits a largely apolitical life of tranquility, with limited needs, and as few changes as are necessary to the conduct of the community. The Utopians are isolated from their neighbours — almost in an Epicurean garden writ large — removed from influence which could foster irrational passions, and being of similar mind (despite the provision for pluralistic beliefs) support each other in their spiritual journey.

By contrast, Europe is insecure and restless, its peoples brought into unnecessary conflict or dispossessed and abused by their rapacious rulers. The justifications of these rulers for their conduct derive from perverse judgement. They have corrupted the Gospel to suit their own interests and can no longer see its message as an indictment of the social order they administer. The Utopians, however, check conclusions derived from right reason against their religious principles so that the two work in harmony to provide an ethos for their just society (161/30-35, 163/21-23). It is not simply that European courts will not apply proper Christian standards to their behaviour, but that they cannot do so from their present position.

Because rulers lack wisdom they perpetuate injustices and remain unamenable to correction from wiser men: "they would never approve the advice of real philosophers because they have been from their youth saturated and infected with wrong ideas" (87/20-22). The most prevalent of these is that the true glory of a king is shown in his martial prowess and conquests. From this evil notion flow innumerable harmful consequences. Yet the part of the counsellor is to reinforce distorted conceptions of virtue rather than to correct them. Imagining himself to be a member of the French court, Hythlodaeus illustrates his case from contemporary international affairs and offers by way of contrast the example of the Achorians. This antipodean people began to suffer the kinds of distress of which Englishmen might justly complain, because of the ambition of their prince for new territory. Hence the Achorians delivered their king an ultimatum: he could choose between his new conquest and them, for "no one would care to engage even a muleteer whom he had to share with someone else" (89/35-91/20).

Yet what would be the response of the French court to his proposals that war be abandoned as fruitless and that the king devote himself to his own people who alone would tax his ability to govern wisely? Morus readily concedes that such advice would be unpopular. Hythlodaeus then goes on to describe other common forms of injustice practised by rulers which courtiers are required to devise or support, such as varying the value of money to the prince's advantage; raising revenues on the pretext of war; enforcing long-forgotten laws; and undermining the independence of judges (91/32-93/36).[27] By these stratagems a king may keep his coffers full, for "no amount of gold is enough for the ruler who has to keep an army" (93/38-39). Moreover, it is argued that a king's security "lies in the fact that the people do not grow insolent with wealth and freedom" (95/5-6).

If Raphael were to utter such opinions at court, or offer the fruits of his experience, such as the wise law of the Macarians limiting the king's treasure and thereby his inclinations to acquisitiveness, with what response would he meet? His hearers would be deaf to him. Morus, however, is not at all surprised: he does not think that

> such ideas should be thrust on people, or such advice given, as you are positive will never be listened to. What good could such novel ideas do, for how could they enter the minds of individuals who are already taken up and possessed by the opposite conviction? In the private conversation of close friends this academic philosophy (*philosophia scholastica*) is not without its charm, but in the councils of kings, where great matters are debated with great authority, there is no room for these notions. (99/1-8)

Hythlodaeus agrees: the objection of Morus simply supports the view that "there is no room for philosophy with rulers." But Morus now insists upon a distinction: he does not advocate an

> academic philosophy which thinks that everything is suitable to every place (but) . . . another philosophy, more practical for statesmen, which knows its stage, adapts itself to the play in hand, and performs its role neatly and appropriately . . . you must not force upon people new and strange ideas which you realise will carry no weight with persons of opposite conviction. On the contrary, by the indirect approach you must seek and strive to the best of your power to handle matters tactfully. What you cannot turn to good you must make as little bad as you can.
> (99/12–101/2)

The arguments of Morus are certainly strong, but Raphael is given the last word. He concedes that his speech "might perhaps be unwelcome," but "cannot see why it should seem odd." What, he asks, is inappropriate about it? Is one to take prevailing standards of conduct as normative, despite the teachings of Christ? The indirect strategy advocated by Morus would be of no avail (103/1–15).

Thus concludes the debate on counsel. Although Morus is prevented from replying to Hythlodaeus, Raphael cannot be said to have won the encounter.[28] Indeed, Bradshaw finds Morus' arguments proof against those of Plato and Hythlodaeus.[29] Neither has persuaded the other to change his mind and the reader is left to determine which of the arguments is stronger according to his circumstances. This, as Perelman has pointed out, is characteristic of dialectic.[30] Yet Raphael is left in a strong position. Although he seems to make the best the enemy of the good, he does present his interlocutors in both inner and outer dialogues with an argument which is troubling: if one is to remain faithful to the teachings of Christ how is one to act in public life? To compromise is to weaken Christian doctrine, which is forbidden; to be faithful is to be ineffective or to mask the iniquities of worse men. On the other hand, Morus has raised an equally haunting problem, that of indifference. Can one be truly Christian if one ignores the evils around one? The opposition between Morus and Hythlodaeus is drawn in masterly fashion, not only because each is given strong arguments, but because these arguments arise out of genuine dialogue where common ground—amongst some talk at cross-purposes—is established.

At the conclusion of the inner dialogue, Morus pronounces "everything" which Hythlodaeus has said as "both wise and witty" (85/39-87/1). The criticisms of European politics are conceded, and hence the need for reform. It is Raphael's examples which are the obstacle. The "novel ideas" embodied in them cannot impress themselves on those whose minds are already possessed of contrary notions. Only in the conversation of friends can they be effective: in the courts of kings they are irrelevant. Given Morus' warm approval of Raphael's anecdote about his visit to Morton, this last statement is surprising: the Cardinal alone of the company was prepared to give consideration to Raphael's novel views. The problem, not explicated by either Morus or Hythlodaeus, but resting upon ground they hold in common, is the replacement of these false notions by true ones. Raphael advocates a radically direct approach based upon what he takes to be the injunction of Christ. Morus is concerned with effective means, and hence favours indirection as likely to be more successful.

Morus takes the distinction between his *philosophia ciuilior* and Raphael's *philosophia scholastica* to mark off their respective positions. Yet Raphael has not proposed an academic philosophy at all. Indeed, the kind of "philosophy" held by both is fully in accord with humanist notions of what should be implied in the term. Erasmus, in the dedicatory epistle to his *The Education of a Christian Prince* refers, like Morus, to the argument of Plato that philosophy must join with government.

By "philosophy" I do not mean that which disputes concerning the first beginnings, of primordial matter, of motion and infinity, but that which frees the mind from the false opinions and the vicious predilections of the masses and points out a theory of government according to the example of the Eternal Power.[31]

The real basis of the difference between Morus and Raphael is not over brands of philosophy, but over ways to impart and implement it. And even here, their failure to resolve the matter is instructive, for they suggest in their conversation a solution to the problem which incorporates both their positions. In fact, the whole Dialogue of Counsel, so often seen as reflecting the debate in More's own mind about whether to enter royal service, raises the prior problem of communication. Quite apart from the criticisms and reforms proposed, the values of proper dialogue are represented in the personae of Morton, Giles, Morus, and even the uncompromising Hythlodaeus.

Morton is the personification of reasonableness in political authority. As Raphael describes him he

> deserved respect as much for his prudence and virtue as for his authority.... His countenance inspired respect rather than fear. In conversation he was agreeable, though serious and dignified.
> (59/26-29)

In discourse with Hythlodaeus, Morton displays the virtues of a willing listener and intelligent conversationalist. His peremptory silencing of the lawyer safeguards the values of conversation while his guarantee to the man to "reserve your right unimpaired till your next meeting" (71/35) demonstrates the extent of his open-mindedness and tolerance.

Peter Giles is also described as a man of charm and virtue whose conversation is polished and inoffensively witty (49/2-12). And Morus himself is an engaging person, eager to hear of Raphael's travels, and even if perplexed by his novel ideas, to learn from him (109/21-26). Hythlodaeus is a more shadowy character, and his earnestness and enthusiasm make him less attractive than his interlocutors.[32] To some he is even dogmatic.[33] Yet, of course, he is a rhetorical device, hardly a character at all in the book of More's first intention. And as a device he has important dialectical functions, as we shall presently see.

∽

More's conception of dialectic is classically humanist, that is, it is at one with rhetoric in being practical and is not restricted to the uses of the schoolmen. More's defence of this conception in his Letter to Dorp is contemporary with the composition of *Utopia* and it is not surprising to find aspects of the former in the latter. Dorp had accused Erasmus of being unable to tell "what distinguishes a dialectician from a sophist..."[34] More rebuts the accusation and turns it back upon Dorp, proposing a wider definition of dialectic on the authority of Lefèvre d'Etaples: "All of our better minds and sounder judgments acknowledge in him a restorer of true dialectic and true philosophy, especially Aristotelian."[35] True philosophy, for More, is not the kind of debate engaged in by scholastics on realism or nominalism, which he finds "highly absurd," but rather fruitful discourse:

In dialectic, by the same token, I should have thought it sufficient to master the nature of words, the force of propositions, and the forms of syllogisms, and at once to apply dialectic as a tool to the other branches of learning.[36]

For More the usefulness of dialectic is vouchsafed in its adherence to ordinary usage:

... the rule of the dialecticians ... is to press us along with true reasoning, to any conclusion, by using the same language we do. ...[37]

The values which suffuse the extraordinary Letter to Dorp[38] are found in the interlocutors in Utopia. If Raphael appears to be impatient, it is because he is acutely aware of the closed-mindedness of so many of his contemporaries, especially amongst scholastic intellectuals. And this is so despite the fact that he does not employ a *philosophia scholastica*, a technical language addressed to absurd problems. Only amongst the likes of Morton, Morus and Giles will he find men willing to be moved "in any direction with reasons that are true." As Germain Marc'hadour has shown, More uses dialogue to pursue the truth and reveal it to others.[39] Opposed to this was a puerile eristic, which Agricola, like Morus, thought should be confined to the schools.[40] The questions of this type of dialectic are intellectual toys like the jewels with which Utopian children play: they appear brilliant but are actually quite worthless.

Hence the adoption of Aristotle's conception of dialectic as reasoning based on "generally accepted" opinion; "a process of criticism wherein lies the path to the principles of all inquiries."[41] It is a practical discipline dealing in probabilities rather than a speculative one concerned with certainties. This conception of dialectic was very different from that which prevailed amongst the scholastic logicians or terminists, whose talk of supposition, ampliation, restriction, appellation, distribution and relatives[42] was the target of humanist criticism. Their theories of the properties of terms were derived from the last six sections of Peter of Spain's *Summulae Logicales*, the so-called *Parva Logicalia* scorned by More and his friends, and held by them to be a pointless addition to Aristotle's *Organon*.[43] This scholastic dialectic was removed from real problems and was set to resolve questions which were not only useless but at times pernicious.[44] From Petrarch on humanists had complained of the invasion of dialectic into the arts,[45] and rebuked its practitioners for claiming bogus certainty on matters of opinion. Hence, in his Letter to Dorp, More makes it clear that he is:

> not criticising all theologians, and I do not condemn all the problems advanced by the moderns; but those which are not at all relevant, which contribute nothing to learning and are a great hindrance to piety. . . . There are however other kinds of problems which treat human affairs seriously, and of divine affairs reverently. Such problems, if they show by their modest behaviour they are more interested in searching for the truth than in gaining a victory by clever debate, provided they do not lay complete claim on anybody, nor hold anyone too long within their grasp . . . problems that are developed in that fashion I am very willing to embrace. . . .[46]

Again we see not only a proper mode of argumentation being proposed, but the appropriate values to go with it.

These same values dictate that the technical vocabulary of the terminist give way to ordinary language. If dialectic is to be useful in reasoning from common opinion, it cannot divorce itself from ordinary usage. *Utopia* itself is proof of this. It speaks to its admittedly restricted contemporary audience in a common tongue. Its manner is conversational not only in the Dialogue, but from the prefatory letters[47] through to the Discourse. And, in attacking the errors of Christendom, it identifies distorted judgement as the problem. The insistence of More and Vives on correct usage of language is parallel with Raphael's on the proper observance of God's laws. Contemporary practice gives twisted meanings to both.[48] For the humanists, a rehabilitation of discourse was necessary, and this meant the assimilation of dialectic to rhetoric or at least the blurring of the boundary between them. Seigel shows that for Valla, the priority of ordinary over technical language was a way "to tie the dialectician firmly to the linguistic standard of the orator."[49] And Vives writes that dialectic "discovers what is true or false or probable in this common speech which everyone uses."[50] Even though, as Kinney shows, More was more moderate than Valla and Vives and wished to retain a role for an Aristotelian dialectic in a restored trivium, rhetoric would still have precedence over grammar and dialectic.[51]

It is evidence of the right judgement of the Utopians that although they have music, dialectic, arithmetic and geometry, and a mastery of these arts comparable with the classical authors, they are ignorant of the *logica moderna*.

> In fact, they have discovered not even a single one of these very ingeniously devised rules about restrictions, ampliations, and sup-

positions which our own children everywhere learn in the *Small Logicals*. In addition, so far are they from ability to speculate on second intentions that not one of them could see even man himself as a so-called universal. . . . (159/28-33)

This right judgement is also manifested in their openness on matters of opinion. Because they have not had the certitude of revealed Christianity, they have relied upon their own reason and experience in deciding religious questions. King Utopus, their founder, wisely allowed for this when he instituted the commonwealth. Not wishing to dogmatise, "he especially ordained that it should be lawful for every man to follow the religion of his choice." More importantly, the values preserved here go beyond toleration, embracing the correct conduct of dialectic and the pursuit of truth. Utopus allowed proselytisers to "strive" for converts

> provided that [they] quietly and modestly supported [their] own reasons nor bitterly demolished all others if [their] persuasions were not successful nor used any violence and refrained from abuse. . . . Moreover, even if it should be the case that one single religion is true and all the rest are false, he foresaw that, provided the matter was handled reasonably and moderately, truth by its own natural force would finally emerge sooner or later and stand forth conspicuously. (221/5-22)

This exemplary attitude of Utopus and his people is to be contrasted with that of the dogmatic lawyer and angry friar at Morton's table, and with the perverse judgements and closed minds of European courts. The Utopians have a dialectical attitude towards religious matters holding that the truth will be exposed in a dialogue of religions. This attitude was common amongst the humanists, and is reflected in the exchange between Morus and Raphael in the Dialogue. It is true that a willingness to attend rather than to object is called for in Morus and his companions, and that Raphael, as the holder of the central position, is not required to be as flexible.[52] Yet the conversation is certainly not an academic one. On the contrary, it provides a dialectical model for the clarification of truth in contrast with the combative, authority-grasping discourse of Morton's hangers-on. And the problem of counsel is resolvable: both parties are right. Christ's words must be adhered to, but it cannot be imparted by dogmatics and it cannot be practised by formulae. Morus is wrong in calling Raphael's philosophy academic, just as he is wrong in calling "civil" that philosophy which is suitable to affairs debated with "great authority" at European courts. Morus and Raphael agree that these courts are in a parlous condition. Great matters are debated with a great show of authority but the function of this discourse is the protection of private interests. Contrary to Morus, it is precisely the kind of conversation conducted amongst friends, as in Morus' garden, that is needed to restore the authority of Christian courts.

On the other hand, Hythlodaeus' insistence on the faithful transmission of God's word does not constitute a fair objection to the "indirect approach" advocated by Morus. Indirection, in which *Utopia* excels, does not mean compromise. On the contrary, ideas which are uncomfortable are more likely to require an indirect approach than those which have been watered down. If judgement is disordered, it will be unable to apprehend the message of Christ in its purity. God, of course, controls the revelation of that message, but as Augustine recognised, He uses human voices, mundane signs, to point to the higher realities behind temporal affairs.[53] If discourse has been rehabilitated by the Incarnation, then the vapid speculations of scholastic theologians, and the superstitions and inanities of ignorant religious and clergy criticized in More's letters to Dorp, Oxford and a Monk, must be replaced with language more faithful to revelation. A reformed dialectic makes possible a clearer understanding of Christ's message. While More assigns everything to the grace of God, he also gives learning a high priority as a way of coming to know Him.[54] It could be argued that the learning of Erasmus applied to the Scripture brought about a more direct acquaintance with God's word; that nothing could be less indirect in intention. But such an argument would adopt the viewpoint of the humanists, and take no account of the opposition of the entrenched interests against which More so brilliantly defended his friend.

More, then, draws out the strengths and shortcomings of Morus and Hythlodaeus on the problem of counsel. If counsel is to be given, its model is presented in dialogue. The point is, of course, that no stated resolution of the problem is presented by More: neither of his characters is victorious. The values of openness and critical enquiry are reflected in the inconclusiveness of the exchange. The reader is left to judge, as in Starkey's *Dialogue* or the school text dialogues of Vives.[55]

Although Hythlodaeus moves without interruption from the topic of counsel to that of communism, both are aspects of the larger problem of reform. Again, the obstacle is a species of false consciousness.[56] Raphael argues that private property allows the accumulation of wealth in few hands, and thereby prevents justice and happiness from being realised in human affairs. Half-measures, such as ceilings on wealth or limitations on expenses incurred in holding public office, would curb the worst excesses. But the fundamental problems of the commonwealth would be left untreated. For these there is only one cure, according to Hythlodaeus, and it must be radical: the common ownership of property (103/24-107/4).

Morus responds with the familiar but powerful objections that incentive to work would be destroyed and people would come to depend on the labour of others; that when rightfully gained property is legally appropriated "bloodshed and riot" will ensue; and that egalitarianism must destroy the authority of magistrates, and hence social order (107/5-16).

Morus' case is strong, as Hexter points out,[57] and Raphael does not attempt to meet it head on. Indeed, he seems almost to have anticipated it and expresses a certain sympathy for those who are unable even to conceive of what he has actually experienced. He has no great difficulty in meeting these *a priori* objections in the telling of his Utopian story. Having been to Utopia he can assist Morus in conceiving of a commonwealth which seems utterly strange from an English perspective and contrary to well entrenched preconceptions about what is possible and what is desirable in social life and political arrangements. Peter Giles actually comes to stand for the traditional counsellor criticised earlier by Raphael (at 59/9-12) when he questions the latter's preference for the New World given the antiquity and accumulated experience of the Old. Yet while Morus and Peter are presented as attached to familiar views and institutions and as in need of illumination, they are also shown to be willing listeners to new ideas. They are more like the Utopians in taking advantage of their opportunity, than like the Europeans Raphael criticises for their hostility to innovation.

Morus and Peter become model listeners for More's audiences. If men of authority and public standing are willing to attend to the tale of Utopia, then there is indeed hope for reform. For, as Raphael points out, it is precisely the receptiveness of the Utopians to the benefits of the discoveries of other nations that is the chief reason why, though we are inferior to them neither in brains nor resources, their commonwealth is more wisely governed and happily flourishing than ours (109/18-20).

Too few critics[58] have given sufficient weight to this statement. It is hidden, as it were, in the shadow of Raphael's diagnosis of the conditions of injustice and poverty. At the very end of Book I, then, the priority of a dialectical attitude is reiterated as the Discourse on Utopia is introduced. The values represented in the conversation of the Dialogue are fundamental to the Utopians, that is, to the best of a commonwealth.

∽

The place of dialectic in Utopia, then, is not based on a characterisation drawn only from one book. There is, of course, the obvious objection that almost the whole of Book II is taken up with Raphael's uninterrupted discourse.[59] Yet it should be remembered that the description of Utopia is a response to the promptings of Morus, and a reply to his challenge to the idea of community of property. Raphael's discourse is an extended justification of his views about the best ordering of a commonwealth. Of course, if Hexter's reconstruction of the composition of *Utopia* is correct, this could not strictly be so: The Discourse would, in More's first intention, have had merely a narrative function. Yet Hythlodaeus is clearly talking to an audience, anticipating their objections and trying to win them in the intimacy of conversation. For example, on the contentious matter of the Utopian attitude to virtue and pleasure, Raphael says: "Whether in this stand they are right or wrong, time does not permit us to examine—nor is it necessary. We have taken upon ourselves only to describe their principles, and not also to defend them" (179/15-18).

This is, of course, disingenuous, but Hythlodaeus is clearly sensitive to his audience. Even if he is personally defensive and politically committed to Utopian principles, he nonetheless respects the autonomy of his interlocutors—their ability to decide on the issues he raises.

As in so much else concerning *Utopia*, opinion is divided about the character of Book II. Surtz has called it a "one-sided dialogue," a distinction Skinner finds too nice.[60] On the other hand, R. J. Schoeck argues that "monologue" is far too conservative a description of Raphael's narrative, a view which receives a good deal of implicit support from recent scholarship.[61] He sees dialogue in broader terms as a formal cause, embracing the obvious "literary" dialogue in which the interlocutors converse; the extended dialogue between *Utopia* and eminent humanists, who ornament it with their letters; and, finally, between European models of political order, and the rhetorically appealing "speaking picture" which is *Utopia*.[62]

Thus one may understand the Discourse, and not only the Dialogue of Counsel, to function dialectically by challenging its European audience to reexamine its own values. This is done in a number of ways. First, as Sylvester has pointed out, one must suspend one's disbelief in order to hear Raphael's tale.[63] Even if one were to be dismissive of the Utopian scheme, it would first be necessary to lower one's guard sufficiently to let the message penetrate. Having heard the story, however, one is prompted to make sense of it, to resolve its paradoxes and ambiguities rather than just to dismiss it. So the Discourse sets up an internal dialogue in the mind of the reader, requiring the reexamination of settled assumptions about issues raised by Hythlodaeus.

This level of dialectic is underpinned by the comparisons and contrasts between the two books of *Utopia*. In the first, pride governs the social and political life of Europe; in the second, it is all but extirpated from the commonwealth of Utopia. The poor labor to enrich the idle in Europe, but few are exempted from work in Utopia, and sloth is unknown. Want and greed go hand in hand in the Old World, but abundance removes covetousness in the New. The Utopians are well housed and fed, and work short hours. Agriculture is fostered, whereas in England agriculture has been impaired by grazing and cottages have fallen into decay. The Utopians try to avoid war at all costs, but European princes see it almost as a duty. Counsels in Utopia are seriously considered and proposals may not be debated on the day they are made, but imprudence nurtured by pride marks the courts of Europe. Treaties are lightly made and broken in Christendom but are never made and hence never broken in Utopia. All of these contrasts, of course, are related to fundamentally differing social structures and value systems: in Europe money and property are the measure of all things, but in Utopia communism institutionalises and supports co-operation and sharing.

Given the forcible critique of European societies in Book I, the reader is confronted with the problem of making sense of the solutions offered by Hythlodaeus in Book II. One can agree up to a point with interpreters like A. R. Heiserman and Robert C. Elliott that *Utopia* is a satire and its institutions are devices to attack the abuses of Christendom.[64] Certainly there is a good deal of satire in the laws and customs of the Utopians: one need only think of their use of gold. But the satirical interpretation is of value mainly in emphasising that *Utopia* is not programmatic; that it cannot be taken as a series of propositions requiring philosophical deliberation or reconciliation.[65] Its shortcoming is that it does not measure the seriousness with which

More's humanist audience viewed his fantasy. Communism, for example, cannot simply be taken to be a satiric inversion of the European obsession for property. Rather, what More does is to bring communism into dialectical opposition to the practice described in Book I to show how an obsession with property is ultimately destructive of the commonwealth. Those who read *Utopia* as a satire give a salutary warning against a programmatic or narrowly philosophical interpretation of the work. Yet it is only because the spirit embodied in Utopian communism was taken seriously by contemporaries of More such as Budé and Busleyden that it could serve as an effective critique of Europe.[66] To acknowledge the importance of the spirit behind More's communism – the positive as distinct from the purely negative satiric aspect – is not to suggest that it embodied that spirit in a form wholly satisfactory to the author[67] or his audience.

Indeed, to ask whether More really advocated communism through the persona of Hythlodaeus or rejected the idea through that of Morus is not so much to miss the point as to be taken in by the fantasy. More denies to his audience a finality on the issues he raises in *Utopia*. While this denial has provoked attempts to anchor the text to formal or biographical details, the rhetoric of the work constantly subverts such attempts, as Elizabeth McCutcheon has demonstrated.

⁓

In a seminal article, McCutcheon has shown that litotes is one of More's favourite rhetorical devices.[68] In general it has the effect of calling attention to particular issues without forcing a judgement upon the reader. As McCutcheon writes, "it can disarm potential opponents and avoid controversy; yet it emphasises whatever it touches."[69] Hence, the enthusiasm with which Hythlodaeus delivers his discourse is persistently qualified. The Utopians live in buildings that are *neutiquam sordida* ("in no way mean," 120/4); their dress is *nec ad oculum indecore* ("not unbecoming to the eye," 126/5); they go to war *non temere* ("not lightly," 201/4–5), and so on. There is a controlled subversion of explicit detail in the description which belies its potential as a blueprint. This is not a complete denial of the idea that reason can produce practicable reforms, as some have argued,[70] but the blurring of a picture which is finally focused in the dialectical engagement of the reader with the text. Hence, in Book I, Morus says that Raphael found in the New World "not a few points from which our own cities, nations, races and kingdoms may take example for the correction of their errors" (55/2-4) without specifying which. Then, at the conclusion of Book II, Morus declares that "not a few" of the Utopian institutions seem absurd, especially "their common life and subsistence" because these destroy the "magnificence, splendor, and majesty" commonly regarded as "the true glories and ornaments of the commonwealth" (245/17-25).[71]

More's use of litotes has parallels in the larger construction of his book. Surtz argues that he subtly undermines his own picture of Utopian felicity "by having the uncompromising Hythlodaeus overstate his case: the Utopians are too good and their institutions run too smoothly."[72] The Utopian commonwealth is defective as a model for Christian societies because it does not have the necessary revelation to correct unaided reason. Quentin Skinner has drawn out the contrasts between this view and that of Surtz's co-editor, J. H. Hexter, which are silently juxtaposed in the Yale edition. Hexter's crucial point, with which Skinner strongly agrees, is that the Utopians, despite their lack of formal doctrine, are truly Christian because of their conduct. Such a daring proposal would thus make even more scandalous the contrast between benighted Christendom and pagan Utopia.[73]

More did believe that reason is not "to be mistrusted where faith standeth not against it." Indeed, pagan societies can reason to high standards of virtue even though prone to infidelity and idolatry,

> whiche was the specyall thyng frome whiche (God) called his chyrche out of the gentyllys / whiche ellys as for morall vertues and polytycal yf they had not lacked the ryghte cause and ende of referryng their actes to god / were many of them not farre vnder many of vs.[74]

The Utopians certainly refer their actions to God and do not mistake temporal felicities for heavenly ones. And, as Skinner points out, they always relate ethical considerations to religious principles.[75] Nevertheless, Surtz is right: the conduct of the Utopians is exaggerated by Christian standards. While it embodies certain truths dear to Christianity, it frequently exceeds a Christian tolerance. It is as though without the correcting guidance of Christ's church the Utopians fall into absurdity.[76]

The exhortations of priests and officials to the incurably ill to seek an end to their sufferings in voluntary euthanasia is repugnant to Christian principles. This practice, supported by Utopian religions (223/21, 223/17) takes to unacceptable lengths the desire of the faithful to join

God in heaven. Utopian laws on marriage are equally contentious. Where Christians would be expected to extend forgiveness to an adulterous spouse, the Utopians permit divorce and remarriage for the innocent party, and commit the offender to life-long disgrace and celibacy (189). Divorce is also permitted on grounds of incompatibility (191/1-9). Utopian laws on the ordination of women reflect, perhaps, More's own high regard for the abilities of women,[77] but they are nonetheless at variance with Christian tradition. While Utopian methods of waging war are calculated to cause as little harm as possible—seeing that "the commonfolk do not go to war of their own accord, but are driven to it by the madness of kings" (205/302-32)—their behaviour nonetheless resembles that of Europe's warrior-princes. They offer rewards to the enemy population for the assassination or surrender of their king and other designated officials (203/36, 205/9). They rekindle old grievances amongst their enemies' neighbours (205/35-39), and, as a matter of course, hire mercenaries (207/9, 209/15). In short, although the Utopians are exemplary in many respects and notably in their willingness to consider differing viewpoints, their institutions cannot serve as a model for Christian commonwealths.

George Logan has recently suggested that Utopia does serve as a model of kinds, a thought experiment in comparative government to determine what is the best state of the commonwealth. In doing so More follows the Greek best commonwealth exercise, testing the limits of human ingenuity in devising a model society even to the point of considering the merits of institutions which the author might not personally approve of. The dialectic in More's version is, unlike that of his Greek models, hidden: we are presented, argues Logan, only with its results. Logan, then, recognizes the dialectical movement and openness of *Utopia*, but assimilates these to modern forms of thought rather than to humanist rhetorical strategies. Hence he takes the concrete detail of *Utopia* to be part of a comparative method, whereas it is better understood as a function of More's use of Ciceronian dialogue.[78] Wilson has contrasted Platonic and Ciceronian styles of dialogue: the former are concerned with eristic, whereas the latter are peirastic, and borrow from the techniques of drama in a way that would be extraneous in a Platonic argument.[79] More has created a thought experiment, but not in the style of a hypothesis to be tested or a model to be evaluated. The details of Utopia are part of his peirastic, a rhetorical device to evade the deficiencies of reason. More's dialectic is not hidden so much as integrated into the rhetoric of dialogue.

Just as the kingdoms of Christendom have twisted the teaching of

Christ in one direction for evil purposes, so the Utopians have unconsciously given their rationally derived principles a utilitarian bias in their search for the good society. As Khanna rightly observes, the contrasts between the two societies do not "lead to an absolute choice" between them.[80] Just as one must decide exactly where to affix a meaning to the indeterminate litotes, so one must also decide where Utopian practice exceeds Christian principles. The Utopians might well be described as "not pagan," but they are also "not Christian." To make this judgement, however, is also to make a judgement of what is proper according to God's law, and hence implicitly to strike a standard for one's own social and political system.

Utopia is an educational device, but not one, as Wayne Rebhorn would have it, which magnifies "the humanist schoolhouse."[81] It is not heavily didactic, but, on the contrary, works through paradox and indirect persuasion to the restoration of truly Christian judgement in political life.[82] More's strategy is not simply to reassert what was familiar to everybody: that Christian precepts ought to be followed; that uncontrolled appetites are the basis of social vices; that fallen nature needs the discipline of external restraints if there is to be peace and justice. There was nothing to be gained from the repetition of moralisms which had lost their force. The distorted judgement of kings and counsellors, religious and clergy had turned Christian principles into an ideology which served their interests and allowed them to sin in comfort.[83] These men had become proud in their vices and were not amenable to correction. Like those who mistake false pleasures for true (171-73), habituation has made bad judgement seem good. The closed fist of logic finds them on their own ground, ready to argue over the merest detail with a righteous importance, yet indifferent to the plight of those they burden and to their own condition as oppressors. But the open palm of rhetoric is more persuasive. It engages the audience, eliciting responses which are not reflexive or learned by rote.

⁂

Utopia is a demonstration of the healing of the understanding which can be wrought through the word. The occasion of this therapy is the encounter with Raphael Hythlodaeus, whose name encodes his mission: Raphael, the healer; Hythlodaeus, speaker of nonsense. Appropriately, the name of Raphael the archangel is associated not only with healing, but with divine healing: healing through the word of God.

Erasmus had a similar idea in mind in dedicating his *Paraphrasis in evangelium Lucae* to Henry VIII. This dedication felicitously combined Henry's interests in medicine and theology, while suggesting that the ultimate healing power—Christ, the Logos—was available to the king through the Gospel. Like More, Erasmus is attempting to instruct in more than platitudinous Christianity: "I send thee Luke the physician, most generous king, not the one whom you used to have previously, but one speaking more clearly and eloquently to Latin ears."[84]

Utopia, then, is a device for penetrating the closed minds of those who hold political power and those who counsel them. It reflects More's recognition that "authority alone could not make men change.... Would not compel them to use reason to reflect upon their problems."[85] Nor could it speak to them of the true values of Christianity when they had come to regard themselves as virtuous according to their own rules. *Utopia* invites its readers to reappraise their values and the relation of those values to practice. Its success may be measured in the variety of critical opinion it has elicited. For, like More's contemporaries, modern readers must locate the meaning of the work in its dialectical structure.

Even as the thunder of the Reformation called forth a strident tone in More, the humanist intellectual did not give way to the ranter sometimes depicted. More used the dialogue form in religious polemics, and as Germain Marc'hadour and K. J. Wilson have shown in discussing *A Dialogue Concerning Heresies*, did so with wit and perception. Like benighted counsellors and tunnel visioned scholastics, heretics were unamenable to the direct persuasions of reason. Scholastic logic would be useless against heresy, so More resorts to the rhetoric of dialogue, a more plausible dialectic. As Wilson writes,

> A disorder in the right relation between faith and reason, heresy must have aroused a unique distaste in the author of *Utopia*.... Heresy implied willful error against reason, yet there remained hope that the method of rational dialectic might, if not overcome error, prevent the faithfull from choosing it.[86]

In this ambition More ultimately failed, but it is an added irony that in *Utopia*, his more practical method should have come to be a byword for impracticable political schemes.

If the problem of counsel is a problem of communication, then *Utopia* goes some way towards a solution. It is a solution suited to a particular period, when a model of open and rational discourse might gain access to the minds of men like Henry or Wolsey. More realised that what is conventionally demanded from counsellors is not edifying advice about just means and good ends but moral and legal justifications of conclusions already reached. Before long, the Erasmianism in which More shared would become similarly prejudiced in the struggles of the Reformation. But when *Utopia* was written, men might still be called to true dialogue and to attack false judgement which took appearances for realities, and, in pride, proclaimed certainties where there could be none. Hence, Raphael and Morus are left in possession of their positions at the conclusion of the book. More has demanded that his audience be the judge, not of who best represents his true views, but of how from their dialectical exchange the commonwealth may be reformed to be truly worthy of the Christian ideal.

University of New South Wales

Notes

I am most grateful to Michael Jackson and especially to Conal Condren, who provided valuable if sometimes unheeded criticism of this paper in an earlier form.

1. "Here I Sit : Thomas More's Genius for Dialogue" in D. Grace and B. Byron, eds., *Thomas More: Essays on the Icon*, Melbourne, 1980.
2. *The Complete Works of St. Thomas More*, vol. 4, ed. E. Surtz, S. J., and J. H. Hexter (New Haven and London, 1965), hereafter cited as CW 4. Citations are by page and line.
3. Ulrich Mölk, "Philologische Bemerkungen Zu Thomas Morus' *Utopia*," *Anglia* 82 (1964): 309-20.
4. A. F. Nagel, "Lies and the Limitable Inane: Contradiction in More's *Utopia*," *Renaissance Quarterly* 26 (1973): 173-80; F. Jameson, "Of Islands and Trenches: Naturalisation and the Production of Utopian Discourse," *Diacritics* (June 1977): 2-21; cf R. M. Adams' notes to his translation of *Utopia* (New York, 1975), 35, 44, 45, 47, 83 and 84.
5. Elizabeth McCutcheon, "Denying the Contrary: More's Use of Litotes in the *Utopia*," *Moreana* 31/32 (1971): 107-21; reprinted in R. S. Sylvester and G. Marc'hadour, eds., *Essential Articles for the Study of Thomas More* (Hamden, Conn., 1977), 263-74.
6. *Utopia: Biography of an Idea* (New York, 1965); CW 4, xv-xxiii.

7. See Elizabeth McCutcheon, "Thomas More, Raphael Hythlodaeus and the Angel Raphael," *Studies in English Literature* 9 (1969): 21-38.
8. CW 4, 21.
9. Cf. Robert Coogan's perceptive "Nunc Vivo ut Volo," *Moreana* 31/32 (1971): 29-45, especially pp. 43-44. Coogan is careful to show that More's *jeu d'esprit* is not merely a play of wit, p. 31. For Wolsey's seriousness about reform see J. J. Scarisbrick, "Cardinal Wolsley and the Common Weal," in E. W. Ives, R. J. Knecht, J. J. Scarisbrick, eds., *Wealth and Power in Tudor England* (London, 1978), 44-67.
10. Karl Kautsky, *Thomas More and His Utopia*, trans. H. J. Stenning (New York, 1927); and, more soberly, Russell Ames, *Citizen Thomas More and His Utopia* (Princeton, 1949).
11. H. Berger, "The Renaissance Imagination: Second World and Green World," *The Centennial Review* 9 (1965): 36-78 R. S. Johnson, *More's Utopia: Ideal and Illusion* (New Haven, 1969); Ward Allen, "Hythloday and the Root of all Evil," *Moreana* 31/32 (1971): 51-59.
12. George Logan, *The Meaning of More's "Utopia"* (Princeton, 1983).
13. *Incomplete Fictions* (Washington, 1985).
14. Measures had been enacted to achieve this, most recently in 1514 and 1515, and in 1517 Wolsey took steps to prosecute them with a commission into enclosures, before which, ironically, More was summoned to appear; Scarisbrick, "Wolsey and the Common Weal," 61; Elton, *Reform and Renewal* (London, 1977), 67-69.
15. Russell Ames, *Citizen Thomas More and His Utopia*, 176; R. P. Adams, *The Better Part of Valor: More, Erasmus, Colet and Vives on Humanism, War and Peace* (Seattle, 1962), 125 ff.; George Logan, *The Meaning of More's Utopia*, (Princeton, 1983), 55 ff.
16. CW 4, ci; *Biography of an Idea*, 73-81.
17. On the dangers of the different vices, More writes, "I surely think there be some who had in good faith made the best merchandise that ever they made in their lives for their own souls, if they changed those spiritual vices of pride, wrath and envy, for the beastly carnal sins of gluttony, sloth and lechery . . . so . . . they could not be ignorant of their own faults." *The Four Last Things*, ed. D.O'Connor (London, 1935), 39.
18. Ibid., 6-7.
19. According to Mannheim, a social analysis is ideological "when we no longer make individuals responsible for the deceptions we detect in their utterances, and when we no longer attribute the evil that they do to malicious cunning. It is only when we . . . seek to discover the source of their untruthfulness in a social factor, that we are properly making an ideological interpretation." *Ideology and Utopia*, trans. L. Wirth and E. Shils (London, 1960), 54.
20. At 63/5-15; 67/2-13 and 14-16; 69/6-10, 14-17 and 23-25; 71/2-4.
21. Cf. *The Four Last Things*: "this deadly sore of wrath, of which so much harm groweth . . . is but a cursed branch . . . of the secret root of pride," 54.
22. See ibid, 41, 42 and 45 for indirect political references.
23. E. Surtz, S. J., *The Praise of Pleasure*, (Cambridge, Mass., 1957); M.-M.

Lacombe, "La Sagesse D'Epicure dans *L'Utopie* de More," *Moreana* 31/32 (1971): 169-82.

24. J. Jones, "The *Philebus* and the Philosophy of Pleasure in Thomas More's *Utopia*," *Moreana* 31/32 (1971): 61-69. Elizabeth McCutcheon gives a recent survey of More's "unstable amalgam" of Epicurean, Stoic, Platonic and Christian moral notions in "More's *Utopia* and Cicero's *Paradoxa Stoicorum*" in R. Keen and D. Kinney, eds., *Thomas More and the Classics*, *Moreana* 86 (1985): 3-22, especially 15 ff.

25. D. Konstan, *Some Aspects of Epicurean Psychology* (Leiden, 1973) 28,30.

26. Ibid., 70,69.

27. Cf. Dudley, *Tree of Commonwealth*, ed. D.M. Brodie (Cambridge, 1948), 28, 34-36, 41 and Erasmus, *Education of a Christian Prince*, trans. L. K. Born (New York, 1936), 215-218.

28. Cf. Hexter, *Biography of an Idea*, 131-32.

29. Brendan Bradshaw, "More on Utopia," *The Historical Journal* 24 (1981): 1-27; especially 22-24.

30. Ch. Perelman writes that "The point of departure for a dialectical argumentation does not consist in necessary propositions valid everywhere and for all time, but in propositions effectively admitted to a given milieu; in a different setting, in a different historical and social context, these propositions may no longer meet with general approval." "The Dialectical Method and the Part Played by the Interlocutor in Dialogue," in *The Idea of Justice and The Problem of Argument* (London, 1963), 166.

31. Pp. 133-34.

32. For example, Johnson, 33, 48; R. S. Sylvester, "Si Hythlodaeo Credimus," in Sylvester and Marc'hadour, 290-301; 296 ff.

33. W.E. Campbell, *More's Utopia and His Social Teaching* (London, 1930), 46; H. W. Donner, *Introduction to Utopia* (London, 1945), 22. For an overview of opinion on Hythlodaeus see Coogan, "Nunc Vivo ut Volo."

34. *In Defense of Humanism: Letter to Martin Dorp, Letter to the University of Oxford, Letter to Edward Lee, Letter to a Monk, The Complete Works of St. Thomas More*, vol. 15, ed. Daniel Kinney (New Haven and London, 1986), p. 14/23-4. Hereafter cited as CW 15.

35. CW 15, 22/16-17.

36. CW 15, 24/24-28.

37. CW 15, 36/9-11.

38. For three excellent discussions of the rhetoric of the *Letter to Dorp* see M. Fleisher, *Radical Reform and Political Persuasion in the Life and Writings of Thomas More* (Geneva, 1973), chap. III; Germain Marc'hadour, "Thomas More convertit Martin Dorp a l'humanisme" in *Thomas More 1477-1977*, Travaux de l'Institut Interuniversitaire pour l'étude de la Renaissance et de l'Humanisme, IV (Bruxelles, 1980), 13-25; and Daniel Kinney, "More's Letter to Dorp: Remapping the Trivium," *Renaissance Quarterly* 34 (1981): 179-210.

39. "Here I Sit," 11, 15, 24 ff.

40. C. R. J. Armstrong, "The Dialectical Road to Truth: The Dialogue," in *French Renaissance Studies 1540-70*, ed. P. Sharratt (Edinburgh, 1976), 36-51; 42.

41. Aristotle, *Topica*, trans. W. A. Pickard-Cambridge, *The Works of Aristotle*, ed. W. D. Ross, 1 (London, 1928); 100a, 30 and 101b respectively. For More's knowledge of Aristotle see T. I. White, "Aristotle and *Utopia*," *Renaissance Quarterly* 29 (1976): 635-75, especially 637; cf. Fleisher, op cit, 91.

42. See W. and M. Kneale, *The Development of Logic* (Oxford, 1962), 246-74.

43. Generally, see the Introduction of Rita Guerlac, *Vives Against the Pseudodialecticians*, and for Vives, 79, 131; for More, CW 15, 29 ff. W. Ong's *Ramus, Method and the Decay of Dialogue* (Cambridge, Mass., 1958) gives a clear and concise account of the logic of Peter of Spain and its humanist critics in chaps. IV and V. Alan Perreiah puts humanist criticisms into perspective in "Humanistic Critiques of Scholastic Dialectic," *The Sixteenth Century Journal* 13 (1982): 3-22.

44. See e.g., Vives' views on the detriment of dialectic to theology, 117.

45. Ibid, 14.

46. *St. Thomas More: Selected Letters*, ed. E.F. Rogers (New Haven and London, 1961), pp. 40-41.

47. For P. R. Allen, the prefatory material extends the conversation: "The world of Utopia becomes an incident in a long discussion; it is not a separate book but the central subject of the conversation – a rather lengthy anecdote told to a group of humanists, all of whom listen to it and comment on it." "*Utopia* and European Humanism: the Function of the Prefatory Letters and Verses," *Studies in the Renaissance* 10 (1963): 91-107; 100.

48. Vives poses the problem of language in much the same way as More raises that of false religious ideas: "What then if a dialectician should investigate the true and false by verbal meanings made up at his pleasure, ignoring the common and current ones? Surely everyone who knew the language would say, 'You are not seeking the truth of our discourse but of your own dreams . . .'" *Against the Pseudodialecticians*, 133.

49. J. E. Seigel, *Rhetoric and Philosophy in Renaissance Humanism* (Princeton, 1968), 162.

50. *Against the Pseudodialecticians*, cf. 49, 77.

51. Kinney, 206-7.

52. Warren Wooden goes much further. He sees in Hythlodaeus the epitome of the scholastic dogmatist. Hence *Utopia* satirizes scholasticism through the figure of Raphael. "Anti-Scholastic Satire in Sir Thomas More's *Utopia*," *The Sixteenth Century Journal* 8 (1977): 29-45.

53. On Augustine's theory of signs and the rehabilitation of discourse see Marcia Colish, *The Mirror of Language* (New Haven and London, 1968), chap. 1.

54. In his Letter to a Monk he makes a spirited defence of Erasmus which is also a strong defence of learning. Erasmus, he tells the monk, has done more for the Church than the monk, ". . . unless you think that anyone's fasts or perfunctory prayers do as much or do such widespread good as so many great volumes, through which the whole world is instructed in righteousness . . ." Due allowance should be made, perhaps, for polemical hyperbole (CW 15, 296/10-13; but cf. 302-4).

55. Cf. the remarks of K. Burton in her introduction to *A Dialogue Be-*

tween *Reginald Pole and Thomas Lupset* (London, 1948), 3; for Vives see *Tudor School-Boy Life*, trans. Foster Watson (1908, reprinted London, 1970). C. J. R. Armstrong observes of Cicero's dialogues, "*all* the speakers are clearly using dialectic, but every man's dialectic has equal rights with every other man's. None is represented as 'victorious' . . . Likewise, each interlocutor remains at the end, as at the beginning, in secure possession of his original opinion. . . . The decision in the matter under discussion . . . is left to someone outside the discussion itself: to you and me, the readers." "The Dialectical Road to Truth," 43. W. J. Kennedy ventures a similar opinion about the conclusion of *Utopia* where More "passes the responsibility [for further discussion] onto the reader . . . ," *Rhetorical Norms in Renaissance Literature* (New Haven and London, 1978), 103.

56. Cf. Fleisher, 132.: "More's problem—everyone's problem—is that the false *image* of things impedes the reception of the truth."

57. *Biography of an Idea*, 36-42.

58. An important exception is Lee C. Khanna: "It is Utopian ability to change, to heed and apply new ideas that Hythloday lauds as their chief quality—not their communism, Epicureanism, nor any of their customs." "*Utopia*: The Case for Open-mindedness in the Commonwealth," *Moreana* 31/32 (1971): 91-105; 94. Cf. Bradshaw, 26-27; Logan, 62.

59. See e.g., Fleisher, 130.

60. CW 4, cxxxix; Q. Skinner, "More's *Utopia*," *Past and Present* 38 (1967): 158-63; 157.

61. See e.g., notes 27, 53 and 60 above, and Elizabeth McCutcheon, *My Dear Peter: The Ars Poetica and Hermeneutics for More's Utopia* (Angers, 1983), 58-68.

62. " 'A Nursery of Correct and Useful Institutions': On Reading More's *Utopia* as Dialogue," in Sylvester and Marc'hadour, 281-89; especially 285-87. Cf. Logan, 61 ff.

63. Sylvester, 292-93. At 292, Sylvester denies that Book II is "dialogue at all, but a fervently eulogistic monologue." He does, however, emphasize that *Utopia* poses a question which "the reader must ponder" rather than providing a solution.

64. A. R. Heiserman, "Satire in the *Utopia*," PMLA 78 (1963): 163-74, especially 172-74; Robert C. Elliott, "The Shape of Utopia," ELH 30, (1963): 317-34.

65. See, for example, Elliott's comments on Surtz's readings of *Utopia*, 317-20. Cf. Lyman Tower Sargent's cautions on the satirical interpretation in "More's *Utopia*: An Interpretation of Its Social Theory," *History of Political Thought* 5 (1984): 195-210; 200; and McCutcheon, *My Dear Peter*, 69. A recent philosophical treatment of *Utopia* which seems a case in point is T. A. Kenyon's "The Problem of Freedom and Moral Behaviour in Thomas More's Utopia," *Journal of the History of Philosophy* 21 (1983): 349-73.

66. See the letters of Budé to Lupset, CW 4, 5-15, especially 9/35-13/2; and Busleyden to More, ibid, 33-37, especially 35/25-37/8; Hexter, *Biography of an Idea*, 44-48; David O. McNeil, *Guillaume Budé and Humanism in the Reign of Francis I* (Geneva, 1975), 30 and 57; and, for a comprehensive

view of humanist attitudes to communism, E. Surtz, *The Praise of Pleasure* (Cambridge, Mass., 1957), chaps. XIV and XV.

67. See More's objections to communism in practice in CW 12, 174 ff., especially 180.

68. She counts one hundred and forty uses in one hundred pages in "Denying the Contrary," 263.

69. Ibid, 267.

70. See Andrew D. Weiner, "Raphael's Eutopia and More's *Utopia*: Christian Humanism and the Limits of Reason," *Huntington Library Quarterly* 39 (1975): 1-27.

71. I have followed McCutcheon's translations because, as she points out, the Yale Edition frequently obliterates litotes.

72. CW 4, cxli-cxlii.

73. Skinner, 160.

74. Complete Works, vol. 6, *A Dialogue Concerning Heresies*, ed. Thomas M. C. Lawler, Germain Marc'hadour, and Richard C. Marius (New Haven and London, 1981), part 1, book 1, chap. 29, 117. Cf. Kenyon, 355 ff.

75. Skinner, 159.

76. Cf. Weiner, p. 13. See also Clare M. Murphy, "Un aspect de 'différance' dans l'*Utopie* de More: 'langue' du Livre I et 'parole' du Livre II," *Autrement Dire* (Presses Universitaires de Nancy) 3-4 (1986-87), 123-33, especially 128-32.

77. Cf. Dudok, *Sir Thomas More and His Utopia* (Amsterdam, 1925), 89, and More's letter to Gonnell (No. 63) on the education of his daughters, *The Correspondence of Sir Thomas More*, ed. Elizabeth Frances Rogers (Princeton, 1947), 120-23.

78. Logan, 59-66, 105, 110, 139-40, 216 ff.

79. P. 49; cf. chap. 1 and 2 passim.

80. Khanna, 93.

81. "Thomas More's Enclosed Garden: *Utopia* and Renaissance Humanism," *English Literary Renaissance* 6 (1976): 140-55; 155.

82. D. B. Fenlon argues that Utopia shows that the *philosophia Christi* was incapable of being invested with social and political content, and that Christian ideals and political reality are incompatible. "England and Europe *Utopia* and Its Aftermath," *Transactions of the Royal Historical Society*, Fifth Series, 25 (1975): 115-35; 124-25.

83. Cf. More's *Letter to a Monk*, Rogers, 124-31.

84. Marjorie O'Rourke Boyle, "Erasmus' Prescription for Henry VIII: Logotherapy," *Renaissance Quarterly* 31 (1978): 161-72; 163.

85. Schoeck, 284.

86. Pp. 152-54.

JEAN-CLAUDE MARGOLIN

Sur l'insularité d'Utopia : Entre l'érudition et la rêverie

> ... Divinités par la rose et le sel
> Et les premiers jours de la jeune lumière,
> Iles !
> ... Ruches bientôt, quand la flamme première
> Fera que votre roche, îles que je prédis,
> Ressente en rougissant de puissants paradis,
> Les Iles du Levant, mères vierges toujours ...
>   Paul Valéry, La Jeune Parque

LES ÎLES ONT TOUJOURS EXERCÉ, sur l'imagination humaine, une étrange fascination.[1] Surtout l'imagination des continentaux qui rêvent aux îles lointaines, inaccessibles, mystérieuses, si différentes, de par leur situation spatiale et leur insertion dans un temps où l'histoire se confond avec le mythe. Sans doute la rêverie des îles, comme la nostalgie, n'est plus aujourd'hui ce qu'elle était hier ou avant-hier, et quand un Boeing 747 survole à dix mille mètres d'altitude la Sicile tricorne, l'étoilement des Cyclades, ou les Iles Marquises, ces formes découpées dans la mer ou dans l'océan, entrevues à travers un hublot, n'ont plus le même pouvoir d'incantation, d'attirance ou de redoutable séduction que l'île des Lotophages pour le curieux et intrépide Ulysse, celle de Robinson, ou, passant, si l'on peut dire, de la légende à la réalité dûment chronologisée, les îles de la Mer Rouge ou du Golfe d'Aden, chères à Alain Gerbaud ou à Henry de Monfreid. Il n'empêche: que les conditions du voyage aient transformé la perception des îles, vues du ciel, en une multiplicité de planches d'un atlas mobile, où le relief sera souvent à peine plus accentué que ces taches brunes, blanches ou bleutées (la neige ou les glaciers) qui figurent sur les cartes des atlas dits scolaires, l'homme ou la femme disponible retrouvera, sans trop de peine, lors d'une rencontre – même abstraite et fugitive – avec les Iles, un peu de cette émotion amoureuse de l'enfant baudelairien, penché sur les cartes géographiques. Il ou elle aura au moins le loisir de rêver sur les noms de ces îles, rêverie d'autant plus féconde et gratifiante que ses connaissances de la géographie et surtout de l'histoire seront limitées: Iles sous le Vent, Açores ou Canaries, Iles de Pâques, Galapagos, et Gorée, "la joyeuse," aujourd'hui "la délaissée," l'Ile au Trésor de Stevenson et l'Ile Mystérieuse de Jules Verne, l'Ile Rose de Charles Vildrac, ou Chypre, que le sourire et la chevelure d'Aphrodite-née-des-flots rend plus présente à notre mémoire érudite et rêveuse que les longs démêlés – parfois sanglants – entre les Grecs, les Turcs et les Chypriotes, du temps de Mgr Makarios III et du débat-combat pour l'*Enosis*. Persistera une vision poétique et affective des îles, pour ceux dont le sort n'est pas lié au destin de ces terres émergeant des flots, et qui préfèrent ignorer l'origine historique de leur nom pour se complaire dans une rêverie intemporelle et fantaisiste qui ajoutera à leur charme en faisant naître dans l'imaginaire des ondes de désir: Marie-Galante, dont le nom, nous apprennent les dictionnaires, lui fut donné en hommage à la Vierge Marie, mais qui évoquera toujours, dans l'inconscient des voyageurs, même les plus austères, pour peu qu'ils aient admiré les toiles de Gauguin et rêvé sur sa vie, je ne sais quel charme ou envoûtement féminin, où l'amour s'unit avec l'insouciance du "carpe diem," dans une parenthèse de la vie "sérieuse," que connut si bien Ulysse, qu'il cédât ou non à la séduction de Calypso, des Sirènes ou de Nausicaa.

Les Iles oubliées où s'écrivit l'histoire: Tel est le titre d'un livre que j'ai découvert récemment au cours d'un vagabondage moins poétique à travers les rayons de la Butler Library, sur le campus de l'Université de Columbia. Il est dû à André de la Far,[2] et il permet au lecteur-rêveur de contourner ou de survoler, en deux heures du temps des horloges, à travers les océans et les mers du globe et dans une remontée du cours de l'histoire, quelques centaines d'îles, petites ou grandes, sauvages, odoriférantes, granitiques ou volcaniques, rondes ou étoilées, plates ou pyramidales, allongées ou trapues, isolées ou rassemblées en archipel. On y apprend des quantités de choses, mais on s'y prend surtout à rêver. Bon exercice de rêverie aussi que cet *Island World*, de

Charles Barrett, qui date de 1944,[3] et qui, simple anthologie des Iles du Pacifique, mêle à des descriptions précises des notations d'une subjectivité dont l'imagination du lecteur prend le relais et qui le met dans les meilleures dispositions du monde pour ouvrir, une fois de plus, ce "libellus vere aureus, nec minus salutaris quam festivus," ou plutôt—car le latin ne nous servira ici que de bouée de sauvetage contre un excès d'imagination—je veux dire "L'île d'Utopie" de Thomas More:[4] cette île d'Utopie, qui ne figure dans aucun des deux ouvrages cités, sur aucun atlas de géographie universelle, mais qui fixe notre regard dès l'ouverture du livre, soit dans la première édition—celle de Louvain en 1516[5]—soit dans l'édition bâloise de 1518.[6] C'est avant tout sur cette image de l'île, dans ses diverses variantes réelles ou imaginaires, ainsi que sur la description littéraire (et littérale) de l'île (sans oublier le quatrain liminaire en langue utopienne)[7] que je fixerai cette rêverie éveillée à prétention philosophique. Deux guides m'accompagneront dans ce parcours: André Prévost, dans son excellente édition-traduction-commentaire de l'*Utopie*,[8] dont l'immense savoir historique, théologique et philologique m'évitera bien des écueils, et Louis Marin (au nom prédestiné!) dont les *Utopiques*[9] et les propres réflexions philosophiques sur la topographie et les origines de l'île seront pour moi un puissant stimulant.

∽

L'immense bibliographie[10] de ce célèbre ouvrage de More fait apparaître un certain nombre d'études portant sur la description de l'île, la gravure liminaire, les rapports entre les aspects topographiques d'*Utopie*, son origine, son gouvernement, et sa fonction politico-sociale. Mais les commentateurs, depuis bientôt cinq siècles, ont si largement insisté—sans doute avec raison—sur le contenu sociologique, philosophique, politique ou religieux, et bien entendu, satirique, de cette oeuvre hors du commun, sans passé véritablement assignable (en dépit de Platon) et sans postérité véritable (en dépit de Bodin ou de Samuel Butler), que la topographie d'*Utopia*, la forme de ses côtes, l'acte de fondation de l'île par le roi Utopus, sont généralement relégués à l'arrière-plan, comme s'il s'agissait de données de fait qui n'ont guère de rapports organiques ou de cause à effet avec les mobiles d'action des Utopiens ou le mécanisme institutionnel de cette République. C'est donc, de façon délibérée, en me fondant essentiellement sur le double paramètre spatial et temporel, que je développerai mes réflexions, tirées d'une observation du dessin de l'île et d'une lecture de sa description, sans me croire d'ailleurs tenu à faire de la gravure de 1516[11] ou de celle, inversée, de 1518,[12] le modèle *ne varietur* de toute représentation visuelle de l'île: certes, n'est pas Holbein qui veut (si tant est que l'auteur de la gravure liminaire de 1518 soit Holbein lui-même, Hans ou peut-être Ambroise),[13] mais pourquoi l'imagination bien réglée d'un lecteur de la fin du XXe siècle (qui pourrait éventuellement avoir quelque talent graphique) ne viendrait-elle pas se substituer à celle de l'artiste rhénan, transportant avec elle un univers culturel fort différent du sien? Quant à Gérard Geldenhauer – à supposer qu'il soit le dessinateur d'Utopia[14] dans la première édition – dont chacun connaît l'intérêt pour l'histoire et la géographie, et les futurs démêlés religieux avec Érasme,[15] il n'a pas une réputation d'artiste telle qu'elle nous contraigne à nous incliner sans broncher sur l'honnête et ronde figure qu'il a dessinée dans un bel élan de solidarité humaniste.

Or donc, larguons les amarres qui nous rattachent trop exclusivement à la terre ferme des études humanistes, cinglons vers *Utopia* en abandonnant sur le continent une cargaison excessive et inutile, et approchons-nous de cette île, en suivant, certes, le récit d'Hythlodée, mais sans nous prendre pour lui, et en posant au dessin de l'île et à sa description les questions qui sont celles d'un lecteur-rêveur de la fin du XXe siècle. Description qui d'ailleurs donne énormément à voir et à entendre (à comprendre), s'il est permis de rappeler que, dans son épître dédicatoire à Jérôme de Busleiden,[16] "Mécène des études et gloire de notre siècle,"[17] Pierre Gilles d'Anvers écrit en toutes lettres: "Je croirais volontiers que Raphaël lui-même a vu moins de choses dans cette île, pendant les cinq années entières qu'il y a passées, que la description de More en laisse voir."[18] Hommage à l'écrivain et au narrateur, dira-t-on avec raison, selon le principe humaniste qu'une bonne description, rehaussée de toutes les ressources de l'art oratoire vaut mieux qu'une expérience vécue, intériorisée, mais qui peut souffrir d'un défaut de *copia* ou d'*ekphrasis*. Mais aussi appel à l'imagination du lecteur face à tout ce que la puissance d'évocation et d'expression de l'écrivain donne à voir. Notons enfin que dans cette même adresse liminaire à Busleiden, Pierre Gilles,[19] ami intime de More (et d'Érasme) et dont la fonction de secrétaire de la ville d'Anvers donne à ce récit océanique et imaginaire sa dimension d'authenticité, insiste sur la brièveté des propos de Raphaël relatifs à la géographie de l'île. Raison de plus pour que nous nous étendions davantage sur cette géographie imaginaire d'Utopia, où la nature et l'art se sont prêté mutuellement appui pour en faire une réalité – j'insiste sur ce mot – exemplaire, en même temps qu'unique en son genre.

I

Espace et topographie d'Utopia

L'habileté de More, avec ses interventions personnelles, soit dans sa lettre-préface à son ami Gilles,[20] soit sans les premières pages du récit lui-même, où il évoque sa présence physique à Anvers, ses rencontres, dont celle d'Hythlodée, a pour résultat que l'île d'Utopie se présente à nous à la fois comme une réalité qui s'intègre dans les récits de voyages et de découvertes de l'époque (le nom de Vespucci est cité dès le début), une île lointaine, encore très mystérieuse, isolée au milieu de l'Atlantique, dans l'hémisphère austral, bien au-delà de l'équateur et de la zone torride des tropiques, à mi-distance de la Flandre et de l'Equateur (vers le 50e parallèle sud), et comme une création littéraire ou philosophique. Elle se situe donc dans un espace à la fois réel et imaginaire. Alors que le récit d'Hythlodée s'inscrit tout naturellement dans le temps – le temps du récit lui-même, et le temps évoqué par l'histoire mythique de l'île – la perception d'Utopia par l'observation du dessin et par la fixation des images que nous suggère la partie descriptive du récit se fait d'une manière globale ou intuitive. Même si nous sommes conduits à suivre *discursivement* le tracé de la côte, le cours des fleuves, et à repérer *successivement* les différentes montagnes ou collines, les divers bourgs ainsi que la capitale Amaurote, ce parcours ne se situe pas dans un temps réel: il analyse simplement, ou examine en détail ce qui nous est donné, ou nous sera redonné dans une synthèse globale. Mais, comme l'a très bien montré Louis Marin,[21] nous ne pouvons pas séparer, ni en droit ni en fait, cette vision instantanée de la carte d'Utopie du récit d'Hythlodée, *alias* More, malgré tous les efforts d'écriture et de mise en scène employés par l'auteur pour se différencier du narrateur, de celui qui a *vu*, qui a *vécu* cinq années dans l'île, qui en est *revenu*, et qui s'en fait, par son récit, le témoin oculaire, existentiel et irremplaçable, celui qui, sur un plan humain, rien qu'humain, apporte aux incroyants ou aux incrédules – ou simplement aux ignorants – la "bonne nouvelle" de cette *Utopia*, qui devait s'appeler, comme on sait, *Eutopia*,[22] le lieu bien situé, ou plutôt, selon l'intuition et la volonté de More, le lieu le meilleur, ou le pays du bonheur. Et l'habile philologue, qui savait donner aux mots leur plénitude de sens et jouer sur la polysémie qui leur est inhérente, pouvait apparemment faire de cette *Eutopie* ou île enchanteresse, l'équivalent ou l'analogue, non pas des Iles Fortunées de la mythologie païenne, mais d'un paradis terrestre: *Eutopia, Evangelia*, ce rapprochement n'a rien qui puisse choquer, même une âme chrétienne.

Le rapprochement que nous venons de faire devrait nous conduire à distinguer entre un espace profane et un espace sacré. Oublions un moment ce que nous savons de More, et surtout de sa destinée future, terrestre et posthume; ne songeons pas, en relisant *Utopia*, que son auteur est devenu un saint de l'Église catholique. Oublions aussi les diverses interprétations du texte, notamment celles qui se situent aux antipodes l'une de l'autre: l'interprétation socio-politique marxisante[23] (qui ne tient aucun compte de la dimension éthico-religieuse de l'oeuvre), l'interprétation purement (ou exclusivement) chrétienne qui ferait de la Cité utopienne l'équivalent ou l'analogue de la Cité de Dieu de saint Augustin. Il semble — et André Prévost l'a bien montré — que dans Utopia et dans le comportement des Utopiens, le profane ne soit jamais exclusivement profane, et qu'en revanche, le sacré ne se situe pas en surplomb, ou dans une transcendance absolue par rapport au profane. Cette distinction d'un double espace n'en est pas moins nécessaire: espace profane, ou plus simplement géographique, dans lequel Utopia va s'insérer, dans une carte du monde où figurent déjà l'île de Ceylan, le port de Calicut, et bien d'autres étapes des voyages au long cours des Vespucci, des Magellan, des Raphaël Hythlodée. Insertion au milieu de l'*évocation* — plutôt que de la *description* — de ces peuples, de ces villes, de ces places-fortes, de cette "vie commerciale intense, terrestre et maritime, qui s'exerce... même avec des peuples très éloignés," car il faut aller vite, et ne pas retarder exagérément l'attente du lecteur, avide de nouveautés. Mais nous voici au Livre second, et à la description proprement dite d'Utopia:

> L'île des Utopiens, dans sa partie médiane (c'est sa plus grande largeur) mesure deux cents milles; elle n'est guère plus étroite ailleurs; elle s'amincit progressivement aux deux extrémités, qui s'incurvent pour dessiner un arc de cercle de cinq cents milles de circonférence et donner à toute l'île l'aspect d'une lune renaissante. Les eaux de la mer pénètrent entre les cornes de ce croissant, distantes de onze milles, plus ou moins, et se répandent dans un immense golfe, entouré de tous côtés, de collines qui arrêtent les vents; elles forment une sorte de grand lac, où le calme est rarement troublé par la tempête, et font du sein de cette terre presque tout entier un port que les navires sillonnent en tout sens, pour le plus grand profit des habitants....[24]

Si je me reporte au dessin de l'édition de 1516 ou à celui de l'édition de 1518 (vraisemblablement dû à l'un des frères Holbein),[25] force m'est bien d'avouer que je ne reconnais guère en eux une représentation fidèle de cette description; ou plutôt, j'aperçois le golfe en forme de croissant de lune sur la gravure de 1516, et non sur celle de 1518. D'où, pour une seconde fois, ma protestation de liberté à l'égard de la représentation visuelle de la description verbale de l'île. Je serais plus "indulgent" pour la représentation du rocher et de la forteresse qui doivent se dresser au milieu de l'étroite passe maritime ("Le goulet, en raison de hauts-fonds d'un côté et de rochers de l'autre, est extrêmement dangereux. A peu près au milieu des passes se dresse un rocher isolé que sa visibilité rend inoffensif et sur lequel est édifiée une tour tenue par une garnison"):[26] rocher et tour sont en effet très visibles sur le dessin dont parle Geldenhauer; quant à celui de Holbein, la tour est beaucoup plus discrète, située sur la partie gauche de la vignette, où pourrait se lire, à la rigueur, une esquisse--difficilement identifiable--de ce "croissant" dont je niais un peu plus haut la représentation.

Comme le fait remarquer Marin dans son exégèse des *Utopiques*, la forme de l'île—côte circulaire, mais étroit goulet qui se contracte ou se dilate selon l'alternance du flux et du reflux—exprime à la fois une volonté d'accueil et un souci de sa propre défense. Volonté d'ouverture au monde extérieur—en l'occurrence aux navigateurs passant à proximité de l'île et souhaitant s'y réfugier en attendant de reprendre le large—et volonté non moins ferme de se protéger contre toute attaque éventuelle venant de la mer.[27] Forme paradoxale de cette île, où la volonté et l'ingéniosité des hommes ont aménagé la géographie naturelle: à la fois tournée vers le dehors et vers le dedans, accueillante—jusqu'à un certain point—à l'expérience et à la culture des autres, mais aussi, et même surtout, soucieuse d'aménager au mieux de ses intérêts les ressources vitales et intellectuelles, affectives et morales, des Utopiens. L'espace et la topographie de l'île ne sont donc pas pour ses habitants des données irréductibles qu'ils subissent et dont ils s'accommodent tant bien que mal. Si l'on songe—nous y reviendrons—à l'acte fondateur d'Utopia, quand le roi Utopus, qui portait déjà dans son nom le destin exceptionnel de son État, décida, d'une manière délibérée, de détacher cette terre, alors intégrée au continent, pour la faire dériver vers ce lieu de nulle part en la transformant dans son essence comme dans sa fonction, et en la faisant sortir d'un âge de l'Histoire—ou d'un temps mythique—pour la faire accéder à un nouvel Âge qui inaugurerait véritablement son destin historique, on reconnaîtra sans peine que la nature n'est pas pour les Utopiens et pour leur chef une divinité devant laquelle on s'incline sans mot dire. L'espace profane de l'île, ses accidents topographiques, orographiques, hydrographiques, et bien entendu ses marques toponymiques, laissent place à une sacralisation.[28] L'acte fondateur d'Utopia et la désignation du nom de l'île et de tous les éléments géographiques dont elle se compose – géographie physique et géographie humaine – ressemble, toutes proportions gardées, à l'acte de dénomination des espèces animales, délégué à Adam par Dieu au début de la *Genèse*. On dirait volontiers que les fleuves, les montagnes, les cités d'Utopia, n'acquièrent, comme les animaux de la Bible, d'existence réelle et une insertion dans l'histoire, qu'à partir du moment où ils sont dénommés avec solennité, et toute la sagesse dont peut être capable un être inspiré: tel était le cas d'Adam, tel nous imaginons qu'ait pu l'être celui d'Utopus.

Une expression, celle de la "lune renaissante"[29] et de son croissant, retiendra notre attention: j'y verrais pour ma part un microcosme linguistico-culturel de la Renaissance, et compte tenu de la mythologie lunaire et de sa fonction dans l'imaginaire de cette époque, une sacralisation de l'espace. Expliquons-nous.

On pourrait, comme l'a fait Stouvenel dans sa traduction de l'*Utopie*,[30] négliger le terme *luna* et s'en tenir simplement à la *forme* du croissant de lune – il traduit: "l'île présente la forme d'un croissant" – mais ce serait une erreur. Car s'il est vrai que le croissant de lune, ou la lune à son premier quartier (la *luna renascens* succède à une "pleine lune" qui, son cycle régulier accompli, s'est en quelque sorte résorbée dans l'immensité du ciel et de la nuit) dessine cette figure que représente la lettre C, et à propos de laquelle les Rhétoriqueurs de la fin du XVe et du début du XVIe siècle ont épilogué à satiété;[31] s'il est également vrai que la description de l'île se veut pleinement réaliste, et que l'on peut voir dans cet aménagement de la côte la preuve de la haute compétence technique des ingénieurs d'Utopia, la référence à la croissance et à décroissance de la lune, et l'allusion à ce bassin d'eau paisible qui ressemble à un lac, mais qui peut se gonfler ou se vider partiellement au gré du flux et du reflux de la mer (commandés, comme on sait, par la lune) me font rêver à quelque immense organisme animal ou à quelque divinité tutélaire, animal femelle, divinité féminine. La lune ne représente-t-elle pas, même aux yeux d'auteurs chrétiens ou de philosophes épris de raison, l'astre féminin, Diane ou Sélènè, Hécate, protectrice des femmes en gésine, dont la fonction, dans le cas qui nous occupe, n'est pas tant d'éclairer[32] (car nous n'envisageons pas de navigation nocturne de la part des Utopiens, ni non plus d'invasion maritime par une nuit sans lune) que de les materner, en quelque sorte? Cette présence discrète de la lune ajoute à la configuration profane de l'île une dimension sacrée.

Je n'ai généralement pour les interprétations psychanalytiques appliquées à des auteurs du passé ou à des textes consacrés par des générations d'exégètes, qu'un intérêt de curiosité marqué d'un léger scepticisme. Mais je me demande si, à partir de cette image d'un espace animé, organique, changeant au rythme de la vie – et de la vie d'un organisme féminin – on ne pourrait pas saisir une nouvelle clé d'interprétation de plus d'un aspect de l'oeuvre de More, sans parler de sa vie personnelle.[33] On me rétorquera que, dans l'organisation de la Cité utopienne, les femmes ne jouent pas un rôle prépondérant: quand une fille est nubile ("ubi foeminae maturuerint"), lit-on au chapitre des rapports mutuels (*De commerciis mutuis*),[34] on la donne à un mari (*collocate maritis*), et il est admis que "les femmes étant plus faibles, elles ne travaillent qu'à la laine et au lin" (à supposer que ce soit le signe d'une parfaite équité envers les femmes que de leur assigner des travaux aussi pénibles qu'aux hommes!) Ce sont les Anciens – entendons les hommes les plus âgés – qui détiennent l'autorité, après le roi bien entendu, les femmes "servent leurs maris," et c'est le père de famille qui se charge de nourrir sa maisonnée. Certes, ce serait, au temps de More, et même encore à bien des égards de nos jours, un autre type d'utopie que de placer les femmes dans une situation d'indépendance ou plutôt de prépondérance par rapport aux hommes, à l'intérieur ou à l'extérieur de leurs familles. Cependant, si l'on veut bien admettre que l'équilibre de l'île et des insulaires tient à un habile et constant dosage entre la nature et l'art (lieu commun, dira-t-on, mais dialectique pensée à nouveaux frais, et comme vécue de l'intérieur), on découvre – ce qui n'a rien pour nous surprendre – que le monde de la nature est celui de la femme, celui de l'art (techniques, organisation étatique, travaux d'intérêt public, etc.) étant celui de l'homme. Mais les prescriptions concernant le mariage, la manière de le contracter, les cas exceptionnels de divorce, tout dans l'organisation de la famille implique une égalité parfaite entre l'homme et la femme. La sévérité à l'égard du viol est le signe d'un respect inhabituel à l'égard de la femme.

Ces remarques nous éloignent de la géographie de l'île et de sa configuration "lunaire." Mais si l'on veut bien admettre cette influence de l'astre féminin sur la vie pratique des Utopiens, et, par le jeu alterné du flux et du reflux de la mer, de proche en proche, les modifications constantes du cours du fleuve Anydre – "le fleuve sans eau" (sa source est peu abondante, dit le texte),[35] que Vossius[36] interprétait dans le sens d'un paradoxe, à l'égal d'Utopia, le pays de nulle part, c'est-à-dire la "non-rivière," on reste fidèle à l'image de cet organisme féminin et nourricier, allaitant en quelque sorte ses enfants, selon les images traditionnelles qui viennent de loin, et où, cette fois, la Lune-Sélènè serait remplacée par Déméter ou Vénus (une Vénus marine, bien entendu). Les commentateurs érudits, ou attentifs au parallèle Utopie-Angleterre, ont montré (comme R. Blunt)[37] que la largeur de l'Anydre, au moment où le fleuve se présente devant la capitale Amaurote—au nom mystérieux, qui a donné matière à bien des exégèses . . . ou au silence des commentateurs, car le grec *amauros*, qui signifie obscur, se contredit lui-même, si tant est que nous ayons, ici encore, un préfixe privatif, puisque *mauros* signifie lui-même obscur![38]—fait immanquablement songer à la Tamise, à Chelsea (résidence de More et de sa famille). Mais cette analogie probable ne doit pas nous empêcher de poursuivre l'image ou la thématique de ces eaux nourricières, navigables, apaisantes, féminines, dont Bachelard aurait pu nourrir sa propre rêverie, si ces eaux fluviales n'avaient pas été aussi rapprochées de la mer, à laquelle il était foncièrement allergique.[39]

Le rapprochement qui a été souvent fait entre l'île d'Utopie et l'Atlantide détermine un espace mythique ou fabuleux dans lequel le lecteur érudit ne se sent pas tout à fait étranger, et qui donne à sa rêverie quelque consistance. Mais l'île d'Atlantide est immense, et ce continent ne peut pas exercer le même pouvoir sur notre imagination:

> Cette île, précise Critias,[40] était alors plus grande que la Libye et que l'Asie réunies. Aujourd'hui qu'elle a été submergée par des tremblements de terre, il n'en reste plus qu'un fond vaseux infranchissable, obstacle difficile pour les navigateurs qui cinglent d'ici vers la grande mer. . . .

Et voici quelques traits descriptifs de l'Attique ancienne, véritable pays de Cocagne, qui, si elle ne présentait pas l'aspect d'une île, mais plutôt d'une presqu'île, en possédait la fertilité et la douceur de vivre paradisiaque:

> La terre de ce pays[41] dépassait, dit-on, en fertilité toutes les autres, en sorte que la contrée était alors capable de nourrir une grande armée, exempte des travaux de la terre. . . . Ce qui en subsiste encore aujourd'hui est sans égal pour la variété et la qualité des fruits, et pour l'excellence des pâturages qu'elle offre à toute sorte de bétail. . . . Détachée tout entière du reste du continent, elle s'allonge aujourd'hui dans la mer, comme l'extrémité du monde. . . . En ce temps-là, encore intacte, elle avait pour montagnes de hautes ondulations de terre: les terres, qu'on appelle aujourd'hui champs de Phelleus, étaient couvertes d'une glèbe grasse; il y avait sur les montagnes de vastes forêts, dont il sub-

siste encore maintenant des traces visibles. . . . La terre donnait aux troupeaux une pâture inépuisable. *L'eau fécondante de Zeus qui s'y écoulait chaque année ne ruisselait pas en vain*, comme aujourd'hui, pour aller se perdre de la terre stérile dans la mer: la terre en avait dans ses entrailles, et elle en recevait du ciel une quantité qu'elle mettait en réserve dans celles de ses couches que l'argile rendait imperméables; elle dérivait aussi dans ses anfractuosités l'eau qui tombait des endroits élevés. *Ainsi, en tous lieux, couraient les flots généreux des sources et des fleuves*. . . .[42]

On aura remarqué que, dans l'Attique ancienne et mythique, les eaux nourricières sont essentiellement celles qui tombent du ciel ou qui jaillissent de la terre, la mer ne représentant que l'extrémité du cours des fleuves. Dans l'île d'Utopie, la localisation d'Amaurote et des autres villes est davantage commandée par les mouvements de flux et de reflux de la mer qui regonfle les rivières, comme l'Anydre, et qui, malgré l'inconvénient de sa salure, ne fait pas obstacle à la purification des eaux des rivières et à leur consommation quotidienne par les Utopiens.

II

Temps mythique et temps historique d'Utopia

Tóte, in illo tempore, en ce temps-là. . . . Ces formules simples et traditionnelles par lesquelles le narrateur—platonicien ou autre—situe la description d'un pays fabuleux, et notamment d'une île lointaine, perdue au milieu des flots, à plusieurs jours, semaines ou mois, de navigation à partir des côtes qui nous sont familières et qui voient se dérouler un temps marqué par une succession d'événements, les uns répétitifs, les autres surgissant dans leur singularité historico-sociale, renvoient à un passé mythique, quand bien même la foule de détails concrets ou de précisions topographiques ou toponymiques, ainsi que la présence vivante du narrateur ("J'y étais," ou "On m'a rapporté") tendraient à faire croire à une continuité historique, un avant et un après.

Or précisément l'avant et l'après d'Utopia marquent une rupture, et non une continuité. A la différence de l'Atlantide et de l'ancienne Attique, dont l'avant et l'après sont marqués par le surgissement de catastrophes ou de bouleversements cosmiques, raz-de-marée ou tremblements de terre, qui modifient du tout au tout la configuration du pays et sa fécondité sans que les hommes aient eu à intervenir (on peut toujours invoquer un dieu!), c'est l'acte volontaire et fondateur d'Utopus qui, comme nous l'avons déjà dit, a détaché l'actuelle Utopia du continent. Ce temps, le narrateur ne l'a pas connu, et il s'en remet aux traditions, à la légende, à l'affabulation: *uti fertur.* "*Ea tellus olim non ambiebatur mari . . .*"[43] Et bien entendu, Utopia ne s'appelait pas alors (*in illo tempore*) Utopia, puisque cette appellation, due au héros éponyme qui a fondé l'île (comme, dans l'histoire des découvertes, des hommes ont donné leur nom aux Iles Marshall ou aux Falkland pour s'en assurer la propriété réelle ou imaginaire, la main-mise, la régence personnelle ou la simple gérance) correspond précisément à sa date d'entrée dans l'histoire et à ses possibilités de communication, d'échanges, de rencontre avec Hythlodée. Elle s'appelait—mais ce n'était pas encore elle!—Abraxa, ou plutôt Abraxas, autre nom assez énigmatique, dont les érudits—et notamment Vossius[44]—nous ont appris le sens probable, par référence à l'hérésiarque Basilides et au système de numération des Grecs qui accordaient aux diverses lettres de l'alphabet une valeur numérique précise: $\alpha = 1$, $\beta = 2$, $\rho = 100$, $\alpha = 1$, $\xi = 60$, $\alpha = 1$, $\sigma = 200$, ce qui donne en tout: $1 + 2 + 100 + 1 + 60 + 1 + 200 = 365$. Contrairement à ce que nous pourrions imaginer, le nombre 365 ne désigne pas celui des jours de l'année, mais, d'après Basilides, les 365 cieux. Abraxas désignerait alors la plus haute sphère céleste, le pouvoir suprême. Etre de raison, être mythique, ce nom nous plonge d'emblée dans un temps qui n'en est pas un, qui n'est pas, en tout cas, un temps vécu par des hommes qui ont une histoire. Mais, dira-t-on, quand s'est effectuée la rupture, l'île à la dérive ne se mit-elle pas à porter un nom étrange, un nom qui n'en est pas un non plus, ou qui porte en lui-même un paradoxe: nom du roi créateur de l'île, certes, mais ce nom n'est-il pas un "non lieu," comme Ulysse, qui se fit appeler Personne (*Oudeis,* en grec) pour les besoins d'une cause précise, ou ce personnage de Hutten, que l'on désigne par *Nemo*[45] (comme le capitaine d'un roman de Jules Verne), nient, par le seul énoncé de leur identité, toute possibilité d'identification personnelle. Bel exemple de *jocoserium* humaniste, jeu auquel Érasme aussi s'entendait bien! Mais surtout, volonté pour un auteur d'assurer une fonction nouvelle à l'utopie: une fonction sociale. Ce qui frappe en effet, dans le récit des modalités de la vie communautaire des Utopiens, c'est leur activité multiforme, réglée selon la sagesse d'un législateur qui connaît bien les ressources de l'homme, selon une division du travail qui se veut rationnelle, et surtout le sens de la durée: une durée elle-même diversifiée, un temps qui exprime un progrès. Vue de l'extérieur (de la mer) par des voyageurs pressés, l'île, avec tous ses accidents et tous ses habitants, paraît figée dans une immobilité, ou, à tout le moins, une existence au ralenti. Mais il n'en est rien. André Prévost écrit justement dans sa longue introduction à son édition d'*Utopia*:

> L'un des préjugés les plus fréquents chez ceux qui analysent l'*Utopie* de More est de voir en elle une société achevée, un modèle que sa perfection même figerait d'une manière définitive. L'Utopien serait le premier étonné d'un tel contresens. Sa communauté politique est une société en marche, ses institutions sont ouvertes aux mutations, ses religions sont en pleine évolution. Bref, l'Utopie vécue, l'Utopie véritable est une réalité inachevée qui porte, inscrite en elle, la nécessité d'un incessant progrès.[46]

Mais voilà: il nous faut nous placer du côté des Utopiens, il nous faut—nous, lecteurs du XXe siècle, ou nous, contemporains de More, attentifs au récit d'Hythlodée—abandonner nos propres "coordonnées," nos "lieux communs," nos instrument de mesure, notre échelle des valeurs, nos préjugés sociaux, raciaux, religieux, pour nous mettre à l'écoute de ces insulaires. Belle leçon d'anticolonialisme, éclatante revanche sur les "conquistadores" d'Amérique dont le comportement violent ou éventuellement naïf est commandé par le préjugé que les Indiens n'ont pas d'histoire, à peine une langue,[47] réduits à une existence précaire au sein d'une nature plus dangereuse que généreuse: la culture, la civilisation, les techniques agricoles ou urbanistiques, la langue, les cadres d'une vie sociale dûment réglementée, et une religion affermie par une longue histoire, seraient l'apanage des Européens, en l'occurrence des Espagnols et des Portugais. Les Utopiens, comme les Indiens, vus de loin et de l'extérieur, ou, si l'on préfère, tenus à distance, n'ont pas d'histoire; ils vivraient dans un éternel présent, soumis seulement au rythme des saisons et au mouvement de la mer, qui fait gonfler ou assécher leurs rivières. Or que nous dit le texte? Tout le contraire! Relisons la fin du Livre I, le récit du marin-philosophe, qui donne à ses contemporains européens une belle leçon de relativité et de modestie:

> S'il faut leur accorder foi, les villes existaient là-bas avant même qu'il y eût des hommes chez nous. . . . D'après leurs annales (car ils ont des annales), avant notre débarquement—ils nous appellent les Ultra-Equinoxiaux—jamais, en quoi que ce fût, ils n'avaient entendu parler de notre monde, si ce n'est qu'il y a douze cents ans [notons la précision], un certain navire, poussé par la tempête, fit naufrage sur les côtes de l'île d'Utopie. Les flots jetèrent sur le rivage quelques hommes, des Romains et des Egyptiens,

qui ne quittèrent jamais plus le pays. Il faut noter quels avantages les Utopiens retirèrent, à force de travail, de cette occasion unique.[48]

Cette antériorité des Utopiens et de leur civilisation par rapport aux Romains et aux Egyptiens, traditionnellement considérés, avec les Grecs, comme les modèles indépassés de la civilisation antique, à l'origine, le christianisme en moins, de la civilisation occidentale, est une belle leçon de solidarité humaine: en bouleversant la traditionnelle succession des "âges du monde," schéma dans lequel la Renaissance est encore l'héritière du Moyen Age, et en faisant des Utopiens une puissance capable d'assimiler Romains et Egyptiens en leur donnant le goût de vivre dans l'île et de renoncer à leur ancienne civilisation, More nous donne une leçon de relativité historique. Il est bien connu que les puissances impérialistes et colonisatrices ont tendance à nier la réalité historique des peuples colonisés, à nier tout progrès matériel ou intellectuel des autochtones et à faire de la date de prise de possession du territoire l'An I de leur histoire et de leur véritable civilisation. La lecture de l'*Utopie* nous contraint à voir les choses dans un sens inversé, ou plutôt—car il n'est pas question de marquer une insolente supériorité sur ces brillantes civilisations méditerranéennes—à nous placer du *point de vue* des Utopiens. D'ailleurs, dans le texte que je viens de citer, les insulaires rendent hommage au degré de civilisation technique des Romains et des Egyptiens, puisqu'ils avouent sans la moindre gêne que leurs visiteurs—notons ce terme—leur ont fourni des explications qui leur permettraient d'assimiler ces connaissances. Ainsi le temps, dans ses différents rythmes, comme l'histoire, dans ses divers accidents, ses lenteurs, ses accélérations, ses continuités et ses ruptures, font-ils intégralement partie de la conception qu'il nous faut avoir d'Utopia. Amaurote, Anydris, Nusquama, Utopos: tous ces termes négatifs et paradoxaux que nous avons recontrés—et qui donnent précisément à l'oeuvre de More sa dimension utopique—ont été créés à l'usage de l'Européen, lecteur du récit d'Hythlodée et des discussions "continentales" qui ont lieu dans les rues d'Anvers ou sur le parvis de la cathédrale Notre-Dame. Mais pour ceux que nous continuerons d'appeler les Utopiens—ils n'ont pas d'autre nom!—cette négativité, cette réalité fantomatique, ce "non-lieu," ce "nulle-part," cette "rivière sans eau" ou cette cité-fantôme, se transforment en éléments pleinement positifs. Ulysse n'est Personne que pour le balourd Polyphème et le subtil lecteur d'Homère; pour lui, il reste bien Ulysse, Ulysse le malin, qui a plus d'un tour dans son sac! Utopos, entouré de ce halo mythique dans lequel nous nous complaisons, est lesté d'un poids humain et politique bien réel. Les travailleurs d'Utopia ne passent pas leur temps à s'interroger sur leur propre nom et sur les toponymes de leur île. D'ailleurs, pourquoi ne pas envisager que l'absence de représentation de cette île sur les cartes maritimes ordinaires, comme ce nom qui n'en est pas un, sont, de la part des insulaires, un système de protection supplémentaire, venant doubler, en quelque sorte, l'étroit goulet et la forteresse qui commande l'entrée du port?

~

Toutes les civilisations ont rêvé d'un Âge d'Or, et la rêverie des Iles a contribué, plus qu'aucune autre, à lui donner, au moins pour un temps, quelque consistance. Âge d'Or, rejeté dans le passé, dans un temps et dans un espace mythiques (l'enfance de l'humanité, qui coïncide parfois si bien avec la rêverie de l'adulte sur sa propre enfance et les "verts paradis" qu'elle fait lever dans son imagination). "En ce temps-là," qu'il s'agisse de l'époque des géants, de l'Attique féconde, des chevaliers errants, ou des Paradis. Âge d'Or, également projeté vers l'avant, et c'est le sens de ces Utopies progressistes au nombre desquelles il faut évidemment ranger l'oeuvre de More. Mais cet Âge d'Or n'adviendra pas au terme de générations successives qui se contenteraient . . . de l'attendre. Non seulement le travail et toutes les formes d'activité sociale et politique sont nécessaires à l'équilibre vital de l'île et de ses habitants, mais c'est cette organisation même, ce réseau de communications interprofessionnelles, intrafamiliales, économiques, etc., qui s'inscrivent dans un temps *historique* et *progressif*, qui expriment la marche vers un prétendu Âge d'Or: car si ce terme veut signifier le repos et la facilité au sein d'une nature féconde qui n'exigerait plus le travail et la peine des hommes, ce n'est pas dans le vocabulaire ou dans la langue des Utopiens qu'on le découvrira. Mais si la convergence de leurs efforts, la sagesse de leurs dirigeants, le réalisme de leur politique extérieure, finissent par exemple par éloigner le spectre de la guerre, comme leur organisation sociale a pu chasser celui de la faim, l'Âge d'Or sera à portée de la main, dans leur volonté même de travailler au bien commun, mais ce sera un Âge d'Or intériorisé. Et leurs aspirations religieuses, la connaissance et la mise en pratique des valeurs évangéliques, donneront à cette histoire humaine et profane, une dimension eschatologique, une sacralisation de leur propre existence.

Les réflexions philosophiques que nous inspire la lecture ou la relecture d'*Utopia* dissiperont-elles la rêverie sur l'île, son dessin, son espace, sa naissance historico-mythique? Le poids des idées fera-t-il chavirer la cargaison d'images ou de fantasmes que nous avions souhaité embarquer avec nous pour le temps court de ce bref essai, et — qui sait? — les déposer ou plutôt, les communiquer en quelque autre esprit? Peut-être. Mais nous ne le déplorerons pas. Les rêves de la nuit sont dissipés au réveil, et malgré les enseignements qu'on en pourrait tirer, il est bon qu'il en soit ainsi. Il est vain de courir après une enfance perdue, quand bien même on nous répètera que nous sommes de notre enfance comme d'un pays. Mais la rêverie sur l'île, quand elle est consciente d'elle-même, peut avoir des effets toniques. Pour nous, amis lecteurs, qui ne voulons être — et qui ne sommes d'ailleurs — ni l'enfant baudelairien penché sur ses cartes, ni le riche amateur de croisière "aux Iles" qui, après avoir débarqué sur l'une d'entre elles et s'être procuré une pleine mallette de produits locaux, s'en revient passer sur son luxueux navire une nuit plus confortable, ni le prospecteur de mines ou de champs pétrolifères travaillant pour une grande firme continentale (et la liste pourrait s'allonger à l'infini!), cette rêverie sur l'île est salutaire, jointe à une réflexion sur le phénomène *naturel et humain* de l'insularité (quand ces îles ne sont pas de véritables continents dont la majorité des habitants n'aperçoivent pas, dans leur vie quotidienne, la mer ou l'océan qui les entourent). Elle nous fait comprendre, à travers l'histoire, la géographie, la littérature universelle, le sentiment d'indépendance — et parfois la revendication d'autonomie — des insulaires, parvenus à un certain stade de la civilisation, même si cette revendication est irréaliste, même si elle s'accompagne souvent d'inadmissibles violences. Elle nous fait comprendre — sinon approuver — un sentiment de xénophobie, dérivé du premier (à moins que ce ne soit l'inverse), et également un désir profondément écologique (mais à "retombées" politiques évidentes) de sauvegarder les traits spécifiques de l'insularité, la conservation de la flore et de la faune, des mœurs traditionnelles, de limiter l' "invasion" des touristes, de renoncer (quand l'île est proche du continent) à tout projet de pont routier qui en abolirait le caractère essentiel, etc. Mais si nos Utopiens sont soucieux, eux aussi, de leur indépendance, si leur haine de la guerre ne va pas jusqu'à risquer de la sacrifier, ils sont profondément accueillants à l'étranger pacifique. Protection de leur insularité, mais échanges avec les autres, dont certains pourront un jour devenir "les leurs," la forme même de l'île, à l'endroit du "croissant de lune" protégé par une tour, nous l'a montré dans toute sa réalité géographique et socio-historique chargée de symboles. Nous pouvons maintenant refermer le livre (pas pour longtemps, sans doute), relire—si nous en avons le goût ou le loisir—Robinson Crusoé, L'Île mystérieuse ou L'Île Rose, retrouver (ou non) nos émotions d'enfance: Thomas More nous a appris pour toujours, grâce à son île, à acquérir, conquérir ou conserver un esprit adulte, capable de réfléchir sur des problèmes d'adultes.

Centre d'Études Supérieures de la Renaissance
Tours

Notes

1. On pourra lire l'intéressante dissertation allemande d'Ursula Stünzi, intitulée Die Insel (Literarische Inseltypen, Université de Zürich, 1973), inspirée principalement par des textes de littérature française. Voir notamment son chapitre sur l'île enchantée ("Die Insel unter dem Banne der Verzauberung"). Dans Le Bel Inconnu de Renauld de Beaujeu, poème médiéval du 13e siècle (éd. C. Hippeau, Paris, 1860, ou "Guinglain ou le Bel Inconnu," éd. G. Perrie Williams, Paris, 1929), une île enchanteresse est gouvernée par la Fée "aux Blanches Mains." Vision panoramique de l'île:

> Uns bras de mer entour coroit,
> Qui tote la vile ceingnoit;
> D'autre part la grans mers estoit,
> Qui au pié del castel feroit.   v. 1863-1867

2. Paris (Ed. A. Bonne) 1968.
3. "An Anthology of the Pacific," Oxford Univ. Press.
4. Malgré mon désir de rester au seuil de l'érudition bibliographique (pour More et l'Utopie, la bibliographie est démesurée), je signalerai le petit volume de Germain Marc'hadour, Thomas More, publié en 1971 dans la collection des "Philosophes de tous les temps" chez Seghers, et l'édition d'Utopia dans le corpus de Yale (The Yale Edition of The Complete Works of St. Thomas More, Vol. IV, edited by Edward Surtz, S. J. and J. H. Hexter, Yale Univ. Press, 1965).
5. Libellus vere aureus, ed. Thierry Martens.
6. De Optimo Reipublicae Statu deque nova insula Utopia..., Bâle, Froben.
7. Ed. de Yale, p. 18.
8. L'Utopie de Thomas More. Présentation, texte original, apparat critique, exégèse, traduction et notes, Paris, Mame, 1978.
9. Utopiques: jeux d'espaces, Paris, Editions de Minuit, 1973.

10. Je renverrai, une fois pour toutes, aux bibliographies dressées dans les éditions de Surtz et de Prévost, ainsi qu'aux bibliographies classiques de R. W. Gibson (*St. Thomas More: A preliminary Bibliography*..., New Haven, Yale Univ. Press, 1961) et de Fr. Sullivan (*Moreana 1478-1945*, Kansas City, Rockhurst College, 1946), la seconde comportant essentiellement une liste des éditions de l'*Utopie* dans les diverses langues.

11. Voir sa reproduction dans Prévost (cf. n. 8 supra), p. 220.

12. Reproduite dans Prévost, p. 333.

13. Voir sur cette discussion, la légende/notice de Prévost, p. 332. Voir aussi les remarques de Surtz dans son édition, p. clxxxviii, et p. 276-77. Les deux "tabulae" sont reproduites sur deux pages, l'une à côté de l'autre, par Surtz (pp. 16-17).

14. A la vérité, si l'on se reporte à l'édition de 1516 et surtout à une lettre écrite par Geldenhauer à son grand ami Érasme, le 12 novembre 1516 (voir P. S. Allen, *Opus Epistolarum* II, ep. 380), il y est question d'un "quidam egregius pictor" dont le nom n'est pas révélé: secret à garder, ou modestie d'un auteur qui se risque à un travail inhabituel?

15. Voir la notice qui lui est consacrée dans *Contemporaries of Erasmus* (ed. P. Bietenholz, t. II, Toronto Univ. Press), 1986, pp. 82-84. Notons qu'il est l'auteur d'un *De situ Zelandiae* (1514) et d'un *De Batavorum insula* (1520).

16. Sur Jérôme de Busleiden (c. 1470-1517), voir *Contemporaries* (cf. n. 15), t. I, 1985, pp. 235-37 et H. de Vocht, *Jérôme de Busleiden, Founder of the Louvain Collegium Trilingue: His Life and Writings*, Turnhout, 1950.

17. A l'extrême fin de la lettre.

18. Trad. Prévost, p. 338 (et p. 15 de l'édition du texte).

19. Sur Pierre Gilles (Aegidius), voir *Contemporaries*, t. I, pp. 235-37. Sur les rapports d'amitié de Gilles et d'Érasme et l'influence d'Érasme dans les milieux humanistes anversois, voir Gilbert Degroote, "Erasmofilie te Antwerpen in de eerste helft van de zestiende eeuw," in *Commémoration nationale d'Erasme*, Bruxelles, Bibliothèque Royale, 1970, pp. 31-51 (résumé en français).

20. "Thomas Morus Petro Aegidio" (voir éd. Prévost, pp. 342-57 et 18-24 de la pagination de l'édition frobénienne de 1518).

21. "Le récit de voyage, écrit-il, est la remarquable transformation en discours de la carte, de l'icône géographique," (cf. n. 9 supra), *op. cit.*, p. 65. Et encore: "L'acteur anthropomorphise le parcours syntagmatique du texte, les toponymes étant les marques simples du parcours" (p. 65).

22. Sur le binôme *Utopia-Eutopia*, voir Surtz, p. 21 ("Eutopia or Happy Land") et p. 279; Prévost, pp. 673-74, et p. 686, n. 1.

23. Par exemple celle de Kautsky, qui a exercé une influence profonde et durable sur des milliers de lecteurs (voir aussi l'*Utopie* des Éditions Sociales).

24. Trad. Prévost, p. 449 (70).

25. Surtz opte pour Ambroise.

26. Prévost, pp. 449-50 (70-71).

27. Voir *Utopiques* (n. 9 supra), p. 137 sqq.

28. Sur cette consécration de l'espace et la sacralisation d'Utopia, on peut songer à l'étude récente de E. N. Genovese, "Paradise and Golden Age: An-

cient Origins of the Heavenly Utopia," in *The Utopian Vision* (Seven Essays on the Quincentennial of Sir Thomas More), ed. by E. D. S. Sullivan, San Diego State Univ. Press, 1983, pp. 9–28. J'ajouterai toutefois que l'essai en question s'oriente dans une direction tout autre.

29. *luna renascens.*
30. Paris, Éditions du Pot Cassé (coll. "Scripta manent"), 1927.
31. Voir à ce sujet, avec la référence à un célèbre texte de Rabelais dans *Gargantua*, nos propres remarques dans l'ouvrage *Rébus de la Renaissance* (Paris, Maisonneuve et Larose, 1986) que nous avons publié, Jean Céard et moi-même (t. I, p. 17 et 43).
32. Le second "luminaire" célébré à l'envi par les philosophes d'inspiration néo-platonicienne ou ficinienne, tel Charles de Bovelles dans son *Liber de Sapiente.*
33. Les femmes—essentiellement ses deux épouses et ses filles, et plus particulièrement Margaret—ont exercé sur son "affectus" une influence considérable.
34. Prévost, p. 480 (86).
35. "Oritur Anydrus . . . modico fonte, sed aliorum occursu fluminum," p. 459 (75). Sur l'Anydre, voir les remarques de Surtz, p. 392, et de Prévost, pp. 676 et 709.
36. *Opera*, 4, 341.
37. "The Glory of Chelsea," *The Fame of Blessed Thomas More*, p. 96.
38. Voir pourtant à ce sujet les explications de Surtz, p. 388. Amaurote serait la Cité fantôme, la Cité-mirage (comme l'Utopie, l'île de nulle part): ici encore, le réel et l'imaginaire se combinent pour créer cette poésie des lointains.
39. Voir son livre sur *L'Eau et les Rêves*, Paris, José Corti, 1942.
40. Voir éd.-trad. A. Rivaud, Paris, Belles-Lettres, 1925, 108e–109a.
41. *Ibid.*, 110e–111d.
42. C'est nous qui soulignons (à deux reprises).
43. Prévost, p. 451 (71).
44. Voir la note de Surtz, p. 386, qui cite Vossius (*Opera* 4, 340), mais aussi Erasme, qui se réfère plusieurs fois à Abraxas (dans son édition des Oeuvres de saint Jérôme, dans la *Moria*, dans sa Correspondance).
45. Voir notre essai, "Le *Nemo* d'Ulrich von Hutten: crise de langage, crise de conscience, crise de société?" in Mélanges offerts à Hans-Gert Roloff, *Virtus et Fortuna*, hrsg. P. Strelka & J. Jungmeyr, 1983, pp. 118–63.
46. Introduction, p. 113.
47. On ne dira jamais assez, dans cette perspective—et dans bien d'autres—l'importance de cette langue utopienne, jetée, dès l'ouverture de l'ouvrage, en pâture à notre curiosité et à nos réflexions philosophico-linguistiques.
48. Trad. Prévost, p. 445 (68).

For the story of this wine cup, see *Moreana* 25.
Pour l'histoire de cette coupe, voir *Moreana* 25.

University of Wisconsin—Parkside
Box No. 2000
Kenosha, Wisconsin 53141-2000

Humanities Division
Telephone: 414-553-2331

7 December 1987.

Germain Marc'hadour, Editor
Moreana
29 rue Volney -- B.P. 808
49005 Angers Cedex
France

My dear Germain,

Today is my daughter Morgan's sixth birthday, and the 46th anniversary of Pearl Harbor : a date to reflect on one of the horrors of modern life, and, through the life of my child, on my hopes for the future. And I bring you greetings from Kenosha where I teach, and from the more familiar sounding (to you) Racine where I live : the former, an American Indian tribal name, and the latter, supplied by early French explorers for the settlement they found at the juncture of the Root River and Lake Michigan. These place names are appropriate locations from which to send greetings. You visited here, and our friendship and mutual study of Thomas More has spanned and connected the New World with the Old.

I recall our first meeting in Chicago when you were visiting the Newberry Library and I, as yet an unpublished novice Renaissance scholar, nervously showed you my manuscript about an unnoticed English translation of Erasmus's *Conjugium* which you encouraged me to send to *Moreana*. How little did I realize then that this Chicago meeting would be but the first of many personal encounters over the next decades ; you were the encouraging voice that prompted me to explore more fully the world of More and his circle.

And then, shortly thereafter, you came to Racine to help us celebrate More's 500th birthday, and talked about St. Thomas More to our community. For months and years afterwards, many who had heard you would ask me when that gentle French priest who spoke so lovingly about St. Thomas More would return. I'm still waiting for that return visit, which I hope will come soon ! I owe you some hospitality.

After all, I was your guest for a week in Angers, sleeping on a cot in the office by night, using your marvellous study by day. I had taken a week from my stay at the Katholieke Universiteit te Leuven to visit, study, and write about Bishop William Barlowe, trying to resolve unsolved problems in his biography and in his relationship to More, and to the Catholic recusants who fled to Louvain. *Moreana* has published the results of some of these studies, but it was in that marvellous library of yours, and in *your* marginalia correcting the errors of others, that I found some clues and hints to solving my scholarly problems.

But that visit also introduced me to you, to your pastoral work (saying early morning Mass for the sisters), to your kindness (awakening me after Mass for breafkast in the garden), to your labors as editor (helping you to translate some German, or to edit a manuscript), and to the life you share with colleagues and friends in Angers. How good it was to meet those associated with the journal, to live for a week at Moreanum, and to feel the energy at the center of activities that produce *Moreana*.

I especially recall a hair-curling drive through town with Jean Rouschausse, the wonderful lunch he had prepared for me, and the good conversation about his work on John Fisher. By observing you work and working with you, I realized how *Moreana*, with its strange but wonderful mixture of impeccable scholarship and world-wide review of things Morean, reflects your own sense of scholarship and love of people.

And this is what I have learned from you and continue to admire : how to combine scholarly dedication and impressive learning that is always tempered by good will and graciousness towards others. Now that you are stepping down as Editor, I hope that I can repay you your lesson by serving *Moreana* well as a member of its Editorial Board, and by my own mentoring of young scholars and lay persons who seek knowledge and insight into the world of Thomas More. My little study group of Catholic lawyers in Racine, for example, has been meeting monthly for most of the year now, and they have decided, partly motivated by their patron saint, to hold a weekend retreat to reflect on the ethical and spiritual dimensions of their profession in relationship to their personal faith. Now, if I can only get them to subscribe to *More ana*....

I trust this letter will find good company among the other words of tribute to you collected in this volume. It is a fitting way for all of us whose lives you have touched to say thank you, Germain. Your life and work have been a model of dedication to scholarly inquiry that studies the past in order to give meaning to the present and hope to the future.

I look forward to our next visit, and close, as usual, with my warmest regards,

Andrew M. McLean
Professor of English and Humanities
Chair, Humanities Department

G. Budé, sketch by Raymond Joly

MARIE-MADELEINE DE LA GARANDERIE

*Guillaume Budé
lecteur de l'*Utopie

COMMENT NE PAS RENDRE grâces à Thomas Lupset? Jeune étudiant servant de courrier entre l'Angleterre et la France, nous lui devons en effet ce joyau dans l'oeuvre de Guillaume Budé, la Lettre à Lupset du 31 juillet 1517, morceau depuis lors presque inséparable de l'*Utopie*![1] Les circonstances sont bien connues. Lupset termine ses études à Paris, tout en veillant conjointement à la publication, chez Guillaume Le Rouge, des traités de Galien traduits par Thomas Linacre, et à celle de la seconde édition de l'*Utopie*, qui sortira, à la fin du mois de septembre, des presses de Gilles de Gourmont.[2] Il a communiqué l'un et l'autre ouvrage à Budé, lequel s'empresse de l'en remercier: une demi-page pour Linacre, plus de quatre pages pour Thomas More. Quatre pages qui, en vérité, ont beaucoup plus à nous apprendre sur Budé que sur More. Budé est certainement un homme qui se plaît à parler de lui-même; mais ici, de manière privilégiée, nous le saisissons, nous le surprenons, dans un moment de détente heureuse, une sorte de rêve éveillé où vibre le pressentiment d'une amitié.

> Ce livre, lance-t-il aussitôt, il n'a pas quitté mes mains, tandis qu'à la campagne je vais, viens, m'active, et donne des ordres aux ouvriers . . . . ; j'ai été si ému par cette lecture, découvrant les moeurs et les institutions des Utopiens, et les méditant, que j'ai presque négligé, voire abandonné, l'administration de mon domaine.   (Y 4, 22; P 4, 5)

Quelque chose s'est donc produit, un coup de foudre en somme, un "suspens de l'ordinaire durée," dirait Valéry.[3] La première manifestation en est un trouble, et comme la fine pointe d'une inquiétude: que suis-je donc en train de faire, m'agitant aux choses du "ménage"? Assurément Budé, qui a naguère si longuement philosophé, au cours de la rédaction de son *De asse*, sur le thème des richesses, ne pense pas faire, quant à lui, mauvais usage des "biens de fortune"; il se voit comme un bon père de famille qu'inspire le souci légitime d'accroître son patrimoine.[4] Et pourtant il s'en faut de peu que ce même Budé ne soit saisi tout à coup par quelque "mauvaise conscience bourgeoise." Atteinte passagère, il est vrai. L'émotion se fraye bientôt une autre voie; elle provoque une vive excitation de l'esprit, qui va se manifester à la fois par une sorte d'allégresse verbale, et par un foisonnement d'idées.

La paix heureuse, l'innocence des Utopiens suscitent d'abord, par contraste, l'évocation de la violence, des empoignades, des vols érigés en pratique légale, dont la société des hommes offre le triste spectacle:

> Aussi bien je voyais que c'était vanités, ces règles et ces pratiques de l'économie domestique, et, de façon générale, tout le soin que l'on prend d'accroître son revenu. Ce soin pourtant, il n'est personne qui ne voie et ne comprenne que, tel un taon intérieur et inné, il pique tout le genre humain. Aussi irai-je presque jusqu'à dire que—il faut bien l'avouer—le but des arts et des sciences qui se pratiquent légitimement dans la société est d'amener chacun à prendre toujours, avec une habileté aussi jalouse que scrupuleuse, quelque chose à son prochain auquel le lient les droits de la citoyenneté et quelquefois ceux de la famille: quelque chose à arracher en tirant, en traînant, en raflant, en reniant; à extirper en pressurant, assommant, dénonçant, extorquant, fouillant, frappant; à soutirer, à subtiliser, à soustraire, à s'approprier, et, tantôt avec la complicité, tantôt avec l'appui des lois, à dérober et à détourner. (Y 4, 27; P 4, 11)

Pour le seul plaisir de l'ouïe, et des yeux, citons ces dernières lignes en latin:

> ... semper abducat, abstrahat, abradat, abjuret, exprimat, extundat, exculpat, extorqueat, excutiat, excudat, subducat, suffuretur, suppilet, inuolet, legibusque partim conniuentibus, partim autoribus, auferat et interuertat.

Nulle part Budé (sinon peut-être dans les descriptions de la chasse qui ornent le *De Philologia*) ne déploie autant de virtuosité stylistique. Or, chez lui, l'écriture précède et porte la pensée. Aussi une méditation sur les rapports du droit et de la morale, rapports qui avaient déjà occupé plusieurs de ses annotations aux *Pandectes*,[5] est-elle lancée et mise sur orbite par cet étincelant "morceau de bravoure."

Viennent alors, jetées sur le papier dans l'émotion de la lecture, des pensées sur la justice. On ne peut se garder de songer à Pascal. . . . Mais où est donc la justice? se demande Budé. Ce n'est pas elle, mais son contraire, sa caricature, une injustice légale, qui se cache derrière le rideau de fumée de la chicane:

> Les usages et les institutions juridiques, nul ne l'ignore, ont fait prévaloir l'opinion selon laquelle les hommes habiles à prendre des cautions, ou plutôt à "prendre" tout court, ces chasseurs à l'affût des citoyens imprudents, ces fabricateurs de formules (c'est-à-dire de faux-fuyants), experts en matière de contrats, ces fauteurs de procès, jurisconsultes d'un droit inversé, renversé, bouleversé, sont regardés comme des pontifes de justice et d'équité. (Y 6, 9; P 4, 5)

Droit inversé dont les détours et les obscurités offrent à ceux qui ont le privilège, jalousement gardé, de savoir s'y retrouver, et de savoir en abuser, l'occasion de s'enrichir. Car tout pouvoir appelle la richesse, et la richesse procure le pouvoir. Et des hommes médiocres

> s'ils tiennent en mains les liens et les filets dans lesquels sont enserrés les patrimoines . . . peuvent posséder à eux seuls le revenu de mille citoyens, et souvent celui de cités entières, voire davantage! (Y 8, 9; P 6, 7)

Car la richesse porte en elle-même sa puissance d'accroissement, et chaque génération peut élever sur l'héritage de ses prédécesseurs de nouveaux biens "pour avoir réussi à évincer voisins, alliés, parents, frères et soeurs." (Y 8, 23; P 6, 24)

Ainsi la méditation de Budé s'achève sur le thème qui l'avait ouverte: la féroce compétition des hommes entre eux, à la poursuite de cet argent qui mène le monde et fausse toute représentation et tout exercice de la justice.

∽

Ce thème appellerait par contraste l'évocation idyllique de l'Utopie. Or il en est autrement, et, de façon inattendue, c'est le nom du Christ qui surgit: *At vero Christus* ..., "Et pourtant le Christ ..." Ce n'est pas seulement un pieux réflexe; car, tout au long de l'analyse décapante qui précède, le Christ, en fait, a été constamment le repère, le phare. Le voici donc sur le devant de la scène:

> Et pourtant le Christ, fondement et arbitre de toute possession, a laissé entre ses disciples un lien de communauté pythagoricienne[6] et de charité, et l'a consacré par un exemple lumineux, lorsque Ananie fut condamné à mort pour avoir violé cette loi. Par cet acte le Christ me semble avoir abrogé, du moins parmi les siens, tous ces volumes chicaniers du droit civil et du droit canon modernes,[7] ce droit qui constitue aujourd'hui la clef de voûte de notre jurisprudence et régit nos destinées.(Y 8, 24; P 6, 26)

Il semble que se soit produit, dans l'inconscient de Budé, une assimilation entre Utopiens et "vrais chrétiens," entre la description d'Hythlodée et le chapitre V des *Actes des Apôtres*. Mais le rapprochement n'est pas sans poser un problème. Car le texte des *Actes* laisse clairement entendre qu'Ananie et Saphire ont été foudroyés pour avoir menti. Pierre précise en effet qu'Ananie n'était nullement tenu de se dépouiller de son bien:

> Pierre dit: "Ananie, pourquoi Satan a-t-il rempli ton coeur? Tu as menti à l'Esprit-Saint et tu as retenu une partie du prix du terrain. Ne pouvais-tu pas le garder sans le vendre, ou, si tu le vendais, disposer du prix à ton gré?"   (*Actes*, 5:3)

Qu'il y eût de la part d'Ananie restriction mentale, c'est bien ce qu'entend Budé quand il déclare que, par ce châtiment, Dieu a rendu inutiles toutes les arguties du droit civil et du droit canonique. Mais son texte demeure ambigu, car il semble bien suggérer aussi que, par la mort d'Ananie et de Saphire, le mode de vie communautaire des premiers chrétiens s'est trouvé comme sacralisé. De sorte que l'on pourrait dire que, dans sa lettre à Lupset, Budé tire l'Évangile (ou plus exactement les *Actes*) à l'*Utopie*, comme réciproquement il tire l'*Utopie* à l'Évangile. La symbiose devient manifeste lorsque, plus loin, Budé énonce les trois principes qui définissent à la fois sagesse chrétienne et sagesse utopienne:

> L'île d'Utopie—j'entends dire Udépotie[8]—a eu la chance extraordinaire, si nous en croyons ce livre, de s'être assimilé, pour la vie publique comme pour la vie privée, les pratiques et l'authentique

sagesse du Christianisme, et de les avoir gardées intactes jusqu'à ce jour; certes, puisqu'elle retient à mains serrées, comme on dit, les trois principes divins: une parfaite égalité en toutes choses, bonnes ou mauvaises, ou, si vous préférez, le partage sans réserve de la citoyenneté; un amour constant et tenace de la paix et de la tranquillité; le mépris de l'or et de l'argent. Or ce sont là, j'ose le dire, les trois démolisseurs de toutes fraudes, impostures, filouteries, supercheries. . . . (Y 10, 1; P 7, 8)

Et les lignes qui suivent sont tout effusion, tout émerveillement: Ah, si ces principes avaient pu être gravés de manière indélébile dans les esprits de tous les autres hommes—dit en substance Budé—comme tout irait mieux! Quantité de livres de droit pourraient être abandonnés aux vers, ou servir dans les boutiques de papier d'emballage. . . . Et ce serait l'âge d'or. . . .

Ce thème de la justice injuste qu'entretiennent les tortueuses complications du droit est, à l'évidence, le leitmotiv de la lettre à Lupset. Budé y revient de manière quasi obsessionnelle. Ce faisant, il oublie, du moins le temps de cette lettre, que le christianisme ne saurait se réduire aux "trois principes divins" qu'il vient d'énumérer, et que, d'autre part, une lecture non-chrétienne de l'*Utopie* est parfaitement possible. Les deux messages ne coïncident pas. . . . Mais à quoi bon pousser si loin l'analyse, alors qu'il s'agit ici, Budé l'a dit d'entrée de jeu, d'une émotion, d'un choc spirituel! L'*Utopie* fascine Budé parce qu'elle propose une exigence absolue, et qui heurte de front, sans laisser place pour aucune voie médiane (comme, par exemple, la recherche d'un usage légitime des richesses), toutes les pratiques de nos sociétés. Si toute propriété privée est vol, que faire, notamment, des deux maisons de campagne qu'il est en train de faire construire sur les terres de Marly et de Saint-Maur qu'il a reçues en héritage? En fait, à cet endroit de sa lettre, Budé ne fait plus retour sur lui-même. Il jouit du "jeu de massacre." Il vit son rêve éveillé. Car il a pris une conscience fulgurante, l'*Utopie* lui servant de révélateur, que le christianisme est nécessairement, intrinsèquement, révolutionnaire; ou, pour dire les choses en termes plus budéiens, que l'Évangile est non seulement *paradoxal*, mais *antidoxal*,[9] tandis que la *doxa*, l'opinion, mène le monde.

∽

L'*Utopie* est donc pour Budé une parabole du royaume de Dieu. Une parabole? Non pas . . . ou plutôt mieux: le royaume de Dieu sur terre. . . . C'est bien ce que semble dire la dernière partie de la lettre. Budé paraît s'y intéresser avec une extrême curiosité à la situation géographique de l'île:

> Quant à moi, j'ai fait des recherches et acquis la certitude que l'Utopie est située en dehors des limites du monde connu, et qu'elle est assurément l'une des Iles Fortunées, et toute proche peut-être des Champs-Élysées; car Hythlodée, au témoignage de More lui-même, n'en a pas encore établi de manière précise la situation.
> (Y 12, 1; P 8, 18)

Au-delà des limites du monde connu, au siècle des grandes découvertes, il peut bien exister quelque îlot suffisamment séparé du reste du monde pour avoir échappé aux "civilisations" destructrices ou corruptrices! On songe aux *Cannibales* de Montaigne, au "bon sauvage" célébré par les missionnaires ou par les philosophes du siècle des Lumières. Et l'on peut songer aussi à l'émerveillement de l'ethnologue moderne qui découvre les rares survivants de peuplades primitives. . . . Budé parle avec tant de naturel de l'île d'Utopie, il rapporte avec tant de sérieux le témoignage d'Hythlodée, que l'on se surprend, non sans stupéfaction, à penser qu'il croit à l'existence réelle de ce lieu béni.

Entrons quelque temps dans cette hypothèse. La logique d'une lecture littérale confère alors à Hythlodée le statut d'un personnage historique (le navigateur, le compagnon d'Améric Vespuce), que Thomas More, tel un journaliste, fait parler. Le seul problème qui peut se poser à l'interprète est celui de bien répartir et apprécier les rôles respectifs du témoignage et du reportage. Budé semble bien rentrer dans une telle logique, quand il souligne à deux reprises, en latin, puis en grec, la modestie de More:

> Manifestement ce fut par scrupule de conscience qu'il ne s'est pas arrogé la part maîtresse, afin qu'Hythlodée, si un jour il se fût décidé à confier lui-même aux lettres ses aventures, ne pût avoir un motif de se plaindre de ce que More ne lui eût laissé qu'une gloire déjà cueillie et déflorée.
> (Y 12, 20: P 9, 14)

Une telle remarque prouve, certes, que Budé perçoit bien que le rôle de "reporter" auquel More prétend se limiter est déjà infiniment plus important qu'il ne semble, puisque ses interventions animent le discours, stimulent les débats, et mettent les audaces en relief par la contradiction. Mais il ne s'ensuit pas, évidemment, que Budé soit dupe du jeu. . . .

Peut-on imaginer en effet que ce savant helléniste n'ait pas été alerté, ne serait-ce que par les étymologies: Amaurote, Anydre, etc.? Au contraire, cet amateur de mystère et d'allégorie[10] ne pouvait qu'être séduit par cette sorte de jeu sérieux que lui proposait l'*Utopie*. D'autant qu'il aime, et sait fort bien, comme il le prouvera dans le *De Philologia*, pratiquer l'ironie et l'humour. Effectivement plusieurs signes manifestent que Budé est entré dans le jeu de More. Il y est même si bien entré qu'il y a joué sa partie. Il a pris son autonomie, et s'est permis d'être à plusieurs égards infidèle au texte de More. Certes on peut penser qu'il a lu un peu trop vite quand il fait d'Hythlodée (Y 12, 14; P 9, 7) le bâtisseur de la cité et le législateur d'Utopie. Mais d'autres infidélités révèlent que Budé s'est si bien laissé emporter par le jeu qu'il se plaît à l'alimenter à son tour, le relançant à sa façon et dans des directions qui lui sont propres. Quelle meilleure preuve peut-on trouver, et de la fécondité de l'invention de More, et de l'affinité et connivence que l'*Utopie* vient de faire éclore entre les deux hommes?

Ainsi, quand Budé feint d'hésiter sur le nom de l'île d'Utopie ("j'entends dire aussi Udépotie..."), il fait évidemment référence au premier titre prévu pour le livre, *Nusquama*, dont Udépotie est la traduction en grec latinisé; il indique ainsi qu'il est au courant de la correspondance sur le sujet entre More et Érasme, et fait entrer, sans le nommer, le grand Érasme dans le tableau. Mais ne semble-t-il pas en même temps donner, avec gentillesse et astuce, une leçon de grec à More?[11] Plus curieuse est la substitution, au nom d'Amaurote, la cité inconnue, invisible, introuvable, du nom d'Hagnopolis. On pourrait être tenté de faire d'Hagnopolis l'équivalent d'Amaurote, en se référant à ἀγνώς = inconnu. Mais ce serait négliger la présence de l'H initial (Budé est trop bon helléniste pour ne pas faire la différence entre l'esprit doux et l'esprit rude). On se voit donc conduit à remonter à ἀγνός = pur, saint, sacré. C'est ce que font aussi bien E. Surtz et J. H. Hexter qu'A. Prévost.[12] Mais, dans cette hypothèse, c'est l'association d'un masculin ἀγνός et d'un féminin πόλις qui a lieu d'étonner. Une autre solution s'offre, me semble-t-il, celle qui verrait dans Hagnopolis la transcription pure et simple d'ἀγνοπόλος, mot rare et poétique—ce qui n'était pas pour déplaire à Budé—et qui signifie pur, comme ἀγνός, mais relève plus précisément du vocabulaire religieux. Dans cette nouvelle hypothèse, c'est la terminaison du mot qui fait difficulté. On ne peut pourtant être insensible au fait que πόλος signifie pôle. Pôle de la pureté, absolu de la pureté, voilà qui convient bien à cette cité,

> Hagnopolis, l'unique, celle qui rassemble et harmonise entre elles les autres cités, et qui, contente de ses usages et de ses biens,

heureuse dans son innocence, mène en quelque
sorte une vie céleste.   (Y 12; P 8)

Enfin, quand on sait à quel point Budé se plaît à la polyphonie, on se prend à penser que ces étymologies diverses interfèrent. Ces termes de structures voisines, ἀγνώς/ἀγνός, πόλις/πόλος, ne voisinent-ils pas dans l'esprit de Budé comme ils voisinent dans les colonnes de nos dictionnaires? Un "plus haut sens" (pour parler comme Rabelais au prologue de son *Gargantua*) s'élabore de leurs rapprochements, ou plutôt de leurs combinaisons. Le "pur" est l'"inconnu" et l'"inconnu" le "pur." Référents négatif et positif se rejoignent. Aussi bien est-ce la loi de la théologie "négative."[13] C'est bien, en fin de compte, de théologie qu'il s'agit ici. Hagnopolis, dans les lettres mêmes de son nom, inclut un message pluriel. C'est une sorte de logogriphe, complexe et mystérieux. Budé, par nature, se porte toujours vers le sublime; et il n'est aucune de ses oeuvres qui ne désigne un pôle mystique.[14] Aussi ne peut-il se garder de substituer à Amaurote, ville fantôme, morne stéréotype,[15] Hagnopolis, la pure, l'absolue.

Mais une telle substitution est-elle volontaire ou involontaire? Si elle est volontaire, nous tenons là une preuve supplémentaire de la participation ludique de Guillaume Budé. Mais si, comme je suis tentée de le croire, la substitution est involontaire, cette participation n'en est que plus patente. Budé fait un rêve qu'élabore presque malgré lui sa lecture très personnelle de l'*Utopie*. Une lecture qui privilégie le Livre I au détriment du Livre II. Une lecture plus accordée aux aspects moraux et religieux qu'aux audaces politiques et sociales, à l'Évangile plutôt qu'à l'utopie (sans majuscule). C'est ce qu'avait déjà montré l'importance inattendue accordée à l'épisode d'Ananie. Tout lecteur séduit par un livre–tel, Budé, lecteur de l'*Utopie*–est à la fois fidèle et infidèle. Il subit un charme qui le rend créatif. Le livre est un miroir qui reflète auteur et lecteur. Une rencontre....

⁓

Budé s'est pris à aimer More en lisant l'*Utopie*. Dans le même temps, un peu plus tôt peut-être, More s'était pris à aimer Budé en lisant le *De asse*. Les deux hommes se connaissaient donc avant de s'être rencontrés. Ils s'appelaient en quelque sorte par leurs livres. Et la lettre à Lupset fut entre eux le premier lien. Lupset évidemment la montra à More. Elle allait, comme on sait, servir de préface à l'édition parisienne de l'*Utopie*. Et More ne se montra pas avare d'autres remerciements. Il envoya à Budé, par l'intermédiaire du même Lupset, un couple de chiens anglais "aussi bons dépeceurs de bêtes que gardiens du logis,"[16] et, présent infiniment plus précieux, "un couple de lettres." Une seule nous a été conservée. On imagine aisément le bonheur qu'elle procura à Budé. Car elle commençait ainsi:

> Toutes vos oeuvres, loin de les lire à la légère, je leur fais place parmi mes études sérieuses et essentielles; mais à votre *De asse*, je m'attarde aussi attentivement qu'aux meilleurs livres des Anciens. . . . Aussi bien n'est-ce pas un livre que l'on peut comprendre à la hâte, et vous l'avez voulu ainsi. . . .   (Rogers, ep. 65)

Et soudain Budé se sentait compris! More ne se bornait pas, en effet, à admirer dans le *De asse* le prodigieux travail scientifique qui avait redonné à la vie antique une réalité concrète et presque palpable, il avait saisi, à travers les digressions du livre, l'intention profonde et la philosophie de Guillaume Budé.[17] Il avait compris aussi quel type d'écrivain était Budé: de ceux qui acceptent d'être difficiles, et qui attendent du lecteur qu'il sache venir à eux et leur prêter longue attention. Enfin il avait perçu que leur condition de laïques, d'hommes mariés, de pères de famille, faisait de l'un et de l'autre des cas assez rares à l'époque, ce qui contribuait encore à les rapprocher.

Ils se rencontrèrent. Ce fut, comme on sait, au Camp du Drap d'Or. Ils ne furent certainement pas déçus, car ces lignes de More disent assez la tristesse de la séparation:
—de Calais, au début de l'été 1520 (Rogers, ep. 96):

> Des lettres de vous, qui me rendraient moins pénible votre absence, je n'oserais en réclamer, si le désir ne m'en pressait vivement. . . .

—de Calais encore, peu de temps après sans doute (ep. 97):

> Je ne sais, cher Budé, s'il est bon de posséder une fois les choses qui nous tiennent à coeur et nous sont chères, alors qu'on ne les peut garder. J'avais pensé que je serais parfaitement heureux s'il m'était donné de voir un jour devant moi Budé, dont la lecture m'avait tracé une merveilleuse image. Quand mon voeu s'est accompli, je me suis vu plus heureux que le bonheur même. Mais . . . notre accointance à peine ébauchée s'est trouvée interrompue, et nous-mêmes, obligés chacun d'accompagner notre prince, avons été entraînés dans des directions différentes, et j'ignore si jamais nous nous reverrons. Plus heureuse avait été la rencontre,

plus grande certes est la tristesse qui m'a envahi depuis ce départ. . . .

Ils ne devaient plus se revoir, et leur correspondance même serait rare, les affaires de leur temps les accaparant et les séparant, sans pourtant que leur amitié perde rien de son évidence. Comme l'avait écrit Budé à More dans sa longue lettre du 9 Septembre 1518 (ep. 66), ils étaient "en quelque sorte nés sous les mêmes astres," ils étaient "venus au monde déjà initiés aux institutions et aux moeurs d'Utopie."

Université de Nantes

Notes

1. Cette lettre ne figure ni dans les recueils d'épîtres latines de Budé, ni dans ses *Opera omnia* (1557). Elle apparaît pour la première fois en 1517, en préface à l'édition parisienne de l'*Utopie*. On la trouve également dans l'édition bâloise (1518), que reproduit, avec traduction française, la savante édition d'André Prévost: *L'Utopie de Thomas More*, Paris, 1978. La première traduction française que nous possédions est celle de Jean Le Blond, qui accompagne la première édition de l'*Utopie* en français (Paris, 1550). Une autre traduction, due à Nicolas Gueudeville, accompagne l'édition de Leyde (1715); elle est reproduite dans *Moreana*, 19/20, p. 43-49. J'ai moi-même, voici plus de quinze ans, traduit sans le publier ce même texte. C'est ma propre traduction que je cite dans le présent article. Que le lecteur veuille bien considérer qu'il ne s'agit point là d'une attitude critique à l'égard de la traduction donnée par A. Prévost. J'éprouve seulement le besoin, après une pratique déjà longue de l'oeuvre de Budé, d'accéder au texte latin par mes propres voies.

Dans le domaine anglo-saxon, la lettre à Lupset a été traduite pour la première fois dans l'édition de J. H. Lupton (Oxford, 1895). Dans l'édition de Yale University Press, *The Complete Works of St Thomas More*, t. 4, ed., E. Surtz et J. H. Hexter, (New Haven and London, 1965), la lettre et sa traduction en langue anglaise occupent les p. 4-15.

Je ferai référence, dans la suite de cette étude:
– par la lettre Y à l'édition de Yale,
– par la lettre P au livre d'André Prévost.
– par O.o., aux *Opera omnia* de Guillaume Budé (Bâle, 1557, 4 vol.), reproduites par Gregg Press (Farnborough, 1966 et 1969).
2. Cf. Y, Introduction, E. Surtz, p. clxxxv-clxxxvii.
3. *Eupalinos, ou l'Architecte*, éd. Gallimard, p. 42.

4. Voir sur ce sujet les lettres de G. Budé:
— à Érasme (7 juillet 1516), *Opera omnia*, Bâle, 1557, reprint Farnborough, Hants, G. B., 1969, p. 368; trad. franç. dans M-M. de La Garanderie, *La Correspondance d'Erasme et de Guillaume Budé* (Paris, 1967), p. 68-69;
— à Louis Budé, son frère (19 janvier 1517), *O.o.*, t. 1, p. 402, lettre grecque, trad. franç. par G. Lavoie, Sherbrooke, 1977, p. 87-93;
— à François Deloynes (29 septembre 1519), *O.o.*, t. 1, p. 95-96;
— à Germain de Brie (5 avril 1520), auquel Budé reproche son goût excessif pour le luxe et les mets délicats, *O.o.*, t. 1, p. 290-95, lettre grecque, trad. franç. G. Lavoie, p. 50-61.
Cf. *De asse*, *O.o.*, t. 2, p. 19.

5. Voir en particulier les annotations aux deux premiers titres: *De justitia et jure*, et *De origine juris*, *O.o.*, t. 3, p. 1-61.

6. Cf. Érasme, *Adages*, 1; et A. Prévost, op. cit., p. 652.

7. *Recentiores*. Budé dénonce d'une part l'altération du droit civil, conséquence de l'accumulation des gloses, et d'autre part la multiplication des décrets pontificaux postérieurs à la compilation de Gratien (Décrétales, Extravagantes, etc.).

8. Transposition de *Nusquama*, nom par lequel More et Érasme avaient primitivement désigné l'Utopie. Cf. le début de la lettre de More à Érasme (Allen, ep. 461): *Nusquamam nostram nusquam bene scriptam ad te mitto*. Voir A. Prévost, op. cit., p. 61-73. Budé avait vraisemblablement eu connaissance de cette variante par Thomas Lupset.

9. Cf. *De transitu Hellenismi ad Christianismum*, éd. de R. Estienne, Paris, 1535, f° 11; *O.o.*, t. 1, p. 142 c.

10. Sur la préférence de Budé pour un style difficile et surchargé de figures, voir M-M. de La Garanderie, "Le style figuré de Guillaume Budé et ses implications logiques et théologiques," in *L'Humanisme français au début de la Renaissance* (Paris, 1973), p. 343-59. Cet article s'appuie en particulier sur la lettre de Budé à Érasme du 26 novembre 1516 (Allen, ep. 493; *O.o.*, t. 1, p. 368), et sur sa lettre à Thomas More du 9 septembre 1518 (Rogers, *The Correspondence of Sir Thomas More* [Princeton, 1947], ep. 66; *O.o.*, p. 245).

11. Le mot Utopie est forgé par More à partir de la négation οὐ et de τόπος. C'est le "non-pays"; tandis qu'Udépotie qui transcrit οὐδέποτε = jamais, est en somme du bon grec. Cf. Germain de Brie, *Antimorus*, f° G 2: ". . . Utopia quoque sua, quam Udepotiam non Utopiam, si quid volebat Graece recte formare, appellare debuit . . ." Cf. aussi la lettre du même Germain de Brie à Erasme (Allen, ep. 1045, 1. 77), lettre publiée à la fin de l'*Antimorus*, f° I 2 v°. Notons qu'en passant d'Utopie à Udépotie, on passe de la négation du lieu à celle du temps; je ne pense pas qu'il faille y voir quelque subtilité; la négation, me semble-t-il, compte seule ici. Sur les échanges entre More et Érasme concernant le titre de l'ouvrage, cf. supra, n. 8.

12. Avec une nuance toutefois: les premiers (Y 275) estiment que Budé se souvient de la cité sainte, τὴν πόλιν τὴν ἁγίαν, la Jérusalem céleste d'*Apocalypse*, 21; A. Prévost suggère (P 8, n. 8) que le choix d'ἁγνός correspond chez Budé au souci de se démarquer du texte de l'*Apocalypse*.

13. Budé pouvait s'être familiarisé avec la pensée que "nous connaissons l'infinité de Dieu par notre impuissance à le comprendre" par la lecture de Charles de Bovelles, dont les traités philosophiques (parmi lesquels le *De nihilo*) étaient parus en 1510 chez H. Estienne, suivis en 1513 et en 1515 chez J. Bade des *Quaestiones theologicae*, et des *Theologicae conclusiones*.

14. Voir *De asse*, O.o., t. 2, p. 308 (la philosophie "sublimipète" et "uranophrone"); *De studio*, éd. de 1532, f° XVI v° et O.o., t. 1, p. 14 d (le mont Hélicon où les Muses "quêtent sur les traces de la nature sensible et de la mathématique les choses célestes. . . , et sur le plus haut sommet duquel la *philothéorie*—c'est-à-dire la contemplation—s'élève, sublime et comme ailée, jusqu'au plus haut de la capacité humaine").

15. Toutefois A. Prévost, op. cit., p. 133, mène sur le mot Amaurote une réflexion qui ne me semble pas fort éloignée de celle qui concerne ici Hagnopolis.

16. Ces mots se trouvent dans la lettre du 12 août 1519 (Rogers, ep. 80 et O.o., t. 1, p. 282), à l'occasion d'un nouveau cadeau de More (des bagues) qui fournissent à Budé un prétexte pour rappeler le premier présent de son ami, et surtout le plaisir qu'il éprouve à recevoir de lui des lettres. Pour la correspondance de Budé et de More, on pourra se reporter à la traduction française que j'ai donnée dans *Moreana*, 19/20, pp. 41-68.

17. Cf. supra, n. 10. Voir aussi "L'harmonie secrète du *De asse* de Guillaume Budé" in *Bull. de l'Assoc. G.B.* 4 (1968), pp. 473-86. Ce dernier article avait fait l'objet d'une sévère critique de Guy Lavoie: "Y a-t-il un secret dans l'architecture du *De asse*?" in *Renaissance and Reformation/Renaissance et Réforme*, nouvelle série de III-1 (1979), pp. 29-43. Lavoie revenait en fait à l'interprétation de L. Delaruelle, *Guillaume Budé, les origines, les débuts, les idées maîtresses* (Paris, 1906), chap. 5. Avec les inévitables nuances qu'impose le temps, je persiste à penser que mon hypothèse— celle d'une unité profonde de l'ouvrage—rendait compte globalement de la *forma mentis* d'un auteur qui pratique couramment le discours allégorique. Et c'est ce que More, me semble-t-il, avait senti.

6 City Road
Dunedin, New Zealand
21 October 1987.

Dear Father,

How many times I skidded the Moreanum bike to a halt at the steps of 29 rue Volney, put my key into the lock of the door with its peeling green paint, and made an unceremonious entry under the welcoming glance of Sir Thomas More, who looks down from the Holbein painting.

A knock at your door always brought a ready « Entrez ! » No matter what learned tome or important footnote you were immersed in for Yale, the enthusiastic greeting was always the same, and the same for all who came. The year Ellen Jones and my sister Therese were there, we told you that a warm welcome must await you « au Ciel ». Before you even get near the Pearly Gates, St Thomas More will be shouting in his best ambassadorial French « Entrez ! ».

There is a busy road which separates the world of Moreanum with its old house, wooden staircase and enclosed garden, from the big, bustling world of « la Catho », the university. New documentalists soon learn the Marc'hadourean theory for crossing the road -- just go straight out, down our steps, and cross immediately.... A similar approach to riding a bicycle in traffic left Ellen and me one day with our hearts in our mouths as you sped off to the Post Office with a bag of fresh-from-the-printer *Moreanas* strapped to your back.

I could never do justice to my thanks for all the kind memories, the people who came through that welcoming door, because you, Father, made it a place they wanted to come to -- the Catho gardener in his sabots with a bunch of Spring flowers, Soeur Marie-Stéphane with her medicine for the sick, a clochard in need of a parapluie or a Bretonne galette, the students and friends from France and far beyond, the gipsy who so wanted to buy your best chair, the Australian pilgrims on their way to Rome in the anniversary year of 1985 ....

Now, from my far away Pacific island, I can only try to say thank you with all my heart for all the love and goodness of a true Abbé that you gave to us.

God Bless you,

Mary O'Neill

ELIZABETH McCUTCHEON

William Bullein's
Dialogue Against the Fever Pestilence:
A Sixteenth-Century Anatomy

REPRESENTED AS "BOTH PLEASANT AND PIETY-FULL," the latter word encompassing notions of the pious *and* the compassionate,[1] William Bullein's *Dialogue Against the Fever Pestilence* is a joco-serious, quirky, and often brilliant work that is important in its own right and for the light it sheds on the development of the utopia and related genres in sixteenth-century England. Bullein, who was related to Anne Boleyn, was born between 1520 and 1530 and died in 1575/6. He was both a cleric and a physician, serving as the rector of Blaxhall, Suffolk, in 1550, and subsequently practicing as a doctor, first in the north of England and later in London, where he was living by 1560.[2] Bullein wrote four books: *The Government of Health* (1558); a collection of works called the *Bulwarke of Defence* (1562); *A Comfortable Regiment Against Pleurisi* (1562); and the *Dialogue*—actually a series of dialogues, although the divisions are unmarked and often abrupt— printed four times between 1564 and 1578.

The *Dialogue* has as its immediate context an outbreak of bubonic plague in London in June, 1563, made worse "by the return of Elizabeth's already infected troops from her ill-fated attack on Le Havre in August of the same year": at least 18,000 people died, according to one source, 20,000 (close to a quarter of London's population), according to another.[3] There are twelve interlocutors: the beggar, Mendicus; the chief speaker, Civis, and his wife, Uxor (later in the *Dialogue* called Susan); their servant, Roger; a rich Italian merchant, Antonius, who is a foil to Civis; the doctor, Medicus, in later editions called Dr. Tocrub (here Bullein is satirizing a well-known doctor in Tudor England); the doctor's apothecary, Crispine; two lawyers, Avarus and Ambodexter, like the doctor out to get the dying merchant's money; a traveller and teller of strange tales, Mendax; a wholly allegorical figure, Death; and Theologus. The action, which is not staged but conveyed through the dialogues (twelve, by my count), opens in London, as the beggar knocks at the door of Civis's house. From there it soon shifts to the house of Antonius, who is dying from the plague and is being treated (and mistreated) by the doctor, eager to accept gold and gifts for medicine and treatments he knows, in this case, are of no avail. As he later tells Crispine: "He loued me as I loued hym, He me for healthe, and I hym for money" (p. 55). In the second part of the *Dialogue* (the last five scenes or episodes), the action shifts to the countryside outside of London, as Civis, Uxor, and Roger leave the plague-filled city. They pass Barnet—now a stop on the London underground—where Uxor's son, Samuel, was wet-nursed, and somewhat further on they stop at an inn for dinner. Here they encounter Mendax, after admiring the walls of the parlor, and learn about a number of marvellous countries. They continue their journey, but soon there is a terrible thunder storm and Mors appears with three darts in his left hand: a black one for pestilence, a blood-red one for war, and a pale one for famine. He strikes Civis, who temporarily has been abandoned by his wife and manservant and realizes that he is dying: "Oh, wretched man that I am; whether shal I fly for succor" (p. 119). Susan and Roger return, and Civis sends Roger to fetch Theologus, who teaches him "the waie to the kyngdome of Christe" (p. 120). Thus the deaths of Antonius and Civis are counterpointed, as are the characters of the doctor and Theologus, the latter presented as a heavenly physician (p. 120). Among other things, then, the *Dialogue Against the Fever Pestilence* is an analysis of the body and the soul and a disquisition on the nature of humankind. Yet larger political and social issues are implicit throughout, since the name of the main interlocutor is Civis, *Citizen*, rather than Everyman. And we become increasingly conscious of the body politic the Tudors called the commonwealth as we move through the *Dialogue*.

When the *Dialogue* was published for the third time, in 1573, there were a number of additions, the most notable being Mendax's description of Taerg Natrib (Great Britain in reverse) and its chief city, Ecnatneper or Nodnol (Repentance or London). This utopian or quasi-utopian description, unnoticed, so far as I can tell, by any of the standard bibliographies of English utopias,[4] could be thought of as the first Renaissance utopia to have been written originally in English. For we can hardly count the allusion to "Eutopia," named, but not otherwise discussed, in Hugh Plat's "merrie tale of Master Mendax" (first printed in 1572), with its comic description of a house "all tylde with tarte" — a metonymomic representation of a Land of Cockaygne.[5] And Bullein's addition clearly precedes a lively utopian or quasi-utopian romance by one T. N., *A Pleasant Dialogue betweene a Lady called Listra, and a Pilgrim. Concerning the Gouernment and Commonweale of the Great Province of Crangalor* (London, 1579), about a happy and blessed land where vice is punished and virtue rewarded, as well as Thomas Lupton's *Siuqila* (London, 1580). Siuqila (Aliquis, in reverse: like Bullein, whom he seems to be imitating, Lupton exploits the antipodean concept) is Omen's (Nemo's) account of Mauqsun (Nusquam), where lords are liberal, ladies courteous, husbands faithful, wives obedient, maidens modest, masters sober, servants diligent, judges equitable, etc. In short, Mauqsun is a place where so "manye thynges are so rare and straunge . . . that me thinkes they should be too good to be true," as Siuqila, who has been looking for a country where the people fear God, love his word, esteem equity, and abhor wickedness, tells Omen.[6]

Wedged into the larger work, along with other bits and pieces, Mendax's utopian description invites the sorts of questions that have perplexed those who have written about the *Dialogue*: just what sort of work is it? And how do we read it? For at every point, the part seems to be larger than the whole, and the *Dialogue* continually threatens to self-destruct — witness to its high energy and tension, from one point of view, or its lack of coherence, from another. According to C. S. Lewis, for example, Bullein "was trying to do too many things at once. He wanted to write prescriptions against the Plague, satire against usurers, satire against lawyers, a Protestant tract, a catalogue of Emblems, and a Dance of Death."[7] In fact, Lewis's list is not complete: the *Dialogue* includes a garden of the muses, an anthology of English poetry, a philosophical discourse on the nature of the soul, beast fables, and an *ars moriendi* and consolation in time of death, as well as a utopia. Bullein anticipates criticism and defends himself by pointing out the value of diversity or variety (p. 1), a privileged concept for the Renaissance writer — think of the sonnet sequence and other instances of mixed forms.[8] But there is also a slap-dash quality about parts of Bullein's work that makes any interpretation of it difficult. What about the interlocutor who suddenly appears in place of Crispine, for example, or the *ad hoc* satire, which can be very rough indeed. And the introduction of utopian material in the 1573 edition clearly disturbs the elegant symmetry of the 1564 text, which comes closer to meeting Lewis's standards.

Lewis, who characterized Bullein's work as "a full-blown Erasmian 'Colloquy,' " admired it insofar as it constituted a "mirror of life."[9] Other readers have argued for a variety of other forms and intentions. Herbert G. Wright, for one, situated the *Dialogue* in its immediate context—the plague of 1563—and stressed its Apocalyptic and biblical quality and "the eloquent passages where he [Bullein] broods on the fading of beauty and the frailty of man." Like C. S. Lewis, though, he insisted that "Bullein's work loses through the introduction of too many themes."[10] By contrast, Baugh reduced the work to its merry tales and quick wit and jests. Thinking of it, primarily, as a "collection of tall tales within a framing narrative" and grouping it with Painter's *Palace of Pleasure*, he thus highlighted the promise of pleasure made on the title-page, like Bullein's nineteenth-century editors, who pointed out that the *Dialogue* is "full of merry tales (pills to purge melancholy at plague-time)" (p. v).[11]

Though not a drama, the *Dialogue* is extremely dramatic, and Routh long ago called it a "drama of death," at the same time emphasizing its satiric element, which "reaches nearly every abuse of the age."[12] Another classic study also related Bullein's *Dialogue* to drama, on the one hand, and social commentary, on the other. Arguing that "the real purpose of the writer is to attack avarice," O. J. Campbell suggested that Bullein (like many other Tudor commentators) responded to the "social and economic evils" of Tudor capitalism and anticipated the satiric comedies of Ben Jonson, who may well be indebted to Bullein for part of the plot in *Volpone*.[13] Perhaps the fullest analysis of both the drama and the satire occurs in a recent study by William C. Boring, who points out how Bullein has "drawn heavily" on morality plays for his characters and compares Civis to Everyman, Uxor to the shrews of the cycles, Ambodexter and Avarus to the Vice, and Mors to his counterpart in *Everyman*. There are social types, as well: Antonius and Mendax are "miser and braggart, respectively."[14] Finally, however, Boring interprets the work as "variations on the theme of *De contemptu mundi*," stressing the contrast between the death of the rich merchant, who, like the doctor, is a "*Nulla fidian*" (*Dialogue*, p. 14), and Civis, who dies confessing his Protestant faith.[15]

The most recent study of the *Dialogue*, by Jacqueline Proust, is a particularly full and provocative reading of it as a "formulation d'une thérapeutique pour l'âme en péril."[16] Emphasizing the dialectical nature of the dialogue, which she divides into two "acts," one in London, one on the road, she argues that what purports to be a medical work, complete with an analysis of symptoms and actual prescriptions for a preventative therapeutic, evolves into another kind of therapeutic which leads to self-examination and self-knowledge. Insisting that Civis's death is the just punishment of his faults—he too much loved the goods of this world—Proust shows how through the questions and answers of the dialogue the symptoms of a truly sick, that is, evil, world are revealed. Finally, each reader is invited to discover who he/she is and to repent, thanks to the homily of Theologus, who delivers the word of God rather than the delusive discourse of men and reminds every reader that true riches are heavenly.

All these readings illuminate important aspects of Bullein's *Dialogue*, yet none actually places it as to its kind or genre, leaving us with a distorted sense of the relationship of one part of the work to another and undervaluing its thematic and formal variety and its fascination with ideas and attitudes. In fact the *Dialogue* is a sophisticated albeit troubled instance of a fictive kind that is sometimes called a Menippean satire, sometimes an anatomy. In his annotated catalogue of Menippean satires, Eugene Kirk includes the *Dialogue*, characterized as "apocalyptic Lucianism."[17] Unfortunately, though, the summary of the work confuses the various speakers and reads too simply and too literally what is densely metaphoric. Certainly the apocalyptic overtones are crucial, and the day of judgment is at hand—literally for Antonius and Civis, by implication for everyone else. Moreover, the idea of judgment is doubly relevant, its application simultaneously satiric and spiritual. Yet the world as a whole does not come to an end, despite Roger's foreboding: "I thinke the daie of Dome is at hande" (p. 78). And the quotidian futures of Civis's wife and himself are the subject of speculation by a sometimes cynical, sometimes naive Roger, whose imagination and desires are only intermittently under control.

In any case, I prefer the term "anatomy," because it is one that sixteenth and seventeenth-century writers themselves used—as Devon L. Hodges has shown, the anatomy became something of a fad in Tudor England[18]—and because it adumbrates both the play between the medical and the moral that Bullein exploits and his role as a writer-anatomist. Indeed, there is some evidence to suggest that the *Dialogue* evolved from the *Anatomie* that Bullein had hoped to include in his *Bulwarke of Defence*. All that actually appeared in 1562 is a single page with a skeleton, each of its bones duly labeled. He explains: "In this place, good reader, but that infortunate happe haue preuented me with lettes . . . I would haue written at length, the whole large *Anatomie of the bodie of mankind.*"[19] The first edition of the *Dialogue* is also accompanied by a skeleton—almost identical to the one in *The Anatomie*, which was taken "either from Vesalius' *Tabulae anatomicae* (1538)" or a plagiarism of it, rather than the more familiar muscle man of 1543.[20] Now, however, the skeleton is heightened emblematically. Standing self-reflexively, one arm supported by a spade, the other thrown open and out (rather than up, as in the earlier, more clearly anatomical work), it challenges us to reflect upon the nature of humankind and his or her temporal end as we gaze upon the "bone-house" or body. Commenting on the title-page from Bullein's *Anatomie*, O'Malley observed: "The use of this skeleton, with its errors of osteology, including the misarticulation of the clavicle, rather than the much superior skeletal figures of Vesalius' *Fabrica* (1543) suggests Bullein's deficiencies in anatomy."[21] But Bullein seems to have been interested in both a naturalistic-scientific perspective (why else label the bones in the earlier *Anatomie*?) *and* a moral-metaphysical one: to know more about the body becomes, paradoxically, a way of knowing more about the soul and the mysteries of the human character. In fact in the *Anatomie* the skeleton was itself accompanied by a biblical motto, "A tergo & a fronte me finxisti," that is (as the King James Bible renders it), "Thou hast beset me behind and before" (Psalm 139).[22] It seems, then, that both illustrations were designed to underscore the implications (medical, moral, and psychological) that the idea of an anatomy represented at a time when dissections were newly performed and there was an intense preoccupation with the nature of human nature.

More particularly, these skeletons visualize the role of the writer as satirist-anatomist, who uses his scalpel to "strip away false appearances and expose the truth,"[23] a truth which can be horrible and often tragic, although in this case it is potentially redemptive, insofar as the satirist-anatomist is also a preacher (and humorist). In a fascinating study of medical metaphors and their relation to satiric theory, Mary Clair Randolph has shown how the Renaissance critic and satirical writer alike thought of satire as a "scourge, a whip, a surgeon's scalpel, a cauterizing iron, a strong cathartic," the satirist himself becoming a barber-surgeon or a "doctour of physik."[24] In sharp contrast with late seventeenth and eighteenth-century satire, concerned primarily with reason and the will and attracted to a quieter "rational" vocabulary of philosophical and psychological terms, Renaissance satire attacks the "ulcers, tetters, and pustules" that symbolize the infection of mankind—infections that it seeks to expose and (perhaps) cure.[25] But while stressing the Renaissance notion of "satire as a sanative agent, a means of curing a man of his moral ills," Randolph admitted that satire also provided an outlet for the satirist's own irritation at certain social conditions.[26] In fact, indignation and frustration over what Bullein calls "ingratitude" in his dedicatory epistle (p. 1; compare the treatment on p. 67) and his outrage over injustice in the commonwealth are major concerns in the *Dialogue*.[27] And the psychological pressure behind such concerns intermittently explodes in controlled violence, as when Uxor describes a picture she doesn't quite understand. What she sees is horrifying—"a mans skin, and tanned, coloured like vnto Leather, with the skin of the handes and feete, nayles and heare remainyng; and the skinne is spread abroad" (p. 84). Civis, always ready with an explanation, tells her that this "is the Skin of a wicked Judge, a Lawier, whiche plaied on bothe handes" and "loued golde aboue God, and crueltie aboue justice" (p. 84). To punish him, the prince (both good and great) "commaunded his Skin to be flaine from his fleshe, he beyng yet leuyng, roaryng, with blood runnyng from his bodie" (p. 84).

In effect, then, Bullein's *Dialogue* is an anatomy twice over; that is, both its matter and its formal structure are the stuff of anatomy or dissection. So Bullein anticipates by close to fifty years the kind of material that appears in Donne's "Anatomy of the World," where the speaker, in some part an anatomist, analyzes the state of a world that is metaphorically (and in some sense literally) sick, dead, "yea putrified," since it has lost its "[i]ntrinsique Balme" and preservative, the young Elizabeth Drury whose death John Donne was mourning in the first of his two anniversary poems.[28] Bullein uses less of the new science than Donne does (this is not surprising, given the state of scientific knowledge in England at the time), and he writes, for the most part, in prose. But the *Dialogue* is a kind of physico-theology, and Bullein, like Donne, is at once a scientist, a satirist, and a preacher, although he is also a humorist.

Similarly, the *Dialogue*, far from being an ill-composed hodge-podge of material, is structurally an anatomy as Northrop Frye has defined it: "a loose-jointed narrative form" that parodies and echoes countless other works and "deals less with people as such than with mental attitudes."[29] A high-energy work and, often, an "encyclopaedic farrago"— Frye himself tactfully speaks of "exhaustive erudition"—the anatomy combines fantasy with morality, at its most concentrated presenting "a vision of the world in terms of a single intellectual pattern."[30] As befits a literary kind that is so encyclopedic and so various, each instance is, to some degree, *sui generis*; Lucian, Petronius, Boethius, Rabelais, Burton, and Swift all wrote anatomies, and each one is patently unlike the others. Yet, like these, the *Dialogue* is an immensely learned work; Bullein echoes and/or parodies almost every English writer who preceded him, as well as the Bible and the classics, and he took the learning seriously enough to include an index with the 1564 editions. The *Dialogue* is also a comic, satiric, sometimes personal or confessional, potentially tragic, medical-spiritual work that addresses—at a critical moment—what is, perhaps, the fundamental issue for the Renaissance: namely, the nature of humankind, both individually and corporately.

Structurally, then, as Proust has indicated, the *Dialogue* can be divided into two large parts, one concerned primarily with the body, the other with the soul, although the first half is also, from one point of view, a parody of the second; like Milton's *Paradise Lost* the *Dialogue* begins with an "anti-form." In this and other ways Bullein transforms a popular medieval debate and articulates a characteristically Renaissance preoccupation.[31] Hence the situation of Antonius, who speaks from what we know is his death bed. The doctor's advice and the many different prescriptions for treating the plague are scientific or medical, by sixteenth-century standards, that is. But the doctor is very like the doctor Chaucer sketched in the General Prologue of his *Canterbury Tales*:

> He kepte that he wan in pestilence.
> For gold in phisik is a cordial,
> Therefore he lovede gold in special.[32]

And Medicus and his apothecary are none too squeamish about the medicine they prepare for the merchant. Similarly the dialogue between doctor and patient concerning the nature of the macrocosm and the microcosm generates a black comedy and an increasingly complex irony that surfaces when the doctor tells the understandably puzzled Antonius that there is a soul in man. For, as the latter remarks, "Why, then there must needes be a greater thing as the cause of euery liuyng soule, which I take to be God, which hath made all thynges; and when you and I talked together you seemed that *Non est deus*" (p. 32). Backtracking, the doctor hastily explains that he follows Aristotle, not the Bible (compare Chaucer's point that the doctor's study "was but litel on the Bible"),[33] which leads the two to something like a catechism (or rather, a parody of the catechism). But this text-book explication of the powers and virtues of the soul (pp. 32–36) moves in an ominously downward cycle. For after this academic and highly arid discussion— compare Theologus' later homily—the two begin to discuss the signs of the plague in what amounts to a dissection of the suffering and infected body, and we hear in vivid detail about cancers, buboes, carbuncles, etc., sometimes having a "crust like vnto the squames or flakes of Iron when thei fall of when the Smith doeth worke, and in colour like ashes . . . by extreme heat and burnyng" (p. 45).

By contrast, there is Civis's anguished cry at the beginning of the second large panel of action, as he hears the "daiely ianglyng and rynging of the belles" and the "diggyng vp of graues" (p. 56). "Alas, what shall I doe to saue my life?" (p. 56). The question, thus put, is ironic: Civis (like Antonius) means life here and now. But Mors will shortly smite him. So, in the course of the second half of the *Dialogue*, he discovers what, in a more abstract sense, he already knows: that "our life" is as a "vapour that appeareth for a little tyme, and afterward vanishe awaie" (p. 56). Thus there are two ways to answer Civis's agonized question. One is medical: hence the *Dialogue* includes prescriptions (in Latin) that the apothecary carefully inscribes in his notebook. The other is spiritual, delivered by Theologus by way of homily and liturgy at the end of the *Dialogue*, which ends with a prayer for the soul that "commeth nowe vnto thee, good Lorde" (p. 134). Medical cures are not ruled out, then, and it is recognized that the plague is spread by natural causes. Yet such cures (which sometimes are fraudulently proffered) are subsumed in spiritual cures, for, as Skelton (who is frequently echoed in the *Dialogue*) wrote, "It is generall / To be mortall."[34] Metaphysically, of course, the two sorts of "life" are interdependent as well, since the corruption, decay, and death of the body are seen as signs of a primal fall. Indeed everyone is metaphorically corrupt (or infected with the plague), having fallen with Adam and Eve at the beginning of time (cf. p. 124). So there is a symbolic allusion in the motto on the clock in the merchant's garden: "*Tempora labuntur*" (p. 18), a motto the doctor interprets in purely naturalistic terms: "What is it a clocke?" (p. 19).

The *Dialogue* begins no less ironically and symbolically. The first words we hear are the beggar's, who cries out, "God saue my gud Maister and Maistresse, the Barnes, and all this halie houshaude, and shilde you from all doolle and shem" (p. 5). The beggar's cry seems conventional enough, individualized only insofar as the accent is that of a man born in Northumberland.[35] But it elicits antithetical responses in Civis and his wife. Civis too was once poor, and he is moved to charity: "I praie you, wife, giue the poore man somethyng to his dinner" (p. 5). But Susan is not about to do anyone's bidding in a hurry: "Softe fire maketh swete Malte: he shall tary my leasure" (p. 6). So the responses to the beggar's cry give us glimpses of character (along with the misogyny that infects so much Renaissance, as well as medieval, satire).[36] But the cry itself has ironic and metaphysical undertones that become wholly overt when, facing certain death, Civis can depend only upon the mercy of God, "purchased by the Sacrifice of Christe" (p. 126): salvation is the Lord's. Here Bullein embodies the Protestant theology of later sixteenth-century England; not even Civis's good deeds will serve, important though the practice of charity is throughout the *Dialogue*.

So we need to look again at Civis's question, now noting its confused (and wholly human) orientation towards the "I." "Alas, what shall I doe to saue my life?" Civis is generally a sympathetic character, although, like many of Lucian's characters, he is something of a know-it-all, given to explaining everything to everyone. He also participates in the general human condition, and we see him placing self-interest ahead of common interest as he flees from the plague-ridden city, taking the keys of his chest and his sturdy steel casket with him (p. 58). This self-centeredness is present everywhere in the dialogue: consider the machinations of the two lawyers for Antonius' estate (like ravens seeking carrion), or the relationship between the unscrupulous doctor and Antonius, or Susan's concern for herself rather than her husband when Mors appears ("Good housband, remember that I am yonge, and with childe" [p. 114]). And it surfaces in a particularly humorous, if blatant, form when Mendax pauses in the middle of his story about the precious stones he and his friends might have gathered (and thus "gotten a worlde"), had they held together "like frendes" (p. 99). But: "Alas, alas, euery man is but for hymself; you maie consider what diuision is" (p. 100). Thus the *Dialogue*'s attack on avarice, greed, and usury is subsumed in a more subtle indictment, part comedy, part lament, and part diatribe, of selfishness and profound self-centeredness, signs of a fundamental corruption of being.

Up to now I have concentrated on microcosmic relationships, which are the dominant ones so far as the action behind the *Dialogue* is concerned. Yet all but one of the interlocutors represent a social or professional type, so that the larger society is never far from the surface of the text. And the macrocosm, that is, the commonwealth, is as sick and corrupt as the individuals and different social groups in it. This point is made again and again by the actual dialogue; Roger pretends, for example, that his master owns the fields they pass by after dinner, a device that allows Bullein to call attention to the sharp practices of the great landowners of England (pp. 112–13). In addition, various images and symbols illuminate issues enacted in the text, adumbrating the condition of the commonweal and linking the individual with the whole. Early on, for instance, the action is interrupted when Crispine describes the merchant's garden, with its powerful, if highly ambiguous, emblems of the human state. Crispine is particularly troubled by the representation of a tiger which is ready to kill a young child. The child has a crown of gold upon his head and holds a globe, called *microcosmos*, which also figures the whole world. Both the doctor and Crispine interpret the emblem, the one stressing the great ancestry of the child, the other the depravation of the commonwealth: "Globus conuersus est: the worlde is chaunged or tourned in suche a common weale" (p. 15). A similar idea is subsequently voiced by Roger, who frequently complains that everything has become monstrous, topsy-turvy. But both readings of the emblem are radically incomplete (begging the question of the nature of the microcosmos), and we are left with an ominous sense of the dangers that threaten the human condition.[37]

As the dialogue continues, the movement between microcosmos and macrocosmos becomes increasingly overt. While Civis, his wife, and Roger are on the road, Roger tells a number of fables, opening up, in yet another form, the question of humankind's behavior. The issue is launched dramatically and wittily—do animals talk? Roger answers affirmatively; after all, his parrot says, "Beware the Catte, and she will call me Roger as plaine as your Maistership" (p. 61). Civis disagrees; animals lack reason, he explains, unlike human beings. But a third answer, at once ironic and dramatic, is suggested by the action of the dialogue and the beast fables that follow. Likewise there are the wise sayings and pictures in the comely parlor of the inn where Civis, Susan, and Roger have dinner with Mendax. Touching the estates and offices, they build up a devastating picture of the corruption that is England as well as a picture of humankind more generally, universalized by way of the ship of fools: "Some there are Kynges, Queenes, Popes, Archbishoppes, Prelates, Lordes, Ladies, Knightes, Gentlemen, Phisicions, Lawiers, Marchauntes, Housebandemen, Beggers, theeues, hores, knaues, &c." (p. 93).

The largest rupture in the text (and most obviously macrocosmic section) is also the most fantastic. The narrator here is the irrepressible Mendax, who wears a green coat, gives the innkeeper's son a piece of unicorn horn—it's good to detect poisons—and is full of wonderful stories about his travels to strange places. Some of his tales appeal, primarily, to our sense of the marvellous; we hear about giants, people with one foot, satyrs, centaurs, etc. Others tap fantasies of the idyllic life—already subverted, however, by the dramatic irony of the rest of the text. Thus Mendax has been to Terra Florida, a never- never land (set in America) that the doctor earlier commented on. Not only is Terra Florida full of "gold & precious stones and Balmes"; "no labour is in that land, long life they haue." But it is, alas, no place for doctors or lawyers, since no one ever gets sick, and there is "no debate nor strife in their common wealthes" (p. 26). Mendax tells about yet another commonwealth, ironically called "good" in the margin (p. 100), which is actually a terrifying anti-utopia, where "women will eate their owne children, and one man an other." There "one is equal with another, the strongest of bodie are chifest, for there al is ruled by force and not through reason, after the maner of Swine" (p. 100).

To such material that sometimes promises (or seems to promise) an easy escape from the exigencies of existence, or else subverts any utopian dream, Bullein added a description of an even stranger country—stranger because it is simultaneously fantastic *and* moral—when he revised his text in 1573. Going by contraries, Taerg Natrib reverses the aberrations that characterize Great Britain. Like More's Utopia, in fact, it is "our Antipodie, foote against foote, in a land like ours, and al had been in one climate, of Riuers, Hilles, and Valies like ours" (p. 105).

The actual description is brief (seven pages of text in the Early English Text Society edition) and scatter-shot, though not as scatter-shot as it appears to be, and More's *Utopia* is a subtext or pre-text that is parodied throughout. What, for example, do the people in Taerg Natrib wear? Mendax's answer is a typical jumble of manners and morals (much indebted to the sumptuary laws of sixteenth-century England) that allows us to place Taerg Natrib vis-à-vis Utopia and other quasi-utopian societies. The people are:

> Verie plain, sauing the nobles, which are riche, in faire attire like angelles. There the women are verie huswifly, the men homely, greate labor, little silke is worne, no ieuels, no light colours, no great hose, no long daggers, no cockscombe feathers, no double ruffes, not many seruyng men, no dising nor unlawfull games; neither coggyng, knauerie, foystyng, or cosenyng. Plaine, plaine; plain both in word and dede. (pp. 110–11)

Plain, albeit hierarchical: such are the hallmarks of the type of ideal society that J. C. Davis calls "the perfect moral commonwealth"—a term to which I will return.

First, though, we need to consider the central issue as Mendax presents it by way of synecdoche: Taerg Natrib is a reformed Protestant commonwealth, symbolized by the way that Ecnatneper or Nodnol keeps the Sabbath. "And as thei doe in this hedde Citie, so all the other Cities doe" (p. 106), Mendax adds, obviously echoing Hythlodaeus' account of Amaurotum. As Mendax tells it, *everyone* ("both man, woman, yong and olde") goes to church on the Sabbath day, hearing "the naked, true, and perfite worde of God." There is: "No flattering in the preacher, neither railing, but teaching truly euery manne his duetie to God, their prince and one to another; the greate curses of the lawe, and sweete promises of the Gospel" (pp. 107–08). Over their city gates and in their churches are the words they live by, from 1 Peter 2: "Honor all men. Love the brotherhood. Fear God. Honor the king" (p. 109). Civis draws the obvious conclusion: "So Goddes lawes and the Princes are obserued in that happie lande" (p. 109). And Mendax also reveals the blessings the happy polity enjoys—speaking (as so often in More's *Utopia*) by way of negation: there is no usury or idleness; no robberies, murders, etc. have been committed for twenty-one years; the judges and lawyers take no fees; everyone lives in peace and quiet. In short, "The effecte that dooe followe is justice, charite, quietnesse. And so God doe cast his blessing vpon them, ij haruestes in one yeere" (p. 109).

In *Utopia and the Ideal Society: A Study of English Utopian Writing: 1516–1700*, J. C. Davis argues that we should distinguish the utopia proper from four alternative types of ideal society—the Land of Cockaygne, the arcadia, millennialism, and "the perfect moral commonwealth, with its insistence upon men's reconciliation with the status quo."[38] For Davis, a utopia is a place that "accepts recalcitrant nature and assumes sinful man."[39] Instead of idealizing man, in other words (by imagining his perfect reformation), a utopia idealizes organization, reorganizing society and its institutions, its aim primarily order rather than happiness.[40] In the perfect moral commonwealth, on the other hand, "existing social arrangements and political institutions" are accepted, and "society is to be made harmonic by the moral reformation of every individual in society, and hence of every class and group."[41] Davis does not mention Bullein's *Dialogue*—the work has generally escaped notice by all but literary critics, despite its popularity throughout the Renaissance—but he does comment on Lupton's

Siuqila, which imitates it.⁴² And certainly the *Dialogue* describes a place where "Goddes lawes and the Princes" are observed with happy results for the commonweal, although not everything is perfect.

Davis's distinctions usefully call attention to the *radical* nature of utopian thought and the simpler and obvious political and social conservatism of a perfect moral commonwealth, which is rearmed morally. Yet both More's Utopia and Bullein's Taerg Natrib are clearly "no places" that reverse the aberrations of the known world; Bullein, like More, has reworked the traditional topos of the *mundus inversus*.⁴³ Moreover, the Utopians, like those who live in Taerg Natrib, have teleological and moral goals to which social goals are finally subordinate, and both societies control morality, albeit in different ways. Nor is either society actually represented as altogether perfect. There is another, perhaps more fundamental problem with the distinctions Davis draws: they work only if we stand *inside* the frame of the imagined society, taking the part for the whole and ignoring the reflexive nature of the text. For Bullein, like More, has written a work that is both a fiction and a metafiction that calls its own status into question, and we cannot ignore the many ways in which he questions his own and other texts and expects readers to do so too.

In *My Dear Peter* I have shown how More invites his readers to play a hypothetical and fictive game by way of his letter to Peter Giles.⁴⁴ Bullein plays an even showier game with his readers (obliquely commenting on the *Utopia*'s conditional discourse, as well). To begin with, there is the name and nature of the narrator, Mendax. He is related to the narrator of Lucian's *True History*. But Bullein probably had the reportorial More's play with mendacity and the fictive in mind when he wrote Mendax's patter. Notice, in particular, how Civis answers Mendax's pointed question about Taerg Natrib: "Is not this well doen, maister *Ciuis?*" (p. 108). "*If this be true* it is a blessed Citie" (p. 108: italics mine). In fact, lying and its cognate, story-telling, are recurrent issues in the *Dialogue*. Mendax himself claims he doesn't lie: "And thus fare you well, for this is true or els I doe lye" (p. 111). So he exploits the liar paradox that Lucian played with and that is at the heart of the reportorial More's truth claims. Roger, by contrast, calls a spade a spade: "I will swear vppon a Booke thy laste woordes are true, and all the reste are lies," he tells Mendax (p. 111). Susan is impatient with all stories: "I praie you geue eare to no suche trifles and lies, good houseband," she urges Civis as he encourages Roger to tell his story about the lion and the mouse (p. 63). But Civis loves a good story as much as Bullein and More do. So he tells Uxor: "It is as good to heare a lye whiche hurteth not as sometyme a true tale that profiteth not" (p. 63), like More echoing Horace on the pleasure and profit of laughter. Likewise Bullein privileges Civis's response to Mendax, for he alone courteously (albeit ironically) plays the game, going so far as to tell Mendax, "Gentleman, fare you well, I dooe giue credite to your tale. You muste bere with my man, he is a verlet, and you a gentleman of great trauel, iudgement, and experience" (p. 111). And once again Bullein echoes More's *Utopia* – this time reminding us of the reportorial More's final address to Hythlodaeus and the many ambiguities implicit in it.

Bullein is also the master of a comic hyperbole that subverts the presumed perfection of Taerg Natrib. According to Mendax, for instance, "there were no people walking abroad in the seruice tyme; no, not a Dogge or a catte in the streate, neither any Tauerne doore open that daie, nor wine bibbyng in them, but onely almose, fasting, and praier" (p. 108), a remark that glances at (and takes the measure of) Hythlodaeus' straight-faced description of Utopia as a place where there is no "license to waste time, nowhere any pretext to evade work – no wine shop, no alehouse, no brothel anywhere, no opportunity for corruption, no lurking hole, no secret meeting place."[45] Finally, there is the irony that Bullein generates by juxtaposition. By inserting a description of a wholly reformed Great Britain in a section devoted to a variety of never-never lands, Bullein suggests that the perfect moral commonwealth is itself a fantasy – as T. N. and Lupton later do. Bullein thus replicates the ambiguity of so much utopian and quasi-utopian discourse. On the one hand, he must have sympathized with the values of Taerg Natrib, a thoroughly reformed Protestant polity. On the other hand, he has no expectation that such a place could exist or would be realized, given his sense of the nature of human nature and the post-lapsarian world. Thus, ironically, Bullein's larger *Dialogue* subverts the very premises of the perfect moral commonwealth, as Davis has defined them: Taerg Natrib may achieve an almost perfect reformation, but Bullein's anatomy undermines any ideas of humankind's perfection or perfectibility. In fact he is more pessimistic about the possibilities of reform than More is in the *Utopia*. Probably he would have emphasized the latter part of the reportorial More's response to Hythlodaeus: "What you cannot turn to good you must at least make as little bad as you can. For it is impossible that all should be well unless all men were good, a situation which I do not expect for a great many years to come!"[46]

Had Thomas More and William Bullein met in Tudor England, they would have been irremediably divided over religious and political issues that manifested themselves in More's execution on Tower Hill, the development of the Tudor monarchy, and the Protestant reformation. Bullein, who was rabidly anti-papal, admired Thomas Cromwell as much as he detested Bishop Bonner, and More appears just once in the *Dialogue*, yoked with John Frith in a collection of paradoxical diptychs on view in the inn beyond Barnet. Yet Bullein was too sharp a reader and too good a parodist of the *Utopia* to have underestimated a text that addresses issues of such fundamental concern to him. Like More, he was passionately interested in the nature of humankind and the question of community. Like More, too, he turned to dialogue and Menippean satire to explore a world where all is, in some sense, topsy-turvy, even though he reversed More's emphasis, concentrating on the microcosm and anatomizing the body and soul of humankind. Finally, like the *Utopia*, Bullein's *Dialogue Against the Fever Pestilence* is simultaneously philosophical and "foolosophical," asking ultimate questions while giving itself to mirth, what Civis calls "the greatest iewll of this world" (p. 71).

University of Hawaii

Notes

1. See *A Short-Title Catalogue of Books Printed in England, Scotland, & Ireland: 1475-1640*, compiled by A. W. Pollard & G. R. Redgrave, revised by W. A. Jackson, F. S. Ferguson, & Katharine F. Pantzer, 2nd. ed., 2 vols. (London: The Bibliographical Society, 1976-1986), 1: 178; and the *Oxford English Dictionary*: pietifull and pitiful.

Citations of Bullein's *Dialogue* are taken from William Bullein, *A Dialogue Against the Fever Pestilence*, ed. Mark W. Bullen and A. H. Bullen (1888; London: Early English Text Society, 1931). This text is particularly useful because it includes material from the editions of 1564, 1573, and 1578. I have also seen the British Library copies of one of the 1564 editions and the 1573 edition.

2. William S. Mitchell, "William Bullein, Elizabethan Physician and Author," *Medical History* 3 (1959): 188-91, and W. H. Welply, "An Unanswered Question: Bullein and Hilton," *Notes and Queries* n. s. 4 (1957): 3-6.

3. Mitchell, 197; Joyce Youings, *Sixteenth-Century England* (Harmondsworth: Penguin Books, 1984), 149-50.

4. Works checked include: Irving D. Blum, "English Utopias from 1551

to 1699: A Bibliography," *Bulletin of Bibliography* 21 (1955): 143-44; Glenn Negley, *Utopian Literature: A Bibliography* (Lawrence: Regents Press of Kansas, 1977); and Lyman Tower Sargent, *British and American Utopian Literature: 1516-1975* (Boston: G. K. Hall, 1979), which skips from More to T. N. and Lupton (see below).

5. Included in Hugh Plat, *The Floures of Philosophie*, ed. Richard Panofsky (Scholars' Facsimiles: Delmar, New York, 1982): 98; see also Richard Panofsky, "An Unknown Sixteenth Century Reference to More's *Utopia*," *Moreana* 19 (1982): 38.

6. Lupton, Sig. Z.

7. C. S. Lewis, *English Literature in the Sixteenth Century, Excluding Drama* (Oxford: Clarendon Press, 1954), 292.

8. Rosalie L. Colie, *The Resources of Kind: Genre-Theory in the Renaissance* (Berkeley: University of California Press, 1973): 76-102.

9. Lewis, 292.

10. Herbert G. Wright, "Some Sixteenth and Seventeenth Century Writers on the Plague," *Essays and Studies of the English Association* n. s. 6 (1953): 42.

11. Albert C. Baugh, *A Literary History of England* (New York: Appleton-Century Crofts, 1948): 413.

12. In *The Cambridge History of English Literature*, ed. A. W. Ward and A. R. Waller, 15 vols. (Cambridge: The University Press, 1907-27), 3: 108-09.

13. Oscar James Campbell, *Comicall Satyre and Shakespeare's "Troilus and Cressida"* (1938; San Marino: Huntington Library, 1970), 18-19.

14. William C. Boring, "William Bullein's *Dialogue Against the Fever Pestilence*," *The Nassau Review* 2 (1974): 34.

15. Boring, 40.

16. J. Proust, "Le dialogue de W. Bullein à propos de la peste (1564): formulation d'une thérapeutique pour l'âme en péril," in *Le dialogue au temps de la Renaissance*, ed. M. T. Jones-Davies (Paris: Centre de Recherches sur la Renaissance, 1984), 59.

17. Eugene P. Kirk, *Menippean Satire: An Annotated Catalogue of Texts and Criticism* (New York: Garland Publishing Company, 1980), item 475.

18. Devon L. Hodges, *Renaissance Fictions of Anatomy* (Amherst: University of Massachusetts Press, 1985), 1. Though Bullein's is among the earliest anatomies and a particularly interesting one, it is nowhere mentioned in this study.

19. Willyam Bulleyn, *Bulleins Bulwarke of Defece* [sic] *Againste All Sicknes Sornes and Woundes* (1562; Amsterdam: Da Capo Press, 1971), Sig. Ii, iv.

20. C. D. O'Malley, "Tudor Medicine and Biology," *Huntington Library Quarterly* 32 (1968-69): 12. For Vesalius' skeleton, see *The Illustrations from the Works of Andreas Vesalius*, ed. J. B. deC. M. Saunders and Charles D. O'Malley (Cleveland: World Publishing Company, 1950), Plate 90. The skeleton accompanying the 1564 editions of Bullein's *Dialogue* is included in Proust, p. 61.

21. O'Malley, "Tudor Medicine," 12.

22. Bullein must have chosen this citation with an eye upon the inscription over the third skeleton from Vesalius' "Tabulae Sex," which reads "Skele-

ton *a Tergo* Delineatvm" (italics mine): see *The Illustrations*, Plate 92. Unlike the anatomist, who can only delineate one view at a time (Vesalius shows the skeleton from front, then side, then back), God's knowledge of humankind is all-encompassing.

23. Hodges, 2.

24. Mary Claire Randolph, "The Medical Concept in English Renaissance Satiric Theory: Its Possible Relationships and Implications," *Studies in Philology* 38 (1941): 125.

25. Randolph, 126.

26. Randolph, 137-38.

27. Involved in the early 1560's in several lawsuits and imprisoned, apparently under false charges, Bullein had compelling personal reasons to attack lawyers and judges; see Mitchell, 190-91.

28. Citations are from John Donne: *The Anniversaries*, ed. Frank Manley (Baltimore: John Hopkins Press, 1963), 69. See too Rosalie L. Colie, " 'All in Peeces:' Problems of Interpretation in Donne's Anniversary Poems," in *Just So Much Honor*, ed. Peter Amadeus Fiore (University Park: Pennsylvania State University Press, 1972), 189-218, and Barbara Kiefer Lewalski, *Donne's "Anniversaries" and the Poetry of Praise: The Creation of a Symbolic Mode* (Princeton: Princeton University Press, 1973), 226-35.

29. Northrop Frye, *Anatomy of Criticism: Four Essays* (1957; Atheneum, New York: Atheneum Press, 1967), 309.

30. Frye, 310-11.

31. For the tradition see Michel-André Bossy, "Medieval Debates of Body and Soul," *Comparative Literature* 28 (1976): 144-63.

32. *The Works of Geoffrey Chaucer*, ed. F. N. Robinson, 2nd ed. (Boston: Houghton Mifflin, 1957), 21.

33. Chaucer, 21.

34. John Skelton, *Poems*, ed. Robert S. Kinsman (Oxford: Clarendon Press, 1969), 9; cf. p. 132 of the *Dialogue*.

35. Each of the interlocutors has his / her own distinct accent; for more on the dialogic "word" see Proust, 62-64. On the importance of the oral in the anatomy, more generally, see Philip Stevick, "Novel and Anatomy: Notes Toward an Amplification of Frye," *Criticism* 10 (1968): 153-65.

36. See John Peter, *Complaint and Satire in Early English Literature* (Oxford: Clarendon Press, 1956), 86-91. The entire fourth chapter, on the moral themes of complaint, illuminates attitudes in Bullein's *Dialogue*.

37. Proust, p. 66, argues that this is the central image of the *Dialogue*.

38. J. C. Davis, *Utopia and the Ideal Society* (Cambridge: Cambridge University Press, 1981), 26.

39. Davis, 36.

40. Davis, 38.

41. Davis, 27.

42. Davis, 29.

43. Thus Darko Suvin terms the utopia an "estranged genre"; see his *Metamorphoses of Science Fiction* (New Haven: Yale University Press, 1979), 53-55.

44. Besides *My Dear Peter* (Angers: *Moreana*, 1983), see Gary Saul Morson, *The Boundaries of Genre: Dostoevsky's "Diary of a Writer" and the Traditions of Literary Utopia* (Austin: University of Texas Press, 1981).

45. *Utopia, The Complete Works of St. Thomas More*, vol. 4, ed. Edward Surtz, S. J., and J. H. Hexter (New Haven: Yale University Press, 1965), 147/21-25.

46. *Utopia*, 101/1-4.

London, 1 December 1987.

Cher Père, Caro Amico,

Have I even told you how patient and « kindly » you have been with an ignorant non-scholar who had to learn everything about Thomas More ; and what a pleasure it has been learning about him from you ? From earliest childhood, his face was more familiar to me than that of any other saint ; the Holbein drawing hanging over my father's desk at home -- for him, *the* model for every government servant ; yet I knew next to nothing about him. And, in addition, you have introduced so many of his friends, both contemporary and present-day, to me. What a privilege ! I know I speak for several English *Amici* when I say this.

How pleasant it was visiting Angers at last in Summer '87 and seeing Moreanum. You were so hospitable to us 5 Londoners, not only in the ordinary way of things but also by celebrating Mass for us at special times. I now realise why Angers is so suitable a place for a Moreanum. It has, on a small scale, what any Londoner hopes to find in any other city : A river with boats ; an avenue of plane trees ; *two* delightful museums ; a castle with wide views from its walls ; broad thoroughfares for traffic and spacious quiet streets for walking in ; and inside 29 rue Volney, that gently curving and elegant staircase looking back to a small garden behind, which was so like a London 18th-century house.

Affectionate prayers *e con omaggio,*

Rosemary Rendel

Christopher Columbus, sketch by Raymond Joly

SILVIO ZAVALA

Aspects de la littérature utopique en Espagne et en Amérique latine

Espagne et Angleterre

ON SAIT LA PLACE OCCUPÉE par la littérature utopique dans le monde de langue espagnole. A titre de preuves, citons les noms de Vasco de Quiroga, de Francisco de Quevedo (dans le commentaire de sa traduction de l'*Utopie* de More [Cordoue, 1637]) et d'autres écrivains dont Francisco López Estrada dresse la liste avec soin dans *Tomás Moro y España, sus relaciones hasta el siglo XVIII* (Madrid, 1980).[1] Andrés Vázquez de Prada, dans *Sir Tomás Moro, Lord Canciller de Inglaterra* (Madrid, 1966; 3e éd. 1975) rappelle qu'au cours de sa vie More côtoya de très près Catherine d'Aragon et Marie Tudor, qu'il a personnellement connues et défendues (p. 14). Aux pp. 26 et suivantes, il présente la bibliographie espagnole. Il rappelle également que les missionnaires espagnols qui, de la Californie à la Terre de Feu, ont enflammé de leur verbe et de leur sang la foi du Nouveau Continent américain, respectaient le programme d'Utopie, et que Quiroga lança un plan audacieux de socialisation chrétienne sur le territoire mexicain (p. 193). Il explique les deux visites de Charles Quint à Londres, en 1520 et 1522 (pp. 231s). Du fait de la nature biographique du livre, l'analyse de l'*Utopie* occupe une place secondaire (pp. 178s, ainsi que les pages indiquées dans la Table des Matières: *Escritos*, p. 546). Mais au chap. VII (pp. 186s.), il fait un examen plus détaillé de cette oeuvre sous le titre de: "El secreto de Utopía." Il déclare que l'*Utopie* ne s'adresse pas aux personnes manquant d'humour ou d'intelligence (p. 189). Il cite Quevedo: "El libro es corto, mas para atenderlo como merece, ninguna vida será larga" (p. 190). Vázquez de Prada le considère pour sa part comme la concrétisation d'un idéal permettant d'aller vers un monde meilleur actuellement inaccessible (p. 191).

Si l'on en juge par les publications récentes dont je me propose de rendre compte ci-après, l'intérêt porté à cette littérature utopique dans le monde de langue espagnole semble toujours aussi vif.

> Demetrio Ramos Pérez, "Sobre el origen de la utopía de Tomás Moro," dans *Homenaje a Antonio Maravall*, Centre de Recherches Sociologiques, Conseil Supérieur de Recherches Scientifiques, Madrid, 1985, Tome III, p. 221 à 235.

L'auteur, grand expert des voyages de découverte, considère plus particulièrement le quatrième voyage transocéanique d'Améric Vespuce, effectué au cours des années 1503-1504, et raconté dans une *Lettera* du 4 septembre 1504 (imprimée en 1505 ou 1506 par Gian Stefano di Carlo di Pavia pour le libraire Piero Paccini). Une version latine en fut réalisée par Jean Basin de Sendacour pour l'humaniste Martin Waldseemüller, et publiée sous le titre de *Quatuor Navigationes*, en avril 1507, en même temps que *Cosmographiae Introductio*. More en eut peut-être connaissance par l'intermédiaire de Pierre Gilles.

Ramos se réfère à un article de 1938 (cité aussi dans *Moreana* 31/32, p. 81-82): George B. Parks, "More's Utopia and Geography," et à Isaac J. Pardo, *Fuegos bajo el agua: la invención de Utopía* (Caracas, La Casa de Bello, 1983), p. 697, chez qui il estime que l'on retrouve, avec beaucoup d'érudition, l'origine et le déroulement de tous les projets de société heureuse qui ont été proposés. Nous reparlerons de ce livre.

Ramos étudie l'influence que put avoir sur More, au moment où il a rédigé *Utopie*, l'oeuvre de Pierre Martyr, dans l'édition de 1511 (dix livres de la première décade du *De Orbe Novo*): rencontre avec le monde amérindien, description des indigènes des Antilles, notamment du caractère extrêmement heureux des Indiens d'Hispaniola. L'Utopie, séparée du continent par un détroit, ressemble à cette île où, en plein âge d'or, une population vit sans vêtements, sans juges, sans livres, en se contentant des produits de la nature, sans interrogation aucune sur l'avenir: en quelque sorte, le message d'un humaniste qui aurait pu être repris par l'autre.

Même s'il est plus difficile que More en ait eu connaissance avant d'écrire son livre, les trois premières décades du *De Orbe Novo* parurent, également en latin, en 1516, à Alcalá de Henares, imprimées par Arnao Guillén de Brocar. Mais déjà dans l'édition de 1511, Pierre Martyr disait que les Indiens vivaient sans vêtements, toutes leurs terres faisant partie du bien public, sans la notion du "ce qui est à moi" et "ce qui est à toi."[2]

Ramos fait remarquer avec finesse que Catherine d'Aragon se trouvait à Londres depuis novembre 1501 (p. 235), et que le mariage de l'Infante espagnole avec l'héritier du trône anglais avait été convenu en 1497 (p. 228) [il eut lieu à Londres le 14 novembre 1501]. Il pense que l'Infante se serait rendue à Londres en emportant avec elle le souci indianiste dont elle s'était imprégnée à la Cour de ses parents, et qu'elle aurait suivi avec attention les nouvelles et les intentions qui émanaient du cercle londonien auquel More n'était pas étranger.

Au Vénézuela: Pardo et l'utopisme

Isaac J. Pardo, *Fuegos bajo el agua, La invención de Utopía*. Fondation La Casa de Bello, Caracas, 1983, 802 p. (Prix National de Littérature, 1984).

D'après ce qu'explique l'auteur du livret d'*Homenaje a Isaac J. Pardo* (La Casa de Bello, Caracas, 1984, p. 21 à 23), Pardo souhaitait initialement présenter au lecteur vénézuélien un personnage de l'histoire mexicaine du 16e siècle, Don Vasco de Quiroga. Ce juriste qui devint évêque, ému par la dureté des Conquistadores, entreprit d'établir des collectivités d'Indiens conformément au modèle suggéré par More dans l'*Utopie*, oeuvre qu'il considérait comme inspirée par l'Esprit Saint pour un gouvernement correct du Nouveau Monde.

A peine avait-il entrepris ce travail que l'auteur vénézuélien eut l'idée de faire précéder le portrait de Quiroga d'une étude sur More et l'*Utopie*, et il estima peu après qu'il était préférable de remonter jusqu'à la *République* de Platon. Au bout de onze ans, il avait écrit huit cents pages d'un livre où Vasco de Quiroga n'est cité que deux fois.

Fuegos bajo el agua–"Feux sous l'eau"–constitue donc une vaste fresque de préliminaires concernant l'utopie à la Renaissance et son influence sur l'histoire de l'Amérique. Mais les préoccupations de Pardo ressortent tout au long des pages de son remarquable travail. Il consacre sa Cinquième Partie (pp. 679 à 748) à Thomas More et à l'*Utopie*.

P. 682, remarque 2, il donne une bibliographie sur Quiroga, à qui le livre de More semblait "tan apropiado . . . para el gobierno del Nuevo Mundo."[3] P. 694, il répète que Don Vasco estimait que More était "inspirado por el Espíritu Santo." P. 758, Pardo écrit à juste titre: "Si la sociedad descubierta por Hitlodeo pudo parecer y parezca todavía indeseable a muchas personas, Vasco de Quiroga, en México y en 1535, estaba en lo cierto al pensar que los indios del Nuevo Mundo, sujetos al yugo de los conquistadores, podrían alcanzar la felicidad si se les ofreciese la manera de vivir en colectividades organizadas según el modelo de *Utopía*." Parmi les tentatives de mise en pratique du modèle utopique dans le Nouveau Monde, il rappelle "el de Bartolomé de las Casas en la costa de Venezuela; los 'hospitales' de Vasco de Quiroga y las ideas milenaristas-joaquinistas de Gerónimo de Mendieta, en México; las Misiones o República de los jesuitas en Paraguay; las frenéticas búsquedas del Dorado o, mejor dicho, de los dorados de América" (p. 762). Il aurait pu ajouter la pénétration pacifique de Las Casas et de ses compagnons dominicains à Vera-Paz de Guatemala, étudiée avec tant de soins par André Saint-Lu.

La partie américaine de l'oeuvre projetée aurait dû inclure des essais sous le titre de "L'Utopie aux Indes," mais l'auteur ne parvint qu'à esquisser l'étude sur Vasco de Quiroga. Pour en revenir aux pages de *Fuegos bajo el agua* écrites sur le sujet qui nous intéresse, nous pouvons noter ce qui suit. L'épigraphe fournie en explication du titre est prise chez Empédocle, *Fragmento 52*: "Muchos fuegos están ardiendo bajo el agua." Au début du texte, p. 13, l'auteur déclare: "Un contemporáneo de Tomás Moro, Hernán Pérez de Oliva, emprendió una *Historia de la Invención de las Indias*, y a finales del siglo XVI cantaba Juan de Castellanos, en sus *Elegías*, la memorable partida de Cristóbal Colón: 'Al occidente van encaminadas / Las naves inventoras de regiones. . . .'"
Il commente: "Inventar significaba entonces, como ahora, crear, imaginar, pero también hallar o descubrir y a pesar de haber caído en desuso esta segunda acepción hemos querido conservar, por considerarla adecuada al tema que nos ocupa, la antigua dualidad en la cual se disfumina la línea divisoria entre lo ideado y lo vivido."[4] Rappelons le sous-titre de l'ouvrage: *La invención de Utopía*.

A la même p. 13, l'auteur explique qu'il tente de réunir les traditions et les légendes les plus anciennes pour remonter au moment où Thomas More, dans son fameux livre, a donné à l'utopique une force qui a conservé toute sa vigueur près de cinq cents ans plus tard, et a créé en même temps un nom qui était appelé à s'imposer à l'échelle universelle. Il aborde alors d'une part les mythes et les oeuvres de poètes et de philosophes: l'utopie en tant que pure essence imaginative; et de l'autre le plan des faits historiques, évolutifs, durs et imparfaits comme la vie elle-même: l'utopie en passe de devenir réalité au prix d'efforts immenses. Apparemment irréconciliables, les deux plans ont cependant coutume de se frôler et de se confondre. Dans l'un comme dans l'autre cas, il s'agit d'imaginations ou de découvertes, c'est-à-dire d'une invention avec toute l'ampleur que nos ancêtres ont donnée à ce terme.

Après un résumé succinct de la vie de More (p. 681 à 694), dans lequel on ne cesse de constater, comme dans tout le reste de l'oeuvre, ses grands dons de narrateur et le soin qu'il met à se fonder sur des informations dûment vérifiées, l'auteur vénézuelien aborde, à partir de la p. 695, l'examen du livre *Utopie*. Il n'omet pas le fait que le Portugais Raphaël Hythlodée intervient dans le dialogue comme accompagnateur d'Améric Vespuce au cours de trois de ses voyages vers le Nouveau Monde (p. 695). More, écrit-il, "bromeaba en serio" (plaisantait avec sérieux), ce qui donne à l'*Utopie* son profond mystère (p. 701).

C'est lorsqu'il examine l'idée de la colonisation, évoquée dans l'*Utopie* (p. 722), que le récit de Pardo revient à l'Amérique: si l'île était surpeuplée, les habitants d'Utopie fondaient une colonie dans un endroit quelconque du continent où il restait encore des terres non exploitées par les autochtones. Pardo rappelle aussi que More justifie cette politique de la façon suivante: si les autochtones refusent l'implantation, une guerre est déclarée, car le fait qu'un peuple qui n'utilise pas la terre, la laissant inféconde et inhabitée, empêche que cette terre soit possédée et mise en valeur par d'autres qui, de par la loi naturelle, doivent se nourrir de cette terre, constitue un motif suffisant de déclaration de guerre. More dit auparavant que ces colonies sont régies par les mêmes lois qu'Utopie elle-même et sont ouvertes à tous les autochtones qui désirent s'y établir. Pour les habitants ainsi unis en une communauté d'institutions et de coutumes, la fusion devenait facile, à l'avantage de tous.

Pardo fait remarquer (p. 723) que le voyage de Christophe Colomb avait fait naître chez les Anglais une passion pour le Nouveau Monde et un grand désir d'aventures. Cette passion touchait la famille de More, dont le beau-frère John Rastell projetait une colonisation en un point de Terre Neuve, la tentative ayant finalement échoué du fait d'une émeute de l'équipage. Pardo cite R. W. Chambers, p. 139 à 142: "Colonisation and transatlantic adventure meant much to the writer of *Utopia*. . . . The Utopians only settle where there is 'much waste and unoccupied ground,' and they admit to full citizenship any of the natives who care to join them." More ne réclamait pas un monopole des droits coloniaux pour l'Angleterre: "If he is staking out a claim, it is for the common body of Christendom." S'appuyant sur Edward Surtz (*Utopia*, Introduction, p. clxxix), Pardo déclare (remarque 141) que les nouvelles du Nouveau Monde et des étonnants habitants parvinrent à More par l'intermédiaire des *Quatuor Navigationes*: "An incident on the fourth voyage furnishes the framework for the whole description of Utopia. Vespucci also supplies various details which, even if found in classical sources as well, help to impart a contemporary atmosphere to hedonism, communism, indifference to gold, dearth of iron, use of feathers, participation of women in war, and friendliness to strangers." Et, par l'intermédiaire de Pierre Martyr: "Anglería pays more attention than Vespucci to native religion, especially to the deity and human immortality."

A la fin de sa lecture intense et mesurée du texte de l'*Utopie*, Pardo déclare: "Así terminaba Hitlodeo el relato de su sorprendente descubrimiento, de su *invención*, como solía decirse entonces" (p. 738). Et quant à l'applicabilité du modèle utopique, il rappelle la pensée de Socrate: "Estamos dispuestos a sostener que hubo, que hay y que habrá un Estado como el nuestro, cuando reine la musa filosófica" (p. 741). Moins catégorique que son maître, More n'a fait que formuler un souhait: "No es hacedero que todo sea bueno, a menos que la humanidad lo sea, cosa que no espero hasta dentro de algunos años" (p. 746).[5]

A partir de la p. 749, nous touchons un point culminant de l'oeuvre, où Pardo examine brièvement l'évolution de la pensée et des faits utopiques suite à la parution de l'*Utopie* en 1516. Il estime que les projets sont, ou ont tenté d'être, des schémas ou des projets visant à satisfaire le plus profond, le plus ancré des désirs humains: jouir du plus grand bonheur possible pour l'ensemble de la société. A la p. 762, il fait brièvement référence à la Constitution des États-Unis d'Amérique et à la Révolution Française; dans la remarque 39, il donne une bibliographie succincte, en s'attachant à Babeuf, qu'il voit "como animador de una utopía dentro de la utopía."

L'auteur aurait pu ajouter l'oeuvre de Bronislaw Baczko, *Lumières de l'Utopie* (Paris, 1978), car, suivant un cheminement différent de celui de Pardo, Baczko met en relief les liens entre la pensée utopique et la réalité historique, à l'époque des Lumières et sous la Révolution Française. On lit, p. 7 de la Préface: "Utopie et Histoire: rapports complexes que ce livre se propose de dégager au travers de l'étude de l'imagination sociale à l'oeuvre au 18e siècle, et notamment au cours de la période révolutionnaire." Comme chez Pardo, le précédent que constitue l'*Utopie* occupe une place appropriée dans l'oeuvre de Baczko.[6]

Viennent ensuite les guerres d'Indépendance et la création des républiques d'Amérique Latine, partie dans laquelle Pardo mentionne l'oeuvre de Miguel Acosta Saignes, *Acción y utopía en el Hombre de las Dificultades* (Casa de las Américas, La Habana, 1977) pour les grandes conceptions utopiques de Simón Bolívar. Il évoque également "El utopismo socialista en América Latina," présenté par Carlos M. Rama à la Bibliothèque Ayacucho (Caracas, 1977), volume consacré à l'*Utopismo socialista, 1830-1893*. Pardo estime que la crise du monde contemporain ne peut être dépassée que par la voie de la pensée utopique, capable d'imaginer et de rendre réel ce qui est apparemment impossible. Il sait que jamais nous n'atteindrons le but, mais que chaque jour nous pourrons nous en approcher davantage (p. 765). Et il pose la question de savoir si la nature humaine permet de réaliser un tel idéal (p. 769). Son vaste examen de l'histoire universelle observée depuis son mirador utopique offre dans une large mesure les éléments positifs et les éléments négatifs des réponses possibles.[7]

L'Équateur face à l'utopisme éclairé

Arturo A. Roig, Université Pontificale Catholique de l'Équateur, "Momentos y corrientes del pensamiento utópico en el Ecuador," dans *Latino América*, Anuario / Estudios Latinoamericanos 14, Université Nationale Autonome de Mexico, Faculté de Philosophie et de Lettres, Mexico, 1981, Centre de Coordination et de Diffusion des Études Latinoaméricaines, p. 51 à 69.

Roig examine le thème de l'utopie dans la pensée d'un écrivain équatorien de la deuxième moitié du 18e siècle: Eugenio Espejo. Il décèle chez Espejo une revalorisation de l'utopisme classique dans l'atmosphère d'utopisme chrétien primitif (p. 65). Dans *El Nuevo Luciano de Quito*, Espejo attaque durement le probabilisme jésuite; il s'y déclare d'ailleurs "vériste," mais avec un certain penchant vers l'utopique. C'est dans le cadre de la réélaboration de la pensée de la Renaissance au cours du 18e siècle que l'on constate le retour à l'*Utopie* de More chez Espejo. Les idées politiques de Voltaire et sa conception de la critique de textes, ainsi que l'ouverture vers le genre utopique consacrée chez l'écrivain français, marquent de leur sceau ce retour d'Espejo.

Philip L. Astuto, autre spécialiste d'Espejo,[8] explique qu'en 1779, il fit circuler sous forme de manuscrit *El Nuevo Luciano de Quito o Desper-*

tador de los ingenios quiteños en nueve conversaciones eruditas para el estímulo de la literatura. Ce dialogue satirique à la manière de Lucien de Samosate préconisait la réforme des études. Espejo critiquait encore l'éducation traditionnelle dans *Marco Porcio Catón* (juin 1780), dont l'autre titre en option est: *O Memorias para la impugnación del Nuevo Luciano de Quito,* afin de désorienter ceux qui tenteraient d'identifier l'auteur. Pour des raisons de polémique, Espejo écrivit une deuxième partie de *El Nuevo Luciano,* sous le titre de *La Ciencia Blancardina,* également sous forme de dialogue, ce après juillet 1780.

Roig indique que, dans ce "Diálogo tercero" (édition de 1912, tome II, p. 99 à 121), Espejo fait une distinction entre la "politique ordinaire" et celle qui doit "aller plus loin et examiner la forme de gouvernement." C'est-à-dire qu'il pose la question de la forme juste de la République. Espejo mentionne ici Voltaire (à qui il attribue l'anti-Machiavel du roi Frédéric de Prusse) et l'*Utopie* de More, car nous voyons dans ces oeuvres où doit se situer la clé, le coeur de celui qui gouverne: faire une politique heureuse, ce mot étant plus longuement expliqué dans l'oeuvre que nous a laissée le pieux chancelier.

Faisant ressortir la mention élogieuse de More dans les écrits de Espejo, Roig commente que chez l'un et l'autre on trouve le lien entre la pensée utopique et le retour à l'Église chrétienne primitive, dans la mesure où Espejo affirme que "para saber esta nobilísima política, es necesario estudiar la Santa Escritura" (p. 67).

Espejo travailla sur une édition de l'*Utopie* incluant les vers où Anemolius déclare que l'île d'Utopie devrait s'appeler *Eutopia,* la ville heureuse. Roig cite dans la traduction anglaise de Paul Turner (Baltimore, 1965), p. 25. Son île n'est alors plus un non-lieu mais un projet de vie communautaire juste.

Si ce lien entre le souvenir de l'*Utopie* de More et l'écrivain équatorien du 18e siècle représente déjà un enrichissement de la littérature utopique en langue espagnole, que l'on avait oublié, on trouve dans l'étude de Roig (p. 61) une autre donnée curieuse relative aux contacts qu'avait eus Vicente Rocafuerte, Équatorien distingué qui représentait le Mexique à Londres, avec le réformateur anglais Robert Owen, en 1828, dans le cadre du projet élaboré par ce dernier en vue d'établir dans les états mexicains de Coahuila et du Texas des "communautés expérimentales socialistes." La requête de Owen date de septembre 1828 et a été publiée dans *Cuadernos Americanos,* Mexico, juillet-août 1949, p. 149 à 154. Les lettres échangées entre Owen et Rocafuerte sont conservées aux Archives Générales du Secrétariat aux Relations Extérieures, Mexico, Dossier H / 554. Rocafuerte admirait les idées de Owen, mais il pensait que son plan était impraticable "du fait de l'état actuel de la population" (Cf. *Utopismo socialista* de Carlos M. Rama, pp. liii–liv de l'Introduction). On sait que Owen avait fondé la communauté de New Harmony, dans l'Indiana, en 1824. Un socialiste de l'école de Charles Fourier, le très actif Victor Considérant, installa sa colonie près de Dallas et put visiter le nord du territoire mexicain, ce qui lui permit d'écrire ses impressions, comme je l'indique dans mon article: "Victor Considérant ante el problema social de México," *Historia Mexicana* 27, VII-3 (El Colegio de México, janvier-mars 1958), 309–28.[9]

Ces quelques informations permettront de rappeler les divers liens qui ont existé au cours des temps entre le Nouveau Monde et la littérature utopique, et de voir dans quelle mesure les nouvelles découvertes inspiraient la littérature utopique, cette dernière venant à son tour influencer la vie du Nouveau Monde.

El Colegio de Mexico, DF

∽

Notes

Traduit de l'espagnol par Danièle Simon.

1. Voir aussi Stelio Cro, *Realidad y utopía en el descubrimiento y conquista de la América Hispana (1492–1682)* (Troy, Michigan, Madrid, 1983), xvii, 273 pages. Introduction par Francisco López Estrada. L'ouvrage comprend quatre parties: I. 16e–17e siècles. L'utopie christiano-sociale (Vasco de Quiroga, p. 53; Bartolomé de Las Casas, p. 68; république chrétienne du Paraguay, p. 78). II. 16e–17e siècles. Les fondements théoriques de l'utopie hispano-américaine. III. L'Âge d'Or et l'utopie en Amérique. IV. 17e siècle. L'utopie systématique. *Sinapia*.

2. En ce qui concerne l'âge d'or chez les Indiens du Nouveau Monde, Ramos consulte *De Orbe Novo* (décade 1, livre II, chap. IV) dans la version espagnole de Joaquín Torres Asensio (Madrid, 1982), pp. 145–46. Il mentionne également décade 1, livre III, chap. VIII, pp. 201–2. Cromberger avait, en 1511, imprimé à Séville dix livres de la première décade, avec le récit du voyage que Pierre Martyr avait fait au Caire en tant qu'ambassadeur des Rois Catholiques, en 1501–1502, et où il est fait référence à l'atmosphère islamique de l'Egypte. Voici les références bibliographiques:

> P. Martyris ab Angleria Mediolanensis (1455–1526): *Opera. Legatio babilonica. Occeanea decas. Poemata*. Cum privilegio. Hispali, 1511. Im-

pressum cum summa diligentia per Jacobum Corumberger alemanum. In-fol. Original: Biblioteca Colombina, Séville. Facsimilé: Library of Congress E 141 A5. 1511 a.
De Orbe novo decades (Petri Martyris Anglerii. Cum ejusdem *Legatione Babylonica.* Edidit Antonius Nebrissensis). Compluti, impr. in contubernio A. Guillelmi, 1516. In-fol. B. N. Paris, Rés. C. 757 (2-3). Et plus tard avec description du titre: *Relationi del S. Pietro Martire, . . . delle cose notabili della provincia dell' Egitto, scritte in lingua latina . . . et hora recate nella italiana de Carlo Passi.* Venetia, G. de' Cavalli, 1564. In-8°. B. N. Paris 03 b.l. Catalogué à la B. N. Paris comme: ANGHIERA (Pietro Martire d').

3. L'auteur m'écrit courtoisement que cette remarque 2 figure "en guise de réparation du fait de son infidélité vis-à-vis du 'tata Vasco.' "

4. "Les navires inventeurs de régions s'acheminent vers l'Occident . . ." – "Inventer signifiait alors, comme à présent, créer, imaginer, mais ce terme signifiait également trouver ou découvrir et, bien que cette deuxième acception soit tombée en désuétude, nous avons tenu à la conserver, parce qu'elle nous semblait appropriée au thème qui nous préoccupe, l'ancienne dualité grâce à laquelle s'estompe la limite entre l'imaginaire et le vécu."

5. On trouvera la phrase en latin à la p. 62 de l'édition de nov. 1518 (p. 432, dans l'*Utopie* éditée par André Prévost, Paris, 1978). Ajoutons à l'excellente bibliographie d'Isaac J. Pardo, p. 779-800, un titre qui aurait tout à fait trouvé sa place à la fin du Cinquième Chapitre de son oeuvre. *Essential Articles for the Study of Thomas More*, edited with an Introduction and Bibliography by R. S. Sylvester and G. P. Marc'hadour (Hamden, Connecticut, 1977). (La série "Essential Articles" a pour "Editor General" Bernard N. Schilling).

6. Voir dans cette oeuvre, à titre d'exemples, les pages 18 à 21, 33, 46 et 59.

7. Francisco López Estrada a commenté l'oeuvre de Isaac J. Pardo, *Fuegos bajo el agua*, dans un compte rendu minutieux publié en langue espagnole dans *Moreana* 91/92 (décembre 1986), p. 103-110. Il souligne le mérite littéraire de l'oeuvre, sa grand portée historique et la "nouvelle compréhension de l'utopie" qu'elle propose compte tenu des circonstances actuelles (p. 109). De nos jours, estime-t-il, l'utopie n'a plus pour fonction d'imaginer l'impossible bonheur collectif qui avait pris racine dans une île inaccessible, pas plus que d'ouvrir un chemin visant à rendre l'homme meilleur; sa fonction actuelle consiste à libérer l'esprit de façon qu'il puisse prévoir les conséquences du grand changement qui est en train de se produire.

8. Auteur de l'article "Eugenio Espejo, a Man of the Enlightenment in Ecuador," *Revista de Historia de América* 44 (1957), pp. 369-91, et du livre: *Eugenio Espejo (1747-1795), Reformador ecuatoriano de la Ilustración* (México, Fondo de Cultura Económica, 1969), 160 p. (Collection Tierra Firme). On en trouvera le compte rendu dans *R.H.A.* 69 (1970), p. 149- 50, par Roberto Moreno. Il existe deux éditions des écrits de Espejo. L'une, *Escritos del Dr. Francisco Javier Eugenio de Santa Cruz y Espejo* (Quito, Imprimerie Municipale, 1912),

2 volumes, est due à Federico González Suárez. La deuxième, qui fut celle consultée par Astuto, nous la devons à Jacinto Jijón y Caamaño et Homero Viteri Lafronte: *Escritos del doctor Francisco Javier Eugenio Santa Cruz y Espejo* (Quito, 1923).

9. L'article fut publié sous le titre: "Victor Considérant et le problème social au Mexique" dans *Revue Historique,* Année 92, tome 239 (Paris, 1968), 19-28.

Père,
en t'offrant ce sacrifice,
nous commémorons ton fils, Jésus.
La mort n'a pu le retenir,
car tu l'as relevé dans l'Esprit de sainteté
et tu l'as exalté comme Seigneur de la création.

Que sa venue dans la gloire nous trouve
toujours vigilants dans la prière,
forts dans l'amour,
et fidèles à la fraction du pain.

VI forts dans l'amour

Father,
we commemorate Jesus, your Son,
as we offer you this sacrifice.
Death could not bind him,
for you raised him up in the Spirit of holiness
and exalted him as Lord of creation.
May his coming in glory find us
ever-watchful in prayer,
strong in love,
and faithful to the breaking of the bread.

St. Ann's Rectory
4001 YUMA STREET, N.W.
WASHINGTON, D.C. 20016

October 16, 1987.

Dear Germain,

The beginning of our friendship corresponds closely with the beginning of the publication of *Moreana*. A quarter of a century ago when I was Pastor of St. Joseph's Parish on Capitol Hill, Washington, D.C., near the Folger Library, you came to visit me and stay with me during your research and your speaking engagements in the Washington area.

By vocation I am a parish priest, as you know, involved in the daily work of ministering to souls. Into our life at St. Joseph's and in the subsequent parishes where I was stationed you brought your scholarly and refreshing conversations, lectures, and example of the industry of a true scholar. Your vocation reminded us parish priests of our studies in seminary days and the life and research of a scholar that was beyond the grasp of a parish priest by his calling. It is so good to be reminded of that life and its fruits by your presence. We couldn't be what you are either by talent or vocation. But your visits and your frequent living with us through those years, while you were in our country, lifted us above the daily routine and spurred us on in the midst of our ministry to find some time for the good, the beautiful and the inspirational by your humble and tireless efforts to speak with us about St. Thomas More, to address our people on matters of the spiritual life (I still have copies of your talks).

May God reward your efforts, not only for scholars but for us who labor in a different section of the Lord's vineyard and for what you have been to us, a true friend and an inspiration.

Looking forward to your next visit, I remain.

Fraternally yours,

William J. Awalt

Rev. Msgr. William J. Awalt
Pastor

Lublin 18.11.1987

Cher Monsieur l'Abbé,

C'est le premier Congrès des Études Néolatines qui m'a donné la possibilité et la chance de vous connaître. Je me rappelle bien deux choses : vos messes dites dans une grande chapelle avec quelques fidèles qui y assistaient et qui très vite se sont sentis très proches ; et, naturellement, votre amour pour Thomas Morus, ainsi que pour tous les amis unis par son nom. Et encore une soirée des amis, vécue comme un mystère. Les mêmes impressions sont restées dans ma mémoire à l'occasion des autres congrès dans les différents pays. Vous étiez toujours très, très occupé et en même temps vous aviez les yeux ouverts pour tous les amis -- un sourire, quelques paroles, chacun se sentait important et cher pour vous. Je crois que le Christ de la même manière passait parmi les gens.

Je me rappelle votre effort pour étudier la difficile prononciation de la langue polonaise quand vous aviez préparé votre court séjour en Pologne. On a aperçu avec étonnement qu'avec les prêtres polonais vous avez concélébré votre messe, priant en polonais quand c'était votre tour.

Un frère parmi les autres, toujours simple, proche -- signe de la bonté, dont la source unique est Dieu le Père.

Je vous souhaite, Cher Monsieur l'Abbé, que votre présence partout où vous irez puisse unir vos amis (= *Amici Thomae Mori*) en les dirigeant vers l'Amour éternel, où nous attend votre et notre patron -- Thomas Morus.

Vôtre in Christo

Krystyna Stawecka

LOYOLA UNIVERSITY OF CHICAGO
JESUIT COMMUNITY

6525 North Sheridan Road   Chicago, Illinois 60626

October 27, 1987.

Dear Germain,

    Best wishes to you on this very happy occasion ! It has been a great privilege to know you and through you to meet so many fine people all over this world.

    I treasure your love of the Church, your scholarship and your kindness to me these many years. Each note that you send to me is always a real pleasure to read and I appreciate your thoughtfulness in often enclosing a new image of Saint Michael for my collection.

    Your patience and fidelity to hard work serve all of us well and may we mirror such example. You evidence special concern for human beings even though so much of your time is controlled by reading manuscripts and writing books.

    The bouquet of accomplishments is great and best of all these « flowers » is your imitation of Christ and your love of His people.

    Félicitations !

Michael Grace, S.J.

ALOÏS GERLO

Érasme conciliateur

Érasme de Rotterdam était continuellement à la recherche du compromis. Il ne voulait pas de rupture avec Rome malgré sa critique sévère, mais ne se laissait pas embrigader. Pour la même raison, il restait en contact par correspondance avec des Réformateurs comme Zwingli, Oecolampade, Melanchthon, Bucer et Capiton, alors qu'il avait déjà pris ses distances envers la théologie réformatrice. Mais il y eut une rupture définitive avec Luther après la dispute sur le libre arbitre. Luther, qui jadis avait appelé Érasme "ornement et espoir de la théologie," dit plus tard: "Érasme est une anguille, personne ne peut l'attraper, sinon le Christ lui-même. *Est vir duplex* (c'est un homme à deux visages)."[1]

Même après sa mort, Érasme conservait des ennemis dans les deux camps. L'image qu'on avait de lui était surtout négative. Aussi bien aux yeux des Catholiques que des Protestants, Érasme était un sceptique, un opportuniste, un faible sinon un lâche.

A notre époque, celle du mouvement oecuménique, l'image est devenue beaucoup plus positive: Érasme est l'homme qui refusa de choisir entre Rome et Wittenberg, parce que des deux côtés il distingua le pour et le contre. Huizinga, dans sa célèbre monographie de 1924, appela Érasme "un maître de la réserve" (*een meester van het voorbehoud*). Néanmoins, son appréciation du Prince de l'Humanisme resta très critique. Beaucoup plus positive est la dernière biographie érasmienne, celle de Cornelis Augustijn.[2] Les dons d'Érasme pour le compromis et la réconciliation y sont considérés comme une grande qualité. Et Augustijn n'est pas seul de cet avis. Dans un article récent intitulé "Érasme aujourd'hui," le professeur Charles Béné pose la question: "Appellera-t-on un jour le XXe siècle le siècle d'Érasme?"[3] Jamais le prestige d'Érasme ne fut aussi grand. Ses *Opera omnia* sont réédités, sa correspondance intégrale fut traduite et commentée en français, et, à l'Université de Toronto, on procède à la traduction anglaise des oeuvres complètes.[4] Chaque année voit la parution de nombreux articles et études sur Érasme et son oeuvre. Le supplément à la *Bibliographie de l'Humanisme des Anciens Pays-Bas*, qui sera publié incessamment,[5] a recensé environ 1200 titres nouveaux depuis 1967. Partout dans le monde les commémorations du 500e anniversaire de la naissance d'Érasme en 1967-1969 et du 450e anniversaire de sa mort en 1986, furent impressionnantes. Elles ont donné et donneront encore lieu à d'importantes publications.

Les réserves d'Érasme envers la Réforme résultaient de son individualisme et de son amour de la liberté. Il sentit que la conduite de Luther et son impérieux besoin de convertir étaient dangereux pour le climat de liberté spirituelle dont lui, Érasme, ne pouvait se passer, et il savait que fanatisme et irréductibilité rendraient les guerres de religion inévitables. A peine dix ans après sa mort, en effet, eut lieu la guerre Schmalkaldienne (1546-1547). Dans la ligne de l'irénisme érasmien, un dernier compromis fut conclu, la Paix d'Augsbourg, qui préconisait la cohabitation des confessions. Adepte de la tolérance érasmienne, Guillaume d'Orange fut néanmoins entraîné dans une lutte âpre et sans merci qui mènerait à l'*Akte van verlatinghe* en 1581 (abjuration de Philippe II) et au meurtre d'Orange lui-même en 1584. Les Guerres de Religion éclataient non seulement aux Pays-Bas mais également en France, et dès 1559 les oeuvres d'Érasme furent mises à l'Index. La scission de l'Église s'avérerait définitive.

Autre aspect de la tolérance érasmienne: bien avant l'apparition de Luther, Érasme avait opté pour la conciliation entre culture antique et théologie, entre littérature classique et Christianisme. Pour lui, il n'existait pas d'opposition irréconciliable entre les deux. Ici également il fut l'homme qui jetait des ponts. Les deux éléments, culture antique et Christianisme, étaient pour lui des piliers équivalents de la culture européenne. De là la synthèse qu'il appelle *philosophia Christi*, c'est-à-dire son Humanisme chrétien, où il refuse de dissocier piété et érudition, prière et raisonnement.

Ses modèles sont Augustin, et aussi Jérôme qui possédait les trois langues: latin, grec et hébreu. Dans une lettre au pape Léon X d'avril

1517,[6] Érasme écrit: "Cette synthèse produira un siècle d'or." Luther, de son côté, apporte confrontation et polarisation. Voilà la raison pour laquelle il n'y eut pas de siècle d'or mais au contraire des conflits religieux interminables, inspirés par un fanatisme effréné.

Le troisième aspect de la tolérance d'Érasme est son pacifisme conciliateur. Dans la deuxième moitié de sa vie, Érasme assistait à la formation des états européens qui, depuis la fin du 15e siècle, se disputaient l'hégémonie en Europe. Si l'on songe qu'encore au 20e siècle les peuples européens se sont massacrés dans deux guerres mondiales — d'aucuns parmi les historiens font état de "guerre civile européenne" — il faut bien constater que la pensée politique d'Érasme fut en son temps quelque peu naïve, quelque peu utopique. Mais cette naïveté n'était pas sans limite comme le prouve son traité *De bello Turcico* (La guerre contre les Turcs), de 1530. Au début, Érasme vit dans cette guerre un acte de pure politique impériale. Plus tard, après la défaite de Mohacs, lorsque les Turcs se trouvaient devant Vienne, sa pensée pacifiste devint beaucoup plus réaliste. Il adjura les princes chrétiens de serrer les rangs, de se réconcilier pour que l'Europe ne soit pas submergée par l'Islam.

Érasme voyait dans la guerre l'ennemi de la culture, inconciliable avec son credo humaniste. Lorsque tout argent va aux armes et au paiement des soldats, il n'y en a plus de disponible pour les arts et les sciences, pour les *bonae literae*, et la grande victime — il l'écrit à plusieurs reprises — est toujours et partout le peuple, le *vulgus*.

Lorsque nous dressons le bilan de l'activité érasmienne, force nous est de constater qu'elle est restée sans résultat, aussi bien dans le conflit religieux que dans le conflit politico-militaire. Il n'a pu empêcher ni la scission de l'Église ni les guerres. Par contre, très réussie fut son activité comme philologue, comme prince de l'Humanisme, dans le domaine de l'histoire culturelle et de l'enseignement. Ici son influence et son effet lointain furent énormes.

Il fut un géant intellectuel, un grand Européen, un des grands fondateurs de la culture occidentale, et les fondements qu'il a posés méritent d'être défendus partout dans le monde, entre autres contre l'obscurantisme de ceux qui, vers 1970, dans plusieurs pays européens, ont décidé d'abolir dans l'enseignement secondaire nos Humanités, tellement imprégnées d'esprit érasmien.

La modération d'Érasme, sa lutte pour la liberté de pensée et la tolérance, son aversion profonde pour la bêtise, sont des valeurs qui, à chaque époque, à chaque phase culturelle, doivent être défendues et renouvelées par des hommes qui, sans être nécessairement de sa trempe et de son envergure, ont à coeur de suivre la voie qu'il a tracée.

Vrije Universiteit Brussel

Notes

Cet article a paru dans *Het Laatste Nieuws*, Bruxelles, sous le titre "Erasmus als bemiddelaar." Il est publié ici avec l'aimable autorisation de l'éditeur.

1. Weimarer Ausgabe Tr 1, 55, 32–33.
2. Beck Verlag, Munich, 1986.
3. *Bulletin* n° 9 (avril 1986) de la Section Isère de l'Association des Membres de l'Ordre des Palmes Académiques, p. 1–10.
4. *Collected Works of Erasmus*, University of Toronto Press, 1974–.
5. par la Classe des Lettres de la "Koninklije Academie voor Wetenschappen, Letteren en Schone Kunsten van België."
6. Allen, *Opus epistolarum D. Erasmi*, t. III, Ep. 566, lignes 31–40.

RAINER PINEAS

Polemical Technique in Thomas More's *The Answere to ... the Poysened Booke*

In December 1533 Thomas More published *The answere to the fyrst parte of the poysened booke, whych a namelesse heretyke hath named the souper of the lorde*. More's work was intended as partial rebuttal to the anonymous *Souper of the Lorde* published in the spring of that year—almost certainly by the reformer George Joye.[1] Since my previous treatments of this controversy have focused either exclusively on Joye or only generally on More's polemics,[2] it is the purpose of this paper to concentrate solely on examining the polemical technique of More's *Answere*.[3] My procedure, therefore, will be to analyze first certain polemical devices which derive from More's real or assumed attitude towards his opponent, then devices occasioned by his opponent's anonymity, then tactics common to all his polemics, and, finally, to consider what conclusions about More can legitimately be drawn from his controversies.

Although some critics have taken at face value More's repeated assertions that his opponent is the most stupid with whom he has ever had to deal,[4] and have therefore dismissed Joye's *Souper* as inept,[5] a closer study of More's polemics would have revealed that such a characterization is a standard ploy of More's polemical technique; the adversary of the moment is always the most stupid More has ever had to refute.[6] That these assertions do constitute a polemical device rather than represent More's actual feelings is borne out by the very fact that More felt compelled to answer Joye's work at all—and that at considerable length.[7] An interesting footnote to More's "invidious comparison" technique is that, so far as English Reformation polemics are concerned, it seems to be original with More. Only one other contemporary polemicist uses the device, namely the reformer John Frith, who seems to have copied it from More, as he apparently did many other controversial techniques.[8]

In contrast to the "invidious comparison" technique, More's insistence that his opponent is wrong about absolutely everything—theology, scriptural exegesis, English grammar and syntax, history, logic, quotations from and interpretations of More's works—is a common contemporary polemical technique, as is the minute dissection of even the most innocent-looking passage in an opponent's work, which facilitates such criticism.[9]

Classical rhetoric commends the effectiveness of demonstrating that there is really no need for demolishing one's opponent, since the very arguments he has introduced to support his case happen to be ones which most refute it.[10] Therefore wherever he can, as part of his general denigration of his opponent's abilities, More contends that the harder the author of the *Souper* attempts to prove his position correct, the more he inadvertently undermines it (CW 11, pp. 15, 145, 156, 183, 195, 198).

Although More had been at least the editor, if not the real author, of Henry VIII's *Assertio septem sacramentorum*,[11] and indisputably the author of the *Responsio ad Lutherum*—published under two different pseudonyms,[12] this did not deter him from making polemical capital out of the anonymity of the author of the *Souper*. Therefore in order to counteract Joye's pun on his name in calling him "M. Mocke" (CW 11, p. 339), as well as to have some kind of appellation for the author of the *Souper*, More refers to him as "Masker" throughout his *Answere*. More's polemical stance is that it is because his opponent is so ashamed of his work that he has kept his identity hidden, and that only the cover of anonymity permits him to write such nonsense as he does (CW 11, p. 12). This device of More's is actually a variation of one of the most common polemical techniques of sixteenth-century religious controversy—one which had important implications for the villains of contemporary polemical and nonpolemical drama—namely, that one's opponent really knows that he is wrong but nevertheless persists in maintaining an evil cause out of inveterate malice.[13] Therefore More pictures the Masker in their dispute as playing with false dice (pp. 13, 57), and under his "vysor of dyssymulacyon" (p. 115) spreading ridiculous lies about Catholic belief and practice. But his most effective polemical use of his opponent's anonymity—and a progression from his dubbing of the adversary as "Masker"—is the accusation that in interpreting the passages in scripture which deal with the Eucharist as referring to Christ's flesh and blood as exclusively allegorical and denying the Real Presence, Joye is guilty of a masker's "iuglynge." Here More is casting back into the teeth of Protestant polemicists the very term they themselves had coined to describe the priestly consecration of the bread and wine, which was eventually the subject of an entire polemical play—*Jacke Jugeler*.[14]

The Yale edition of More's *Answere* correctly points out that More "wishes . . . not merely to correct, but to humiliate and expose the Masker . . ." (p. lxxii), and indeed this was More's standard intention in polemics, no matter what the identity of his adversary. As part of this effort to demolish his opponent More seems to have invented a rhetorical device expressive of the paradoxical attitude that even if his opponent were right in details, he would remain wrong in his conclusion. I find this technique in neither classical rhetoric nor contemporary polemicists, except in Frith, who again probably copied it from More. If there is one controversial technique which can be called the hallmark of More's polemics it is this one; it is at once indicative of his compulsion to leave no stone uncast and at least a partial explanation for the immoderate length of his diatribes. For example:

> But now good chrysten readers all this exposicyon, were it neuer so trew, neuer so comely, nor neuer so cunnyngly handeled/ yet were it . . . very farre from the purpose (p. 17).

Again:

> . . . whan these heretikes proue that the blessed sacrament is called bred, they proue nothing agaynst vs. For they that call it brede declare yet that in dede it is not brede but the body of Chryste. And whan they proue that it is called a fygure/they proue no thynge agaynste vs (p. 54).

And again:

> And veryly yf he so mene, he hath a madde menynge. And yf he mene not so: than hath he a madde maner of spekynge. And yet bysyde that hys menynge is as madde that waye as the tother (pp. 139-140).

The third passage is but one of the many instances in both his *Answere* and his other polemical treatises in which More criticizes his opponent's language—a standard ingredient of sixteenth-century controversy.[15] In one of the few places where the now obviously exhausted More recaptures the brilliance of his earlier polemics, he "mistakes" as perplexity concerning correct English what is, in fact, Joye's attack on More's daring to criticize the English of Tyndale's New Testament translation. In *The Confutacyon of Tyndales Answere* More had criticized Tyndale's English, claiming that "nay" and "yea" should be used to answer a question posed in the affirmative, while "no" and "yes" should be reserved for a question put in the negative (*CW* 8, pp. 231-232). Now it so happens that Joye's favorite polemical device is what I have elsewhere called "ironic refrain,"[16] —the derisory repetition of what he regards as his opponent's most foolish expressions—and he uses this technique in the *Souper* in mockery of what he considers More's pedantic criticism. At the end of a passage attacking More's view of the Eucharist, Joye leaves his opponent with a question to answer in either the affirmative or the negative: ". . . yf he say no or nay then scripture is playn agenst him. Io. 6. 10. 15 yf he saye ye or yisse . . . ," then More will get into even greater difficulty (*CW* 11, p. 310). More brilliantly pretends to misunderstand Joye's point and reminds his readers that he had previously criticized Tyndale's English and had worked out a rule for Tyndale to determine when to use which adverb:

> Nowe mayster Masker whan he wrote hys boke, neyther hauynge my boke by hym, nor the rule by hart thoughte he wolde be sure that I sholde fynde no such faute in hym/ and therefore on the tone syde for the answere, assygneth ye and yes both/ and on the tother syde bothe naye and no/ leuynge the choyce to my selfe, whyche he durst not well take vpon him, lest he myght shew therin suche congruytie in the Englyshe tonge, as he sheweth in some other thynges wherin he speketh englyshe as congrewe, as a man myghte that hadde lerned his englishe in a nother lande (*CW* 11, pp. 158-159).

It is, perhaps, surprising that More would undertake to set up rules of grammar and usage for English, in which no written rules as yet existed. He can certainly be mistaken, as he was in taking Joye to task for misusing the word "dissemble."[17] And he himself can certainly write awkward English: ". . . you haue sene me done myracles . . ." (p. 39); ". . . wold you not labour to hym. . . . and therfore labour to hym . . ." (p. 40); ". . . that you maye be lerned by his wurkynge to fayth . . ." (p. 48); ". . . whiche wold make myne answere ouer long to brynge them in all . . ." (p. 100).

We have noted above how More pretended to mistake Joye's meaning in the yes/yea and no/nay issue; such "mistakes" were again common weapons in the arsenals of More and other contemporary polemicists.[18] For instance, in a derogatory reference to Catholic belief in the Real Presence, Joye, commenting on John 6, says of Christ's declaration:

> The brede whiche I shal geue you, is my flesshe. . . . yf he had so ment as More meanethe, that he wolde haue bene conuayed & conuerted, as oure iuggelers sleyghly can conuaye hym wyth a fewe wordis, into a syngynge lofe orels, as the thomisticall papistis saye, bene inuisyble wytheal hys dymencioned body vnder the forme of brede transsubstauncyated into it. . . (CW 11, p. 309).

Contrary to the Yale edition's note on More's response to this passage, nowhere does More seize "upon the illogicality of the Masker's sloppy language in 'convayeth and conuerteth' " and nowhere does More suggest that "the two terms are contradictory" (p. 273). What he does claim through a minute dissection of Joye's terms is that Joye has shamelessly saddled him with views of the Eucharist Joye knows he, More, does not hold—namely Luther's view and/or Joye's own Zwinglian view! (p. 130). That More's minute dissection of Joye's language is made only to facilitate the accusation detailed above is indicated both by the patent absurdity of More's pretended misunderstanding of his opponent's meaning and by the evidence of his correct understanding at the beginning of the discussion, namely, that Joye is talking about the Catholic view of "the conuersyon of the brede and wyne into the blessed body and bloude of Chryste in the blessed sacrament . . ." (p. 129).

A variation of pretending to mistake an opponent's meaning or position is actually to distort it, and More does this quite frequently in his *Answere*. For instance, More's assertion that although the reformers originally taught justification by faith alone, Catholics have so confuted them that they are now ashamed to teach that doctrine (p. 37), or that Luther himself had abandoned it (p. 119) must be included among those matters that for More were "easier . . . to wish for . . . than to have any hope of seeing realized" (*Utopia*, CW 4, p. 247). Nor does More's assertion that Tyndale broke his vow of celibacy and was "gone ofter than onys a woynge" (p. 106) agree with the facts. Furthermore, Joye was not an "aduersary of the blessed sacrament" (p. 51) but of the doctrine of the Real Presence, and much of the patristic "proof" More cites to support his interpretation of the scriptures is as ambiguous as the scriptural passages it is supposed to elucidate (See, especially, pp. 63–67).

One should hasten to add that misrepresenting an opponent's position was by no means unique either to More or the Church he was defending; the practice was again a commonplace of polemics, indulged in by both Catholics and Protestants.

The same was certainly true of scriptural mistranslation and paraphrase for polemical purposes, of which there are quite a number of examples in More's *Answere*. For instance, when More promises to translate with commentary John 6:37 and following, he so intertwines text and commentary that it is impossible to distinguish one from the other. In the process he manages to slip into this melange the Catholic doctrine of the Real Presence and the Catholic teaching on the relationship of works to faith as necessary for salvation (pp. 43–46). Again, in citing I Corinthians 11:23 to support the contention that the traditions of the Church are equal in authority to the scriptures, More correctly cites the Latin—"*Ego enim accepi a domino quod et tradidi vobis*"—which he then mistranslates as "For I haue receyued the thynge of oure lorde by tradycyon, without wrytyng the which I haue also delyuered vnto you" (p. 127). There is no justification in the Latin for "by tradycyon without wrytyng." Then, to reinforce his point, More adds a patently incorrect interpretation to his mistranslation: "As though he wold say, as I haue receyued it by tradycyon or delyuery of our lord, so without wrytyng I haue deliuered it by tradicion to you" (p. 127).[19]

Let us now consider two larger elements in More's work. The first of these is the question of More's audience and the appropriateness of More's *Answere* to the immediate situation. More determined that the *Souper* needed a response because he correctly judged it to be very dangerous work, but it is difficult to understand in what way he thought the *Answere* was a suitable work for popular polemics and how it fulfilled his commission to "show to simple and unlearned men the cunning malice of the heretics . . . ."[20] In spite of the lavish praise the Yale edition has bestowed on More's work, much of it—especially the entire first book—is astonishingly self-indulgent. How, for instance, to quote from the Yale edition, were the "simple and unlearned" supposed to comprehend the following?

> More's exposition insists upon the rich unity of all God's works. Eating the bread of Christ's godhead through faith and eating his eucharistic body in the host are the equally important con-

stituents of the effectual working of the sacrament and the miracle of incorporation. . . .He [More] lingers lovingly, for example, on the unity of persons in the Trinity. . . .

Nowhere is More's emphasis on divine wholeness and harmony more pronounced than in the passages dealing with incorporation . . . . The sacramental reality of our incorporation into Christ's living body is also a sacramental sign for our incorporation into his mystical body. . . .

He [More] delights in erecting complex theological and moral distinctions upon the formulas provided by John 6 . . . .Similarly, in looking at a variant reading of John 6:51, More relishes a possible congruity between the working of the scripture and the structure of theology (pp. lxvi–lxix).

If one did not know better, one might be tempted to conclude that More has given up, that the burden has become too heavy, that he has decided—in the end—to please at least himself. Whatever the reason, and that need not be anything more esoteric than hurry and fatigue, this is a far cry from the sparkle of the 1529 works, *A Dialogue concernynge Heresyes* and *The Supplicacion of Soules*.

The other subject which must be discussed is More's view of heresy. There cannot be the slightest doubt that by the time he came to write the *Answere* More regarded as heresy any denial of even a minutia of orthodox belief, including the literal truth of every part of the scriptures—anyone who claims the Samson story is only allegorical, "hym wold I reken, for an heretyke to" (p. 19)—"raylynge agaynst images, purgatory, and prayenge to sayntes" (p. 99), creeping to the cross, giving reverence to relics, "our ladys psalter, &. . .bedys" (p. 186), denying the need for pilgrimages, in short, absolutely everything the Church teaches, "the whole thynge reueled by god vnto his chyrche" (p. 110).

It is equally clear that by 1533 More regarded as "deuylysshe" anyone who insisted that the Church was wrong about anything (p. 128), and that it was the height of irresponsibility on the part of both the civil and ecclesiastical authorities not to extirpate such people along with the books they disseminated (pp. 6, 9).

Unless one wishes to go beyond the evidence, what one may conclude from the foregoing is that as More saw the position he was trying to defend overrun by the marital ambitions of Henry VIII and the anti-clerical legislation sponsored by the King's chief minister, Cromwell (who, two years after More's death, admonished the English bishops no longer to rely on "unwritton verytes"[21]), More desperately redoubled his single-handed efforts and ended up trying to defend *everything*. Ironically, what he was defending were very often the same practices his "derelyng" Erasmus, in a more tranquil period, had satirized. This was poor polemics, but it was politics, not polemics, which finally defeated More, who—certainly to a much greater extent than his opportunistic royal master—really deserved the title "Defender of the Faith."

York College
City University of New York

Notes

1. On the authorship of the *Souper*, see Michael Anderegg, "The Probable Author of *The Souper of the Lorde*: George Joye," in Thomas More, *The Answer to a Poisoned Book*, ed. Stephen M. Foley and Clarence H. Miller, in *The Complete Works of St. Thomas More* 11 (New Haven and London, 1985), 343-74. Hereafter cited as *CW* 11.

2. See Rainer Pineas, "George Joye's Controversy with Thomas More," *Moreana* 38 (1973), 27-36, and *Thomas More and Tudor Polemics* (Bloomington and London, 1968).

3. Such an analysis has already been attempted in the Yale edition of the *Answere*. See *CW* 11, lxi-lxxviii.

4. *CW* 11, pp. 7, 73, 108, 120-21, 142, 143, 190.

5. Ibid.

6. See Thomas More, *Responsio ad Lutherum*, ed. John M. Headley, in *CW* 5 (New Haven and London, 1969), Pt. 1, 6/27-29, 8/8-12, 10/28-12/5; *The Confutation of Tyndale's Answer*, ed. Louis A. Schuster, Richard C. Marius, James P. Lusardi, and Richard J. Schoeck, *CW* 8 (New Haven and London, 1973), Pt. 2, 831/8-15, 832/35-37, 863/23-34, 839/23-26; *The Workes...in the Englysh tonge*, STC 18076 (London, 1557), pp. 294-95, 306-7.

7. See Anderegg's more accurate assessment of the *Souper* in *CW* 11.

8. See Rainer Pineas, "Polemical Technique in the Works of John Frith," *The Crane Review* 7 (1964), 105-16.

9. See the polemics of Bale, Barnes, Becon, Brixius, Gardiner, Luther, and Turner. *CW* 11, pp. 8, 9, 97, 101, 107, 110, 113, 126, 196.

10. See Quintilian, *Institutio Oratoria*, V. xiii. 17; also Thomas Wilson, *The Arte of Rhetorique*, STC 258000 (n. p., 1560), pp. 144, 149.

11. *Tudor Polemics*, pp. 16-17.

12. Ibid., pp. 14-15.

13. For nonpolemical drama, see Rainer Pineas, "The Morality Vice in *Volpone*," *Discourse* 5 (1962), 451–59; for polemical drama, Pineas, *Tudor and Early Stuart Anti-Catholic Drama* (Nieuwkoop, 1972).

14. Ibid., pp. 7–8; *CW* 11, pp. 121, 133, 134.

15. See, for instance, Bale, *A mysterye of Iniquite*, STC 1303 (Geneva, 1545), sigs. B6, G6, I1v; Joye, *George Ioye confuteth Vvinchesters false Articles*, STC 14826 (Antwerp, 1543), sigs. C2, U4.

16. "George Joye's Controversy with Thomas More," p. 28.

17. See *CW* 11, p. 126 and note. The Yale edition, nevertheless, lists this as "another error" in Joye's English (p. lxxx).

18. Recommended by Quintilian (*Inst. Orat.* VI.iii.84–85), this technique of intentional "misunderstanding" was used with great effect by John Bale, among others; see Bale, *The Apology of Johan Bale agaynste a ranke Papyst*, STC 1275 (London, c. 1550), sigs. H4–H5v, K1, Q1–Q1v.

19. This kind of scriptural manipulation for polemical advantage was, again, a tactic indulged in by both Catholics and Protestants, the most notorious examples being provided by the Reformer John Bale. See Rainer Pineas, "Polemical Use of the Scriptures in the Plays of John Bale," *Nederlands Archief voor Kerkgeschiedenis*, 66 (1986), 187 ff.

20. See *Tudor Polemics*, p. 39.

21. See Alistair Fox and John Guy, *Reassessing the Henrician Age* (Oxford: Basil Blackwell Ltd., 1986), p. 202. In the *Souper*, Joye had derided More's contention that there were certain "vnwrytten verities" necessary to be believed for salvation. See *CW* 11, pp. 311, 312, and 314.

PARISH OF ST. DUNSTAN WITH HOLY CROSS, CANTERBURY

September 23rd, 1987.

Our Dear Germain,

It is a great pleasure and honour for me to be asked to give a tribute to you and I feel in your case I might quote the Latin -- 'Pro tanto quid retribuamus'. You have given us all so much not only in Scholarship but in other ways that many of us will feel it impossible to thank you adequately.

A great person for me and my family is one who has not only the gifts of the Spirit but has the unique ability to be at ease and have control over any situation in life. This is not so easy to attain, yet I and my wife and family have felt that you showed this spiritual greatness.

It was always a pleasure to have you as our guest at the Vicarage and, as you know, we treated you as you would always want to be treated, as one of the family.

In our wonderful conversations with you, whether philosophic or light hearted, we were happy to sit at the feet of our Gamaliel and listen. We were well rewarded.

Thank you, Germain, for the sincere interest you have taken in us, as a family, over the years -- especially in John and Christina. How fortunate they are to have met you and been influenced for good by you as they both now set out on their adult life.

Betty and I shall never forget your help and encouragement when I inaugurated the 'Friends of St. Dunstan's' as far back as 1971.

We remember with gratitude your interest in the annual Thomas More Commemoration services and the links we forged in bringing together so many distinguished speakers. You own addresses in St. Dunstan's in 1980 and last year 1986 will never be forgotten. Indeed thanks to you and Moreana, *St. Dunstan's, as a Church, is firmly established in the hearts and minds of many all over the world.*

However, as a family, our best recollections of you will be always in the context of our home : The conversations over a meal, interspersed with our laughter, and with the portraits of Thomas More looking down benignly upon us. Or out in the garden taking those never to be forgotten photos and trying to get Angus, our very independently minded West Highland terrier, to join the group !

Then there were excursions into the lovely Wealden countryside to visit friends and places of More interest in Tenterden. Remember ? All such homely experiences are now part of our lives and we, as a family, shall treasure them as we hope you will too.

So Betty, with her smile which you admired so much, John and Christina and myself, we all send you our love, gratitude, best wishes and God's Blessing upon you now and always.

As always,

Yours,

Hugh and Betty
John and Christina

LOUIS L. MARTZ

Thomas More: The Search for the Inner Man

MOST OF US, I IMAGINE, HAVE HELD IN OUR MINDS an image of Thomas More shaped directly or indirectly by the classic biography by R. W. Chambers, or influenced by the similar figure created by Robert Bolt in *A Man for All Seasons*: the image of a man humane, wise and witty, honest in his work as judge and lawyer, devoted to and loved by his family and friends, but underneath all this, a man of conscience so strong that he would die rather than bend his beliefs to suit the demands of a ruthless tyranny.

But this image has recently become a matter of severe debate, mainly because of the studies of G. R. Elton and the massive new biography of More by Richard Marius.[1] The debate has extended far beyond the walls of academe, until it has come to influence a recent production of *A Man for All Seasons*. This is clear from an interview in the *New York Times* with Philip Bosco, who played the role of More in the New York production of 1987. Bosco was in 1961 an understudy for the roles of Henry VIII and Norfolk in Paul Scofield's production of the play. But Bosco now questions the interpretation of More that he watched so intently from the wings twenty-five years ago: "Mr. Bosco knows," we read in the *Times*, "through rehearsal talk about the play's period, that Mr. Bolt's image of Sir Thomas More is conspicuously lacking warts. He also knows that the figure who was to achieve sainthood was immoderately proud of his high position in the realm and fierce, indeed, bloodthirsty on the subject of heretics."[2]

"Rehearsal talk" has apparently been affected by the new biography, for this view of More's treatment of heretics, disseminated long ago by Foxe's *Book of Martyrs*, and laid to rest for a while by modern scholars, is vehemently resurrected by Marius as a basic theme: "His fury at the Protestant heretics . . . has a touch of hysteria about it, and although we may exonerate him from old charges that he tied heretics to a tree in his yard at Chelsea and beat them, he was if anything inclined to an even greater savagery against them, for he cried for them to be burned alive, and he rejoiced when some of them went to the fire. This fury was not a bizarre lapse in an otherwise noble character; it was almost the essence of the man" (p. xxiv). Clearly this view goes far beyond the recognition of certain blemishes in the complexion: it offers a radical alteration in our image of the man.

Now it is true that More frequently declared that those convicted of heresy were "well and worthily burned"—but these words seem to me to represent the grim approval of a judge concerning the well-deserved punishment of a criminal who has committed what More calls the worst of crimes—the crime of leading other souls to eternal perdition. "And for heretikes as they be," says More, "the clergy dothe denounce them. And as they be well worthy, the temporaltie doth burne them. And after the fyre of Smythfelde, hell dothe receyue them / where the wretches burne for euer."[3] In passages such as this I do not hear a note of hysteria or rejoicing, but rather a tone of fearsome warning and somber satisfaction at finding justice done.

More did pursue rigorously those suspected of heresy; he questioned them, according to his own account, with a mixture of severity and charity, and he turned them over to the religious authorities for trial when he found his suspicions warranted. This is what his duty required under the statutes of the realm, and it was certainly a duty that More willingly performed. More himself makes his participation clear in his *Apology*. Here, for example, is how he describes the way in which he apprehended Thomas Philips "of London letherseller":[4]

> Whom when I was chauncellour, vpon certayn thynges y^t I found out by [i.e., concerning] him, by thexamynacyon of dyuerse heretyques whome I hadde spoken wyth, vppon the occasyon of the heretyques forboden bokes, I sent for / and when I hadde spoken wyth hym, and honestely intreated hym one day or twayn in myne house, and laboured about his amendement in as harty louynge maner as I coulde: when I perceyued fynally the person suche that I coulde fynde no trouth, neyther in his worde nor

his othe, and saw the lykelyhed that he was in the settynge forth of such heresyes closely [i.e., secretly], a man mete and lykely to do many folke myche harme: I by endenture delyuered hym to his ordynary [i.e., to the ecclesiastical authority].(CW 9.126)

It is essential to note that responsibility was shared, for it may be thought that More was primarily responsible for the increase in the pursuit of heretics about the year 1529, when More became Lord Chancellor. But the increase occurred because the examples of heresy, in printed books and in people, were increasing rapidly, and Henry VIII, at this very moment, was beginning to show his increasing willingness to listen to those of heretical persuasion, in his frustration over the divorce, in his anxiety to have a male heir, and especially an heir by Anne Boleyn.

Those clerics who were supporting the divorce, such as Stokesley, could demonstrate their basic orthodoxy by hunting out heretical books and people. Meanwhile, those who opposed the divorce, such as More and Tunstall, could, by pursuing heresy, remind Henry of the dangers of heresy and of Henry's own earlier enmity toward Luther, as demonstrated in the famous "King's Book," Henry's *Assertio*, a book of which More constantly and shrewdly reminds the King.

The pursuit of heretics continued after More's resignation, and after his death, though usually now for different reasons: though the basic cause was religious, the charge now was usually treason, refusing to accept Henry's supremacy over the Church. We are told that in the five years following April 1535 (three months before More's execution) Thomas Cromwell engaged in vigorous personal prosecution of those suspected of continuing to support the papacy, and during those five years "something like sixty-five" people suffered the "horrible execution" decreed for treason.[5] This figure, of course, does not include the thirteen or fourteen Anabaptists condemned in May 1535, or the Nun of Kent and her five followers, condemned a year earlier, nor does it include the several hundred who were executed for their part in the Pilgrimage of Grace. We should compare these figures with the fact that More "was personally involved" in prosecuting only three out of the six cases of heresy in all of England that led to burning during the three years of his chancellorship.[6]

My point is not to show that one party was worse than another. No doubt More and his party – the faction working behind the scenes to oppose the divorce – would have been equally ruthless had they been able to summon equal power. My point is simply that the political procedures of the age were cruel and ruthless on either side, and that therefore it is difficult to argue that Thomas More's prosecution of those he suspected of heresy was any more severe than Thomas Cromwell's prosecution of those he suspected of treason. For both it was a grim matter of quelling what they, for different reasons, saw as seditious. Let us lay aside, then, this ancient and unfounded charge against More.

I should like to try another approach, implicit in the visual images of More and his family presented by Hans Holbein. Consider first the pen and ink drawing preserved in the museum at Basel and presented by More to Erasmus as a token of friendship (Figure 1). Let me first introduce the characters. Starting from the left, More's daughter Elizabeth; next to her, More's foster-daughter, Margaret Giggs, leaning over to point out a place in a book to More's father, Judge John More; seated next, Thomas More, aged fifty; in between Sir John and Sir Thomas, the small figure of the young lady destined to carry on the male line: More's ward, Anne Cresacre, soon to marry More's son John, standing next to his father. The burly figure facing us by the doorway is More's fool, Henry Patenson. Below him, seated, More's daughter Cecily, with a rosary in her left hand. Prominent in the right foreground, More's favorite child Margaret Roper and at the far right, More's second wife, Dame Alice, significantly kneeling at a *prie-Dieu*, with her eyes cast down upon an open book which we assume must be a prayer book of some kind. The cross on the chain before the book adds to the devotional atmosphere. And now we note that all the books that the characters are holding are quite small and seem to be prayer books. Larger books are lying upon the floor, or on the shelf by the window, temporarily laid aside, it would seem. Perhaps Margaret Giggs is pointing out the place in the prayer book for a service that is about to begin.

But if so, why is not Sir Thomas kneeling to lead the service, as his wife is kneeling? I think he is about to do so. Notice the low footstool near More's feet, which from an aesthetic point of view serves neatly to center and focus the scene. But what purpose might it serve in the scene's dramatic moment? Is More about to leave his seat, kneel upon the stool, and lead a service of devotion? Note too the angle of the stool's placement: it is in line with the direction in which some of the figures are gazing—towards the viewer's right. What are they gazing at? What would More, kneeling on the footstool so centrally placed, look at as he leads the service? Something is beyond the drawing that we cannot see: perhaps an altar with a crucifix upon it, or a painting on the wall. In any case it seems beyond doubt that the drawing presents the group as a devotional service is about to begin.

Figure 1. Hans Holbein the Younger, *Thomas More and his Family*. Kupferstichkabinett der Öffentlichen Kunstsammlung Basel.

Now there are at Windsor Castle two drawings of More by Holbein, one of which is closely allied to the image of More in this drawing of the devotional group, while the other is the prototype of the famous oil portrait now in the Frick Collection. We need to compare these closely. The prototype of the Frick painting presents an image of firm control (Figure 2). The large black hat dominates the face, set down low upon the brow, and the hair, cut short, is firmly restrained within the hat. The facial expression is resolute, suitable to a lawyer, judge, royal counsellor, and statesman. The furred gown (hiding the hair shirt) shows his high estate, giving further support to the firm countenance. Experts in art much prefer this drawing to the other: after all, it is more thoroughly done: the hair and robe are colored. The other Windsor drawing (a lightly tinted sketch, Figure 3) has been called feebler, less skillfully done.[7] It may be weaker, in some sense, but is it less skillful? It is in every way more relaxed, more open: the hat is softer and reveals more of the forehead, while the long hair flows out freely from beneath it on each side. We see the face of a man unguarded, open, vulnerable, seeking, devotional in its mood. Even the lack of color in the robe adds to this effect, for we cannot see this man's worldly status: it is of no importance. Perhaps we tend to underrate the skill of Holbein here because we are so accustomed to the More of the Frick portrait, with its stern, strong, formidable guise. Holbein, in the devotional drawing of More, seems to have given us a rare glimpse of the unguarded More, the inner man seeking the strength of his faith to support him. Here is the sensitive, humane, and humanist More who loves his Latin and his Greek, also the More who in his youth said his prayers at the Charterhouse, the More who might have been a churchman. He chose to follow the career of lawyer, judge, and statesman represented by the facial expression and the robe and the regalia found in the Frick portrait. But underneath lies the sensitive, seeking spirit of the religious devotee, the humanist, the lover of ancient languages.

It is the humanist scholar that we find in the great tempera portrait of the family by Holbein, now destroyed, but extant to some degree in the apparently faithful replica made by Rowland Locky about 1593.[8] The devotional atmosphere of the drawing is here removed. Dame Alice, in accordance with a note written by Holbein on the Basel sketch, is now sitting, not kneeling. Cecily's rosary is gone. The footstool is gone. Most of the books visible are now much larger, and some of them can be identified. Elizabeth has under her right arm a book labeled as Seneca's Epistles, while the book on Margaret's lap is open to a readable page in the fourth act of Seneca's *Oedipus*. One of the

Figure 2. Hans Holbein the Younger, *Sir Thomas More*. Windsor Castle, Royal Library; copyright Her Majesty Queen Elizabeth II.

Figure 3. Hans Holbein the Younger, *Sir Thomas More*. Windsor Castle, Royal Library; copyright Her Majesty Queen Elizabeth II.

books on the sideboard is labeled as Boethius' *Consolation of Philosophy*. Margaret Giggs has changed places with Elizabeth, and one may see a certain propriety in the fact that no one is pointing out the place in a classical book to Sir John, who did not at all approve of his son's attraction to the life of humanist learning. A figure has been added — More's secretary, leaning in the doorway. The whole scene is now that of More's little "Academy," where the women were able to read Latin as well as the men. It is the atmosphere More evokes in the delightful letter that he wrote to his children from Court in 1521. It is in Latin, though some of the children addressed were only twelve or thirteen, but if they could not read Latin easily by then there was no hope for them. Nevertheless, I will quote in translation:

Thomas More to his Whole School Greeting.

See what a compendious salutation I have found, to save both time and paper, which would otherwise have been wasted in listing the names of each one of you in salutation, and my labor would have been to no purpose, since, though each of you is dear to me by some special title, of which I could have omitted none in an ingratiating salutation, no one is dearer to me by any title than each of you by that of scholar. . . . But I think you have no longer any need of Master Nicholas, since you have learned whatever he had to teach you about astronomy. I hear you are so far advanced in that science that you can not only point out the polar star or the dog star, or any of the ordinary stars, but are able also . . . to distinguish the sun from the moon! Onward then in that new and admirable science by which you ascend to the stars! But while you gaze on them assiduously, consider that this holy time of Lent warns you, and that beautiful and holy poem of Boethius keeps singing in your ears, teaching you to raise your mind also to heaven, lest the soul look downwards to the earth, after the manner of brutes, while the body is raised aloft.

Farewell, all my dearest.
From Court, the 23rd March[9]

As Chambers has shown, we will never understand More unless we give full weight to his love of humanist learning. But what then shall we make of his youthful sojourn with the monks of the Charterhouse, of the hair shirt, and of the practice of whipping the flesh reported by Roper? It has been argued that these ascetic practices indicate More's longing for the life of a medieval monk and his sense of guilt that sexual desire had led him to marry and lead a life in the world.[10] But such severities could serve also to mortify the pride of worldly place as More advanced in the King's service, and we know for a fact that More, as his prosperity increased, wrote a long meditation on the seven deadly sins, showing, as St. Bernard and many others had shown, that the primary sin, the root of all the others, was pride.[11]

We need to examine closely the events of More's early life to see what evidence there is to support the oft-repeated view that More longed for the monastic life. Harpsfield, following Roper and family tradition, probably gives the best account, and from it we gather that More, during the years roughly from 1500 to 1504, when he was twenty-two to twenty-six years old, was attempting to maintain at least four simultaneous concerns: practice in the law, study of Greek, study of theology, and religious devotion. After his boyhood training in the household of Archbishop Morton, later Cardinal Morton (strongly praised in the *Utopia*), More was sent at Morton's urging to Oxford.

> This Cardinall then that had raysed both to himself and others such an expectation to this childe, being nowe more and more carefull to haue him well trayned vp, that his goodly budd might be a faire flower, and at length bring forth such fruit as he and the others expected and looked for, thought it best he should be sent to the Vniuersite of Oxforde, and so he was; where, for the short time of his abode (being not fully two yeres) and for his age, he wonderfully profited in the knowledge of the latin and greeke tonges; where, if he had setled and fixed himselfe, and hadd runne his full race in the study of the liberall sciences and diuinitie, I trowe he would haue beene the singuler and the onely spectacle of this our time for learning.[12]

And surely something in this line is what Morton would have had in mind when he recommended Oxford for the boy: a distinguished career as a scholarly man of the Church, leading perhaps to political involvement such as Morton himself had known.

More's father had quite different ideas, as Harpsfield goes on to tell:

> But his father minded that he should treade after his steppes, and settle his whole minde and studie vpon the lawes of the Realme. And so being plucked from the vniuersities of studies and learninges, he was sett to the studies of the lawes onely of this Realme. (p. 12)

Although More pursued his legal studies vigorously, nevertheless, Harpsfield adds,

> he cutt off from the studie of the lawe muche time, which he employed to his former studies that he vsed in Oxforde; and especially to the reading of St Augustine *de Ciuitate Dei*, which though it be a booke very harde for a well learned man to vnderstande . . . yet did Master More, being so yonge, being so distracted also and occupied in the studie of the common lawes, openly reade [i.e., give lectures on] in the Churche of St Laurence in London the bookes of the saide St Augustine *de Ciuitate Dei*, to his no small commendation, and to the great admiration of all his audience. His lesson [i.e., his lecturing] was frequented and honoured with the presence and resort, as well of that well learned and great cunning man, Master Grocin (with whom and with Master Thomas Lupsett he learned the greeke tonge) as also with the chiefe and best learned men of the Citie of London.
> (pp. 13-14)

(Harpsfield is wrong with regard to Thomas Lupset here; at this time More was actually learning Greek from Thomas Linacre.)

At the same time he was not only pursuing his career in law but was also active as a Burgess of Parliament, incurring the enmity of Henry VII in 1504 by his opposition to a subsidy, and he was also performing devotions with the monks of the Charterhouse.

> And all this while was he vnmaried, and seemed to be in some doubt and deliberation with himselfe what kinde and trade of life he should enter, to folowe and pursue all his longe life after. Surely it seemeth by some apparant coniectures that he was sometime somewhat propense and inclined either to be a priest, or to take some monasticall and solitary life; [note the alternative that Harpsfield here allows] for he continued after his foresaide reading fowre yeres and more full vertuously and religiously in great deuotion and prayer with the monkes of the Charterhouse of London, without any maner of profession or vowe, [and here again Harpsfield allows for an alternative set of choices] eyther to see and proue whether he could frame himselfe to that kinde of life, or at least for a time to sequester himselfe from all temporall and worldly exercises. (p.17)

Now these devotions at the Charterhouse must have gone on concurrently with his work as a lawyer, for there is no evidence at all that he gave up his legal profession to enter upon a concentrated four-year retreat. As Harpsfield suggests at the end of the passage just quoted, it appears that More used the Charterhouse as a place for meditation and prayer concerning his vocation, to perform what were later called "exercises of election"—spiritual exercises performed in order to see if he would follow a religious or a secular career. But because he chose the Charterhouse as the place to pursue these meditations does not necessarily indicate (as Harpsfield realized) a tendency toward the monastic life.[13] Everything else we know of More's activity during these early years of his life would indicate the opposite, would indicate that he is tending toward a scholarly life in the world, such as his good friends Colet and Grocyn and Linacre and Erasmus were pursuing—a career in orders that would satisfy his religious instinct as well as his love of scholarship and literature, a career that might well lead to high office in the Church, and important influence in the affairs of state. Think perhaps of More as Bishop of London, Archbishop of York, Archbishop of Canterbury—positions in which his legal training would also be of great advantage. We may well believe that More would have reached such high office. It seems more likely that this sort of career was in More's mind than the monastic life. Harpsfield and others, I think, have put far too much weight upon two later utterances of More in moments of great stress.

> Himselfe saide also afterwarde, when his daughter Margarete Roper . . . escaped against all expectation . . . of a most daungerous sicknes, that if she had dyed, he would neuer haue intermedled with any worldly affaires after. Furthermore, being prisoner in the towre, he tolde his said daughter that his short penning and shutting vp did litle greeue him; for if it had not beene for respect of his wife and children, he had voluntarily longe ere that time shutt him selfe in as narrowe or narrower a roome then that was. (pp. 17–18)

But these are later thoughts, twenty-five or thirty years later, and the last, especially, is a bitter thought in a time of complete political failure. These thoughts bear little weight when we are considering the options of this gifted young man, protégé and admirer of Cardinal Morton, a young man whose studies in the law, in language, in divinity, could well combine in distinguished service for the Church in the active life. But More, after four years of hesitation and meditation, chose to marry and to stay with the law. Why did he do so? I think it was not only because he suffered from sexual desire, though no doubt this played a part in his decision. It seems likely that he wished to raise a family and continue his father's line, in accordance with the duty of an elder son. And this was also, we certainly may believe, the vehement desire of the strong-minded father whom he loved and honored. The report of Erasmus that More gave up thoughts of the priesthood because he wanted a wife must be taken in the known context of his father's very strong pressures in the secular direction and More's sense of family duty.[14]

The decision to pursue a secular career in the law instead of an active career in the church may have had important implications for More's later activities and ultimate death. As he watched one bishop after another, and in the end even Warham and Tunstall, bow to the pressures of the King, what would the inner man have felt? Had I been there in churchly power could I have helped to turn affairs another way? Had I been there in that Convocation that bowed to Henry's threats and signed the Submission of the Clergy—had I been there in a post of power, could I perhaps have helped to turn the vote another way? We do not know what would have happened if a strong Archbishop had led the opposition to Henry at this point. As it was, perseverance to the death was perhaps, in More's view, the only way in which he could make amends to God for being absent from the churchly hierarchy in its time of gravest need. But before this end he could work closely with the clergy by writing treatises against heresy.

Fury against heresy there certainly was in his writings, but this quality needs to be combined with the humane, humanist, Socratic portrait drawn by Chambers, and with the devotional, humanist, juridical, and statesmanlike portraits drawn by Holbein. But how can this be done? How can one defend or explain the violence of More's manner in his works of religious controversy? Professor Elton has put the problem well:

> As William Ross, defending Henry VIII against Luther, he matched Dr. Martin in violence of abuse, a remarkable achievement. His controversial manners were bad: in his exchanges with Tyndale, he generally proved the more scurrilous of the two, and he was savage to St. German who had not been savage at all.[15]

It is good to remember that More thus began his career in religious controversy by combating Luther on behalf of Henry, whose *Assertio* against Luther had been attacked by Luther in a treatise of which it has been said: "It is unlikely that any tract addressed to any king in Christian Europe had ever been as insulting, as vitriolic, as obscene as Luther's little book."[16] One might even say that More picked up his bad manners in controversy by consorting thus with Luther. More's job, willingly undertaken, to be sure, was to bespatter Luther with the same muck that Luther had hurled at Henry—only more of it. The justification for such excesses on both sides has been well stated by a later expert in religious controversy who expressly takes Luther as his model, arguing from the example of the prophets and Christ himself "that there may be a sanctifi'd bitternesse against the enemies of truth."[17]

> Wee all know that in private and personall injuries, yea in publique sufferings for the cause of Christ, his rule and example teaches us to be so farre from a readinesse to speak evil, as not to answer the reviler in his language though never so much provok't. Yet in the detecting, and convincing of any notorious enimie to truth and his Countries peace [what More called "seditious heresy"], especially that is conceited to have a voluble and smart fluence of tongue . . . I suppose and more then suppose, it will be nothing disagreeing from Christian meeknesse to handle such a one in a rougher accent, and to send home his haughtinesse well bespurted with his owne holy-water. . . . And although in the serious uncasing of a grand imposture . . . there be mixt here and there such a grim laughter, as may appear at the same time in an austere visage, it cannot be taxt of levity or insolence: for even this veine of laughing . . . hath oft-times a strong and sinewy force in teaching and confuting; nor can there be a more proper object of indignation and scorne together then a false Prophet taken in the greatest dearest and most dangerous cheat, the cheat of soules.[18]

That, of course, is John Milton defending his own vituperative style. The example of Milton shows that what we are watching here is a tradition of "sanctifi'd bitternesse" that runs from Luther and More on to Milton and Salmasius. This is, alas, the common practice of gifted religious humanists in verbal conflict. More and Milton and other devout humanists are using their command of good Latin and colloquial English as weapons against what they regard as deadly enemies of truth, and nothing can be too vile to sling against such vileness: the whip of cords, ingeniously and cruelly knotted, must be used to drive these evil-doers out of the temple. We should not think of the Renaissance humanist as a peaceful person. He is an expert in language, not in self-control.

To say, however, that such vituperative violence in writing represents the real Thomas More, the inner man, this seems to me as wrong as if we were to say that Milton's prose propaganda represents the real Milton, the inner man, rather than *Paradise Lost*.[19] For More is writing propaganda in the basic sense of that word, *de propaganda fide*, writing to advance a certain faith or cause: and in that aim, it is no part of the writer to point out that there is much to be said for the other side. It seems to me naive to complain that More, in these writings, is unfair to the opposition, that such procedure, though appropriate to a lawyer arguing a case, is disappointing in a saint.[20] What then shall we say of St. Augustine in his polemics against the Pelagians or the Manichaeans? Even an Augustine, in polemical writing, must constrict his whole nature: the writer of polemic is, of necessity, ungenerous and unfair. The writing of propaganda delimits the expression of the whole being; and that is why, as Alistair Fox has said in his judicious and penetrating study of More's controversial writings, More cannot display his awareness of the paradoxes and ambiguities of life, and thus appears increasingly unhappy, bitter, sometimes desperate, at his "nadir," in his role as a polemicist.[21] For More the task of controversial writing, I believe, came into deep conflict with the sensitive inner self that Holbein found, unguarded, in one of the Windsor drawings.

We note, for example, in the *Apology*, how he seems to realize that his polemical rhetoric has carried him too far in something that, as he remembers, he has said about Frith. He says that someone told him "that Fryth labored so sore that he swette agayne, in studyeng and wrytyng agaynst the blessed sacrament." More then picks up the image of the sweat and creates a bitter contrast between Frith's sweat and the bloody sweat of Christ in the Garden of Gethsemane: "I wolde some good frend of hys shold shew hym, that I fere me sore that Cryst wyll kyndle a fyre of fagottes for hym, & make hym therin swete the bloude out of hys body here, and strayte frome hense send hys soule for euer into the fyre of hell."

More seems to realize the words are rhetorically too strong, for he then goes on to say:

> Now in these wordes I neyther ment nor meane, that I wold it were so. For so help me god and none otherwyse, but as I wolde

> be gladde to take more laboure, losse, and bodyly payne also, thenne peraduenture many a man wolde wene, to wynne that yonge man to Cryste and his trewe fayth agayne / & therby to preserue and kepe hym from the losse and perell of soule & body bothe. (CW 9.122)

Or again, in the forty-ninth chapter of the *Apology*, in the midst of his final attack on St. German's treatise, More declares:

> As touchynge heretykes, I hate that vyce of theyrs & not theyr persones / and very fayne wolde I that the tone were destroyed, and the tother saued. And that I haue toward no man any other mynde then thys, (howe lowdely so euer these blessed newe bretherne the professours & preachers of verytye bylye me) yf all the fauour and pytye that I haue vsed amonge theym to theyre amendement were knowen, yt wolde I warraunt you well and playne appere / wherof yf it were requysyte I coulde bryng forth wytnesses mo then men wold wene. (CW 9.167)

Still, it is argued that, aside from Martin Luther, his only peer in vituperation, More shows intemperance in language to an unusual degree. In a sense this is true. More is wittier, more clever, more gifted in his sardonic command of language than most writers of controversy. His vituperation stands out because of this literary power, not because of any unusual vindictiveness in his person. His opponents would have shown equal vituperative power if they had had the ability to do so. And Luther did. But Tyndale surely, you might argue, was a verbal artist of the very greatest power, as his translation of the Bible proves: he had consummate skill in rendering profound thought in common language. But in vituperation Tyndale has no gift: he tries, but he sounds only petulant; his strength lies elsewhere. We can see this in the exchanges between More and Tyndale set forth in More's *Confutation of Tyndale's Answer*.

When Tyndale tries to be vituperative, More can perform cadenzas around him, as when Tyndale scornfully refers to Erasmus as More's "darling," and More launches off into that brilliant cascade of rhetorical buffoonery on the theme of "Erasmus my darling" (CW 8.177), or when Tyndale unwisely brings in the "filthy idol Priapus" to ridicule the sacrament of confession, and thus gives More another chance to take off on the theme of Luther, his nun, and the "abominable bichery" of the newly married priest[22](CW 8.207). On the other hand, when Tyndale is setting forth reformed doctrine in his style of sturdy, simple eloquence, More's answers frequently are labored and he comes out second best.[23]

As for More's savagery against the mild St. German, we may well wonder about the mildness of this "pacifier," as More calls him, and we may understand More's sarcasm in the *Apology* when he takes this mild, pacific pose to be a mask that guards a ruthless attack upon the privileges of the Church. More seems to suspect that this anonymous treatise "concerning the division between the spirituality and temporality"—almost certainly the work of Christopher St. German, as More almost certainly realized—was part of an official campaign designed by Thomas Cromwell to undermine the Church and in the end take over most of its powers and properties.[24] It is against this threat that More adopts the device of writing his own *Apology*: his defense of his own writings and actions against the heretics. Tacitly, More is saying, this treatise on the division represents everything that I have tried to combat. Suspecting, though, that this publication is coming from a source quite close to the throne, More, in his usual devious way, does not compose his *Apology* as a direct attack on St. German's *Division*. No, he brings in this attack only by the way, as part of a long list of charges that have been brought against him by "the brethren." "For they fynde fyrste for a great fawte, that my writyng is ouer longe, and therfore to tedyouse to rede. For whyche cause they say they will neuer ons vouchsaufe to loke theron"(CW 9.5). This charge seems to have hit a sore spot in More, for he keeps returning to it, and indeed, who can deny that the *Confutation* is over-long? In spite of their declaration that they will never look upon the book, the brethren seem to have found lots of particular flaws within the text.

> ... they fynde a greate fawte, that I handle Tyndale and Barons theyr two newe gospellers, with no fayrer wordes nor in no more courteyse maner.
>
> And ouer thys I wryte they say in such wyse, that I shew my selfe suspecte in the mater & parciall toward the clergy.
>
> And than they saye that my wurkes were wurthy myche more credence, yf I had wryten more indyfferentely, and had declared and made open to the peple the fawtes of the clergy.

Now, at last, after these preliminaries he comes to St. German's treatise. "And in this poynt they laye for a sample the goodly and godly mylde & gentle fashyon vsed by hym who so euer he was, that now lately wrote ye boke of the deuisyon bytwene the temporaltye and the spyrytualty / whyche charytable mylde maner they say that yf I had vsed, my wurkes wold haue ben redde both of many mo, & wyth mych better wyll"(CW 9.5). He then adds a few other charges. But More delays dealing with St. German's treatise until eight and one half chapters have elapsed—forty pages, a quarter of the *Apology*. And although he spends most of the remaining three-quarters of the *Apology* attacking this treatise, he says that he is not going to do so. On page sixty-one,[25] for example, he says: "But for as mych as the touchynge of ye boke is here not my principal purpose / I wil therfore not peruse it ouer & touch euery point therof. Whyche yf I wolde, I coulde I thynke well make men se, y^t very fewe partes therof had eyther such cherite or such indifferencye therin, as not onely the new naughty bretherhed bosteth, but some good folke also take yt at a superfycyall redynge." He then, of course, proceeds to prove exactly this. It turns out that he has, well, one more thing, and one more thing, to add against it until the *Apology*, after one hundred and twenty pages almost entirely concerned with St. German's treatise, comes to the forty-ninth chapter, which opens with words that have the effect of a double-take: "And thus good crysten readers I make an ende of this mater, the boke I meane of thys dyuysyon"(CW 9.167). And then after four more pages of making an end, wholly concerned with denouncing St. German's book, he adds a final two-page chapter coming back to "the last fawt that the brethern fynde in my bokes."

More's *Apology* is thus composed according to a series of maneuvers designed to distract readers from thinking that this treatise on the division is something that he is deliberately attacking; no, his attack happens only by the way, in defense of himself and as an example of how misguided and perhaps well-intentioned people may help to spread trouble even though they mean to pacify:

> For trouth it is that murmur & dyssensyon (god knoweth how it begonne) agaynste the clergye is a greate waye gone onward in his vnhappy iourney / and maye by suche maner and meane of pacyfyenge, within short processe be conuayed rounde aboute the realme, and leue no place in peace. Not y^t I wolde thynke the man that made that boke to be of suche malycyouse mynde, as wyllyngly to sowe dyssensyon / but that as me semeth he taketh at the lest wise vnware a wronge waye towarde the contrary / and that the maner of his handelynge is farre from such indyfferencye as he sholde vse, that wolde make a loue day and appease any murmur and grudge of the laye people agaynste the prestes.(CW 9.54–55)

The *Apology*, with its pervasive irony and indirection, is one of More's most skillful pieces of improvised ordering, under the appearance of a casual disorder. Its mode of indirection takes us back to that famous passage in More's *Utopia*, where the character named Morus is trying to persuade Hythlodaeus that philosophers should take part in the councils of kings. In answer to Hythlodaeus' stern objection, this character called More argues:

> . . . by the indirect approach you must seek and strive to the best of your power to handle matters tactfully. What you cannot turn to good you must make as little bad as you can. For it is impossible that all should be well unless all men were good, a situation which I do not expect for a great many years to come!

But Hythlodaeus then gives the grim prophetic answer a dozen years before More's troubles began:

> As to that indirect approach of yours, I cannot see its relevancy. . . . At court there is no room for dissembling, nor may one shut one's eyes to things. One must openly approve the worst counsels and subscribe to the most ruinous decrees. He would be counted a spy and almost a traitor, who gives only faint praise to evil counsels.[26]

In the end More's indirect approach could not conceal from Cromwell and the King his bitter and continuing opposition to what they were attempting to achieve. He went to his death because his enemies saw him as a spy and a traitor, but like the martyrs to the other faith, though in another sense, he too died well and worthily.

Yale University

Notes

This essay is based upon the R. W. Chambers Memorial Lecture delivered at University College, London, in February, 1987, with major revisions and additions derived from a lecture delivered at Yale University in March, 1988, as part of a symposium on More.

1. G. R. Elton, "Thomas More, Councillor," in *St. Thomas More: Action and Contemplation*, ed. R. S. Sylvester (New Haven: Yale University Press,

1972), pp. 87-122; included in Elton, *Studies in Tudor and Stuart Politics and Government*, 2 vols. (Cambridge: Cambridge University Press, 1974), I, 129-54; "The Real Thomas More?" in *Reformation Principle and Practice*, ed. Peter Newman Brooks (London: Scolar Press, 1980), pp. 23-31. Richard Marius, *Thomas More*, New York: Knopf, 1984.

2. New York *Times*, January 4, 1987, Section H, p.5.

3. *The Complete Works of St. Thomas More* (New Haven: Yale University Press, 1963-), 8.590. (Referred to hereafter as *CW*.) The passage is cited by Marius, p. 406.

4. More is here explaining why he "advised and helped" to have Philips sent to the Tower instead of to the bishop's prison; it was, he says, because he feared that Philips might commit suicide in the bishop's prison and thus bring about another anti-clerical uproar such as attended the death of Richard Hunne, which More believed to be a suicide: see *CW* 9. 126-27.

5. G. R. Elton, *Reform and Reformation* (London: Arnold, 1977), pp. 191-92.

6. J. A. Guy, *The Public Career of Sir Thomas More* (New Haven: Yale University Press, 1980), pp. 166-67.

7. See *Holbein and the Court of Henry VIII* (Catalogue of an Exhibition in The Queen's Gallery, Buckingham Palace, 1978), p. 28, Item 2. Also K. T. Parker, *The Drawings of Hans Holbein in the Collection of His Majesty the King at Windsor Castle*, second ed. (Oxford and London: Phaidon Press, 1945), p. 36, Item 2.

8. See the discussion and reproduction of this painting in Stanley Morison, *The Likeness of Thomas More* (New York: Fordham University Press, 1963), pp. 18-25. For further illustrations and details of the lettering on the books see M. W. Brockwell, *Catalogue of the Pictures at Nostell Priory (1913)*, pp. 79 ff.

9. Thomas More, *Selected Letters*, ed. Elizabeth Frances Rogers (New Haven: Yale University Press, 1961), pp. 146-47.

10. See Elton, "The Real Thomas More?"; Marius, pp. xxi-xxiii and chapter 3, "Priesthood or Marriage."

11. See his treatise on the "last things," dated "around" the year 1522 in Rastell's edition of More's *Works*, 1557.

12. Nicholas Harpsfield, *The life and death of S[r] Thomas Moore*, ed. Elsie Vaughan Hitchcock (London: Early English Text Society, Oxford University Press, 1932), p. 12.

13. Thomas Stapleton, in the latest of the three early lives of More, is responsible for much of the emphasis upon More's desire to become a monk and for his alleged regret about his decision to marry. After saying "he was far more zealous to become a saint than a scholar," and stressing his ascetic practices, Stapleton adds: "For the religious state he had an ardent desire, and thought for a time of becoming a Franciscan. But as he feared, even with the help of his practices of penance, that he would not be able to conquer the temptations of the flesh that come to a man in the vigour and ardour of his youth, he made up his mind to marry. Of this he would often speak in after life with great sorrow and regret, for he used to say that it was much

easier to be chaste in the single than in the married state." *The Life and Illustrious Martyrdom of Sir Thomas More*, trans. Philip E. Hallett (London: Burns Oates, 1928), pp. 9–10. But, as Hallett notes, Stapleton's "primary object was not to write a history, but rather a devotional work for the edification of his readers" (p. ix). The life is the third of three saints' lives in his Latin work *Tres Thomae* (1588), the other saints being Thomas the Apostle and Thomas à Becket.

14. See the famous letter of Erasmus to Ulrich von Hutten, 23 July 1519. The passage concerning More's decision to marry needs close examination: "Interim et ad pietatis studium totum animum appulit, vigiliis, ieiuniis, precationibus aliisque consimilibus progymnasmatis sacerdotium meditans. . . . Neque quicquam obstabat quo minus sese huic vitae generi addiceret, nisi quod vxoris desyderium non posset excutere. Maluit igitur maritus esse castus quam sacerdos impurus." He performed various spiritual exercises, "meditating upon priesthood." "Nothing stood in the way of giving himself to this kind of life, except that he was not able to shake off his desire for a wife. Therefore he chose to be a chaste husband rather than an impure priest." Erasmus provides the witty interpretation in the last sentence. See Erasmus, *Opus Epistolarum*, ed. P. S. Allen et al. 12 vols. (Oxford: Clarendon Press, 1906–58), IV, 17–18.

15. Elton, *Studies in Tudor and Stuart Politics and Government*, I, 149.

16. Marius, p. 280.

17. John Milton, *Apology*, in *Complete Prose Works*, ed. Don M. Wolfe et al., 8 vols. (New Haven: Yale University Press, 1953–82), I, 899–903.

18. Milton, Preface to *Animadversions*, *Complete Prose Works*, I, 662–64.

19. See Marius, p. 289: "Unpleasant as it is, the *Responsio ad Lutherum* brings us as close to the real Thomas More as anything else he wrote until that time. Here he had the freedom to be himself, unfettered by the formal demands art made in his *History of King Richard III* or *Utopia*. He was where he could pour out the deepest passions of his soul in the belief that those passions coincided exactly with the will of God." Also pp. 338–39, where Marius speaks of the "parade of English polemical works from More's pen that for all their ferocity and dreary dullness still offer the most significant literary monument we have to his mind and heart." One result of this view in the Marius biography is the decision to treat More's account of the Richard Hunne case in the context of More's early career, that is, in 1514–15, when the Hunne case caused anti-clerical disturbances. More's satirical account of the witnesses in the case (CW 6. 316–30) dates from 1529, when he wrote it as part of his *Dialogue Concerning Heresies*: the satire ridicules the flimsy grounds of gossip that can lead to anti-clerical uproar. The passage tells us much about More's satirical wit as a polemicist; it tells us little, in my view, about his heart, and certainly nothing about his early years.

20. See Marius, p. 339.

21. Alistair Fox, *Thomas More: History and Providence* (New Haven: Yale University Press, 1983), pp. 111–205.

22. I am not convinced that More's frequent repetition of this charge shows

any peculiar sexual obsession. In the *Confutation* these repetitions are part of a larger pattern of rhetorical repetition. As he explains in the *Apology* (*CW* 9. 8-10), he has designed the *Confutation* so that each section will contain within itself the essential elements of his argument against Tyndale; hence he repeats within each section the same elements of confutation—in a way that is bound to be wearisome in consecutive reading of the whole treatise. The theme of the breaking of priestly vows by marriage is thus bound to recur, partly because it provides a riposte against the reformers' charges of moral laxity in the Roman church, and partly because it provides such a fertile field for the play of More's earthy, mordant wit. (See my essay "More as Author: The Virtues of Digression," *Moreana* 16 (1979), 105-19.)

23. See, for example, the passage (*CW* 8.403-4) where Tyndale gives a rousing statement of the central principle of Reformation doctrine, justification by faith, and More's answer seems to falter and ramble.

24. See Alistair Fox, pp. 187-98.

25. My pagination is given according to the edition of the *Apology* in *CW*.

26. *CW* 4. 99-103.

Soeur Anne-Marie MARC'HADOUR
Congrégation de St Joseph de Cluny
97360 MANA (Guyane Française)

Mana le 4 septembre 1987.

Mon cher Germain,

De tout coeur, merci de ton envoi d'images de Fatima, du timbre de Sainte Thérèse d'Avila... J'aime ce timbre, rappel silencieux de la grande contemplative, protectrice de notre Ordre.

Je reviens de Sinnamary où j'ai fait ma retraite annuelle chez les Franciscaines Missionnaires de Marie, retraite prêchée par le Père Boisvert, canadien.... Me re-voici dans mon cadre habituel de la Communauté et de l'école où en ce moment, nous faisons des travaux : la réfection des peintures de la façade et du pignon s'impose.... En regardant ce bâtiment, je repense que c'est toi, qui, en 1948, as lancé une souscription afin de nous permettre d'en commencer la re-construction... Il fallait, en effet, abattre l'école primitive, en bois, vieille de 120 ans ... Nous étions pauvres .... Ce geste, je ne l'ai jamais oublié ; dans nos archives, le texte de la souscription demeure, témoin de ta charité inventive qui ne se contente pas de paroles .

Le Père Pédrono (morbihannais comme nous), vient d'être nommé Curé de Saint-Laurent et de Mana... Missionnaire dans l'âme, il a le souci de ceux qui ne sont pas encore dans le bercail... de nos plus proches voisins : les Indiens : « ...leur apprendre à prier dans leur langue ... Mais qui va faire cette traduction ? ». Ma réponse ne s'est pas fait attendre : - Père, mon frère a vécu 3 mois ici, il avait le même souci que vous et, aidé par deux jeunes Galibis, Paul et Félix, avait traduit en indien, les principales prières ... J'ai les textes... De même, mon frère voulait que les indiens entendent, dans leur langue, la PAROLE DE DIEU lue à la messe du dimanche. Il se rendait dans la semaine, au village, pour assurer cette traduction. Il n'avait qu'une voiture de fortune pour arpenter cette mauvaise piste longue de 17 km... Régulièrement, à son retour, il me disait : -- « Annick ; encore un miracle, je n'ai pas eu de panne !! ». Germain, j'admirais ton zèle, ton courage; sans t'en rendre compte, tu transmettais ta « flamme », j'ai accueilli la lumière, elle ne saurait s'éteindre ...

Un jour, je revenais avec toi d'un village indien... Dans la voiture, avec nous : un groupe d'européens... A côté de moi : un jeune homme noir. Je ne sais comment, la conversation s'est portée sur les gens du pays... Des mots, des phrases assez humiliantes ont été prononcées. Arrivés à la maison, tu n'as pas craint de me dire ce que tu pensais : -« j'avais honte d'entendre ainsi parler devant ce jeune noir, nous sommes ici pour servir ces gens-là, pour nous occuper d'eux et non pour nous croire supérieurs à eux .... ». Là, vois-tu, je découvrais la bonté de ton coeur, ton « non-racisme », ton souci de relever celui qui était abaissé... Il y a de cela 17 ans, la leçon porte son fruit, je ne l'oublie pas et je dis : « Louange à Toi, Jésus, Tu as donné à Germain un coeur semblable au tien ... Louange à Toi, Marie, Tu formes le coeur de tes prêtres sur le Modèle Divin ».

Assez souvent, je traverse la PLACE DE L'ÉGLISE, passant devant le buste de notre Fondatrice : la Bienheureuse ANNE-MARIE JAVOUHEY. Je n'y passe jamais sans penser à toi. Pourquoi ? Te souviens-tu que, ne voulant jamais lui tourner le dos, tu faisais le tour du buste en voiture, afin de passer devant celle qui fut de Mana
« la Fondatrice et la Mère »
- détail dira-t-on ... galanterie d'amoureux !, mais le respect, l'amitié ne se traduisent-ils pas par ces 1000 détails qui tissent notre vie de relations, laissant deviner une délicatesse de coeur, fruit du Saint-Esprit...

Tu vois qu'aujourd'hui, nous avons re-vécu un peu ces longues semaines passées ensemble... sans le savoir, tu jetais des semences... tant et si bien que les braves Mananais me demandent encore : - « Et votre frère ? ... » Je leur réponds : - « il ne vous oublie pas ».

A travers l'Océan, reçois donc, avec la brise, le souvenir reconnaissant et affectueux de ta soeur qui t'embrasse bien fort.

Soeur Anne-Marie Marc'hadour

Statue du XVe siècle, polychrome, artiste inconnu. Sainte Anne, seule achevée, ressemble à l'arbre de Jessé, dont sortent, comme une branche et un scion, Marie et l'enfant Jésus.

Wooden statue, 15th-century, polychrome, artist unknown. Saint Anne holds the Virgin, who holds the infant Jesus: a matrilineal Jesse Tree.

L'Université Catholique de l'Ouest, Oratoire. Photo par Pierre Gosselin.

Dr. Nancy Ruthford Sodeman
419 Valley Cove
Richardson, TX 75080

October 5, 1987.

Dear Germain,

How astonishing that life so quickly ebbs into backwater if one isn't careful. Before this happens, I must let you know what you have meant to me. I would forever rue the day that I mused about what a grand fellow you are but did not write to tell you before it was too late. Now I write honoring you for your twenty-five years of publishing *Moreana* and thanking you for your longstanding friendship.

First of all I recall meeting you in Georgia where I was writing my dissertation on Thomas More. You took precious time to read it, to make suggestions and put me in touch with a fine Morean scholar, Dr. Walter Gordon, at the University of Georgia. You wrote to my committee at Georgia State to commend my work and to encourage them to complete their critique so that, finally, I was able to win my doctorate. What a fine friend and scholar to have on hand at such a crucial time.

Also, while in Georgia I remember our having been at a meeting in Conyers at the Monastery of the Holy Spirit from which we journeyed to Atlanta in search of the stomping ground of Martin Luther King. My friend, the famed political cartoonist with the *Atlanta Constitution,* Baldy (Clifford Baldowski), could not arrange a meeting for us. But he did suggest visiting a restaurant in the vicinity where we ate a typical Black meal : cornbread, collard greens, chitlings and chicken. The experience meant much to me. Having lived seventeen years in the South after my childhood in Minnesota, I had a quaint but sympathetic attitude about our then still segregated brothers. Your attempt to walk in their shoes and to eat their food renewed my hope. The dignity and the destiny of the Blacks were obviously your own anxious concern. It was good to see and feel.

Another fond remembrance is your visit to Texas. What a joy to see you and introduce you to the family before my husband, Walter, died and to my favorite Jesuit, Fr. Bob MacCown (now writing and teaching media skills to fellow priests and nuns in Brazil).

These are simply highlights of what you mean to me. Many other examples come to mind ; but I need to keep this note short. Blessings on you and thank you especially for your twenty-five-year dedication to *Moreana*. Through this means you have kept the world in communication, inspiring us to look to Thomas More as an example. Thanks for being YOU.

Fondly,

Nancy

Abbé Marc'hadour made another visit to Dallas and Richardson, April 9-10, 1989.

LÉON-E. HALKIN

Érasme contre la liturgie?

On pourrait penser qu'Érasme ne veut rien comprendre à la liturgie, tant il loue la piété personnelle et la prière privée.[1] Par ailleurs il est vrai que le début du seizième siècle ne privilégie pas souvent la prière officielle de l'Église.[2] Ne nous étonnons donc pas de ne point trouver sous la plume d'Érasme un éloge soutenu de la liturgie.

Toutefois rien dans les textes ne permet de conclure qu'Érasme demeure fermé à la prière publique de l'Église et aux cérémonies liturgiques. Je voudrais, à travers quelques-uns de ses écrits, montrer qu'il connaît, pratique et apprécie les prières du missel et du bréviaire.

Religieux à Steyn, Érasme chante les heures monastiques et possède un bréviaire. Prêtre, il célèbre la messe. Lorsqu'il dit adieu au cloître, il emporte son bréviaire et nous savons qu'il dit parfois la messe.[3] Quand il perd son bréviaire il en est affecté.[4] En 1502, il demande à un ami de lui acheter un psautier.[5] En 1511, nous le voyons à la messe à Cambridge.[6] En 1518, il va à la messe à Cologne[7] et, revenu malade à Louvain, il ne sort que pour la messe.[8] A Bâle, il souffre, vers la fin de son séjour, de ne plus pouvoir assister à l'office dans une église. Sans doute dit-il la messe dans sa chambre qui est devenue son oratoire: *cubiculum nobis pro templo est.*[9]

En ce qui concerne le bréviaire, son livre d'heures, Érasme en énumère avec compétence toutes les parties, des matines aux complies.[10] Il y retrouve à toutes les pages des textes de l'Écriture Sainte. Quelques années plus tard, dans son *De praeparatione ad mortem*, il utilise des sources liturgiques.[11] Un article plein de verve de l'abbé Marc'hadour montre que, même dans ses lettres familières, Érasme introduit des réminiscences liturgiques, dans un contexte parfois déconcertant. A l'archevêque Warham, il décrit son cheval:

> S'il n'est pas vraiment beau, il est bon. Tous les péchés capitaux lui manquent, sauf la gourmandise et la paresse. En outre il est orné de toutes les vertus du bon confesseur: il est pieux, prudent, humble, réservé, sobre, chaste et tranquille.

Or cette série d'épithètes vient de l'office du Commun des Confesseurs! Sûr d'être compris par son correspondant, Érasme les emploie avec une désinvolture bien ecclésiastique et un humour très personnel.[12]

Dans l'oeuvre immense d'Érasme, le mot "liturgie" semble absent. Il se lit pourtant dans le titre du petit volume de 1523, rédigé pour son ami Théobald Bietricius, curé de Porrentruy: *Virginis Matris apud Lauretum cultae liturgia*.[13] Dans ce cas, "liturgie" est synonyme de messe, alors que ce que nous appelons habituellement "liturgie" est exprimé ailleurs par *solennes Ecclesiae preces*.[14]

Une messe en l'honneur de Notre-Dame de Lorette! Il est permis de s'étonner de ce zèle imprévu. Érasme, fidèle à lui-même, ne cautionne pas la légende de la *santa casa*. Il a sans doute voulu manifester sa maîtrise dans un genre aussi exceptionnel que la composition d'une messe votive. Belle occasion en outre d'enseigner par l'exemple ce que doit être un culte vraiment chrétien, replaçant la Vierge Mère dans l'économie de la Rédemption! D'un écrit de circonstance, il a tiré une leçon de piété mariale, conformément à ses convictions profondes.

L'oraison de la messe est révélatrice des intentions de l'auteur: "Nous vénérons la Mère à cause du Fils." La page d'évangile est celle des noces de Cana, un texte qui célèbre la bonté et l'humilité de la Vierge. Le sermon, ajouté dans la seconde édition, n'est pas moins érasmien: Marie, servante du Seigneur et modèle de disponibilité.[15]

Une *Missa* figure parmi les oeuvres de saint Jean Chrysostome publiées par Érasme. Il s'agit de la célèbre *Liturgie de saint Jean Chrysostome*. Cette traduction est une oeuvre médiocre et entachée d'erreurs. Elle remonte sans doute aux dernières années du quinzième siècle, alors que le grec d'Érasme était encore hésitant.[16]

Ces deux écrits mineurs mis à part, il n'est guère question du culte public de l'Église dans les écrits d'Érasme. Ses lettres et ses traités abondent en notations péjoratives sur les "cérémonies." On aurait tort d'en conclure qu'il rejette les cérémonies liturgiques et particulièrement la messe.[17] Bien sûr, il critique tout ce qui dans la prière, publique ou privée, est machinal. Il craint l'obscurcissement de la piété et même, en certains cas, la contagion de la superstition, voire de la magie. L'authenticité de la prière est à ce prix.

Érasme veut que le cadre de la prière publique soit adapté à sa fin. De ce souci procèdent ses critiques les plus nettes. Puisque les églises doivent être réservées au culte divin, Érasme proscrit les jeux et les spectacles qui les encombrent parfois. Il demande que, pendant la messe, les fidèles ne bavardent pas, qu'ils ne se promènent pas dans l'église et ne se réfugient pas sur le parvis.[18] De même, il écarte les chants à la Vierge, du moins quand ils se font durant la consécration.[19] Enfin il blâme vigoureusement les prêtres qui ne disent la messe que pour le bénéfice matériel qu'ils en retirent. Pour ces prêtres médiocres il emploie le verbe péjoratif *missare*, "vivre de la messe!"[20]

Dans le colloque intitulé *Pietas puerilis*, le jeune Gaspard s'efforce de s'unir au prêtre et de comprendre ce qu'il lit, particulièrement l'épître et l'évangile. Si le prêtre ne se fait pas entendre, Gaspard utilise un livre contenant les lectures du jour. Il écoute pieusement le sermon et fuit toute superstition.[21]

Le *Modus orandi Deum*, publié à Bâle en 1524, est la principale contribution d'Érasme à l'art de la piété.[22] La liturgie, il faut le reconnaître, occupe peu de place dans ce petit traité de caractère pastoral. Le chrétien doit prier sans cesse et en toute circonstance.

Érasme propose donc à ses lecteurs de beaux développements sur la prière de Jésus, l'oraison dominicale et la prière des disciples. La Bible, d'une part, et les prières de l'Église, d'autre part, offrent un choix presque inépuisable d'élévations de l'âme vers Dieu. Le *Modus orandi* recommande d'utiliser les oraisons liturgiques, de préférence en langue vulgaire, ce qui aiderait les laïcs à mieux s'associer au prêtre durant la messe. Ceux qui agissent autrement et oublient ce que fait le prêtre à l'autel *Ecclesiae sunt, non Ecclesia*.

En 1533, le *De sarcienda Ecclesiae concordia* reprend l'essentiel du programme de son auteur: primauté de l'Évangile, mission de l'Église, oecuménisme actif, purification des institutions et de la piété.[23] Érasme soumet ses réflexions au jugement de l'Église et il évoque, entre autres, ce qui concerne la messe:

S'il s'y est glissé, dit-il, quoi que ce soit de superstitieux ou d'indigne, il est normal que l'on y remédie, mais je ne vois pas ce qui justifierait l'exécration que certains lui vouent aujourd'hui.[24]
La messe comporte le chant d'un psaume, qu'on appelle introït, une doxologie, une oraison, des cantiques sacrés. On fait ensuite

la lecture d'écrits prophétiques ou apostoliques, c'est l'épître; on lit l'évangile, on fait une profession de foi catholique. Vient ensuite l'action de grâces appelée eucharistie et une pieuse commémoration de la mort du Seigneur. De nouveau des prières, parmi lesquelles la prière que le Seigneur nous a apprise. Puis le symbole de la paix chrétienne, suivi bientôt de la communion, à laquelle succèdent un cantique sacré et une prière. Le tout se termine lorsque le prêtre, prenant en quelque sorte le peuple sous sa protection, le remet à Dieu et le lui recommande par la bénédiction, engageant les fidèles à persévérer dans leurs dispositions de piété et de charité mutuelle. Qu'y a-t-il dans tout cela qui ne soit pieux et ne mérite le respect?

Deux mots de conclusion. Pour Érasme, comme pour toute la tradition catholique, le missel et le bréviaire sont d'admirables instruments de la piété s'ils sont lus avec attention, médités avec respect et vécus dans la foi.

Fidèle à l'enseignement de Platon, Érasme pense que les cérémonies sont précieuses en ceci qu'elles peuvent élever les âmes des choses visibles aux choses invisibles.[25] Encore faut-il que ces cérémonies, aussi riches de sens qu'elles soient pour les croyants, conservent une tenue digne de leur objet. Tel est le leitmotiv des réflexions d'Érasme sur la piété.

Université de Liège

Notes

1. On a été jusqu'à reprocher à Érasme "son dédain de la piété catholique traditionnelle, en affectant de ne parler à Dieu qu'avec des textes bibliques." Cf. H. Busson, *Littérature et théologie*, p. 81, Paris, 1962.
2. Saint Ignace, qui avait abandonné le chant choral, fut accusé de manquement à l'esprit liturgique. Cf. L. Peeters, *Spiritualité ignacienne et piété liturgique*, Tournai, 1914. Josse Clichtove, contemporain d'Érasme, est exceptionnellement intéressé par la liturgie. Cf. J.-P. Massaut, *Josse Clichtove, l'humanisme et la réforme du clergé*, t. 2, p. 285, Paris, 1968.
3. Allen, *Opus epistolarum*, 154, 18–21.
4. Allen, 95, 6 et 18.

5. Allen, 169, 4-5.
6. Allen, 232, 6.
7. Allen, 867, 68.
8. Allen, 867, 249-50.
9. Allen, 2134, 201; 2136, 23.
10. *Opera omnia Desiderii Erasmi Roterodami* (= A.S.D.), t. V-1, p. 134, l. 467-71 (*Modus orandi*).
11. Remarques de A. Van Heck dans son édition: A.S.D., t. V-1, pp. 331, 333.
12. Tous les textes sont réunis par G. Marc'hadour, "Le Nouveau Testament dans la correspondance d'Érasme," dans l'ouvrage collectif *La Correspondance d'Érasme et l'épistolographie humaniste*, p. 68, Bruxelles, 1985.
13. A.S.D., t. V-1, p. 87.
14. A.S.D., t. V-1, p. 144, l. 831. Le mot *liturgia* se retrouve à la dernière ligne de la préface de l'édition de 1525: A.S.D., t. V-1, p. 96, l. 41. J'ai noté dans l'*Exomologesis* l'expression "liturgia vespertina." Cf. *Desiderii Erasmi Roterodami opera omnia*, t. 5, col. 159 D. Érasme appelle aussi "liturgia" la messe de saint Jean Chrysostome. Cf. ma note 16.
15. A.S.D., t. V-1, p. 99.
16. Paris, 1536. Cf. A. Jacob, *L'édition érasmienne de la Liturgie de saint Jean Chrysostome*, dans *Italia medioevale e umanistica*, t. 19, p. 291-324, Padoue, 1976. Ailleurs Érasme appelle cette λειτουργία "officium Chrysostomi" ou "Graecorum liturgia." Cf. Allen, 467, 21 et 916, 33.
17. J. Chomarat, *Grammaire et rhétorique chez Érasme*, t. 1, p. 651, 652, 698, 699, Paris, 1981. Sur les cérémonies qu'Érasme rejette, voir mon article "La piété d'Érasme," dans la *Revue d'histoire ecclésiastique*, t. 79, p. 684, n. 2. J'ajoute un texte significatif de l'*Enchiridion militis christiani*. Cf. H. Holborn, *Desiderius Erasmus Roterodamus ausgewählte Werke*, p. 66, l. 4-25, Munich, 1933.
18. *Desiderii Erasmi Roterodami opera omnia*, t. 7, f^{oxx}3vo. Allen, 2205, 85-92; 2284, 118-21, 153-54.
19. Allen, 2284, 133-35. Cf. J.-Cl. Margolin, *Érasme et la musique*, Paris, 1965.
20. Allen, 2853, 12.
21. A.S.D., t. I-3, p. 176, l. 1663-68, 1672-74; p. 177, l. 1715. Holborn, *op. cit.*, p. 73 et 249. Allen, 1333, 198-200.
22. A.S.D., t. V-1, p. 111-76.
23. A.S.D., t. V-3, p. 257-313. L'extrait cité est p. 307-8.
24. Érasme écrit à Louis Ber en 1529: "Je n'ai jamais méprisé et je n'ai jamais enseigné qu'il fallait mépriser les constitutions et les rites de l'Église." Cf. Allen, 2136, 209-10.
25. A.S.D., t. V-1, p. 166, l. 579-80.

Angers, November 17, 1987.

Dear Germain,

This special occasion has given me the opportunity to tell you how much your friendship has meant to us since our first dinner in April 1974. Your reputation as a teacher, lecturer, writer, scholar and specialist of Thomas More and the Renaissance is very well known and I have great admiration for your achievement. But there is something else that I want to bring to light. These accomplishments, your many pursuits, have never deterred you from your first calling -- the priesthood. Roger loved to say that to be present when Germain was celebrating the Eucharist was a spiritual experience. All our friends, Catholic or not, who attended a Celebration concurred with him and with me. Obviously, the most important role in your life has remained that of a priest, a minister to human spiritual needs.

From the time we returned to Angers in May 1983 to 28 December, 1984, the day Roger died, your assiduity and your devotion to Roger during his long and difficult illness were remarkable. I wish I could tell you how your almost daily visits were precious to Roger and to me. The courage and serenity which were his during the last few months of his life were in great part due to you, to your prayers and to the Faith and Hope that you instilled into him. You must know how much I too depended on those few minutes you spent with us and the strength I derived knowing that you were only a phone call away anytime -- day or night.

Thank you, Germain, for being what you are, all that you are.

Je t'embrasse,

Thérèse

BRIAN F. BYRON

From Essence to Presence:
A Shift in Eucharistic Expression Illustrated
from the Apologetic of St. Thomas More

One of the many benefits of my providential choice of St. Thomas More as a subject for a doctoral thesis was my coming into contact with the Moreanum of Angers and its founder Germain Marc'hadour. Since 1965 he has enriched my life with his scholarship, his organization and his friendship. I have had the honour of being his guest several times and his host once. My visits to Angers have always been joyous and inspiring. His visit to Australia in 1978 for the quincentenary of More's birth is still having its effects. As a fellow priest I appreciate his love of the Mass and his writings on More's eucharistic devotion. I know he has a special place in his thoughts for the priest-members of the Amicale. As I write I have on my desk a postcard from Angers signed by Father Gregory Meere, Germain, Beatrice Lemasson and Mary O'Neill on 19 September 1986. Greg died suddenly shortly afterwards on his way home on 27 September in Los Angeles. He would want to be closely associated with the honouring of Germain at this high point in his illustrious career.

The central part of the present article was delivered as a paper at the International Conference on More and St. John Fisher at Chelsea in 1985. We were allowed only twenty minutes on that occasion so I had to be succinct. I may now be allowed additional words of explanation though I fear they will still not be enough. I hope to have the opportunity of dealing comprehensively with the subject at book-length.

The title I have given this essay is meant to describe a change that gradually came into eucharistic theology—a change from expressions of identity (or essence) to those of presence. "Essence" is from the Latin *esse*, the copulative "to be." This copulative *esse* is to be distinguished from the substantive *esse* meaning "to exist." "Presence" is from *prae-esse*, "to be before," in which *esse* has the substantive meaning. By using More's catena of patristic texts as an example, I indicate that there was a gradual change from the copulative *esse* to the substantive *preesse* in regard to the Eucharist. The verb "to be" as used of the Eucharist in the New Testament is always the copula. Thomas More uses the words of the Fathers in his efforts to prove eucharistic realism. I believe he succeeds. But he, like most in his time, expresses it in terms of *presence*. Is there any difference? Maybe we should look at the evidence first. What follows in the next section is the text of the paper I delivered at Chelsea in July 1985.

I

One of the most bitter debates between Catholics and Christians of the reformed traditions from the time of Luther until the mid-twentieth century was that over the Eucharist. Any possibility of reconciliation seemed impossible until in recent decades the miracle of the Ecumenical Movement replaced diatribe with dialogue and invective with agreed statements. Amongst these, of particular note are the Anglican Roman Catholic International Commission (ARCIC) and World Council of Churches' Faith and Order Commission (Lima) reports, which aim to by-pass the stalemates of the Reformation era by reformulating doctrine in uncontroversial language. My general objective in this paper is to further this wonderful enterprise. I believe that several important misconceptions had imperceptibly altered the formulation of eucharistic doctrine by the late scholastic period. I believe that some of these were not detected by either side at the time of the Reformation and, unfortunately, they are still undetected by most people and hence continue to cloud our understanding of the Eucharist today.

Thomas More and John Fisher provide us with a fair sampling of the Catholic apologetic of the Eucharist at the time of the Reformation. Studies have already been done on the treatment of the eucharistic sacrifice by these two defenders of the Catholic faith. It has also been shown that both men had a good understanding of the best scholastic explanation of the Real Presence and utilized it skillfully.[1] I am going to suggest, however, that there was one flaw in the scholastic theory which More and Fisher did not consider.

In my opinion there were, over the centuries, several shifts in the meaning of key expressions in eucharistic theology. I will concentrate in this paper on only one of them, namely, the shift from expressions which designate *identity* to those which designate *presence*. More's last extensive writing on the Eucharist provides us with patristic citations with which I can illustrate the *fact* that a change in *expression* had crept in. I maintain that the change in expression reveals a change in conception.

The shift from expressions of *identity* to those of *presence* is in my mind very significant. It gave rise unconsciously to an erroneous comprehension of the sacrament. More importantly I believe that this wrong comprehension still constitutes a problem in eucharistic theology and ecumenical dialogue today. We are still asking the wrong questions at the very beginning.

I limit myself to the late work of More, *A Treatise Upon the Passion*, because it provides sufficient material for me to illustrate my claim.[2] This particular work, unlike More's earlier eucharistic writings, is a relatively calm, invective-free exposition of the Catholic position. In it More is at pains to show that the Church's doctrine was at his time identical with that of the early Fathers. In conjunction with "the old holy doctors" he held to the realism of the eucharistic formulas. He utilized scholastic theory to show the intrinsic possibility of that position. This in turn led him into the intricacies and subtleties which the Reformers found so repugnant, but which they did not always manage to avoid themselves. I will first examine More's catena of patristic texts by which he sought to prove the continuity of Catholic doctrine from the earliest times. I will indicate the gradual change in expression. Then I will suggest how the change caused the setup which triggered the Reformation dispute.

More's series of citations begins with St. Ignatius of Antioch (d. 107) and concludes with St. Anselm (d. 1109). More's technique, as in so many of his other works, is to quote the (Latin) text and then to give his own English translation. His objective is to uphold the Catholic, realist understanding of the Eucharist and to refute a purely symbolic sense. More does this by indicating the expressions in which the Fathers assert that the Eucharist *is* the body and blood of Christ and those which describe the *eating* and *drinking* of Christ's body and blood. Expressions describing the *change* of bread and wine into the body and blood of Christ are also highlighted.

Let us look more closely at the expressions used by Fathers whom More quotes as witnesses of the Catholic tradition. He begins, as I said, with St. Ignatius who writes of "The bread of life, which *is* the flesh of Christ" (to use More's own translation, emphasis mine) (CW 13, 161). Next he cites St. Justin the Martyr: "So this food . . . we be taught that it *is* the flesh and blood of the same Jesus incarnate" (CW 13, 161; emphasis mine.) Again he quotes Irenaeus, "How shall it appear to them to be true, that the eucharistical bread upon which thanks be given, *is* the body of their Lord . . .?" (CW 13, 161; emphasis mine.)

Note then that these first three Fathers give their witness to faith in eucharistic realism by affirming *what the eucharist is* as distinct from what the scholastics were to assert later, viz, that the Body of Christ is *present* or is "contained" in the Eucharist.

More proceeds over a well-worn track to other familiar early Christian writers: Tertullian's famous words regarding the nourishment of our *bodies* by the Eucharist are rendered: "The flesh [i.e., our flesh] eats the body and blood of Christ that the soul also may be made fat of God." Origen is invoked to prove that in Communion we "eat and drink the body and blood of our Lord" (CW 13, 162). Cyprian too is cited: he repeats the words of institution in two forms, one in the Synoptic tradition, the other affected by the Johannine: "This is (saith he) my body"; "this is my flesh and this is my blood . . ." (CW 13, 163).

Passing on to Hilary, More translates that writer's proof of the hypostatic union from the analogy of the Eucharist. Hilary concludes, in More's translation: "Of the truth and verity therefore of his flesh and his blood, is there now no place left for any man to doubt: for now both by the word of our Lord himself, and by our faith also, verily is it his flesh and verily is it his blood, and these two received and drunken bring this to pass, that both we be in Christ and Christ in us" (CW 13, 165).

Eusebius Emesenus (i.e., of Emesa in Syria), who died in 359, is quoted by More in a Latin text which, if authentic, must be one of the earliest to introduce the term "substance." More translates: "For the invisible priest by his word and secret power, doth change and convert the visible creatures into the substance of his body and blood . . ."; "When the creatures which are to be consecrated by the heavenly words, are set upon the holy altars, there is the substance of bread and wine. But after the words of Christ there is the body and blood of Christ" (CW 13, 165–6).

We may pass quickly over More's references to Basil and Hesychius, though we may note the latter's conception of the eucharistic action in terms of sanctification of the elements (CW 13, 166-67).

Ambrose is brought forward next as another witness of eucharistic realism: "The sacrament before it be consecrate is bread. But when Christ's words be come to it, it *is* the body of Christ" (CW 13, 167; emphasis mine).

John Chrysostom's eucharistic realism is sometimes thought to be extreme and so he provides additional ammunition for More. Jerome is also cited but there is not much detail. Cyril is next: he compares Communion between Christ and us in the Eucharist to the joining of two pieces of melting wax (CW 13, 167-68).

Next comes Augustine: his famous misunderstanding of the title of Ps 33 (34), "Ferebatur in manibus suis," is applied to Christ at the Last Supper: "Christ bare himself in his own hands, when he commended his body and said on this wise, this is my body. For Christ bare that body in his hands" (CW 13, 168-69).[3] Augustine's witness to the eucharistic fast also confirms the tradition of realism: "The body of our Lord should be received and taken into the mouth of a Christian man before any bodily meat" (CW 13, 169-70).

Gregory compares the blood of Christ to that of the paschal lamb: ". . . which blood is put upon both the posts, when it is drunken and received, not only by the mouth of the body, but also by the mouth of the heart . . ." (CW 13, 169).

Saint Bede (c673-735) gets closest to a scholastic expression: "There appeareth the form of bread where the substance of bread is not" (CW 13, 170).

Theophilactus, a Byzantine exegete of the eleventh century, appears to have a theology typical of other Eastern Fathers: More translates a passage of his: "Furthermore, saying, this is my body, he sheweth that the bread which is sanctified upon the altar, is the very body of our Lord, and not a figure answering to it. For it is changed by an unspeakable working, although it seems bread to us that be weak, and abhor to eat raw flesh, specially the flesh of man, and, therefore, it appeareth bread, but it is flesh." (More's translation omits a sentence which would have strengthened his case even further: "Non enim dixit, Hoc est figura, sed hoc est corpus meum" [CW 13, 170].)

And the Englishman by adoption, Anselm, also in the eleventh century uses the terms, "species" and "substance," which were to be universally adopted by the scholastic tradition. More renders an extract from "the second book of the body and blood of our Lord": "In those kinds of bread and wine, either there is no substance, or else it is the substance of our Lord's body and blood" (CW 13, 170).

This virtually ends the evidence from the Fathers. More summarizes his argument by asserting that all these writers professed the same faith as the Church of his day. But in doing so he uses an expression which none of the early Fathers used, viz. ". . . *in* this blessed sacrament *is* the very body and the very blood of Christ . . ."; and later ". . . no man gainsaying the very blessed body and blood to be *therein* . . ." (CW 13, 171). As he goes on, More quietly changes to the more common scholastic expression when he speaks of "the *presence* of Christ's very body and blood in the blessed sacrament" (CW 13, 174).

Hence in the citations I have given, More exemplifies the shift which I claim occurred over the centuries from the original expressions denoting *identity* to those signifying *presence within*. In other words, the scholastics evidently considered to be synonymous the two statements: "This is my body" and "My body is in this." Their theological theory was geared entirely to prove the intrinsic possibility of the second statement, while they thought it justified a realistic interpretation of the first. The scholastics had, however, inverted subject and predicate apparently without realizing it. St. Thomas Aquinas came close to noting this when, in refuting consubstantiation, he reminded us that the words of consecration were "hoc est corpus meum"; "This is my body," not "Here is my body" (S. Th 3 q.75 a.2).

If one were to ask why this shift took place I would point to the need to make sense of the strong traditional belief in eucharistic realism coupled with another shift from the Semitic concept "flesh" to the holistic term "body." This latter claim is more difficult to document and substantiate and obviously time does not allow me to attempt it now, but I guess it is the real reason why the scholastics conceived the problem the way they did, i.e., in terms of presence. In doing this they took something consequential as essential.

I am of the opinion that a new theology of eucharistic realism is necessary and possible. There have been a number of fresh approaches by Catholic theologians in recent decades but to my mind they fail. Some of them do so because they also centre around the problem of presence. Certain transcendental theories seem to me to be obscurantist—a thing which More would never have countenanced! A good theology of the Eucharist must start from an accurate statement of the problem, a precise analysis of the terms and the sentences used as its basis; there should moreover be the provision of illuminating analogies related to an intelligible philosophy and to a culture.

Thomas More and his scholastic mentors had every right to theologize about the Eucharist using the current philosophical world-view. To my mind, however, they got themselves into difficulties by starting with the wrong questions—questions about presence rather than identity. Here I will attempt to explain what I think are the implications of the fact demonstrated above.

II

To my mind St. Thomas More proved the realism (as opposed to a simple symbolism) of the eucharistic faith of the Fathers from their writings. But his citations illustrate that there was a change in the statements about the Eucharist. Instead of the primary statements in his own theology being about the identity of the eucharistic signs, they became statements about the Body of Christ and its presence within the signs. Is there a difference? Yes. One can argue thus:

This is the Body of Christ
This is present
Therefore the Body of Christ is present

But one cannot argue:

The Body of Christ is present
This is present
Therefore this is the Body of Christ.[4]

The right question to ask about the Eucharist is not therefore: how can the Body and Blood of Christ be present in the host and cup? This was the sort of question the scholastics asked. The Reformers did not perceive this inaccuracy and many theologians today still have not realized it is a wrong start. The right question to begin with is surely, in what sense is the bread of the Eucharist the Body of Christ? In what sense is the content of the cup the Blood of Christ? The scholastics got sidetracked somewhere with the problem of how the whole Body of Christ could fit into the dimensions of the host and how it can be in many places at once. These questions had not preoccupied patristic writers.

Is it possible to build up a theology of eucharistic realism, compatible with Catholic doctrine, that is based on essence rather than presence? Many who have tried to provide an alternative to the scholastic synthesis have had their efforts condemned. However, let us accept the challenge, albeit with caution.

We must realize that Christianity was born in a *Semitic* culture. The later cultures which came into vogue sometimes failed to appreciate that the conceptualizations and thought patterns of the original Scriptures were different from their own and ended up with some erroneous conclusions.

In regard to the Eucharist we must remember that the Semitic mind tended to conceive things in an elemental as opposed to a holistic way. So, for example, man is spoken of as "flesh and bone," "flesh and blood," etc. Possibly the evangelist John's version of the Eucharist (Chap. 6) in terms of *flesh* and blood, rather than *body* and blood, is the original. The question of the *ipsissima verba* of Jesus in regard to the Eucharist has been thoroughly examined by Joachim Jeremias.[5]

Without going into detail I can remind readers that both the elemental term "flesh" and the holistic term "body" are found in early eucharistic texts. Sometimes both terms are used anarthrously in Greek texts—an indication of an elemental understanding. Of course Latin did not have either a definite or indefinite article, a factor which I believe helped to confuse matters further. There are nuances of meaning which depend on articles or their absence which can be lost in Latin. English, like other modern languages, can express such nuances.

For example, take the sentences: "We ate the lamb," "We ate a lamb," "We ate lamb." The last anarthrous usage designates what I am calling an elemental concept as opposed to a holistic one. This elemental sense corresponds with the idea of substance as understood in ordinary speech.

It seems to me that in the movement from the original Semitic concept, through Greek to Latin, the conception of the Eucharist in elemental terms tended to be replaced with a holistic sense. The trend was somewhat modified by the introduction of the term "substance" in the phrase "the substance of the body of Christ" in the West, though this in turn became obscure with the attribution to it of subtle and esoteric meanings. This was particularly true when it was coupled with the scholastic concept of accidents. Without making a general judgment on the philosophical validity of the substance-accidents analysis, I want to claim that "substance-appearances" is a better pairing for a discussion of the Eucharist.

I would like to argue first that appearances are not the same as accidents. As understood in the scholastic system at least, accidents are an objective constituent of being. They give rise to impressions in an observer. Appearances, however, allow for a subject observing reality to be confused and err. Let me illustrate: a snake may have the appearance of a stick and an observer may assume that it is a stick. The snake certainly does not have the *accidents* of a stick; it has its own. But it may have a stick's appearances. There is no falsehood in reality ("*ens et verum convertuntur*") but there is the possibility of deception through ambiguity. Nature's camouflage is an obvious example. It works because the unwary does not take the whole context into account.

I believe that the Eucharist is better analysed along these lines. The bread and wine of the Eucharist are assumed by the Person of the Word-Jesus. They are possessed through the sending of the Holy Spirit and are identified thereby as substance of his Body and Blood. They do not undergo any physical or physiological change. They must retain their forms as bread and wine to be suitable as our food and drink. A person not knowing the faith and liturgical context would from appearances conclude that they are merely bread and wine. But this would be erroneous.

One implication of the use of the traditional word "substance" is that the bread and wine can be the "stuff" of the Body and Blood of Christ without being a *part*. They become simply substance. The consecrated bread and wine are the Body and Blood *substantially*. They retain the appearances of bread and wine but those who know the full context by faith, who know of the words of consecration and the history behind them, will know that they are something far greater. Sharing in the humanity of Christ they are the sign and instrumental cause of His grace.

I have argued above that a viable ontology (to use Paul VI's term) of the Eucharist must start from the New Testament's expressions. As the quotations from St. Thomas More exemplify, these expressions of identity were repeated by the Fathers, who displayed a belief in realism without using either the expression or concept of "presence." "Essence" is the primary foundation of this ontology. I accept that the concept "presence" may be introduced as a secondary one, as a consequence. But what the Eucharist *is*, is what is present. The presence of the Person Jesus in the Eucharist has to be mediated through the consecrated species if it is to be specifically eucharistic. (The Person of Jesus as God is of course present everywhere.) If we want to assert the presence of the *whole* Jesus – Body, Blood etc. – we have to move out of physics into metaphysics. The scholastics rightly stated that this presence follows "the manner of substance." The principle, *totum in toto et totum in qualibet parte*, applies to substance in natural objects. For example, the substance *marble* is completely verified in this statue both in the whole and in any part. The *whole* statue is marble, and any part, e.g., the head, is marble. This metaphysical principle applies to the host and the consecrated wine.

In an article published some years ago I suggested other analogies explaining the essence of the Eucharist and consequent presence of Christ.[6] These were various kinds of what I called "real tokens." Examples of these: samples; first fruits; a token force; representative teams; Adam in whom all sinned; Christ in whom all are saved, etc. Vatican Council II added another: the Universal Church is present in the local Church (*Lumen Gentium*, n.26).

Given the above understanding of the term *substance* and its use with regard to the Eucharist there is no difficulty with the traditional term "transubstantiation." That term, accused by some of being a neologism, has antecedents dating to the Greek Fathers, as Paul VI pointed out in his encyclical *Mysterium fidei* where he gives parallels: change, transform, transelement (par 47). Thomas More's catena of texts also provides examples.[7]

Disputes about the meaning of the sentences in the New Testament describing the Eucharist intensified at the time of the Reformation. Henry VIII attacked Luther's explanation, Luther counterattacked and More took up the King's part in his *Responsio*.[8] Luther and Zwingli had a heated conversation on the issue, making no impression on each other. Not only were there differences between realists and pure symbolists, but among the realists themselves. One reason for this was that their conception of realism was in terms of presence: Luther proposed the presence of the Body and Blood with the bread and wine; More in the scholastic tradition thought of presence in the accidents of bread and wine. I am suggesting that by making the concept "presence" central and formally dominant they were causing difficulties and thence disagreement. As I have said, they asked the wrong question, viz "How is Christ present in the Eucharist?" Centuries before, Augustine had asked, "How is bread His Body? How the chalice His Blood?"[9] These I believe are better questions. (However, Augustine's answer may not have been so satisfactory!)

In what sense is the eucharistic bread the Body (or Flesh) of Christ? The wine His Blood? In answering, the first choice is between symbolic and real. Zwingli opted for the purely symbolic. If he is right there is no metaphysical problem. However, as More demonstrates, there is a strong tradition, not only of symbolism, but also of realism, both in East and West. Together with some other recent writers, I am going to opt for symbolic realism.

Unfortunately, or maybe fortunately, in the history of thought there have been several concepts of what is "real." Pilate's question, "What is truth?" is not so inane. There is the Aristotelian concept of truth, which is the correspondence of the mind with reality; there is the Platonic which finds reality in a transcendent world of which the things of this world are only a shadow; there is the phenomenological or personalist idea that reality is judged by relationship to man. No doubt there are others. Studies have been made of the meaning of the word "real" or "true" in John's Gospel. These are relevant to the Eucharist because of the words, "My Flesh is true food, My Blood true drink" in Chapter 6:55. John's concept of the true or real is not Aristotelian but is nearer to the Platonic, though influenced by his Semitic and Christian background.[10]

The doctrine of the Eucharist had travelled a long way before the Reformation: from a Semitic mentality, through Greek and Latin thought into scholasticism. Even in the last two centuries there have been fresh attempts to explain the Eucharist influenced by modern physics and philosophies, some of them bizarre,[11] some reasonable but still deemed insufficient by Church authorities.[12]

Gleaning from what I think to be true and seeking to avoid errors and inaccuracies, I would submit briefly my own conclusions.

As liturgical and some patristic formulas indicate, the bread and wine are sanctified by the Holy Spirit. This has the effect of making them the Body and Blood of Christ. The sanctified bread and wine *are* the Body and Blood of Christ. They are possessed and owned by the Person of the Word: this is *My* Body. The Person of Christ communicates truth and grace by the medium of the sacrament, the words and the elements. The bread and wine do not change physically or physiologically but in their natural form are the Flesh/Body and Blood. How? Substantially. The bread and wine, without changing form, become the substance of the Body and Blood. By substance I mean the stuff, matter, the elements. In the Semitic idiom flesh and blood were the elements of humanity. They had their original crude meaning but more abstractly they signified humanity, the human element or medium, sometimes with moral or other overtones.

So far I have not used the term or concept of "presence." It is a term that has been given a very important role in the Catholic and ecumenical theology of the Eucharist as well as in the Magisterium as late as the encyclical *Mysterium fidei* of Paul VI. Having seen what the eucharistic Bread and Wine *are* ontologically, we can bring in secondary and chronologically and logically later ideas which must flow from the primary and original ones.

The Eucharistic Bread and Wine, the sacramental Body and Blood, "contain" the whole Christ, not physically, but following the nature of a sign. "Sacramenta sunt in genere signi," as Aquinas says.[13] Not *any* sign, not a mere sign, but in the case of the Eucharist we are dealing with a "real sign." I have suggested above examples of real signs or real tokens as analogies. A mere token would be such things as flags, rings, red lights. A real token is one which shares the nature or quality of what is symbolized, e.g., a representative, a sample. The Eucharist transcends this category of course, but I think it gives us the genre. The substances of bread and wine, having been consecrated by the invocation of the Holy Spirit, are possessed by the Word, Who is the Person of Jesus, and ontologically are thereby made substance of His Body and Blood, without being incorporated in any way such as digestion, but by being made real symbols in which His whole being can be said to be present and operative, communicating truth (as sign) and grace (as cause). The elements are the eucharistic *verbum visibile* (Augustine) by which the Father speaks to us and offers His love.

The ontological problem of the Eucharist has in a sense been an unfortunate area for confusion and controversy, distracting from its more important spiritual message. Whilst some would spurn it as less worthy of our attention than many other problems affecting Christianity and mankind, it has been central, indeed for some, the epitome of the difference between Catholicism and the Reformation. This was true for Thomas More, Martin Luther, William Tyndale, Thomas Cranmer and others of their time. Many today, both Catholic and Protestant, still give it a high priority in confessional differences.

Thomas More and Germain Marc'hadour, whilst reverencing the concerns of metaphysics, would prefer to contemplate the devotional aspects of the Eucharist.[14] Yet the memory of past bitterness suggests that it is better to heal the wounds of division than risk them festering under the surface. The present essay is offered in that belief.

Our Lady Queen of Peace Church
Gladesville, Australia

Notes

1. Edward Surtz, S.J., *The Works and Days of John Fisher*, Harvard University Press, Cambridge, Mass, 1967, especially Chap. 8, "Answering Oecolam-

padius on the Real Presence"; John Jay Hughes, *Stewards of the Lord*, Sheed and Ward, London, 1970, especially Chap. 7, "The Catholic Apologetic for the Mass in England"; Walter Gordon, "Selected Problems in Thomas More's Controversy with John Frith," *Harvard Theological Review* 69 (April 1976) 131-49; Walter Gordon, "A Needle in a Meadow: A Missing Reference in the More-Frith Controversy," *Moreana* 52 (November 1976) 19-22.

2. *A Treatise Upon the Passion*, The Yale Edition of the Complete Works of St. Thomas More, Vol. 13, ed. Garry E. Haupt (New Haven and London: 1976). All further references to this work will be given in parentheses in the body of my text as CW 13. I have modernized the spelling.

3. See Germain Marc'hadour, *The Bible in the Works of St. Thomas More*, Part I (Nieuwkoop: B. De Graaf, 1969) 131. David feigned madness in the presence of Achish, ruler of Gath, a Philistine city. This incident is narrated in 1 Sam 21, 11-16, and follows David's visit to Ahimelech. The phrase corresponding to *Ferebatur in manibus suis* ("He walked on his hands") is not found in the title of most versions.

4. The Holy Spirit is also present in the Eucharist but one cannot argue, "therefore, this is the Holy Spirit."

5. *The Eucharistic Words of Jesus* (London: SCM Press, 1966). See especially pp. 198-201.

6. Brian Byron, "The Eucharist—A Real Token," *The Clergy Review* 56 (1971) 331-42.

7. E.g., Eusebius Emesenus, *A Treatise*, CW 13, p. 165.

8. The Yale Edition of the Complete Works of St. Thomas More, Vol. 5, ed. John M. Headley (New Haven and London: 1969) 449 ff.

9. Rouët de Journel, *Enchiridion Patristicum*, Herder 1953, 1154: "Quomodo est panis corpus eius? Et Calix, vel quod habet calix, quomodo est sanguis eius?"

10. See a good summary in J. McKenzie, *Dictionary of the Bible* (London: Geoffrey Chapman, 1965), 901-3.

11. Walter Gordon discusses a theory in "Time Space in the Eucharist," *Downside Review* (April 1977): 110-17.

12. Pope Paul VI, *Mysterium fidei*, 1965, pars. 10 and 11.

13. S. Th 3 q 60 a 1.

14. During his visit to Sydney in 1978 Germain gave me a copy of a Holy Hour he had composed using More's devotional writings on the Eucharist.

4 Fisher Close, Middx UB6 9UF
Greenford, Angleterre.

Cher Monsieur l'Abbé,

Si c'est bien St. Thomas More qui m'a poussée d'abord vers le catholicisme, c'est vous, mon père, que j'ai à remercier pour m'avoir précipitée dans l'église catholique... car sans ce que vous avez fait par un beau dimanche au mois de juin 1986, je serais sans doute restée encore comme une nageuse au bord de l'eau, ayant peur de me mouiller les pieds !

J'étais venue à Angers pour passer une semaine au Moreanum, et le premier dimanche de ma visite, vous m'aviez invitée à assister à la messe que vous alliez célébrer dans le petit oratoire de l'Université Catholique. A l'époque, je connaissais la messe déjà bien, car j'avais l'habitude d'y aller en Angleterre, mais souvent en regrettant de ne pas être parmi ceux qui avaient le droit de recevoir le Saint Sacrement. Toutefois, pendant cette messe vous m'avez offert l'hostie comme aux autres, et je l'ai reçue presqu'automatiquement, comme dans un rêve.... et c'est ainsi, mon père, que sans le savoir, vous m'avez donné ma première communion -- une communion qui m'a unie définitivement à l'église catholique, de la façon la plus concrète.

Plus question maintenant de me tenir à l'écart -- il m'a fallu régulariser la situation le plus tôt possible. Alors, une fois revenue en Angleterre, je me suis adressée à Rosemary Rendel, qui a trouvé un très bon prêtre au London Oratory pour m'instruire... et je suis enfin devenue catholique le 14 février 1987. Je n'aurais jamais cru que cela m'aurait apporté tant de joie -- une joie renouvelée le 22 juin 1987 à Paris, lorsque j'ai reçu le Saint Sacrement de votre main, cette fois sans aucune irrégularité.

Voilà ce que vous avez fait pour moi, Monsieur l'Abbé, et je vous en serai reconnaissante toute ma vie.

Je vous écris ce témoignage en français, car j'ai l'habitude de me servir de cette langue pour vous parler et vous écrire. C'est dommage que vous n'êtes pas auprès de moi en ce moment, pour corriger mes erreurs !

Avec toute mon affection et mes amitiés, et mes meilleurs voeux pour l'avenir, je vous quitte, cher Monsieur l'Abbé, en vous remerciant encore une fois pour m'avoir mise sur le bon chemin !

le 24 octobre 1987.

Hazel M. Allport.

We pray for those here present
and all whose lives bring hope to this world.
Lord of the living and the dead,
awaken to the undying light of pardon and peace
those fallen asleep in faith,
...
Gather them all into communion
with Mary, the Mother of God,
and with all your saints.

VII Into Communion…With all your Saints

Nous prions pour ceux qui sont ici présents
et pour tous ceux dont la vie apporte de l'espoir à ce monde.
Seigneur des vivants et des morts,
réveille à la lumière sans déclin du pardon et de la paix
ceux qui se sont endormis dans la foi,
...
Rassemble-les tous dans la communion
avec Marie, la Mère de Dieu,
et avec tous tes saints.

UNIVERSITY OF TSUKUBA

Institute of History and Anthropology

Sakura, Niihari
Ibaraki, 305, Japan

Germano Mercatori, C.P.D.

Ever since we met you for the first time in South Bend in 1965, you have personified for Margaret & me the gentleman scholar one always wants to be with.

You left the same impression, I am sure, with our Japanese amici Mori who had the pleasure & privilege of meeting you here in Japan during your 1978 Far Eastern journey. We also cherish the memory of yr beautifully celebrating Holy Mass using Thomas More's "Mirrour of Vertue" chalice at our home in Tsukuba.

Amice suavissime atque doctissime Mori omnium amicorum, vale feliciter mi Germane amicissime,

Tsukubae, xi. Novembris A.D. MCMLXXXVII

Totus ex animo tuus
Paulus Akio Canada

MARION LEATHERS KUNTZ

Angela da Foligno:
A Paradigm of Venetian Spirituality
in the Sixteenth Century

WHEN FIRST I READ FATHER GERMAIN MARC'HADOUR'S study, "Thomas More and His Foursome of 'Blessed Holy Women',"[1] I was happy to be reminded of some of the feminine saints whose lives had impressed More: Anastasia, Hildegard von Bingen, Bridget of Sweden, and Catherine of Siena. I am happy also to recall that with the exception of Saint Anastasia, these holy women are the same ones whose influence upon More's contemporary Guillaume Postel cannot be minimized. In place of St. Anastasia, the woman who completes Postel's quaternary of "blessed holy women" is Angela da Foligno, whose name appears often in the writings of Postel. Angela's saintly life and teachings reveal the theme of love which was also common to the four admired by More.

Other associations make Angela a fitting subject for an essay honoring Father Germain. Like him, Angela was a Franciscan tertiary. And as 1985 was an important year for those devoted to More, so it was also for those devoted to Angela. In 1985 there were celebrations to mark the fiftieth anniversary of the canonization of More and of John Fisher, and there were celebrations to extol the life and work of the blessed Angela da Foligno. Perhaps the most significant of these was the publication of the first critical edition of Angela's writings.[2] On their return trip from Rome to Angers in May 1985, Father Germain and his group of pilgrims stopped for two days in Assisi, significant not only for St. Francis but also for Angela, who had her first mystical experience while on a pilgrimage to Assisi. More and Postel themselves shared many ideas, and Postel's admiration of More and his family was expressed in print. More is mentioned in the *Appendix* to the *Chronicon* of Ioannes Carion of which Postel is the author.[3] In Postel's *Les tres merveilleuses victoires des femmes* . . . (*The Most Marvelous Victories of Women*. . .) he wrote of women who were distinguished not only in divine letters but also in humane letters. Among those whom Postel named were "the three daughters of the late M. Thomas Morus . . . ."[4]

This study then is offered with humility and affection to a modern day scholar and saintly man in the hope that the life and influence of Angela da Foligno will become for him another example of "blessed holy women."

The facts of Angela's life are incompletely known, but she was born probably in 1248 into a wealthy family of Foligno; she lived in Foligno until her death in 1309 and is buried there in the Church of Saint Francis. The cult of Angela was officially validated by Pope Clement XI in 1701. Her feast day with Mass and Office is celebrated in the Franciscan Order every year on the fourth of January. The title of Beata was granted to her without a regular canonical process (*Libro* 40–41).

Michele Faloci Pulignani, one of her modern biographers, has noted: "If the city of Foligno is known in all the world—at least in the Christian world—the reason is that there was born, and there died six centuries ago a woman named Angela. No one has recorded her family name, as no one remembers the cognomen of Francis of Assisi."[5] She was a woman devoted to things of the world, and she took great pleasure in luxuries. Although married and the mother of numerous children, Angela was more dedicated to pleasure than to her duties as wife and mother. Abbé Ferré, one of her more authoritative biographers, described her as "a woman who loved the world and an easy-going life, who loved good cheer and pleasure, with a cultivated and open mind, impulsive and headstrong, of a somewhat restive temper, a sharp tongue, quick in repartee."[6] Her life of pleasure, however, did not bring satisfaction. When she began to feel some remorse, she prayed to Saint Francis to provide a confessor who could truly understand and who could beg for the grace of total forgiveness (Ferré viii). Saint Francis answered her prayer: when she entered the Cathedral of Foligno, a Franciscan was preaching, and suddenly she decided that this man was to be her confessor (Pulignani x–xi).[7] The Franciscan friar, Fra Arnaldo, like Angela a native of Foligno, became her spiritual father and a significant influence on her life. After meeting Fra Arnaldo,

Angela determined to live a better life, but her commitment was coupled with grief. At the same time that she renounced some of her luxuries she lost by death her mother, her husband, and her children. Her grief was somewhat assuaged, however, by her increasing spirituality. She sold her property and possessions and journeyed to Assisi to beg acceptance in the Third Order of Saint Francis. She took the habit of the penitents of Saint Francis in 1290 or 1291, when she was about forty-two years old. During her sojourn in Assisi a strange occurrence befell Angela. As she entered the Basilica of Saint Francis to venerate his tomb, "she was overcome by so violent an attack of crying and of nerves that, like a mad woman, she threw herself on the ground wailing and weeping, causing a great commotion. The brothers and the devout gathered around her, waiting until she became calm after that so strange outburst. Fra Arnaldo, her kinsman, at that time continued to remain in the convent at Assisi, since he considered it prudent to distance himself from the scene and await a conclusion to the event" (Pulignani xi).

Then Fra Arnaldo reprimanded Angela for her strange behavior and urged her companions not to accompany her again to Assisi. After some time, however, Fra Arnaldo returned to Foligno and desired to question Angela about the causes of her behavior at Assisi. Angela refused to reveal the causes until Fra Arnaldo agreed not to reveal "that which the Beata was calling 'the divine secret'. . ." (Pulignani xii). Then Angela began to explain how the Holy Trinity had taken possession of her and forced her to cry out, "Unknown love, you do not believe me! Why do you leave me? Why? Why? Why?" (Ferré ix). Angela spoke in Italian, and Arnaldo transcribed her words in Latin. Angela and Arnaldo "were distressed and uncertain if those revelations were true and whether Fra Arnaldo had interpreted those words correctly or not. They asked God for a sign (Ferré xiii) and then a divine voice was heard to say: "All which has been written in that little book is in accordance with my will; it has also proceeded from me, and I shall affix my seal to it" (Pulignani xiii).

Angela's sanctity became so well known through her writings and through her life of charity that a number of Tertiaries, men and women, gathered around her to advance in holiness (Baumann 98).[8] Later she established at Foligno a community of sisters who chose the cloistered life because they wanted to devote themselves fully to works of charity. In addition, Angela was "the head of a group of theologians and philosophers, a group without laws and statutes; very many people from Italy and other countries came to this group to be enlightened by her, whether by the spirit or by the intellect. One in the group was the celebrated Fra Ubertino da Casale, who came from Paris to Foligno to be illuminated by her." Fra Ubertino also noted that ascetics and mystics from over the Alps were seeking her counsel. Consequently, she was constrained to write many letters to personal friends and to groups (Pulignani x).

The fame of Angela da Foligno was spread not only by her disciples but also by her writings, which were dictated by Angela and recorded by Fra Arnaldo. *Angela De Fvlginio, in qvo ostenditvr Nobis vera via qua possumus sequi vestigia nostri Redemptoris* (*Angela of Foligno, in which is shown to us the true path by which we can follow the steps of our Redeemer*) enjoyed numerous editions, the first of which was anterior to 1500, although no one has seen this edition. The first known publication was printed at Toledo by Cardinal Ximenes. The second edition was that of Venice, issued in 1521 by the priest, Paolo Roselli, who wrote a beautiful preface in Latin and Greek and dedicated his edition to Suor Angelica, abbess of Santa Lucia in Venice (Pulignani xvii). Throughout the centuries there have been numerous translations into Italian, French, Spanish, Catalan, German, English, Danish; in our own century a new version in Italian was published at Florence in 1922. In 1985 a critical edition in Latin and Italian was published at Assisi.[9]

The influence of Angela da Foligno and an interpretation of her book are worthy of a monograph. In the present consideration, however, we shall investigate the influence of the Blessed Angela on Venetian piety as it relates specifically to Mother Zuana, the Virgin of Venice whose life was heralded by Guillaume Postel. Recently we have discovered that Lodovico Domenichi also wrote a biography of Giovanna (Zuana).[10] We cannot say with certainty when Postel first became aware of the writings of Angela da Foligno, but we may surmise that it was during his second Venetian sojourn in 1547–49. In his book, *Les tres merveilleuses victoires des femmes du nouveau-monde*, (*The Most Marvelous Victories of Women of the New World. . .*), published in 1553, he wrote: "Whoever is desirous of learning and has read the Evangelical doctrine which was divinely revealed to blessed Angela da Foligno will see that, except for Jesus Christ and his apostles, there never was a doctor or preacher in the world who came close to it [her doctrine]. Saint Catherine of Siena's is comparable" (Sig. Bii^v).[11]

Postel's admiration for Angela de Foligno did not decline, and he often mentioned her as one of the women who had been illuminated by God.[12] In 1577, in letters to Jacopo Corbinelli, Postel again spoke of Angela Fvlignea, "whose goal is the witness of returning the highest love of God through Christ which has been placed in Poverty, Scorn, and Pain; and by bearing these calmly there is the greatest virtue, in contradiction to the Riches, Pleasures, and Honors of this world."[13] In 1578, during Postel's confinement in the monastery of Saint Martin des Champs, Corbinelli wrote to Vincenzo Pinelli to request for Postel the *Tesori di sapienza evangelica* (*Treasures of Evangelical Wisdom*) of Angela da Foligno.[14] The request by Corbinelli indicates that Postel continued to cherish the life and teachings of the Beata Angela, even as his own life was drawing to a close. We shall endeavor to pinpoint in this study which teachings of Angela appealed to Postel to the extent that they became for him a paradigm for the spiritual life and for universal restitution; in addition, we shall compare the teachings of Angela da Foligno in relation to those of the Virgin of Venice whom Postel called the "madre del mondo" (mother of the world), and whose life he extolled as that in which Christ dwelled most fully.

After Saint Francis had appeared to Angela in a dream and after her conversion, Angela sold all her goods, distributing the proceeds to the poor. She then devoted herself to a life of perfect poverty. Her poverty defined the love which she demonstrated to all, especially to the lepers whom she nursed in the hospital of Foligno. Angela "saw Christ in the sick, and through the sweetness which she experienced with them she was as if sharing in the sweetness of Christ."[15] A characteristic note of her spirituality is its Christocentrism, which permeates her whole spiritual journey. "The Cross, for Angela, is the fountain of purification and transformation of the Soul. In the warm embrace of the company of Christ one finds His poverty, pain, and scorn. Love's action, which is the action of Christ, carries one to mystical union with Him" (*Biblioteca Sanctorum*, 1187). The Cross of Christ becomes a leit-motif for Angela's teachings. On the title page of several editions of her book, Angela is pictured carrying a large cross; she holds in her hands flagella indicating Christ's shame, which she wishes to emulate. In the foreground are two crowns of thorns, one for Christ, one for Angela. In the background of the engraving is a ladder by which one may ascend to God through suffering the poverty, pain, and scorn of His Christ. The engraving is bounded on three sides by the words, *summa paupertas, summus dolor*, and *summus despectus*. According to Angela's teachings, only through living the highest poverty, the highest pain, and the highest scorn can one ascend to God through Christ.[16]

The life and work of the blessed Angela revealed a mystical journey which was guided by three successive transformations of the soul:

the transformation in the humanity of Christ, the transformation in the divinity of Christ with the first infusion, the transformation in God with the most perfect union. This last grade corresponds to the consummate union such as that enjoyed by St. Teresa de Jesús, St. John of the Cross, the Venetian Virgin, and Postel himself.

The principles upon which Angela based her program for the spiritual life are also found in Venetian spirituality, especially in the Quattrocento and Cinquencento, and this would be expected, since Franciscan spirituality played a prominent role in Venetian piety.[17] There are, however, specific aspects of Angela's piety which are peculiarly hers and which reappear in the teachings of the Virgin of Venice and her chosen "figliolo," Guillaume Postel.

The foundation upon which Angela based her spiritual journey was the pure and true love of God. Throughout her writings Angela proclaims a love in which the lovers are truly united, man with God, God with man. In a vision the Holy Spirit spoke to Angela about love:

> and there is no one who can excuse himself from that love, because every person can love God; and He does not require anything except that the soul seek and love Him, because He truly loves the soul, and He is the very love of the soul. . . .He was explaining his passion and other things which He did for us; and He was adding: See if there is anything in me except love; and my Soul was very certainly understanding because He was nothing except love. . . .Therefore He was saying again to me: my daughter who is sweet to me, love me, because you are loved much more than you love me. My beloved, love me; and He was saying: great is the love which I have for the soul which loves me without malice.[18]

This is the passionate, all consuming love of God which guides mankind to the true *cognitio Dei*. This knowledge of God, gained through divine illumination and through the grace of God, is followed by love which transforms the lover into the beloved. Angela writes:

> . . . so the soul united with God through the perfect grace of divine love becomes as if wholly divine and transformed in God; without a change of its own substance the soul transforms itself completely in its life in the love of God and becomes as if totally divine. Lo, how great a good does the knowledge of God bring to us; indeed it is necessary . . . that, in the path of God and in him who wishes to have God, the knowledge of God precedes,

and afterwards love which transforms the lover into the beloved follows. . . .(*Angela de Fvlginio* 250-51).[19]

Angela's emphasis upon knowledge of God (*cognitio dei*) as a prerequisite for transforming love is significant, since it demonstrates that the mental and spiritual faculties are interdependent: knowledge of God effects love of God; to love God one must know God.

This mystical transformation into a unity of love became for Angela a *societas* in which the lover must share the life of the other. The *societas* of Christ was granted by God the Father, and Christ was never without that *societas*. Angela described this "society" as follows:

> Moreover, the Society which God the Father Almighty willed according to His own wisest dispensation, that His own most beloved son would have in that world, is this: first, the most perfect, continuous and highest poverty; second, the most perfect, continuous and highest grief. That was the Society with which Christ was associated throughout His life to give to us the example of choosing and esteeming and enduring, even unto death, this Society above all other things (*Angela de Fvlginio* 259).[20]

The way of poverty (*povertà*), scorn (*disprezzo*), and pain (*dolore*) is the only direct route (*via recta*) by which the soul may approach God. This path is the ladder by which man ascends and joins the *societas Christi*. When the soul of Christ, according to Angela, was associated with the highest *dolore* and was united to the human body and to divinity, it was at once filled with the highest wisdom and immediately Christ became a *viator* (wayfarer) and a *comprehensor* (one who has obtained knowledge). For each man to participate in the *societas Christi* he must take upon himself the characteristics of the beloved, that is, the *povertà*, *disprezzo*, and *dolore* of Christ (*Angela de Fvlginio* 285). Only through these associations of Christ can man become a *viator* and *comprehensor*. Angela in her final admonition to her "sons and daughters" urged them to judge no sinner since God would lead them all back into his fold; rather each man should practice mutual love and profound humility. She then reiterates the inheritance of the *via recta*:

> And I leave to you my whole inheritance, which is also the inheritance of Jesus Christ: namely, poverty, pain and scorn, that is, the life of Christ (*Angela de Fvlginio* 428).

The influence of Angela da Foligno on Guillaume Postel can be ascertained not only by his statements about Angela which have been cited above, but more significantly by his use of the theme of *povertà, disprezzo*, and *dolore* in relation to the Virgin of Venice and to his own philosophy of restitution.[21] Indeed almost every teaching of Angela can be found in the writings of Postel.

Postel's relationship to the Virgin of Venice paralleled in several aspects the relationship of the Blessed Angela and Fra Arnaldo. In 1547 in Venice Postel met at the Ospedaletto of Saints John and Paul a woman known only as Giovanna. Like Angela, the family name of Giovanna was unknown, even to Postel. The history and teachings of this amazing woman Postel unfolds specifically in three books *Les tres merveilleuses victoires des femmes. . .* , (*The Most Marvelous Victories of Women*), *Le prime nove del altro mondo* (*The First New Things of the other World*) and *Il libro della divina ordinatione* (*The Book of the Divine Ordination*), and in countless other writings. Giovanna spent all of her time and efforts in work among the poor and sick of Venice. About 1520 she began to feed the poor and care for the sick in a temporary shelter near the Church of Saints John and Paul. She convinced some wealthy Venetians that they should practice the charity of Christ by building a permanent shelter for the sick and homeless (Kuntz 69-92).[22] So great was the Venetian Virgin's devotion that her temporal body was filled with the spirit of God and the living Christ dwelled most fully within her person (Kuntz 77-79). Because her heart and soul were consumed by the living Christ, she gave herself completely to Him. Therefore, to serve Christ she spent her life in service to others. In following the path of Christ and service to Him her own life reflected the *povertà, disprezzo*, and *dolore* of Christ, the same characteristics advocated by Angela da Foligno as necessary for participation in the *societas* of Christ.[23] When Postel first met the Virgin of Venice and heard her prophecies about the restitution of all things, he, like Fra Arnaldo in regard to Angela, doubted that an unlearned woman could be truly illuminated with the spirit of God. However, after searching out a brother at the Church of San Francesco della Vigna who had heard her confessions and who had confirmed to Postel the divine voice speaking through this woman, Postel realized that the prophecies spoken by Giovanna were "of power and supernatural virtue" (*Le prime nove . . .* , sig. Biii) Again and again Postel tells the story of her divine immutation in 1540 in Venice:

> Thus in 1540 in the year of salvation and of the restitution of the first or higher part, a mystery happened, and the spiritual or heavenly body of Christ descended into the very holy virgin,

Johanna by name, an attendant of the Xenodocheus, next to the church of John and Paul at Venice. Before she died she was ordered by God to reveal this mystery to me, as if to her own first born, about seven years after it happened, so that in my own time I might make it clear to the whole world.[24]

Postel himself received a divine immutation in 1552, when the heavenly body of the Venetian Virgin in whom Christ dwelled descended into the old body of Postel and made him a new man with reason restored (Kuntz 101-108). Postel was chosen by the Venetian Virgin because of a divine impulse, similar to that which led the Blessed Angela to Fra Arnaldo. Postel makes clear, however, that the Virgin of Venice, his Madre Giovanna or Zuana, received the indwelling of Christ's presence because she possessed love toward God in the highest degree and revealed this love by practical charity toward all people (Sloane ms. 1411, fol. 439). Love, according to Postel, is the highest goal of divine and human law (*Idem*, fol. 438ᵛ). Because of her love of God and her expression of this love the Venetian Virgin became the fulfillment of the law and true bride of Christ. The Venetian Virgin as the spouse of Christ represented both wisdom and love which, in union, are the foundation of Christ's church (*Le prime nove. . .*, sig. Kiii). Postel, in describing the highest grade of love and wisdom found in the Venetian Virgin, links her with other illuminated women who have the same virtues; among the first of these is the blessed Angela da Foligno. Postel writes:

> May they know how it is necessary in every way that this Restitution of everything, destroyed by Satan, have its basis in the same Principle, or rather in the most perfect Love which has already been demonstrated by countless women such as the Sibyls and many others; and especially by the blessed Angela of Foligno, by Saint Catherine of Sienna, by Saint Hildegard, and by Mathilda, Bridget and others whose writings seem inferior to no Doctor. Since through the way of Love not only men but much more clearly women are illuminated by the act of perfect intelligence of the word of God, Christ has wished in His own Bride and Mother of the World [Giovanna] to show the height of the power of the Intellect of true Wisdom joined with the highest grade of Love so that this Fourth Principle and Foundation of His own Church be and become similar to the other two most kindred, that is, to Judaism and to Christianity.[25]

So influenced was Postel by the Venetian Virgin that he adopted her teachings as his own "platform of restitution," namely, *Amor dei, vnitiua virtus, Charitas in proximum,* and *virtus diffusiua sui*: love of God, unifying virtue, Charity toward one's neighbor, and virtue diffusive of itself (Sloane ms. 1411, fol. 439ᵛ). These are also the themes which are constantly found in the teachings of Angela da Foligno. Postel felt compelled to make Mother Johanna's teachings known because of the Truth which they revealed. He wrote that "such a great burden lies upon me that there will be woe upon me if I do not evangelize this [her teaching]" (Sloane ms. 1411, fol. 439ᵛ). Postel often wrote that his Madre Giovanna was able to interpret the most obscure passages in the *Zohar*, although she was untutored in the ancient languages. One of the most significant effects of his relationship with the Venetian Virgin was Postel's increasing interest in Hebrew sources. Postel also wrote that the doctrine of the *prisci theologi*, the ancient theologians, had been revealed to the Venetian Virgin as also the *Dottrina Sibyllina*, the Sibylline Doctrine (*Le prime noue* . . . , sig. Kiiii).[26] The understanding of Hebrew sources by the Venetian Virgin raises the question of the use of Hebrew sources by the Blessed Angela whose teachings appear to have influenced the Venetian Virgin and subsequently Postel, but this line of investigation must wait for future research.[27]

We may assume that the teachings of Angela da Foligno became known to Postel during his association with the Venetian Virgin in Venice between 1547 and 1549. Since Mother Giovanna had a Franciscan confessor before Postel's arrival, she could easily have heard about the Franciscan Tertiary Angela from the brothers of San Francisco della Vigna. In addition, the theme of Love expressed by the virtues of *povertà, dolore,* and *disprezzo* – the major theme of Angela da Foligno – does not become central to Postel's thought before his meeting with the Venetian Virgin in 1547. *Amor, povertà, dolore,* and *disprezzo* appear as major themes in Postel's books and manuscripts in 1553, about six years after his meeting with the *Madre del mondo* and about one year after his divine "immutation" by the "Mother of the World," the Venetian Virgin. Related to the theme of love is pardon, and Postel constantly speaks of the need to forgive (Kuntz 45–46; Sloane ms. 1411, fol. 396–396ᵛ). Angela likewise speaks of pardon in relationship to love.

Whereas we can only speculate how the teachings of Angela da Foligno became known to Postel, there is clear evidence that the teachings of Angela had profound influence on Guillaume Postel and appear often in his writings. We reiterate these specifically:

(1) The Love of God and charity toward all men, the central theme of Angela's teachings, become the basis of Postel's prophecies about the restitution of all things.

(2) Poverty, pain, and scorn are the virtues which best express the love of God. Angela wrote: "And I leave to you my whole inheritance, which is also the inheritance of Christ Jesus, namely: poverty, pain and scorn, that is, the life of Christ" (*Angela de Fvlginio* 428). In countless references Postel links *caritas* with *paupertas, dolor,* and *probrum* or *despectum,* and all are essential for the restitution of all things. In a significant passage he wrote:

> ... It is necessary that all who truly will understand this mystery of the Restitution of all things and truly proclaim it from the soul be so moved . . . toward all men on account of the heavenly Father that not only do they desire to die for those individuals either in Poverty, Scorn, or Pain and are altogether ready to live in extreme Love, but also to pardon completely and to bear toward others their faults. . . .[28]

(3) Knowledge of God as knowledge of truth, and vice versa, is expressed by Angela and also Postel (*Angela de Fvlginio* 248–57; Sloane ms. 1411, fol. 391).

(4) The idea of Christ as *viator* and *comprehensor* is related by Angela to Christ's infusion with the highest wisdom.[29] Similarly, Postel, after his infusion with the presence of Christ in the spiritual form of the Venetian Virgin, believed that his reason was restored to its state before the Fall and that he was not only a *viator* but also a *comprehensor*.[30]

(5) The idea of *societas* which Angela described was the *societas divina* in which Christ participated from the moment of his conception. This *societas* which the Father willed for His beloved Son was that of *perfectissima, continua et summa paupertas, perfectissimus, summus, et continuus despectus,* and *perfectissimus continuus et summus dolor.* Angela also noted: "that Christ had been associated with this society throughout His life" (*Angela de Fvlginio* 259). Postel used the word *societas* to indicate the *persona* or that part of human nature which is weaker and joined to matter and for which God created the universe (Sloane ms. 1411, fol. 379ᵛ). Postel also related the *Societas Jesu*, to which Society he belonged from 1544–1547, to the ideas of *povertà, dolore,* and *disprezzo*. In an autograph manuscript of 1560 Postel wrote: ". . . Romam

veni deductus a Iesuitis ut ibi cum illis agerem Probro Paupertatique [Dolore]." (. . . I came to Rome drawn by the Jesuits so that I might live there with them in Scorn, Poverty, and Pain.)[31]

This initial study on the relation of Blessed Angela da Foligno to Venetian spirituality as revealed in the Venetian Virgin and in Guillaume Postel has noted numerous strands of Postel's thought which have their source in the teachings of Beata Angela da Foligno. As a tribute to Angela and as one final indication of Postel's debt to her we cite from his *Description et Charte de la Terre Saincte (Description and Map of the Holy Land)*, 1553: "Bethany was a place about two short miles from Jerusalem, where were located in part the possessions of this glorious and Holy family, Mary Magdalen and Martha, and Lazarus their brother, where with the first compendium of his Church it pleased God to give substance to the true Etymology of the name Bethany which means House of Poverty, Pain, and Scorn."[32]

Georgia State University

Notes

1. Germain Marc'hadour, "Thomas More and His Foursome of 'Blessed Holy Women'" in *Thomas-Morus-Gesellschaft Jahrbuch 1983/84*, ed. Hermann Boventer (Düsseldorf: Triltsch, 1984), 113–30.

2. *Il Libro della Beata Angela da Foligno*, Edizione critica, Ludger Thier OFM and Abele Calufetti OFM editors (Grottaferrata Romae: Editiones Collegii S. Bonaventurae ad Claras Aquas, 1985). I am deeply indebted to Fra Giuseppe of the Church of San Francesco, Foligno, and to Dottore Leonello Radi, Direttore Generale della Cassa di Risparmio di Foligno, for making a copy of this important text available to me. All subsequent references to this work will be incorporated into the text.

3. *Ioannis Carionis mathematici Chronicorum libri tres. Appendix eorum, quae a fine Carionis ad haec vsque tempora contigere.* (Venetiis: Ex Officina Eramiana Vincentii Valgrisii, 1553), 463.

4. *Les tres merveilleuses victoires des femmes du novveav monde,.* . . (Paris, Iehan Gueullart, 1553) sig. Biiii[v]. All subsequent references to this work will be indicated in parentheses in the text.

5. *L'autobiografia e gli scritti della Beata Angela da Foligno. Pubblicati e annotati da un codice sublacense per cura di Mons, M. Faloci Pulignani.* Tradotti da Maria Castiglione Humani con prefazione di Giovanni Joergensen (Città

di Castello: Casa editrice "Il Solco," 1932), vii. All subsequent references to this work will be given in parentheses in the body of the text as Pulignani. Also see Rudolph M. Bell, *Holy Anorexia* (Chicago: University of Chicago Press, 1985), 105–13, for some interesting comments about Angela.

6. "Une femme amie du monde et de la vie facile, amie de la bonne chair et du plaisir, un esprit cultivé et ouvert, une nature pleine d'abandon, impulsive et tenace, un tempérament quelque peu frondeur, une langue sarcastique et prompte à la riposte." *Le livre de l'expérience des vrais fidèles: texte latin publié d'après le manuscrit d'Assise*, par M. J. Ferré traduit avec la collaboration de L. Baudry (Paris: E. Droz, 1927), vii. All subsequent references to this work will be indicated in parentheses within the text as Ferré.

7. See also Émile Baumann, *L'anneau d'or* . . . (Paris: B. Grasset, 1924), 88–89. All subsequent references to this work will be cited as Baumann within the text.

8. "Ceux qu'Angèle appelle ici ses frères et ses fils étaient des moines, surtout des franciscains, peut-être quelques mondains convertis, dont elle dirigeait la vie spirituelle. Catherine de Sienne aura de même autour de sa figure séraphique des contemplateurs et des disciples. Les doctes venaient chercher auprès d'Angèle, la théologie infuse, celle qu'on n'apprend pas dans les livres. Les mondains lui demandaient le secret de la conversion parfaite; ils touchaient en l'approchant les délices de la pauvreté, la paix d'une vie simplifiée par la pénitence; et les illuminations de ses extases ressemblaient à une descente du Paradis sur un visage humain."

"Those whom Angela here calls her brothers and her sons were monks, especially Franciscans, perhaps some converted worldlings, whose spiritual life she directed. Catherine of Siena was likewise to have contemplators and disciples round about her Seraphic figure. The learned came to get from Angela the infused theology which books do not teach. Worldly people asked her for the secret of a perfect conversion; in approaching her they felt the pleasures of poverty, the peace of a life which had been simplified by penitence; and the illuminations of her ecstasies resembled Heaven's descent upon a human face."

9. The text was actually printed at Assisi, Tipografia Porziuncola, in the series listed above, note 2.

10. See my soon to be published article in *Studi Veneziani* on "The Biography of Giovanna Veronese by Lodovico Domenichi."

11. "qui haura, auec desyr d'apprendre leu la doctrine Euangelique Diuinement à la beata Angela de Foligni reuelée, Voira qu'il ny eut jamais sauf Jesus Christ et ses Apostres docteur ne prescheur au monde qui approchast d'elle. Le semblable est de celle de saincte Catherine de Siene. . . ."

12. See, for example, *Le Prime Noue del altro mondo* (Padova?, 1555) sig. Kii[v]. All subsequent references to this work will be cited in the text as *Le prime noue* . . .

13. Postel's letters to Corbinelli are published in *Dantis Aligerii praecellentissimi poetae De VVLGARI Eloqventia. Libri Duo* (Parisiis, 1577), 65–75. See p. 71 for Postel's statements about Angela: "cuius scopus est, summi erga Deum

amoris, per Christum referendi, testimonium positum in Paupertate, Probro, et Dolore, vbi tolerando aequanimiter, summa virtus est, contra Diuitias, Delicias, et Honores huius mundi."

14. Rita Calderini De-Marchi, *Jacopo Corbinelli et les érudits Français d'après la correspondance inédite Corbinelli-Pinelli (1566–1587)* (Milano: Ulrico Hoepli, 1914), 150, n. 3.

15. *Bibliotheca Sanctorum* (Roma: Istituto Giovanni XXIII nella Pontificia Università Lateranense, 1961), 1187. All subsequent references to this text will appear in parentheses in the text.

16. On the title page of the 1521 Venetian edition Angela is pictured holding in her hands the cross of Christ and some branches of myrrh.

17. See for example Silvio Tramontin, "La Cultura monastica del Quattrocento dal primo patriarca Lorenzo Giustiniani ai Camaldolesi, Paolo Giustiniani e Pietro Quirini," in *Storia della Cultura Veneta*, 3/1, (Vicenza: Neri Pozza, 1980), 431–57; Vittore Branca, "L'Umanesimo veneziano alla fine del Quattrocento, Ermolao Barbaro e il suo circolo," *Storia della Cultura Veneta* 3/1, 123–75; Aldo Stella, "Movimenti di riforma nel Veneto nel Cinque-Seicento," *Storia della Cultura Veneta* 4/1, 1–21; *Venezia e Lorenzo Giustiniani*, a cura di Silvio Tramontin con la collaborazione di Franco Donaglio (Venezia: Comune di Venezia. Ufficio Affari Istituzionali, 1981). *Renovatio Urbis: Venezia nell'età di Andrea Gritti (1523–1538)*, a cura di Manfredo Tafuri (Roma: Officina Edizioni, 1984); Margaret King, *Venetian Humanism in the Age of Patrician Dominance* (Princeton, N. J.: Princeton UP, 1986).

18. "Et non est aliquis qui possit se excusare de isto amore, quia omnis persona potest amare Deum: et ipse non requirit aliud, nisi vt anima requirat, et diligat eum, quia ipse veraciter diligit eam et ipse est amor animae: . . . explicabat passionem et caetera quae pro nobis fecit: et subiungebat. Vide ergo si in me est aliud nisi amor: et comprehendebat anima mea certissime, quod ipse non erat nisi amor. . . . Dicebat igitur mihi iterum: filia mea dulcis mihi ama me, quia tu es multo plus amata, quam tu ames me. Amata mea, ama me: et dicebat. Immensus est amor quem habeo animae quae me diligit sine malicia." *Angela de Fvlginio, in quo ostenditur nobis vera via qua possumus sequi vestigia nostri Redemptoris* (Parisiis, Apud Guillelmum Chavdiere, 1598), 66–67. Subsequent references to this work will be given in parentheses in the body of the text, cited as *Angela de Fvlginio.* . . ."

19. ". . . sic anima vnita cum Deo per gratiam perfectam amoris diuini, quasi tota diuina efficitur, et in Deum transformatur, non mutata propria substantia sed transformat se totam in sua vita in Dei amore, et quasi tota fit diuina. Ecce quanta bona affert nobis cognitio Dei, oportet enim . . . quod in via Dei et in eo qui Deum vult habere, quod eius cognitio praecedat, et postea sequatur amor qui transformat amantem in amatum:. . . ."

20. "Societas autem quam Deus pater Altissimus secundum suam sapientissimam dispensationem voluit, vt filius suus dilectissimus haberet in isto mundo, haec est. Primo perfectissima, continua et summa paupertas. Secundo perfectissimus summus et continuus despectus. Tertio perfectissimus continuus et summus dolor. Ista fuit societas a qua Christus fuit associatus in tota sua

vita, vt exemplum nobis tribueret hanc super omnia eligendi et diligendi et tolerandi vsque ad mortem. . . ."

21. For Postel's concept of man as *viator* and *comprehensor* because of Christ in his person, see M. L. Kuntz, *Guillaume Postel, Prophet of the Restitution of All Things* (The Hague, Martinus Niihoff, 1981). All subsequent references to this work will be indicated in the body of the text as Kuntz.

22. Also see M. L. Kuntz, *Guglielmo Postello e la 'Vergine Veneziana.' Appunti storici sulla vita spirituale dell' Ospedaletto nel cinquecento*, Quaderni 21 (Venezia: Centro Tedesco di Studi Veneziani, 1981); "Guillaume Postel and the World State: Restitution and the Universal Monarchy," *History of European Ideas*, 4/3, part 1, 309–11; 4/3, part 2, 449–53 (1983).

23. Note Postel's words in *Les tres merveilleuses victoires des femmes*, sig. D-iiii: "Ainsi comme la souueraine Authorité a esté par le Nouueau Adam au Monde replantée, soubz le tiltre de POVRETE DOVLEVR et MESPRIS, pour confondre les Sataniques et Babyloniques princes, qui se voulantz deifier et faire proprietaires de ce monde, veulent en Richesse auaricieuse, en VOLVPTE vitupereuse, et en HONNEURS indeuz au monde commander. Pour ceste cause ma tressaincte Mere IOCHANNE ha en telle POVRETE DOVLEVR et MESPRIS comme son Espoux voulu passer ceste vie, sans soy donner à cognoistre à aultre personne du monde qu'à moy, et ce par l'expres commandement de IESVS mon Pere, qui luy hauoit ainsi expressément ordonné."

"Thus as the sovereign Authority was put back again into the world by the New Adam, under the sign of POVERTY PAIN and SCORN, so as to confound the satanic princes of Babylon, who aspiring to self-deification and an appropriation of this world, want to govern as its wealthy misers, vile voluptuaries, and so-called "Worshipfuls." For that cause my very holy mother JOHANNA has wanted, like her Spouse, without allowing anyone else in the world but me to know her, to spend this life in POVERTY PAIN and SCORN, and this by the special commandment of JESUS my Father, who had expressly ordered her to do so."

24. "Anno itaque salutis et primae siue superioris partis Restitutae 1540 innotuit et in Sacrosanctam virginem Iochannam nomine, Xenodochii iuxta Iohannis et Pauli templum Venetiis erecti ministram descendit spirituale siue coeleste Christi corpus, cuius mysterium iussa est coelitus antequam euolaret in Coelum mihi tanquam eius primogenito reuelare septem aut circiter annis postquam accideret ut suo tempore toti illud patefacerem orbi." The British Library, Sloane ms. 1411, fol. 431^v. All subsequent references to this ms. will be incorporated into the body of the text, cited as Sloane ms. 1411.

25.". . . Cognoschino come è ad ogni modo necessario che questa RESTITVTIONE d'ogni cosa per Satanasso destruita habbia il suo fondamento per uia del medesimo Principio cioe, di perfetissimo Affetto Hauendo dunque gia mostrato per innumerabili Donne, come erano le Sibylle, et altre infinite, et massimamente per la beata Agniola da Foligno per S. Catarina da Siena, per S. Hildegarda, et Mechtilda, Brigita et altre li cui scritti si uedono à niuno Dottore inferiori, come per la via dello Affetto non solamente gli huomini ma molto piu chiaramente le Donne sono illuminate, per la consumatione della perfetta intelligentia del verbo di Dio, Christo ha uoluto nella sua Sposa et Madre del mondo, mostrar il colmo della possanza di detto Intelletto o uera Sapienza congiunto col sommo grado dell'Affetto, accioche questo Quarto Principio et Fondamento della sua Chiesa sia et si uegga essere simile à gli altre doi prossimi cioe il Giudaico et il Christiano." *Le prime nove*,... sigs, Kii^v–Kiii.

26. Also see Kuntz, *Guillaume Postel*, 82–86.

27. On the topic of love in Medieval Judaism, see Georges Vajda, *L'Amour de Dieu dans la théologie juive du moyen âge* (Paris: Librairie Vrin, 1957).

28. "... necesse est omnes qui sunt revera hoc mysterium intellecturi, et reuera Restitutionis omnium ex animo assertores erga omnes homines ... esse ita affectos propter communem patrem coelestem, ut non tantum cupiant ... mori pro illis singulis aut in Paupertate Probro Dolore et excessiua Charitate viuere sint omnino paratissimi, sed maxime excusare et supportare erga alios eorum vitia...." Sloane ms. 1411, fol. 396.

29. "In illo enim momento quo fuit anima illa humano corpori et diuinitati vnita, statim, fuit repleta summa sapientia: et ideo Christus statim fuit viator et comprehensor: ...." *Angela de Fvlginio*, 285.

30. Note Postel's words, Sloane ms. 1411, fol. 362–362^v: "... in tali me gradu Intelligentiae constitui [Christus] voluit, ut comprehensor in via et non tantum viator videar et sic cuilibet poscenti demonstrari valeam."

31. The British Library, Sloane ms. 1412, fol. 313^v.

32. "Bethanie estolt vn lieu viron deux petitz mille de Ierusalem, lá ou estoit vne partie des possessions de celle glorieuse et Saincte familie Marie Magdelene, et Marthe, et Eleazare leur frere, lá ou il pleut a Dieu planter auec le premier racoeuil de son Eglise la vray Etymologie du nom de Bethanie qui signifie Maison de Pauurete, Douleur, et Mespris" (sig. cv). It is interesting to point out that André Thevet in his *Cosmographie du Levant*, the first edition of which was published in 1554, a year later than Postel's reference to Bethanie as the home of *povertà, dolore*, and *disprezzo*, wrote: "... pour y fonder la vray Bethanie, cestadire, la maison de poureté, douleur, et mespris...." ("... so as to found the real Bethany there, that is to say, the house of poverty, pain, and scorn....") For the text of Thevet, see *Cosmographie du Levant*, ed. Frank Lestringant (Genève: Librairie Droz, 1985), 178.

Cracovie-Washington D.C.
Novembre 1987.

Cher Germain,

Vous avez trouvé le plus beau titre de gloire de votre vie dans la propagation et le renouvellement, dans le monde entier, de la gloire de St Thomas More. Les érudits et les magistrats de plusieurs pays, sur tous les continents, respectent votre travail et vous en sont reconnaissants. Grâce à ce labor impiger, *quotidien, multiple, vous tenez devant leurs regards cette personnalité unique qui inspire courage, loyauté, probité, amour des lettres et de ce qui les surpasse, le sens de l'humour et tant d'autres valeurs, en un mot le portrait vivant et historiquement exact d'un savant, chancelier et un saint de la Renaissance.*

Ce portrait, surgissant sur les pages de vos Moreana, *montre comment ce grand homme, régissant les hautes affaires d'un royaume, savait s'affirmer essentiellement égalitaire et apprécier les gens humbles, les détails de la vie de tous les jours (y compris ceux de la vie de famille). A la manière, si vous voulez, de son Maître Suprême qui* in altis habitat et humilia respicit in caelo et in terra. *Ce serviteur à la cour du roi, passant quelques années sous le toit des Chartreux, donc orienté vers l'observation du rituel, patron de l'art, était aussi, suivant la formule de C.S. Lewis,* a great commoner, *l'auteur d'une constitution (fictive) basée sur un libre choix. Contemporain de certains représentants des ordres mendiants, il se sentait peut-être en sympathie avec certaines de leurs idées : indubitablement il gérait de grandes sommes -- et savait aussi mépriser l'or.*

Il n'y a donc pas de contradiction dans le fait que vous êtes savant Morien qui marche, nous nous apercevons, dans les pas du Poverello. *Sans fortune, presque à la merci du moment, vous avez trouvé tant de fois des solutions et des moyens pour continuer votre oeuvre (de dimensions mondiales) et même supporter les besogneux. Comment y arriviez-vous ? C'est votre secret. Nous voulons vous dire notre admiration.*

Qui dit (de vous ou d'un autre) imitateur Morien de S. François dit aussi, à bon escient ou non, internationaliste. Vous en êtes un des plus sincères, pour qui tous *sont des* amici. *Ce n'est pas sans grande importance de nos jours, remplis d'exemples de fanatisme et d'acharnement. Vous élargissez les coeurs ! Continuez.*

Janina Scraniecka-Mroczkowska Przemysław Mroczkowski
Thomas Mroczkowski. Université de Cracovie

Przemysław Mroczkowski

PRINCETON UNIVERSITY PRESS

PRINCETON - NEW JERSEY 08540

October 1, 1987.

Dear Germain,

    When my Doktorvater, Dick Sylvester, set me on the path of More studies two decades ago, he supplied me with an illuminating guide in the form of Joaquin Kuhn's brief essay on the Dialogue of Comfort *in a little journal called* Moreana. *If, as I learned, the* Dialogue *was a* consolatio scripturarum, *then I needed to learn more about its author's biblical sources. And thus I discovered that* mercator Mori, Germain Marc'hadour.

    Gradually (by installments) I became aware of a vast enterprise, a kind of scholarly Utopia, industriously cultivating the works of Thomas More. Through your own labors you made these scholars colleagues. Your Moreanum radiates a spirit of cooperation, embracing even those controversialists who linger at its margins. In revealing More you have helped us in ways too personal to relate to find our own better nature. So continuing, may our Lord bless and protect you and all of us in the company of His saint and under the shield of His inscrutable wisdom.

    Yours,

    Jay

    Jay Wilson
    Director of Rights

· William Roper ·

CHARLES BÉNÉ

Cadeau d'Érasme à Margaret Roper: Deux hymnes de Prudence

IL PEUT PARAÎTRE SURPRENANT QU'ERASME ait dédicacé à Margaret Roper, fille aînée de More, les Commentaires de deux hymnes de Prudence:[1] c'est pour une jeune femme de dix-huit ans qu'il s'est arraché à des travaux – et des soucis – qui l'écrasent, afin de répondre à une demande instante, et d'offrir en primeur à une jeune maman le commentaire d'un poète chrétien.

Sans doute, la famille More tient une place de choix dans le coeur d'Erasme: depuis 24 ans déjà, il a découvert Thomas More, et c'est dans sa maison qu'il a composé, au retour d'Italie, son célèbre *Eloge de la Folie*.[2]

Cet attachement, qui se double d'une grande estime, a naturellement rejailli sur les enfants du magistrat, et on peut en suivre la permanence à travers les biographies qu'Erasme a composées de son ami. Margaret est à peine âgée de 14 ans lorsque Erasme, dans sa lettre de Juillet 1519 à Ulrich de Hutten, en fait une première mention, associant l'aînée à ses soeurs, Elisabeth et Cécile, et à son jeune frère John. Il est cependant significatif qu'Elisabeth, comme d'ailleurs dans la dédicace des oeuvres d'Aristote à John More, verra son prénom transformé en Aloysia, et cette confusion, qui est simple inadvertance, montre au moins qu'Erasme faisait quelque différence dans son affection pour les enfants de More.[3]

La lettre à Guillaume Budé, écrite en 1521 (Margaret a alors 16 ans), évoque avec admiration l'éducation que Thomas More assure à ses enfants, et cette fois il cite exactement les prénoms, auxquels il ajoute Margaret Giggs, la fille adoptive. A l'occasion d'une lettre composée par chacun des enfants, et envoyée sans retouches par leur père à Erasme, leur éminent correspondant y exprime son admiration pour la sûreté de leur latin, la profondeur et la finesse du contenu des lettres.[4] Considération qui se manifestera par la dédicace d'ouvrages composés par Erasme lui-même.

C'est curieusement à John More, le cadet, qu'il fera sa première dédicace. De fait, en lui envoyant, en Juin 1523, le commentaire de la *Nux Ouidii*, c'est à un tout jeune homme, âgé de quinze ans, et qui a besoin d'être encouragé dans ses études, qu'il s'adresse. Aussi n'hésite-t-il pas à faire jouer l'émulation en faisant un éloge vibrant de ses "dulcissimae sorores," marquant que par leur culture, leurs qualités, elles risquent de le laisser derrière elles, avec leur avantage d'être un peu plus grandes et plus âgées. Mais si elles pourront rivaliser avec Cornélie, la mère des Gracques, c'est à lui, John, de rivaliser avec son père, qui ne souhaite, d'ailleurs, que d'être dépassé par son fils.[5] Le texte choisi n'a rien de grave, ni de sérieux: mais il fallait tenir compte de l'âge et des goûts du jeune homme, et ne pas le rebuter par un texte trop pesant.

L'affection qui attache Erasme à Margaret Roper est d'une autre nature. Il semble bien que la fille aînée, et la préférée de Thomas More, soit aussi la préférée d'Erasme.

L'étude du Commentaire des deux hymnes de Prudence, l'hymne de Noël et celui de l'Epiphanie, qui a suivi de quelques mois à peine la dédicace de la *Nux Ouidii* à John More, fait apparaître, par le texte choisi, par le caractère même du commentaire, d'inspiration beaucoup plus spirituelle, que ces ouvrages ne sont guère comparables. Le cadeau à Margaret apparaît, en même temps qu'un témoignage d'affection, une oeuvre de pédagogue, soucieux d'instruire une élève de choix, et qui met en valeur les divers aspects de l'humanisme érasmien.

I

Un témoignage d'affection

Témoignage d'affection d'abord, et on ne peut qu'être saisi par l'extrême élégance de la lettre-dédicace.[6]

Ces commentaires, adressés à la "très chaste" Margaret Roper, n'oublient pas les soeurs de la jeune femme. Déjà s'adressant à John More, il évoquait ses *dulcissimae sorores*. Ici, ce sont leurs lettres, malheureusement perdues, qu'Erasme mentionne, en en faisant l'éloge: "si naturelles, si fines, si naïves, si pleines d'affection," éloge qui deviendra ensuite celui des enfants eux-mêmes, qualifiés, selon l'expression de Paul, de γνήσια τέκνα,[7] tant les enfants sont fidèles aux éminentes qualités de leur père.

Aux soeurs de Margaret, Erasme associera son mari, William Roper. Compliment suprême: Erasme affirmera que par sa pureté de moeurs, sa douceur, sa modestie, si Roper n'était son mari, c'est vraiment un frère qu'il serait (*germanus videri posset*), tant ses qualités sont celles de la famille More!

Même délicatesse dans l'évocation de cette première naissance: "Ton mari t'a donné ces prémices tant souhaitées de votre union"; puis, double correction: "ou, si tu préfères, c'est toi qui les lui as données," et enfin: "ou, pour dire plus exactement, c'est chacun de vous deux qui a donné à l'autre ce petit enfant" (*vterque dedit alteri* παιδίον).[8] Et le mot qui, chez Luc, sert à désigner Jésus, permet à Erasme de proposer en cadeau au jeune ménage "un autre enfant, Jésus," ce qui le conduit alors à faire l'éloge du couple. Eloge singulier, puisqu'Erasme évoque en même temps leur pureté, leur concorde, leur sérénité, leur simplicité, mais qui va bien au-delà, puisqu'il n'hésite pas à affirmer "qu'on trouverait difficilement, même parmi ceux qui ont fait voeu de virginité, des personnes qui oseraient se comparer à eux."

Cette attitude affectueuse, si profondément marquée par la délicatesse, se retrouve dans la conduite même du commentaire. Erasme présente à Margaret Roper un auteur nouveau, et il n'oublie pas qu'il s'adresse à une jeune femme qui a encore bien des choses à apprendre. Le savant Rotterdamois se transforme donc en pédagogue attentionné, pour que son "élève" soit à même de mieux comprendre—et de mieux goûter—celui qu'il n'hésite pas à appeler *Pindarum nostrum*. Leçons qui peuvent paraître bien austères au lecteur moderne mais Erasme a souci de tout exposer clairement à une élève de choix.

Ainsi, la première page du Commentaire de l'hymne de Noël peut surprendre. Erasme ne dit rien sur l'auteur, ni sur les circonstances de la composition, mais il propose, ex abrupto, un véritable cours sur le poème iambique. Il remonte à ses origines, à ses premiers emplois (satire violente, hymnes guerriers), puis à son utilisation dans l'élégie. En présentant les hymnes d'Ambroise, nouvelle digression savante sur l'emploi de la penthémimère, rythme que l'on retrouve chez Prudence. Dernier développement enfin sur les substitutions de mètres, tels le spondée ou le dactyle, les règles de leur emploi, et les effets musicaux obtenus.[9]

Leçon qui frappe par sa richesse, mais aussi par le sens pédagogique. Ainsi, pour expliquer l'usage de la penthémimère, il n'emploie pas moins de trois exemples tirés de l'hymne d'Ambroise *Deūs creātor ōmnium*, où les deux iambes, suivis d'un demi-mètre (penthémimère), se ferment sur un dactyle.

Si le cours de versification, qui au long du commentaire est complété par d'utiles remarques sur la quantité des voyelles, et l'usage de Prudence,[10] est surtout limité aux premières pages, Erasme sera amené à développer plus largement ses considérations sur la science des astres.

L'hymne de Noël leur donne une place de choix, car l'allongement des jours, après le solstice d'hiver, symbolise parfaitement l'arrivée de la vraie lumière, Jésus, venu pour éclairer les ténèbres où le monde est plongé.[11] On retrouvera dans le Commentaire de l'hymne de l'Epiphanie de nouveaux développements sur l'astronomie—et l'astrologie. C'est d'abord un exposé sur les phases de la lune, puis sur les étoiles fixes, les astres errants, et les comètes annonciatrices de malheurs. Erasme complète ses explications astronomiques par une étude de l'influence, bonne ou mauvaise, de certaines constellations (Pléiades, par exemple).[12]

Leçons de prosodie et véritable cours sur la poésie iambique; leçons d'astronomie qui n'oublient pas l'astrologie antique: on pourrait évoquer de même, avec référence à Laurent Valla, telle leçon de grammaire sur l'emploi correct de *quamlibet*, ou ces développements sur les arbres et les parfums, avec références à Pline l'Ancien.[13]

Plus importantes, pour suggérer cette liberté dont Erasme use envers Margaret, nous paraissent les faiblesses "visibles" des deux commentaires. Erasme a dit à Margaret, dès les premières lignes de la lettre-dédicace, dans quelles conditions il s'est mis au travail: "Mais, pour que vous n'ayez pas le sentiment d'avoir parlé à un sourd, j'ai volé à mes travaux, où je suis enseveli, quelques maigres instants de loisir, pendant cette période de Noël."[14] Ainsi, première constatation, pressé d'offrir deux commentaires pour Noël, Erasme ne s'est pas donné le temps d'établir une édition critique du texte de Prudence.

Il pouvait en effet, en 1524, disposer de deux éditions, l'une parue à Deventer en 1497, l'autre à Venise, chez Alde, en 1501. Sans doute aurait-il pu consulter tel ou tel manuscrit, pour restaurer un texte dont il note lui-même les faiblesses.[15] Or il n'en a rien été. Malgré son silence, on a tout lieu de penser qu'Erasme avait sous les yeux l'édition de Deventer, dont il reproduit certaines erreurs (*pudicae*, "Hymne de Noël," v. 58; *quaternis petris*, "Epiphanie," v. 175), mais dont il corrige deux fautes qui rendaient le texte inintelligible ("Noël," v. 114, 115):

les formes *quae sit . . . quae te* sont corrigées par Erasme avec cette remarque: *hoc carmen a sciolo deprauatum restitui*.[16]

C'est sans doute la hâte et le manque de temps qui expliquent également la dissemblance des deux commentaires. Celui de l'hymne de Noël, sans doute composé le premier, est d'une grande richesse, par ses annotations et ses références de tout ordre. Il occupe d'ailleurs, dans l'édition Leclerc, une douzaine de colonnes pour un poème de 116 vers. Mais lorsqu'il s'est agi de commenter l'hymne de l'Epiphanie, Erasme a dû se rendre compte qu'il avait présumé de son temps. Il lui a fallu abréger, réduire certaines observations à quelques mots, si bien que le commentaire est parfois plus bref que le texte lui-même. Erasme d'ailleurs a le premier noté cette différence, puisque, si le premier Commentaire est appelé *commentarius*, le deuxième prend plus modestement le nom de *commentariolus*.[17]

II

L'oeuvre humaniste

On a pu déjà entrevoir dans ces commentaires le pédagogue attentionné, soucieux de former une élève de choix en même temps que d'éclairer un texte nouveau. Ils révèlent à la fois une attitude presque paternelle et une certaine familiarité d'Erasme à l'égard de sa filleule. Ce n'est pas tout. Les deux commentaires — mais plus particulièrement l'hymne de Noël, beaucoup plus développé — font apparaître en outre l'humanisme d'Erasme, dans toute sa richesse et sa complexité: commentaire savant, mais surtout commentaire spirituel; références nombreuses à l'Antiquité, mais plus encore à l'Ancien et au Nouveau Testament; permanence enfin d'une certaine tradition médiévale qui peut surprendre chez un novateur comme Erasme.

Pindarum nostrum: Erasme affiche, dès le premier vers commenté, son admiration pour Prudence.[18] Pour la première fois, il compose le commentaire d'un poète d'inspiration chrétienne, et il n'hésite pas à le comparer au plus prestigieux des lyriques grecs: Pindare. Le possessif *nostrum* montre bien que c'est en chrétien qu'il se place, et qu'il le revendique à ce titre.

Peut-être sera-t-on surpris, et du choix de Prudence, et de l'admiration que révèle cette épithète flatteuse? Ce serait oublier qu'Erasme n'a jamais cessé de dire son admiration pour les poètes d'inspiration chrétienne. Ses premières lettres, ses premiers poèmes l'exprimaient déjà.

Lui-même, dans une lettre à H. de Bergen, en 1496, avouait sa préférence pour un Paulin de Nole, un Juvencus ou un Prudence; il donnait à Baptiste le Mantouan le titre de "Virgile chrétien," lui prédisant une gloire égale à celle de Virgile; et sur la foi d'Agricola, il appelle Lactance "le Cicéron chrétien."[19]

Mais c'est un fait qu'il a toujours gardé une admiration particulière pour Prudence. Dès ses premiers poèmes, les réminiscences sont nombreuses et si, comme le note C. Reedijk,[20] c'est sans doute dès ses années de Collège à Deventer qu'il le découvrit, cela pourrait expliquer qu'Erasme n'ait pas cherché ailleurs l'édition de Prudence qu'il voulait commenter. Fidélité qui ne se démentira pas, puisqu'en 1528, composant le *Ciceronianus*, Prudence a plus de prestige à ses yeux même qu'un poète chrétien comme Sannazar: "Je préfèrerais de beaucoup un seul hymne de Prudence sur la naissance de Jésus aux trois livres de Sannazar." Car s'il lui sait gré d'avoir osé traiter un sujet chrétien, il lui reproche, en faisant intervenir Phébus et Protée, Hamadryades et Néréides, de traiter en païen un sujet chrétien.[21]

Si Erasme élève Prudence au rang de Pindare, c'est d'abord qu'il le considère comme un poète inspiré. Le premier mouvement:

Quid est quod arctum circulum. . . ?

lui paraît propre au genre prophétique (et de fait, bien des prophéties de l'Ancien Testament commencent par une interrogation brutale),[22] à quoi il ajoute: "et je ne doute pas qu'il est lui-même inspiré par Dieu." D'autre part, son interprétation de la période de la naissance de Jésus, le solstice d'hiver, fait apparaître "l'homme pieux" qui accorde une signification spirituelle au choix de la période: le Christ, la vraie lumière, paraît dans le monde au moment où les jours vont recommencer à croître.[23]

Erasme, dans le commentaire proprement dit, reste fidèle à l'humanisme traditionnel en faisant largement appel à l'Antiquité, qu'il s'agisse du vocabulaire ou des idées exprimées. Ainsi, le *dulcis pusio* (doux petit enfant) est illustré par les *dulces liberos* d'Horace; l'évocation du chaos qui précède la création amène trois vers des *Métamorphoses* d'Ovide; les ennuis de la gestation [*fastidia*] sont illustrés par Virgile:

Matri longa decem tulerunt fastidia menses,

et l'annonce du nouvel âge d'or, par le célèbre passage des *Bucoliques*.[24]

Mais les références antiques, dans l'interprétation spirituelle, n'ont là qu'une valeur d'appoint, car c'est à la Bible surtout qu'Erasme fait appel pour commenter dignement cet hymne de Noël. L'avènement du Christ et de la lumière évoquent Isaïe et Zacharie; l'anthropomorphisme de Dieu est expliqué par les Psaumes; la création de la lumière évoque la Genèse; l'avènement du nouvel âge d'or, surtout, fait intervenir Isaïe, auquel sont associés Joël et Amos.

Mais si l'Ancien Testament occupe naturellement la première place, les épîtres de Paul et de Pierre, et surtout l'Apocalypse, tiennent naturellement une large place.[25] Au total, commentaire très spirituel qui, conformément à une doctrine déjà exposée dans l'*Enchiridion*, n'utilise les auteurs anciens que dans la mesure où ils annoncent, ou préfigurent, le message divin.[26]

Cette présence de l'humanisme n'exclut pas un certain nombre de "fidélités" à la tradition médiévale. Ainsi, Erasme accepte des étymologies qui peuvent paraître aujourd'hui contestables. Evoquant les Scythes, les Goths ("plus semblables à des pierres ou à des rochers qu'à des hommes"), il émet l'hypothèse que c'est peut-être de là que vient le nom donné aux Saxons (*a saxis*).[27] Mais lorsqu'il suggère que *fastidium* peut être un amalgame de *fastu* et de *taedium*, on est bien obligé de constater que cette hypothèse se retrouve chez nos étymologistes modernes.[28]

Fidélité encore à la tradition médiévale au sujet de l'âge du monde. En effet, si le Moyen-Age avait adopté deux chronologies, selon que l'on suivait la tradition hébraïque (3952 ans) ou la Septante (5228 ans) Erasme, suivant la tradition d'Isidore de Séville, qui était la plus communément admise, adopte le chiffre de 5228 ans, pour la mort du Christ, ce qui donne, pour le temps de sa naissance, 5199 ans. Il est donc inexact de dire, comme le note un critique moderne, qu'après le 12e siècle, rien ne devait rester de cette tradition.[29] Mais pouvait-on s'attendre à la retrouver chez Erasme?

Plus curieuse est cette tradition qui suggérait que la semence du fils de Dieu avait pénétré dans le sein de la Vierge Marie par l'oreille. Erasme l'adopte, ainsi que l'accouchement "sans lésion, sans douleur," précisant que même si les évangélistes ne le disent pas ouvertement, il est "plus légitime, et plus pieux, de le croire, puisque c'est là l'enseignement des Pères les plus savants et les plus saints." Cette tradition, qui sera maintenue au 17e siècle à travers les traductions françaises du *De Partu Virginis* de Sannazar, n'est pas étrangère à une plaisanterie de Molière fort mal reçue par ses censeurs.[30]

Erasme enfin reprend à son compte cette ancienne tradition qui faisait figurer auprès de la crèche un boeuf et un âne. Il marque nettement que les Saintes Lettres ne l'indiquent nulle part, mais il l'explique par Isaïe: *Cognouit bos possessorem, et asinus praesepe Domini sui . . .* (Is 1.3), mais plutôt que d'adopter l'interprétation d'Origène et de Jérôme, où le boeuf symbolisait Israël et l'âne les nations païennes, il préfère garder l'interprétation de Prudence.[31]

Ces notations, et d'autres encore, concernent surtout le langage théologique (e.g., "hypostase," à propos des cadeaux des Rois mages qui s'adressent aux trois "natures" de Jésus). Mais plus d'un passage de la dédicace ou du commentaire permet de retrouver l'Erasme de toujours, à travers des thèmes qu'il n'a cessé de reprendre dans toute son oeuvre.

Ainsi en est-il de la critique du paganisme. En évoquant ces peuples qui adoraient des statues de pierre ou de bois, il fait écho au Psaume 113 dont il fait une sorte de paraphrase.[32] Lorsqu'il décrit ces nations qui choisirent comme dieux protecteurs des singes, des chiens ou des serpents, on peut penser au panthéon égyptien. Mais lorsque, pour comble d'aveuglement, il présente les sacrifices de parents, ou d'enfants, comment ne pas penser aux moeurs de la Grèce primitive, dont Homère et Euripide, par exemple, se font les échos? On retrouvera semblable critique dans le commentaire du Psaume IV, publié en 1525, mais plus développée. Aux boeufs, singes ou serpents, il ajoutera crocodiles et dragons. Surtout, évoquant les sacrifices humains, il citera explicitement l'exemple d'Agamemnon.[33]

C'est dans la lettre-dédicace que l'on retrouve surtout les thèmes préférés d'Erasme. Dans la critique du célibat ecclésiastique, par exemple, critique discrète, sans doute: (Jésus) ne dédaignera pas d'être chanté par de tels époux, qui donnent l'exemple d'une telle pureté, d'une telle concorde, d'une telle sérénité, qu'on trouverait difficilement des gens qui oseraient se comparer à eux, même chez ceux qui ont fait voeu de virginité.[34]

Cette critique du monachisme n'est pas nouvelle: on la retrouve dans la plupart des publications d'Erasme, mais on touche ici une des sources de cette défense du mariage et de la critique des voeux monastiques, à travers cet éloge adressé à Margaret et à son mari. En fait, n'est-ce pas d'abord au foyer de Thomas More qu'Erasme a découvert la sainteté dans le mariage? Il n'a cessé d'en prendre la défense, et même d'en faire l'éloge, de l'*Encomium Matrimonii* (1518) à l'*Institutio Christiani matrimonii* (1526), sans oublier les colloques matrimoniaux (1523).[35] Si Thomas More avait offert à Erasme, à peine sorti du monastère, ce témoignage vécu de la sainteté du mariage, on devine la joie d'Erasme de retrouver chez la fille aînée les mêmes qualités que chez le père.

Cette critique du célibat ecclésiastique est souvent doublée d'une dénonciation de l'ignorance des moines. Déjà, dans l'*Eloge de la Folie*, il avait stigmatisé, avec quelle vigueur, ces moines qui estiment que "la plus haute piété est de ne rien savoir, pas même lire. . . ." Il reprendra en 1524 cette critique d'une manière beaucoup plus fine dans le célèbre colloque "Le Père abbé et la femme instruite." Que Magdalia représente Margaret Roper, cela paraît une évidence au savant traducteur des *Colloques*, Craig Thompson. "Magdalia" avait le double avantage d'évoquer Margaret (familièrement "Meg") et de permettre à Erasme d'évoquer à loisir les filles de son ami, non seulement Margaret, mais aussi Elisabeth et Cécile, ce qui n'aurait pas été aussi aisé si une "Margaret" avait eu la parole.[36]

Enfin, lorsque Magdalia cite quelques exemples de femmes cultivées, les filles de Willibald Pirckheimer, celles d'Ambroise Blaurer, elle propose—est-ce un hasard?—le meilleur commentaire des dernières lignes de la lettre dédicace: "Il existe, écrit Erasme, même en Allemagne, des familles célèbres qui préparent, non sans succès, ce que vous réalisez avec tant de bonheur." Mais avant tous ces exemples, c'est celui de la Reine elle-même qu'il cite, "Catherine d'Aragon, vraie Calliope de ce choeur très saint," qu'il qualifiait déjà, dans une lettre, d'*egregie doctam, cuius filia scribit bene latinas epistolas*.[37]

Ces hymnes enfin, qu'Erasme adresse à Margaret et à son mari, lui donnent l'occasion de redire ce que représente pour lui la vraie musique. Car ce commentaire de Prudence n'est pas une simple oeuvre scientifique: les hymnes de Noël et de l'Epiphanie sont destinés à servir de chants de louange pour Jésus, celui qui doit devenir, "le véritable Apollon de leurs travaux intellectuels." Ces deux hymnes remplaceront, sur les lèvres de la jeune maman, ces chants grossiers que mères ou nourrices chantent pour les enfants. "Car seul, ajoute-t-il, il est digne d'être continuellement célébré sur la lyre, les flûtes ou la voix humaine, mais surtout, précise-t-il, avec les sentiments harmonieux d'une âme inspirée par la piété."[38]

De fait, Erasme n'a jamais cessé d'opposer cette vraie musique, la seule qui plaît à Dieu, à un usage trop extérieur, trop bruyant, trop païen, de la musique prétendue sacrée.

Déjà, éditant les oeuvres d'Arnobe, Erasme avait défini la vraie musique. Il reprendra ce thème dans les Commentaires des Psaumes, dénonçant, dans celui du Psaume IV, danses, chants et gesticulations, ou la violence des trompettes et des orgues. Il souligne que la seule musique agréable à Dieu, c'est une âme, devenue instrument, en harmonie avec l'esprit de Dieu: remarques qui forment la conclusion du Commentaire du Psaume 14, véritable testament spirituel d'Erasme, par la date de sa publication (1536).[39]

Erasme n'en restera pas à ces deux dédicaces, l'une, de la *Nux Ouidii* à John More, l'autre, du Commentaire de deux hymnes de Prudence à Margaret Roper.

Huit ans plus tard, c'est au même John qu'il dédiera les oeuvres d'Aristote,[40] occasion pour lui de faire un véritable éloge de la philosophie du Stagirite. Aussi en souligne-t-il la grande valeur morale: Aristote enseigne à vivre, et à bien vivre. Mais cette dédicace, véritable Préface de l'édition, souligne la richesse de l'oeuvre, en offre un classement détaillé, aborde l'étude des principales éditions, dont il fait l'examen critique. Dédicace qui corrige de manière évidente ce que la *Nux Ouidii* pouvait présenter de plus terre à terre, dans le sujet comme dans le traitement, et il montre en même temps en quelle estime il tenait ce fils de Thomas More, appelé naturellement à marcher sur les traces de son père.

La fidélité d'Erasme envers Margaret s'exprimera autrement. En 1529 par exemple, c'est-à-dire six ans plus tard, adressant à Thomas More une lettre grave, où il évoque en particulier ses démêlés avec les partisans de Luther, il joint une lettre personnelle à Margaret, pour la remercier du tableau d'Holbein représentant la famille More. Son regard s'est porté d'abord sur Margaret: "Je n'ai reconnu personne mieux que toi." Evoquant son ouvrage sur la *Veuve chrétienne*, il refait l'éloge des belles-lettres, "parure dans le bonheur, consolation dans le malheur." C'est Margaret enfin qu'il charge de transmettre la lettre à ses soeurs, de saluer Dame Alice, la deuxième épouse de More, de transmettre à John ses voeux, et de saluer W. Roper, son mari.[41]

Cette considération toute spéciale d'Erasme pour l'aînée des enfants de More trouvera sa justification dans la première traduction anglaise faite par Margaret de la *Paraphrase du Pater Noster* d'Erasme, et surtout par son attitude aimante et courageuse, pour ne pas dire héroïque, au moment de l'emprisonnement et du supplice de son père. Rarement si haute amitié aura été si bien placée, et on ne sait qui en a été le plus enrichi, de Margaret ou d'Erasme.

Université de Grenoble

Notes

1. *Commentarius in Hymnum Prudentii de Natali Pueri Jesu*, LB V 1337–1348. *Commentariolus in Hymnum Prudentii de Epiphania Jesu Nati*, LB V 1349–1357.

L'édition critique est en préparation dans le cadre des oeuvres complètes d'Erasme, Amsterdam (*ASD*).

2. L'*Eloge de la Folie*, préparé pendant le voyage de retour d'Italie (Juillet 1509), sera rédigé chez Thomas More, dans sa maison de Bucklersbury, à la fin de l'année.

3. Erasme présente la famille de More dans quatre lettres: à U. de Hutten, 1519 (Allen L. 999); à G. de Brie, 1520 (L. 1117); à G. Budé, 1521 (L. 1233); à J. Faber, 1532 (L. 2750). Pour la confusion des prénoms, voir L. 999, l. 175 et L. 2432 (à John More), l. 306.

4. Cf. Allen L. 1233, ll. 52–77.

5. Cf. Allen L. 1402, ll. 31 et 58–64.

6. Les notes renvoient au texte de Allen L. 1404, p. 366–67.

7. γνήσια τέκνα: "authentiques enfants." Paul emploie ces termes en 1 Tm. 1.2 et Tit. 1.4.

8. παιδίον: l'expression, en grec dans le texte, est empruntée à Luc 1.59, 86; 2.18; 2.40. Elle annonce le rapprochement de Thomas, le fils de Margaret, avec Jésus.

9. Cf. *LB* V 1337 C–1339 A.

10. Cf. *LB* 1341 E F: remarques sur *sophia, idola, paraclitus,* et *callebas*.

11. Cf. *LB* 1339 B–1340 AB.

12. *LB* 1349 F–1350 A (Lune); 1350 F–1315 A (Etoiles); 1351 B (influences des astres).

13. *Quamlibet, quanquam, quamuis* 1341 DE; *amomum, balsamum* 1346 A.

14. Allen L. 1404.

15. Outre ces deux éditions, il existe aujourd'hui plus de 90 manuscrits des *Hymnes* de Prudence. Il est probable qu'Erasme aurait pu en consulter quelques-uns, s'il en avait eu le loisir.

16. *pudicae* 1344 B; *quaternis petris* 1356 C; *quae sit . . . quae te* 1348.

17. *Commentariolus* figure dans le titre 1349 A, et dans la dernière ligne 1357 C.

18. *LB* 1340 A.

19. Cf. C. Reedijk, *The Poems of Erasmus*, Leiden, 1956; C. Béné, *Erasme et saint Augustin*, Genève 1969, pp. 45–48, et Allen L. 49, ll. 96–103.

20. Cf. C. Reedijk, op. cit., p. 100.

21. Cf. Gambaro, *Il Ciceroniano*, Brescia, 1965, ll. 4028–38 et 4046–47.

22. Cf. Is. I.2; Lam. 1.1; 2.1; 4.1. Racine conservera ce mouvement pour la prophétie de Joad (*Athalie* III, 7, v. 1139ss).

23. *LB* 1339 AB.

24. Horace, 1340 E; Ovide 1342 C; Virgile, 1344 A; Virgile (âge d'or) 1344 C.

25. Ancien Testament: 1339 D; 1341 C; 1342 A; 1345 AB; Nouveau Testament: Paul 1344 D, 1345 E; Pierre 1348 C; Apocalypse 1344 D.

26. *Enchiridion Militis Christiani*, éd. Holborn, München, 1933, p. 64, ll. 14–26.

27. *LB* 1345 D.

28. *fastidium LB* 1344 A. Cf. Ernout et Meillet, *Dict. Etym. de la langue latine*, Paris, 1939, p. 335.

29. *LB* 1342 E. Cf. Bernard Guenée, *Histoire et culture historique dans l'Occident médiéval*, Paris, 1980, pp. 148-54.
30. *LB* 1340 E. Molière, *Ecole des Femmes* I, v. 162-64. Voir aussi Gaston Hall, "L'Allusion chez Molière," in *Mélanges Scherer*, Nizet, 1986, pp. 333-39.
31. *LB* 1346 C, et K. L. Schmidt, "Prudentius und Erasmus über die Christuskrippe mit Ochs und Esel," in *Theologische Zeitschrift*, Basel 5 (1949), pp. 469-71.
32. *Hypostasis: LB* 1352 F; paganisme: *LB* 1339 C; Ps. 114 (Vulg. 113) v. 4-8.
33. *Commentarius in Ps. IV, ASD* V-2, p. 206, l. 420.
34. Allen L. 1404.
35. Cf. E. V. Telle, *Erasme et le septième sacrement*, Droz, Genève, 1954.
36. *Stultitiae Laus, ASD,* IV-3, 1979, p. 160, ll. 529-31; C. Thompson, *The Colloquies of Erasmus*, Chicago, 1965, p. 218.
37. Cf. Allen L. 2133 (à J. Vergara), ll. 105-6.
38. Cf. Allen L. 1404. ll. 15-19.
39. Cf. Allen L. 1304 (à Adrien VI), ll. 425-44; Ps. IV, *ASD*, V-2 (1985), p. 248, l. 795; Ps. XIV, *ASD*, p. 313, ll. 889-92; p. 316, 994-1000.
40. Allen L. 2432, ll. 1-90.
41. Allen L. 2212, ll. 10; 26-34.

CLARENCE H. MILLER

∽

Erasmus's Poem to St. Genevieve: Text, Translation, and Commentary

As A TOKEN OF ESTEEM AND AFFECTION for Germain Marc'hadour, I have chosen to present and translate Erasmus' poem to St. Genevieve, partly because Germain himself has written with learning and enthusiasm about "blessed holy women"[1] and partly because St. Genevieve, protectress of France and patroness of Paris, was the spiritual protégée of St. Germain d'Auxerre. According to a life of Genevieve written about 520, eighteen years after her death,[2] St. Germain and St. Loup de Troyes, two renowned and holy bishops, visited Nanterre, Genevieve's birthplace, on their way to Britain, where they intended to help put down the Pelagian heresy. They were greeted by a crowd of villagers, among whom Germain singled out the child Genevieve as one who seemed destined for a holy and wonderful life. He asked her whether she wished to become the bride of Christ. She said she did and confirmed her assent on the following day, when St. Germain found on the ground a bronze coin inscribed with a cross which he gave her to wear as a sign of her commitment. Later she officially took her vows before the bishop of Paris.[3] After her parents died, she went to live with her godmother in Paris. When she began to be admired for her holiness, she was, not unsurprisingly, attacked by backbiters, who were rebuked by St. Germain when he visited Paris a second time. Finally a conspiracy was hatched to kill her, either by stoning or drowning; but she was saved by a messenger sent from Auxerre by St. Germain.[4]

The anonymous author of the *vita* never knew St. Genevieve personally, and he collected his information mainly from oral reports. He is mostly interested in miracles and unfortunately gives us little of the flavor of her personality. Even eighteen years (to say nothing of 50 or 70 years, for she lived to be 80) is enough time for a solid core of miracles to gather colorful embellishments. If some of the miracles did not happen precisely as they are described, they should have. Once, a woman stole Genevieve's shoes. When the thief got home, she was suddenly struck blind. Realizing that this was heaven's vengeance for her crime, she took the shoes back and threw herself at Genevieve's feet, begging to be forgiven and have her sight restored. Genevieve, smiling, kindly took her by the hand, raised her up, made the sign of the cross on her eyes, and the thief could see as well as before.[5] One would like to know what was behind Genevieve's smile. Another time, as she was standing in the doorway of the house where she lived, she saw a girl[6] carrying a bottle. She asked the girl what she had there. The girl replied, a bottle she had just bought from some merchants. But Genevieve saw the devil himself lurking in the mouth of the bottle, whereupon she blew on it, made the sign of the cross, and drove away the devil, who broke off the mouth of the bottle in his flight. Everyone was amazed that even the devil couldn't hide from her.[7] Life was devilishly difficult in Merovingian times, and it is not surprising that many of her miracles were directed against devils, especially diabolical possession.[8]

Her first miracle was perhaps her most touching. Not long after she first spoke with St. Germain, her mother, setting off to church on a feastday, ordered Genevieve to stay behind (perhaps for a good reason — the *vita* does not say). Genevieve wept and begged to go along, and when she wouldn't give up, her mother lost patience and slapped her cheek. Her mother was instantly struck blind and remained so for 21 months, until one day she sent Genevieve to the well to draw water. Genevieve hurried off to the well, but when she got there she paused and burst into tears because she blamed herself for her mother's blindness. When she stopped crying, she filled the bucket, took it home, and made the sign of the cross over it. Her mother washed her eyes with the water and could see a little bit. It took two or three more washings before her sight was completely restored.[9]

During her long life St. Genevieve cured many people, mostly of blindness, deafness, paralysis (from which she herself once suffered), muscular contractions, and diabolical possession.[10] In 1129 the victims of a plague which brought with it a burning fever ("ignis sacer" or "mal des ardents") were cured when the body of St. Genevieve was carried in procession to Notre Dame, where the sick had been gathered together.[11] This famous miracle is frequently referred to in medieval hymns,[12] and it was probably because of it that Erasmus's mind instinctively turned to her when he was suffering from a quartan fever in Paris late in 1496 or early in 1497.[13]

In January 1497 he wrote to a friend: "Lately I fell into a quartan fever, but have recovered health and strength, not by a physician's help (though I had recourse to one) but by the aid of St. Genevieve alone, the famous virgin, whose bones, preserved by the canons regular, daily radiate miracles and are revered: nothing is more worthy of her, or has done me more good."[14] A little over a year later, when the fever had recurred, he wrote to James Batt: ". . . I clearly felt the symptoms of the nocturnal fever which two years since all but laid me in the grave. I am combating it with all the proper precautions and with the aid of physicians, but am hardly out of danger, for my health is still in a very unreliable condition. If this fever attacks me once again, then, my dear Batt, it will all be over with your friend. Nevertheless I do not altogether despair, for I trust in St. Genevieve, whose ready help I have more than once enjoyed; particularly since I have obtained the services of William Cop, a physician who is not merely highly skilled in his profession but friendly and loyal and, a most uncommon thing, devoted to the Muses."[15]

In 1532 Erasmus had the poem printed in its own quarto volume in Freiburg im Breisgau. In 1529 he had left Basel because of the reformation there (which included some iconoclastic refusal to venerate the saints).[16] He had probably written it not long before it was printed.[17] It was the only poem Erasmus published all by itself, and he must have had a high regard for it to single it out in this way. No doubt he also thought that he would not have truly fulfilled his promise unless he not only wrote but also published the poem. One of the things he could give to Genevieve by 1532 was a very large readership. In the concluding lines he turns the long delay into a courtly compliment to Genevieve's mercy, but Genevieve also got a better poem than she probably would have if Erasmus had kept his promise in 1497.

In 1489, while he was still in the monastery at Steyn, Erasmus and his young friend Cornelius Gerard produced a self-conscious and high-flown dialogue in asclepiadean strophes concerning the religious uses of poetry (Reedijk, Nos. 14-15). The predictable upshot of it all, conveniently confirmed by Jerome himself at the end of the dialogue, was that it is permissible and even edifying to read and write good (that is, classical) poetry on religious themes—to claim the spoils of Egypt for true religion. On Erasmus's part, there were a few polished and pleasing results from this resolution: the hymns to Ann, Gregory, Michael, Gabriel, Raphael, and all the angels.[18] But he also turned out in the nineties a batch of melodramatic, overblown productions: poems on the earthquake and the darkness of the sun at the crucifixion and on the harrowing of hell, a poem on the Christmas scene (pretty in a Franciscan sort of way), and a sapphic paean to Mary, which makes its 400-line way to the annunciation by way of the creation (truly *ab ovo*), the fall, and a heavenly "consult" between God the Father and the Son, until finally Gabriel makes his announcement in eight sapphic strophes, not even allowing Mary to speak her one line but simply anticipating it.[19] It is not pleasing to think of what Erasmus might have done in 1497 with the ample historical material from the early *vita* of Genevieve.[20]

After about 1500 Erasmus did not devote his energies to poetry but to biblical, patristic, and classical studies (in about that order of priority). But he did write, often on demand, a considerable amount of occasional verse, including a few satiric squibs, many epitaphs, a few poems on places, and many epideictic pieces on men and books. His poems came down to earth and became more precise and conversational. If we may compare great things with small, he moved into something like Yeats's middle period. In 1513 he wrote to Andrea Ammonio:[21] "I myself have always liked verse that was not far removed from prose, albeit prose of the first order. . . . I take the greatest pleasure in rhetorical poems and in poetical rhetoric, such that one can sense poetry in the prose and the style of a good orator in the poetry. And whereas some other men prefer more exotic elements, my own very special approval goes to your practice of depending for your effects on the bare narrative and your concern for displaying the subject rather than your own cleverness.[22] This is the kind of poetry Erasmus himself had learned to write when he fulfilled his promise to Genevieve.

Apart from the invocation (lines 1-4) and the graceful conclusion (lines 109-14), the poem is divided into four parts, as I have indicated by the paragraphing in the translation. The first part uses the course of the Seine to locate precisely the important places associated with St. Genevieve: her abbey, the cathedral of her co-patroness Mary, the church of St. Denis (which she inaugurated), and her birthplace Nanterre. It is especially appropriate to St. Genevieve because she herself sailed on this part of the Seine.[23] It enables Erasmus to contrast the countryside, the orchards, the vineyards, the fields, and the little village with the teeming metropolis of Paris; after all Genevieve was a country girl who lived most of her life in the big city. The leisurely meandering of the river is reflected in the long, sinuous sentence winding through lines 1–18.[24] The next section takes up the dual patronage of Paris. The two ladies do not quarrel over precedence, as high-born rulers are likely to do. It is as if the Defense Department and the Department of Health and Human Services were in complete harmony. And the two ladies also manage to make church and state into balanced powers. These harmonies are expressed in the parallel and balanced clauses of lines 33–39 and 43–45. Finally, almost reluctantly like the river, Erasmus gets down to the matter at hand as he nostalgically looks back at his illness of 35 years ago, recollecting in tranquillity his emotions then and even earlier when he was a boy. Here the style is easy, relaxed, conversational—we are in the everyday, realistic world of the colloquies. And this change was deliberate, for surely Erasmus is indulging in mild and self-deprecating irony when he tells us he is now going to give us a "lofty song" or "paeana" (line 49). "Paean" was the term he used in the title of his high-flying poem to Mary (Reedijk, No. 19), but the following presentation of the cure is down-to-earth and factual, quite unlike the earlier paean. Erasmus seems to be implying: if you wish to report a miracle, give us the details, credible evidence, and a reliable witness like William Cop—little of which can be found in the *vita* of Genevieve or the medieval hymns in praise of her. The fourth section propounds the perfectly orthodox and traditional teaching that miracles are the work of Christ, not of his saints, but there is a certain emphatic tenseness here because of the curtness of the sentences and the repetitions in lines 102–3 and 105–06. The tension is resolved in the two brief, beautiful, and (dare we call them) metaphysical metaphors of the sun seen through glass and the spring water flowing through conduit pipes. Surely the implied message here is as much for the protestants as the catholics: if you reject what Christ performs through and for his saints, you reject him.

I have not included in the commentary the echoes from classical poems given in Dr. Reedijk's notes. Some are not very close in phrasing[25] and others express such general or commonplace ideas that they do not create much resonance. When Erasmus says "Proin erat in votis mihi mors" ("Therefore I desired to die," line 60), the echo (if there is one) of Horace looking at his country estate and saying with satisfaction "Hoc erat in votis" ("This is what I wanted," *Satires* 2.6.1) seems remote and not very relevant.[26] But two echoes that Dr. Reedijk notes (lines 47-8 and 65) and one he does not (line 36) suggest that Erasmus did intend us to call to mind the Dido episode in Virgil's *Aeneid*. Mary is said to "fondle the wretched in her bosom" ("fovet gremio," line 36); Virgil uses the phrase "gremio fovet" (*Aeneid* 1.718) to describe Dido fondling the disguised Cupid in her bosom as she takes in her destructive and poisonous passion for Aeneas.[27] Erasmus says it is time for him to "give thanks" ("grates / Persoluam," lines 47-48) to Genevieve; Aeneas uses the same phrase in thanking Dido for her hospitality (*Aeneid* 1.600). And Erasmus says in his silent prayer to Genevieve that during her lifetime she was accustomed to "helping miserable people" ("miseris succurrere," line 65); in her reply to Aeneas' speech of thanks, Dido invites him into her palace, saying that she herself has suffered and hence has learned to "help miserable people" (*Aeneid* 1.630). These allusions provide overtones of a contrast between the love and compassion of Mary and Genevieve, who provide Paris with peace and harmony, and Dido, whose love and compassion ruined her own city and almost prevented the founding of Rome.

The Latin text given here is taken from a xerox of the first edition.

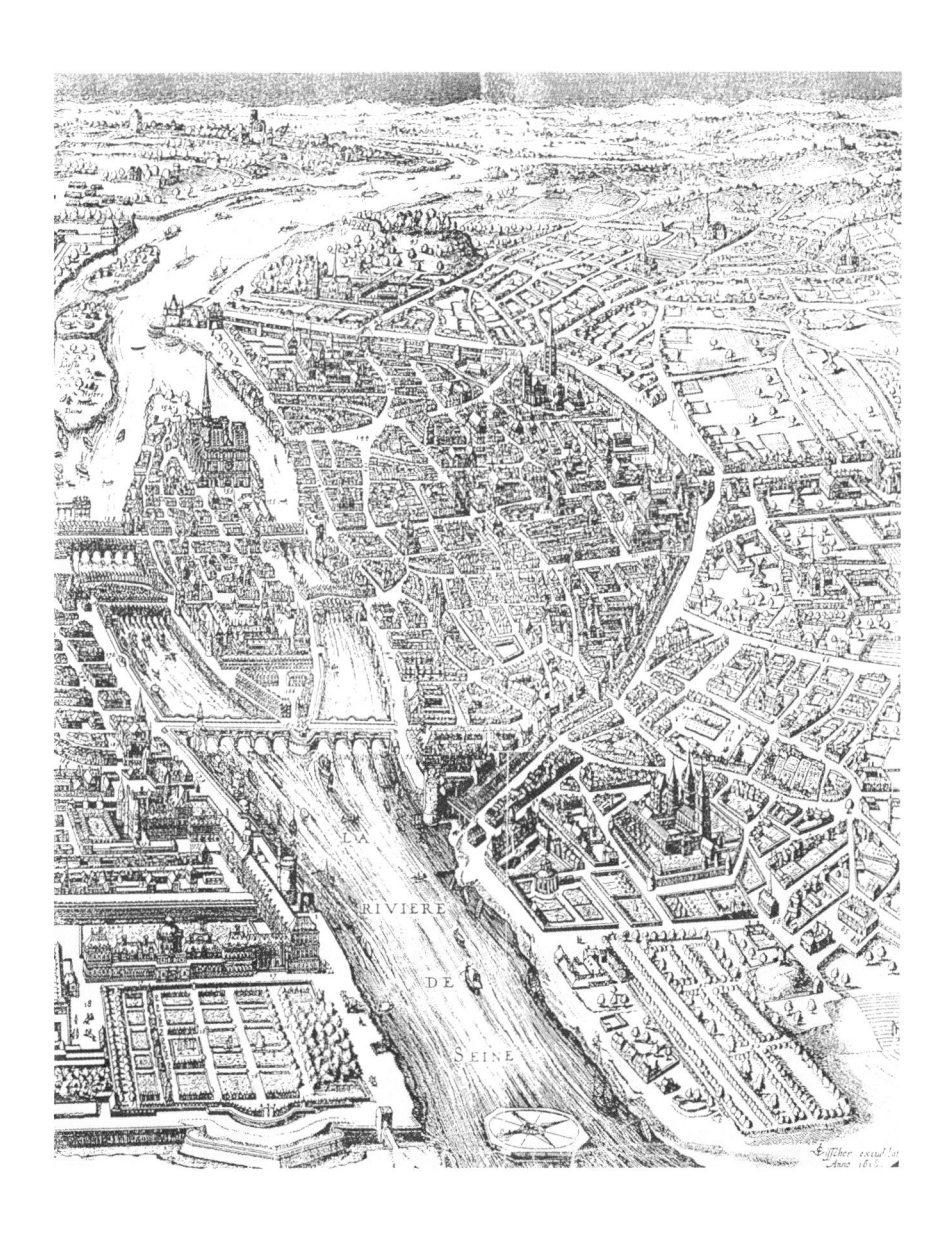

Part of a map of Paris (engraved by Visscher in 1618) showing the Abbey of St. Genevieve and Notre Dame. The river is flowing west, toward the viewer.

Des. Erasmi Roterodami diuae Genouefae praesidio a quartana febre liberati, Carmen votiuum. Nunquam antehac excusum. (Freiburg im Breisgau: Ioannes Emmeus, 1532.)[28]

[sig. a2]
Diua pij uatis uotiuum soluere carmen
Qui cupit, aspirans uotis sterilem imbue uenam
Mentis, & ut te digna canat, tu suggere uires
Protectrix Genouefa tuae fidissima gentis,
Gallia quam late triplici discrimine secta   5
Porrigitur: sed praecipue tibi pars ea cordi est,
Sequana qua hospitibus factus iam animosior undis,
Matrona quas defert, fluuioque admiscet amico,
Pomiferos per agros, per prata uirentia, perque
Vitiferos colles, adopertaque frugibus arua,   10
Vitreus incedit & ad amplam Parisiorum
Metropolim properans, ad leuam pronus adorat
Arcem virgo tuam, mox brachia diuidit, atque
Virgineae matris spatiosam amplectitur aedem:
Ac flexu augustam ueneratus supplice diuam,   15
In sese redit, adque tui cunabula partus,
Ac praedulce solum quo sacra infantula primos
Vagitus dederas, festinat alacrior amnis.
Viculus est humilis, sed tali prole beatus:
Huc igitur properans, obiter uicina salutat [sig. a2v]   20
Phana dicata tibi, Celtarum lux Dionysi.
Hac regione diu sinuosis flexibus errans,
In se uoluitur atque reuoluitur, ora subinde
Ad cunas Genouefa tuas, urbemque relictam
Reflectens, dicas inuitum abscedere flumen.   25
Est merito cunctis uenerabile Namethodorum,
Cui licet hospitibus monumenta ostendere prisca
Ortus diua tui, fontemque liquore salubri
Vndantem. At potius bis terque quaterque videtur
Praeside te felix populosa Lutetia uirgo,   30
Cuius tutelam pariter cum uirgine matre
Iugibus excubijs peragis: nec enim illa grauatur
Muneris eiusdem collegam: tu quidem in alta
Sublimis specula late cirumspicis agros,
Ac mala propulsas charis minitantia Gallis: 35
Illa fouet gremio miseros, mediamque per urbem

A poem by Desiderius Erasmus of Rotterdam
in fulfillment of a vow made to St. Genevieve,
whose protection freed him from a quartan fever.
Never printed before.

Look with favor, holy lady, on the desires of a devoted poet who wishes to fulfill his vow by writing the promised poem; enrich his depleted poetic vein and lend him the power to write a poem worthy of you,[29] O Genevieve, most faithful protectress of your people, as far as France, divided into three sections,[30] extends, but you are most concerned about that part[31] where the Seine,[32] growing more vigorous as he plays host to the waters which the Marne yields and mingles with his river friend,[33] proceeds[34] glassy-smooth through orchards, through flourishing meadows, through the vineyards on the hillsides and the fields covered with crops, and, as he hurries on to the large metropolis of Paris, he bend down in reverence to your citadel on the left hand, O virgin; then he spreads his arms and embraces the grand sanctuary of the virgin-mother; and, bending humbly in veneration of that holy and majestic lady, the river collects himself together[35] and eagerly hastens on to the cradle of your birth and the most sweet soil where you as a holy little babe gave forth your first cries.[36] The village is a humble one, but it is blessed in having such offspring. And so, hurrying along toward that village, he salutes in passing the nearby church dedicated to you, Denis, light of the Celts.[37] As he pursues for a long time his wandering, winding way in this region, he bends back on himself time and again, turning his head repeatedly toward your cradle, Genevieve, and the city he has left behind; you would say that the river was unwilling to depart.

Nanterre is deservedly venerated by everyone, since it can display to its visitors the ancient monuments of your birth, holy lady, and your spring, flowing with healing waters.[38] But happy indeed, thrice happy and more, O virgin, is populous Paris, which you continuously protect and guard,[39] together with the virgin-mother.[40] For she takes no umbrage at sharing her office with a colleague. You, to be sure, high in your lofty watchtower, look around far and wide over the fields and repel any evils that threaten your dear Frenchmen;[41] she fondles the wretched in her bosom[42] and hears the woeful cries of the poor

Audit egenorum ploratus: hic quoque natum
Clementem mater referens, nihilo secus ac tu
Sponsa tuum Genouefa refers mitissima sponsum.
Interea paribus studijs defenditis ambae 40
Germanos Druidas, ac maiestate senatum
Regali, sed christophilum super omnia regem,
Illos qui populo reserent oracula mentis
Diuinae, hos uarijs ut mixtam gentibus urbem
Aequo iure regant. Est uestri muneris ergo [sig. a3] 45
Nulla quod hoc aeuo respublica floreat usquam
Prosperius. Sed tempus adest, ut carmine grates
Persoluam Genouefa tibi pro munere uitae,
Ac paeana canam, multis e millibus unus
Quos ope praesenti seruasti. Languida febris 50
Triste tenaxque malum, quod quarto quoque recurrit
Vsque die, miseros penitus peruaserat artus.
Consultus medicus sic consolatur, abesse
Diceret ut uitae discrimen, sed fore morbum
Lentum. Mox haec uox me non secus enecat, ac si 55
Dixisset, prius atque quater sol occidat, alta
In cruce pendebis. Siquidem est renouata cicatrix,
Dum mihi post multos animus reminiscitur annos
Quod puerum toto febris me haec torserat anno.
Proin erat in uotis mihi mors, quia tristius omni 60
Morte malum medicus denunciat. Hic mihi numen
Diua tuum uenit in mentem, simul optima quaedam
Spes animum reficit, tacitoque haec pectore uoluo:
Virgo sponsa deo gratissima, corpore terram
Quum premeres, semper miseris succurrere sueta, 65
Et nunc plura potes, postquam te regia coeli
Coepit, & es Christo sponso uicinior, huc huc
Flecte oculos Genouefa tuos, & corpore febrim
Pellito: me studijs, sine queis nec uiuere dulce est,
Obsecro restituas. Etenim leuius puto, uitam [sig. a3v] 70
Exhalare semel, quam lento arescere morbo.
Quod tibi pollicear, nihil est, nec tu indiga nostri es.
Quod superest, grato recinam tibi carmine laudes.
Vix ea fatus eram, nullo cum murmure linguae,
Verum intra arcanae mecum penetralia mentis, 75
Prodigiosa loquar, sed compertissima, stratis
Exilio, reddor studijs, uestigia nulla

in the midst of the city, a mother who represents here also her merciful son, just as you, espoused to Christ,[43] represent your spouse[44] by your great kindness. At the same time you are both equally diligent in protecting true priests,[45] and the parliament with its regal majesty, and above all the Christ-loving king:[46] the priests, so that they can reveal to the people the mysteries of the divine mind; the secular rulers, so that they may rule over the city with equal justice for all its mixed and diverse inhabitants. And so it is a gift from both of you that in this age there is nowhere a more flourishing commonwealth.

But now it is time, Genevieve, that I direct my poem to giving you thanks for saving my life, time that I sing a lofty song to celebrate your making me one of the thousands you have saved by being at hand with your help. An enervating fever, a grievous and persistent affliction, which also returns every fourth day,[47] had completely pervaded the limbs of my suffering body. The physician I consulted consoled me by saying that my life was not in danger but added that this was a lingering disease. Thereupon I found those words of his as devastating as if he had said "before the fourth sun set you will be hanging high on the cross." For his words opened up an old wound, as my mind went back to what had happened many years ago when as a boy such a fever as this had tortured me for a whole year. Therefore I desired to die because the physician had pronounced for me a fate worse than any death. At that point, holy lady, your heavenly power came into my mind, a vague but powerful hope refreshed my spirit, and I silently turned over in my heart such thoughts as these: "O virgin spouse most pleasing to God, when your bodily footsteps pressed down on the earth, you were always[48] helping miserable people, and now you can do even more, now that the royal court of heaven has received you and you are closer to your spouse Christ.[49] Hither, turn your eyes hither, O Genevieve, and drive this fever out of my body. Restore me, I beg you, to my studies, without which life itself has no sweetness. For I think it would be easier to breathe out all my life at once than to wither away with this slow disease. What I can promise you is nothing, nor do you have need of anything from us. All that remains is to promise to compose a poem of gratitude in praise of you." I had hardly said this—with no murmuring or movement of the tongue, but deep within the secret recesses of my mind—when (what I am going to say is miraculous but quite well established), when, I say, I sprang up from my bed, went back to my studies, felt no trace of

Sentio languoris, nec inertis taedia febris.
Septima lux aderat, qua se quartana recurrens
Prodere debuerat, sed corpus alacrius omne 80
Quam fuit ante uiget. Medicus redit, atque quid actum
Miratur, uultum speculatur, & ore latentem
Explorat linguam, tum quem uesica liquorem
Reddiderat, poscit: quin brachia denique summis
Pertentat digitis: ubi nullas comperit usquam 85
Morbi relliquias: & quis deus, inquit, Erasme
Te subito fecit alium? Quis corpore febrim
Depulit, ac uatem me, quo de gaudeo, uanum
Reddidit? Is quisquis diuûm fuit, arte medendi
Plus nostra, fateor, multo ualet: haud ope posthac 90
Nostra opus est. Nomen medici uis nosse? Guihelmus
Copus erat, iam tum florens iuuenilibus annis
Me quamuis aetate prior, perfectus ad unguem
Dotibus ingenij, sophiaeque mathemata callens,
Vt si quisquam alius: senio nunc fessus in aula [sig. a4] 95
Francisci regis, procerum inter lumina, cunctis
Charus adoratur, fruiturque laboribus actis.
Hic igitur mihi testis erit grauis, atque locuples
Munere diua tuo reuocatae uirgo salutis.
Quanquam quicquid id est, autori gloria Christo 100
In solidum debetur, honosque perhennis in aeuum.
Muneris huius erat, quod uiua Deo placuisti,
Muneris eiusdem est, quod mortua pluribus aegris
Praesidio es. Sponso sic uisum est omnipotenti.
Per te largiri gaudet sua munera, per te 105
Gaudet honorari: ueluti lux ignea Phoebi
Per uitrum splendet iucundius, ac ueluti fons
Per puras transfusus amat manare canales.
Hoc unum superest, ut te precer optima uirgo,
Ne mihi sit fraudi, quod tanto tempore uotum 110
Soluere distulerim. Patere hanc accedere laudem,
Tot titulis Genouefa tuis, ut castior usquam
Nulla fuit, toto non ulla modestior orbe,
Sic nec in aethereis clementior ulla feratur.

FINIS

exhaustion nor any of the deadening weariness of the fever. The seventh day dawned, when the quartan fever was supposed to return, but my whole body felt more active and vigorous than it had before. The physician came back and was amazed at what had happened. He looked over my face and examined my tongue in the recesses of my mouth,[50] and then he asked for some of the fluid produced by my bladder. Finally he even tested my arms with his fingertips.[51] When he found no remaining traces of the disease, "Erasmus," he said, "what god has so suddenly made you into another person? Who drove the fever out of your body and made me—much to my delight—a false prophet? Whichever god it was, he can do far more, I confess, than my skill in healing. After this there will be no need for my help." Do you want to know the name of the physician? It was William Cop, at that time still young and vigorous, though somewhat older than I was, his intellectual endowments honed razor-sharp and conversant with learning and wisdom on a par with anyone.[52] He is now old and weary, at the court of king Francis, among the luminaries of the nobility; beloved and venerated by all, he enjoys the fruits of his past labors. This man, therefore, will be my weighty and substantial witness of how you, O holy virgin, gave me the gift of recovered health.

But whatever it is, the glory of it belongs entirely to its source, Christ; to him be the honor for ever and ever.[53] It was his gift that while you were alive you were pleasing to God. It was his gift that after your death you were the refuge of many sick people. Such was the pleasure of your almighty spouse. He rejoices in dispensing his gifts through you. He rejoices in being honored through you, just as the burning light of Phoebus shines through glass more pleasantly,[54] and just as a spring delights in pouring itself out through clean conduits.[55]

All that remains, O best of virgins, is for me to beg that I suffer no harm because I put off fulfilling this vow for so long. To your many titles of praise, Genevieve, allow this one to be added: as no one in the whole world was more chaste, no one more modest than you were, so let no one among the saints in heaven be considered more merciful than you.[56]

THE END

I append here the text and a translation of a long and somewhat diffuse explanatory note on lines 66–67 of Erasmus's poems, arguing that saints are more powerful in heaven than on earth. It was printed in *Des. Erasmi Roterod. Carmen D. Genovefae Sacrum. D. Genouefae vita ex martyrologiis & historiis excerpta. De eadem carmen D. Herici Benedictini Altissiodorensis. Scholion ad idem Erasmi carmen de ss. precibus* Parisiis, Apud viduam Guil. Morelij, in Graecis typographi Regij. 1566. (sigs.

Scholion ad illud, *Et nunc plura potes, &c.*

Sic Hieronymus ad Paulam suam, in eius ad Eustochium epitaphio, Praesens facilius, quod postulas, impetrabis. Et hoc argumento cùm patres alij, tum S. Bernardus[58] libenter vtitur, Ex tribus, inquiens, quae in festiuitatibus Sanctorum vigilanter considerare debemus, auxilium imprimis sancti est, quia qui potens fuit in terra, potentior est in caelis ante faciem Domini Dei sui. Si enim dum hîc viueret, misertus est peccatoribus, & orauit pro eis, nunc tantò amplius, quanto verius agnoscit miserias nostras, orat pro nobis Patrem: quia beata illa patria charitatem eius augmentauit, non immutauit, & nunc potius induit sibi viscera misericordiae, cùm stat ante fontem misericordiae. Et rursus,[59] sedet veteranus Christi miles, debita iam suauitate & securitate quietus. Securus quidem sibi, sed nostri solicitus. Non enim cum putredine carnis simul se exuit visceribus pietatis, nec sibi sic induit stolam gloriae, vt nostrae pariter miseriae, suaeque ipsius misericordiae obliuionem indueret. Non est terra obliuionis, quam Sancti anima inhabitat, non terra laboris, vt occupetur in ea: non denique terra, sed caelum est. Nunquid caelestis inhabitatio animas, quas admittit, indurat, aut memoria priuat, aut pietate spoliat? Fratres, latitudo caeli dilatat corda, non arctat: exhilarat mentes, non alienat: affectiones extendit, non contrahit. Et ab An[b3]gelico nostri praesidio sic argumentatur, superni spiritus, nunquid quia caelos ab initio incolunt, terras despiciunt? nunquid quod semper vident faciem patris,[60]

b2v–b4v)⁵⁷ The author, identified only as "C. D.," seems to have been a somewhat defensive Catholic theologian who could write passable "Ciceronian" Latin (but by then who couldn't?). His admiration for St. Bernard suggests that he may have been a Cistercian. Since Hericus Benedictinus' poem ended near the top of the third page of an eight-page gathering, one may wonder if the scholium was provided to fill up the rest of the pages.

A Scholium on the passage
"And now you can do even more, etc." [lines 66–67]

This is what Jerome says to Paula, in the funeral eulogy he sent to Eustochium: "Now that you are present, you can more easily obtain what you ask for."⁶¹ This argument is freely used both by other fathers and also by St. Bernard, where he says: "Of the three things which we ought to consider alertly on the feastdays of the saints, the chief point is help from the saint, because a person who was powerful on earth is more powerful in heaven before the face of his lord God. For if he was merciful to sinners and prayed for them while he was alive, now he will pray for us to the Father so much the more, as he more truly recognizes our miseries, since that blessed homeland did not change but increased his charity and his feelings of mercy are now more intense when he stands before the fountain of mercy."⁶² And again: "The veteran soldier of Christ now sits quietly, having earned his sweet security. About himself, of course, he is secure, but he is anxious about us. For he did not put off the bowels of pity together with the rottenness of the flesh, nor did he put on for himself the stole of glory in such a way as to take on at the same time forgetfulness of our misery and of his own mercy. It is not an earthly land of forgetfulness that the soul of a saint inhabits; it is not an earthly land of labor, that he should be occupied there; in fact, it is not an earthly land, but heaven. Are we to believe that a heavenly dwelling-place hardens the souls it receives or deprives them of memory or strips them of affection? Brothers, the expanse of heaven does not contract but rather expands the heart; it does not alienate but enlivens the mind; it does not stunt but extends the affections." And from the angels' protection of us, he argues thus: "Are we to believe that because the spirits lived high up in heaven from the beginning, they despise the earth? That because they always behold the face of the Father, they put aside

ministerium euacuat pietatis? Quid ergo? Angeli succurrunt hominibus, & qui ex nobis sunt, nesciunt nos: nec norunt tam compati, in quibus passi sunt & ipsi? Qui dolores nesciunt suos, sentiunt tamen nostros, & qui venerunt de magna tribulatione, non recognoscunt iam in quo fuerunt? Et alibi paucis,[63] Omnino valde potens est in caelis, qui tam magnus & potens extitit in terris, secundum magnitudinem gratiae magnitudine gloriae exaltatus. Loquitur autem illic de mirifico sanctorum, erga nos patrocinio, vt & aliàs,[64] Quis scit si idcirco sublatus fuerit, vt nos suis intercessionibus protegat apud Patrem? Vtinam ita sit. si enim tantae charitatis erat, dum esset nobiscum, vt omnia quae ad necessitatem corpoream spectant, libentius mihi quàm sibi cederet: quantò magis nunc, cùm illi summae charitati, Deo, inhaeret, maiorem habet in me gratiam et charitatem? Nec ita pòst, Vtilitatis etiam propriae consideratio exultandum nobis suggerit et laetandum,[65] quòd tam potens suos patronus, tam fidelis ad caelestem curiam praecesserit aduocatus, cuius et feruentissima charitas obliuisci nequeat filiorum, & probata sanctitas obtineat gratiam apud Deum. Quis enim nunc sanctum minus aut posse prodesse, aut suos diligere suspicetur? Profectò cum prius diligeretur, certiora nunc suae dilectionis experimenta capit: & cùm dilexisset suos, in finem dilexit eos. Absit autem vt tua nunc, ô anima sancta, minus efficax aestimetur oratio, quando praesenti viuidius supplicare est maiestati, nec iam in fide ambulas, sed in specie regnas. Absit vt imminuta, nedum exinanita tua illa tam operosa charitas reputetur, cùm ad fontem ipsum charitatis aeternae procumbis, pleno hauriens ore, cuius & ipsa prius stil-[b3v]licidia sitiebas. Non potuit morti cedere charitas, fortis vt mors,[66] imò & morte ipsa fortior. Et ad id, Inuenerunt me vigiles, qui custodiunt ciuitatem.[67] Sed enim, quinam, ait,[68] illi sunt vigiles, à quibus inuentam se sponsa perhibet? Nempè Apostoli & Apostolici viri: verè hi sunt, qui ciuitatem custodiunt, id est, eam ipsam quam inuenerunt Ecclesiam, eóque vigilantius, quò nunc temporis grauius periclitantem conspiciunt, à malo vtique domestico & intestino, sicut scriptum est, Inimici hominis domestici eius.[69] Neque enim pro qua ad sanguinem vsque restiterunt, suo derelinquunt patrocinio destitutam, sed eam protegunt & custodiunt die ac nocte, id est, in vita et in morte sua. Et

their loving service? What then? Do angels serve us, and those who are like us do not know us and have so thoroughly forgotten how to have compassion on those among whom they themselves suffered? They know no pain themselves, but they are sensible of ours. They came from great tribulation, and are they now oblivious of where they were?"[70] And briefly in another place: "A person who was so great and powerful on earth is certainly very powerful in heaven, where he is exalted by the greatness of glory according to the greatness of grace."[71] Moreover, he is speaking there about the marvelous assistance the saints give us, as he is in another place: "Who knows if the reason he was taken from us was to protect us by his intercession with the Father? Would that it were so, for if while he was with us he had such great charity that he granted all bodily necessities more willingly to me than to himself, how much more, now that he is fixed in that highest charity, God, how much more favor and charity does he have toward me?"[72] And afterwards, to paraphrase:[73] Also the consideration of what is useful to us suggests that we should exult and rejoice because such a powerful patron, such a faithful advocate, has gone ahead of his loved ones to the court of heaven,[74] for his most fervent charity cannot forget his sons, and his proven sanctity obtains grace with God. For who will suppose that now the saint is either less able to do good or less loving of his own? Indeed, since he was loved before, he now receives even more certain proofs of his love; and since he loved his own, he loved them to the end.[75] Far be it from us to think that now, O holy soul, your prayer is less efficacious, since it is more true to life to supplicate the majestic king in his very presence and now you do not walk in faith but reign by seeing. Far be it from us to think that that very active charity of yours is lessened or even weakened, now that you have prostrated yourself at the very fountain of eternal charity, drinking mouthfuls of what you once thirsted for as it fell drop by drop. Charity cannot yield to death; it is strong as death, nay it is even stronger than death. And on the passage "The watchmen who guard the city found me," he says: "For who are those watchmen who found the spouse, as she says. They are, namely, the apostles and apostolic men. Truly they are the ones who guard the city, that is, the very one they found, the church, and they do so all the more vigilantly in that they now behold her in a time of grave danger, beset, as it were, by evils from within her household, as it is written, 'A man's enemies are his household servants.' For they do not leave her, for whom they stood firm even to shedding their blood, destitute of their assistance, but they protect and guard her day and

si preciosa in conspectu Dei mors sanctorum eius,[76] non ambigo quin tantò in morte potentius id agant, quantò in ipsa etiam confortatus est principatùs eorum.[77] Sic ista asseris, ait quis, ac si oculis tuis videris ea: sunt autem ab humanis seclusa conspectibus. Cui ego, Si oculorum tuorum testimonium fidele putas, testimonium Dei maius est. Ait verò, super muros tuos, Hierusalem, constitui custodes tota die & tota nocte, im [sic] perpetuum non tacebunt.[78] Sed de Angelis, inquis, id dictum est, Non abnuo: Omnes sunt spiritus administratorij.[79] At quis me prohibeat itidem & de istis sentire, qui potentia quidem minimè iam ipsis Angelis impares sunt, affectu autem & misericordia, eò nobis forsitan germaniores, quò natura coniunctiores? Iunge earundem passionum & miseriarum tolerantiam, in quibus nos pro tempore adhuc versamur. Nihilnè amplius miserationis pro nobis vel solicitudinis operabitur in mentibus sanctis, quod & se transisse per eas proculdubiò meminerunt? Nonnè illa ipsorum vox est, Transiuimus per ignem & aquam, & adduxisti nos in refrigerium?[80] Quid? Ipsi transierunt, & nos in mediis ignibus vel fluctibus derelinquent? nec saltem manum porrigere dignabuntur [b4] periclitantibus filiis? Non est ita. Bene tecum agitur, ô mater Ecclesia, in loco peregrinationis tuae. De caelo & terra venit auxilium tibi. Qui custodiunt te, non dormitant, nec dormiunt custodes tui, Angeli sancti, vigiles tui spiritus & animae iustorum. Non errant qui te ab vtrisque inuentam spiritibus, senserint ab vtrisque pariter custodiri. Hactenus Bernardus, recentior quidem fortassis, sed veterum nullo vitae vel morum sanctimonia inferior, vel in praecipuis Ecclesiae dogmatibus minus purus ac solidus. Cuius in hoc etiam ratio & firmissima est, & in scripturis fundatissima. Cùm enim oratio pro alio vel facta vel facienda ad dilectionis, quam proximo debemus, rationem pertineat, & ex charitate fraternitatis prodeat et proueniat: charitas autem donorum Dei et charismatum longè maximum,[81] aliis tàm multis alioquin in patria euacuandis, abolendis, cessaturis, adeò illic non excidat aut intercidat, vt ibi demùm perficiatur: quantò ergo ciues maioris, & quàm in via fuerunt, perfectioris ibidem sunt charitatis, tantò magis pro nobis viatoribus

night, that is, in life and in their death. And if the death of his saints is precious in the sight of God, I have no doubt that in death they have all the more power to do it inasmuch as their preeminence is confirmed even in death itself. 'You assert these things,' someone says, 'as if you saw them with your own eyes; but they are hidden from the sight of man.' To such a person I say: if you think the testimony of your own eyes is trustworthy, the testimony of God is greater. But he says, 'I will place guards on your walls, Jerusalem, all day and all night; they will never be silent.' 'But this,' you say, 'is spoken of the angels.' I do not deny it: for they are all ministering spirits. But who is to forbid me to understand it likewise of those who in power, certainly, are hardly unequal to the angels themselves but who in affection and mercy are perhaps all the more brotherly to us inasmuch as their nature is more joined to ours? Add that they have suffered the same passions and miseries in which we, for the time being, are still involved. Do not the minds of the saints feel any more pity and solicitude for us because they remember, as they undoubtedly do, that they too passed through these troubles? Are not those words their very own: 'We have passed through fire and water, and you brought us to a place of refreshment.' What? They themselves passed through, and will they abandon us in the midst of the fire and the waves? and will they not even deign to reach out a hand to their sons who are in danger? It is not so. It is well with you, O mother church, in the place of your pilgrimage. From heaven and earth help comes to you. Those who guard you are not drowsy, your guards do not sleep, the holy angels, those watchful spirits of yours, and the souls of the just. It is not wrong to think that you were found by both kinds of spirits and are likewise guarded by both kinds."[82] This is what Bernard has to say – to be sure, a rather recent writer, perhaps, but not at all inferior to any of the ancient fathers in sanctity of life and conduct nor any less pure and solid in the principal dogmas of the church. And in this matter his reasoning is most firm and well grounded in the scriptures. For since prayers said or to be said for another belong to the order of the love which we owe our neighbor and come forth and arise from charity for our brothers, and since charity is by far the greatest of the gifts and charisms of God, and since, though so many other gifts will be put aside, will cease and be eliminated in our homeland, charity will be so far from disappearing or dying there that it will be finally perfected there, it follows that, to the degree that the charity of the citizens of heaven is greater and more perfect there than it was when they were on their earthly pilgrimage, they pray all the more for us pilgrims and

orant, & salutem nostram desiderant: quòque Deo sunt coniunctiores, ac magis intimi, hoc etiam eorum orationes sunt efficaciores. Sint haec quidem scholastica, sed nihilo vera minus, orthodoxa & fortia, si non diserta, inquit ille.[83] Nec est cur offendant patroni, aduocati, intercedendi, & siqua alia huiusmodi vocabula. Est magis cur ea benignè interpretemur, cùm apud neminem veterum Catholicorum Graecorum et Latinorum eadem non occurrant adeò nullo Christi Domini aduocati, interpellatoris, intercessoris, mediatorisque nostri praeiudicio, nullàue contumelia, vt idem beatus pater audeat vbi suprà, & sic ratiocinetur, Non est discipulus contra magistrum, non potest sanctus quicquam facere, nisi quod magistrum viderit facientem, Opera quae ille facit, & hic fecit similiter (de oratione, [b4v] seu nostri compassione loquitur vir pius, ne quis cauilletur) iam caelos ingressus quos antè apertos beatis oculis suspiciebat, verè nunc reuelata facie speculatur gloriam Dei, absorptus quidem, sed non oblitus clamorem pauperum, &c. Amant ergo, & proin cum Christo & nobiscum, vt ita dicam, coorant, & multa nobis exorant & impretrant. Haec satis uel potius nimis quàm pro scholio: nec enim hac de re tractatum in praesentiarum institui. Vt igitur ad poetam redeamus, Credamus ei non vt olim pueriliter fortè colloquenti aut confabulanti, sed seniori iam, & se, & nos ad mortem sic inter alia praeparanti, Efficacius, inquit, solatium est, si cogitet aegrotus vniuersam Ecclesiam esse pro suo membro solicitam. Cùm autem Ecclesiam dico, quàm beatam, qumàque [sic] numerosam societatem dico, quae prophetas, quae Apostolos, quae tot martyrum ac virginum examina, tot animas Deo charas complectitur. Haec vniuersa sodalitas pro vno quolibet Christi membro periclitante orat assiduè, suisque meritis (en merita, & quidem aliena alios iuuantia) ac precibus laborantem subleuat. Et aliquantò pòst, Mea sententia praesentius remedium est aduersus desperationem, si laboranti ponatur ob oculos totius Ecclesiae communio, quae latissimè patet, complectens quicquid ab initio mundi fuit piorum hominum qui Deo placuerunt: quo in contubernio sunt et Angeli. Tota haec sodalitas votis ac precibus adiuuat laborantem, speciosa expectans speciosam. Cur abijciat clypeum, qui tam numerosas copias habet auxiliares? Nec procul ab opusculi fine, Atque ita sibi diffisus, fretus immensa Dei mi-

desire our salvation and that, the closer and more intimate they are with God, the more efficacious also are their prayers. Granted that this is quite scholastic, but it is nonetheless true, orthodox, and firm, if not elegant, as he says.[84] Nor is there any reason why the words "patron," "advocate," "interceding," and suchlike, should give any offense. Rather there is good reason why we should interpret them generously, since there is no ancient Catholic writer, Greek or Latin, who does not use them, with no prejudice or scorn of our lord Christ as our advocate, spokesman, intercessor, and mediator, so that the same blessed father [Bernard] dares to speak as above and reasons thus: "No disciple is against his master; a saint cannot do anything except what he has seen his master doing. The deeds which he does Christ likewise did (the pious man is speaking of prayer or compassion for us, lest anyone cavil).[85] Having entered the heavens which opened before so that his blessed eyes could see them, he now truly beholds the glory of God with the veil removed from his face; he is swallowed up indeed, but has not forgotten the cries of the poor, etc."[86] They do love, therefore, and together with Christ and with us they co-pray, so to speak, and by their prayers they prevail and gain many things for us. This is enough, or more than enough, for a scholium, for I did not set out to write a treatise about the matter on this occasion. And so, to return to the poet, let us believe him, not when he is writing perhaps childish confabulations or colloquies, as he once did, but when in his old age he wrote to prepare himself and us for death[87] (among other things). "It is a quite effective consolation," he says, "if a sick man should think that the whole church is solicitous about its member. But when I say 'church,' what a happy and populous society I am speaking of, one which embraces the prophets and the apostles, so many swarms of martyrs and virgins, so many souls dear to God. This whole company prays constantly for whatever member of Christ is in danger, and by their merits (notice merits, and indeed the merits of one person helping others)[88] and prayers they relieve the afflicted one."[89] And a little further on: "In my opinion it is a quite applicable remedy against despair if the communion of the whole church is held up before the eyes of the afflicted one, a communion in the very widest sense, including all holy men who have pleased God from the beginning of the world and having the angels also in its household. This whole company, a beautiful body hoping to be beautiful, helps the afflicted one with wishes and prayers. Why should anyone who has such numerous troops in reserve, throw away his shield?"[90] And not far from the end of the work: "And thus, having no confidence

502 ~ *Erasmus's Poem to St. Genevieve*

sericordia, Christi meritis, ac sanctorum suffragijs, contrito corde, cum religiosa fiducia dicat, In manus tuas Domine, commendo spiritum meum, &c. Haec ad Erasmicum de D. Genouefa carmen occurrebant ineunte anno, Lutetiae, in aedibus Rhemaeis C. D. 1566.

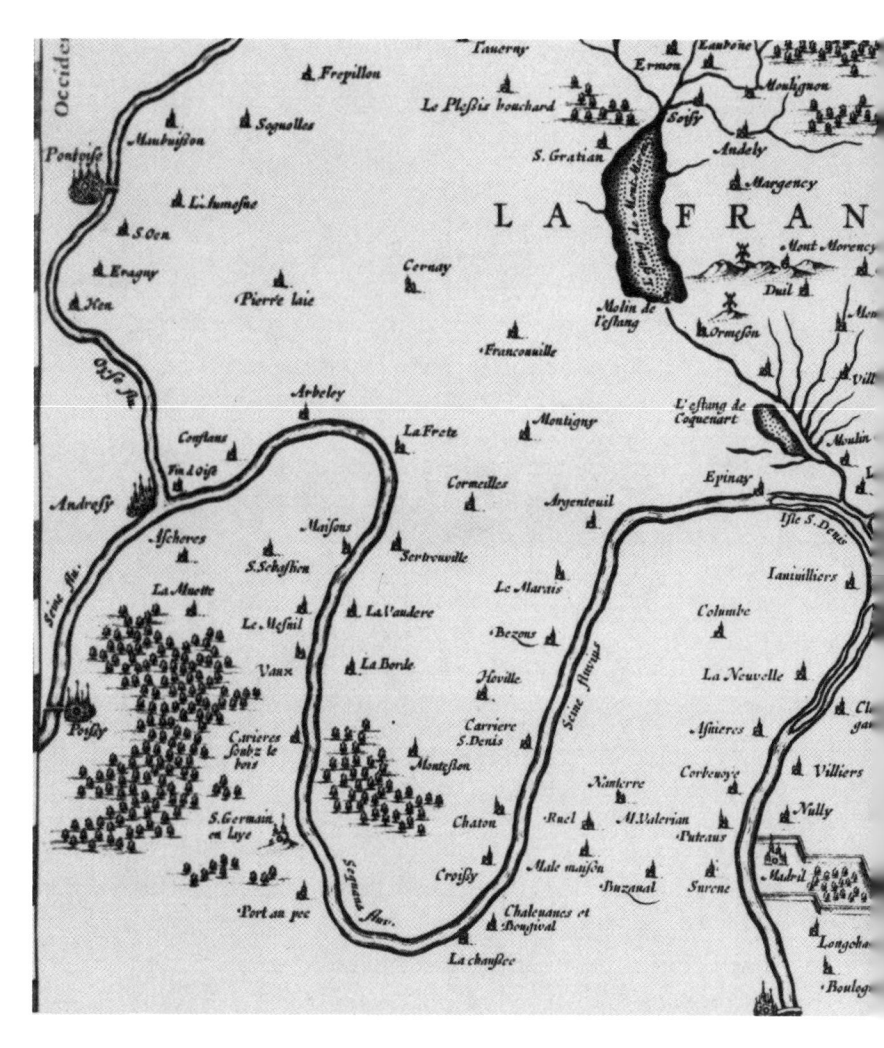

Part of a map of L'Isle de France showing the junction of the Marne and the Seine (right), Paris, Isle S. Denis, and Nanterre (Johan Blaeu, *Le Grand Atlas*, Amsterdam, 1663; rpt. in 12 vols. Theatrum Orbis Terrarum, 1967; vol. 7).

in himself, let him rely on the immense mercy of God, the merits of Christ, and the prayers of the saints; with a contrite heart and with religious confidence let him say 'Into your hands, O lord, I commend my spirit,' etc."[91] These thoughts about Erasmus' poem on St. Genevieve occurred to me at the beginning of the year, in Paris, at the house of Rhemus[?] C. D.[92] 1566.

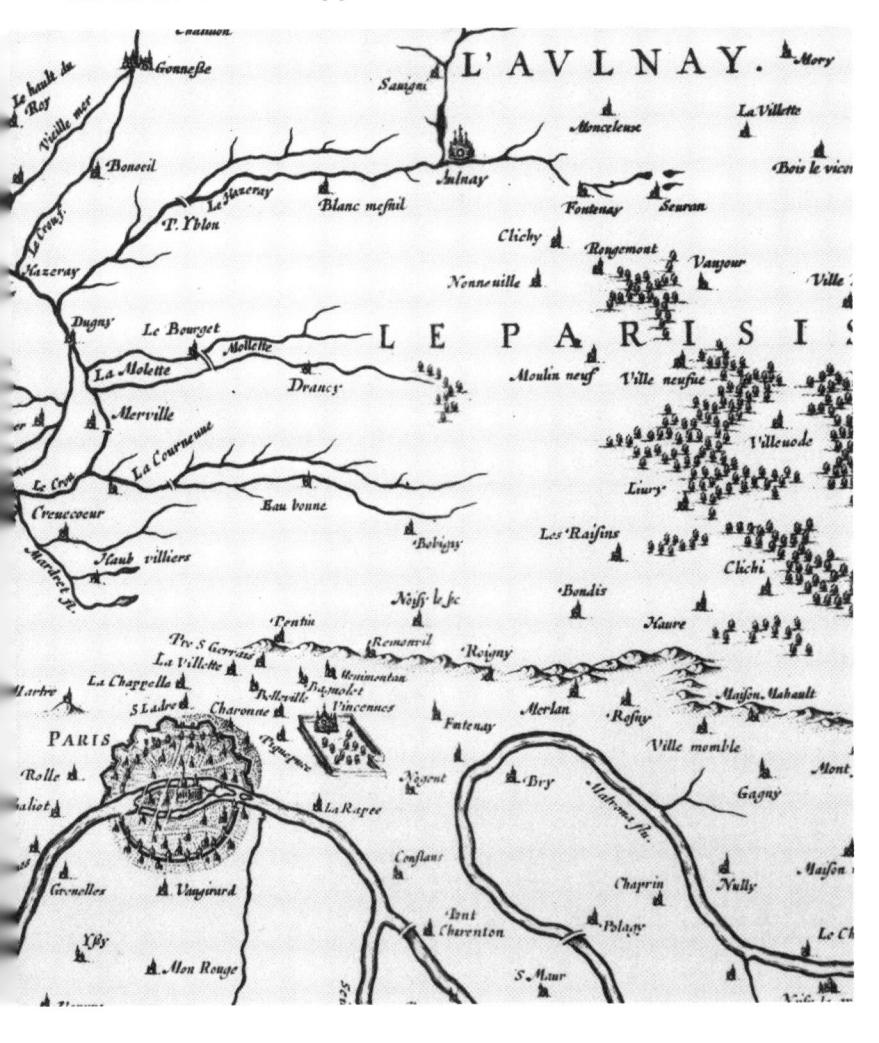

Finally I append a French translation by Paschal Robin, Seigneur de Faux, printed in 1586 as a part of a collection of material on St. Genevieve gathered by Fr. Pierre Le Juge, a canon regular at Genevieve's abbey.[93]

Ie ne tairay point aussi en ce present traitté, le beau miracle fait la en personne de Didier Erasme de Roterodam, qui viuoit du temps du grand Roy François, lors qu'l estoit Escolier, & dont il faict mention au cinquiesme tome de ses oeuures, Ainsi qu'il s'ensuit: [p. 124. The Latin poem follows on pp. 124–126v]

[The translation follows on pp. 126v–135v.] Ces vers ont esté traduits de Latin en François par Paschal Robin Seigneur de Faux, Angeuin,[94] en la maniere qui sensuit [for s'ensuit].

O Saincte Geneuiefue, à qui ie m'estudie
D'offrir ces vers promis, que mon cueur te dedie,
Fauorise mes voeuz, arrosant le canal
De mon esprit tary, tant que d'vn chant égal
A tes merites saincts, re [for ie] raconte ton aide.   5
Donne m'en le pouuoir, toy qui seurement aide
Le peuple qui t'inuoque en tous les saincts endroits,
Par où s'estend la foy et sceptre des François.
Mais sur tout celuy-la t'est aymé, par où Seine
Roulle ses flots meslez auec la blanche areine   10
De Marne, qui l'accroist & l'accolle à trauers
Les vergers pommoneux, et parmy les prez vers,
Et entre les coustaux renommez les plus noble
En fertiles, & beaux, & genereux vignobles:
Et par où ce grand fleuue & superbe & luysant   15
Va d'vn cours plantureux les plaines arrosant,
Qui foisonnent de fruicts, & tranchant la contree.
Se haste d'aller faire à Paris son entree,
Paris chef des citez, où du gauche costé
Ses ondes à l'approche adorent la cité[95]   20
Où sur toutes paroist l'Eglise nostre Dame;
Et à coup se fendant ses riues il entasme,
Et comme auec deux bras les serre estroictement,
Et d'vn deuot repli se fléchist humblement
Deuant la vierge mere en sa plaisante islette   25
Puis retournant à soy d'vne course plus preste.
Il vogue alaigrement au tres-plaisant terroir,

Où tu nasquis heureuse, en tres-heureux manoir
Dans vn petit village heureux par ton issuë,
Où se tournant ondeux en passant il saluë 30
Le Monastere sainct, sepulchre des grans Rois,
Sacré à Sainct Denis, Apostre des Gaulois,
Par ces vallons retorts il se recourbe & erre,
Et se recostoiant arrose en fin ta terre
Des ondes, qu'il respand des cornes de son front, 35
Et dirois que ses flots à regret s'en reuont.
A bon droict les François honnorent tous Nanterre,
Qui faict monstre aux passans, au milieu de sa terre,
O saincte, des ton bers, et des sainctes liqueurs
De la fontaine viue & propice aux langeurs: 40
Mais par sus tous Paris, peuplade nompareille,
Se sent infiniment heureuse par ta veille
Et patronage, ô vierge, où c'est que ta part
Auec la vierge mere vn bon heur se depart,
Sans qu'elle soit en rien ialouze qu'auec elle 45
Tu faces la dedans garde perpetuelle
Là bien hault esleuee à la cyme du mont
Tu descouures de loign les plaines iusqu'au fond,
Et repousses les maux, qui menacent la France,
Mais icelle au milieu de la ville s'auance 50
D'embrasser en pitié les habitans piteux,
Oyants les pleurs, & cris des pauures souffreteux:
Et là comme elle suit son cher fils pitoiable,
Tu l'imites aussi, son espouse amiable.
Tandis, vous defendez ensemble en voeux pareils 55
Les saincts estats vnis, le Conseil des Conseils,
Le Parlement sacré, mais sur tout la Prouince,
Et le Roy tres-Chrestien et tres-Auguste Prince:
Les vns qui sainctement decouurent les secrets,
Au peuple tres-deuot, des mysteres secrets, 60
Les autres qui par loix equitables regissent
La ville, où maintes gens, meruelle se pollicent,
C'est donc de vos bienfaicts, qu'on ne voit auiourd'huy
Peuple florir ailleurs au dessus de cestuy,
Mais, ô Saincte, il est temps que ie te remercie 65
Pour auoir recouuert par tes merites vie,
Et veux vn entre mille & mille retirez
De mort par ton secours, t'offrir ces vers sacrez.

L'hyuernalle frisson d'vne fieure infuyable,
Qui le quatriesme iour reuient presque incurable, 70
M'auoit desia passé iusques au fond des os,
Lors que le medecin, requis pour mon repos,
Me console et promet, que telle maladie
Ne sera qu'ennuyeuse, & sans perte de vie.
Il m'esiouyt autant, que s'il m'eust en effect 75
Dict que dans quatre iours ie pendrois au gibet,
Car il me semble aduis, que le mal recommence,
Quand apres si longs ans i'ay bien la souuenance
Que ce feu langoureux en ma prime verdeur
Me geina tout vn an, dont ie n'auois au coeur 80
Que desir de la mort, laquelle bien que blesme,
N'est si triste qu'vn mal dict du medecin mesme,
Alors, ô saincte vierge, il me souuint de toy,
Et d'vn espoir tres-bon ie confirmé ma foy,
Remuant en mon coeur ces secrettes pensees: 85
O espouse de Dieu, qui vierge luy agrees,
Et qui durant qu'icy ta vie eust si beau cours
Soulois tousiours donner aux malades secours,
Et qui peux ores plus, apres que le ciel mesme
T'a donné pres de Dieu ta demeure supresme: 90
Icy, icy regarde, & chasse de mon corps
La lente fieure quarte & la banny dehors:
Rend moy ie te supply, et moymesme à mon liure,
Sans la ioye duquel ie ne sçaurois plus viure.
Car ie pense qu'il est plus aisé de mourir 95
Vne fois, que fieureux par tant de iours languir:
Mais ce n'est rien qu'icy ie te face promesse,
Aussi tu n'as besoin de nostre petitesse,
Au reste ie chanteray le los de ton bien faict.
A peine sans parler i'auois ce voeu parfaict, 100
Mais sans plus à part moy au secret de mon ame,
Ie diray grand merueille, & si n'y aura blasme.
Ie retourne à l'estude et dispost et gaillard,
Sans aucun sentiment de langeur de ma part,
Ny de lentes frissons de la fiéure ocieuse. 105
Sept iours passoient desia, quand la fiéure odieuse
Se deuoit remonstrer, mais tout le corps deuient
Plus frais qu'au parauant, le medecin reuient
Admirant le miracle, il me visage en face,

Il visite ma langue, & faict produire en face 110
De l'vrine qu'il voit, puis me taste le poux,
Et me trouuant tout sain, il dict; Qui t'a recoux
De la fieure si tost, Erasme, et qu'elle [for quelle] grace,
Et quel Dieu t'a rendu le bon air de ta face?
Quiconque est le bon sainct, qui t'a si bien guery, 115
Il en sçait plus que moy, bien que ie sois nourry
En l'art de medecine, & n'en as plus affaire,
Le nom du Medecin ie ne veux iamais taire:
C'est Guillaume le Cop, lequel estoit alors
En la fleur de ses ans, ieune encor de corps, 120
Mais plus aagé que moy, et vieil es bonne [for bonnes] lettres,
Philosophe parfaict, entre les plus grands maistres:
Auiourd'huy tout chenu, & chargé de vieux ans,
Il est presqu'adoré de tous les courtisans,
Prés du grand Roy François entre les plus illustres, 125
Comme vn astre ecclatant de mille & mille lustres.
Et ioüit là du bien de ses diuins labeurs,
Dignement respecté des Princes & Seigneurs.
Or ie produiray donc deuant ta saincte image,
(O vierge mon secours) son graue tesmoignage: 130
De la santé receuë, & de la vie encor
A la débilité de mon fragile corps:
Combien que tout l'honneur de ce bien appartienne
Du tout à Iesus Christ, mais (vierge tres-Chrestienne)
Il t'a donné cet heur auecques luy là haut, 135
Pour luy auoir compleu au monde comme il faut,
C'est de sa grace aussi, qu' aprés ta chere vie,
Quoy que morte, tu peux guerir la maladie,
Comme par charité tu feis en ton viuant.
C'est ainsi que le veut ton espoux tant pouuant, 140
Il luy plaist d'eslargir par toy ses dons & graces,
Et de se veoir loüé par toy en tant de places,
Prenant plaisir de luyre au temple transparant,
De ton corps qu'il esleut, comme vn iour esclairant
Au trauers de la vitre, & comme vne fontaine 145
Pousse par des canaux sa source pure & saine,
De poinct me reste seul, que i'obtienne de toy
Par tres-humble priere, ô vierge, que sur moy
Ce blasme ne soit mis, dequoy par si long terme
I'ay différé ce voeu, payé de foy tres-ferme. 150

Endure ie te prye qu'il te soit adiousté
Ce beau Cantique deu à ton los merité,
Et à tant de blasons, d'honneurs, & de loüanges,
Et tiltres de ton nom, que les peuples estranges
Ny Latins, ny Gregois, ny autres nations   155
Ne congneurent iamais plus de perfections
En vierge de renom, que par ta modestie,
Et par ta chasteté la grace est departie
A ton pouuoir, parmy les bien heureux esprits.
Et qu'autre que toy n'est plus douce en Paradis.   160

Notes

1. See his "Thomas More and His Foursome of 'Blessed Holy Women' " in *Thomas-Morus-Gesellschaft Jahrbuch 1983/84*, ed. Hermann Boventer (Düsseldorf, 1984), pp. 113–30.

2. One form of the life is given in *Acta sanctorum*, 65 vols. (Antwerp, Paris, Rome, Brussels, 1643–1940), 1, 138–47. A slightly different recension has been edited by Bruno Krusch in *Passiones vitaeque sanctorum aevis Merovingici et antiquiorum aliquot* in *Monumenta Germaniae historica: scriptorum rerum Merovingicarum*, vol. 3 (Hannover, 1896), pp. 204–38 (hereafter cited as MGH). A third recension has been edited by Karl Künstle (Leipzig, 1910). There is still no scholarly consensus about the priority among the three recensions, but the acrimonious arguments of Krusch against the authenticity of the life have been refuted by several scholars, and there is no reason not to believe the author of the life when he says that he composed it eighteen years after Genevieve's death. For a convenient summary of the lively and protracted disputes about the life, see E. Vacandard, *Études de critique et d'histoire religieuse: quatrième série*, 2nd ed. (Paris, 1923), pp. 261–66; Vacandard also paraphrases and analyzes the life itself (pp. 65–124).

3. *Acta sanctorum*, 1, 138 (MGH, 215–18).

4. *Acta sanctorum*, 1, 139 (MGH, 219–20).

5. *Acta sanctorum*, 1, 140 (MGH, 225).

6. In other versions it is a man.

7. *Acta sanctorum*, 1, 142, 147 (MGH, 235).

8. It would not matter if some of the victims were suffering from psychotic delusions because actually curing a psychosis would be almost as miraculous as exorcising the devil.

9. *Acta sanctorum*, 1, 138 (MGH, 217–18). That the cure was not immediate and sensational lends credibility to the story.

10. *Acta sanctorum*, 1, 141–51 (MGH, 225–38).
11. *Acta sanctorum*, 1, 151–52 (not in MGH).
12. *Analecta hymnica*, ed. Clemens Blume and Guido Maria Dreves, 55 vols. (Leipzig, 1886–1922), 8, 136; 39, 145; 46, 262; 49, 327; 55, 167.
13. Erasmus might also have later felt a special affinity for St. Genevieve because a man was once cured of kidney stones, from which Erasmus suffered over the years, through her intercession (*Acta sanctorum*, 1, 143; MGH, 237).
14. *The Collected Works of Erasmus*, vol. 1 (Toronto and Buffalo, 1974), trans. R. A. B. Mynors and D. F. S. Thomson, annotated by Wallace K. Ferguson, pp. 105–6 (hereafter cited as CWE). "Nuper in quartanam incideramus, sed conualuimus confirmatique sumus non opera medici, tametsi adhibeamus, sed vnius diuae Genouefae, virginis nobilissimae, cuius ossa penes canonicos regulares seruata cotidie monstris choruscant et adorantur: nihil illa dignius, mihi salutarius" (*Opus epistolarum Des. Erasmi Roterodami*, ed. P. S. Allen, 12 vols. (Oxford, 1906–1958), 1, 164–65 (hereafter cited as "Allen"). Erasmus himself was a member of the canons regular and hence should have been all the more familiar with Genevieve.
15. CWE, 1, 250–51. ". . . ita sum ea nouitate offensus, vt nocturnae illius febris, quae nos ante biennium Orco fere demiserat, manifesta vestigia senserim: nos contra omni cura medicorumque opibus pugnamus, vixque effugimus. Dubia enim adhuc plane valetudine sumus. Quod si denuo ea febris me arripuerit, actum de tuo, mi Batte, fuerit Erasmo. Non pessima tamen in spe sumus, diua Genouefa freti, cuius praesentem opem iam semel atque iterum sumus experti: maxime medicum nacti Guilhelmum Copum non modo peritissimum, verumetiam amicum, fidum et Musarum, quod rarissimum est, cultorem" (Allen 1, 286).
16. See Hans R. Guggisberg, *Basel in the Sixteenth Century* (St. Louis, 1982), pp. 25, 29–30.
17. But it is quite unlikely that the flooding of the Seine in January 1530/31 had anything to do with the writing of the poem, as Dr. Reedijk suggests in his edition of *The Poems of Desiderius Erasmus* (Leiden, 1956), p. 351 (hereafter cited as "Reedijk"). See note 49, below. In his article "Erasmus' 'Carmen Votivum' ter ere van Ste-Geneviève," *Hermeneus*, 58, (1986), N. van der Blom argues very tenuously (from the imagined content of two non-extant letters) that Erasmus wrote the poem in the middle of May 1532.
18. Nos. 17, 22, 34–37 in Dr. Reedijk's edition.
19. Nos. 19–21, 33. Prof. Harry Vredeveld, in a forthcoming publication, will give some reasons to think that Nos. 19–21 were written in 1499, not 1489 (as Dr. Reedijk suggests.)
20. More than one medieval hymn included many episodes from the *vita*: see *Analecta hymnica*, 18, 77–80; 43, 152–54; 46, 261–64.
21. Whom he praised in one of his most elegant poems (Reedijk, No. 91).
22. CWE 2, 270–71. "Mihi semper placuit carmen quod a prosa, sed optima, non longe recederet. . . . Me vehementer delectat poema rhetoricum et rhetor poeticus, vt et in oratione soluta carmen agnoscas et in carmine rhetoricam phrasin. Aliis longius petita placent; at mihi vel praecipue probatur quod

orationem ex ipsis rebus sumis, nec tam studiosus es ostentandi ingenii quam ostendendae rei" (Allen, *1*, 545).

23. See note 32, below.

24. The comma, instead of a semicolon, in line 13 seems to signal that we are not really beginning a new sentence, even though there is no conjunction.

25. Those at lines 22, 67-68, and 72.

26. So too with the echoes at lines 73, 74, and 100.

27. In her instructions to Cupid Venus says that Dido will "take him to her bosom" ("gremio accipiet," *Aeneid* 1.685).

28. The copy is in the Houghton Library at Harvard University. I have expanded the abbreviations (except for "&") and omitted the accent marks placed over the letters which precede an enclitic *-que*. Sometimes, when a period or question mark clearly ending a sentence is followed by a word beginning with a lower-case letter, I have silently capitalized it. I have also emended "febrin" to "febrim" in line 87 and have added a period at the end of line 104. In "Towards a Definitive Edition of Erasmus' Poetry," *Humanistica Lovaniensia* 37 (1988), 171, Prof. Harry Vredeveld notes that Dr. Reedijk's edition wrongly prints "referent" for "reserent" in line 43.

29. The translation does not try to present the wordplay on "votiuum" (done in fulfillment of a vow) and "votis" (desires) or the v-alliteration in the first three lines.

30. Caesar, *Gallic Wars* 1.1.1

31. In medieval hymns St. Genevieve is invoked as the protectress of France, but especially of Paris (*Analecta hymnica*, 39, 144; 42, 209).

32. Genevieve herself sailed on this part of the Seine. During a famine in Paris she sailed up the Seine to Arcis near Chaumes to get food. On the way she encountered a tree that had caused boats to sink; by her prayers it was miraculously uprooted. On another occasion, as she was returning from Nanterre by boat, eleven grain boats with which she was sailing threatened to capsize in a high wind. She saved the fleet by her prayers. See her *vita* in *Acta sanctorum*, 1, 141-42 (MGH, 229-31).

33. In concept, though not in language, Erasmus takes his cue here from Ausonius' description of the confluence of the Sauer with the Mosel and that of the Mosel with the Rhine (*Mosella* 354-58, 418-30). At first glance I thought that the harmonious blending of the Seine (Sequana) and the Marne (Matrona) was an anticipation of the cooperation of the two patronesses, but Erasmus makes Sequana, which is usually feminine, masculine (under some metrical constraint in "factus"), and Matrona is usually masculine. There's simply no telling about rivers. But it is also fitting, I suppose, that the gallant and manly river should pay his homage to the two noble ladies.

34. In the Latin here (line 11) and at line 87 the first syllable of the third foot is short instead of long. Erasmus is following the custom of lengthening a short syllable before a masculine caesura—a practice that has some classical precedents but was sometimes followed excessively in the middle ages. Erasmus was not fussy about such things, but one imagines that he could

have avoided them here if he had really wanted to. Is it significant that they occur in passages where a river rolls on its way and Cop asks in amazement what has happened to Erasmus?

35. The Latin "In sese redit" also implies that he came back to his senses after the ecstatic vision of the Blessed Virgin.

36. The Latin "infantula" (derived from "infans," the root meaning of which is "speechless") suggests that all the babe can do is cry because it cannot speak.

37. Genevieve, who was especially devoted to St. Denis, thought to be the first bishop of Paris (d. 258), persuaded the clergy and people of Paris to build a basilica dedicated to him and his fellow martyrs Rusticus and Eleutherius on the Ile S..Denis. Genevieve obtained a couple of miracles to get the work started and to keep it going (*Acta sanctorum*, *1*, 139-40; MGH, 221-24).

38. The subterranean grotto where St. Genevieve withdrew to pray and the nearby well from which she drew water for her mother's eyes were still places of pilgrimage a century ago; see Auguste Vidieu, *Sainte Geneviève, patronne de Paris et son influence sur les destinées de la France* (Paris, 1884), p. 364.

39. Her body was kept in the gothic abbey at Mont Ste. Geneviève, which in Erasmus' time belonged to the Augustinian canons regular, Erasmus' own order. The Collège de Montaigu, where Erasmus resided as a student in 1496, was on the site of the present-day Bibliothèque Ste.-Geneviève, very near the church of Ste. Geneviève. In the eighteenth century the gothic church was replaced by what is now the Panthéon, which was secularized first in 1791 and finally in 1885. The relics were destroyed in 1871.

40. In medieval hymns St. Genevieve is frequently invoked as co-patroness of Paris, together with Mary (*Analecta hymnica*, 8, 132, 135; *39*, 144; *42*, 209; *49*, 327).

41. The high central tower of the abbey church, which was quite near the city wall, looked out over the fields south of the city. When Attila was approaching Paris, the people wanted to pack up what they could and take refuge elsewhere. Genevieve persuaded the men to stay and the women to fast and pray with her. Attila passed by Paris and plundered the very places to which they would have fled (*Acta sanctorum*, *1*, 139; MGH, 219).

42. In the statues of the virgin at the cathedral of Notre Dame in Paris, Mary fondles the Christ child in her bosom or on her lap. But Christ identified himself with the suffering (Matt. 25:35-40). Also, the poor must have congregated around the cathedral to beg alms.

43. "Sponsa Christi" is a usual title for a virgin saint, but in medieval hymns it seems to be applied to St. Genevieve with unusual frequency (*Analecta hymnica*, 8, 132-33, 135; *9*, 140; *18*, 77-80; *29*, 104; *42*, 210; *43*, 154-55; *46*, 262), perhaps because of the vivid scene near the beginning of her *vita* where St. Germain picked her out of a crowd as a little girl and asked her whether she wished to become the bride of Christ (*Acta sanctorum*, *1*, 138; MGH, 215-18).

44. In a medieval trope St. Genevieve is called "christifera" (Christ-bearer); see *Analecta hymnica*, *49*, 364.

45. In "Notes on Some Poems of Erasmus," *Daphnis*, 16 (1987), 611–13, Prof. Harry Vredeveld gives evidence to show that Dr. Reedijk (in spite of the emphatic agreement of James Hutton in his review of Dr. Reedijk's edition in *Erasmus: Speculum Scientiarum*, 11, 1958, 34, and the tentative assent of Jean-Claude Margolin in "Paris through a Gothic Window at the End of the Fifteenth Century: A Poem of Erasmus in Honor of St. Geneviève" in *Res Publica Litterarum: Studies in the Classical Tradition*, 1, 220, note 66) is wrong to suggest that "Germanos Druidas" is a caustic allusion to the theologians of the Sorbonne, meaning something like "lamas of the first water" (p. 353)—a position reaffirmed by Dr. Reedijk in *Actes du Congrès Érasme de Rotterdam 1969* (Amsterdam and London, 1971), pp. 181–82. The usage of Erasmus' contemporaries shows that it simply means "genuine priests," the same priests who (two lines later) explain religious mysteries to the people. The French translator of 1586 also takes the phrase in a straightforward way (see line 56, below). N. van der Blom (*Hermeneus*, 58, 193 and note 8) pointed out that "Druidas" was not satiric in a poem which calls St. Denis "Celtarum lux"; but he suggests that "Germanos" means "brothers" and translates "De broeders de Druiden"; but this interpretation is highly unlikely in this context and is not supported by the examples he gives in note 8.

46. The kings of France had the title "most Christian."

47. As N. van der Blom pointed out (*Hermeneus*, 58, 198, note 16), a quartan fever occurred on the fourth day only if one counts the day of its onset as the first day; we would say it recurs every three days.

48. N. van der Blom (*Hermeneus*, 58, 198, note 17) states that "sueta" here is vocative, but it is perhaps less strained simply to understand "eras" (as N. van der Blom does in his own translation).

49. Dr. Reedijk (p. 354) notes that at the time of Erasmus' fever the Seine had flooded so that the shrine of St. Genevieve was carried in procession to Notre Dame. He suggests (and Jean-Claude Margolin seems to agree with him in *Res Publica Litterarum*, 1, 210) that the meaning of the lines is "apparently that as Ste G. is now enjoying the hospitality of the Virgin, she is nearer to Christ than normally and therefore more powerful." N. van der Blom (*Hermeneus*, 58, 198, note 17) briefly expressed his disagreement. And in fact the context and the language preclude such an interpretation. The contrast is between the time when Genevieve pressed the earth with her feet and the time when she is in heaven ("coeli"). And "regia coeli" cannot refer to Mary herself (who can be called "regina" but not "regia," which cannot mean "queen") nor to her church (which is not in heaven). In fact the phrase "regia coeli" is borrowed from Virgil (*Aeneid* 7 [not 8, as Dr. Reedijk has it].210), where it refers specifically to a heavenly, not an earthly, palace. Besides, the position of the relics of Genevieve has no bearing on her closeness to Christ. See the scholium which follows this translation and the French translation of 1586 (lines 89–90, below). A medieval hymn comes close to Erasmus's meaning: "Standing before the face of the king, reconcile us to the king" (*Analecta hymnica*, 43, 140). Thomas Aquinas points out that we have all the more reason to call upon the saints when they are in heaven than we do when

they are on earth because they are more acceptable to God (*Commentary on the Sentences*, IV, d. 45, q. 3, a. 2). But he also says that the saints themselves, on earth or in heaven, do not have the power to perform miracles; that power is God's alone and the saints are its instruments (*Summa theologiae*, 2a-2ae, q. 178, a. 1). But the saints in heaven are also more perfectly conformed to the divine will (*Commentary on the Sentences*, IV, d. 45, q. 3, a. 1). Thomas More also makes the point that the saints in heaven are more willing and able to help than they were when they lived on earth, though he recognizes that they do so not by their own power but by their intercession. See his *A Dialogue concerning Heresies*, The Yale Edition of the Complete Works of St. Thomas More, volume 6, ed. Thomas Lawler, Germain Marc'hadour, and Richard Marius (New Haven and London, 1981), part 1, 211/20-212/28.

50. Did he make him say "ah?"

51. Was he checking for swelling, or taking his pulse? The French translator ("taste le poux," line 111) chooses the latter.

52. William Cop, who died on 2 December 1532, not long after Erasmus's poem was first published, had studied at the University of Basel (and probably at other universities) for some seven years before he became a doctor of medicine at Paris on 17 May 1496, about a year before he treated Erasmus's fever; see *Contemporaries of Erasmus: A Biographical Register of the Renaissance and Reformation*, ed. Peter G. Bietenholz and Thomas B. Beutscher, 3 vols. (Toronto, Buffalo, London, 1985-1987), 1, 336-37.

53. Compare *Virginis et martyris comparatio*: Quidquid enim in Sanctis gloriosum est, Christi munus est (For whatever is glorious in the saints is the gift of Christ); see *Opera omnia*, ed. Jean Leclerc, 10 vols. (Louvain, 1703-6), 5, 590B.

54. Not until the fifteenth century was the art of making more or less clear glass rediscovered in Venice; most of the glass with which Erasmus would have been familiar was colored or tinted.

55. Line 108 imitates the sound of rushing water tamed in a channel. I think of the old fountains in public squares with their spout pipes flowing.

56. On one occasion Genevieve interceded for a servant who had angered his master by his misdeeds. When the master obstinately refused her, she left in sadness. When the master arrived home he was suddenly overtaken by a deadly fever. Foaming and burning with fever, he threw himself at the saint's feet. She cured him and he forgave his servant (*Acta sanctorum*, 1, 147; MGH, 233).

57. I am deeply grateful to Prof. Jacques Chomarat, who clearly and precisely copied by hand the scholium from the copy in the Bibliothèque Nationale in Paris. Later I checked the text against a xerox of the copy in the Houghton Library at Harvard University. I have expanded all abbreviations except "&."

58. *Sidenote*: Serm. in vigil. SS. Petri et Pauli.

59. *Sidenote*: Serm. 2. de S. Victore.

60. *Sidenote*: Matt. 18[:10].

61. Ep. 108 (*Epitaphium Sanctae Paulae*) 32 in *Eusebii Hieronymi Epistulae*,

ed. Isidore Hilberg, Corpus Scriptorum Ecclesiasticorum Latinorum, vol. 56 in three parts (Vienna and Leipzig, 1910-1918), part 2, p. 350. Eustochium was the daughter of Paula, who was celebrated in the funeral eulogy.

62. *Sancti Bernardi Opera*, ed. J. Leclercq, C. H. Talbot, and H. Rochais, 8 vols. (Rome, 1957-77), 5, 185-86.

63. *Sidenote*: Serm. de S. Benedicto.

64. *Sidenote*: Serm. in obitu deuoti Humberti.

65. *Sidenote*: Serm. 2. in transitu.S. Malach.

66. *Sidenote*: Cant. 8[:6].

67. *Sidenote*: Cant. 3[:3].

68. *Sidenote*: Serm. 77.

69. *Sidenote*: Mich. 7[:6].

70. *Sancti Bernardi Opera*, 6, 34-35.

71. *Sancti Bernardi Opera*, 5, 6-7.

72. *Sancti Bernardi Opera*, 5, 446.

73. This is the best I can do with the puzzling phrase "Nec ita post." In Bernard the paraphrase does not follow shortly after the preceding quotation. Perhaps the scholiast means: "And that it is not so [that is, that the saints forget us, he says] later."

74. He seems to be paraphrasing the following sentence from Bernard's second sermon on St. Malachy: "Laetemur, inquam, et exultemus, quia caelestis illa curia ex nobis habet cui sit cura nostri, qui suis nos protegat meritis, quos informavit exemplis, miraculis confirmavit" (*Sancti Bernardi Opera*, 5, 54). The following sentences sound as if they might be Bernard's, but they are not in that sermon or in any of the other works mentioned in the sidenotes.

75. John 13:1.

76. *Sidenote*: Psal. 115[:15].

77. *Sidenote*: Psal. 138[:17].

78. *Sidenote*: Esa. 62[:6].

79. *Sidenote*: Hebr. 1[:14].

80. *Sidenote*: Psal. 65[:12].

81. *Sidenote*: 1. Cor. 13[:13].

82. *Super Cantica sermo 77, Sancti Bernardi Opera*, 2, 263-64.

83. *Sidenote*: Cypria. lib. & epist. 2.

84. Cyprian, *Ad Donatum* 2 in *S. Thasci Caeceli Cypriani opera omnia*, ed Wilhelm Hartel, Corpus Scriptorum Ecclesiasticorum Latinorum, vol. 3 in 3 parts (Vienna, 1868- 71), part 1, p. 4. Cyprian's words are: "denique accipe non diserta, sed fortia." The formulation of the sidenote seems to depend on the fact that in the sixteenth century *Ad Donatum* was sometimes considered to be a separate *libellus* and was sometimes placed second among the epistles.

85. The scholiast's parenthesis guards against a misunderstanding: the saint could pray and feel pity, as Christ did, but he could not perform miracles by his own power, as Christ did.

86. *Sancti Bernardi Opera*, 6, 35.

87. He refers to Erasmus' *De praeparatione ad mortem* (1533).

88. In his parenthesis the scholiast is emphasizing the Catholic implications of Erasmus words.

89. *Opera omnia Desiderii Erasmi Roterodami*, ed. Jan H. Waszink et al., 10 vols. (Amsterdam, 1969– ; hereafter cited as ASD), group V, vol. 1, *De preparatione ad mortem*, ed. A. van Heck, 368/667–73.

90. ASD V-1, 380/997–1002. It is characteristic of the scholiast that he omitted the following sentence, which ends the paragraph: "Si spem facit vnius monasterii deprecatio, in hoc numero sunt vniuersa monasteria."

91. ASD V-1, 390/237–40.

92. I have not been able to identify C. D. or *aedes Rhemaeae*. Though *Rhemaeus* is not a recognized adjectival form referring to Reims, I have wondered if the house might belong to the archbishop of Reims, the primate of France and sometimes its chancellor.

93. *L'histoire de Saincte Geneuiefue, Patronne de Paris, prise & recherchee des vieux liures escris à la main, des histoires de France, & autres autheurs approuuez. Plus. Vn brief recueil & discours des choses antiques & signalees de la dicte maison. Ensemble. L'histoyre propre & office de ladicte Saincte. Par F. Pierre le Iuge, Parisien, Religieux en l'Abbaye de Saincte Geneuiefue.* (Paris: Henry Coypel, 1586). Once more I am deeply grateful to Prof. Jacques Chomarat for carefully copying the translation by hand from the copy in the Bibliothèque Nationale in Paris. Later I checked the text against a microfilm of the copy in the British Library. With one exception I have not included the sidenotes, which simply identify places.

94. Thus he was a native of Anjou, the center of which is Angers, the home of Fr. Marc'hadour and *Moreana*.

95. The translator wrongly took "arcem" as referring to Paris rather than to the Abbey of St. Genevieve. The sidenote a little lower explains: "*Paris* enclos de la riuiere de Seine voy le Misopogon de Julian l'Apostat."

FRANCISCO LÓPEZ ESTRADA

Tomás Moro en un Libro de Fray Alonso de la Torre, cartujo sevillano

LAS BIOGRAFÍAS DE TOMÁS MORO dan noticias sobre la relación que tuvo con la Orden de los Cartujos; esto ocurrió en la época de sus estudios, en la juventud.[1] Ya en la última parte de su vida, Moro pudo saber que los Cartujos habían adoptado una postura como la suya en lo referente a los designios de Enrique VIII, y algunos murieron afirmándose en su adhesión al catolicismo.

Esta relación obtuvo en España una cierta resonancia, y fue ocasión para establecer un dato más que añadir a la presencia de Tomás Moro en España y en la América de habla española.[2] Encontré un testimonio de la misma en la obra escrita por un monje de la Cartuja de Sevilla,[3] fray Alonso de la Torre, que profesó en el monasterio de Nuestra Señora de las Cuevas en 1606 y fue allí monje, procurador y vicario, y luego pasó a ser procurador, presidente y Rector de la filial de Cazalla de la Sierra, en donde murió en 1650. La Cartuja de Sevilla contaba con una buena biblioteca,[4] que, en lo quedase de ella, pasó en 1835 a la Biblioteca Provincial y después a la actual Universitaria de Sevilla. Este monasterio, fundado a fines del siglo XIV, estaba situado en el barrio de Triana, junto al Guadalquivir, y en el siglo XVI llegó a ser uno de los más activos de la Orden; Colón tuvo buenas relaciones con estos cartujos, y estableció allí su panteón familiar. En este Monasterio Fray Alonso de la Torre tuvo medios para realizar sus libros; es un escritor laborioso y consecuente, cuyas obras apenas se conocen, pues no llegaron a publicarse y permanecieron manuscritas en la Biblioteca de la Cartuja sevillana. Se trata de libros escritos para sus hermanos de la Comunidad y referentes a episodios de la historia de la Orden; en ellos encontramos estas referencias a Tomás Moro, de las que daré una breve noticia y también una muestra de la obra escrita en la parte relativa a Moro.

Fray Alonso de la Torre tuvo ocasión, en su obra religiosa, de ocuparse de la desgraciada fortuna de los cartujos ingleses que habían padecido martirio por orden de Enrique VIII; y junto con ellos también lo hizo de John Fisher, el obispo de Rochester, y de Tomás Moro, como ocurre en las crónicas de estos hechos de la historia de la Europa moderna. Por fortuna, el manuscrito de esta obra es de los que se han conservado, y hoy lo guarda la Biblioteca de la Universidad de Sevilla (sign. 330/170). Tiene un título breve, en la parte superior del primer folio, que es: *Historia de los Martires de la Cartuxa de Inglaterra*.

Y otro título extenso en el folio tercero como portada del libro:

La vida y martirio, | *de tres Padres Priores de la* | *Cartuxa D. Joan Houthon:* | *D. Roberto Laurens: Don* | *Agustin Vuebiter y de quince Religiosos Monges y frailes de la dicha* | *Cartuxa, y la del Obispo Roffense, y Thomas Moro: y* | *sus Martirios, y de Reginaldo Monge de Sancta Brigida, y Fray* | *Joan Forésto Confessor dela Reyna Doña Cathalina.* | *Todos fueron martiriçados por el Rey Enr-* | *rique Octauo, por la defension de la Sancta* | *Fé Catholica y Primado del* | *Romano Pontífice* | *J.H.S.* | *Por el P. Don Alonso dela Torre Monge professo en la Car-* | *tuja delas Cuevas de la Ciudad de Sevilla.* |

Fray Alonso de la Torre escribe su libro basándose en la información que recoge de las obras sobre el asunto; estas fuentes informativas están escritas en latín, y su labor resulta ser la de un traductor que acomoda las obras de sus fuentes a la lengua española, procurando constituir una obra con un sentido de unidad, adecuada para sus fines y los lectores a los que se la dedica; de su cuenta sólo son los comentarios piadosos que acompañan esta urdimbre de la obra ajena. Por esto declara al comienzo de su libro en la dedicatoria "al cristiano y piadoso lector": "La historia de la vida y martirio de los santos mártires se escribió en latín para que todas las naciones y lenguas la gozasen, traduciendo cada uno en la suya . . ."[5] A él le tocó pasar la historia a la lengua española,[6] tal como manifiesta en el prólogo, en el que explica la intención que le guiaba. Fray Alonso de la Torre escribe su obra con intención piadosa para que aproveche a las diferentes clases de gentes a las que se dirigía. Así, en primer lugar, los cartujos ingleses son ejemplo para los monjes de su tiempo. Después, el obispo Fisher lo es para los prelados eclesiásticos. Y, finalmente, Tomás Moro se presenta como un ejemplo para la gente civil, para los casados; y también pone de relieve el virtuoso comportamiento de la familia de Moro en el hogar y en el trabajo: "en él [pueden hallar modelo] los abogados, los consejeros y ministros reales; en él, los gobernadores, jueces y presidentes; y todos en él, un invencible mártir." Y luego señala la fuente de la obra:

> Toda esta historia es sacada de la que escribe en latín el padre don Mauricio Chauncy, monje de la misma Cartuja de Londres, como testigo de vista; y como por brevedad toca solamente las causas de tantas calamidades que fueron las segundas bodas de Enrique VIII y después el cisma sucintamente, pero como yo las saco en nuestra lengua vulgar, digo todo aquello que hubo y es necesario para esta historia, tomando algunos capítulos [. . .] de la historia que escribió el padre Pedro de Ribadeneyra, de aquel tiempo, y está bien trabajada y dispuesta y sacada de graves autores. . . .[7]

Fray Alonso de la Torre nos da a conocer los libros que sirven como base del suyo: uno de ellos es el de Fray Mauricio Chauncy (1509-1581)[8] y el otro, el del Padre Pedro de Ribadeneyra, (1527-1611);[9] y urde así, con la paciencia y voluntad de un cartujo que labra todos los días su espacio de huerta, un libro que quiere servir, al mismo tiempo, como información sobre los frailes mártires de su Orden, y como ejemplo de piedad para eclesiásticos y civiles, conjuntamente.

Nos importa el libro en lo que toca a Tomás Moro, pues añade una obra más a las que difundieron por España las noticias de su vida y muerte. El capítulo XX trata "De los ilustres varones don Juan Fisher [Fischero lo llama], obispo rofense y Tomás Moro y de su martirio y causas por qué murieron"; y el XXI, "De otras muchas cosas muy notables de la vida y del martirio de Tomás Moro, excelente mártir del Señor". De este conjunto daré una muestra[10] de la versión de Fray Alonso; escojo la parte que toca al juicio de Tomás Moro.

Capítulo 21. Del martirio de Tomás Moro y combates.

[fol. 66] . . . Después que estuvo casi catorce meses en la cárcel, el primer día del mes de julio del dicho año [1535] fue llevado de la Torre de Londres delante los jueces por el Rey señalados. Iba sustentándose con el báculo en tan largo camino, el cuerpo debilitado y flaco por la grave enfermedad y cárcel, pero con mucha alegría en su rostro, sin señal de alguna tristeza o turbación.

Lo primero, le fueron recitados los capítulos de los crímenes que se le oponían; luego, el Cancelario que sucedió a Tomás Moro y Duque de Norfolk le habló de esta manera:

—Ves, Moro, que tú ciertamente en esta parte contra la real Majestad gravemente has pecado, pero, no obstando esto, confiamos tanto de la clemencia y benignidad del mismo Rey, que si quisieres arrepentirte, y ésta tu temeraria opinión, a la cual pertinacísimamente te has allegado, la trocares en mejor, alcanzarás fácilmente remisión y perdón de tu delito.

A estas cosas respondió Moro:

—Magníficos varones, a vosotros -dice- hago gracias y agradezco esta vuestra benevolencia para conmigo. Pero aquello sí lo pido y ruego al omnipotente, óptimo y máximo Dios: que yo, ayudado con su favor, pueda perseverar en esta mi opinión hasta la muerte. Cuanto a las acusaciones con quienes soy onerado, pertenece, merécelo y temo, que o el ingenio o la memoria o las palabras basten para la declaración, como si solamente impida la proligidad de los artículos y grandeza, mas también la larga detención en la cárcel y la enfermedad y flaqueza del cuerpo que ahora me tiene y padezco.

Entonces por mandado del Magistrado le fue traída una silla en la cual se sentase; en esta manera prosiguió su razonamiento:

—Cuanto a la primera parte de la acusación pertenece, la cual tiene que "yo para que más mostrase la maledicencia de mi ánimo contra el Rey en contención de su segundo matrimonio, perpetuamente haber contradicho y repugnado a su Serenísima Majestad", ninguna otra cosa tengo que responder, sino aquello que antes he dicho, y haber hecho eso apretándome la conciencia, porque no quería ni debía celar y encubrir a mi Príncipe la verdad; lo cual, sino hubiera hecho principalmente en negocio de tanto memento donde pendía la honra del Príncipe y la tranquilidad y quietud del Reino, entonces y en tal artículo verdaderamente hubiera sido lo que ahora se opone: malévolo, pérfido y traidor. Por este delito (si acaso se puede llamar delito) he padecido gravísimas penas, despojado de todos mis bienes y hacienda, aplicados al fisco, sentenciado a perpetua cárcel en que [he] estado ya quince meses enteros. [fol. 66v.] Empero, dejadas todas estas cosas, tan solamente responderé a aquellas que de este negocio son las principales. Decir que yo he merecido la pena y castigo que pone la constitución o estatuto hecho en estas Cortes próximo pasadas estando yo en la cárcel, así como con malicioso ánimo y pérfido, traidoramente haya dicho mal quitando la fama, honra y dignidad a la Real Majestad, las cuales cosas le eran a él dadas por la dicha constitución con consentimiento de todos, conviene saber: que allí el Rey es declarado debajo de Jesucristo por suprema cabeza de la Iglesia de Inglaterra; y ante todas cosas, lo que oponéis y de que me hacéis cargo, que yo ninguna cosa quisiese responder al Secretario del Rey y al venerable Consilio de su Majestad cuando me preguntaba cuál por ventura fuese mi sentencia de aquel decreto, respondí que yo ya estaba muerto al mundo, ni semejantes negocios me quería más inquietar, mas tan solamente meditar en la Pasión de Nuestro Señor Jesucristo; a lo cual ya claramente respondo que por semejante silencio mío no es lícito a vosotros ni podéis condenarme a muerte, porque ni vuestro decreto ni algunas leyes del mundo pueden condenar alguno por el silencio a muerte, mas tan solamente por el dicho o por el pecado cometido. Porque de las cosas ocultas sólo Dios juzga.

Entonces el Procurador del Rey, tomando la palabra:

—Semejante silencio—dice—era algún cierto indicio y oscura significación de algún maligno pensamiento contra el mismo decreto, por causa y razón que todo súbdito sincero y fiel al Rey, si del dicho decreto sería preguntado, está obligado, fuera de toda disimulación y fingimiento, responder que el dicho edicto y mandado del Rey es bueno, justo y santo.

Entonces Tomás Moro:

—Mas si—dice—es verdadero lo que el derecho común tiene: "el que calla consentir parece," este mi silencio más aprobó este vuestro decreto que lo enflaqueció. Y a lo que dices que todo fiel súbdito es obligado que responda que el edicto del Rey es bueno, si fuere preguntado, respondo que el súbdito de buena fe, más obligado está a Dios, a la conciencia y a su ánima que a alguna cosa en este mundo, y muy principalmente si es tal la conciencia, cual es la mía [fol. 67] que ninguna cosa de ofensa y estropiezo, ninguna de discordia y división entre los ciudadanos cause o engendre para su Príncipe y Señor, por esto, por cosa cierta, os puedo decir y afirmar que a ningún hombre en este negocio he descubierto y declarado mi conciencia.

[Sigue hablando Tomás Moro] Cuanto al segundo capítulo de la acusación a que ahora llego, por el cual soy argüido y acusado haber yo maquinado contra la dicha constitución y decreto vuestro porque yo haya escrito ocho pares de epístolas al obispo rofense [John Fisher, obispo de Rochester], con las cuales le haya animado contra este edicto, cierto con ansia y vehemencia desearía que las tales epístolas aquí públicamente se presentasen, mas porque, como vosotros decís, fueron quemadas por el obispo, yo, pues, de mi voluntad os referiré el argumento de las epístolas. En algunas de ellas se trataban cosas familiares, como nuestra antigua costumbre, comunicación y amistad pedía. Una de aquellas tenía la respuesta para la epístola del mismo obispo, por la cual saber deseaba de qué manera yo respondería en la cárcel cuando primero fuese examinado y preguntado sobre el dicho decreto. Al cual respondí que yo había desonerado mi conciencia y seguido la razón, y por eso, para que él mismo, de la misma manera hiciese, aconsejaba. Esta fue, así Dios me sea propicio, la sentencia de mis epístolas, por la cual causa de estas epístolas no puedo, por vuestro decreto, ser condenado a muerte.

[Sigue hablando Tomás Moro:] Lo que al tercero artículo pertenece, el cual contiene que yo cuando del senado era examinado, haber respondido que vuestro decreto era semejante al cuchillo cortador de dos filos, para que el que le obedeciese, peligrase de la salvación de su ánima, y el que le contradijese, perdiese la vida, y las mismas cosas haber yo respondido al Obispo rofense así como decís. De lo cual parece que estas cosas entre nosotros de pensado y con ánimo deliberado se trataban respondiendo el uno y el otro de la misma manera; a estas cosas respondo que yo simplemente, mas debajo de condición haber hablado, conviene saber, si hubiese algún estatuto semejante al cuchillo agudo y de dos filos, del cual por ningún modo alguno de los hombres podría huir que no caiga en el uno u otro filo, demás de esto que haya respondido el Obispo rofense, no sé; y puede ser que haya respondido de la misma manera si sus palabras convenían con las mías. Esto en ninguna manera se hizo por conspiración, mas antes por semejanza de los ingenios y doctrina. Brevemente esto tened por cierto [folio 67v.] que yo nunca maliciosamente he hablado contra vuestro decreto alguna cosa. Con todo en el ínterin pudo ser que muchas cosas se hayan depravadamente referido a la real Majestad para mover odio contra mí.

Después de estas cosas, fueron llamados por un ministro público doce varones según la costumbre de aquella gente, a los cuales fueron entregados los artículos sobre los cuales consultasen y juzgasen por ventura Moro maliciosamente hubiese pecado contra el decreto. Estos, como por una cuarta parte de hora se apartasen, volvieron a los Príncipes y jueces delegados y pronunciaron y declararon que Tomás Moro es digno de muerte; notable cosa dentro de un cuarto de hora negotio tan grave, hecho tan depriesa.

Luego el Cancelario pronunció la sentencia, según la forma del dicho decreto: "que fuese arrastrado, ahorcado y dejado caer de la horca, y desentrañado estando aún vivo, y que le cortasen la cabeza en los lugares que mandase el Rey." Esta fue la sentencia que se dio contra Tomás Moro, no por otra culpa sino por haber callado primero y después dicho la verdad al Rey, por haberle sido ministro fiel y leal consejero y por haber tenido cuenta con Dios y con su conciencia como más largamente se refiere en sus descargos, aunque esta sentencia tan rigurosa y cruel después se moderó y trocó en que le cortasen la cabeza, más por la costumbre que hay en el Reino de Inglaterra que a las personas en sangre o en dignidad ilustres que mueren por la justicia, les cortan la cabeza, que no por la clemencia y benignidad del Rey.

Entonces Tomás Moro, con grande alegría, dice:

—Ahora que estoy condenado a muerte, y como hombre que está a la puerta de ella, para desonerar mi conciencia libremente, os diré qué siento de vuestro decreto. Yo, por la gracia de Dios, siempre he sido católico y nunca me he apartado de la comunión y obediencia del Papa, cuya potestad entiendo que es fundada en el derecho divino y que es legítima, loable y necesaria, aunque vosotros temerariamente la habéis querido abrogar y deshacer con vuestra ley. Siete años he estudiado esta materia y revuelto muchos libros para entenderla mejor, y hasta ahora no he hallado autor santo y grave ni antiguo ni moderno [fol. 68] que diga que en las cosas espirituales que tocan a Dios, hombre y príncipe temporal pueda ser cabeza y superior de los eclesiásticos que son los que las han de gobernar. También digo que el decreto que habéis hecho ha sido muy mal hecho porque es contra el juramento que tenéis hecho de no hacer jamás cosa contra la Iglesia católica, la cual por toda la Cristiandad es una e individua, y no tenéis vosotros todos autoridad para hacer leyes ni decretos ni concilios contra la paz y unión de la Iglesia universal. Esta es mi sentencia, esta es mi fe, en la cual moriré con el favor de Dios.

Apenas había dicho estas palabras Tomás Moro, cuando todos los jueces a grandes voces comenzaron a llamarle traidor al Rey, y particularmente el Duque de Norfolk le dijo:

—¡Cómo declaráis vuestro mal ánimo contra la majestad del Rey!

Y él respondió:

—No declaro, señor, mal ánimo contra mi Rey, sino mi fe y la verdad. Porque en lo demás yo soy tan aficionado al servicio del Rey, que suplico a nuestro Señor que no me sea más propicio a mí ni de otra manera me perdone, que yo he sido a su Majestad fiel y afectuoso servidor.

Entonces el Cancelario, interrumpiendo las palabras de Tomás Moro, le dijo:

—¿Vos queréis ser tenido por más sabio y de mejor conciencia que todos los obispos, abades y eclesiásticos, que todos los nobles, caballeros y señores y finalmente que todo el Reino?

A esto respondió Tomás Moro:

—Señor, por un obispo que vos tenéis de vuestra parte, tengo yo ciento de la mía, y todos santos; por vuestros nobles y caballeros, tengo yo toda la caballería y nobleza de los mártires y confesores; por un concilio vuestro (que sabe Dios cómo se ha hecho), están en mi favor todos los concilios generales que en la Iglesia de Dios se han celebrado mil años ha; y por este vuestro pequeño Reino de Inglaterra, defienden mi verdad los Reinos de España, Francia, Italia y todas las otras provincias, potentados y Reinos amplísimos de la Cristiandad.

Oyendo estas palabras que había dicho Tomás Moro delante del pueblo, pareciendo a los jueces que no ganarían cosa alguna para sus intentos, le mandaron apartar, habiéndole dado la sentencia de muerte. Acabado esto, le tornaron a la cárcel. [fol. 68v.]

Llevándole, salió al camino su hija Margarita, muy querida de él, a la cual había enseñado la lengua latina y griega. Ella, no haciendo caso de sí ni del lugar público ni de las circunstancias, rompió por medio de los soldados encendida por el demasiado amor y deseo de su padre para pedirle su bendición y ósculo de paz; el cual dio el padre a su hija con mucho amor y ternura, y, abrazada al cuello de su padre, con las muchas voces, suspiros y lágrimas declaraba el sin medida dolor y pena de su corazón; y como lo tuviese algún poco tiempo muy apretadamente abrazado, y por el dolor apenas ya podía hablar, el padre, con permisión de los soldados, la consoló de esta manera:

— Margarita, hija, ten fuerte ánimo, no te aflijas y atormentes más; así ha parecido a Dios. Ya tiempo antes sabes los secretos de mi corazón.

Después, habiendo caminado el padre diez o doce pasos, otra vez abrazó Margarita a su padre, ya como por despedida. Allí el santo varón, sin derramar lágrimas, sin alguna perturbación de rostro, le dijo tan solamente estas palabras:

—Anda, vete enhorabuena y ruega a Dios por la salvación de mi ánima.

Aquí cada uno considere consigo mismo cuán traspasado fue el corazón de Tomás Moro con tan fuerte cuchillo de piedad.

Vuelto a la cárcel, diose más a la oración y contemplación, recreando su santa ánima el Señor con muchas y suavísimas consolaciones divinas; y algunas veces tomaba una sábana y se envolvía en ella como quien se amortaja a sí mismo. Y en vida meditaba y se ensayaba en lo que después de la muerte le había de suceder.

El día antes que le sacasen al martirio, escribió con un carbón, porque no tenía pluma, una carta a su hija Margarita en que le decía el deseo grande que tenía de morir el día siguiente y ver a nuestro Señor, por ser el día de la octava del príncipe de los Apóstoles San Pedro, pues moría por la confesión de su Primado y cátedra apostólica y víspera de la traslación del glorioso mártir santo Tomás que en su vida había sido siempre su abogado; y así se hizo como él lo deseaba, porque a los seis días de julio padeció.

Salió de la cárcel en la plaza de la Torre de Londres flaco, descolorido y consumido del mal tratamiento de la larga prisión que había padecido, y con la barba muy crecida, llevando una cruz colorada en la mano, levantados los ojos al cielo y vestido de una ropa muy pobre y vil de un criado suyo, porque queriendo él salir con una ropa honrada de chamelote que le había enviado a la cárcel su amigo Antonio Bonvisi, italiano, así por hacerle del placer [fol. 69] como por darla al verdugo en pago de la buena obra que de él recibía, fue tan grande la codicia o maldad del carcelero, que se la tomó y le obligó a salir vestido de la manera referida. Pero para Tomás Moro fue esta ropa servil y afrentosa muy excelente y preciosa y como de fiestas y bodas, sí por haberse con ella semejado a Cristo pobre, como por haber bebido el cáliz del Señor y gozado por aquel traje de las bodas del cordero. Cuando le llevaban a la muerte, una mujer, movida de compasión, le ofreció una copa de vino y él agradecióselo; no la quiso tomar, y dijo que a Cristo, nuestro Redentor, hiel le habían ofrecido en su bendita Pasión y no vino.

Estando en el lugar del martirio, acabadas sus oraciones, llamó por testigos de la fe católica en que moría a todo el pueblo encargándole que rogase a Dios por el Rey y protestando que moría como fiel ministro suyo, pero más de Dios, que es el Rey de los Reyes. Después, pidiéndole el verdugo perdón, le besó con grande amor y ternura y le dio cierta moneda de oro, imitando a San Ciprián, y le dijo estas palabras:

—Vos me haréis hoy la mejor obra que hasta ahora me ha hecho hombre ni me podrá hacer.

Y encomendándose a todos los circunstantes rogasen a Dios por él, tendió la cerviz al cuchillo, con el cual el sayón cortó aquella cabeza de justicia, verdad y santidad, llorando todos y pareciéndoles que no había sido quitada la cabeza a Moro, sino a todo el Reino.

Quedó Enrique muy contento como si fuera oficio de la cabeza de la Iglesia, cual él se tenía, quitar cabezas a varones tan insignes en todo género de letras y virtud, aunque escriben que cuando le trajeron la nueva de la muerte de Tomás Moro estaba jugando y que se volvió a Ana Bolena, que estaba sentada junto a él, y le dijo:

—Vos sois la causa de la muerte de este hombre.

Y que luego se levantó del juego y se entró en su cámara y lloró muchas lágrimas, como dicen que lo hace el cocodrilo cuando ha muerto y comido algún hombre.

Margarita en esta ocasión se mostró de mucho ánimo, y así deseó y procuró enterrar a su padre decentemente, porque supo que el cuerpo del Obispo rofense había sido arrojado en la hoya sin clérigo, sin cruz y sin una sábana, y que no había habido quien osase enterrarle por la tiranía del Rey. Temiendo que no sucediese otro tanto a su padre, y no habiendo en su casa lienzo en que envolverle ni dineros con que comprarlo, entró en una tienda [fol. 69v.] y concertó las varas de lienzo que le parecieron bastantes para aquel oficio de piedad, y queriendo que se lo diesen fiado, echó acaso mano a la faltriquera y halló el justo precio para pagar el lienzo que había comprado sin faltarle ni sobrarle un maravedí. Y animada con este milagro, envolvió el cuerpo de su padre, no atreviéndose alguno a estorbarla por ser mujer e hija de tal padre, y cumplió con la obligación que a padre y a santo mártir se debía.

La cabeza de este santo mártir estuvo casi un mes sobre un asta en la puente de Londres por mandado del Rey, y cuando la hubieron de quitar y echar en el río, la misma Margarita se dio tan buena maña, que la hubo en su poder, tan fresca y hermosa que parecía viva, sino que los pelos de la barba, que cuando vivía Tomás Moro comenzaban a emblanquecer, después de muerto estaban como rubios. Se refiere que, recelosos los crueles ministros del Rey Enrique, que, y mucho más en él, no sucediese con la cabeza de Tomás Moro lo que con la del Obispo rofense según se ha dicho en el capítulo diez y ocho antes de este, la cocieron en agua muy caliente para desecarla y afearla, y así causase mucho horror, pero con todo eso les salió al contrario, pues a cabo de tanto tiempo estaba tan fresca y hermosa, como viva y aun remozada, pues los pelos blancos se tornaron de color de oro, significando el grande tesoro de aquella santa cabeza.

Esta es una muestra del libro del cartujo del Monasterio sevillano de Nuestra Señora de las Cuevas. Hay que estudiar esta obra de Fray Alonso de la Torre en cuanto a la relación con sus fuentes, y establecer el carácter de su versión; no se trata de un escritor de alta calidad, sino de un modesto artesano de la traducción, que escribe con dignidad y decoro. La misma Biblioteca Universitaria de Sevilla conserva otra obra suya manuscrita: una Historia de San Bruno,[11] con caracteristicas semejantes a la *Vida y martirio*... que trato aquí. Considerando la limitación propia de este artículo, aquí sólo he querido dar una primera noticia del libro de fray Alonso de Torre, y he señalado su relación con Tomás Moro en un libro español, escrito en la gran biblioteca del Monasterio de Santa María de las Cuevas en Sevilla; queda por hacer el estudio del mismo y la coordinación de las fuentes. En cuanto al texto elegido como muestra, digo que es una versión más del juicio de Tomás Moro, estudiado por J. D. M. Derrett,[12] al que sigue la condena y ejecución de Moro.

La obra de Fray Alonso de la Torre obtuvo una difusión limitada y pertenece a la literatura religiosa, pero un esfuerzo intelectual de esta naturaleza es posible que lograse algún eco en la cultura sevillana de los Siglos de Oro. En efecto, en Sevilla se había escrito y publicado un libro sobre Tomás Moro; su autor fue el gran poeta sevillano Fernando de Herrera (1534-1597) y su título: *Tomás Moro*, impreso primero en Sevilla, 1592, y luego en Madrid, 1617. No sabemos qué atrajo hacia la vida de Moro a un poeta de la personalidad recogida como es la de Herrera; en el librillo—pues es de pocas páginas—Herrera nos presenta a un héroe moderno en una circunstancia histórica difícil. Es una historia literaria, la biografía de un moderno, tan ejemplar para él como la de un antiguo griego o romano. Herrera es un buen escritor, de cuidada retórica, que escribe sobre una vida real, situada en un tiempo histórico y cercano, de una actualidad próxima. La obra, redactada en prosa, resulta en cierto modo anómala con la mayor parte de su creación literaria, de índole poética, y siempre hay que plantearse la pregunta de cuál fue el motivo que lo llevó a redactar su *Tomás Moro*. Se sabe que quiso escribir una *Historia General*, y por esa parte cabe pensar en que sintió especial curiosidad (afición de ánimo y obligada piedad, confiesa en el libro) por el Canciller inglés. Quiero aquí insinuar tan sólo que la biblioteca del Monasterio de Santa Fe pudo ser en Sevilla un hogar cultural, donde las noticias sobre Inglaterra estarían ampliamente documentadas. Herrera pudo encontrar en los libros de esta biblioteca información sobre el caso inglés. No sabemos hasta qué punto pudo serle accesible esta biblioteca por su condición de clérigo beneficiado de la parroquia de San Andrés o (lo que me parece más propio) por medio de alguno de los nobles sevillanos, benefactores de la Cartuja. El temperamento de Herrera era adecuado para acercarse a unos frailes callados como los Cartujos, y la biblioteca estimo que sería abundante en libros de humanidades; el Monasterio de Santa Fe hubo de ser un lugar muy propio para informarse sobre las cuestiones de la historia de Inglaterra que habían causado tan honda repercusión en la espiritualidad europea. Fray Alonso de la Torre, a fines del siglo XVI y comienzos del XVII, lo tuvo muy presente en su obra religiosa, y en el Monasterio de las Cuevas o en Cazalla encontró los libros adecuados para emprender una obra como la que llevó a cabo. En este Monasterio un gran artista, Francisco de Zurbarán, pintó entre 1630 y 1635 tres extraordinarios cuadros sobre asuntos cartujos ("San Bruno y el Papa," "San Hugo en el refectorio de los cartujos" y "La Virgen amparando a los cartujos"), hoy en el Museo de Bellas Artes de Sevilla. Zurbarán dedicó también su pintura a los cartujos ingleses, como es el cuadro dedicado a fray John Houghton, el prior de Londres, en el Museo de Bellas Artes de Cádiz. En este caso el arte de la pintura excedió con mucho al literario.[13]

Quede esta repercusión enunciada sólo en principio y añadida la noticia de otro libro, escrita en lengua española y también en Sevilla, en el que, con intención apologética, se trata de Tomás Moro.

Universidad Complutense de Madrid

༄

Notas

1. R. W. Chambers, *Tomás Moro* [1936] (Buenos Aires: Editorial Juventud, 1946), 74; Ernest Edwin Reynolds, *Santo Tomás Moro* [1953] (Madrid: Rialp, 1959), 66–68; Andrés Vázquez de Prada, *Sir Tomás Moro, Lord Canciller de Inglaterra* (Madrid: Rialp, 1962), 61–66.

2. Francisco López Estrada, *Tomás Moro y España* (Madrid: Publicaciones de la Universidad Complutense, 1980).

3. Véase Baltasar Cuartero y Huerta, *Historia de la Cartuja de Santa María de las Cuevas, de Sevilla, y de su filial de Cazalla de la Sierra* (Madrid: Real Academia de la Historia, 1950), II: 697–702. Una información general sobre la Cartuja en España, en Ildefonso M. Gómez, *La Cartuja en España* (Salzburg: Analecta Cartusiana, Universität, 1984).

4. Información bibliográfica, en Albert Gruys, *Cartusiana* (Paris: CNRS, 1977), II: 363-64. El Monasterio sufrió graves daños en la época de la invasión de Napoleón, y después de la exclaustración, en 1838, se instaló en su recinto la fábrica de cerámica llamada de la Cartuja; sobre su actual estado, véase Alfredo J. Morales y otros, *Guía artística de Sevilla y su provincia* (Sevilla: Diputación Provincial, 1981), 248-51.

5. *Historia de los mártires* . . ., prólogo, folio a.

6. La parte correspondiente a esta Historia ocupa hasta el folio 101. A continuación sigue otra traducción referente al mismo asunto: *Historia de doze martires cartuxanos que en Ruremunda* [Roermonde] *ducado de Geltria* [Geldern], *año de mil quinientos setenta y dos, acabose felizmente su pelea. Escrita en latín y compuesta por el venerable padre don Arnoldo Habensis, doctor en Teología y Prior de la Cartuxa Gandense y traduzida en lengua vulgar española por el padre Alonso de la Torre.* Sin numeración. Después de esta historia, siguen otros textos con notas sobre la orden cartuja, disciplina, observancia, varones ilustres y casas de la misma.

7. *Historia de los mártires* . . ., folio c, vuelto.

8. La *Historia* de Chauncy se publicó en Maguncia, 1550, y en otras partes; hay una edición española, de Burgos, 1583: Maurice Chauncy, *Historia Aliquot Nostri Saeculi Martyrum cum pia, tum lectu iucunda, nunc denuo typis excusa* . . . (Burgis: Apud Philipum Iuntam, 1583). Toma el texto de la edición de 1550 y añade una carta-prefacio de Theotonio de Bragança, Obispo de Evora en Portugal. Tomo el dato de *NUC*, vol. 104, n. 684; se conserva un ejemplar en la New York Public Library. Para datos del autor, véase A. Gruys, *Cartusiana*, op. cit., I: 64.

9. La obra de Ribadeneyra se titula *Historia eclesiástica del Cisma del reino de Inglaterra* (Madrid, I, 1588; II, 1593), y puede leerse en dicho autor, *Historias de la Contrarreforma* (Madrid: BAC, 1945), 851-1326, con estudio de Eusebio Rey. Esta obra procede de la latina de Nicolás Sander, *De origine ac Progressu Schismatis Anglicani*, con las adiciones de E. Rishton y P. Persons, como se indica en el estudio.

10. Transcribo el texto en la ortografía académica actual; voy indicando los folios del fragmento. Lo que va encerrado dentro de los corchetes es añadido mío.

11. *Historia | dela vida del glorioso | Patriarca | San Bruno y principios | Dela sagrada orden de | Cartuxa | Que el fundó. Y de otras vidas de muchos sanctos hijos suyos | y de otras muchas cosas notables dela dicha orden, sacadas de diuersos | Auctores dela misma orden, y de otros de fuera.| Por el Padre Don Alonso de la Torre Monge Professo | Dela Cartuxa de Nª. Sª. delas Cuevas | de Seuilla. |*. Es el manuscrito 333-185, Biblioteca Universitaria de Sevilla.

12. J. Duncan M. Derrett, "Neglected Versions of the Contemporary Account of the Trial of Sir Thomas More," *Bulletin of Institute of Historical Research* 38 (1960): 202-23. Sobre el juicio, véase Ernest E. Reynolds, *The Trial of St. Thomas More*, (London: Burns and Oates, 1964). Hay que notar la gran difusión que tuvo el relato del proceso de Moro por Europa. Referente a España,

el poeta Herrera tomó el relato de Sander (véanse las notas de mi edición del *Tomás Moro*), y la parte del proceso y muerte de Moro aparece en una *Relación* de Simancas y en un pliego suelto en forma de *Carta*; y llegó a ser conocido por el escritor Francisco de Quevedo. Véanse mis artículos "La difusión por España de las noticias sobre el proceso y muerte de Santo Tomás Moro," *Homenaje al Profesor Alarcos* (Valladolid: Universidad, 1966), II: 289-300; y "Quevedo y la *Utopía* de Tomás Moro," *Homenaje al profesor Giménez Fernández* (Sevilla: Universidad, 1967), 155-96.

13. Sobre la temática cartujana en Zurbarán, véase Paul Guinard, *Zurbarán et les peintres espagnols de la vie monastique* (Paris: Les éditions du temps, 1960).

Summary

Professor López Estrada adds to the evidence of the presence of Thomas More in Spain with the discovery of a manuscript of Fray Alonso de la Torre in the University of Seville library, *Historia de los Martires de la Cartuxa de Inglaterra*, and the reproduction of the section of that manuscript dealing with the trial and execution of More. The author was a Carthusian monk who professed in Seville in 1606 and died in 1650. The dedication of his work to his "Christian and pious reader" explains that he has used the Latin sources to retell the story in Spanish for the edification of his countrymen, clergy and laity alike. The excerpt included in this article not only confirms his pious purpose but indicates his use of sources still to be identified. Professor López Estrada speculates on the usefulness of the manuscript as a clue to the role of the Carthusian library in the cultural life of Seville. Could it have had some connection with the writing of *Tomás Moro* (1592), the only prose work of the great Seville poet, Fernando de Herrera? Attention is also called to the paintings of Carthusians by Zurburán, one of which portrays the English Prior John Houghton, listed in Fray Alonso's long title as "D. Joan Houthon." R. H. K.

Résumé

Le professeur López Estrada ajoute aux documents sur la présence de Thomas More en Espagne un manuscrit découvert dans la bibliothèque de l'Université de Séville. Il s'agit de Fray Alonso de la Torre,

Historia de los Martires de la Cartuxa de Inglaterra. L'auteur reproduit une partie du manuscrit traitant du procès et de l'exécution de More. Alonso était un chartreux qui prononça ses voeux en 1606 et mourut en 1650. La dédicace de son oeuvre à son "pieux lecteur chrétien" explique qu'il a utilisé les sources latines pour raconter de nouveau l'histoire en espagnol pour l'instruction de ses compatriotes, aussi bien clergé que laïcs. L'extrait compris dans cet article confirme non seulement son but pieux mais indique aussi son usage de sources qui restent encore à identifier. Le professeur López Estrada s'interroge sur l'utilité du manuscrit comme indice du rôle de la bibliothèque carthusienne dans la vie culturelle de Séville. Se peut-il qu'il y ait un certain rapport avec la composition de *Tomás Moro* (1592), la seule oeuvre en prose du grand poète sévillan, Fernando de Herrera? Ne manquons pas enfin d'attirer l'attention du lecteur sur les tableaux des chartreux par Zurbarán; l'un des portraits représente le prieur anglais John Houghton, qui figure d'ailleurs dans le long titre de Fray Alonso sous le nom de "D. Joan Houthon."

H. D. R.

Anne de Bretagne, sketch by Raymond Joly

Briollay, December 3rd 1987.

Dear G.M.,

It was exactly 16 years ago that I heard of you when I was searching desperately in Paris for ANY work written by Sir Thomas More in order to start my maîtrise at Nanterre Paris X. All I could find was the Penguin translation of *Utopia* and the Yale volumes of *Responsio at Lutherum*. Having been told by a friend that the world's greatest authority on Thomas More lived in Angers, I finally plucked up courage to write to this great man for his advice on finding the books I needed. By return of post, your niece, Elizabeth, replied that you had just departed for a lecture tour around the United States and would not be returning to France for another 6 months. My heart sank in despair -- how could I possibly do any research without any documentation ? To my amazement, within a week, I received (by post) the huge volume of More's *The Dialogue Concerning Tyndale* with a short note from Elizabeth explaining that you had authorized her to lend me this precious book of yours which was the ONLY copy in France. This spontaneous generosity and trust in an unknown, obscure student miles away, completely overwhelmed me and I was determined that once I had finished my memoire, I would come directly to Angers to return the book in person and to show you how grateful I was for your precious help.

It was a warm and pleasant day in August when we rang at the shabby door of 29 rue Volney. I had expected to find some imposing Professor presiding behind a superb desk in a palatial office. The contrast was all the more startling when this beaming, little modest man jumped up to make us welcome, made us sit down on his narrow divan bed (scattering first the proofs and letters which always clutter it up) and plied us (especially my 2 little boys) with the famous Breton biscuits from Hennebont. This world authority was in fact the most generous and warmest friend one could wish for. Your trust in human nature is as natural as a bird's song in spring. On meeting you for the first time, I really understood Christ's saying « knock and it shall be opened unto thee ». In this self-centered world, you *were* and *are* the ever-open door. You do not know how to say « No » and everyone who knocks at your door is received with the same warm welcome, the same spontaneous generosity.

Since September 1974, I have had the privilege of coming to that open door many a time for refuge and strength especially when my own teaching chores become a burden. And you have often been the welcome guest in our house enlightening our family circle with your amazing mine of knowledge. The climax of our long friendship was the joy of your baptising our first grandchild, Clara, last Easter (87) on the eve of Palm Sunday. « Suffer the little children to come unto me » you seemed to say as you cuddled Clara in your arms. Clara is the light of our world and you have become the predominant light of all the *Amici* in the World of Thomas More -- May your « rayonnement » continue to shine among us all for many years to come.

With affectionate thanks for your loyal friendship,

Anne Payan

Since the time her grandmother wrote this letter, Clara has welcomed a little brother, Thomas More Payan, into the family circle.

Alors, enfin, la création entière sera une
et toute division guérie,
et nous chanterons à l'unisson ta louange
par ton Fils, Jésus-Christ.
...

Amen.

VIII Epilogue

Then, at last, will all creation be one
and all divisions healed,
and we shall join in singing your praise
through your Son, Jesus Christ.
...

Amen.

Garden City, le 11.5.87.

Cher Tonton Germain,

Nous voici déjà à la fin de 1987, une année comme bien d'autres et cependant tout à fait spéciale pour toi et tous les Amici qui vont célébrer le 25ème anniversaire de *Moreana* en 1988.

J'ai peine à croire qu'il y a 20 ans déjà, je commençais mes études d'anglais à la Catho. Je ne t'ai jamais dit combien j'appréciais le fait que tu savais si bien être un oncle affectueux, attentif et toujours prêt à écouter l'étudiante pas très studieuse que j'étais.

Tu as toujours été présent pour chaque grand moment de ma vie. Baptême, communion solennelle, fiançailles, mariage. Aucune occasion n'est passée sans que tu sois là pour nous bénir et partager notre joie. Et puis le cycle a recommencé avec Grégory et Mélanie... De plus, le fait que nous soyons tous les deux nés le 16 avril, est à mes yeux quelque chose de tout à fait unique, qui nous lie tout spécialement.

Nous espérons que ton prochain voyage aux USA passera par New York. Tu sais qu'Anita se fait un grand plaisir de te recevoir chez elle, pour te permettre de te reposer et de travailler en paix, loin du bruit et des distractions de notre maison.

En attendant de te revoir bientôt, mille baisers affectueux de la part d'Anita, Lonny, Grégory et Mélanie.

Maryvonne

Abbé Marc'hadour a eu des réunions joyeuses avec sa nièce, leur famille, et leurs amis, en novembre 1988 et mars et mai 1989.

Thomas More, sketch by Raymond Joly

RICHARD J. SCHOECK

*Moreans from Chambers to Marc'hadour:
Some Recollections and Reflections*

A HISTORY OF RECENT SCHOLARSHIP of Thomas More needs to be written, but this is not the place for such an effort. Rather, I should like to do two things: first, to offer a passing glance at More scholars who preceded my generation and whose efforts contributed so greatly to our own—those giants upon whose shoulders we pygmies have stood (how otherwise could we see farther than they were able to?). Following this excursus I shall offer some personal recollections and reflections on Germain Marc'hadour and the Yale Edition of the Complete Works of St. Thomas More.

Before I left Notre Dame in 1959 to work for a year at Yale on the More Edition, I had a long conversation with Father Philip Hughes about Reformation scholarship and the study of More. That superb raconteur had many stories about the older English Moreans—like Father T. E. Bridgett, who did his work at the British Museum during lunch hours in order to continue his parish duties—and about others like Henry de Vocht at Louvain (where Hughes had done his studies as *archiviste*). One of his anecdotes speaks volumes about the lack of support that those older scholars who were priests had had to confront. "After the first volume of *Reformation in England* appeared," Hughes told me, "I sent a copy to my bishop and in a week or so was asked to appear in his ·. I was naive enough to think that now, at long last, I would be given recognition. Instead, the moment my foot stepped across the threshold, he fixed me with a glaring look and pointed an accusing finger: 'Hughes, I've long suspected that you were neglecting your parish duties. Now I have proof of it!' " In spite of such lack of support somehow that generation managed to do its research and produce scholarly, foundational work: this is the story of the liturgical scholar Edmund Bishop, a layman, as well as religious like Fathers Bridgett and Hughes. Small wonder that the best that was available for More studies before 1935 was the 1557 *Workes* instead of a modern edition, plus the biography of More by Bridgett, and a rather small scattering of studies. More scholarship lacked even the basic tools that were then available for the study of Erasmus, for there had been the splendid early eighteenth-century edition by LeClerc at Leiden, the bibliography by Vander Haeghen in 1893, and excellent biographies by Preserved Smith and Johan Huizinga in the early 1920s.

Even Roman Catholic institutions in the 1950s did all too little teaching of the works of More—I was not encouraged to teach a course built around his writings at Notre Dame and had to wait until I moved to Toronto for that opportunity. But at Cornell, that home of Preserved Smith and of much fine scholarship on Erasmus, I had been told that I was wasting my time with minor figures like More and Erasmus—this in late 1954. Times have changed, and one notes with a deep sense of rightness that a kind of scholarly justice is being done by the Catholic University of America Press in its decision to publish the works of William Tyndale.

Foundations for the flowering of More studies after 1935 were international. There was Professor R. W. Chambers and a small circle in London which produced solid editions in the Early English Text Society of the Tudor lives of More by Harpsfield, Roper and Ro. Ba. This English scholarship tended to see More and his achievement as largely literary and in the light of the British universities' reading of English literature, and it is not to be wondered that R. W. Chambers, a superb teacher at London (in the W. P. Ker tradition of seeing the whole sweep of a literature, for Chambers lectured on English literature from *Beowulf* to modern, as his splendid collection of essays entitled *Man's Unconquerable Mind* testifies), should have argued so vigorously for the continuity of English prose with More's efforts in the vernacular providing the key hinge in the development from medieval to Tudor. Certain key elements in that thesis have been challenged—not unlike Chambers' undue weighting in his trenchant argument for the arrest of Tudor humanism under Henry VIII, challenged, largely convincingly, by Douglas Bush in a now classic polemical essay first published in the *University of Toronto Quarterly* in

1939. More scholarship was no longer cold ashes left over from the Reformation, and it could now be seen that the issues radiating outward from questions about More's humanism were weighty indeed and had profound implications for all Tudor studies.

In effect, J. K. McConica's fine monographic study of *English Humanists and Reformation Politics under Henry VIII and Edward VI* (Oxford, 1965, and reviewed by me in this journal in that year), adjudicates the quarrel between Chambers and Bush. Toronto with its unrivalled medieval studies at the Institute and with its great strengths in Renaissance studies as exemplified by such products as Bush and Woodhouse, then later Arthur Barker, might well have been the home of a More Edition, as it later became the home of the Collected Works of Erasmus after 1969.

For many years the biography of More by Chambers has served us well: it covered the life and career of Thomas More more thoroughly than previous lives; it was far better documented and subsumed much original archival research; and it was neither patronizing nor excessively hagiographic. The bulk of R. W. Chambers' research was naturally done in London; but he spent some time in the United States, and a story is told of Chambers at the Huntington Library in San Marino, California, during the final year before the completion of the biography. An expedition was organized by staffers to take Professor Chambers to see the Grand Canyon (though another version I have heard has it that they went to Yosemite); a wag arranged that Chambers would be in a white Cadillac following a lead car. As the vehicles pulled in each time for refueling, going and returning, the service attendant was slipped a dollar bill and told that an English-looking gentleman was sitting in the rear seat of the white Cadillac following. That Englishman was to be asked, "Aren't you Professor Chambers of London?" and after the affirmative reply he was to be questioned, "And how is your biography of Thomas More coming?" Chambers (who may well have been playing a straight face) exclaimed upon his return to the Huntington, "Everyone in the Southwest seems to know about Thomas More and my biography!"

The foundations of which I have been speaking were English and American, and they were also continental. One must speak of French and Belgian scholars: of the work of H. de Vocht at Louvain, and Marie Delcourt, whose excellent edition of the Latin text of *Utopia* still stands on my shelves beside that of Surtz—or it did, before I packed away my library in the process of moving to Trier for a couple of years. The importance of Pierre Mesnard must be recognized, both for More and Erasmus studies (Margaret Mann Phillips—whose recent loss we lament deeply, personally and professionally—has spoken of his great encouragement in her studies of Erasmus) and Mesnard is a vital figure for sixteenth-century studies in France, in his own scholarship and through his splendid foundation at Tours. In the French scholarly tradition that has produced so many great *seiziémistes* (and there is time to mention only Jean-Claude Margolin in this context), More is read in a significantly different milieu—owing to the force of the scholarship of Mesnard, Renaudet, Bataillon, and others. Germain Marc'hadour has written elsewhere of his mentor Mesnard, and I should like to place in the record at this point a personal remembrance of the gentleness, civility and scholarship of Marcel Bataillon.

There were many exemplars of fine scholarship in the Netherlands, of course, where the achievement of Erasmus has never been forgotten; and in Germany one thinks of such names as Kautsky, Oncken and Ritter that have contributed especially to our continuing reading and understanding of *Utopia*, even when (as with Kautsky) their interpretations challenged traditional readings. Here too the angle of reading differed from the Anglo-American, for these interpretations tended to be political, or politico-philosophical, rather than literary or theological.

And in North America there was the work of a number whose efforts before 1959 were largely uncoordinated, but whose enthusiasm and dedication were well-nigh inspiring. Frank and Majie Sullivan (at Loyola in Los Angeles) dreamed of an edition of More, but alas, only their bibliographical work reached publication. Frank Sullivan was for a time connected with the Yale Edition, but resigned. At Yale Father E. J. Klein, who had published a volume in the E. E. T. S. on a contemporary of Thomas More, labored to do an edition; but he worked singlehandedly and the effort was too much for his health. However, those efforts and his collections of early editions led to the founding of the Yale Edition with the generous support of the Grace Foundation, and later of the N. E. H. Here should be mentioned the ambitions of A. W. Reed, Chambers and others—there were certain connections with Downside and lines of Roman Catholic scholarship in England (as I reported many years ago in *The Month*)—to achieve a facsimile printing and scholarly edition of More, which would have been too expensive after World War II, with skyrocketing printing costs, even if part of that aborted edition had not been lost in the London Blitz of (I think) 1942.

The name of Craig R. Thompson earns a high place in this brief discussion, because his early work on Lucian illuminated both More and Erasmus studies, and in a unique measure he has continued over a long span to contribute to both the Yale Edition of More (with his volume on Lucian) and the Toronto Edition of Erasmus (with his volumes as editor of literary and educational writings, CWE 23 and 24, and his forthcoming volumes on the *Colloquies*). Elizabeth F. Rogers began her work on the Correspondence of Thomas More under the inspiration and with the encouragement of P. S. and Helen Allen, whose consummate edition of the Latin letters of Erasmus—begun as long ago as 1906 and completed only in 1958—still stands as a model of philological scholarship to satisfy the rigorous standards of even a Scaliger or a Casaubon. The Rogers *Correspondence* has been a necessary tool for forty years, and her desire to provide a needed new edition of the Correspondence resulted at least in the extremely useful volume of *Selected Letters*. The memory of her indomitable dedication and courage, in the face of blindness and despite a brutal mugging in New York, insures her place in a gallery of More scholars; and she was honored by an early special issue of *Moreana* (15/16, November 1967).

All of us who have worked in More studies owe much to these figures, giants indeed, and it seems to me an essential part of the humanistic enterprise to recognize our debts to our predecessors (and to transmit that recognition to our students), and then to accept all that is implied in seeing our own work as a part of a continuum. We who teach and publish today are neither the first to interpret More nor shall we be the last. But this is not the occasion to address the question of tradition—though I have touched upon it in a recent Erasmian study of "*Translatio Studii* and *Studia Humanitatis*" in *Classical and Modern Literature* in 1987—nor is it the time to speak of the threats to a viable sense of tradition that impinge upon us now from a number of directions, as More and Erasmus also experienced analogous threats.

To turn to the second part of my little *esquisse*: the Yale Edition and Father Germain Marc'hadour. The Edition—or the More Project as it came to be known in the halls of Sterling Library at Yale (where it quickly took its place alongside other, older projects like the Boswell edition and the Benjamin Franklin papers)—has been the center of More research for the English-speaking world of scholarship, and it has deeply influenced More studies everywhere. No one has served more prodigiously than Germain Marc'hadour in being an apostle to the rest of the world carrying the message of More's character, his rôle, and his achievements.

The history of the beginnings of the Yale Edition of the Works of St. Thomas More has been well told by Roy Watkins in the *Yale Univer-*

sity Library Gazette, and I shall not try to retell it [See Richard Marius's "Looking Back."—Ed.]. With an executive committee that at that time included W. K. Wimsatt, Louis L. Martz, Frank Levan Baumer, and Roy Watkins (then Reference Librarian of Yale), Richard Sylvester was chosen as the Executive Secretary—but of course he was more than that, as we all knew: he was the lifeblood of the edition, and he was its intelligence and spirit. Yet one must add a commemoratory note on William Wimsatt, a man of great and wide learning and acumen, whose wise counsel was vital in the setting up of the edition and in guiding it through its early years. A giant physically as well as in literary achievement, he was one of the most generous of men with his time and support. In the summer of 1959 a *TLS* piece of mine had spoken of Wimsatt's "quasi-philosophical jargon," and the first day we met and walked to lunch he growled (from his great height), "What's this about my jargon?" I explained, gave examples, and contrasted a philosophical piece of his in *New Scholasticism* which did not have jargon; he was satisfied; and thereafter we were good friends.

The first scholar to take up residence at Yale as a fellow in the More Edition was Edward Surtz, who was completing his splendid work on *Utopia* during the calendar year 1959—his two previous volumes of interpretation had carried *Utopia* scholarship a very large step forward. Arriving as I did in early September 1959, I was the second More fellow, and I overlapped for one semester with Father Surtz; I soon learned that he played a mean game of squash, and I found him to be a delightful dinner companion nearly every night of the week. He was totally dedicated to his work on More; and our talk and the privilege of reading his manuscript of *Utopia* (to which J. H. Hexter, the historian, contributed an historical introduction), allowed me to see first-hand and in process Surtz's meticulous scholarship and his *ordonnance* of a wealth of documentation. Although a Jesuit he might well have had carved above his desk the Benedictine *laborare est orare*. Edward Surtz has also already been memorialized in a special issue of *Moreana* (31/32, November 1971).

Much of the esprit and the ambiance of scholarship in the More Project was born that year through discussions among the editors, with Richard Sylvester, and with Yale scholars like Wimsatt, E. D. Hirsch, and others. But simply to say this is not enough. One must recall the neglect of More in American universities, and one must appreciate the need to approach More's complex and manifold *oeuvre* with all of the humility of a highly trained specialist (or apprentice-scholar!) who has to move out of the circle of his expertise to edit and comment on those More writings which cut across literature and history, theology and politics. Our discussions bridged gaps, provided vital leads, and gave us confidence to go on. It was at about that time (1960 and shortly thereafter) that J. B. Trapp and Father Marc'hadour arrived in Sterling Library, after the departure of the immensely civil and widely learned Father Surtz.

There was what soon became the "middle generation" of More editors: Garry Haupt, John Headley, Frank Manley, Richard Marius, Hubertus Schulte Herbrüggen, and these were quickly followed by others, mostly younger ones. Some of that "middle generation" have been taken off into other areas of Renaissance or Reformation studies; one thinks of Erasmus' reply to the news that More had been named to the King's Council: *ademptus es*—you have been snatched from us and good letters. But the service of Joe Trapp (for one) as librarian and now director of the Warburg Institute in London has been immense in itself, and his generosity of time and counsel has contributed greatly to the work of many other scholars.

Germain Marc'hadour came quietly on the scene, although there were a few sparks in the first meeting of him and Elizabeth Rogers, who was not happy to have errors and omissions in her *Correspondence* pointed out to her by this effervescent young French scholar. It was clear from the outset that his special knowledge of More and the Bible added a great measure of support to the work of all of us. Ever since he first appeared in the rooms of the More Project in Sterling, he has been an essential part of the Yale Project, with his steadiness of purpose and his quiet, warm devotion to St. Thomas More. His contributions to the annual More Luncheons at New Haven and to many conferences on More around the world have been memorable. *Moreana* is in fact a center for French, and of course wider, studies of More, and he animates 29 rue Volney as the *genius loci* that he is.

I recall having the pleasure of introducing Father Marc'hadour to an audience in Toronto, and I spoke of him as a true *peregrinus*, having met him in New Haven, San Francisco, the Huntington and the Folger, Oxford and Angers, of course. Quickly Father Marc'hadour retorted, "Only one *peregrinus* could have been in all of those places in order to introduce another!" But he has been in many places, and he has always made a deep and lasting impression upon his audiences—whether students at St. Michael's, Florida, or Notre Dame, or general audiences of adults or specialized gatherings as of lawyers in various cities. He is a scholar-priest who incarnates the *caritas* that we recognize as one of the marks of Thomas More's greatness, his true nature as a living man who became a saint.

I remember too being at his *soutenance* twenty years ago at the Sorbonne, where a rather large audience gathered in the formidable Louis-Liard salon with its huge portraits of Racine and other greats of French letters staring down at us. The *soutenance* went on, as they did in those days, and after it was all over and we were walking together for dinner (at a nearby restaurant around the corner from the Librairie Vrin), I asked him what he thought, seeing those portraits looking down at him. "What portraits?" he replied, for his concentration, then, as usually, had been total.

One more story about GM must be added. One summer he was pastoring at Thame in Oxfordshire, not far from Oxford, and I wanted to phone him from London to let him know the time of arrival next day; but lacking the name of the parish priest I could not phone and had to send a telegram in care of the Presbytery. Next day on arrival I learned that the telegram had just been delivered, addressed to:

Father Marcador
The Presbyterian
Thame

He laughed, of course, and I hope that he kept the telegram as a souvenir — a post-Reformation souvenir, perhaps?

At the turn of this century into the next we shall look back upon a solid number of volumes in the Yale Edition and a goodly number of studies of many kinds. Germain Marc'hadour will have paid his dues several times over in that scholarly enterprise. But he has also served — perhaps most deeply, most lastingly — in reminding us of the essential Christianity of More, and by example as by word of the centrality of *caritas* and joy in that Christianity.

Universität Trier

Lódź, le 12 Octobre 1987.

Mon Cher Ami,

Nos relations amicales remontent à l'année 1971, au premier Congrès des Études Néolatines, organisé par M. Jozef IJsewijn à Leuven. Je me rappelle votre conférence concernant Thomas More pendant ce Congrès. Depuis nous nous sommes rencontrés pendant tous les Congrès jusqu'au dernier à Wolfenbüttel (12-16 Août 1985). Les « adorateurs » de Thomas More y parlaient souvent de ce martyr. Nos collègues vous apprécient toujours comme aumônier des néolatinistes. Les messes que vous célébrez pendant tous les Congrès nous émeuvent profondément. On pense aux groupes des chrétiens de l'antiquité. Vos conférences consacrées à Thomas More sont aussi de grande valeur. C'est vous qui avez inspiré l'édition de Moreana *en langue française et anglaise -- presque cent numéros jusqu'à présent. Cette revue est très utile et très instructive et c'est une initiative bien à propos de rendre honneur au Fondateur et Directeur de* Moreana.

Monsieur l'Abbé Germain Marc'hadour, Fondateur et Rédacteur de Moreana *vivat crescat floreat.*

Jerzy Starnawski

Los Angeles, California
September 21, 1987.

Dear M. l'Abbé,

It gives me great pleasure to think back over our years of happy association, from the appearance of the first volume of *Moreana*, the organ of the Amici Thomae Mori, and the almost simultaneous appearance of the first of our seven volume bibliography, *Moreana, Materials for the Study of Saint Thomas More.* That is now complete or as complete as I am able to make it without the aid of my beloved co-author Frank, but may your *Moreana* go on forever, bringing more information, interest, and devotion to our dear saint.

These are bitter-sweet memories because on the occasions when we met, Frank and I were together -- when you visited Loyola University of Los Angeles, and we chatted in the patio of the now enlarged library of the even more enlarged University with the added name of Marymount and the inclusion of women students.

And then there were the times when we met at the Huntington Library in San Marino, that treasure of scholar's delight. Robert Kinsman, another devoted Huntingtonian, told us of a week-end you spent with his family.

I am no longer able to get to the Huntington but I shall always cherish the days spent there and the friends and associates of those days as the happiest of my California years.

So God bless you, dear co-worker in the cause of saint Thomas More, and please include in your prayers a transplanted Saint Louisan who remembers you fondly.

Most affectionately,

Majie Padberg Sullivan

Majie Padberg Sullivan
(Mrs. Frank Sullivan)

Angers, 22 novembre 1987.

Cher Monsieur l'Abbé,

*En tant qu'*Amica *de la première heure, je m'en voudrais de ne pas m'associer à l'hommage qui vous est rendu à travers ce numéro de* Moreana.

Vous vous souvenez ? C'était en 1960 : un Père Capucin m'avait pressentie pour que j'apporte mon aide à la préparation d'une exposition Thomas More.

J'hésitai avant de donner une réponse positive, car m'occuper d'une exposition représentait une tâche toute nouvelle pour moi... mais pourquoi ne pas tenter l'expérience ?

Thomas More ? Bien sûr, je savais la place éminente qu'il tenait près d'Henry VIII ; son Ile d'Utopie ne m'était pas inconnue, non plus que son portrait par Holbein. Cependant, j'ignorais tout de sa personnalité et de son oeuvre littéraire. Une occasion s'offrait de les mieux connaître. Et c'est ainsi que le 2 avril, en la fête de St François de Paule, fondateur des Minimes et contemporain de More, je sonnai à la porte du 29 rue Volney : un large sourire « ensoutané » m'accueillit et je me trouvai dans un bureau où documents et livres envahissaient, outre la table de travail, les murs, le sol, le lit et les quelques sièges répartis dans la pièce.

Embauchée sur-le-champ, j'allais très vite aussi découvrir la vaste érudition, la simplicité toute franciscaine de mon nouveau « patron » et, non sans quelque inquiétude -- tant elle me semblait parfois téméraire -- son absolue confiance dans la Providence.

La préparation de « l'Expo » représentant une lourde tâche, on fit appel à la collaboration de mes parents.

Dans les quelques lignes que vous aviez bien voulu consacrer à la mémoire de mon père, vous écriviez : « notre ami... à notre exposition de mai 1960, se révéla comme « the man for all seasons » ou « for all jobs »... aussi prêt à transporter des caisses dans sa 2 CV qu'à vérifier les références bibliques ou classiques, à quoi l'aidait sa connaissance du latin, du grec et de la liturgie... Des amici *de tous pays se sont assis à sa table... »*

Et voici quelques mois, lors de l'inhumation de ma mère, vous évoquiez ses talents artistiques et la façon dont elle les mit au service du Moreanum.

De justesse, tout fut en place pour l'inauguration de l'Exposition, qui ferma ses portes après avoir accueilli de nombreux visiteurs.

A vrai dire, cette Exposition connut un prolongement en 1962, lors de la quinzaine Thomas More organisée à Bruxelles, manifestation qui servit de cadre à la création des Amici Thomae Mori. *Afin d'assurer le bon fonctionnement de l'amicale, un secrétariat fut mis en place à Angers : cela signifiait que je restais au service de Thomas More !*

Dès septembre 1963 paraissait le premier numéro de Moreana, *dont la dactylographie sur stencil (et le machine ne ressemblait en rien à la Compugraphic !), n'alla pas sans poser quelques problèmes.*

Pendant cette période s'élaborait votre thèse : Thomas More et la Bible, *à laquelle, avec la collaboration de mon père, je fus particulièrement heureuse d'apporter mon concours. Elle me permit de faire connaissance avec l'anglais du 16e siècle dans cette merveilleuse édition de 1557 des* English Workes.

Time Trieth Truth...

Les années ont passé, au cours desquelles le cercle des Amici *n'a cessé de s'élargir, regroupant des amitiés chaleureuses et fidèles -- solides comme le granit breton -- à l'image même de celui qui les fait éclore à profusion et les entretient précieusement, tant il est vrai que peuvent s'appliquer à vous les paroles qu'Érasme dédiait à Thomas More : « On le dirait né et mis au monde pour l'amitié ; il la cultive avec une absolue sincérité qui n'a d'égale que sa ténacité. Et il n'est pas homme à redouter le trop grand nombre d'amis, cette polyphilie qu'Hésiode n'apprécie guère. Il n'exclut personne de ces liens sacrés. »*

Je suis sûre qu'en pensent à vous... à Angers... à travers le monde, chaque amicus, *chaque* amica *salue de ses applaudissements les paroles du grand Rotterdamois.*

Marie-Paule Bataille

January 10, 1988.

Dear Father Marc'hadour,

Happy New Year and Congratulations on the 25th Anniversary of *Moreana*. I think that it is very meaningful to begin the new year with a letter to you -- for with each new year one looks back to try to recapture a bit of the flavour of the past, to savour it even as we try to incorporate it into the present and to remember it and preserve it for the future. It is now at least 20 years or more since first we met, on your first trip to America and your first visit to the embryonic More project. I remember that Dick announced that you would be coming to dinner and I was aghast ! What, entertain a real Frenchman, with a house full of babies, no help & no money ! Horrors ! I know that I cooked up a storm that day not realising that you were, as you announced at the table that evening, « every bit as happy to have a bowl of oatmeal as anything fancy ! » Ah yes, that was one of the first impressions I had of you and from that moment you became very much a part of our lives and more like a family member than many actual relatives. Certainly Dick spent many hours & days with you, in person or by letter, and your file of correspondence from him must be voluminous indeed. From that very first meeting until the very last days of his life, Dick was in constant touch with you, usually happily, often chidingly but always, always you were a presence. Certainly the children grew up hearing about you, and enjoying your visits and somewhat bemused as well as amused by the flying-around French priest whom they would usually call « Father Butterfly ». On our first trip to Europe after Patrice's death, in 1965, I was not the least bit amazed to find myself with 2 children living in a house with Spanish nuns in Angers -- that way we were all looked after while the men went off and worked. « Women's Lib » was a long way away, and a good thing too, because it was during that visit that the Thomas More Prayerbook came to light and found its way thus to the Beinecke Library.

That is many years ago and throughout the years you were a part of all that went on in the lives of the Sylvesters, the few joys, the many sorrows, the triumphs and the tears. Since Dick's death, our communications have been rare, but I very much enjoyed my visit to you in Angers last year while I was teaching at HEC in France. I enjoyed seeing friends in Angers as well as knowing that *Moreana* was still alive and well. I know that were Dick still among us he would want to be among the first to congratulate you on these 25 years and to wish you many more. And for myself, I wish you all the best and greet you most affectionately. Bonne Chance et Bonne Année,

Joy Sylvester (Mrs Richard S. Sylvester)

Joy Sylvester (Mrs Richard S. Sylvester)
c/o Dept. of Romance Languages
Univ. of No. Carolina - Chapel Hill
Chapel Hill, No. Carolina 27514.

RICHARD MARIUS

Looking Back

THE YALE EDITION OF THE COMPLETE WORKS of St. Thomas More has lived in symbiosis with *Moreana* over the past twenty-five years. Father Marc'hadour's first issue of *Moreana* appeared in 1963, the same year that Richard S. Sylvester's edition of More's *History of King Richard III* emerged from Yale University Press, first of those volumes in Yale blue that has become so familiar through the intervening years.

Until his untimely death in 1978 Dick Sylvester used *Moreana* to publish his annual report on the progress of the Yale edition. Clarence Miller followed his example, and for many years Father Marc'hadour opened its pages to the *dicta* of the Yale editors as they unearthed their discoveries in the vast mine of More's prodigious output.

To peruse the pages of both the Yale Edition and of *Moreana* is to resurrect memories of the living and the dead. In the Yale Edition we have the measured scholarly result of much dogged labor; in *Moreana* we have not only scholarship, but thanks to the informal notes that Father Marc'hadour included from the beginning, we catch personal glimpses of hard-working people, and we see something of the development of their interests in both More and the sixteenth century.

In retrospect what strikes me most is how young we all were at the start of this enterprise. When I met Dick Sylvester in November 1959, he was about thirty-three years old, already distinguished by his definitive edition of Cavendish's *Life* of Thomas Cardinal Wolsey in the

Early English Text Society series. Dick was ensconced with an efficient German secretary in a largish room on the third floor of Sterling Library. He was a tall and slender man, a chain smoker who sat near an open window even on a sharp, cold day so the smoke from his cigarette would drift outside. The room was lined with shelves piled up with thin black boxes that held photostats of the various editions of More's works. (In those days had we heard the name Xerox, we might have supposed it to refer to a new bleach intended like Clorox to be used in washing machines.)

Dick had a marvelous ability to gather a team of young people around him and make them loyal not only to the edition but also to himself. Joe Trapp from the Warburg Institute was there in 1959 on one of the fellowships the More project was able to give in those years. He was about Dick's age, and he came and went in athletic silence, taking long legged strides that sometimes made the hem of his overcoat fly out behind him. I thought he was a dour sort and hardly dared to interrupt him in his swift passage through the corridors of Sterling. One of the later delights of my life was to discover that he possesses a quick and sometimes rollicking wit and that he is an avid fan of the Rugby Team the All Blacks from his native New Zealand and that he and his wife Elaine are among the most hospitable people on earth.

My major professor at Yale was Roland Bainton, and one of his students, John M. Headley, had a year's fellowship working on the *Responsio ad Lutherum*. He was about thirty then, with reddish hair and serious ways, and we shared several summers of work as the project moved first to the fourth floor of Sterling and then finally to the three rooms it occupied for so long on the second floor. One summer afternoon when we were working alone, John in one room and I in another, we fell into a whistling competition, one of us whistling the tune to one operatic aria and the other responding with the tune of another. Finally a harassed looking woman from the Benjamin Franklin Project around the corner came down very angrily and asked the More editors to shut up, because our whistling was disturbing the entire floor. Despite his seriousness at work, John could erupt in a long, rising laugh that ended in a shout of mirth. Somehow the More project of my memories always rings with laughter.

Louis Martz was the patriarch of the edition, the person who got it established at Yale and who chose Dick to be the executive editor. Since he was only in his forties when the edition began, he was a young patriarch, always somewhat aristocratic in his bearing with penetrating blue eyes and a perpetual expression of serious inquiry and good humor.

I thought that he and Dick worked so well together because they were both devoted to the text. How does scholarship proceed? You discover who a writer is by looking at his text. You find the right text, cleansed of errors in transmission, and you read it again and again and again to find the writer's thought not as other people have interpreted it but as that writer has put it down himself. The text, of course, never gives us in itself the answers to all the questions we may bring. The reader is left to infer a complete picture from the fragments of life represented by the text. In that regard Louis was always an active reader, never merely presenting the text but wrestling with it and making something of it. I still remember with pleasure his lecture on the *Dialogue of Comfort* one cold December afternoon in a Yale Law School auditorium.

The principle of beginning with the text was especially important in the developing history of the Yale edition. Thomas More comes down to us surrounded by such contradictory mythologies that getting to the "real" More is a little like trying to find an airport in a dense fog. I was never able to decide fully in my own mind whether Robert Bolt's *A Man for All Seasons*, which played on Broadway with Paul Scofield as More in 1962, was boon or disaster to More studies. Scofield's stunning dramatic performance, first in the play and then with lesser power in the film, turned More into an icon, and icons are usually set too high in walls and are too glittering to be studied easily by mortals of ordinary stature. The sudden attention to More now made our own studies more respectable; people stopped assuming that those of us who said we were working on Thomas More were laboring on the Irish poet. Unfortunately that attention also meant that many people already knew what we were supposed to find when we studied More. We were supposed to find Robert Bolt's More who, of course, was William Roper's More translated to stage with one of the best actors in the English speaking world taking the leading role. The attention of Dick Sylvester and Louis Martz to the primacy of the text kept us on course.

As I recall, Father Marc'hadour appeared on the scene about the time of my last year at Yale in 1962. I do not know how he and Dick met, but their mutual affection was warm and constant through the years. I encountered him first as a soft-voiced priest who spoke slowly and deliberately in both French and in English and who conveyed the pleasant sense that he thought carefully about everything he said. For some reason I have always thought of him partly in terms of the *Journal d'un Curé de Campagne* by Georges Bernanos and *Le Petit Prince* by Antoine de St. Exupéry. Yet beneath his outward gentleness he has always maintained a steely devotion to Thomas More.

Father Marc'hadour was, I think, somewhat older than Dick Sylvester, abstemious when the rest of us were not, amused when the rest of us were raucous. I believe that his *gravitas* always made him seem a little older than he in fact was. But in any case age was only relative; we were all young, and we were immersed in Thomas More. Father Marc'hadour and Joe Trapp gave us an international dimension at a time when not even the English were especially interested in More studies. Dick went over to Angers once during these years and gave one lecture on More and another on Robert Frost. He kept on the wall near his desk until his death the poster announcing these lectures.

It was intriguing to me that a French priest should be so devoted to an English saint and so easy to engage in conversation. It is embarrassing to report that Father Marc'hadour was the first Catholic priest with whom I ever had a conversation, this despite my having been at the University of Strasbourg for a year studying the Reformation, having spent a summer at Sens south of Paris, and having been two or three years in the Yale graduate school when we met. No Catholics lived in the rural Tennessee where I grew up. In France I had frequently sat in on the Mass, especially in early mornings on bicycle trips through the glorious French countryside, and I had twice been to Lourdes, observing in a mixture of reverence and curiosity the solemn dawn liturgy for the critically ill that begins the day at the famous grotto where Bernadette saw her visions. But I had never exchanged more than three or four sentences with a priest. (I never met Father Edward Surtz, one of the editors of the *Utopia*.) We talked easily enough, but I discover after all these years that some southern formality towards the clergy makes me address him as "Father Marc'hadour" in English or "Mon Père" in French and never as "Germain."

In 1963 after teaching English for a summer in the French town of Brive-la-Gaillarde, I returned to Paris and went to the publishing house of J. Vrin near the Sorbonne and purchased from Monsieur J. Vrin himself Father Marc'hadour's great chronology of More's life, the *Univers*, whose covers I have long since worn away. It is a beautifully produced work, and I recall how Monsieur Vrin stood looking over my shoulder on a brilliantly sunny day and grumbled about the cost even while he expressed great satisfaction with the book. I praised the book lavishly but walked out into the splendid morning feeling that M. Vrin was not convinced that all that white space was necessary.

In 1962 Jim Lusardi, Louis Schuster, R. J. Schoeck, and I were formally commissioned to edit the *Confutation*. (Dick thought we would have it done by 1967. It finally appeared in three thumping volumes in 1973!) Frank Manley and Garry Haupt were hard at work on their volumes, and Clarence Miller came to do the work on the wondrous *De Tristitia Christi*, discovered as though by a miracle in Valencia. When Davis Harding died, Tom Lawler came on to work with Father Marc'hadour and me on the *Dialogue Concerning Heresies*. We gathered in the summer and toiled patiently and happily together. Jim and I shared living quarters one summer in Dick's office in, I think, Timothy Dwight College. I slept on the couch, and Jim bunked on a cot spread in the middle of the floor.

We all seemed to live on coffee. The coffee pot perpetually hot in the More Project produced what was doubtless the strongest and most horrible brew I have ever drunk. At times to this day I wonder why I am no longer able to stay awake until 4:00 in the morning and rise at 7:30 for a full day's work, and I think the reason for my sluggishness is that the More Project coffeepot has gone out of my life. At times we worked at cultivating Father Marc'hadour's ascetic ways. For a time when he was giving up cigarettes, Frank Manley chewed tobacco. I recall those occasions when a carload of editors pulled up at a traffic light and Frank leaned out with as much dignity as he could to spit a jet of tobacco juice into the street. None of us had much money. We sometimes treated ourselves to beer in the evening. Dick decided at one point that we could all economize by buying something called "Tudor Beer," the house brand of a supermarket. It was wretched stuff. The only good thing that could be said of Tudor Beer was that it made the project coffee taste like the elixir of life, and I quietly poured a lot of Tudor Beer into the grass of this or that place where we were having our long evening talks, doubtless inflicting permanent damage on the ecology of New Haven. Altogether we enjoyed a kind of academic Camelot of a sort that perhaps only the young can have.

In December the project sponsored an annual lecture open to anyone interested in Thomas More—something of a test of endurance for all of us since the lecture was always given in a very warm room after a huge lunch that had been preceded by limitless cocktails. I delivered the lecture of 1966 in Yale's Hall of Graduate Studies. Roland Bainton was there, sitting off to my right in a window seat, making a sketch of me which now hangs on the wall of my study in my house—a thin, stoop-shouldered Richard Marius with unruly hair looking very earnest and almost grim because he was so frightened by the crowd of luminaries. Dick Sylvester sat in the front row looking pleased. Louis Martz dozed off, making me envious because he was getting a nap and I was having to lecture. Leicester Bradner, who had worked on Thomas More while most of the rest of us were still children, was also there looking wonderfully benign and wise. Father Marc'hadour and Stefan Kuttner, editor of *Traditio*, were both present and both came up afterwards and asked if they could have the lecture for their publications. I split it between them—a fact that may indicate that the lecture was far too long for a Saturday afternoon! My article in *Moreana* was out first and so represents my first scholarly publication on More apart from two or three reviews.

The lectures were always best when an editor spoke on work he was doing on one of the volumes. Then the discussion was stimulating and enriching because we were all living in Thomas More's texts, and we could argue about conclusions and add to the information the lecturer had given us. We dispersed only when people looked anxiously at watches and noted timetables and trains about to leave, and we always broke up with loquacious regret. I still recall the enthusiasm with which we greeted Craig Thompson's opinion that though *Utopia* might be Platonic in parts and Aristotelian in parts and medieval in parts, it was Morean in the whole.

The steady progress of the edition brought out friendly divisions among the editors. I think that Dick Sylvester, Father Marc'hadour, and Louis Martz loved More while the rest of us found him merely absorbing. More had the Utopians believe that they were surrounded by the dead, and something of that same view turns up in his feeling about the saints of the church. For some, including some of the More editors, More seems very near, a presence, a friend. For others of us he is much like a character in a Tolstoy novel—infinitely complex and magnetic in his capacity to make us want to understand him in all his variety and subtlety even while we recognize that we can never reduce him to one principle or find the incidents of his life strung along one thread.

In October of 1970 the More Conference of St. John's University in Queens brought Louis Martz, Father Marc'hadour, Dick Schoeck, and G. R. Elton together to read papers under Dick Sylvester's presiding hand. Several of the editors were asked to make spontaneous responses to the papers. The audience was not large. But it was enthusiastic, and the meeting was one of those exciting occasions that live in memory. Elton brought to the conference a revisionist view of More based on his reading of More himself—evidence that once a text becomes widely distributed, no one can control how others will read that text. Dick Sylvester leaned over to me as Elton sat down and whispered, "Get up and refute him." I only laughed.

Father Marc'hadour did debate him gently. It was an electric occasion. Elton represented a kind of Hegelian antithesis to the traditional thesis about More, and he and others writing from outside the circle of More editors have done much to stir a dialogue about More that continues unabated to this day as we seek some synthesis. The St. John's conference was a benchmark not only in the growing interest in More stirred by the combined efforts of the More editors and *Moreana* but also of the necessary, friendly debate about More that eventually had to come. Aristotle held that the rhetor should never undertake to argue a topic for which there was not an opposing view. His counsel holds for scholars once substantial knowledge—such as a body of accessible text—becomes available about a scholarly subject. Debate is not only inevitable; it is desirable, and if Thomas More were not debatable, he would not be interesting. In that respect, the St. John's conference and the animated discussion between Elton and Father Marc'hadour was a great event.

In the summer of 1974 my wife Lanier and my sons Richard and Fred detoured through New Haven to picnic with the Sylvesters on our way to a bicycle trip in France. We all sat happily around a long table in the Sylvester yard, talking in the warm evening air. A few weeks later, Lanier, the boys, and I pedaled into Angers after a long swing out of Paris and down the Loire and had a picnic with Father Marc'hadour in his garden—where we discovered his passion for artichokes.

In 1975 Dick Sylvester came down with stomach cancer. An operation that autumn only put off the inevitable. The cancer came back in 1977, and Dick died in July 1978. Until the last he kept up his indefatigable correspondence, and I am one of at least two people who returned from his funeral to find letters that he had written to us a few hours before the end.

We all gathered around Dick in those last years, and we were brought together again—older, sharing memories now more than experience. Only a couple of weeks before Dick's death, nearly all the surviving editors assembled at the triumphal Georgetown Conference to commemorate the 500th anniversary of More's birth. Now a glittering constellation of scholars from within the edition and from without gathered to pay homage not only to the scholarly enterprise revolving around More but also to Dick. Thomas More studies were no longer a cottage industry; they represented a truly international enterprise. Dick received an honorary doctorate from Georgetown University on June 22 and delivered his last lecture, seated in a chair because he was too weak to stand. We gave him a standing ovation, and afterwards a great crowd of us sat around him on a stone porch outside in the warm night air, unwilling to let him or the occasion go.

Clarence Miller and Louis Martz are nobly bringing the More Project to a grand conclusion, aided by young scholars such as Steve Foley, Dan Kinney, and Ralph Keen, who were little children when the project began. *Moreana* continues, and Father Marc'hadour continues to add to More's *Univers*.

Just before his death, More expressed his hope that he, his friends, and his enemies might be merry together in heaven forever and ever. It is a nice sentiment for this quarter-century mark of our various publications. I suspect that in that event, every one of us — both those who love Thomas More and those merely devoted to studying him — will have to endure his fairly lengthy seminar on the places where we all got him wrong. Perhaps, too, he will be able to tell us some places where he got it wrong himself. However that might be, our experience through these swift years has shown that we can all be merry together.

Harvard University

COLLEGE OF THE HOLY CROSS
WORCESTER, MASSACHUSETTS 01610-2395

January 15, 1988.

l'Abbé Germain Marc'hadour
Moreana
29 rue Volney -- B.P. 808
49005 Angers CEDEX, France

Dear Germain :

I hope I will not embarass you if I use this occasion to recall some special moments over the years when you touched so deeply my life and the lives of my wife and children. I first met you on Dick Sylvester's order when I was a graduate student at Yale. Father Marc'hadour is coming, he said, and you must *see him. After your lecture at More House, the Catholic Chapel at Yale, I had only a few moments to shake hands amidst the crowd of well-wishers. A few years passed before I met you again in another crowd on a bus taking us to lunch at the St. John's University More Conference in October, 1970. Somehow you glimpsed me in the pack and greeted me with a wave and cheery « Tom Lawler. » How startled I was that you remembered me after your brief encounter some years before and how pleased with that instant recognition.*

Then came that lovely April at the Folger (in 1972 I think) when we were working together on A Dialogue Concerning Heresies. *When I stumbled on a problem in the text I could go down from my table in the reading room to your hideaway in the stacks and you would soon have me on the right way again. But we were not always working. Sometimes we extended lunch and strolled across the Washington Mall to the main post office so you could decorate your letters to France with the latest U.S. issues. Once you had a chest cold and my children brought you a basket of fruit ; but you took only one pear and saved it all week-end for your lunch Monday at the Folger. In these small ways we came to know you, although I never could adequately explain to my children why you had waited three days to eat the pear you singled out with such evident anticipation.*

Another cherished memory is of your visit to Holy Cross. You were pleased with the window of More in the Chapel and then we proceeded to my afternoon Renaissance class where you explicated the Tower Prayer before the main event of your evening lecture. After class I invited the students to join us for dinner and most of them overcame their shyness and went off with us to a Lebanese restaurant in the back alleys of Worcester. As we were about to go in, you spotted three small boys across the street fighting in front of a shabby three-decker tenement. « Watch », I said to the student beside me, « Father Marc'hadour will break that up and have them make peace. » As you came back to us the student said to me, « It was just like Alyosha with the small boys in the first chapters of The Brothers Karamazov. *» So I had been thinking myself, and so it was.*

Last spring from Good Friday through Easter Monday you took the « American family » with you on your rounds about Angers : Good Friday and Easter Vigil liturgies at the home for aged nuns, the pontifical mass at the Cathedral and vespers at a cloistered convent on Easter Sunday. It was another lovely April and our first trip to France. Before we came to Angers we had been to Notre Dame and Chartres, Vézelay and Fontenay Abbey, the medieval hospital at Beaune with the Last Judgment Altar piece by Roger Van Der Weyden. We had been « going on pilgrimage » and finally arrived at 29 Rue Volney. The weather was fair and we ate outside in your garden -- cold chicken and artichokes and galettes from Brittany. We were profoundly touched. I felt that I had taken wife and daughters Kate and Meg into some inner circle of peace which would always be with them.

One afternoon as he paced about the entrance corridor to the More Project in Sterling Library at Yale (stretching his legs after an afternoon behind the desk) « our boss » Dick Sylvester had given me another order. « You must see Germain in his lair at Angers », he said, and then continued « I love him this side of heaven. » And in this, as so much else, he spoke for us all.

With gratitude and love,
Tom Lawler

The Lawlers, with their daughter Meg, visited Abbé Marc'hadour again on December 11, 1988, for a liturgy at Christ the King Church in Kingston, RI, and a seafood dinner and very cold run on the beach at Galilee.

ST. JOSEPH'S
HOPE ROAD,
SALE, CHESHIRE.
M33 3AD.

19 Oct. '87

My dear Germain,

The summer of 1984 found you spending your August here at St Joseph's ; though it must be admitted that your time was divided between the parish and the John Rylands Library on Deansgate. You were working on one of the introductory chapters for *The Supplication of Souls* in the great Yale edition.

To situate More's work in its sixteenth-century context you spent every weekday afternoon reading all the Rylands Library had on purgatory from the sixteenth century. The lot. And then there was the day a librarian returned after spending a considerable sum on a further such work from this period. He was concerned lest it was too expensive, and not an important work. As he talked to the staff, one of the young women at the counter told him that there was a foreign scholar reading all the library had in this field. They checked your library card and found who you were, and whom they were entertaining. And then you reassured the librarian -- an excellent purchase of an important work.

Like many of your friends I look forward to *The Supplication of Souls,* and when it does come, for me it will always ring of August 1984. May you, *Moreana* and the Yale Edition all flourish.

Sincerely,

John P. Marmion

GABRIEL GUILLAUME

Décennies de voisinage et de compagnonnage

BIEN AVANT L'AN 40 J'AVAIS entendu parler avec éloge de Germain Marc'hadour: un as, un crack, un caïd pour transposer en langage d'étudiants lyonnais des années 50, un surdoué en langage non moins moderne. Comme il avait fait ses études secondaires au Petit Séminaire de Sainte Anne d'Auray, séminaire qui accueillait les élèves originaires de la partie bretonnante du Morbihan, tandis que les Gallos, dont j'étais, s'orientaient spécialement vers Ploërmel, je le rencontrai pour la première fois au Grand Séminaire de Vannes à l'automne de 1939.

Unissant par je ne sais quelle supputation linguistique le nom et la renommée, je m'imaginais que l'abbé [maradur] ou [max-] était d'une taille, d'une carrure, d'une corpulence analogue à celle d'un condisciple ploërmelais qui s'appelait [mōdėgèr], et qui avait aussi l'avantage d'un droit et d'une auréole d'aînesse, c'est-à-dire celui d'être d'une classe au-dessus de la mienne. Ce fut pour moi une certaine surprise de découvrir, sur la cour transformée en terrain de jeu, un athlète, vif certes, mais plutôt du genre petit David. . . .

L'ordination sacerdotale de G. M. fut préparée par une retraite écourtée mais, je présume, intensive, au retour d'examens de licence en Sorbonne. A la date marquante, 18 juin 1944, où dans la chapelle de Notre Dame du Mené il était ordonné prêtre, je m'engageais comme sous-diacre: "Vinctus Christi, laetus servi." Dans la liturgie de 1945 la messe solennelle comportait diacre et sous-diacre. Pour une grand-messe que je chantai à Anetz sur Loire, demeure de ma famille depuis quelques années après son départ de St. Martin sur Oust, j'eus l'honneur d'avoir l'ami Germain, étudiant à Angers, comme sous-diacre; le prédicateur du jour fut le chanoine Dréano.

Quels furent nos rapports dans les années où G. M. enseignait à Pontivy, ayant à instruire (ce qui, allait de soi), et à discipliner (ce qui, paraît-il, faisait parfois problème) plusieurs classes du Collège Saint Ivy? Une rencontre eut lieu à Paris. Le jeune professeur d'anglais, affamé de savoir, s'était orienté vers une licence de lettres classiques. Dans mon discours de soutenance de thèse j'ai pu rappeler une divergence de traduction, entre les candidats que nous étions au certificat de latin: il s'agissait de quelque potentiel ou irréel. D'autre part j'ai retrouvé, au dos d'une image qui reproduisait en traduction anglaise une définition du sacerdoce par Lacordaire, ces lignes d'une écriture qui n'a guère changé depuis quarante ans:

> To my most dear
> Gabriel Guillaume,
> as a token
> of my warm friendship
> in Our Lord,
> Who is the Word made flesh,
> & in Our Lady,
> Who is the Seat of Wisdom.
>
> 1st Friday of July 1943
> St Ivy School.
> Germain Marc'hadour

C'est en 1951 que je commençai mon enseignement à la Faculté libre des Lettres d'Angers, après deux années de formation (et de recherche) spécialement à Lyon. Le département d'anglais ayant besoin d'accroître son corps professoral, je signalai l'abbé Marc'hadour à Mgr. Joseph Pasquier, recteur de l'Université Catholique de l'Ouest. L'évêque de

Vannes, Mgr. Le Bellec, m'avait laissé partir facilement de son diocèse. Il n'en fut pas de même pour l'abbé G. M.: le recteur alla le pleurer auprès de notre évêque. L'élu (non candidat), appelé à une vocation nouvelle dans la même ligne, a rapporté que ses amis le plaignirent, en même temps que, je suppose, ils le félicitèrent: un prêtre aller enseigner de l'anglais en Faculté! De la philosophie, passe encore. . . . Evidemment la carrière du disciple de Saint Thomas More et du maître mondial des études moriennes est une apologie, une réponse éclatante à des apitoiements confraternels.

Déménageant de Pontivy en taxi familial, G. M. ne faisait d'abord qu'une escale à Angers, en 1952. Il devint élève de la Catho de Lyon, où j'avais moi-même, en sus d'études de linguistique romane, suivi un cours de philologie anglaise du Chanoine Fafournoux. Ensuite, outre Manche, il conquit d'autres grades, *summa cum laude*, en phonétique anglaise. . . . Je saurais dire d'autres souvenirs sur l'achat d'une maison rue Pascal, sur la venue à Angers de la maman de G. M. et sur son décès, sur l'installation au célèbre – du moins *extra pagum andegavensem* – 29 rue Volney.

Individuum est ineffabile; certains le sont plus que d'autres. Continuant de choisir, avec la même loupe égocentrique, quelques dates et faits, je dirai que G. M. a été pour moi un initiateur en organisation de sessions – lui, d'anglais, et moi, l'année suivante, à partir du français, en grammaire comparative et analyse textuelle: c'était en 1956, 1957, 1960, 1961. Je me rappelle une exposition Thomas More, avec des calligraphies de Mme Madeleine Bataille, dans la grande salle du palais universitaire, petite serre qui préparait l'éclosion du banyan morien.

Si ces lignes étaient un portrait, plutôt qu'un égrènement de souvenirs, j'aurais à dire mon admiration pour le professeur d'anglais, phonétique et philologie, etc., pour l'immense travail qui conduit à son centième numéro une revue de haut standing, revue qui dévore son directeur sans entamer sa vitalité. Il me faudrait savoir dire aussi – last but not least – une fraternité eucharistique (un agenouillement commun près du tabernacle transcende de longues discussions religieuses), la richesse de ses conseils, l'intérêt de réponses, parfois plus ou moins convaincantes, mais toujours suggestives et bénéfiques, aux multiples questions que je lui aurai posées au cours de trois, sinon quatre ou cinq, décennies de voisinage.

Grand merci donc à l'avocat-conseil et au stimulateur de prière, de travail et d'initiatives, de son voisin de 27 rue Volney.

Université Catholique de l'Ouest

MOREANA

Organe de l'Association AMICI THOMAE MORI
A Bilingual Quarterly
29 Rue Volney - B.P. 808
49005 ANGERS CEDEX, France
Tél. : 41.88.83.98

Past Presidents : *E.E. Reynolds (d. 1980), Richard S. Sylvester (d. 1978)*
President : *Nicolas Barker*
Past Vice-Presidents : *Marialisa Bertagnoni, Ward S. Allen*
Vice-President : *Hermann Boventer*

Direction de **Moreana**	: *Germain Marc'hadour*
Administration	: *Henri Gibaud*
Edition de la **Gazette**	: *Marie-Claude Rousseau*
Assistanat	: *Marcel Le Ny*
Photocomposition	: *Béatrice Lemasson*

NATIONAL SECRETARIES

British Isles : *Rosemary Rendel*
CRS, 114 Mount Street, London W1Y GAH

North America : *Brother Michael Grace, S.J.*
Loyola U., 6525 N. Sheridan Road, Chicago, IL 60626

FILIALES. DAUGHTER SOCIETIES.

Amici Thomae Mori, Sezione italiana, 17 via Pantano, 20122 Milano.
Japan Thomas More Society, c/o *Moreana's* editor Paul Akio Sawada.
Thomas More Society of America, Box 65175, Washington D.C. 20035.
Thomas-Morus-Gesellschaft, Hubertushöhe 9, Bensberg,
5060 Bergisch-Gladbach.

Subscription outside France

Individual members	US	$	38.00
Librairies & Institutions	US	$	56.00
Life members	US	$	800.000
Back issues of *Moreana*	US	$	10.00
Single issues of the Gazette	US	$	12.00
Utopia special	US	$	17.00

Abonnement pour la France

Membres individuels	200 F.
Bibliothèques & Collectivités	260 F.
Membre à vie	4500 F.
Le cahier isolé de *Moreana*	60 F.
L'exemplaire de la Gazette	70 F.
Le cahier *Utopie*	80 F.

Cheques can be made payable to National Secretaries or to Amici Thomae Mori
Chèques à l'ordre de AMICALE THOMAS MORE :
C.C.P. Nantes 2694-22 J. ou C.I.O. Angers 299054656U.

Dépôt légal : 1ère et 2ème trimestre 1989.

EDITORIAL BOARD ★ COMITÉ DE LECTURE

Ward S. Allen, Jefferson Davis Highway, Rt 3, Box 3, Auburn, AL 36830, USA
Marialisa Bertagnoni, Via del Teatro Olimpico, 36100 Vicenza, Italia.
Franz Bierlaire, Quai Orban 42/051, 4020 Liège, Belgique.
Peter G. Bietenholz, U. of Saskatchewan, Sask., Canada S7N OWO.
J.M. de Bujanda, Centre Renaissance, U. de Sherbrooke, Québec, Canada J1K 2R1
Charles Clay Doyle, Dept of English, U. of GA, Athens, GA 30602, USA.
André Godin, 155 rue Saint-Martin, 75003 Paris, France.
Damian Grace, P.O. Box 1, Kensington, New South Wales, Australia 2033.
Jacques Gury, 26 rue de Kératry, 29200 Brest, France.
Ralph Keen, 1540 N. State Parkway, Chicago, IL 60610, USA.
Elizabeth McCutcheon, 3618 Woodlawn Terrace, Honolulu, HI 96822, USA.
Andrew M. McLean, Dept of English, U. of WI at Parkside, Kenosha, WI 53140, USA
Clarence H. Miller, Dept of English, St Louis U., St Louis, MO 63108, USA.
Clare M. Murphy, 33 Starr Drive West, Apt. 5, Narragansett, RI 02882, USA.
Anne Lake Prescott, 81 Benedict Hill Rd, New Canaan, CT 06840, USA.
André Prévost, 16 avenue des Fleurs, 59110 La Madeleine, France.
Angele Botros Samaan, 15a Haroun Street, Dokki, Cairo, Egypt.
P. Akio Sawada, Tsukuba U., Tsukuba, 305 Ibaraki, 300.31 Japan.
Richard J. Schoeck, Postfach 3825, Universität Trier, 5500 Trier, Germany.
J.B. Trapp, Warburg Institute, Woburn Square, London WC1H OAB, England.

★ ★ ★

• *Moreana,* the bilingual (French and English) quarterly of Thomas More Studies, serves as bulletin to the International Association *Amici Thomae Mori.*

• The Association *Amici Thomae Mori* was born at Brussels on 29 December 1962. *Moreana* No. 1 appeared in September 1963. The journal's aim is to provide a forum for research and discussion about the world of More, with which it assumes its readers to be basically acquainted.

• Submissions should be sent to the director, or to any member of the Editorial Board. Kindly provide three copies of the manuscript.

• To subscribe to *Moreana*, send your cheque to the Secretary, B.P. 808, 49005 Angers Cedex, France, or to one of the National Secretaries (addresses on back page).

• Le Moreanum angevin, qui publie *Moreana*, appartient à la F.I.S.I.E.R. (Fédération Internationale des Instituts de la Renaissance). Il reçoit l'aide du C.N.R.S. et est un des constituants de l'I.R.F.A. (Institut de Recherche Fondamentale et Appliquée) à l'Université Catholique de l'Ouest.